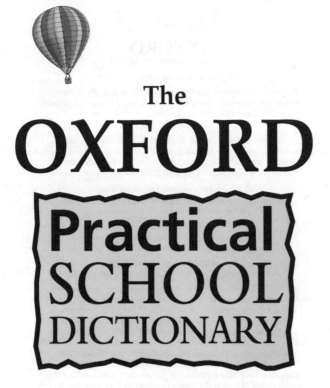

The
OXFORD
Practical
SCHOOL
DICTIONARY

Chief Editor
Robert Allen

OXFORD
UNIVERSITY PRESS

OXFORD

UNIVERSITY PRESS

Great Clarendon Street, Oxford OX2 6DP

Oxford University Press is a department of the University of Oxford.
It furthers the University's objective of excellence in research, scholarship,
and education by publishing worldwide in

Oxford New York

Athens Auckland Bangkok Bogotá Buenos Aires Calcutta
Cape Town Chennai Dar es Salaam Delhi Florence Hong Kong Istanbul
Karachi Kuala Lumpur Madrid Melbourne Mexico City Mumbai
Nairobi Paris São Paulo Singapore Taipei Tokyo Toronto Warsaw

with associated companies in Berlin Ibadan

Oxford is a registered trade mark of Oxford University Press
in the UK and in certain other countries

British Library Cataloguing in Publication Data available

hardback ISBN 0-19-910799-8
export ISBN 0-19-910800-5

1 3 5 7 9 10 8 6 4 2

Typeset by Pentacor plc, High Wycombe
Printed in Great Britain

Preface

The aim of the Oxford Practical School Dictionary is to explain in a clear and straightforward style the meanings and use of the English words that children aged 8 and upwards are likely to come across and want to use. When a word falls outside the normal range but needs to be included, it is marked as '(not an everyday word)' when it is more formal or technical than normal, and '(informal)' when it is more colloquial than normal.

A major innovation of this edition is the inclusion of additional items of information about words and their use, over and above their meaning and the other information a dictionary ordinarily gives. Many of these items deal with word origins (*Bible*, *Celsius*, *checkmate*, *demon*, *electricity*, *graffiti*, *paradise*, the names of the days and months, etc.), others with aspects of usage (*aboriginal*, *billion*, *ditto*, etc.), and others again with examples of special language features (*acronym*, *anagram*, *consonant*, *fable*, etc.).

In writing the new text I have made extensive use of the British National Corpus, a language database containing 100 million words of written and spoken English of all kinds assembled by a consortium of publishers and academic institutions. This material offers rich insights into the ways in which words are used and the typical contexts in which they occur. Study of the Corpus, as well as of children's literature (both traditional and modern), has been especially important in devising the example sentences, which achieve a naturalness that is not possible solely on the basis of the compiler's intuition.

Of the many people who helped me in writing this dictionary I should like to thank especially Jessica Feinstein, who read a first version of the text and made many important suggestions to improve it. I should also like to thank all those teachers who answered extensive questionnaires on the selection and presentation of information in dictionaries for children.

Robert Allen

Pronunciation

The pronunciation of difficult words is given in round brackets after the headword. A stressed syllable is shown by bold type, and certain special sounds are shown in the following ways:

oo shows the sound as in **soon**

uu shows the sound as in **book**

th shows the sound as in **th**in

th shows the sound as in **th**is

zh shows the sound as in vi**s**ion and mea**s**ure

Word Origins

Where do the words we use come from? Why are some very short and others long and difficult to say and spell?

Some English words are very old and were used in a form of the language called Old English, which the Anglo-Saxons used (and so it is sometimes called Anglo-Saxon). Most of the pronouns (*I, you, he, me, she, we*, and so on) come from Old English. Here are some examples of other common words that come from Old English:

a	fly	man	slide
and	forbid	merry	son
come	give	milk	south
daughter	glad	mother	sparrow
do	glass	must	step
down	go	name	tail
each	hand	narrow	the
ear	hen	neck	thing
east	honey	north	tool
edge	it	or	town
elbow	itch	oven	up
enough	keep	post	west
fall	kettle	right	what
far	law	ring	when
father	learn	self	where
fetch	leather	sell	which
field	leave	ship	who

Some words are from Norse, the language used by the Vikings who settled in parts of Britain in the ninth and tenth centuries (the 800s and the 900s). Here are some examples of these:

anger	flat	skull	trust
birth	leg	take	ugly
dirt	mistake	they	want
egg	odd	thrust	window

Other words come from Latin and Greek words. Many of these were brought into English by the Normans, who invaded England under William the Conqueror in 1066. The Normans spoke a form of French, and many of their words came from words in Latin and Greek. Here are some examples of words that have come into English in this way:

accuse	crown	foreign	noble
active	cruel	gentle	person
beauty	deceive	herb	possible
button	desire	lemon	precious
ceiling	empire	logic	river
common	enjoy	medicine	save
council	face	minister	serve

Some modern words have come straight from other languages, such as French, German, Italian, Persian, and Turkish. Here are some examples:

anorak	Eskimo	lager	German
banana	Spanish or Portuguese	safari	African languages
		sauna	Finnish
bazaar	Turkish	ski	Norwegian
bungalow	Indian languages	spaghetti	Italian
café	French	yacht	Dutch

Some words are made by joining together other English words. These are often called compounds. For example:

footprint newspaper paintbrush

Some words have interesting stories behind them, for example:

deadline *noun* (plural **deadlines**) a time by which you have to do something
A deadline was once a real line drawn round a prison. Prisoners were shot if they stepped over it.

Wednesday *noun* (plural **Wednesdays**) the fourth day of the week
Wednesday is an Anglo-Saxon name honouring the god Odin or Woden.

You will find these stories and some others given in the dictionary.

Grammatical Terms

The following list contains vocabulary that teachers and children can use to talk about language.

adjective a word that describes a person or thing, for example *red* or *big*

adverb a word that tells you about a verb or adjective, for example *slowly* or *very*

alphabet the letters used in a language arranged in a special order

alphabetical order the usual order in which words are arranged in lists and dictionaries, A, B, C, D, E, and so on

capital letter a large letter, A, B, C, and so on, used at the start of a name or a sentence

conjunction a word like *and* or *but* that joins phrases and parts of a sentence together

consonant any of the letters b, c, d, f, g, h, j, k, l, m, n, p, q, r, s, t, v, w, x, y (as in *yell*), z

definite article the word *the*

exclamation a word or phrase you say out loud to show surprise, fear, or pain, or other feelings, for example *oh!* or *ouch! aha! pooh! ugh!*

grapheme a unit of writing that expresses an individual sound; for example, there are three graphemes in the word *cat* (*c, a,* and *t*) and three graphemes in the word *cough* (*c, ou, gh*)

homograph a word that has the same spelling as another word but has a different meaning, for example *bat* (for hitting a ball) and *bat* (an animal)

indefinite article the word *a* or *an*

interjection another word for exclamation

letter one of the symbols used for writing words, a, b, c, d, e, and so on

lower case	a small form of a letter, a, b, c, and so on
noun	a word that stands for a person, place, or thing. A common noun stands for a whole kind of things or people, for example *girl, horse, town, table*; a proper noun is the name of one person or thing and begins with a capital letter, for example *Rachel, London, Concorde*
onset	see **syllable**
phoneme	a letter or group of letters that stands for a sound in a word
plural	the form of a word when it means more than one person or thing, for example *houses, carts, children,* and *they*
preposition	a word such as *for, on, in,* and *over,* which shows how one word is connected with another word, as in *put the book on the shelf*
pronoun	a word such as *I, me, he, her, them,* and so on, which you use instead of a noun
sentence	a group of words that form a statement, question, or command, usually beginning with a capital letter and ending in a full stop, question mark, or exclamation mark
singular	the form of a word when it means only one person or thing, for example *house, cart,* and *child*
syllable	a word or part of a word that has a separate sound when you say it; for example, *mouse* has one syllable and *el-e-phant* has three syllables. The first part of a syllable is called the onset; for example in the syllable *dog, d* is the onset.
upper case	another term for capital letter
verb	a word that shows what someone or something is doing, for example *be, do, come, talk, want*
vowel	any of the letters a, e, i, o, u, and sometimes y (as in *rhyme*)
word	a set of sounds or letters that has a meaning and is written with a space before and after it. There are seven words in this sentence.

Some Common Prefixes

A prefix is a group of letters joined to the beginning of a word to change its meaning, for example *re-* in **recapture** (= to capture again) and *un-* in **unknown** (= not known).

Here are examples of some common English prefixes:

co-	together	coeducation
de-	undoing or taking away	de-ice
dis-	not	dishonest
dis-	taking away	disconnect
ex-	that used to be	ex-president
in-	not	incorrect
mis-	wrong	misbehave
non-	not	non-existent
over-	too much	overdo
poly-	many	polygon
pre-	before	prehistoric
re-	again	recapture
un-	not	unknown
under-	not enough	underdone

Some Common Suffixes

A suffix is a group of letters joined to the end of a word to change its meaning, for example -er in **baker** (= someone who bakes bread) and -ness in **kindness** (= being kind).

Here are examples of some common English suffixes:

-able	able to be	eatable
-er	someone who does something	baker
-er	more	nicer
-ess	a female	lioness
-est	most	nicest
-ish	rather like	childish
-ize or **-ise**	used to make verbs	criticize, televise
-less	not having, without	helpless
-ly	used to make adverbs	bravely
-ment	used to make nouns	amusement
-ness	used to make nouns	kindness
-or	someone who does something	sailor
-ous	used to make adjectives	dangerous
-ship	used to make nouns	friendship

Dictionary Features

Headword: the first word in each entry.

Forms of adjectives: comparative and superlative forms.

Part of speech: noun, verb, adjective, adverb, etc.

Use label: e.g. (not an everyday word).

Definition: the meaning of the headword.

Number before definitions: used when a word has more than one meaning.

Verb forms: present tense; present participle; past tense and past participle.

Example: how a word is used.

Derivative: a word with a meaning connected with the headword's meaning.

Plural of noun: all regular and irregular plurals are given.

Illustration: adding more information to definitions.

Pronunciation: how to say a word.

able *adjective* (**abler, ablest**) **1** having a special talent or skill ► *Some of the more able pupils do extra reading.* **2** having the oppotunity to do something ► *They said they were not able to stay any longer.* **ably** *adverb*

abstract *adjective* to do with ideas and not with physical things ► *People enjoy abstract paintings as much as portraits and landscapes.*

abundant *adjective* (not an everyday word) large in amount, plentiful **abundance** *noun*

account *noun* (*plural* **accounts**) **1** a story or description of things that have happened **2** an amount of money kept in a bank or building society **3** a statement of the money that someone owes
account *verb* (**accounts, accounting, accounted**) account for to be or give an explanation of something ► *It was difficult to account for such a huge hole in the road.*

acknowledge *verb* (**acknowledges, acknowledging, acknowledged**) (not an everyday word) **1** to admit that something is true **2** to express thanks for something you have received **acknowledgement** *noun*

acne *noun* (*pronounced* **ak**-ni) a skin disease with red pimples on the face

acorn *noun* (*plural* **acorns**) the egg-shaped seed of an oak tree

acoustics *plural noun* (*pronounced* a-**koo**-stiks) **1** the qualities that make a room good or bad for hearing clearly **2** the science of sound

x

Aa

a *adjective* (called the *indefinite article*)
1 any; one ▶ *Have you brought a book
with you?* 2 each, every ▶ *They see us once
a month.*

aback *adverb* **taken aback** rather surprised
or shocked

abacus *noun* (*plural* **abacuses**) a frame
with rows of sliding beads, used for
counting

abandon *verb* (**abandons, abandoning,
abandoned**) 1 to go away and leave a
person or place ▶ *The villagers had
abandoned their homes after the
earthquake.* 2 to stop doing something
before you have finished it ▶ *The search
was abandoned after dark.* **abandon ship** to
leave a sinking ship and get into the
lifeboats

abbey *noun* (*plural* **abbeys**) a place where
monks or nuns live or used to live

abbot *noun* (*plural* **abbots**) the head of an
abbey of monks

abbreviation *noun* (*plural* **abbreviations**)
a short way of writing something ▶ *PC is
an abbreviation of 'personal computer'.*

abdicate *verb* (**abdicates, abdicating,
abdicated**) to give up being king or queen

abdomen *noun* (*plural* **abdomens**) the
part of the body that contains the stomach

abide *verb* **cannot abide** cannot stand
someone or something

ability *noun* (*plural* **abilities**) the
knowledge or skill that helps you to do
something

ablaze *adjective* burning brightly

able *adjective* (**abler, ablest**) 1 having a
special talent or skill ▶ *Some of the more
able pupils do extra reading.* 2 having the
opportunity to do something ▶ *They said
they were not able to stay any longer.* **ably**
adverb

abnormal *adjective* not normal, unusual
abnormality *noun* **abnormally** *adverb*

aboard *adverb* on a ship or train or plane

abolish *verb* (**abolishes, abolishing,
abolished**) to get rid of a rule or custom
▶ *Some people would like to abolish
television licences.* **abolition** *noun*

abominable *adjective* very bad or wicked

aboriginal *noun* one of the original
inhabitants of a country
Aborigines is also used for the early inhabitants of
Australia.

abortion *noun* (*plural* **abortions**) an
operation to remove an unborn child
(foetus) from a woman's womb

about *preposition* and *adverb* 1 nearly,
roughly 2 to do with

above *preposition* and *adverb* 1 higher than
2 more than

abreast *adverb* side by side

abroad *adverb* in a foreign country

abrupt *adjective* 1 sudden and unexpected
▶ *His uncle often had abrupt changes of
mood, smiling one moment and scowling the
next.* 2 unfriendly and short-tempered in
the way you speak

abscess *noun* (*plural* **abscesses**) a painful
swelling on the body, full of pus

abseil *verb* (**abseils, abseiling, abseiled**) to
lower yourself down a steep cliff or rock
by sliding down a rope

absent *adjective* not at the place where you
should be **absence** *noun* **absentee** *noun*
someone who is absent

absent-minded *adjective* forgetting
things easily

absolute *adjective* total, complete ▶ *The
house was an absolute mess.* **absolutely**
adverb completely

absorb *verb* (**absorbs, absorbing, absorbed**) to soak up liquid **absorbent** *adjective* able to soak up liquid **absorbing** *adjective* interesting

absorbed *adjective* very interested in something ▸ *The old woman was absorbed in some needlework.*

abstain *verb* (**abstains, abstaining, abstained**) to decide not to do something you have a right to do ▸ *Many people will abstain from voting.*

abstract *adjective* to do with ideas and not with physical things ▸ *People enjoy abstract painting as much as portraits and landscapes.*

absurd *adjective* silly or ridiculous **absurdity** *noun*

abundant *adjective* (not an everyday word) large in amount, plentiful **abundance** *noun*

abuse *verb* (**abuses, abusing, abused**) (*pronounced* a-**bewz**) 1 to use something wrongly and harm it 2 to hurt someone or say unpleasant things about them **abuse** *noun* (*plural* **abuses**) (*pronounced* a-**bewss**) 1 wrong use of something 2 unpleasant words about someone 3 harm or cruelty done to someone

abusive *adjective* saying unpleasant or insulting things

academic *adjective* to do with learning in a school or university

academy *noun* (*plural* **academies**) a college or school

accelerate *verb* (**accelerates, accelerating, accelerated**) to go faster **acceleration** *noun* **accelerator** *noun* a device in a car to make it go faster

accent *noun* (*plural* **accents**) 1 the way that people pronounce words 2 a special mark put over a letter, e.g. the é in *café*

accept *verb* (**accepts, accepting, accepted**) 1 to take something when someone offers it to you 2 to agree that something is true ▸ *I accept that I may have been wrong.* **acceptance** *noun*

acceptable *adjective* all right, satisfactory

access *noun* (*plural* **accesses**) a way to reach a place ▸ *A narrow lane was the only access to the village.*
access *verb* (**accesses, accessing, accessed**) to get information stored in a computer

accessible *adjective* easy to reach or get near to

accession *noun* (*plural* **accessions**) the time when a new king or queen begins ruling ▸ *Tomorrow is the anniversary of the Queen's accession.*

accessory *noun* (*plural* **accessories**) an extra part or item that goes with something else

accident *noun* (*plural* **accidents**) something bad or unwelcome that happens by chance **accidental** *adjective* happening by chance **accidentally** *adverb*

accommodate *verb* (**accommodates, accommodating, accommodated**) to provide someone with a room or a place to sleep **accommodation** *noun* a place to live or stay

accompany *verb* (**accompanies, accompanying, accompanied**) 1 to go with someone 2 to happen at the same time as something else ▸ *They heard loud talking accompanied by laughter.*

accomplish *verb* (**accomplishes, accomplishing, accomplished**) (not an everyday word) to do something successfully **accomplished** *adjective* able to do something well **accomplishment** *noun* something you do well

accord *noun* (*plural* **accords**) of your own accord willingly and without being asked

accordingly *adverb* (not an everyday word) 1 as a result; therefore 2 in a way that is suitable ▸ *Frank was doing harder work now and being paid accordingly.*

according to in someone's opinion, as someone says ▸ *The party's tomorrow, according to Duncan.*

accordion *noun* (*plural* **accordions**) a musical instrument like a large concertina with a set of small piano keys at one end

account *noun* (*plural* **accounts**) **1** a story or description of things that have happened **2** an amount of money kept in a bank or building society **3** a statement of the money that someone owes

account *verb* (**accounts, accounting, accounted**) **account for** to be or give an explanation of something ▸ *It was difficult to account for such a huge hole in the road.*

accountant *noun* (*plural* **accountants**) a person whose job is to help people to organize their money **accountancy** *noun*

accumulate *verb* (**accumulates, accumulating, accumulated**) (not an everyday word) to collect together or pile up **accumulation** *noun*

accurate *adjective* correct, done exactly and carefully **accuracy** *noun* **accurately** *adverb*

accuse *verb* (**accuses, accusing, accused**) to say that someone has done something wrong **accusation** *noun*

accustomed *adjective* (not an everyday word) **be accustomed to** to be used to something

ace *noun* (*plural* **aces**) **1** a playing card with an A in the corner and a picture of the suit in the centre **2** a serve in tennis that is so good that the other player cannot reach the ball **3** someone or something very clever or skilful

ache *noun* (*plural* **aches**) a dull steady pain
ache *verb* (**aches, aching, ached**) to feel an ache

achieve *verb* (**achieves, achieving, achieved**) to do something by your own effort **achievement** *noun* something you achieve

acid *noun* (*plural* **acids**) a chemical that contains hydrogen and causes chemical change
acid *adjective* sour or bitter to taste **acidic** *adjective* **acidity** *noun* the level of acid in a substance

acid rain *noun* rain that contains harmful acids from waste gases in the air

acknowledge *verb* (**acknowledges, acknowledging, acknowledged**) (not an everyday word) **1** to admit that something is true **2** to express thanks for something you have received **acknowledgement** *noun*

acne *noun* (*pronounced* **ak-ni**) a skin disease with red pimples on the face

acorn *noun* (*plural* **acorns**) the egg-shaped seed of an oak tree

acoustics *plural noun* (*pronounced* **a-koo-stiks**) **1** the qualities that make a room good or bad for hearing sound clearly **2** the science of sound

acquaintance *noun* (*plural* **acquaintances**) someone you know slightly

acquainted *adjective* (not an everyday word) **be acquainted with** to know someone or something slightly

acquire *verb* (**acquires, acquiring, acquired**) (not an everyday word) to obtain something **acquisition** *noun*

acquit *verb* (**acquits, acquitting, acquitted**) to decide that someone is not guilty of a crime in a law trial **acquittal** *noun*

acre *noun* (*plural* **acres**) (*pronounced* **ay-ker**) an area of land equal to 4,047 square metres or 4,840 square yards

acrobat *noun* (*plural* **acrobats**) an entertainer who gives displays of difficult jumping and balancing **acrobatic** *adjective* **acrobatics** *plural noun* the exercises that an acrobat does

acronym *noun* (*plural* **acronyms**) (*pronounced* **ak-ron-im**) a word or name that is formed from the first letters of other words
Here are some examples of acronyms:
Nato = *North Atlantic Treaty Organization*,
Aids = acquired immune deficiency syndrome,
radar = radio detection and ranging.

across *adverb* and *preposition* from one side of a thing to the other

act *noun* (*plural* **acts**) 1 something that someone does 2 an item of entertainment in a show ▸ *The next act will be a conjuror.* 3 one of the main sections of a play or opera 4 a law passed by a government **put on an act** to pretend to be something that you are not, to show off

act *verb* (**acts, acting, acted**) 1 to do something or behave in a certain way ▸ *The police acted very swiftly.* 2 to be an actor or actress

action *noun* (*plural* **actions**) 1 something that someone does 2 fighting in a battle ▸ *James's grandfather had died in action in France.* **out of action** not working properly

activate *verb* (**activates, activating, activated**) to start a machine or device working

active *adjective* busy and energetic **actively** *adverb*

activity *noun* (*plural* **activities**) 1 doing things 2 something you do, such as a sport or hobby

actor *noun* (*plural* **actors**) someone who takes part in a play or film

actress *noun* (*plural* **actresses**) a girl or woman who takes part in a play or film

actual *adjective* real, really happening ▸ *The story is based on actual events.*

actually *adverb* really, in fact

acupuncture *noun* a way of curing disease or taking away pain by sticking needles into parts of the body

acute *adjective* 1 sharp or severe ▸ *The pain in Henry's arm was acute.* 2 clever, quick to understand something **acute accent** a mark (´) put over a letter as in *café* **acute angle** an angle of less than 90 degrees

AD is short for *Anno Domini*, which means 'in the year of the Lord'. It is used with dates that come after the birth of Jesus Christ, for example AD 1066 is the year of the Battle of Hastings.

ad *noun* (*plural* **ads**) (informal) an advertisement

Adam's apple *noun* the lump at the front of a man's neck

adapt *verb* (**adapts, adapting, adapted**) 1 to make something suitable for a new purpose 2 to become used to a new situation or way of life ▸ *They adapted to life in the country very quickly.* **adaptation** *noun*

adaptable *adjective* able to adapt or become suitable for different things

adaptor *noun* (*plural* **adaptors**) a device for connecting different pieces of electrical equipment

add *verb* (**adds, adding, added**) 1 to put numbers together to make a bigger number 2 to mix one thing with another, for example in a recipe **add up** to make a bigger number or total

adder *noun* (*plural* **adders**) a small poisonous snake

addict *noun* (*plural* **addicts**) someone with a habit they can't give up, for example taking drugs or drinking alcohol **addicted** *adjective* **addiction** *noun*

addition *noun* (*plural* **additions**) 1 adding things together 2 something that has been added **in addition** also, as well

additional *adjective* extra, added on

additive *noun* (*plural* **additives**) a chemical that is added to food

address *noun* (*plural* **addresses**) 1 the details of the place where someone lives 2 a speech

address *verb* (**addresses, addressing, addressed**) 1 to write the address on a letter or parcel 2 to speak formally to a person or group of people

adenoids *plural noun* the small spongy lumps of flesh at the back of your nose

adequate *adjective* just enough, sufficient

adhere *verb* (**adheres, adhering, adhered**) (not an everyday word) to stick to something

adhesive *noun* (*plural* **adhesives**) something that you use to stick things together, such as glue or paste
adhesive *adjective* sticky ▸ *adhesive tape*

Adi Granth *noun* (*pronounced* ah-di grunt) the holy book of the Sikhs
Adi Granth is an ancient Sanskrit name meaning 'first book'.

adjacent *adjective* next to something
▸ *There is a river adjacent to the golf course.*

adjective *noun* (*plural* **adjectives**) a word that describes something, for example *red* and *big* in the sentence *The red house is big.*

adjust *verb* (**adjusts, adjusting, adjusted**) to change something slightly to make it right or to make it work better **adjustment** *noun* a small change you make to something

administration *noun* (*plural* **administrations**) managing and running something, such as a country or a business **administrator** *noun*

admirable *adjective* worth admiring; excellent **admirably** *adverb*

admiral *noun* (*plural* **admirals**) an officer of the highest rank in the navy

admire *verb* (**admires, admiring, admired**) to like someone or something or to think they are very good or very beautiful
▸ *This is a good spot to admire the view over the valley.* **admiration** *noun* **admirer** *noun*

admission *noun* (*plural* **admissions**) 1 something that someone admits or confesses 2 being allowed to go into a place ▸ *The museum has half-price admission for students.*

admit *verb* (**admits, admitting, admitted**) 1 to let someone into a place 2 to confess something or agree that it is true
▸ *Frances admitted she had been playing by the river.*

admittance *noun* being allowed to go into a private place

admittedly *adverb* although it is true
▸ *Admittedly it's cold but I'd still like to go out.*

ado *noun* **without more ado** without any more fuss or delay

adolescent *noun* (*plural* **adolescents**) a young person who is almost an adult **adolescence** *noun*

adopt *verb* (**adopts, adopting, adopted**) 1 to take a child into your family 2 to use an idea or suggestion **adoption** *noun*

adorable *adjective* lovely, beautiful

adore *verb* (**adores, adoring, adored**) to love someone or something or admire them very much **adoration** *noun*

adorn *verb* (**adorns, adorning, adorned**) to decorate something or make it pretty **adornment** *noun*

adrift *adverb* and *adjective* drifting; off course

adult *noun* (*plural* **adults**) a fully grown person or animal

advance *noun* (*plural* **advances**) 1 a forward movement 2 improvement or progress 3 a loan of money **in advance** beforehand

advance *verb* (**advances, advancing, advanced**) to move forward

advanced *adjective* 1 a long way forward
▸ *The building work is at an advanced stage.*
2 more difficult or more highly developed
▸ *Freda is doing an advanced course in computing.*

advantage *noun* (*plural* **advantages**) something useful or helpful **take advantage of** 1 to treat someone unfairly when they are not likely to complain 2 to get the benefit of something ▸ *We ought to take advantage of the cheap rail fares.*
advantageous *adjective* useful, giving an advantage

Advent *noun* in the Christian Church, the period before Christmas

adventure noun (plural **adventures**) an exciting or interesting event or journey **adventurous** adjective liking to do exciting things

adverb noun (plural **adverbs**) a word used to describe a verb or adjective, such as slowly or very

advert noun (plural **adverts**) (informal) an advertisement

advertise verb (**advertises, advertising, advertised**) to tell people about something you want to sell to them, for example in a newspaper or on television

advertisement noun (plural **advertisements**) a notice or picture, or a short television film, that advertises something

advice noun something you say to someone to help them

advisable adjective sensible, worth doing

advise verb (**advises, advising, advised**) to tell someone what you think they should do

aerial noun (plural **aerials**) a wire or metal rod for receiving or sending radio or television signals

aerobics plural noun energetic exercises that strengthen your heart and lungs

aeroplane noun (plural **aeroplanes**) a vehicle with wings and one or more engines, which can fly

aerosol noun (plural **aerosols**) a container that lets out its contents in a fine spray

affair noun (plural **affairs**) 1 something that happens, an event ▸ The rest of the game was a rather dull affair. 2 a person's private matter or business

affect verb (**affects, affecting, affected**) to make a difference to something or someone, for example by harming them ▸ The dust may affect your lungs.

affection noun (plural **affections**) love or fondness **affectionate** adjective showing love or fondness

afflict verb (**afflicts, afflicting, afflicted**) (not an everyday word) to cause someone to suffer pain or trouble **affliction** noun something that someone suffers

afford verb (**affords, affording, afforded**) to have enough money or time for something

afloat adjective and adverb floating; on water or at sea

afraid adjective 1 frightened 2 sorry ▸ I'm afraid I've spent all your money.

afresh adverb again; in a new way ▸ Let's start afresh.

after preposition and adverb later; later than

afternoon noun (plural **afternoons**) the time from midday or lunchtime until evening

afterwards adverb at a later time

again adverb 1 once more; another time 2 as before ▸ She'll soon be well again.

against preposition 1 touching ▸ A bicycle was standing against the wall. 2 opposed to, not liking ▸ We're all against smoking here.

age noun (plural **ages**) 1 the length of time that a person or animal has been alive 2 a period of history ▸ the Bronze Age **ages** (informal) a long time ▸ We've been waiting ages.
age verb (**ages, ageing, aged**) to become old

aged adjective 1 (pronounced ayjd) having the age of ▸ The boy, aged 9, had not been in trouble before. 2 (pronounced ay-jid) very old ▸ We saw an aged man.

agent noun (plural **agents**) 1 someone whose job is to organize things for customers ▸ We booked our holiday with a travel agent. 2 a spy ▸ Jim's uncle had been a secret agent. **agency** noun an agent's office or business

aggravate verb (**aggravates, aggravating, aggravated**) 1 to make something worse 2 (informal) to annoy someone **aggravation** noun

aggressive *adjective* 1 likely to attack people 2 strong, forceful ▸ *The champion played aggressive tennis and kept his title.* **aggression** *noun* **aggressor** *noun*

aghast *adjective* shocked or horrified

agile *adjective* able to move quickly and easily **agility** *noun*

agitated *adjective* worried and anxious ▸ *As the traffic got worse the driver became more and more agitated.* **agitation** *noun*

ago *adverb* in the past ▸ *She died long ago.*

agony *noun* (*plural* **agonies**) great pain or suffering **agonizing** *adjective*

agree *verb* (**agrees, agreeing, agreed**) 1 to think the same as someone else 2 to be willing to do something ▸ *The boy agreed to come along and help.* 3 to suit someone or be good for someone ▸ *Spicy food doesn't agree with her.* **agreement** *noun*

agreeable *adjective* friendly or pleasant ▸ *We spend an agreeable afternoon in the park.*

agriculture *noun* farming, cultivating the land **agricultural** *adjective*

aground *adverb* stuck on the bottom of a river or the sea in shallow water ▸ *A large ship ran aground off the American coast during the summer.*

ahead *adverb* 1 forwards, in front 2 into the future

aid *noun* (*plural* **aids**) 1 help 2 money or food or other help sent to another country 3 something that helps ▸ *By the time he was fifty he needed to use a hearing aid.* **aid** *verb* (**aids, aiding, aided**) to help someone

Aids or **AIDS** *noun* (short for *acquired immune deficiency syndrome*) a disease which destroys the body's ability to protect itself from other diseases

ailing *adjective* ill or suffering, usually for a long time ▸ *For many years he lived with his ailing mother.*

ailment *noun* (*plural* **ailments**) (not an everyday word) a minor illness

aim *verb* (**aims, aiming, aimed**) 1 to point a gun or other weapon at someone 2 to try or intend to do something 3 to throw something or kick it in a particular direction

aim *noun* (*plural* **aims**) 1 what someone plans to do 2 pointing a weapon in a particular direction

aimless *adjective* not having a plan or purpose **aimlessly** *adverb*

air *noun* (*plural* **airs**) 1 the mixture of gases which surrounds the earth and which people breathe 2 a gentle tune 3 the feeling a place gives you ▸ *The house has an air of mystery.*

air *verb* (**airs, airing, aired**) 1 to put clothes in a warm place to finish drying 2 to let fresh air into a room 3 to tell people your views or opinions about something ▸ *The meeting gave people a chance to air their feelings.*

airborne *adjective* 1 flying in an aeroplane or helicopter 2 carried by the air

aircraft *noun* (*plural* **aircraft**) an aeroplane or helicopter

air force *noun* (*plural* **air forces**) the aircraft that a country uses for fighting wars, and the people who fly them

airline *noun* (*plural* **airlines**) a company that takes passengers and cargo to places by aircraft

airmail *noun* mail that is sent by air

airport *noun* (*plural* **airports**) a place where aircraft land and take off, with passenger terminals and other buildings

airship *noun* (*plural* **airships**) a large balloon with engines, designed to carry passengers or cargo

airtight *adjective* forming a seal, or having a seal, so that air cannot get in or out

airy *adjective* (**airier, airiest**) with plenty of light and fresh air ▸ *He led us into a bright airy kitchen.* **airily** *adverb* in a casual or light-hearted way ▸ *She waved her hand airily and said she didn't want to know.*

aisle noun (*plural* **aisles**) (*rhymes with* mile) a passage between rows of seats in a church, theatre, or cinema, or on an aeroplane

ajar *adverb* and *adjective* slightly open
▸ *Please leave the door ajar.*

alarm *verb* (**alarms, alarming, alarmed**) to frighten someone or make them anxious

alarm *noun* (*plural* **alarms**) 1 a warning sound or signal 2 a sudden feeling of fear or anxiety ▸ *A hand touched her shoulder, making her cry out in alarm.*

alarm clock *noun* (*plural* **alarm clocks**) a clock with a loud ring or bleep to wake you up

alas *interjection* (old use) something you say when you are sad

album *noun* (*plural* **albums**) 1 a book in which you keep a collection of things like photographs or stamps 2 a collection of songs on a CD, record, or tape

alcohol *noun* a clear liquid made by fermenting sugar or starch and used in drinks like beer and whisky, which makes people drunk if they drink too much

alcoholic *adjective* containing alcohol

alcoholic *noun* (*plural* **alcoholics**) someone who cannot stop drinking alcohol

alcove *noun* (*plural* **alcoves**) a space at the side of a room where the wall is set further back than the main part

ale *noun* (*plural* **ales**) a kind of beer

alert *adjective* watching out and ready to act ▸ *She was tired but had to stay alert while she drove us home.*

alert *verb* (**alerts, alerting, alerted**) to warn someone about a danger

algebra *noun* (*pronounced* **al-ji-bra**) a kind of mathematics in which letters and symbols are used to represent numbers

alias *noun* (*plural* **aliases**) (*pronounced* **ay-li-as**) a false name that someone uses instead of their real name

alibi *noun* (*plural* **alibis**) (*pronounced* **al-i-by**) information showing that someone suspected of a crime was not there when the crime was committed ▸ *Luckily we both had a good alibi for the night of the robbery.*

alien *noun* (*plural* **aliens**) (*pronounced* **ay-li-en**) someone from another country or (in stories) from another world

alien *adjective* foreign; from a strange place ▸ *The lights in the sky might have been from an alien spaceship.*

alight *adjective* on fire, burning

alike *adjective* similar, like each other ▸ *The three youngest brothers all looked alike.*

alike *adverb* in the same way ▸ *The twins always dress alike.*

alive *adjective* living, existing

alkali *noun* (*plural* **alkalis**) (*pronounced* **al-ka-ly**) a substance that neutralizes acids or that combines with acids to form salts **alkaline** *adjective*

all *adjective* and *adverb* and *noun* the whole of something; every person or thing ▸ *That is all I know.* ▸ *All my books are in the desk.* ▸ *She was dressed all in white.*

Allah the Muslim name for God

allege *verb* (**alleges, alleging, alleged**) (*pronounced* **a-lej**) to say that someone has done something without proving it ▸ *The woman alleged that someone had run off with her shopping bag.* **allegation** *noun* an accusation

allegiance *noun* (*plural* **allegiances**) (*pronounced* **a-lee-jans**) loyalty to a king or queen or to someone in authority

allergic *adjective* (*pronounced* **a-ler-jik**) becoming ill when you touch or eat a particular thing ▸ *I'm afraid I am allergic to cats.* **allergy** *noun*

alley *noun* (*plural* **alleys**) 1 a narrow street or passage 2 a place where you can play skittles or bowling

alliance *noun* (*plural* **alliances**) an agreement between countries to support each other

alligator *noun* (*plural* **alligators**) a large reptile like a crocodile, found mainly in America

allotment *noun* (*plural* **allotments**) a small piece of ground which someone rents and uses for growing vegetables, fruit, or flowers

allow *verb* (**allows, allowing, allowed**) 1 to let someone do something 2 to provide an amount of money for some reason ▸ *They only allowed £5 for bus fares and it wasn't enough.*

allowance *noun* (*plural* **allowances**) a sum of money that is given regularly to someone ▸ *Kate's Mum gave her a monthly allowance for clothes.*

alloy *noun* (*plural* **alloys**) a metal formed by mixing other metals ▸ *Brass is an alloy of copper and zinc.*

all right *adjective* satisfactory; in good condition ▸ *He put his hand on her arm and asked her if she was all right.* ▸ *All right, I'll sit on the floor over here.*

all-rounder *noun* someone who is good at different things

ally *noun* (*plural* **allies**) (*pronounced* **al**-I) a person or country that helps or supports another

almighty *adjective* 1 having total power 2 (informal) very great or loud ▸ *The door crashed against the wall with an almighty bang.*

almond *noun* (*plural* **almonds**) (*pronounced* **ah**-mond) a flat oval nut that you can eat

almost *adverb* very nearly but not quite ▸ *Jane jumped forward and almost banged her head on the glass.*

alone *adjective* and *adverb* without any other people or things, on your own ▸ *As soon as Mark opened the door he knew he was not alone.*

along *preposition* and *adverb* 1 from one end of something to the other ▸ *The nurse was pushing a trolley along the corridor.* 2 going somewhere with someone ▸ *Our friends enjoyed the outing and were glad we had taken them along.*

alongside *preposition* and *adverb* beside something and close to it

aloud *adverb* in an ordinary voice that people can hear

alphabet *noun* (*plural* **alphabets**) the letters used in a language arranged in a special order **alphabetical** *adjective* **alphabetically** *adverb*

already *adverb* by or before now ▸ *When the phone rang, Claire had already left the house.*

Alsatian *noun* (*plural* **Alsatians**) (*pronounced* al-**say**-shan) a large strong dog with a thick coat and a long pointed nose

also *adverb* as an extra, besides ▸ *We also need some bread.*

altar *noun* (*plural* **altars**) a table or raised surface in a church or temple, used in religious ceremonies or to perform sacrifices

alter *verb* (**alters, altering, altered**) to change something slightly to make it more suitable ▸ *The dress was too long and her mother had to alter it.* **alteration** *noun*

alternate *adjective* (*pronounced* ol-**ter**-nat) every other one ▸ *I visit my grandparents on alternate weekends.* **alternately** *adverb* one after the other in turn

alternative *noun* (*plural* **alternatives**) (*pronounced* ol-**ter**-na-tiv) something you can choose or use instead of something else ▸ *Blinds are a good alternative to curtains in kitchens and work-rooms.*

alternative *adjective* for you to choose instead of something else ▸ *There is an alternative route if you don't want to go through London.*

although *conjunction* even though ▸ *Although the sun was shining, it was still cold.*

altitude *noun* (*plural* **altitudes**) the height of something above sea level

altogether *adverb* **1** completely ▸ *The excuse was not altogether convincing.* **2** as a total, in all ▸ *We made £50 altogether at the cake sale.*

aluminium *noun* a silver-coloured metal that is light in weight

always *adverb* **1** all the time, at all times **2** often, constantly ▸ *The family always go for a long walk on Sundays.* **3** whatever happens ▸ *I could always sleep on the floor.*

am a form of the verb **be** used when the person speaking is referring to himself or herself

a.m. short for Latin *ante meridiem*, which means 'before midday'. You use it to show the time in the morning. ▸ *Wake me at 7 a.m.*

amalgamate *verb* (**amalgamates, amalgamating, amalgamated**) to join things together to form one thing

amateur *noun* (*plural* **amateurs**) (*pronounced* **am-a-ter**) someone who does something because they enjoy it, and not for money ▸ *The orchestra was a mixture of amateur and professional musicians.*
amateur *adjective* done by amateurs

amaze *verb* (**amazes, amazing, amazed**) to surprise or astonish someone very much ▸ *We were amazed that our phone bill was so low.* **amazement** *noun*

ambassador *noun* (*plural* **ambassadors**) an official who is sent to represent a country in another country

amber *noun* **1** a hard clear dark yellow substance often containing fossils of insects and used for jewellery **2** a yellowish colour

ambiguous *adjective* having more than one possible meaning, uncertain ▸ *The words of the song were rather ambiguous.* **ambiguity** *noun*

ambition *noun* (*plural* **ambitions**) **1** a strong desire to be successful in life **2** something you want to do very much ▸ *Polly's ambition was to become a doctor like her mother.* **ambitious** *adjective* having a lot of ambition

amble *verb* (**ambles, ambling, ambled**) to walk along gently without hurrying

ambulance *noun* (*plural* **ambulances**) a special vehicle for carrying sick or injured people

ambush *noun* (*plural* **ambushes**) a surprise attack from a hidden place
ambush *verb* (**ambushes, ambushing, ambushed**) to attack someone in an ambush

amend *verb* (**amends, amending, amended**) to change a piece of writing so that it is better or more accurate **amendment** *noun*

amiable *adjective* friendly, good-tempered **amiability** *noun* **amiably** *adverb*

amicable *adjective* friendly **amicably** *adverb*

amid or **amidst** *preposition* in the middle of, among

ammonia *noun* a gas or liquid with a sharp smell, used to make cleaning liquids

ammunition *noun* bullets, shells, and other objects fired from guns

amnesty *noun* (*plural* **amnesties**) a promise to free prisoners or to pardon people who have broken the law

amoeba *noun* (*plural* **amoebas**)
(*pronounced* a-**mee**-ba) a tiny creature
made of one cell, which can change shape
and split itself in two

among or **amongst** *preposition*
1 surrounded by, in the middle of ▶ *The
heron dived and disappeared among the
reeds.* 2 between ▶ *They decided to divide
the money amongst themselves.*

amount *noun* (*plural* **amounts**) how much
of something there is ▶ *We were alarmed
at the amount of blood running down
Jennifer's face.*
amount *verb* (**amounts, amounting,
amounted**) to add up to a total ▶ *The
train fares amounted to over half the cost of
the trip.*

ample *adjective* (**ampler, amplest**) more
than enough, plenty ▶ *There was food in
the fridge and an ample supply of coal and
logs in the shed.* **amply** *adverb* generously;
with plenty

amplifier *noun* (*plural* **amplifiers**) a piece
of electronic equipment for making music
or other sounds louder

amplify *verb* (**amplifies, amplifying,
amplified**) to make sounds louder or
stronger

amputate *verb* (**amputates, amputating,
amputated**) to cut off a part of the body
when it is diseased **amputation** *noun*

amuse *verb* (**amuses, amusing, amused**)
1 to make someone laugh or smile 2 to
find pleasant things to do ▶ *I had been
quietly amusing myself for several minutes.*
amusing *adjective*

amusement *noun* (*plural* **amusements**)
1 something pleasant that you do to pass
the time 2 being amused; laughing or
smiling

anaemia *noun* (*pronounced* a-**nee**-mi-a)
a poor condition of the blood that makes
you pale and tired **anaemic** *adjective*
suffering from anaemia

anaesthetic *noun* (*plural* **anaesthetics**)
(*pronounced* an-iss-**thet**-ik) a drug or gas
that makes you unable to feel pain

anagram *noun* (*plural* **anagrams**) a word
or phrase made by mixing up the letters of
another word or phrase
Here are some examples of anagrams: **carthorse** for
orchestra, **groan** for **organ**, **ideals** for **ladies**, and
nameless for **salesmen**; an example of a phrase is
they see for **the eyes**.

analyse *verb* (**analyses, analysing,
analysed**) to examine something carefully
to find out about it **analytic** or **analytical**
adjective **analyst** *noun* someone who does
an analysis of something

analysis *noun* a detailed study or
examination of something

anarchy *noun* a situation in which no one
obeys the laws and government of a
country **anarchist** someone who thinks
anarchy is a good thing

anatomy *noun* the study of the parts of
the body **anatomical** *adjective*

ancestor *noun* (*plural* **ancestors**)
someone from your family who lived in
the past **ancestral** *adjective* **ancestry** *noun*
a person's ancestors

anchor *noun* (*plural* **anchors**) a heavy
object with hooks at the end that is
dropped from a ship to stop it from
moving **anchorage** *noun* a place where
ships can stay

ancient *adjective* belonging to times that
were long ago ▶ *The walls of the cave were
covered with ancient carvings.*

and *conjunction* a word used to link other
words and phrases

anemone *noun* (*plural* **anemones**)
(*pronounced* a-**nem**-on-i) a small flower
with the shape of a cup

angel *noun* (*plural* **angels**) a being that
some people believe in, who is a
messenger of God **angelic** *adjective* kind
and beautiful

anger *noun* a strong feeling that you want
to quarrel or fight with someone

angle *noun* (*plural* **angles**) the space
between two lines or surfaces that meet

angling *noun* the sport of fishing with a
fishing rod

angry *adjective* (**angrier, angriest**) feeling or showing anger, cross **angrily** *adverb*

anguish *noun* great sorrow or mental pain ▸ *The man screwed up his face in anguish and let out a long moan.* **anguished** *adjective*

animal *noun* (*plural* **animals**) a being that is alive and can move and feel, such as a horse, elephant, whale, fish, bird, or insect

animation *noun* a way of making films using still pictures or puppets so they appear to move

aniseed *noun* a seed with a strong sweet taste like liquorice

ankle *noun* (*plural* **ankles**) the joint that connects your leg with your foot

annexe *noun* (*plural* **annexes**) (*pronounced* **an-eks**) a building added to a larger building

annihilate *verb* (**annihilates, annihilating, annihilated**) (*pronounced* a-ny-il-ayt) to destroy something completely or kill a large number of people **annihilation** *noun*

anniversary *noun* (*plural* **anniversaries**) a day each year when you remember something special that happened on the same date in an earlier year

announce *verb* (**announces, announcing, announced**) to say something important to a group of people **announcement** *noun* something announced in a newspaper or on television **announcer** *noun* someone who announces something, especially on radio or television

annoy *verb* (**annoys, annoying, annoyed**) to make someone feel cross about something

annual *adjective* happening or coming every year **annually** *adverb* every year

annual *noun* (*plural* **annuals**) a book that comes out with different contents each year

anonymous *adjective* (not an everyday word) without the name of the author or writer being known ▸ *Frances received an anonymous letter.* **anonymously** *adverb*

anorak *noun* (*plural* **anoraks**) a thick warm waterproof jacket with a hood

anorexia *noun* (*pronounced* an-er-eks-ee-a) an illness that makes you not want to eat **anorexic** *adjective*

another *adjective* and *pronoun* **1** an extra or additional thing ▸ *Would you like another drink?* **2** a different person or thing ▸ *If that one doesn't work try another.*

answer *noun* (*plural* **answers**) **1** what you say when someone asks you a question or writes to you ▸ *She told me to think about it and give her an answer tomorrow.* **2** an idea or suggestion that solves a problem or difficulty

answer *verb* (**answers, answering, answered**) **1** to give someone an answer ▸ *At the end of her talk the speaker said she'd answer any questions.* ▸ *The boy left the room without answering her.* **2** to pick up a telephone when it rings

ant *noun* (*plural* **ants**) a small crawling insect that lives in large groups

antagonize *verb* (**antagonizes, antagonizing, antagonized**) (not an everyday word) to make someone feel anger towards you **antagonism** a feeling of anger

Antarctic or **Antarctica** *noun* the area round the South Pole

antelope *noun* (*plural* **antelope** or **antelopes**) a graceful animal like a deer, found in Africa and parts of Asia

antenna *noun* **1** (*plural* **antennae**) a feeler on the head of an insect or shellfish **2** (*plural* **antennas**) an aerial

anthem *noun* (*plural* **anthems**) a religious or patriotic song

anthology *noun* (*plural* **anthologies**) a collection of poems, stories, or songs in one book

anticipate *verb* (**anticipates, anticipating, anticipated**) to expect something and be ready for it ▸ *The police were anticipating trouble at the football match.* **anticipation** *noun*

anticlimax *noun* (*plural* **anticlimaxes**) a disappointing ending or result ▶ *The weather was beautiful but the outing itself proved to be an anticlimax.*

anticlockwise *adverb* and *adjective* moving in the opposite direction to the hands of a clock

antics *plural noun* strange or amusing behaviour ▶ *I was watching the antics of a seabird that had found a crab.*

antidote *noun* (*plural* **antidotes**) something which takes away the bad effects of a poison or disease

antiquated *adjective* old-fashioned ▶ *The people who bought the house threw out the antiquated old boiler and put in smart new central heating.*

antique *noun* (*plural* **antiques**) (*pronounced* an-**teek**) something that is old and valuable

antiseptic *noun* (*plural* **antiseptics**) a chemical that kills germs

antler *noun* (*plural* **antlers**) the branched horns of a deer

anvil *noun* (*plural* **anvils**) a large block of iron on which a blacksmith hammers metal into shape

anxious *adjective* **1** worried and nervous ▶ *I was anxious about singing on stage.* **2** eager to do something ▶ *Her mother was anxious to get to work and couldn't wait any longer.* **anxiety** *noun* a feeling of being worried

any *adjective* **1** one or some ▶ *Is there any milk?* **2** no matter which ▶ *Come any day you like.* **3** every ▶ *Any fool can do that!*

any *adverb* at all; in some degree ▶ *Is it any good?*

anybody *noun* and *pronoun* any person

anyhow *adverb* **1** in any case ▶ *It's raining, anyhow.* **2** whatever happens ▶ *Anyhow, I'm not going to stay.* **3** (informal) carelessly, without much thought ▶ *Books were placed anyhow on the shelves.*

anyone *noun* and *pronoun* any person

anything *noun* and *pronoun* any thing

anyway *adverb* whatever happens; whatever the situation may be ▶ *The shops are probably closed, but let's go anyway.*

anywhere *adverb* in any place or to any place

apart *adverb* **1** away from each other; separately ▶ *The friends were living apart now.* **2** into pieces ▶ *They tried to build a tree house but the sides kept falling apart.*

apartment *noun* (*plural* **apartments**) a flat or set of rooms

ape *noun* (*plural* **apes**) an animal like a monkey without a tail, such as a gorilla or a chimpanzee

apex *noun* (*plural* **apexes**) the highest point of something

apologetic *adjective* saying you are sorry **apologetically** *adverb*

apologize *verb* (**apologizes, apologizing, apologized**) to say you are sorry **apology** *noun*

apostle *noun* (*plural* **apostles**) in Christianity, one of the twelve men sent out by Christ to teach people

apostrophe *noun* (*plural* **apostrophes**) (*pronounced* a-**pos**-tro-fi) a punctuation mark (')
An apostrophe is used to show that letters have been left out, as in *don't* and *she'll*. It is also used with *s* to show who owns something, as in *the woman's hat* (one woman), *the boys' books* (more than one boy).

appal *verb* (**appals, appalling, appalled**) to shock someone very much ▶ *The violence appalled everyone.* **appalling** *adjective* dreadful, shocking

apparatus *noun* a set of equipment used in a scientific experiment or to do a special task

apparent *adjective* 1 clear, obvious ▸ *It soon became apparent that they had taken the wrong road.* 2 appearing to be true ▸ *We were surprised by their apparent wealth.*

apparently *adverb* as it seems, so it appears ▸ *The house was apparently empty.*

appeal *verb* (**appeals, appealing, appealed**) 1 to ask for something you need ▸ *The hospital is appealing for money to build a new kidney unit.* 2 to interest or be attractive to someone ▸ *The idea of going to bed early didn't appeal to us much.* 3 to ask for a decision made in a lawcourt to be changed in a higher court

appeal *noun* (*plural* **appeals**) 1 what makes something interesting ▸ *I can't see the appeal of collecting stamps.* 2 asking for something you need

appear *verb* (**appears, appearing, appeared**) 1 to become visible ▸ *A ship appeared on the horizon.* 2 to seem ▸ *They appeared very anxious.* 3 to take part as an actor in a film or play

appearance *noun* (*plural* **appearances**) 1 coming into sight ▸ *The appearance of the bus was a great relief.* 2 what someone or something looks like ▸ *Dolly checked her appearance in the mirror.*

appease *verb* (**appeases, appeasing, appeased**) to make someone less angry with you by giving them what they want **appeasement** *noun*

appendicitis *noun* a disease of the appendix

appendix *noun* 1 (*plural* **appendixes**) a small tube leading off from the intestines in the body 2 (*plural* **appendices**) an extra section at the end of a book

appetite *noun* (*plural* **appetites**) a desire for food

appetizing *adjective* looking good to eat

applaud *verb* (**applauds, applauding, applauded**) to show that you like what someone has done, usually by clapping **applause** *noun* clapping or cheering

apple *noun* (*plural* **apples**) a hard round fruit with red, green, or yellow skin

appliance *noun* (*plural* **appliances**) a machine or device

apply *verb* (**applies, applying, applied**) 1 to write formally to ask for a job 2 to put something on something else ▸ *We need to apply another coat of paint.* 3 to be relevant ▸ *These rules apply to you too.* **application** *noun*

appoint *verb* (**appoints, appointing, appointed**) to choose someone for a job

appointment *noun* (*plural* **appointments**) 1 an arrangement to meet or visit someone 2 a job or position

appreciate *verb* (**appreciates, appreciating, appreciated**) 1 to enjoy or be grateful for something ▸ *It is good to perform for people who appreciate good singing.* 2 to increase in value **appreciation** *noun* **appreciative** *adjective* enjoying or valuing something ▸ *I enjoy playing to an appreciative audience.*

apprehensive *adjective* nervous and afraid **apprehension** *noun*

apprentice *noun* (*plural* **apprentices**) a young person who is learning a trade or craft **apprenticeship** *noun*

approach *verb* (**approaches, approaching, approached**) to come near to a person or place

approach *noun* (*plural* **approaches**) 1 a way or road leading up to a building ▸ *The approach to the house had trees on each side.* 2 a way of dealing with a task or problem ▸ *Let's try a different approach.*

appropriate *adjective* suitable

approve *verb* (**approves, approving, approved**) to think that someone or something is good or suitable **approval** *noun*

approximate *adjective* roughly correct but not exact ▸ *The approximate cost of the trip will be £50.* **approximately** *adverb*

apricot *noun* (*plural* **apricots**) a juicy orange-coloured fruit like a small peach

April *noun* the fourth month of the year
The word **April** may come from a Latin word *aperio* meaning 'to open', referring to the opening of flowers in spring.

apron *noun* (*plural* **aprons**) a piece of clothing worn over the front of your body to protect your clothes

apt *adjective* (not an everyday word)
1 likely to do something ▸ *The younger children are apt to wander off.* **2** suitable ▸ *Let's find some apt pieces of music for the party.*

aptitude *noun* (not an everyday word) a natural ability to do something well

aquarium *noun* (*plural* **aquariums**)
1 a glass tank for keeping live fish
2 a building in a zoo in which fish are kept

aquatic *adjective* to do with water; living in water ▸ *A fish tank always looks better with a few aquatic plants.*

aqueduct *noun* (*plural* **aqueducts**) a bridge that carries water across a valley

Arab *noun* (*plural* **Arabs**) a member of a people living in Arabia and other parts of the Middle East and North Africa

Arabic *noun* the language of the Arabs

arabic figures or **arabic numerals** *plural noun* the figures 1, 2, 3, 4, and so on (compare *Roman numerals*)

arable *adjective* suitable for growing crops

arbitrary *adjective* (*pronounced* ar-bi-trer-i) (not an everyday word) done or chosen at random or without a proper reason ▸ *The decision to punish everyone seemed arbitrary and unfair.*

arc *noun* (*plural* **arcs**) part of the circumference of a circle, a curve

arcade *noun* (*plural* **arcades**) a covered place to walk, with shops down each side

arch *noun* (*plural* **arches**) a curved structure that helps to support a bridge or building

arch *verb* (**arches, arching, arched**) to make a curved shape ▸ *The cat stretched and then arched its back.*

archaeology *noun* (*pronounced* ar-ki-ol-o-ji) the study of ancient people from the remains of their buildings and other objects that have survived **archaeological** *adjective* **archaeologist** *noun* someone who studies archaeology

archbishop *noun* (*plural* **archbishops**) the chief bishop of a region

archer *noun* (*plural* **archers**) someone who shoots with a bow and arrows

archery *noun* the sport of shooting with a bow and arrows

archipelago *noun* (*plural* **archipelagos**) (*pronounced* ar-ki-**pel**-ago) a group of islands

architect *noun* (*plural* **architects**) (*pronounced* ar-ki-tekt) someone whose work is to design buildings **architecture** *noun*

Arctic *noun* the area round the North Pole

are a form of the verb **be**

area *noun* (*plural* **areas**) **1** the size of a surface, measured in square metres, square yards, or other units **2** a part of the surface of something **3** a part of a place or region ▸ *Jan's family has just moved to a smarter area.*

arena *noun* (*plural* **arenas**) (*pronounced* a-ree-na) a place where a sports event takes place

aren't short for *am not* or *are not* ▸ *Aren't I allowed to come?* ▸ *They obviously aren't interested.*

argue *verb* (**argues, arguing, argued**) **1** to disagree or quarrel with someone **2** to give reasons for something ▸ *She argued that flying is safer than going by train.*

argument *noun* (*plural* **arguments**) a disagreement or quarrel

arid *adjective* (not an everyday word) dry and barren ▸ *The film was set in an arid desert landscape.*

arise *verb* (**arises, arising, arose, arisen**) to begin or become known ▸ *Some confusion has arisen over what exactly happened.*

aristocracy *noun* (*plural* **aristocracies**) the people from important families who often have titles such as *Lord* and *Lady* **aristocrat** *noun* a nobleman or noblewoman **aristocratic** *adjective*

arithmetic *noun* the study of using numbers **arithmetical** *adjective*

ark *noun* (*plural* **arks**) in the Bible, the ship in which Noah and his family escaped the Flood

arm *noun* (*plural* **arms**) 1 the part of your body between your shoulder and your hand 2 the sleeve of a coat or dress 3 something that works like an arm or sticks out like an arm

arm *verb* (**arms, arming, armed**) 1 to give someone weapons 2 to prepare for war

armada *noun* (*plural* **armadas**) (*pronounced* ar-mah-da) a fleet of warships

armadillo *noun* (*plural* **armadillos**) a South American animal with a shell of bony plates

armaments *plural noun* weapons and equipment for fighting

armchair *noun* (*plural* **armchairs**) a chair with supports on each side to rest your arms on

armed forces *plural noun* the army, navy, and air force of a country

armful *noun* (*plural* **armfuls**) as much of something as you can hold in your arms ▸ *Mary came back with an armful of twigs from the garden.*

armistice *noun* (*plural* **armistices**) an agreement to stop fighting in a war or battle

armour *noun* a metal suit or covering to protect people or equipment in battle **armoured** *adjective*

armpit *noun* (*plural* **armpits**) the hollow part under your arm at your shoulder

arms *plural noun* (not an everyday word) weapons ▸ *Our government is selling arms to other countries.*

army *noun* (*plural* **armies**) a large number of soldiers ready to fight

aroma *noun* (*plural* **aromas**) (*pronounced* a-roh-ma) a pleasant smell of food or cooking

arose past tense of **arise**

around *adverb* and *preposition* round or about

arouse *verb* (**arouses, arousing, aroused**) 1 to make someone wake up 2 to stir up feelings

arrange *verb* (**arranges, arranging, arranged**) 1 to put a number of things in the position you want 2 to plan or organize an event or meeting **arrangement** *noun*

arrest *verb* (**arrests, arresting, arrested**) to take someone prisoner because they may have committed a crime

arrest *noun* (*plural* **arrests**) an act of arresting someone

arrive *verb* (**arrives, arriving, arrived**) 1 to reach a place at the end of a journey 2 to happen or take place ▸ *The day of the outing arrived.* **arrival** *noun*

arrogant *adjective* proud and conceited in an unpleasant way **arrogance** *noun* **arrogantly** *adverb*

arrow *noun* (*plural* **arrows**) 1 a long thin pointed stick you shoot from a bow 2 a sign in the shape of an arrow, used to show a direction

arsenal *noun* (*plural* **arsenals**) a place where weapons and ammunition are kept

arsenic *noun* a strong poison

arson *noun* the crime of deliberately setting fire to a building

art *noun* (*plural* **arts**) 1 making things of beauty such as drawings, paintings, sculptures, or music 2 a special skill

artery *noun* (*plural* **arteries**) one of the tubes that carry blood from your heart to parts of your body

artful *adjective* clever at deceiving people **artfully** *adverb*

arthritis *noun* (*pronounced* arth-ry-tiss)
a disease that makes joints in your body
painful and stiff **arthritic** *adjective*

article *noun* (*plural* **articles**) 1 an object
that you can touch or pick up 2 a piece of
writing published in a newspaper or
magazine

articulated lorry *noun* (*plural*
articulated lorries) a large lorry in sections
with joints between them, so that it can
turn more easily

artificial *adjective* made by human beings
and not by nature **artificially** *adverb*

artillery *noun* (*plural* **artilleries**)
1 a collection of large guns used by an
army 2 the part of an army that uses them

artist *noun* (*plural* **artists**) someone who
paints or produces works of art **artistic**
adjective showing beauty and imagination
artistry *noun* the skill of an artist

as *conjunction, adverb,* and *preposition*
linking words and phrases ▸ *As it's late,
we'd better not stay.* ▸ *He fell over as he was
crossing the road.* ▸ *It is not as hard as you
think.*
You use **as** to make special phrases called *similes*,
for example *as green as grass* and *as cold as ice.*

asbestos *noun* a fireproof material that is
made up of fine soft fibres

ascend *verb* (**ascends, ascending,
ascended**) to climb or go up **ascent** *noun*

ash *noun* (*plural* **ashes**) 1 the powder that
is left after something has been burned 2 a
tree with silvery bark and winged seeds

ashamed *adjective* feeling guilty or upset
about something you have done

ashore *adverb* on the shore

aside *adverb* to one side; away

ask *verb* (**asks, asking, asked**) 1 to speak to
someone so as to get information from
them or to get them to do something ▸ *I'll
ask them what time the bus goes.* 2 to say
that you want something ▸ *Ask for a
drink.* 3 to invite someone ▸ *Did you ask
them to our party?*

asleep *adverb* and *adjective* sleeping

aspect *noun* (*plural* **aspects**) (not an
everyday word) a particular way in which
you think about something ▸ *The book
deals with every aspect of keeping birds.*

asphalt *noun* (*pronounced* **ass**-falt) a
sticky black stuff like tar, which is mixed
with gravel to make a hard surface for the
ground

aspirin *noun* (*plural* **aspirins**) a drug used
to relieve pain or reduce fever

ass *noun* (*plural* **asses**) 1 a donkey
2 (informal) a fool ▸ *Shaun, you are an
ass!*

assassinate *verb* (**assassinates,
assassinating, assassinated**) to kill
someone important **assassin** *noun* a person
who assassinates someone **assassination**
noun

assault *noun* (*plural* **assaults**) a sudden or
violent attack on someone
assault *verb* (**assaults, assaulting,
assaulted**) to attack someone violently

assemble *verb* (**assembles, assembling,
assembled**) 1 to make something by
putting the parts together 2 to bring
people or things together 3 to come
together in one place

assembly *noun* (*plural* **assemblies**)
1 a gathering of people for a meeting or
discussion 2 putting the parts together to
make something

assert *verb* (**asserts, asserting, asserted**)
(not an everyday word) to say something
strongly and clearly **assertion** *noun*
something you say clearly and strongly
assertive *adjective* speaking or behaving
firmly and with authority

assess verb (**assesses, assessing, assessed**)
to form an opinion about something by
studying it carefully ▶ *Some officials came
to assess the flood damage.* **assessment**
noun

asset noun (*plural* **assets**) something
useful or valuable

assign verb (**assign, assigning, assigned**) to
give something to someone as a share or
duty ▶ *A different teacher is assigned to
each subject.*

assignment noun (*plural* **assignments**)
a piece of work that someone is given to
do

assist verb (**assists, assisting, assisted**) to
help someone in a practical way **assistance**
noun practical help **assistant** *noun*
someone who gives help, especially as
their job

associate verb (**associates, associating,
associated**) (*pronounced* a-**soh**-shi-ayt) to
connect things in your mind ▶ *I associate
July with sun and holidays.*

association noun (*plural* **associations**) an
organization for people sharing an interest
or doing the same work

assorted adjective of various sorts; mixed
assortment noun a mixture

assume verb (**assumes, assuming,
assumed**) to think or say something
without being sure of it ▶ *I assume you
will be coming tomorrow.* **assumption** noun
something you assume

assure verb (**assures, assuring, assured**) to
tell someone something definite ▶ *He
assured us we had a good chance of seeing a
badger.* **assurance** noun

asteroid noun (*plural* **asteroids**) a small
planet

asthma noun (*pronounced* **ass**-ma)
a disease which makes breathing difficult
asthmatic adjective

astonish verb (**astonishes, astonishing,
astonished**) to surprise someone very
much **astonishment** noun

astound verb (**astounds, astounding,
astounded**) to amaze or shock someone
very much

astray adjective go **astray** be lost or mislaid

astrology noun the study of the
movements of planets and stars and how
these may affect people's lives **astrologer**
noun someone who studies astrology
astrological adjective

astronaut noun (*plural* **astronauts**)
someone who travels in a spacecraft

astronomy noun the study of the sun,
moon, planets, and stars **astronomer** noun
someone who studies astronomy
astronomical adjective

at preposition showing where someone or
something is ▶ *I was at home and not at
the shops.* ▶ *He turned round to look at her.*

ate past tense of **eat**

atheist noun (*plural* **atheists**) someone
who does not believe that there is a God
atheism noun

athlete noun (*plural* **athletes**) someone
who is good at athletics or other sports

athletics plural noun physical exercises
and sports such as running and jumping
athletic adjective

atlas noun (*plural* **atlases**) a book of maps

atmosphere noun (*plural* **atmospheres**)
1 the air around the earth 2 a feeling you
get in a room or at a place ▶ *The
classroom was large and the atmosphere
was good to work in.* **atmospheric** adjective

atom noun (*plural* **atoms**) 1 the smallest
possible part of a chemical element
2 a tiny part of something **atomic** adjective

atom bomb or **atomic bomb** noun
(*plural* **atom bombs** or **atomic bombs**) a
bomb that explodes from the energy made
by splitting atoms, and has nuclear fallout

atrocious adjective (*pronounced* a-**troh**-
shus) wicked, terrible

atrocity *noun* (*plural* **atrocities**) a terrible and cruel act, such as the killing of a large number of people

attach *verb* (**attaches, attaching, attached**) to fix or fasten one thing to another **attachment** *noun* an extra part fitted to a machine or tool

attack *verb* (**attacks, attacking, attacked**) to try to hurt someone with violence or with angry words
attack *noun* (*plural* **attacks**) 1 an act of attacking someone 2 a sudden illness or pain

attain *verb* (**attains, attaining, attained**) (not an everyday word) to reach or achieve something ▶ *Three clarinet pupils attained Grade 3 last term.* **attainment** *noun* something you have achieved

attempt *verb* (**attempts, attempting, attempted**) to make an effort to do something
attempt *noun* (*plural* **attempts**) making an effort to do something ▶ *They will make another attempt to go round the world in a balloon.*

attend *verb* (**attends, attending, attended**) 1 to be present at a meeting or event 2 to be a pupil or student at a school or college **attend to** 1 to deal with someone or something 2 to listen to what someone is saying **attendance** *noun* being present at a meeting or event

attendant *noun* (*plural* **attendants**) an official whose job is to help people

attention *noun* giving care or thought to someone or something

attentive *adjective* listening carefully ▶ *Most of the audience was attentive but some people were chatting or fidgeting.*

attic *noun* (*plural* **attics**) a room or space under the roof of a house

attitude *noun* (*plural* **attitudes**) 1 the way you think or behave ▶ *People have different attitudes about how to spend their holidays.* 2 the position of your body ▶ *She was sitting in an awkward attitude.* .

attract *verb* (**attracts, attracting, attracted**) 1 to seem pleasant to someone or something and get their attention or interest ▶ *Nuts are hung in the branches to attract birds.* 2 to pull something by a physical force like magnetism **attraction** *noun* the power to attract someone; something that is pleasant or interesting

attractive *adjective* pleasant or interesting **attractively** *adverb*

auburn *adjective* reddish-brown

auction *noun* (*plural* **auctions**) a sale at which things are sold to the person who offers to pay the most money **auctioneer** *noun* someone in charge of an auction

audible *adjective* loud enough to be heard **audibly** *adverb*

audience *noun* (*plural* **audiences**) the people watching or listening to entertainment such as a concert or film

audio *noun* (*pronounced* **aw-di-oh**) music and sound produced by electronic equipment such as CD players

audition *noun* (*plural* **auditions**) a test to see if a performer is suitable to act in a play or film or to sing in a choir

auditorium *noun* (*plural* **auditoriums**) (*pronounced* **aw-dit-or-i-um**) the part of a theatre or concert hall where the audience sits

August *noun* the eighth month of the year
The word **August** comes from the name of the Roman Emperor Augustus. It became the name of the Roman month in 8 BC because it was thought to be his lucky month.

aunt *noun* (*plural* **aunts**) the sister of your mother or father, or your uncle's wife

au pair *noun* (*plural* **au pairs**) (*pronounced* **oh-pair**) a young person from another country, who lives with a family and helps in the house

authentic *adjective* real, genuine **authenticity** *noun*

author *noun* (*plural* **authors**) a person who writes a book or play or poem **authorship** *noun*

authority noun (plural **authorities**) 1 the power to give orders to other people ▶ *The police have the authority to search suspects.* 2 a group of people who have the power to make decisions ▶ *Our local authority runs a recycling scheme.* 3 an expert on a subject ▶ *Dave is an authority on tropical fish.*

authorize verb (**authorizes, authorizing, authorized**) to give official permission to someone to do something

autistic adjective having a disability that makes someone unable to communicate with other people **autism** noun

autobiography noun (plural **autobiographies**) the story of a person's life that is written by that person **autobiographical** adjective

autograph noun (plural **autographs**) the name of a famous person written in their own handwriting

automatic adjective 1 working by itself without being controlled by human beings 2 done without thinking ▶ *It is automatic to screw up your eyes in bright light.* **automatically** adverb by automatic means

automation noun (pronounced aw-tom-ay-shun) the use of machines instead of people to do work in factories

automobile noun (plural **automobiles**) (in America) a car

autumn noun (plural **autumns**) (pronounced **aw-tum**) the season between summer and winter, when leaves fall off the trees **autumnal** adjective

available adjective able to be found or used ▶ *The theme music is now available on a CD.* **availability** noun

avalanche noun (plural **avalanches**) (pronounced **av-a-lahnsh**) a sudden heavy fall of snow and ice down the side of a mountain

avenge verb (**avenges, avenging, avenged**) to do harm to someone for something bad they have done to you or to someone else

avenue noun (plural **avenues**) a wide street with trees down each side

average noun (plural **averages**) the number you get by adding several amounts together and dividing the total by the number of amounts, for example the average of 2, 4, 6, and 8 is 5

average adjective of the usual or ordinary standard; normal, ordinary ▶ *On an average day the store will get about two thousand customers.*

average verb (**averages, averaging, averaged**) to have as an average ▶ *The amount we spent averaged £100 a week.*

aviary noun (plural **aviaries**) a place where birds are kept

avid adjective keen, eager ▶ *Susan is an avid reader but her sister is not so keen.*

avoid verb (**avoids, avoiding, avoided**) to keep yourself away from someone or something ▶ *He used country roads to avoid the traffic.* **avoidance** noun

await verb (**awaits, awaiting, awaited**) to wait for someone or something

awake adjective not sleeping

awake verb (**awakes, awaking, awoke, awoken**) to wake up

awaken verb (**awakens, awakening, awakened**) to wake up

award noun (plural **awards**) a prize or special payment given to a person

award verb (**awards, awarding, awarded**) to give someone an award

aware adjective knowing about something ▶ *I was soon aware of something running through the grass.* **awareness** noun

away adverb at a distance or somewhere else ▶ *If any food is left over we have to throw it away.*

away adjective not at home

awe noun fear and wonder ▶ *The mountains filled him with awe.*

awful adjective 1 (informal) very bad; very great ▶ *Sharon had an awful pain in her stomach.* 2 causing fear or horror ▶ *Everyone agrees that war is awful.*

awfully adverb (informal) very, extremely ▶ *It's awfully late.*

awhile adverb for a short time

awkward *adjective* **1** difficult to use or cope with ▸ *The doors were narrow and awkward to get through.* **2** embarrassed and uncomfortable ▸ *John felt awkward in a bow tie.*

awoke past tense of **awake** *verb*

awoken past participle of **awake** *verb*

axe *noun* (*plural* **axes**) a tool for chopping wood

axis *noun* (*plural* **axes**) an imaginary line through the centre of an object that turns ▸ *The earth rotates on its axis once every 24 hours.*

axle *noun* (*plural* **axles**) the rod through the centre of a wheel, on which it turns

Bb

babble *verb* (**babbles, babbling, babbled**) to talk quickly in a way that is difficult to understand

baboon *noun* (*plural* **baboons**) a large kind of African monkey

baby *noun* (*plural* **babies**) a very young child

babyish *adjective* silly and childish

babysit *verb* (**babysits, babysitting, babysat**) to look after a child while its parents are out **babysitter** *noun* someone who babysits

bachelor *noun* (*plural* **bachelors**) a man who is not married

back *noun* (*plural* **backs**) **1** the part of your body between your shoulders and your bottom **2** the upper part of a four-legged animal's body **3** the part of a thing that faces away from the front ▸ *Jack walked towards the back of the house.*

back *adverb* to where someone or something has come from ▸ *We all went back into the living room.*

back *verb* (**backs, backing, backed**) **1** to move backwards **2** to support someone or give them help

backbone *noun* (*plural* **backbones**) the bones down your back, the spine

background *noun* (*plural* **backgrounds**) **1** the part of a scene or picture that looks farthest away **2** the things that happened before an event and help to explain it **3** a person's family and education

backing *noun* **1** support or help **2** a musical accompaniment, especially for a singer

backpack *noun* (*plural* **backpacks**) a bag that you carry on your back while walking or travelling

backstroke *noun* a stroke you use when swimming on your back

backward *adjective* **1** facing the back **2** slow in learning

backwards *adverb* **1** towards the back **2** from the end to the beginning ▸ *Count backwards from 100 to 1.*

bacon *noun* smoked or salted meat from the back or sides of a pig

bacteria *plural noun* tiny organisms that can cause diseases

bad *adjective* (**worse, worst**) **1** of the kind that you do not want or like, the opposite of 'good' **2** wicked or naughty **3** not fit to eat ▸ *Some meat had been left in the sun and had gone bad.*

badge *noun* (*plural* **badges**) a small piece of metal or cloth you pin to your clothes to tell people something about you ▸ *I got a badge for swimming 100 metres.*

badger *noun* (*plural* **badgers**) a grey animal with a white stripe along its nose, which lives underground and is active at night

badger *verb* (**badgers, badgering, badgered**) to pester someone

badly *adverb* **1** in a bad way ► *She slept badly and felt tired the next day.* **2** very much ► *If you want something badly enough you usually get it.* **badly off** poor or unfortunate

badminton *noun* a game in which players use rackets to hit a light object called a *shuttlecock* backwards and forwards over a high net

baffle *verb* (**baffles, baffling, baffled**) to puzzle someone completely

bag *noun* (*plural* **bags**) a container made of soft material, for carrying things

bag *verb* (**bags, bagging, bagged**) to get hold of something or take it ► *Jane always managed to bag the best place.*

bagel *noun* (*plural* **bagels**) a hard ring-shaped bread roll

baggage *noun* the luggage you take on a journey

baggy *adjective* (**baggier, baggiest**) hanging loosely ► *He was wearing a baggy sweatshirt.*

bagpipes *plural noun* a musical instrument you play by blowing air into a bag and squeezing the air out through a set of pipes with finger holes

bail¹ *noun* money paid to a lawcourt so that an accused person can go free until their trial **bail out** to help or rescue someone who is in trouble

bail² *noun* (*plural* **bails**) one of the two small pieces of wood placed on top of the stumps in cricket

bail³ *verb* (**bails, bailing, bailed**) to scoop water out of a boat and over the side

bait *noun* food put on a hook or in a trap to catch fish or animals

bait *verb* (**baits, baiting, baited**) **1** to torment a person or animal **2** to put bait on a hook or in a trap, to catch fish or animals

bake *verb* (**bakes, baking, baked**) **1** to cook food in an oven **2** to make clay hard by heating it in an oven **3** to become very hot in the sun

baker *noun* (*plural* **bakers**) someone whose job is to make or sell bread and cakes

bakery *noun* (*plural* **bakeries**) a place where bread and cakes are made or sold

balance *noun* (*plural* **balances**) **1** a device for weighing things, with two trays hanging from the ends of a horizontal bar **2** a person's feeling of being steady ► *He lost his balance and tipped the chair over.* **3** the amount of money you have left after you have spent some of it

balance *verb* (**balances, balancing, balanced**) to keep something steady without it falling ► *Mum was watching television, balancing a tray on her knee.*

balcony *noun* (*plural* **balconies**) **1** a platform with a railing built out from the wall of a building, which you reach from an upstairs window **2** the upstairs part of a cinema or theatre

bald *adjective* (**balder, baldest**) not having much hair or any hair

bale¹ *noun* (*plural* **bales**) a large bundle of hay or straw or paper tied up tightly

bale² *verb* (**bales, baling, baled**) **bale out** to jump out of an aircraft with a parachute

ball *noun* (*plural* **balls**) **1** a round object used in many games **2** something such as string wound round to form a ball **3** a grand or formal dance

ballad *noun* (*plural* **ballads**) a simple song or poem that tells a story

ballerina *noun* (*plural* **ballerinas**) (*pronounced* bal-e-**ree**-na) a female ballet dancer

ballet *noun* (*plural* **ballets**) (*pronounced* **bal**-ay) a type of entertainment performed on stage, telling a story or expressing an idea in dancing and mime

balloon *noun* (*plural* **balloons**) 1 a small rubber pouch that you fill up with air or gas and use as a toy or for decoration 2 a large round or pear-shaped bag filled out with a light gas or hot air, so that it can carry people into the air 3 an outline in a strip cartoon containing the words the characters are saying

ballot *noun* (*plural* **ballots**) (*pronounced* **bal**-ot) a method of voting in secret by writing your vote on a piece of paper

ballpoint *noun* (*plural* **ballpoints**) a pen that writes with a tiny ball round which the ink flows

ballroom *noun* (*plural* **ballrooms**) a large room where dances are held

balsa *noun* (*pronounced* **bol**-sa) a kind of light wood used to make models

bamboo *noun* (*plural* **bamboos**) a tall plant with hard hollow stems

ban *verb* (**bans, banning, banned**) to forbid something ▸ *Large lorries have been banned from the town centre.*

banana *noun* (*plural* **bananas**) a tropical fruit with a yellow skin

band *noun* (*plural* **bands**) 1 an organized group of people ▸ *On their journey they met a band of travellers.* 2 a group of musicians 3 a circular strip of something

band *verb* (**bands, banding, banded**) **band together** to be friends or form a group

bandage *noun* (*plural* **bandages**) (*pronounced* **ban**-dij) a strip of material for binding a wound

bandit *noun* (*plural* **bandits**) an outlaw

bandstand *noun* (*plural* **bandstands**) a platform for a band playing music outdoors

bandy *adjective* (**bandier, bandiest**) (describing a person's legs) curving outwards at the knees

bang *noun* (*plural* **bangs**) 1 a sudden loud noise 2 a heavy blow or knock

bang *verb* (**bangs, banging, banged**) 1 to hit or shut something with a bang 2 to make a loud noise

banger *noun* (*plural* **bangers**) 1 (informal) a firework that explodes 2 (slang) a sausage 3 (slang) a noisy old car

bangle *noun* (*plural* **bangles**) a band of metal, wood, or plastic worn as an ornament round your arm

banish *verb* (**banishes, banishing, banished**) to send someone away as a punishment ▸ *He was banished from the court for offending the Queen.* **banishment** *noun* being banished

banister *noun* (*plural* **banisters**) a rail with upright supports at the side of a staircase

banjo *noun* (*plural* **banjos**) a musical instrument with a round body and metal strings that you pluck

bank *noun* (*plural* **banks**) 1 a business which looks after people's money 2 the ground beside a river or lake 3 a piece of raised or sloping ground 4 a mass of clouds 5 a row of lights or switches

bank *verb* (**banks, banking, banked**) 1 to put money in a bank 2 to lean over while changing direction ▸ *The little plane banked to the left.* **bank on** to rely on someone or something ▸ *Julia was banking on the boys coming in to help.*

bankrupt *adjective* unable to pay all the money you owe **bankruptcy** *noun*

banner *noun* (*plural* **banners**) 1 a flag 2 a large sign or piece of cloth with a slogan or message on it, carried in a procession

banquet *noun* (*plural* **banquets**) (*pronounced* **bank**-wit) a grand dinner for a large number of people

baptism *noun* (*plural* **baptisms**) the ceremony of admitting a person into the Christian Church by sprinkling them with water or dipping them into water **baptize** *verb* to perform baptism on a person

bar *noun* (*plural* **bars**) **1** a long piece of a hard substance **2** a counter or room where drinks and refreshments are served **3** one of the short equal sections into which music is divided ▸ *A waltz has three beats in a bar.*

bar *verb* (**bars, barring, barred**) **1** to fasten a door or window with a bar **2** to prevent someone from entering or from taking part in something ▸ *All three of them were barred from the library for the rest of the term.*

barbarian *noun* (*plural* **barbarians**) an uncivilized or savage person

barbaric or **barbarous** *adjective* savage and cruel **barbarism** *noun* or **barbarity** *noun* savage cruelty

barbecue *noun* (*plural* **barbecues**) **1** a grill for cooking food over burning charcoal outdoors **2** a party at which food is cooked outdoors

barbed wire *noun* strong wire with sharp twisted spikes on it, used to make fences

barber *noun* (*plural* **barbers**) a person whose job is to cut men's hair

bar code *noun* (*plural* **bar codes**) a code of lines and spaces printed on goods so that they can be identified by a computer

bare *adjective* (**barer, barest**) **1** not having any clothing or covering **2** empty or almost empty ▸ *They were surprised to find the house bare and everyone gone.* **3** only just enough ▸ *We've only got room for the bare essentials.*

barely *adverb* only just; with difficulty ▸ *I reached home with barely enough time to eat.*

bargain *noun* (*plural* **bargains**) **1** an agreement to buy or sell something **2** something bought at an unusually low cost

bargain *verb* (**bargains, bargaining, bargained**) to argue over the price of something

barge *noun* (*plural* **barges**) a long flat-bottomed boat used on rivers and canals

barge *verb* (**barges, barging, barged**) **barge in** to rush into a place or bump clumsily into someone

bark *noun* (*plural* **barks**) **1** the sharp loud sound made by a dog **2** the rough outer covering of a tree

bark *verb* (**barks, barking, barked**) to make the sound of a dog

barley *noun* a cereal plant with a seed used for food and for making malt

barley sugar *noun* a sweet made from boiled sugar

barmaid or **barman** *noun* (*plural* **barmaids, barmen**) a person who serves drinks in a bar or pub

bar mitzvah *noun* (*plural* **bar mitzvahs**) a religious ceremony for Jewish boys who have reached the age of 13

barn *noun* (*plural* **barns**) a large farm building used for storage

barnacle *noun* (*plural* **barnacles**) a shellfish that attaches itself to rocks and the bottoms of ships

barometer *noun* (*plural* **barometers**) (*pronounced* **ba-rom-it-er**) an instrument that measures air pressure and indicates changes in the weather

baron *noun* (*plural* **barons**) a nobleman

baroness *noun* (*plural* **baronesses**) **1** a noblewoman **2** a baron's wife or widow

barracks *noun* (*plural* **barracks**) a group of buildings where soldiers live

barrage *noun* (*plural* **barrages**) (*pronounced* **ba-rahzh**) **1** a round of heavy gunfire **2** a dam or barrier across a river

barrel *noun* (*plural* **barrels**) **1** a container for liquid, with flat ends and curved sides **2** the metal tube of a gun, through which the shot is fired

barren *adjective* not able to produce any crops or fruit ▸ *It was a landscape of jagged mountain peaks and barren slopes.*

barricade *noun* (*plural* **barricades**) a barrier, especially one put up quickly to block a street

barricade *verb* (**barricades, barricading, barricaded**) to block or defend a place with a barrier

barrier *noun* (*plural* **barriers**) a fence or railing put up to stop people getting past

barrister *noun* (*plural* **barristers**) a lawyer who works in the higher courts of law

barrow *noun* (*plural* **barrows**) 1 a small cart 2 an ancient mound of earth over a grave

barter *verb* (**barters, bartering, bartered**) to exchange goods for other goods, without using money

base *noun* (*plural* **bases**) 1 the bottom part of something, or the part on which something stands 2 a place from which military or police operations are controlled

base *verb* (**bases, basing, based**) to use one thing as a starting point for developing another ▸ *The story is based on actual events.*

baseball *noun* (*plural* **baseballs**) an American game like rounders, in which the players run round a series of four 'bases' to score points

basement *noun* (*plural* **basements**) a part of a building below the ground floor

bash *verb* (**bashes, bashing, bashed**) (*informal*) to hit someone or something hard

bashful *adjective* shy ▸ *The youngest children looked nervous and bashful.*

basic *adjective* forming the first or most important part of something ▸ *The course gave them a good basic training.*

basically *adverb* essentially, mainly ▸ *Basically they want their money back.*

basin *noun* (*plural* **basins**) 1 a deep round dish 2 a large container to hold water for washing in 3 the area of land where a river's water comes from

basis *noun* (*plural* **bases**) 1 something that forms a start or foundation ▸ *These players will be the basis of a new team.* 2 the way in which something is arranged or organized ▸ *The girls are willing to help on a regular basis.*

bask *verb* (**basks, basking, basked**) to lie comfortably in sunshine or warmth

basket *noun* (*plural* **baskets**) a container for carrying or holding things, made from woven strips of hard straw or wood

basketball *noun* a game between two teams, in which players score goals by throwing a ball through a high net

bass *noun* (*plural* **basses**) (*pronounced* bayss) 1 a musical instrument that produces the lowest notes, especially a double bass or a bass guitar 2 a male singer who sings the lowest notes

bassoon *noun* (*plural* **bassoons**) a woodwind musical instrument that plays low notes

bat¹ *noun* (*plural* **bats**) a piece of wood of a special shape used to hit the ball in games such as cricket and baseball **off your own bat** (*informal*) without any help from other people

bat *verb* (**bats, batting, batted**) to use a bat in a ball game

bat² *noun* (*plural* **bats**) a flying mammal that looks like a mouse with wings

batch *noun* (*plural* **batches**) a set of things made at one time

bated *adjective* **with bated breath** waiting anxiously

bath *noun* (*plural* **baths**) 1 a large container you fill with water and get into to wash 2 the water you put into a bath ▶ *She went into the bathroom and ran a bath.*

bath *verb* (**baths, bathing, bathed**) to have a bath, or give someone a bath

bathe *verb* (**bathes, bathing, bathed**) (*pronounced* bay*dh*) 1 to swim in the sea or a river 2 to wash a part of your body gently

bathe *noun* (*plural* **bathes**) a swim

bathroom *noun* (*plural* **bathrooms**) a room for having a bath or a wash

baton *noun* (*plural* **batons**) a short stick, for example one used to conduct an orchestra or one used in a relay race

batsman *noun* (*plural* **batsmen**) someone who is batting in cricket or another ball game

battalion *noun* (*plural* **battalions**) a large group of soldiers in the army

batten *noun* (*plural* **battens**) a flat strip of wood

batter *verb* (**batters, battering, battered**) to hit someone or something hard and often

batter *noun* a mixture of flour, eggs, and milk, that you mix together and use for cooking pancakes

battering ram *noun* (*plural* **battering rams**) a heavy pole used in the past to break through the walls and gateways of a city or fort

battery *noun* (*plural* **batteries**) 1 an object that holds electricity and is used in electrical devices 2 a series of cages in which animals are kept close together on a farm 3 a set of devices, especially a group of large guns

battle *noun* (*plural* **battles**) a fight between armies

battlefield *noun* (*plural* **battlefields**) a place where a battle is fought or was fought

battlements *plural noun* the top of a castle wall with openings for shooting arrows

battleship *noun* (*plural* **battleships**) a large heavily armed warship

bawl *verb* (**bawls, bawling, bawled**) to shout or cry loudly

bay *noun* (*plural* **bays**) 1 a place by the sea or a lake where the shore curves inwards 2 an alcove or compartment

bayonet *noun* (*plural* **bayonets**) a steel blade fixed to the end of a rifle and used for jabbing

bazaar *noun* (*plural* **bazaars**) 1 a sale to raise money for charity 2 a covered market in eastern countries

BBC short for *British Broadcasting Corporation*

BC short for *before Christ*. It is used with dates that come before the birth of Jesus Christ. ▶ *Julius Caesar came to Britain in 55 BC.*

be *verb* (**I am; you are; he, she,** or **it is; we are; they are; I, he, she,** or **it was, we were, you were, they were**) 1 to exist or happen ▶ *The plates are in the cupboard.* ▶ *There was a game on Saturday.* 2 to have a particular name or description ▶ *This is my Mum.* ▶ *The town is very busy.*

beach *noun* (*plural* **beaches**) the part of the seashore close to the sea, covered with sand or pebbles

beacon *noun* (*plural* **beacons**) a light used as a warning signal

bead *noun* (*plural* **beads**) 1 a small piece of coloured glass or other hard material with a hole through it, threaded on a string or wire to make a necklace 2 a small drop of liquid ▶ *There were little beads of sweat above his eyebrows.*

beady *adjective* (**beadier, beadiest**) like beads, especially describing eyes that are small and bright

beagle *noun* (*plural* **beagles**) a small hunting dog

beak *noun* (*plural* **beaks**) the hard horny part of a bird's mouth

beaker *noun* (*plural* **beakers**) 1 a tall drinking mug without handles 2 a glass container for pouring liquids in science laboratories

beam *noun* (*plural* **beams**) 1 a long thick bar of wood or metal 2 a ray of light or other radiation

beam *verb* (**beams, beaming, beamed**) 1 to smile happily 2 to send out a beam of light or radio waves

bean *noun* (*plural* **beans**) 1 a kind of plant with seeds growing in pods 2 the seed or pod of this kind of plant, eaten as food

bear¹ *verb* (**bears, bearing, bore, borne**) 1 to carry or support something 2 to be able to put up with something or someone ▶ *The old man couldn't bear the thought of going back alone.* 3 to produce children ▶ *Their grandmother had borne seven sons.* 4 to produce fruit or crops

bear² *noun* (*plural* **bears**) a large heavy animal with thick fur and sharp hooked claws

bearable *adjective* that you are able to be bear; tolerable ▶ *His headache was bearable now.*

beard *noun* (*plural* **beards**) the hair that grows on a man's cheeks and chin **bearded** *adjective* having a beard

bearings *plural noun* where you are or which direction you are going in ▶ *Once she got her bearings she could head for home.*

beast *noun* (*plural* **beasts**) 1 a wild animal 2 (informal) a person you think is cruel or unkind

beastly *adjective* (**beastlier, beastliest**) (informal) horrid, unkind

beat¹ *verb* (**beats, beating, beat, beaten**) 1 to hit a person or animal many times with a stick 2 to do better than another person or team in a game and win it 3 to stir a cooking mixture hard so that it becomes thicker 4 to shape or flatten something by hitting it many times 5 to make regular movements ▶ *My heart beat faster with the excitement.* **beat up** to attack someone very violently

beat *noun* (*plural* **beats**) 1 the regular rhythm or stroke of your heart 2 a strong rhythm in music 3 the regular route of a police officer

beautiful *adjective* very attractive or pleasing to look at **beautifully** *adverb*

beauty *noun* (*plural* **beauties**) 1 the very pleasant appearance or sound that something has ▶ *They enjoyed the beauty of the sunset.* 2 a particularly beautiful person or thing

beaver *noun* (*plural* **beavers**) 1 a brown furry animal with strong teeth and a long flat tail, which builds dams in rivers 2 a member of the most junior section of the Scout Association

became past tense of **become**

because *conjunction* for the reason that ▶ *They were upset because the money had gone.* **because of** for the reason given; on account of ▶ *I remembered the man because of his bald head.*

beckon *verb* (**beckons, beckoning, beckoned**) to make a sign to someone, asking them to come to you

become *verb* (**becomes, becoming, became, become**) to start being something described ▶ *As Toby became tired the job became a lot harder.*

bed *noun* (*plural* **beds**) 1 a piece of furniture for sleeping on 2 a part of a garden where plants are grown 3 the bottom of a river or the sea

bedclothes *plural noun* sheets, blankets, and pillows for using on a bed

bedding *noun* things for making a bed, such as a mattress and blankets

bedraggled *adjective* (*pronounced* bi-**drag**-uld) wet and dirty

bedridden *adjective* (*pronounced* bed-**rid**-en) too ill or injured to get out of bed

bedroom *noun* (*plural* **bedrooms**) a room for sleeping in

bedspread *noun* (*plural* **bedspreads**) a covering to put over the top of a bed

bee *noun* (*plural* **bees**) a flying insect that makes honey

beech *noun* (*plural* **beeches**) a tree with smooth bark and shiny leaves

beef *noun* the meat of an ox, bull, or cow **beefy** *adjective* big and strong

beehive *noun* (*plural* **beehives**) a box for keeping bees in

been past participle of **be**

beer *noun* (*plural* **beers**) an alcoholic drink made from malt and hops

beetle *noun* (*plural* **beetles**) an insect with hard shiny covers over its wings

beetroot *noun* (*plural* **beetroot**) a dark red vegetable from a root plant

before *adverb*, *preposition*, and *conjunction* 1 at an earlier time; already ▶ *Tamsin realized she'd been to the house once before.* ▶ *They came the day before yesterday.* ▶ *Let me know before you leave.* 2 in front of ▶ *He stood up before the whole school.*

beg *verb* (**begs, begging, begged**) 1 to ask people in the street to give you money 2 to ask someone seriously or desperately for something ▶ *He begged the old woman to let him go into the house.*

began past tense of **begin**

beggar *noun* (*plural* **beggars**) someone who lives by begging

begin *verb* (**begins, beginning, began, begun**) to start; to do the first thing **beginner** *noun* someone who is learning to do something **beginning** *noun* the start of something

begun past participle of **begin**

behalf *noun* **on behalf of** for someone ▶ *Mr Kemp was buying the jewellery on behalf of the museum.*

behave *verb* (**behaves, behaving, behaved**) 1 to act in a certain way ▶ *They thought she had behaved like a fool.* 2 to show good manners ▶ *George sometimes found it difficult to behave.* **behaviour** *noun* how someone behaves

behead *verb* (**beheads, beheading, beheaded**) to cut off someone's head, as a form of execution

behind *adverb* and *preposition* 1 at or to the back ▶ *The others are a long way behind.* ▶ *She hid behind a tree.* 2 not making good progress; late ▶ *I'm behind with my work.* ▶ *He's behind the rest of the class in French.* 3 supporting ▶ *We're all behind you.*

behind *noun* (*plural* **behinds**) your bottom

beige *noun* and *adjective* (*pronounced* bayzh) a fawn colour

being *noun* (*plural* **beings**) a living person or animal

belch *verb* (**belches, belching, belched**) 1 to let wind noisily out of your stomach through your mouth 2 to send out thick smoke or fumes

belch *noun* (*plural* **belches**) the act or sound of belching

belief *noun* (*plural* **beliefs**) something you believe is true

believe *verb* (**believes, believing, believed**) 1 to think that something is true 2 to think that someone is telling the truth **believe in** to think that something exists or is important ▶ *David said that he believed in ghosts.*

bell *noun* (*plural* **bells**) a hollow metal object that rings when it is struck

bellow *verb* (**bellows, bellowing, bellowed**) to roar or shout

bellows *plural noun* a device for blowing out air, especially into a fire to make it burn more strongly

belly *noun* (*plural* **bellies**) 1 your stomach 2 the part underneath the body of a four-legged animal

belong *verb* (**belongs, belonging, belonged**) **1** to be what someone owns ▸ *The pencil belongs to me.* **2** to have a proper place ▸ *The butter belongs in the fridge.*

belongings *plural noun* the things that you own

beloved *adjective* (*pronounced* bi-**luvd** or bi-**luv**-id) loved very much

below *preposition* lower than, under ▸ *Jim's uncle lives in the flat below us.*
below *adverb* at a lower point, or to a lower point ▸ *He had climbed on the roof and was hurling stones into the street below.*

belt *noun* (*plural* **belts**) **1** a strip of leather or other material worn round the waist **2** a long narrow area ▸ *They could see a belt of trees on the other side of the hill.*
belt *verb* (**belts, belting, belted**) (*informal*) **1** to hit someone hard **2** to move very fast ▸ *He saw the bus coming and belted along to catch it.*

bench *noun* (*plural* **benches**) **1** a long hard seat for several people **2** a long table for working at

bend *verb* (**bends, bending, bent**) **1** to make something curved or crooked **2** to become curved or crooked ▸ *The shelves started to bend under the weight of so many books.* **3** to move the top of your body downwards ▸ *Molly bent down to pick up the cat.*
bend *noun* (*plural* **bends**) a part where something curves or turns

beneath *preposition* and *adverb* under ▸ *Beneath the soil there is clay.*

benefit *noun* (*plural* **benefits**) **1** something that is useful or helpful ▸ *Having so many shops is one of the benefits of living in the city.* **2** money paid by the government to help people who are poor, sick, or out of work **beneficial** *adjective* useful; giving a benefit

bent *adjective* curved or crooked when it should be straight

bequeath *verb* (**bequeaths, bequeathing, bequeathed**) (*rhymes with* breathe) to leave something to someone in your will **bequest** *noun* something bequeathed in a will

bereaved *adjective* sad or suffering because a close relative has recently died **bereavement** *noun* being bereaved

beret *noun* (*plural* **berets**) (*pronounced* berr-ay) a soft round flat hat

berry *noun* (*plural* **berries**) a small juicy fruit containing seeds

berserk *adjective* go berserk to become extremely angry and violent

berth *noun* (*plural* **berths**) **1** a sleeping place on a ship or train **2** a place where a ship is tied up

beside *preposition* next to; close to ▸ *The little house stood beside a lake.* be beside yourself to be very excited or upset ▸ *We were beside ourselves with worry.*

besides *preposition* in addition to ▸ *Who can come besides you?*
besides *adverb* also ▸ *I don't mind coming for a swim. Besides, it will do me good.*

besiege *verb* (**besieges, besieging, besieged**) (*pronounced* bi-**seej**) to surround a place with troops to force the people living there to surrender

best *adjective* and *noun* most excellent; most able to do something
best *adverb* in the best way; most ▸ *We'll do what suits you best.*

best man *noun* a male friend of the bridegroom who helps him at his wedding

best-seller *noun* (*plural* **best-sellers**) a book or other product that has sold in very large numbers

bet *verb* (**bets, betting, bet** or **betted**) **1** to guess what the result of a race or event will be. You win money if you are right and lose money if you are wrong **2** (*informal*) to say you are sure about something ▸ *I bet I'm right.*
bet *noun* (*plural* **bets**) an agreement you make when you bet money

betray *verb* (**betrays, betraying, betrayed**) **1** to do someone harm when they are expecting your support **2** to reveal something you are trying to keep hidden ▸ *The look on Jim's face betrayed his true feelings.* **betrayal** *noun* betraying someone

better *adjective* and *adverb* **1** more excellent ▶ *Her Mum has got a better job.* ▶ *This road is the better of the two.* **2** well again after an illness ▶ *I hope you are better now.* **3** more well ▶ *I'll try to do it better next time.*

better *verb* (**betters, bettering, bettered**) to improve on something

between *preposition* and *adverb* **1** in the space or time dividing two things ▶ *The train runs between London and Brussels.* ▶ *The buildings were side by side with a tall fence between.* **2** comparing one thing with another ▶ *There's not much difference between the two prices.* **3** among, sharing ▶ *Share these comics between you.*

beware *verb* be careful ▶ *Beware of strangers.*

bewilder *verb* (**bewilders, bewildering, bewildered**) to puzzle someone completely **bewilderment** *noun* being bewildered

bewitch *verb* (**bewitches, bewitching, bewitched**) to put a magic spell on someone

beyond *preposition* and *adverb* **1** farther on ▶ *Don't go beyond the end of the road.* ▶ *They walked down the lane and into the darkness beyond.* **2** more than ▶ *The result of the game was now beyond doubt.*

biased *adjective* unfair because you prefer one person or side to another

bib *noun* (*plural* **bibs**) a piece of cloth or plastic put under a baby's chin during meals to protect its clothes

Bible *noun* (*plural* **Bibles**) the holy book of Christians and Jews **biblical** *adjective* to do with the Bible
The word **Bible** comes from a Greek word meaning 'book'.

bicycle *noun* (*plural* **bicycles**) a vehicle with two wheels that you ride by turning pedals

bid *verb* (**bids, bidding, bid**) to offer an amount of money for something

bid *noun* (*plural* **bids**) **1** an offer of money for something **2** an attempt ▶ *His bad behaviour was just a bid for attention.*

bide *verb* (**bides, biding, bided**) **bide your time** to wait for something to happen that will help you

big *adjective* (**bigger, biggest**) **1** more than the normal size; large **2** important ▶ *The big moment had come.* **3** elder ▶ *They didn't realize that Jack had a big brother.* **biggish** *adjective* fairly big

bike *noun* (*plural* **bikes**) (informal) a bicycle or motorcycle

bikini *noun* (*plural* **bikinis**) a two-piece swimming costume worn by women and girls

bilge *noun* (*plural* **bilges**) the bottom of a ship, where water collects

bilingual *adjective* speaking two languages well

bill *noun* (*plural* **bills**) **1** a piece of paper showing how much money you owe for something **2** a new law before it is discussed in parliament **3** a poster **4** a bird's beak

billiards *noun* a game played with long sticks (called *cues*) and three balls which you have to hit into pockets round the edge of a long cloth-covered table

billion *noun* (*plural* **billions**) a thousand million (1,000,000,000) or sometimes a million million (1,000,000,000,000)
People often say **billions**, meaning very many, and then the exact number does not matter.

billow *verb* (**billows, billowing, billowed**) to rise up or move like waves on the sea ▶ *Gusts of wind were sending smoke billowing back into the room.*

billy goat *noun* (*plural* **billy goats**) a male goat

bin *noun* (*plural* **bins**) a deep container for storing things or for putting rubbish in

binary *adjective* made up of sets of two or of two parts

binary system *noun* a system of expressing numbers by using only the digits 0 and 1. For example, 21 is written 10101.

bind *verb* (**binds, binding, bound**) **1** to tie things up or tie them together **2** to fasten material round something **3** to fasten the pages of a book in a cover

bingo *noun* a game in which players have cards with numbered squares, which they cover or cross out as numbers are called out. The first person to have all the numbers wins the game.

binoculars *plural noun* an instrument with lenses for both eyes, which you look through to make distant objects seem nearer

biodegradable *adjective* able to be broken down by bacteria in the environment

biography *noun* (*plural* **biographies**) the story of a person's life **biographer** *noun* a person who writes a biography **biographical** *adjective* to do with biography

biology *noun* the science or study of living things **biological** *adjective* to do with biology **biologist** *noun* a person who studies biology

bionic *adjective* worked by electronic devices, and imitating a living being

biplane *noun* (*plural* **biplanes**) a plane with two sets of wings, one above the other

birch *noun* (*plural* **birches**) a tall tree with shiny bark and slender branches

bird *noun* (*plural* **birds**) a feathered animal with two wings and two legs

birth *noun* (*plural* **births**) the beginning of a person's life, when they come from their mother's womb

birthday *noun* (*plural* **birthdays**) the anniversary of the day you were born

birthmark *noun* (*plural* **birthmarks**) a mark which has been on someone's body since they were born

birthplace *noun* (*plural* **birthplaces**) the place where someone was born

biscuit *noun* (*plural* **biscuits**) a flat thin piece of crisp baked pastry like a hard cake

bishop *noun* (*plural* **bishops**) **1** a clergyman in charge of all the churches in a city or district **2** a chess piece shaped like a bishop's hat

bison *noun* (*plural* **bison**) a wild ox with shaggy hair

bit[1] *noun* (*plural* **bits**) **1** a small piece or amount of something **2** the part of a horse's bridle that is put into its mouth **3** the part of a tool that cuts or grips **a bit** slightly ▶ *She felt a bit nervous.*

bit[2] past tense of **bite** *verb*

bitch *noun* (*plural* **bitches**) a female dog, fox, or wolf

bite *verb* (**bites, biting, bit, bitten**) **1** to cut or hold something with your teeth **2** to sting or hurt ▶ *What a biting wind!*
bite *noun* (*plural* **bites**) **1** an act of biting **2** a mark or spot made by biting ▶ *He was getting fed up with all the insect bites.*

bitter *adjective* **1** tasting sour and unpleasant **2** feeling angry and envious ▶ *People who suffer bad injuries can become quite bitter.* **3** extremely cold ▶ *The weather turned cold with bitter winds.*

black *adjective* (**blacker, blackest**) **1** of the darkest colour, like coal or soot **2** having dark skin **3** angry and gloomy ▶ *His grandfather had come home in a black mood.* **blackness** *noun*
black *noun* the darkest colour, like coal or soot

blackberry *noun* (*plural* **blackberries**) a sweet black berry that grows on wild brambles

blackbird *noun* (*plural* **blackbirds**) a dark songbird found in countries of Europe

blackboard *noun* (*plural* **blackboards**) a dark board for writing on with chalk

blackcurrant *noun* (*plural* **blackcurrants**) a small black fruit that grows on bushes

blacken *verb* (**blackens, blackening, blackened**) **1** to make something black **2** to become black

black eye *noun* (*plural* **black eyes**) an eye with heavy bruises round it

black hole *noun* (*plural* **black holes**) a region in space with such strong gravity that no light escapes

blackmail *verb* (**blackmails, blackmailing, blackmailed**) to threaten to tell a secret about someone unless they pay you money

blackout *noun* (*plural* **blackouts**) **1** a time when lights are left turned off or are not working **2** losing consciousness or memory for a short time

blacksmith *noun* (*plural* **blacksmiths**) someone who makes and repairs things made of iron, and fits shoes on horses

bladder *noun* (*plural* **bladders**) the baglike part of your body in which urine collects before you pass it out of your body

blade *noun* (*plural* **blades**) **1** the sharp part of a knife or other cutting tool **2** the flat wide part of an oar or propeller **3** a long narrow leaf of grass

blame *verb* (**blames, blaming, blamed**) to say that someone has done something wrong ▸ *Who can blame her for being angry?*
blame *noun* the feeling of being blamed for something

blancmange *noun* (*plural* **blancmanges**) (*pronounced* **bla-monj**) a pudding like a jelly made with milk

blank *adjective* **1** having nothing written or drawn on it **2** showing no interest or expression ▸ *Mark looked blank and shook his head.*

blanket *noun* (*plural* **blankets**) **1** a large piece of thick cloth, used as a warm covering for a bed **2** a thick covering or layer ▸ *In autumn the ground will be covered with a blanket of leaves.*

blare *verb* (**blares, blaring, blared**) to make a harsh loud sound

blasphemous *adjective* (*pronounced* **blas-fe-mus**) disrespectful about holy things **blasphemy** *noun*

blast *noun* (*plural* **blasts**) **1** a sudden loud noise ▸ *The referee gave a long blast of his whistle.* **2** a strong rush of wind or air **3** an explosion

blast *verb* (**blasts, blasting, blasted**) to blow something up with explosives

blast-off *noun* the launch of a spacecraft

blaze *verb* (**blazes, blazing, blazed**) to burn or shine brightly
blaze *noun* (*plural* **blazes**) a bright flame or light

blazer *noun* (*plural* **blazers**) a kind of jacket, often with a badge on the front and worn as uniform

bleach *noun* (*plural* **bleaches**) a strong liquid used to clean things or make clothes white
bleach *verb* (**bleaches, bleaching, bleached**) to make something white

bleak *adjective* (**bleaker, bleakest**) **1** cold and dreary ▸ *The countryside looked cold and bleak.* **2** without hope ▸ *The future is looking bleak.*

bleary *adjective* (**blearier, bleariest**) not able to see clearly ▸ *Tom's bleary eyes had filled with tears.*

bleat *verb* (**bleats, bleating, bleated**) to make the cry of a sheep or goat
bleat *noun* (*plural* **bleats**) a bleating sound

bleed *verb* (**bleeds, bleeding, bled**) to lose blood

bleep *verb* (**bleeps, bleeping, bleeped**) to make a short high sound
bleep *noun* (*plural* **bleeps**) a bleeping sound

blemish *noun* (*plural* **blemishes**) a mark or spot that spoils something

blend *verb* (**blends, blending, blended**) to mix things together smoothly or easily
blend *noun* (*plural* **blends**) a smooth mixture

bless *verb* (**blesses, blessing, blessed**) **1** to wish someone well or bring them happiness **2** to call someone holy

blessing *noun* (*plural* **blessings**) **1** a prayer or act of blessing someone **2** something you are glad of or happy about ▸ *Being left out of the team turned out to be a blessing in disguise.*

blew past tense of **blow** *verb*

blight *noun* (*plural* **blights**) an evil influence or disease

blind *adjective* (**blinder, blindest**) 1 unable to see 2 without thought or understanding

blind *verb* (**blinds, blinding, blinded**) to make someone blind

blind *noun* (*plural* **blinds**) a screen for a window

blindfold *noun* (*plural* **blindfolds**) a piece of cloth used to cover someone's eyes to stop them seeing

blindfold *verb* (**blindfolds, blindfolding, blindfolded**) to cover someone's eyes with a blindfold

blink *verb* (**blinks, blinking, blinked**) to shut and open your eyes quickly

bliss *noun* great happiness **blissful** *adjective* very happy

blister *noun* (*plural* **blisters**) a swelling like a bubble under the skin

blitz *noun* (*plural* **blitzes**) a sudden violent attack, especially from aircraft

blizzard *noun* (*plural* **blizzards**) a heavy windy snowstorm

bloated *adjective* swollen or puffed out

blob *noun* (*plural* **blobs**) a small round lump of a thick liquid

block *noun* (*plural* **blocks**) 1 a solid piece of something hard such as wood 2 something that stops people or things getting through 3 a large building or group of buildings with streets all around it

block *verb* (**blocks, blocking, blocked**) to get in the way of something ▸ *A stone slab blocked our progress.*

block capitals or **block letters** *plural noun* large capital letters

blockade *noun* (*plural* **blockades**) a siege of a city or town

blockage *noun* (*plural* **blockages**) something that gets in the way or stops things moving

blond or **blonde** *adjective* (**blonder, blondest**) fair-haired
You use **blond** when you are talking about a boy or man, and **blonde** when you are talking about a girl or woman.

blonde *noun* (*plural* **blondes**) a fair-haired girl or woman

blood *noun* the red liquid that flows through your veins and arteries **bloody** *adjective*

bloodhound *noun* (*plural* **bloodhounds**) a large breed of dog which can track people over long distances by following their scent

bloodshed *noun* the killing and injuring of people

bloodshot *adjective* (describing your eyes) streaked with red from being strained or tired

bloodstream *noun* the blood flowing round your body

bloodthirsty *adjective* (**bloodthirstier, bloodthirstiest**) enjoying killing and hurting people

bloom *verb* (**blooms, blooming, bloomed**) to produce flowers

bloom *noun* (*plural* **blooms**) a flower

blossom *noun* (*plural* **blossoms**) a flower that grows on a fruit tree in the spring

blossom *verb* (**blossoms, blossoming, blossomed**) 1 to produce blossom 2 to do well, to thrive ▸ *Her career blossomed when she moved to the city.*

blot *noun* (*plural* **blots**) a spot or stain made by ink

blot *verb* (**blots, blotting, blotted**) to make a blot on something **blot out** to remove a mark or writing or make it invisible

blotch *noun* (*plural* **blotches**) an untidy patch of colour **blotchy** *adjective*

blouse *noun* (*plural* **blouses**) a loose type of shirt worn by women and girls

blow *verb* (**blows, blowing, blew, blown**)
1 to let air out from your mouth or nose
2 to make something by blowing ▸ *The children were blowing bubbles.* 3 to make a sound with a whistle, trumpet, or horn
blow away or **blow off** to be driven away in the wind **blow up 1** to destroy something with an explosion 2 to fill something with air

blow *noun* (*plural* **blows**) 1 a hard knock or hit 2 a piece of bad luck that you are not expecting ▸ *The news came to her as quite a blow.* 3 the action of blowing

blue *adjective* (**bluer, bluest**) 1 having the colour of a clear sky 2 sad and miserable
blue *noun* the colour of a clear sky **out of the blue** with no warning ▸ *He just turned up out of the blue one day.*

bluebell *noun* (*plural* **bluebells**) a blue wild flower

blues *plural noun* a type of jazz music that is slow and sad **the blues** a sad feeling

bluff *verb* (**bluffs, bluffing, bluffed**) to make someone think you know something or can do something when you can't
bluff *noun* (*plural* **bluffs**) something you say to bluff someone, for example a promise or threat that you do not really mean

blunder *noun* (*plural* **blunders**) a silly mistake
blunder *verb* (**blunders, blundering, blundered**) to make a silly mistake

blunt *adjective* (**blunter, bluntest**) 1 having an edge that is not sharp enough for cutting 2 saying what you think without being polite about it

blur *verb* (**blurs, blurring, blurred**) to make something unclear or smeared
blur *noun* (*plural* **blurs**) a smudge or smear **blurred** *adjective*

blush *verb* (**blushes, blushing, blushed**) to become slightly red in the face when you are embarrassed
blush *noun* (*plural* **blushes**) a slightly red colour in your face

blustery *adjective* very windy

boa constrictor *noun* (*plural* **boa constrictors**) a large South American snake that crushes its prey

boar *noun* (*plural* **boars**) 1 a wild pig 2 a male pig

board *noun* (*plural* **boards**) 1 a long flat piece of wood 2 a flat piece of wood or cardboard used for something special, such as a noticeboard or a chessboard 3 daily meals given in return for money or work 4 a group of people who run a business **on board** on a ship, plane, or train
board *verb* (**boards, boarding, boarded**) 1 to get on a ship, plane, bus, or train at the start of a journey 2 to rent a room and have your meals at a place

boarder *noun* (*plural* **boarders**) 1 a child at a boarding school 2 a lodger

boarding school *noun* (*plural* **boarding schools**) a school in which the pupils live during the term

boast *verb* (**boasts, boasting, boasted**) to talk proudly about something you own or something good you have done **boastful** *adjective* liking to boast

boat *noun* (*plural* **boats**) a vehicle that floats and travels on water

bob *verb* (**bobs, bobbing, bobbed**) to move gently up and down, like something floating on water

bobsled or **bobsleigh** *noun* (*plural* **bobsleds** or **bobsleighs**) a large sledge with two sets of runners

bodice *noun* (*plural* **bodices**) the upper part of a dress

bodily *adjective* to do with your body
bodily *adverb* with the whole body; as a whole ▸ *She would have to carry him bodily and she wasn't sure if she was strong enough.*

body *noun* (*plural* **bodies**) 1 the flesh and bones and other parts of a person or animal 2 a dead person or corpse 3 the main part of something 4 a group of people or things in one place

bodyguard *noun* (*plural* **bodyguards**) a guard who protects an important person from being attacked

bog *noun* (*plural* **bogs**) an area of wet spongy ground **boggy** *adjective* wet and spongy, like a bog

bogus *adjective* false; not genuine ▸ *He gave a name that turned out to be bogus.*

boil[1] *verb* (**boils, boiling, boiled**) **1** to heat a liquid until it bubbles and gives off steam **2** to start bubbling, like water **3** to cook something in boiling water **be boiling** (*informal*) to be very hot, like the weather

boil[2] *noun* (*plural* **boils**) a painful swelling on the skin

boiler *noun* (*plural* **boilers**) a container for heating water or making steam

boiling point *noun* (*plural* **boiling points**) the temperature at which something boils

boisterous *adjective* noisy and lively

bold *adjective* (**bolder, boldest**) **1** brave and adventurous **2** clear and easy to see

bollard *noun* (*plural* **bollards**) a short thick post put in the road to control traffic

bolt *noun* (*plural* **bolts**) **1** a sliding metal bar for fastening a door or window **2** a thick metal pin for fastening things together **3** a flash of lightning
bolt *verb* (**bolts, bolting, bolted**) **1** to fasten a door or window with a bolt **2** to run away in panic, as a horse does **3** to eat food too quickly

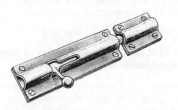

bomb *noun* (*plural* **bombs**) a container filled with explosives for blowing things up
bomb *verb* (**bombs, bombing, bombed**) to attack people or places with bombs
bomber *noun* an aircraft that drops bombs, or a person who plants bombs

bombard *verb* (**bombards, bombarding, bombarded**) **1** to attack a place with heavy gunfire **2** to direct a large number of questions or complaints at someone
bombardment *noun* a heavy attack with guns

bond *noun* (*plural* **bonds**) **1** something that binds or ties people **2** something that brings people together, such as a common interest

bondage *noun* being a slave

bone *noun* (*plural* **bones**) one of the hard pieces of a skeleton **bony** *adjective* thin and hard, like a bone

bonfire *noun* (*plural* **bonfires**) a large fire lit out of doors

bonnet *noun* (*plural* **bonnets**) **1** the cover over the front part of a car **2** a round hat worn by babies and tied under the chin

bonus *noun* (*plural* **bonuses**) an extra payment or reward

boo *verb* (**boos, booing, booed**) to shout disapproval

booby prize *noun* (*plural* **booby prizes**) a prize given to someone who comes last in a race or competition

booby trap *noun* (*plural* **booby traps**) a hidden bomb or trap designed to hit or injure someone when they do not expect it

book *noun* (*plural* **books**) a set of sheets of paper fastened together inside a cover, for reading or writing on
book *verb* (**books, booking, booked**) **1** to reserve a place in a theatre or hotel, or a seat on a train **2** to record something in a book or list

bookcase *noun* (*plural* **bookcases**) a piece of furniture with shelves for holding books

booklet *noun* (*plural* **booklets**) a small book with paper covers

bookmaker *noun* (*plural* **bookmakers**) a person whose business is taking bets

boom *noun* (*plural* **booms**) **1** a deep hollow sound **2** a time when people are well off **3** a long pole at the bottom of a sail to keep it stretched
boom *verb* (**booms, booming, boomed**) **1** to make a deep hollow sound, like a large gun **2** to be prosperous ▸ *Business is booming again.*

boomerang *noun* (*plural* **boomerangs**) a curved stick which returns to its thrower if it misses the target. It is used as a hunting weapon by Australian Aboriginals.

boost *verb* (**boosts, boosting, boosted**) to increase the amount or power of something ▸ *The band's record sales were boosted after they won eight awards.*

boot *noun* (*plural* **boots**) **1** a tall heavy shoe that covers the ankle or leg **2** the space for luggage at the back of a car
boot *verb* (**boots, booting, booted**) **1** to kick someone hard **2** to switch on a computer and start it

booth *noun* (*plural* **booths**) a small compartment for a special purpose, such as making a telephone call

booty *noun* goods that have been taken in a war

border *noun* (*plural* **borders**) **1** the line where two countries meet ▸ *They reached the Spanish border after dark.* **2** a line round the edge of something **3** a flower bed

bore[1] *verb* (**bores, boring, bored**) **1** to drill a hole through something **2** to make someone feel tired and uninterested
bore *noun* (*plural* **bores**) a dull or uninteresting person or thing **boredom** *noun* a feeling of being bored

bore[2] past tense of **bear** *verb*

boring *adjective* dull and uninteresting

born *adjective* **be born** to start your life

borough *noun* (*plural* **boroughs**) (*pronounced* **bu-ro**) an important town or district with its own local council

borrow *verb* (**borrows, borrowing, borrowed**) to use something that belongs to someone else and then return it to them

bosom *noun* (*plural* **bosoms**) a woman's breasts

boss *noun* (*plural* **bosses**) (informal) a person in charge of other people
boss *verb* (**bosses, bossing, bossed**) (informal) to give people orders

bossy *adjective* (**bossier, bossiest**) (informal) fond of giving people orders

botany *noun* the study of plants **botanical** *adjective* to do with botany or plants **botanist** *noun* someone who studies plants

both *adjective* and *pronoun* two, not just one ▸ *We want them both.*
both *adverb* You use **both** with **and** to say two things about something or someone. ▸ *He is both friendly and helpful.*

bother *verb* (**bothers, bothering, bothered**) **1** to make someone worry about something ▸ *The noise outside was beginning to bother them.* **2** to take the trouble to do something ▸ *You needn't bother to wait for me.*
bother *noun* trouble or worry

bottle *noun* (*plural* **bottles**) a glass or plastic container with a narrow neck, for holding liquids
bottle *verb* (**bottles, bottling, bottled**) to put something in a bottle **bottle up** to keep something you are worried about to yourself

bottleneck *noun* (*plural* **bottlenecks**) a place where traffic is held up by a hazard or obstruction

bottom *noun* (*plural* **bottoms**) **1** the lowest point of something **2** the farthest end of a garden, away from the house **3** the part of your body that you sit on

bough *noun* (*plural* **boughs**) (*rhymes with* cow) a large branch of a tree that reaches out from the trunk

bought past tense of **buy** *verb*

boulder *noun* (*plural* **boulders**) a large smooth stone on the ground

bounce *verb* (**bounces, bouncing, bounced**) to spring back when thrown against something, like a rubber ball
bounce *noun* (*plural* **bounces**) **1** a bouncing movement **2** liveliness or energy **bouncy** *adjective* lively, energetic

bound[1] past tense of **bind** *verb*

bound[2] *adjective* **bound for** travelling towards a place ▸ *The cattle were put on a truck bound for Colombo.* **bound to** having to or likely to ▸ *She knew that something good was bound to happen.*

bound[3] *verb* (**bounds, bounding, bounded**) to run with leaping steps
bound *noun* (*plural* **bounds**) a long leap

boundary *noun* (*plural* **boundaries**) 1 a line that marks an edge or limit 2 a hit to the outer edge of a cricket field

bounds *plural noun* **out of bounds** describing a place where you are not allowed to go

bouquet *noun* (*plural* **bouquets**) (*pronounced* boo-**kay** or boh-**kay**) a prettily tied bunch of flowers

bout *noun* (*plural* **bouts**) (*pronounced* bowt) 1 a period of illness ▸ *They are both suffering from a mild bout of sunstroke.* 2 a boxing or wrestling fight

bow[1] *noun* (*plural* **bows**) (*rhymes with* go) 1 a knot made with loops 2 the stick used for playing a stringed instrument such as a violin or cello 3 a weapon for shooting arrows, made of a thin stick bent back to hold a tight string

bow[2] *verb* (**bows, bowing, bowed**) (*rhymes with* cow) to bend your body forwards as a polite gesture
bow *noun* (*plural* **bows**) (*rhymes with* cow) 1 the movement you make when you bow ▸ *The pianist gave a bow.* 2 the front part of a ship

bowels *plural noun* the long tubes in your body that carry waste food for passing out of the body

bowl[1] *noun* (*plural* **bowls**) a deep round dish

bowl[2] *verb* (**bowls, bowling, bowled**) 1 to send the ball towards the batsman in cricket 2 to get the batsman out by hitting the wicket with the ball **bowler** *noun* the player in cricket who is bowling

bowling *noun* an indoor game in which you roll a heavy ball down an alley to knock down skittles placed upright at the other end

bowls *plural noun* an outdoor game played on a smooth piece of grass, in which you roll heavy balls towards a white target ball called the *jack*

box *noun* (*plural* **boxes**) 1 a container made of wood or cardboard 2 a hut or shelter ▸ *a sentry box.* 3 an evergreen shrub
box *verb* (**boxes, boxing, boxed**) to fight with the fists

boxer *noun* (*plural* **boxers**) 1 a person who boxes for sport 2 a large dog with short brown hair

Boxing Day *noun* (*plural* **Boxing Days**) the first weekday after Christmas Day

box office *noun* (*plural* **box offices**) a place where you can buy tickets for the theatre or cinema

boy *noun* (*plural* **boys**) a male child or young man **boyhood** *noun* the time of being a boy **boyish** *adjective* like a boy

boycott *verb* (**boycotts, boycotting, boycotted**) to refuse to have anything to do with something or someone

boyfriend *noun* (*plural* **boyfriends**) a male friend or lover

bra *noun* (*plural* **bras**) (short for *brassière*) a piece of clothing worn by women under their other clothes to support their breasts

brace *noun* (*plural* **braces**) 1 a tool for holding something in place 2 a wire device for straightening the teeth

bracelet *noun* (*plural* **bracelets**) a small band or chain worn round the wrist

braces *plural noun* a pair of stretching straps worn over the shoulders to hold your trousers up

bracken *noun* a kind of fern that grows in the open country

bracket *noun* (*plural* **brackets**) 1 a punctuation mark used in pairs to separate words or figures. Brackets are round ( ) or square [ ]. 2 a support for something attached to a wall

brag *verb* (**brags, bragging, bragged**) to boast

braid *noun* (*plural* **braids**) 1 a plait of hair 2 a ribbon or band used for decoration

braille *noun* a system of writing or printing using raised dots, which blind people can read with their fingers

Braille is named after a French teacher called Louis Braille, who was blind from the age of three and invented the system. He died in 1852.

brain *noun* (*plural* **brains**) the part of your body inside your head that controls what you do and is used for thinking **brains** intelligence

brainwave *noun* (*plural* **brainwaves**) a clever idea that you get suddenly

brainy *adjective* (**brainier, brainiest**) (informal) clever, intelligent

brake *noun* (*plural* **brakes**) a part of a vehicle for making it stop or slow down
brake *verb* (**brakes, braking, braked**) to slow down by using the brakes

bramble *noun* (*plural* **brambles**) a prickly bush with blackberries growing on it

branch *noun* (*plural* **branches**) 1 a part like an arm that sticks out from the trunk of a tree 2 a part of a railway, river, or road that leads off from the main part 3 a part of a large organization
branch *verb* (**branches, branching, branched**) to form a branch **branch out** to start to do something new

brand *noun* (*plural* **brands**) a particular make or kind of goods
brand *verb* (**brands, branding, branded**) to mark sheep or cattle with a hot iron

brandish *verb* (**brandishes, brandishing, brandished**) (not an everyday word) to wave something about

brand-new *adjective* completely new

brandy *noun* (*plural* **brandies**) a strong alcoholic drink made with wine

brass *noun* 1 a yellow-gold metal made by mixing copper and zinc 2 musical instruments made of brass, such as trumpets and trombones **brassy** *adjective*

brave *adjective* (**braver, bravest**) ready to face anything dangerous or difficult **bravery** *noun*
brave *noun* (*plural* **braves**) a Native American warrior

brawl *noun* (*plural* **brawls**) a noisy quarrel or fight

brawn *noun* physical strength **brawny** *adjective* having a strong body and muscles

bray *verb* (**brays, braying, brayed**) to make a loud noise like a donkey

brazen *adjective* bold and shameless

breach *noun* (*plural* **breaches**) a gap or break

bread *noun* food made by baking flour and water, usually with yeast

breadth *noun* (*plural* **breadths**) the width of something from side to side

break *verb* (**breaks, breaking, broke, broken**) 1 to make something go into several pieces by hitting it or dropping it 2 to stop working properly 3 to fail to keep a promise or obey a rule 4 to change suddenly ▶ *At the end of August the weather broke.* 5 to do better than someone else's record in sport or other activities **break down** to stop working properly **break in** to force your way into a building to steal from it **break out** to start and spread rapidly, like a fire or disease **break up** 1 to separate, when friends leave one another 2 to finish school at the end of term

break *noun* (*plural* **breaks**) 1 a broken place; a gap 2 a short rest from work

breakable *adjective* easy to break, fragile

breakage *noun* (*plural* **breakages**) something that is broken ▶ *All breakages must be paid for.*

breakdown *noun* (*plural* **breakdowns**) 1 the sudden failure of a car or machine to work ▶ *We had a breakdown on the way back and had to walk.* 2 an illness in which you become depressed and unable to cope with life

breaker *noun* (*plural* **breakers**) a large wave in the sea

breakfast *noun* (*plural* **breakfasts**) the first meal of the day

breakthrough *noun* (*plural* **breakthroughs**) an important discovery or step forward

breakwater *noun* (*plural* **breakwaters**) a wall built out into the sea to protect the coast from heavy waves

breast *noun* (*plural* **breasts**) **1** one of the two parts on a woman's chest that can produce milk **2** a person's or animal's chest

breaststroke *noun* a swimming stroke you do on your front, by pushing the arms forward and bringing them round and back

breath *noun* (*plural* **breaths**) (*pronounced* breth) the air that you breathe in and out **out of breath** gasping for air after hard exercise

breathalyser *noun* (*plural* **breathalysers**) an instrument for measuring the amount of alcohol in someone's breath **breathalyse** *verb* to test someone's breath with a breathalyser

breathe *verb* (**breathes, breathing, breathed**) (*pronounced* breeth) to take air into your lungs and send it out again

breather *noun* (*plural* **breathers**) (informal) a short rest

bred past tense and past participle of **breed** *verb*

breech *noun* (*plural* **breeches**) the part of a gun barrel where the bullets are put in

breeches *plural noun* (*pronounced* brich-iz) (not an everyday word) trousers, especially trousers that fit tightly at the knee

breed *verb* (**breeds, breeding, bred**) **1** to produce children or young animals **2** to keep animals so as to get young ones from them

breed *noun* (*plural* **breeds**) a kind of animal

breeze *noun* (*plural* **breezes**) a gentle wind **breezy** *adjective* slightly windy

brew *verb* (**brews, brewing, brewed**) **1** to make beer **2** to make tea or coffee **3** to start to develop ▸ *It looked like trouble was brewing.*

brewery *noun* (*plural* **breweries**) a place where beer is made

bribe *noun* (*plural* **bribes**) money or a gift offered to someone to make them do something

bribe *verb* (**bribes, bribing, bribed**) to offer someone a bribe **bribery** *noun* bribing someone

brick *noun* (*plural* **bricks**) **1** a block of hard baked clay used in building **2** something else with the same shape

bride *noun* (*plural* **brides**) a woman on her wedding day

bridegroom *noun* (*plural* **bridegrooms**) a man on his wedding day

bridesmaid *noun* (*plural* **bridesmaids**) a girl or woman who helps the bride at her wedding

bridge *noun* (*plural* **bridges**) **1** a structure built over a river, railway, or road to allow people to cross it **2** the high platform above the deck of a ship, from where the ship is controlled **3** the bony upper part of your nose **4** a thin strip of wood over which the strings of a violin or guitar are stretched **5** a card game rather like whist

bridle *noun* (*plural* **bridles**) the part of a horse's harness that controls its head

bridle path *noun* (*plural* **bridle paths**) a path for people riding horses

brief *adjective* (**briefer, briefest**) lasting a short time **briefly** *adverb*

briefcase *noun* (*plural* **briefcases**) a flat case for keeping documents and papers in

briefs *plural noun* short underpants or knickers

brigade *noun* (*plural* **brigades**) **1** a unit in the army, larger than a battalion **2** a group of people in uniform, for example the fire brigade

brigadier *noun* (*plural* **brigadiers**) an army officer who commands a brigade and is higher than a colonel

brigand *noun* (*plural* **brigands**) a robber or bandit

bright *adjective* (**brighter, brightest**) **1** giving a strong light; shining **2** clever **3** cheerful **brightly** *adverb*

brighten *verb* (**brightens, brightening, brightened**) 1 to make something brighter 2 to become brighter

brilliant *adjective* 1 very bright and sparkling 2 very clever 3 (informal) really good or enjoyable **brilliance** *noun*

brim *noun* (*plural* **brims**) 1 the edge round the top of a cup or glass 2 the part that sticks out round a hat

brimming *adjective* completely full **brimming over** overflowing

brine *noun* salt water

bring *verb* (**brings, bringing, brought**) to come to a place having something or someone with you ▶ *Shall I bring the picnic things?* **bring about** to make something happen **bring up** 1 to look after a child until he or she is grown up 2 to mention something

brink *noun* the edge of a steep or dangerous place

brisk *adjective* (**brisker, briskest**) quick and lively **briskly** *adverb*

bristle *noun* (*plural* **bristles**) a short stiff hair **bristly** *adjective* having many bristles

British *adjective* from or to do with Great Britain

Briton *noun* (*plural* **Britons**) someone born in Great Britain

brittle *adjective* (**brittler, brittlest**) hard and easy to break or snap

broad *adjective* (**broader, broadest**) wide and large ▶ *He had broad shoulders.* **broaden** *verb* to make something broader

broadcast *noun* (*plural* **broadcasts**) a radio or television programme

broadcast *verb* (**broadcasts, broadcasting, broadcast**) to transmit a broadcast or take part in one **broadcaster** *noun*

broadside *noun* (*plural* **broadsides**) a round of firing by all the guns on one side of a ship

brochure *noun* (*plural* **brochures**) a pamphlet containing information

broke¹ past tense of **break** *verb*

broke² *adjective* (informal) not having any money

broken past participle of **break** *verb*

broken home *noun* (*plural* **broken homes**) a family in which the parents have separated

bronchitis *noun* (*pronounced* brong-ky-tiss) a lung disease that makes it hard to breathe and makes you cough

bronze *noun* 1 a yellow-brown metal made by mixing copper and tin 2 a yellow-brown colour

brooch *noun* (*plural* **brooches**) (*rhymes with* coach) a piece of jewellery that you pin on to your clothes

brood *noun* (*plural* **broods**) a number of young birds hatched together

brood *verb* (**broods, brooding, brooded**) 1 to sit on eggs to hatch them 2 to keep on worrying about something

broody *adjective* (**broodier, broodiest**) thinking and worrying about things

brook *noun* (*plural* **brooks**) a small stream

broom *noun* (*plural* **brooms**) 1 a brush with a long handle for sweeping 2 a shrub with yellow, white, or pink flowers

broth *noun* (*plural* **broths**) a thin kind of soup

brother *noun* (*plural* **brothers**) a boy or man who has the same parents as you

brother-in-law *noun* (*plural* **brothers-in-law**) the brother of someone's husband or wife, or the husband of someone's sister

brought past tense and past participle of **bring**

brow *noun* (*plural* **brows**) 1 your forehead 2 your eyebrow 3 the top of a hill

brown *adjective* (**browner, brownest**) having the colour of earth or toast

brown *noun* the colour of earth or toast

Brownie *noun* (*plural* **Brownies**) a junior member of the Guides

browse *verb* (**browses, browsing, browsed**) 1 to read or look at something casually 2 to feed on grass or leaves

bruise *noun* (*plural* **bruises**) a dark mark that appears on your skin when it is hit or hurt

bruise *verb* (**bruises, bruising, bruised**) to get a bruise on your skin

brush *noun* (*plural* **brushes**) 1 a tool with hairs or bristles for sweeping, painting, or arranging your hair 2 a fox's bushy tail

brush *verb* (**brushes, brushing, brushed**) 1 to use a brush on something ▸ *She quickly brushed her hair and rushed down to meet her friends.* 2 to touch something gently as you pass it

brutal *adjective* savage and cruel **brutality** *noun* savage cruelty **brutally** *adverb* in a cruel way

brute *noun* (*plural* **brutes**) 1 a cruel person 2 an animal

BSE short for *bovine spongiform encephalopathy*, a disease that kills cattle by attacking their nerves and making them stagger about. It is also called **mad cow disease.**

bubble *noun* (*plural* **bubbles**) 1 a thin clear ball of liquid filled with air or gas 2 a small ball of air in a liquid

bubble *verb* (**bubbles, bubbling, bubbled**) to make bubbles

bubbly *adjective* (**bubblier, bubbliest**) 1 full of bubbles, like fizzy water 2 cheerful and lively

buccaneer *noun* (*plural* **buccaneers**) a pirate

buck *noun* (*plural* **bucks**) a male deer, rabbit, or hare

buck *verb* (**bucks, bucking, bucked**) to jump with the back arched as a horse does **buck up** (informal) to start hurrying

bucket *noun* (*plural* **buckets**) a container with a handle, for carrying liquids

buckle *noun* (*plural* **buckles**) a clip at the end of a belt or strap for fastening it

buckle *verb* (**buckles, buckling, buckled**) 1 to fasten something with a buckle 2 to bend or give way under a strain

bud *noun* (*plural* **buds**) a flower or leaf before it has opened

Buddhism *noun* (*pronounced* **buud**-izm) a religion that started in Asia and follows the teachings of Buddha **Buddhist** *noun* someone who believes in Buddhism

budding *adjective* likely to do well ▸ *Their other daughter is a budding journalist.*

budge *verb* (**budges, budging, budged**) to move ▸ *A small boy had stopped halfway down the stairs and refused to budge.*

budgerigar *noun* (*plural* **budgerigars**) (*pronounced* **bud**-jer-i-gar) an Australian bird often kept as a pet in a cage

budget *noun* (*plural* **budgets**) a plan for earning and spending money carefully

budget *verb* (**budgets, budgeting, budgeted**) to plan how much you are going to spend

budgie *noun* (*plural* **budgies**) (informal) a budgerigar

buffalo *noun* (*plural* **buffalo** or **buffaloes**) a wild ox with long curved horns

buffer *noun* (*plural* **buffers**) something that softens a blow or collision, especially a device on a railway engine or wagon or at the end of a railway line

buffet *noun* (*plural* **buffets**) (*pronounced* **buu**-fay) 1 a café or place for buying drinks and snacks 2 a meal at which you serve yourself

bug *noun* (*plural* **bugs**) 1 a tiny insect 2 (informal) a germ that makes you ill ▸ *I may have a tummy bug.* 3 (informal) a hidden microphone 4 a fault or problem in a computer program that stops it working properly

bugle *noun* (*plural* **bugles**) (*pronounced* **byoo**-gul) a brass musical instrument like a small trumpet **bugler** *noun* someone who plays the bugle

build *verb* (**builds, building, built**) to make something by putting the parts together **build up 1** to become larger or stronger ▸ *The traffic was steadily building up.* **2** to make someone healthier and stronger ▸ *Regular exercise will build you up.* **builder** *noun* someone who builds houses and other buildings

build *noun* (*plural* **builds**) the shape and size of your body

building *noun* (*plural* **buildings**) something built with walls and a roof, such as a house or an office block

bulb *noun* (*plural* **bulbs**) **1** the glass part of an electric light **2** the round underground part of some plants, with a shape like an onion

bulge *noun* (*plural* **bulges**) a swelling **bulge** *verb* (**bulges, bulging, bulged**) to stick out or swell

bulk *noun* **1** a thing's size, especially when it is large **2** most of something ▸ *The bulk of the population live in cities.*

bulky *adjective* (**bulkier, bulkiest**) taking up a lot of space

bull *noun* (*plural* **bulls**) the male of some large animals, especially an ox

bulldog *noun* (*plural* **bulldogs**) a large powerful dog with a short thick neck

bulldozer *noun* (*plural* **bulldozers**) a heavy vehicle with caterpillar tracks, used to clear or flatten land

bullet *noun* (*plural* **bullets**) a small piece of metal fired from a gun

bulletin *noun* (*plural* **bulletins**) a short news announcement

bullfight *noun* (*plural* **bullfights**) in Spain, a public entertainment in which men challenge bulls, and sometimes kill them **bullfighter** *noun* someone who takes part in a bullfight

bullion *noun* gold or silver bars

bullock *noun* (*plural* **bullocks**) a young bull

bull's-eye *noun* (*plural* **bull's-eyes**) the centre of a target

bully *noun* (*plural* **bullies**) someone who uses their strength to frighten or hurt weaker people
bully *verb* (**bullies, bullying, bullied**) to hurt or frighten people who are weaker

bulrush *noun* (*plural* **bulrushes**) a tall reed which grows in water or on boggy land

bumble-bee *noun* (*plural* **bumble-bees**) a large bee

bump *verb* (**bumps, bumping, bumped**) to knock against something accidentally
bump *noun* (*plural* **bumps**) **1** an accidental knock **2** a swelling or lump

bumper *noun* (*plural* **bumpers**) a bar along the front or back of a motor vehicle to protect it from damage
bumper *adjective* extra large or good ▸ *This year's bumper prize is a holiday in the south of France.*

bumpy *adjective* (**bumpier, bumpiest**) **1** having a lot of bumps **2** with a lot of jolts and jerks ▸ *We had a bumpy ride along the old track.*

bun *noun* (*plural* **buns**) **1** a small sweet bread roll **2** a hairstyle made by winding long hair into a round shape at the back of the head

bunch *noun* (*plural* **bunches**) **1** a number of things joined or tied together ▸ *People left bunches of flowers at the spot where the accident happened.* **2** (*informal*) a group of people

bundle *noun* (*plural* **bundles**) a collection of things tied or wrapped together
bundle *verb* (**bundles, bundling, bundled**) **1** to tie or wrap things loosely **2** to push someone hurriedly somewhere ▸ *The kidnappers bundled her into the passenger seat of the van.*

bung *noun* (*plural* **bungs**) a stopper for a bottle or barrel
bung *verb* (**bungs, bunging, bunged**) to block something up

bungalow *noun* (*plural* **bungalows**) a house with all the rooms on the same level

bungle *verb* (**bungles, bungling, bungled**) to do something badly and clumsily

bunk or **bunk bed** *noun* (*plural* **bunks, bunk beds**) a bed with another bed above it or below it

bunker *noun* (*plural* **bunkers**)
1 a container for storing coal or wood
2 a hollow filled with sand on a golf course
3 an underground shelter

bunsen burner *noun* (*plural* **bunsen burners**) a gas burner with an adjustable flame used in laboratories
It is named after a German scientist called Robert Bunsen, who died in 1899. It is now normally spelt with a small *b*.

buoy *noun* (*plural* **buoys**) (*pronounced* boi) a floating object in the sea, used as a marker or warning sign

buoyant *adjective* able to float

burden *noun* (*plural* **burdens**) 1 a heavy load 2 something unwelcome that you have to do

bureau *noun* (*plural* **bureaux**) (*pronounced* **bewr-oh**) an office or department ▸ *A food information bureau is offering advice on diets.*
Bureau is a French word, and this is why the plural ends in *x* and not *s*.

burglar *noun* (*plural* **burglars**) someone who breaks into a building to steal things **burglary** *noun* the crime of stealing things from a building **burgle** *verb* to steal from a building

burial *noun* (*plural* **burials**) burying a dead body

burly *adjective* (**burlier, burliest**) big and strong

burn *verb* (**burns, burning, burnt** or **burned**)
1 to damage or destroy something by fire or strong heat 2 to be on fire; to give off flames 3 to feel very hot **burner** *noun* the part of a lamp or cooker that makes the flame

burn *noun* (*plural* **burns**) 1 an injury caused by fire or strong heat 2 the firing of a spacecraft's rocket

burp *verb* (**burps, burping, burped**) to belch
burp *noun* (*plural* **burps**) a belch

burrow *noun* (*plural* **burrows**) a hole dug by a rabbit or fox for shelter

burrow *verb* (**burrows, burrowing, burrowed**) 1 to dig a burrow 2 to dig or search deeply ▸ *He burrowed in his pockets to find a pound coin.*

burst *verb* (**bursts, bursting, burst**) 1 to break apart suddenly 2 to make something break apart 3 to start doing something suddenly ▸ *He threw back his head and burst out laughing.*

burst *noun* (*plural* **bursts**) 1 a split caused by something bursting ▸ *There's a burst in one of the pipes.* 2 something short and quick ▸ *We heard a burst of machine-gun fire in the distance.*

bury *verb* (**buries, burying, buried**) to put something under the ground

bus *noun* (*plural* **buses**) a large road vehicle for carrying passengers

bush *noun* (*plural* **bushes**) a plant like a small tree with a lot of stems or branches **the bush** wild land in Australia or Africa

bushy *adjective* (**bushier, bushiest**) thick and hairy ▸ *You can tell a fox by its bushy tail.*

business *noun* (*plural* **businesses**) (*pronounced* **biz-niss**) 1 an activity that someone does to make money ▸ *The company does good business abroad.* 2 an organization that makes money by selling goods or services ▸ *His uncle ran a small engineering business in Birmingham.* 3 what concerns a person and no one else ▸ *It was none of Jane's business, but she still wanted to know more.* **businesslike** *adjective* well organized and practical

busker *noun* (*plural* **buskers**) someone who plays music in the street for money

bust[1] *noun* (*plural* **busts**) 1 a woman's bosom 2 a statue of a famous person's head and shoulders

bust[2] *adjective* (informal) broken or burst

bustle *verb* (**bustles, bustling, bustled**) to be rushing about in a busy way

busy *adjective* (**busier, busiest**) 1 having a lot to do 2 full of people and activity **busily** *adverb*

busybody *noun* (*plural* **busybodies**) someone who interferes in other people's affairs

but *conjunction* a linking word ▸ *I wanted to go but I couldn't.*

but *preposition* except ▸ *There's no one here but me.*

butcher *noun* (*plural* **butchers**) someone who works in a shop that cuts and sells meat

butt[1] *noun* (*plural* **butts**) 1 the end of a weapon or tool that has its handle 2 a large barrel for holding water

butt[2] *verb* (**butts, butting, butted**) to hit someone hard with the head or horns **butt in** to interrupt suddenly or rudely

butter *noun* a fatty yellow food made from cream

buttercup *noun* (*plural* **buttercups**) a yellow wild flower

butterfly *noun* (*plural* **butterflies**) an insect with large white or coloured wings

butterscotch *noun* a kind of hard toffee

buttocks *plural noun* the part of your body you sit on, your bottom

button *noun* (*plural* **buttons**) 1 a small round object sewn on clothes and used to fasten parts together 2 a small knob you press to work a machine

button *verb* (**buttons, buttoning, buttoned**) to fasten something with buttons

buttress *noun* (*plural* **buttresses**) a support built against a wall

buy *verb* (**buys, buying, bought**) to get something by paying for it **buyer** *noun* someone who buys something

buzz *verb* (**buzzes, buzzing, buzzed**) to make a sharp humming sound, like the sound of bees

buzz *noun* (*plural* **buzzes**) a buzzing sound **buzzer** *noun* an electronic device that makes a buzzing noise

buzzard *noun* (*plural* **buzzards**) a large bird of prey

by *preposition* and *adverb* 1 near, close ▸ *Sit by me.* 2 before ▸ *Will the car be ready by tomorrow?* 3 using; by means of ▸ *He made some money by working in a pub in the evenings.* **by and large** mostly, on the whole

bye *noun* (*plural* **byes**) a run scored in cricket when the batsman has not touched the ball

by-election *noun* (*plural* **by-elections**) an election in one place only, when an MP has died or resigned, and not in the whole country

bypass *noun* (*plural* **bypasses**) a road that takes traffic past a congested area

byte *noun* (*plural* **bytes**) a unit in computing that measures data or memory

Cc

C is short for **Celsius** or **centigrade** and is used to show temperatures. ▸ *The temperature is 16° C.*

cab *noun* (*plural* **cabs**) 1 a taxi 2 the place for the driver in a lorry, bus, train, or crane

cabbage *noun* (*plural* **cabbages**) a large round vegetable with green or purple leaves

cabin *noun* (*plural* **cabins**) 1 a hut or shelter 2 a room or compartment on a ship or aircraft

cabinet *noun* (*plural* **cabinets**) 1 a cupboard with shelves and doors 2 the most senior members of the government

cable *noun* (*plural* **cables**) 1 a thick rope, wire, or chain 2 a telegram sent overseas

cable television *noun* a television system using underground cables to send the sound and pictures

cackle *verb* (**cackles, cackling, cackled**) to make the clucking sound of a hen
cackle *noun* (*plural* **cackles**) **1** the clucking of a hen **2** a loud silly laugh

cactus *noun* (*plural* **cacti**) a prickly plant that grows in hot dry places

cadet *noun* (*plural* **cadets**) a young person being trained to join the armed forces or the police

cadge *verb* (**cadges, cadging, cadged**) to get something you want by asking for it in a blunt or direct way

café *noun* (*plural* **cafés**) (*pronounced* **kaf-ay**) a place that sells drinks and snacks

cafeteria *noun* (*plural* **cafeterias**) (*pronounced* kaf-e-**teer**-i-a) a café where customers serve themselves from a counter

cage *noun* (*plural* **cages**) a container made of bars or wires, in which birds or animals are kept

cagoule *noun* (*plural* **cagoules**) a waterproof covering for the top half of the body

cake *noun* (*plural* **cakes**) **1** a sweet food made by baking a mixture of flour, eggs, fat, and sugar **2** a small block of soap

caked *adjective* covered with something that has dried hard, like mud

calamity *noun* (*plural* **calamities**) a disaster

calcium *noun* a chemical element contained in teeth and bones, and also in chalk and limestone

calculate *verb* (**calculates, calculating, calculated**) to work something out by arithmetic or with a calculator **calculation** *noun*

calculator *noun* (*plural* **calculators**) an electronic device for doing sums

calendar *noun* (*plural* **calendars**) a list of the days of the year arranged in weeks and months

calf *noun* (*plural* **calves**) **1** a young cow or ox **2** a young whale or seal **3** the back part of your leg below your knee

call *verb* (**calls, calling, called**) **1** to shout out or speak loudly **2** to telephone someone **3** to ask someone to come to you **4** to visit someone ▸ *Harriet's mother called the next day.* **5** to give someone or something a name ▸ *Why did you call your cat Albert?* **6** to describe someone or something in a certain way ▸ *I don't call that working.* **call off** to cancel something that was planned
call *noun* (*plural* **calls**) **1** a shout or cry **2** a short visit **3** a telephone conversation

calling *noun* a person's profession or job

callous *adjective* not caring; cruel

calm *adjective* (**calmer, calmest**) **1** quiet and still ▸ *a calm sea.* **2** not anxious or excited ▸ *Please keep calm.* **calmly** *adverb*
calm *verb* (**calms, calming, calmed**) to become calm, or to make someone calm

calorie *noun* (*plural* **calories**) a unit for measuring the energy produced by food

calves plural of **calf**

camcorder *noun* (*plural* **camcorders**) a portable video camera that can also record sound

came past tense of **come**

camel *noun* (*plural* **camels**) a large animal with a long neck and one hump (an **Arabian camel**) or two humps (a **Bactrian camel**) on its back

camera *noun* (*plural* **cameras**) a device for taking photographs, films, or television pictures

camouflage *noun* (*pronounced* **kam-o-flah**z*h*) a kind of disguise that makes things look like part of their surroundings

camouflage *verb* (**camouflages, camouflaging, camouflaged**) to disguise something with camouflage

camp *noun* (*plural* **camps**) a place where people live in tents or huts for a short time

camp *verb* (**camps, camping, camped**) to live in a camp **camper** *noun*

campaign *noun* (*plural* **campaigns**) a series of activities that you plan when you want to achieve or win something ► *They started a campaign to ban smoking on the buses.*

campaign *verb* (**campaigns, campaigning, campaigned**) to carry out a plan of action

campus *noun* (*plural* **campuses**) the buildings and grounds of a college or university

can¹ *verb* (*present tense* **can**; *past tense* **could**) 1 to be able to do something ► *Can you help me?* ► *They can speak three languages.* 2 to be allowed to do something ► *Can I go home now?*

can² *noun* (*plural* **cans**) a sealed metal container holding food or drink

canal *noun* (*plural* **canals**) an artificial water channel for boats or for irrigating crops

canary *noun* (*plural* **canaries**) a small yellow songbird

cancel *verb* (**cancels, cancelling, cancelled**) 1 to say that something planned will not happen after all 2 to stop an order or instruction 3 to mark a ticket or stamp so that it cannot be used again **cancellation** *noun*

cancer *noun* (*plural* **cancers**) a disease in which a harmful growth forms in a part of the body

candid *adjective* saying what you think, frank

candidate *noun* (*plural* **candidates**) 1 someone who applies for a job 2 someone you can vote for in an election 3 someone taking an exam or test

candle *noun* (*plural* **candles**) a stick of wax with a wick through it, giving light when it burns

candlestick *noun* (*plural* **candlesticks**) a holder for a candle

candy *noun* (*plural* **candies**) a sweet

cane *noun* (*plural* **canes**) a long thin stick of bamboo

canine *adjective* to do with dogs

cannibal *noun* (*plural* **cannibals**) a person who eats human flesh **cannibalism** *noun*

cannon *noun* (*plural* **cannon** or **cannons**) a large heavy gun

cannonball *noun* (*plural* **cannonballs**) a large ball fired from a cannon

cannot can not ► *I cannot believe it.*

canoe *noun* (*plural* **canoes**) a light narrow boat driven with paddles **canoeing** *noun*

canopy *noun* (*plural* **canopies**) a cover over a throne or bed

can't short for *can not* ► *I can't believe it.*

canteen *noun* (*plural* **canteens**) 1 a restaurant for workers in a factory or office 2 a box containing a set of cutlery

canter *verb* (**canters, cantering, cantered**) to ride a horse at a gentle gallop

canvas *noun* (*plural* **canvases**) a kind of strong coarse cloth

canyon *noun* (*plural* **canyons**) a deep valley with steep sides and a river running through it

cap *noun* (*plural* **caps**) 1 a soft hat with a peak 2 a cover or top

capable *adjective* able to do something well **capability** *noun* **capably** *adverb*

capacity *noun* (*plural* **capacities**) 1 the ability or power to do something ▸ *They have a great capacity for hard work.* 2 the amount that something can hold ▸ *The jug has a capacity of two litres.*

cape *noun* (*plural* **capes**) 1 a piece of high land sticking out into the sea 2 a cloak

caper *verb* (**capers, capering, capered**) to jump about playfully

capital *noun* (*plural* **capitals**) 1 the most important city in a country or region 2 money invested to start a business or to make more money

capital letter *noun* (*plural* **capital letters**) a large letter such as A, B, C

capital punishment *noun* punishment by putting someone to death

capsize *verb* (**capsizes, capsizing, capsized**) to overturn in a boat in the water

capsule *noun* (*plural* **capsules**) 1 a hollow pill filled with medicine for swallowing 2 a small spacecraft that separates from a larger rocket

captain *noun* (*plural* **captains**) 1 an officer in charge of a ship or aircraft 2 an officer in the army or navy 3 the leading player in a sports team

caption *noun* (*plural* **captions**) the words printed beside a picture to explain it

captivating *adjective* charming and attractive

captive *noun* (*plural* **captives**) a person or animal that has been captured **captivity** *noun*

capture *verb* (**captures, capturing, captured**) 1 to catch or imprison a person or animal 2 to take a place by force

car *noun* (*plural* **cars**) 1 a motor vehicle for about four or five people 2 a railway carriage ▸ *The fast train has a buffet car.*

caramel *noun* (*plural* **caramels**) 1 burnt sugar used to give a sweet taste to food 2 a soft toffee

carat *noun* (*plural* **carats**) a measure of how pure gold is

caravan *noun* (*plural* **caravans**) 1 a vehicle towed by a car and used for living in 2 a large number of people travelling together in the desert

carbon *noun* a chemical element found in charcoal, graphite, diamonds, and other substances

carbon dioxide *noun* a colourless gas breathed out by humans and animals

carbon monoxide *noun* a poisonous gas found in the exhaust fumes of motor vehicles

carburettor *noun* (*plural* **carburettors**) a device for mixing fuel and air in a petrol engine

carcass *noun* (*plural* **carcasses**) the body of a dead animal or bird

card *noun* (*plural* **cards**) 1 a piece of stiff paper 2 a playing card 3 cardboard 4 a folded piece of card you use to send greetings ▸ *a birthday card* 5 a small piece of plastic with your name and other information on it, issued by a bank or shop ▸ *a credit card*

cardboard *noun* thick stiff paper

cardigan *noun* (*plural* **cardigans**) a knitted jacket

cardinal *noun* (*plural* **cardinals**) a senior priest in the Roman Catholic Church

care *verb* (**cares, caring, cared**) to feel interested or concerned about something or someone **care for** to look after someone ▸ *Rob's sister has a job caring for old people.*

care *noun* (*plural* **cares**) 1 worry or trouble ▸ *She tripped along without a care in the world.* 2 serious thought or attention ▸ *They did the work with great care.* 3 protection or supervision ▸ *In the end they left the child in the care of a nanny.*

take care of to look after someone or something ▸ *I said I'd take care of the cat while they are away.*

career *noun* (*plural* **careers**) the way you earn a living and make progress in your job

career *verb* (**careers, careering, careered**) to rush along wildly

carefree *adjective* without worries or responsibilities

careful *adjective* taking care, paying attention to something **carefully** *adverb*

careless *adjective* not taking care; clumsy

caress *verb* (**caresses, caressing, caressed**) to touch someone gently and fondly

caretaker *noun* (*plural* **caretakers**) someone who looks after a large building such as a church or school

cargo *noun* (*plural* **cargoes**) goods carried in a ship or aircraft

Caribbean *adjective* (*pronounced* ka-ri-bee-an) from the West Indies or to do with the West Indies

carnation *noun* (*plural* **carnations**) a garden flower with a sweet smell

carnival *noun* (*plural* **carnivals**) a festival with processions of people in fancy dress

carnivore *noun* (*plural* **carnivores**) (*pronounced* **kar-ni-vor**) an animal that eats meat **carnivorous** *adjective*

carol *noun* (*plural* **carols**) a joyful Christmas hymn

carp *noun* (*plural* **carp**) a freshwater fish

carpenter *noun* (*plural* **carpenters**) someone who makes things out of wood **carpentry** *noun*

carpet *noun* (*plural* **carpets**) a thick soft covering for a floor

carriage *noun* (*plural* **carriages**) 1 one of the parts of a train where passengers travel 2 a passenger vehicle pulled by horses

carrot *noun* (*plural* **carrots**) a long thin orange-coloured vegetable

carry *verb* (**carries, carrying, carried**) 1 to lift something and take it somewhere 2 to be heard a long way away ▸ *The sounds carried for miles.* **carried away** very excited **carry on** to continue doing something ▸ *Carry on reading to the end of the chapter.* **carry out** to do something you are meant to do ▸ *They hoped to carry out the work in their spare time.*

cart *noun* (*plural* **carts**) a small vehicle for carrying loads

cart *verb* (**carts, carting, carted**) (informal) to carry something heavy or tiring ▸ *The child came back, carting a telephone directory.*

carthorse *noun* (*plural* **carthorses**) a large heavy work-horse

cartilage *noun* (*pronounced* kar-ti-lij) tough flexible tissue attached to a bone

carton *noun* (*plural* **cartons**) a lightweight cardboard or plastic box

cartoon *noun* (*plural* **cartoons**)
1 a drawing that is funny or tells a joke
2 a series of drawings that tell a story
3 a film made from a series of drawings, so that the characters appear to move

cartridge *noun* (*plural* **cartridges**) 1 the case containing the explosive for a bullet or shell 2 a container holding film for a camera or ink for a pen

cartwheel *noun* (*plural* **cartwheels**) a somersault done sideways, with your arms and legs spread wide

carve *verb* (**carves, carving, carved**) 1 to cut and shape wood or stone to make something artistic 2 to cut meat into slices

cascade *noun* (*plural* **cascades**) a waterfall or a series of waterfalls

case *noun* (*plural* **cases**) 1 a bag or container for carrying things 2 an example of something existing or happening ▸ *It might be another case of chickenpox.*
3 something investigated by the police or by a lawcourt ▸ *He didn't want to have his name mentioned in a murder case.* 4 the facts or arguments used to support something ▸ *She made a good case for getting some extra money.* **in case** because something may happen ▸ *Anna crept to the back door, tiptoeing in case her Mum heard her.*

cash *noun* money in coins and banknotes
cash *verb* (**cashes, cashing, cashed**) to exchange a cheque for cash

cashier *noun* (*plural* **cashiers**) someone in charge of the money in a bank, office, or shop

cask *noun* (*plural* **casks**) a barrel

casket *noun* (*plural* **caskets**) a small box for jewellery

casserole *noun* (*plural* **casseroles**) 1 a dish with a lid for cooking food in an oven 2 food cooked in a dish of this kind

cassette *noun* (*plural* **cassettes**) a sealed case containing recording tape or film

cast *verb* (**casts, casting, cast**) 1 to throw something 2 to shed something 3 to make a metal or plaster object in a mould
cast *noun* (*plural* **casts**) 1 an object made in a mould 2 the actors in a play or film

castanets *plural noun* two pieces of wood or ivory held in one hand and clapped together to make a clicking sound, as in Spanish dancing

castaway *noun* (*plural* **castaways**) a shipwrecked person

castle *noun* (*plural* **castles**) 1 a large old building with thick walls and fortifications to protect people in it from attack 2 a piece in chess, also called a *rook*

castor *noun* (*plural* **castors**) (*pronounced* kah-ster) a small wheel on the leg of a piece of furniture

castor sugar *noun* fine white sugar

casual *adjective* 1 not deliberate or planned ▸ *It was just a casual remark.* 2 informal; suitable for leisure time ▸ *They were all wearing casual clothes.* 3 not regular or permanent ▸ *Jim was looking for casual work on a building site.* **casually** *adverb*

casualty *noun* (*plural* **casualties**) someone killed or injured in war or in an accident

cat *noun* (*plural* **cats**) 1 a small furry animal kept as a pet 2 a larger member of the same family, for example a lion, tiger, or leopard

catalogue *noun* (*plural* **catalogues**) a list of goods for sale or of books in a library

catamaran *noun* (*plural* **catamarans**) a boat with two hulls fixed side by side

catapult *noun* (*plural* **catapults**) a forked stick with elastic attached, used for shooting pellets or small stones

catarrh *noun* (*pronounced* ka-tah) a sticky stuff you get in your nose and throat when you have a cold

catastrophe *noun* (*plural* **catastrophes**) (*pronounced* ka-**tas**-tro-fi) a great disaster **catastrophic** *adjective*

catch *verb* (**catches, catching, caught**) 1 to get hold of something that is moving 2 to discover someone doing something wrong ▸ *In those days anyone caught begging was sent to prison.* 3 to get an illness from someone else 4 to be in time for a bus or train before it leaves 5 to manage to hear something someone says ▸ *I'm afraid I didn't catch your question.* 6 to get your clothes entangled in something ▸ *She caught her jersey on a rose thorn.* **catch fire** to start burning **catch on** (informal) to become popular **catch up** to reach someone ahead of you
catch *noun* (*plural* **catches**) 1 catching something ▸ *Dave made a brilliant catch.* 2 something you catch ▸ *They had a large catch of fish.* 3 a hidden difficulty or snag ▸ *The car was so cheap there had to be a catch.* 4 a device for keeping a door or window closed

catchy *adjective* (**catchier, catchiest**) pleasant and easy to remember ▸ *The song has a catchy tune.*

category *noun* (*plural* **categories**) a group or division of similar people or things

cater *verb* (**caters, catering, catered**) cater for to provide something for people ▸ *The library caters for all ages.* **caterer** *noun* someone who provides food for a group of people

caterpillar *noun* (*plural* **caterpillars**) the long creeping larva of a butterfly or moth

cathedral *noun* (*plural* **cathedrals**) the main church of a region, with a bishop in charge of it

Catherine wheel *noun* (*plural* **Catherine wheels**) a round firework that spins round

Catholic *adjective* belonging to the Christian Church that has the Pope as its head
Catholic *noun* (*plural* **Catholics**) a member of this Church

catkin *noun* (*plural* **catkins**) a fluffy flower that hangs down from a willow or hazel

cattle *plural noun* cows and bulls

caught past tense and past participle of **catch** *verb*

cauliflower *noun* (*plural* **cauliflowers**) a vegetable with leaves round a large head of white flowers

cause *noun* (*plural* **causes**) 1 what makes something happen, a reason ▸ *The cause of the fire was faulty wiring.* 2 an aim or purpose ▸ *They were raising money for a special cause.*
cause *verb* (**causes, causing, caused**) to make something happen

caution *noun* (*plural* **cautions**) 1 being careful 2 a warning
caution (**cautions, cautioning, cautioned**) to give someone a strong warning

cautious *adjective* avoiding risks, careful ▸ *Anna took a cautious step towards the edge of the pool.* **cautiously** *adverb*

Cavalier *noun* (*plural* **Cavaliers**) a supporter of King Charles I in the English Civil War

cavalry *noun* soldiers on horseback

cave *noun* (*plural* **caves**) a large hole under the ground or in the side of a hill or cliff

caveman *noun* (*plural* **cavemen**) a person who lived in a cave in prehistoric times

cavern *noun* (*plural* **caverns**) a deep dark cave

cavity *noun* (*plural* **cavities**) a hollow space or hole

CD short for **compact disc**

CD-ROM short for *compact disc read-only memory*, a system for storing information to be displayed on a VDU screen

cease *verb* (**ceases, ceasing, ceased**) to stop doing something

ceaseless *adjective* not stopping

cedar *noun* (*plural* **cedars**) an evergreen tree with hard wood

ceiling *noun* (*plural* **ceilings**) (*pronounced* see-ling) the top surface of a room

celebrate *verb* (**celebrates, celebrating, celebrated**) to hold a party or have fun on a special occasion ▸ *The villagers celebrated the end of the war by singing and dancing.* **celebration** *noun*

celebrity *noun* (*plural* **celebrities**) a famous person

celery *noun* a vegetable with crisp white or green stalks

cell *noun* (*plural* **cells**) 1 a small room, especially in a prison or monastery 2 a tiny part of a living creature or plant 3 a device for producing electric current

cellar *noun* (*plural* **cellars**) an underground room for storing things

cello *noun* (*plural* **cellos**) (*pronounced* **chel**-oh) a large stringed musical instrument, held between the knees and played with a bow

cellular *adjective* having many cells or holes ▸ *Bella covered the baby with a cellular blanket.*

cellulose *noun* a tissue that forms the main part of all plants and trees

Celsius *adjective* using the scale for measuring temperature that shows 0 degrees for freezing water and 100 degrees for boiling water
Celsius is named after a Swedish scientist called Anders Celsius, who died in 1744. This scale is also called **centigrade**, and another scale is called **Fahrenheit**.

Celtic *adjective* (*pronounced* **kel**-tik) to do with the people or languages of Wales, Scotland, and Ireland

cement *noun* 1 a mixture of lime and clay mixed with water to make concrete and join bricks together 2 a strong glue

cemetery *noun* (*plural* **cemeteries**) (*pronounced* **sem**-e-tri) a place where people are buried when they have died

censor *verb* (**censors**, **censoring**, **censored**) to look at films, plays, and books and take out parts that might offend people **censorship** *noun*

censure *noun* criticism or disapproval

census *noun* (*plural* **censuses**) an official count of the number of people in a place

cent *noun* (*plural* **cents**) a coin and unit of money in America and some other countries

centenary *noun* (*plural* **centenaries**) the hundredth anniversary of something important

centigrade *adjective* another word for **Celsius**

centimetre *noun* (*plural* **centimetres**) a measure of length, one-hundredth of a metre

centipede *noun* (*plural* **centipedes**) a small long creature with many legs

central *adjective* at or near the centre of something **centrally** *adverb*

central heating *noun* a system of heating a building by heated pipes and radiators

centre *noun* (*plural* **centres**) 1 the middle of something 2 an important place 3 a building or place for a special purpose ▸ *They've built a new visitor centre near the site of the battle.*

centurion *noun* (*plural* **centurions**) an officer in the ancient Roman army

century *noun* (*plural* **centuries**) 1 a period of a hundred years 2 a score of a hundred runs in cricket

ceramics *plural noun* objects made of pottery

cereal *noun* (*plural* **cereals**) 1 a grass that produces grain used for food 2 a breakfast food made from grain

ceremony *noun* (*plural* **ceremonies**) (*pronounced* **se**-ri-mo-ni) an important event such as a wedding, funeral, or coronation **ceremonial** *adjective*

certain *adjective* 1 sure, not having any doubt 2 known but not named ▸ *A certain person was here this morning.* **certainly** *adverb* **certainty** *noun*

certificate *noun* (*plural* **certificates**) an official document that records something important

CFC short for *chlorofluorocarbon*, a gas that damages the ozone layer

chaffinch *noun* (*plural* **chaffinches**) a small songbird

chain *noun* (*plural* **chains**) 1 a row of metal rings, called links, fastened together 2 a connected series of things ▸ *The chain of helpers were swinging buckets of water from hand to hand.*

chair *noun* (*plural* **chairs**) a seat with a back

chalet noun (plural **chalets**) (pronounced **shal**-ay) a small wooden house, especially in Alpine regions

chalk noun (plural **chalks**) 1 a soft white rock 2 a stick of a similar rock, used for writing on blackboards **chalky** adjective

challenge verb (**challenges**, **challenging**, **challenged**) to invite someone to perform a feat or take part in a fight **challenger** noun

challenge noun (plural **challenges**) something difficult that someone has to do

chamber noun (plural **chambers**) (old use) a room

champagne noun (pronounced sham-**payn**) a bubbly white French wine

champion noun (plural **champions**) 1 the person who has beaten all the others in a sport or competition 2 someone who fights for a cause ▶ He was always a champion of fair working conditions.

championship noun (plural **championships**) a competition to find the best player or team in a game or sport

chance noun (plural **chances**) 1 a possibility or opportunity ▶ Thursday is our only chance to see the eclipse. 2 the way things happen accidentally ▶ The two boys met by chance on the beach. **take a chance** to take a risk

chancellor noun (plural **chancellors**) an important government or legal official

Chancellor of the Exchequer noun the minister of the British government in charge of finances and taxes

chandelier noun (plural **chandeliers**) (pronounced shan-de-**leer**) a set of lights hanging from a ceiling

change verb (**changes**, **changing**, **changed**) 1 to make someone or something different 2 to become different ▶ When they went back to the place years later it had changed a lot. 3 to exchange one thing for another ▶ Stella wanted to change her dress before going out.

change noun (plural **changes**) 1 the process of changing 2 the money you get back when you give more than the right money to pay for something 3 something different ▶ Let's go out for a change. 4 a set of fresh clothes

changeable adjective likely to change, often changing ▶ The weather is changeable at this time of year.

channel noun (plural **channels**) 1 a stretch of water joining two seas ▶ the English Channel. 2 a way for water to flow along or for ships to travel on 3 a television station

chant noun (plural **chants**) a group of words that is sung over and over again

chant verb (**chants**, **chanting**, **chanted**) to sing or say words in a special rhythm

chaos noun (pronounced **kay**-oss) complete disorder or confusion ▶ A burst water pipe was causing traffic chaos. **chaotic** adjective

chapel noun (plural **chapels**) a small church or room for worship

chapter noun (plural **chapters**) a section of a book

char verb (**chars**, **charring**, **charred**) to scorch something

character noun (plural **characters**) 1 the kind of person you are 2 a person in a story or play 3 a letter or number used in printing

characteristic noun (plural **characteristics**) something that makes a person or thing different from others

characteristic adjective typical

charades noun (pronounced sha-**rahdz**) a game in which you have to guess a word from other players' acting

charcoal noun a black substance made by burning wood slowly

charge noun (plural **charges**) 1 a price or fee 2 a statement that someone committed a crime 3 an attack in a battle 4 the amount of an electric current **in charge of** responsible for someone or something

charge verb (**charges**, **charging**, **charged**) 1 to ask a price for something 2 to accuse someone of committing a crime 3 to rush to attack the enemy in battle 4 to put an electric current into a battery

chariot noun (*plural* **chariots**) a horse-drawn vehicle used in ancient times for fighting and racing **charioteer** noun someone who drove a chariot

charity noun (*plural* **charities**) 1 giving money and help to other people 2 an organization that helps people in need **charitable** *adjective* kind and generous

charm noun (*plural* **charms**) 1 being pleasant and attractive 2 a magic spell 3 something small that you wear or carry to bring good luck
charm verb (**charms, charming, charmed**) 1 to give someone pleasure or delight 2 to put a spell on someone

charming *adjective* pleasant and attractive

chart noun (*plural* **charts**) 1 a large plan or map 2 a diagram or list of information

charter noun (*plural* **charters**) an official document explaining someone's rights or giving them permission to do something
charter verb (**charters, chartering, chartered**) to hire an aircraft or vehicle

chase verb (**chases, chasing, chased**) to go quickly after a person or animal to try to catch them up

chasm noun (*plural* **chasms**) (*pronounced* **ka**-zum) a deep opening in the ground

chat verb (**chats, chatting, chatted**) to talk to someone in a friendly way
chat noun (*plural* **chats**) a friendly talk **chatty** *adjective*

château noun (*plural* **châteaux**) (*pronounced* **shat**-oh) a castle or large house in France
Château is a French word, and this is why it has an accent on the first *a* and the plural ends in *x* and not *s*.

chatter verb (**chatters, chattering, chattered**) to talk a lot about unimportant things

chauffeur noun (*plural* **chauffeurs**) (*pronounced* **shoh**-fer) someone who is paid to drive a car for someone

cheap *adjective* (**cheaper, cheapest**) 1 low in price; not expensive 2 not well made or of good quality

cheat verb (**cheats, cheating, cheated**) to trick someone or behave dishonestly
cheat noun (*plural* **cheats**) someone who cheats

check verb (**checks, checking, checked**) 1 to make sure that something is correct or all right 2 to make someone or something stop or slow down
check noun (*plural* **checks**) 1 the process of checking something ▸ *Joan made a quick check that the room was still tidy.* 2 a position in chess in which the king is threatened by another piece and has to escape 3 a pattern of squares

checkmate noun (*plural* **checkmates**) a winning position in chess when the other player's king cannot escape from check
The word **checkmate** comes from the Persian words *shah mat* which mean 'the king is dead'.

checkout noun (*plural* **checkouts**) the place where you pay for your shopping in a supermarket or a large shop

check-up noun (*plural* **check-ups**) a careful check by a doctor or dentist

cheek noun (*plural* **cheeks**) 1 the side of your face below your eye 2 being rude or impolite **cheeky** *adjective* rude or impolite

cheer verb (**cheers, cheering, cheered**) 1 to shout loudly in support of someone 2 to comfort or encourage someone **cheer up** to become more cheerful
cheer noun (*plural* **cheers**) a shout praising or supporting someone

cheerful *adjective* happy and bright **cheerfully** *adverb*

cheese noun (*plural* **cheeses**) a solid food made from milk **cheesy** *adjective*

cheetah noun (*plural* **cheetahs**) a large spotted animal of the cat family, which can run very fast

chef noun (*plural* **chefs**) (*pronounced* shef) the chief cook in a hotel or restaurant

chemical noun (*plural* **chemicals**) a substance used in chemistry
chemical *adjective* to do with chemistry or made by chemistry

chemist *noun* (*plural* **chemists**) **1** someone who makes and sells medicines **2** an expert in chemistry

chemistry *noun* the study of what substances are made of and how they react with one another

cheque *noun* (*plural* **cheques**) a piece of paper telling a bank to pay money to someone

cherish *verb* (**cherishes, cherishing, cherished**) to look after something lovingly

cherry *noun* (*plural* **cherries**) a small bright or dark red fruit with a stone

chess *noun* a game for two players played with sixteen pieces each on a board of 64 squares

chest *noun* (*plural* **chests**) **1** a large strong box **2** the front part of your body between your neck and your waist

chest of drawers *noun* (*plural* **chests of drawers**) a piece of furniture with drawers for holding clothes

chestnut *noun* (*plural* **chestnuts**) **1** a hard brown nut **2** the tree that produces this kind of nut

chew *verb* (**chews, chewing, chewed**) to grind food into pieces between your teeth

chewing gum *noun* a sticky flavoured gum that you chew without swallowing

chick *noun* (*plural* **chicks**) a young bird

chicken *noun* (*plural* **chickens**) **1** a young hen **2** meat from a hen

chickenpox *noun* a disease that gives you red itchy spots on your skin

chief *noun* (*plural* **chiefs**) a leader or ruler

chief *adjective* most important

chiefly *adverb* mainly, mostly

chieftain *noun* (*plural* **chieftains**) the chief of a tribe or clan

child *noun* (*plural* **children**) **1** a young person; a boy or girl **2** someone's son or daughter

childhood *noun* (*plural* **childhoods**) the time when you are a child

childish *adjective* silly and immature

childminder *noun* (*plural* **childminders**) a person who is paid to look after children while their parents are at work

chill *noun* (*plural* **chills**) **1** a cold feeling **2** a cold that makes you shiver

chill *verb* (**chills, chilling, chilled**) to make something cold

chilly *adjective* (**chillier, chilliest**) **1** slightly cold **2** unfriendly

chime *noun* (*plural* **chimes**) a sound made by a bell

chime *verb* (**chimes, chiming, chimed**) to make a ringing sound

chimney *noun* (*plural* **chimneys**) a tall pipe or passage that carries away smoke from a fire

chimney pot *noun* (*plural* **chimney pots**) the piece of pipe at the top of a chimney

chimpanzee *noun* (*plural* **chimpanzees**) a type of African ape

chin *noun* (*plural* **chins**) the part of your face under your mouth

china *noun* thin and delicate pottery, or cups and plates made from it

chink *noun* (*plural* **chinks**) **1** a narrow opening ▸ *Jane noticed a light through a chink in the curtains.* **2** a light ringing sound ▸ *They could hear the chink of coins.*

chip *noun* (*plural* **chips**) **1** a small piece broken off something **2** a small piece of fried potato **3** a small piece of silicon containing electric circuits and used in computers

chip *verb* (**chips, chipping, chipped**) to knock a small piece off something

chirp *verb* (**chirps, chirping, chirped**) to make short sharp sounds like a small bird

chirpy *adjective* (**chirpier, chirpiest**) (informal) lively and cheerful

chisel *noun* (*plural* **chisels**) a tool with a sharp end for shaping wood or stone

chisel *verb* (**chisels, chiselling, chiselled**) to shape or cut something with a chisel

chivalry *noun* **1** polite and helpful behaviour **2** the behaviour and rules followed by medieval knights **chivalrous** *adjective*

chlorine *noun* a strong-smelling chemical used to kill germs in water

chocolate *noun* (*plural* **chocolates**) a sweet brown food made from cocoa powder

choice *noun* (*plural* **choices**) **1** the process of choosing or the power to choose ▶ *You have the choice whether to go or not.* **2** all the things you can choose from ▶ *The shop has a good choice of sandwiches.* **3** what someone chooses ▶ *The Lake District is a good choice for an outdoor holiday.*

choir *noun* (*plural* **choirs**) a group of singers, especially in a church

choke *verb* (**chokes, choking, choked**) **1** to be unable to breathe properly **2** to stop someone breathing properly

cholera *noun* (*pronounced* **kol-er-a**) a severe infectious disease

cholesterol *noun* (*pronounced* **ko-less-te-rol**) a substance in the cells of your body which helps to carry fat in the bloodstream

choose *verb* (**chooses, choosing, chose, chosen**) **1** to decide to have one person or thing rather than another **2** to make a decision about something ▶ *Mary came, but her sister chose to stay at home.*

chop *verb* (**chops, chopping, chopped**) to cut something into pieces with an axe or knife

chop *noun* (*plural* **chops**) **1** a chopping blow **2** a thick slice of meat with a bone in it

chopper *noun* (*plural* **choppers**) a small axe

choppy *adjective* (**choppier, choppiest**) fairly rough with small waves ▶ *a choppy sea.*

chopsticks *plural noun* a pair of thin sticks used for eating Chinese or Japanese food

choral *adjective* (*pronounced* **kor-al**) for a choir or chorus

chord *noun* (*plural* **chords**) (*pronounced* kord) a group of musical notes sounded together

chore *noun* (*plural* **chores**) (*pronounced* chor) a boring or difficult task

chorus *noun* (*plural* **choruses**) (*pronounced* **kor-us**) **1** a choir **2** a piece of music sung by a choir **3** the words repeated after every verse of a song or poem

chose past tense of **choose**

christen *verb* (**christens, christening, christened**) to baptize a child in a Christian Church **christening** *noun*

Christian *noun* (*plural* **Christians**) someone who believes in Jesus Christ and his teachings

Christian *adjective* to do with Christ or Christians

Christianity *noun* the religion of Christians, following the teachings of Jesus Christ

Christmas *noun* (*plural* **Christmases**) the time of celebrating the birth of Jesus Christ on 25 December

chrome or **chromium** *noun* a shiny silvery metal

chromosome *noun* (*plural* **chromosomes**) the part of an animal cell that carries the genes

chronic *adjective* lasting a long time ▶ *Their uncle was suffering from a chronic liver disease.* **chronically** *adverb*

chronicle *noun* (*plural* **chronicles**) a list of events with their dates

chronological *adjective* arranged in the order in which things happen **chronologically** *adverb*

chrysalis noun (plural **chrysalises**) (pronounced **kris**-a-lis) the form that a caterpillar changes into before it becomes a butterfly or moth

chrysanthemum noun (plural **chrysanthemums**) a garden flower that blooms in autumn

chubby adjective (**chubbier, chubbiest**) rather plump

chuck verb (**chucks, chucking, chucked**) (informal) to throw something carelessly

chuckle verb (**chuckles, chuckling, chuckled**) to laugh quietly

chum noun (plural **chums**) (informal) a friend

chunk noun (plural **chunks**) a thick lump **chunky** adjective

church noun (plural **churches**) a building where Christians worship

churchyard noun (plural **churchyards**) the ground round a church, used as a graveyard

churn noun (plural **churns**) 1 a large container for milk 2 a machine for making butter

chutney noun a strong-tasting mixture of fruit and peppers in a sauce, eaten with meat

cider noun an alcoholic drink made from apples

cigar noun (plural **cigars**) a roll of pressed tobacco leaves for smoking

cigarette noun (plural **cigarettes**) a small thin roll of shredded tobacco in thin paper for smoking

cinder noun (plural **cinders**) a small piece of partly burned coal or wood

cinema noun (plural **cinemas**) a place where people go to see films

circle noun (plural **circles**) 1 a round flat shape, like a coin or wheel 2 the upper floor in a cinema or theatre

circle verb (**circles, circling, circled**) 1 to move in a circle ▸ *Birds were circling in the sky.* 2 to go round a place ▸ *A row of beach chairs circled the edge of the pool.*

circuit noun (plural **circuits**) (pronounced **ser**-kit) 1 a circular line or journey 2 a racecourse 3 the path of an electric current

circular adjective going round like the edge of a circle

circulate verb (**circulates, circulating, circulated**) to move around and come back to the beginning ▸ *Blood circulates around your body.* **circulation** noun

circumference noun (plural **circumferences**) the distance round a circle

circumstance noun (plural **circumstances**) a fact or event that affects something ▸ *He was doing a good job under difficult circumstances.*

circus noun (plural **circuses**) a show with clowns, acrobats, and sometimes animals, usually performed in a large tent

cistern noun (plural **cisterns**) a water tank

citizen noun (plural **citizens**) 1 someone who has the right to live in a particular country ▸ *They are American citizens.* 2 someone who lives in a town or city **citizenship** noun

citrus fruit noun (plural **citrus fruits**) a fruit such as an orange, lemon, or grapefruit

city noun (plural **cities**) a large or important town

civil adjective 1 to do with the citizens of a place 2 to do with the ordinary people and not those who are in the armed forces 3 polite, courteous

civilian noun (plural **civilians**) someone who is an ordinary citizen and not in the armed forces

civilization *noun* (*plural* **civilizations**) an organized society or culture ► *They were reading about ancient civilizations.*

civilized *adjective* living in a well organized society

civil rights *plural noun* the rights of citizens to be free and equal

civil service *noun* the people who work for the government, helping to run the country

civil war *noun* (*plural* **civil wars**) a war fought between people of the same country
Famous civil wars are the English Civil War (1642–51) and the American Civil War (1861–65).

claim *verb* (**claims, claiming, claimed**) 1 to ask for something when you think it belongs to you ► *You can claim the money for your train fares.* 2 to state something clearly ► *They claimed they had been at home all evening.*

claim *noun* (*plural* **claims**) something you claim

clam *noun* (*plural* **clams**) a large shellfish

clamber *verb* (**clambers, clambering, clambered**) to climb over difficult ground using your hands and feet ► *We clambered over the slippery rocks.*

clammy *adjective* (**clammier, clammiest**) damp and slimy

clamp *noun* (*plural* **clamps**) a device for holding things together

clamp *verb* (**clamps, clamping, clamped**) to fix a clamp on something, especially on a vehicle so that it cannot move

clan *noun* (*plural* **clans**) a group of related families with the same name

clang *verb* (**clangs, clanging, clanged**) to make a noisy ringing sound

clank *verb* (**clanks, clanking, clanked**) to make a loud sound like heavy pieces of metal banging together

clap *verb* (**claps, clapping, clapped**) to make a noise by hitting the palms of your hands together, especially to show that you have enjoyed something

clap *noun* (*plural* **claps**) 1 a round of clapping ► *They gave the winners a loud clap.* 2 a sudden sound of loud thunder

clarify *verb* (**clarifies, clarifying, clarified**) to explain something so that it is easier to understand **clarification** *noun* words that explain something

clarinet *noun* (*plural* **clarinets**) a woodwind instrument with a low tone **clarinettist** *noun* someone who plays a clarinet

clarity *noun* clearness

clash *verb* (**clashes, clashing, clashed**) 1 to make a loud sound like cymbals banging together 2 to have a violent fight or argument ► *Supporters clashed with police outside the ground.* 3 to look ugly or unattractive together ► *The reds and pinks in the room clashed terribly.* 4 to happen at the same time as something else, so that you cannot do both ► *The town fair clashes with my holiday this year.*

clash *noun* (*plural* **clashes**) 1 a clashing sound 2 a fight or argument

clasp *verb* (**clasps, clasping, clasped**) to hold something or someone tightly

clasp *noun* (*plural* **clasps**) 1 a device for fastening things 2 a tight grasp

class *noun* (*plural* **classes**) 1 a group of similar people, animals, or things 2 a group of children or students who are taught together 3 a lesson in school 4 a system of different ranks in society

classic *noun* (*plural* **classics**) a book, film, or story that is well known and thought to be very good and important

classic *adjective* very good and important

classical *adjective* 1 to do with the ancient Greeks and Romans 2 to do with older or more serious forms of music

classify *verb* (**classifies, classifying, classified**) to put things in classes or groups **classification** *noun*

classroom *noun* (*plural* **classrooms**) a room in a school where you have lessons

clatter *verb* (**clatters, clattering, clattered**) to make a loud noise like things being banged together

clause *noun* (*plural* **clauses**) 1 a part of a sentence with its own verb 2 a section of a legal document

claw *noun* (*plural* **claws**) a sharp curved nail that some birds and animals have on their feet

clay *noun* a sticky kind of earth, used for making bricks and pottery

clean *adjective* (**cleaner, cleanest**) 1 free from dirt and stains 2 fresh, not yet used ► *She started to write her story on a clean page.*
clean *verb* (**cleans, cleaning, cleaned**) to make something clean

cleaner *noun* (*plural* **cleaners**) 1 a person who cleans inside houses and offices 2 a substance you use to clean something

cleanse *verb* (**cleanses, cleansing, cleansed**) (*pronounced* klenz) to clean something and make it pure

clear *adjective* (**clearer, clearest**) 1 easy to see or hear or understand ► *Jenny's voice was clear and bright.* 2 easy to see through ► *One window had clear glass so you could see into the room.* 3 free from things that get in the way ► *Keep a space clear to sit down on.*
clear *verb* (**clears, clearing, cleared**) 1 to take things away to make a space ► *They cleared a space on the floor to sit on.* 2 to become clearer ► *After the storm, the sky began to clear.* 3 to jump over an obstacle without touching it **clear up** to make things tidy

clearing *noun* (*plural* **clearings**) an open space in a wood or forest

clench *verb* (**clenches, clenching, clenched**) to close your teeth or fingers tightly

clergy *plural noun* the priests and other officials of a Christian church **clergyman** *noun* **clergywoman** *noun*

clerk *noun* (*plural* **clerks**) (*pronounced* klark) someone in an office who deals with letters and papers

clever *adjective* (**cleverer, cleverest**) 1 quick to learn and understand things; skilful 2 done with skill ► *That was a clever trick.*

click *verb* (**clicks, clicking, clicked**) to make a short sharp sound
click *noun* (*plural* **clicks**) a clicking sound

client *noun* (*plural* **clients**) a customer of a bank, or of a lawyer or other professional person

cliff *noun* (*plural* **cliffs**) a steep rock face on the coast

climate *noun* (*plural* **climates**) the normal weather in a particular area

climax *noun* (*plural* **climaxes**) the most exciting and important part of a story or series of events

climb *verb* (**climbs, climbing, climbed**) 1 to go up something steep 2 to grow or rise upwards **climb down** to go down something steep **climber** *noun*
climb *noun* (*plural* **climbs**) an act of climbing ► *We got tired on the long climb up the hill.*

cling *verb* (**clings, clinging, clung**) to hold on or stick closely ► *Paula's wet trousers were still clinging to her legs.*

clinic *noun* (*plural* **clinics**) a place where people see doctors for advice or treatment

clink *verb* (**clinks, clinking, clinked**) to make a short ringing sound, like a coin being dropped

clip *noun* (*plural* **clips**) 1 a fastener for keeping things together 2 a short piece from a film or television programme
clip *verb* (**clips, clipping, clipped**) 1 to fasten things with a clip 2 to cut something with shears or scissors

clipper *noun* (*plural* **clippers**) a fast sailing ship

cloak *noun* (*plural* **cloaks**) a loose outdoor coat with no sleeves

cloakroom *noun* (*plural* **cloakrooms**) 1 a place where you can leave your coat 2 a lavatory

clock *noun* (*plural* **clocks**) an instrument that shows the time

clockwise *adverb* and *adjective* moving in the same direction as the hands of a clock

clockwork *noun* a device for making some clocks and toys work, using a spring which you wind up

clod *noun* (*plural* **clods**) a lump of earth

clog *verb* (**clogs, clogging, clogged**) to block something up

clog *noun* (*plural* **clogs**) a wooden shoe

cloister *noun* (*plural* **cloisters**) a covered passage round a courtyard of a cathedral or monastery

clone *noun* (*plural* **clones**) an animal or plant made from the cells of another animal or plant, so that it is identical

clone *verb* (**clones, cloning, cloned**) to produce a clone of something

close¹ *adjective* (**closer, closest**) (*pronounced* klohss) 1 near ▶ *They have moved to a new house close to the supermarket.* 2 careful and detailed ▶ *The girls came in to take a closer look.* 3 having a strong relationship ▶ *The boys had been close friends for several years.* 4 without much room to spare ▶ *The car squeezed into the garage but it was a close fit.* 5 without much difference between the winner and the others ▶ *The race was very close.*

close *adverb* (**closer, closest**) (*pronounced* klohss) at a close distance ▶ *Some noisy geese were following close behind.*

close² *verb* (**closes, closing, closed**) (*pronounced* klohz) 1 to shut something 2 to bring an end to a meeting or event

close down to stop operating a business

close-up *noun* (*plural* **close-ups**) (*pronounced* **klohss**-up) a photograph or film taken from a short distance

clot *noun* (*plural* **clots**) a lump of thick liquid like blood or cream that has become nearly solid

clot *verb* (**clots, clotting, clotted**) to form into clots, like blood or cream

cloth *noun* (*plural* **cloths**) 1 material woven from wool, cotton, or some other fabric 2 a piece of this material 3 a tablecloth

clothe *verb* (**clothes, clothing, clothed**) (*pronounced* klohth) to put clothes on someone

clothes *plural noun* things that you wear

clothing *noun* clothes

cloud *noun* (*plural* **clouds**) 1 a mass of water vapour floating in the air 2 a mass of smoke or dust in the air **cloudless** *adjective*

cloudy *adjective* (**cloudier, cloudiest**) 1 full of clouds 2 hard to see through ▶ *The glass contained a cloudy liquid.*

clout *verb* (**clouts, clouting, clouted**) to hit someone hard

clover *noun* a small wild plant with leaves in three parts

clown *noun* (*plural* **clowns**) 1 a circus performer who dresses up and wears bright face paint 2 an amusing or silly person

club *noun* (*plural* **clubs**) 1 a heavy stick 2 a stick with a special head for playing golf 3 a group of people who meet together 4 a playing card with the shape of a black clover-leaf printed on it

club *verb* (**clubs, clubbing, clubbed**) to hit someone hard with a heavy stick

cluck *verb* (**clucks, clucking, clucked**) to make a noise like a hen

clue *noun* (*plural* **clues**) something that helps you to solve a puzzle or a mystery

clump *noun* (*plural* **clumps**) a group of trees or plants growing close together

clumsy *adjective* (**clumsier, clumsiest**) careless and awkward **clumsily** *adverb* **clumsiness** *noun*

clung past tense and past participle of **cling**

cluster *noun* (*plural* **clusters**) a group of people or things close together

cluster *verb* (**clusters, clustering, clustered**) to form a close group

clutch *verb* (**clutches, clutching, clutched**) to grab hold of something

clutch *noun* (*plural* **clutches**) 1 a pedal in a motor vehicle which you press when you change gear 2 a set of eggs in a nest

clutter *noun* a lot of things left around untidily

cm short for **centimetre** or **centimetres**

Co. short for **company**

coach *noun* (*plural* **coaches**) 1 a more comfortable type of bus used for long journeys 2 a carriage of a railway train 3 a carriage pulled by horses 4 a sports instructor

coach *verb* (**coaches, coaching, coached**) to instruct or train people in a sport

coal *noun* (*plural* **coals**) a hard black mineral used as fuel

coarse *adjective* (**coarser, coarsest**) 1 rough, not delicate or smooth 2 rude or offensive ▸ *You have a very coarse sense of humour.*

coast *noun* (*plural* **coasts**) the seashore and the land close to it

coast *verb* (**coasts, coasting, coasted**) to ride downhill without using power **coastal** *adjective* to do with the seashore

coastguard *noun* (*plural* **coastguards**) someone whose job is to keep watch on coasts

coat *noun* (*plural* **coats**) 1 a piece of outdoor clothing with sleeves, worn over other clothes 2 a covering of something liquid such as paint

coat *verb* (**coats, coating, coated**) to cover something with a liquid such as paint

coating *noun* (*plural* **coatings**) a covering or layer of paint or other liquid

coax *verb* (**coaxes, coaxing, coaxed**) to persuade someone gently or patiently

cobbles *plural noun* a surface of cobblestones **cobbled** *adjective*

cobblestone *noun* (*plural* **cobblestones**) a small smooth and rounded stone once used to pave streets in towns

cobra *noun* (*plural* **cobras**) (*pronounced* koh-bra) a poisonous snake

cobweb *noun* (*plural* **cobwebs**) a fine sticky net spun by a spider to trap insects

cock *noun* (*plural* **cocks**) a male adult chicken or other bird

cock *verb* (**cocks, cocking, cocked**) 1 to turn your eye or ear in a particular direction 2 to make a gun ready to fire

cockerel *noun* (*plural* **cockerels**) a young cock

cockle *noun* (*plural* **cockles**) a type of shellfish

cockney *noun* (*plural* **cockneys**) someone born in the East End of London
The word **cockney** comes from an older English word meaning 'cock's egg', which became an unkind word for someone who lived in a city.

cockpit *noun* (*plural* **cockpits**) the place in a light aircraft where the pilot sits

cockroach *noun* (*plural* **cockroaches**) a dark brown beetle usually found in dirty parts of a building

cocky *adjective* (**cockier, cockiest**) (informal) conceited and cheeky

cocoa *noun* (*plural* **cocoas**) 1 chocolate powder made from the seeds of a tree called a cacao tree 2 a hot drink made with cocoa powder

coconut *noun* (*plural* **coconuts**) a large round nut that grows on palm trees, with a hairy skin and containing a milky juice

cocoon *noun* (*plural* **cocoons**) the covering round a chrysalis

cod *noun* (*plural* **cod**) a large sea fish that you can eat

code *noun* (*plural* **codes**) 1 a set of signs and letters for sending messages secretly 2 a set of rules ▸ *Drivers have to learn the Highway Code.*

code *verb* (**codes, coding, coded**) to put a message into code

coeducation *noun* teaching boys and girls together **coeducational** *adjective*

coffee *noun* (*plural* **coffees**) a hot drink made from the roasted and crushed beans of a tropical shrub

coffin *noun* (*plural* **coffins**) a long box in which a dead person is buried or cremated

cog *noun* (*plural* **cogs**) a wheel with teeth round the edge so that it can turn another wheel

coil *noun* (*plural* **coils**) a circle or spiral of rope or wire

coil *verb* (**coils, coiling, coiled**) to wind a rope or wire into a coil

coin *noun* (*plural* **coins**) a piece of money made of metal

coinage *noun* a system of money

coincide *verb* (**coincides, coinciding, coincided**) (not an everyday word) to happen at the same time as something else ▶ *Unfortunately, the rain coincided with the guests' arrival.*

coincidence *noun* (*plural* **coincidences**) two things happening by chance at the same time ▶ *It was just a coincidence that Martha was in town on the same day as me.*

coke *noun* a solid fuel made from coal

cold *adjective* (**colder, coldest**) 1 low in temperature, not hot or warm 2 unfriendly or unkind

cold *noun* (*plural* **colds**) 1 cold weather or temperature 2 an illness that makes your nose run and gives you a sore throat

cold-blooded *adjective* 1 having blood that changes temperature according to the surroundings 2 cruel, ruthless

collaborate *verb* (**collaborates, collaborating, collaborated**) to work together with someone **collaboration** *noun*

collage *noun* (*plural* **collages**) (*pronounced* **kol-ahzh** or kol-**ahzh**) a picture made by putting together scraps of paper and other things

collapse *verb* (**collapses, collapsing, collapsed**) 1 (used about a building) to fall down in pieces 2 (used about a person) to faint; to fall down exhausted

collapsible *adjective* able to be folded up

collar *noun* (*plural* **collars**) 1 the part of a shirt or coat that goes round your neck 2 a band that goes round an animal's neck

collect *verb* (**collects, collecting, collected**) 1 to gather or bring things together ▶ *We collected the dead leaves into a large heap.*

2 to come together ▶ *A crowd was collecting outside the hospital.* 3 to make organized sets of things you are interested in, such as coins or stamps 4 to go and fetch someone or something ▶ *Mum had to collect Jane from the station.* **collection** *noun* **collector** *noun*

college *noun* (*plural* **colleges**) a place where people can continue to study after they have left school

collide *verb* (**collides, colliding, collided**) to hit something while you are moving ▶ *The car collided with a lorry which was travelling in the opposite direction.*

collie *noun* (*plural* **collies**) a breed of sheepdog with a pointed muzzle and long hair

collision *noun* (*plural* **collisions**) a crash between moving vehicles

colon *noun* (*plural* **colons**) a punctuation mark (:) used to separate one part of a sentence from another

colonel *noun* (*plural* **colonels**) (*pronounced* **ker-nel**) an army officer higher than a major

colony *noun* (*plural* **colonies**) 1 a country that has people who have settled from another country and is governed by that country 2 a group of people or animals living together **colonial** *adjective* **colonize** *verb*

colossal *adjective* huge, enormous

colour *noun* (*plural* **colours**) 1 red, green, blue, and the other effects of light, produced by rays of different wavelengths 2 the use of all colours, not just black and white ▶ *Is this film in colour?*

colour *verb* (**colours, colouring, coloured**) to add colour to something, especially by using paints **coloured** *adjective*

colour-blind *adjective* unable to see some colours or to tell the difference between them

colourful *adjective* 1 having a lot of colour 2 lively ▶ *The film was a colourful story of life on board a pirate ship.*

colt *noun* (*plural* **colts**) a young male horse

column *noun* (*plural* **columns**) 1 a pillar 2 a strip of printing in a book or newspaper 3 something long and narrow, such as rising smoke

coma *noun* (*plural* **comas**) (*pronounced koh-ma*) a state of being deeply unconscious for a long time

comb *noun* (*plural* **combs**) 1 a tool with teeth for making your hair tidy 2 the red crest on a chicken's head
comb *verb* (**combs, combing, combed**) 1 to tidy your hair with a comb 2 to search a place carefully for something lost

combat *noun* (*plural* **combats**) a fight or battle
combat *verb* (**combats, combating, combated**) to try to get rid of something bad or unwanted ▶ *We need to combat violent crime in the area.*

combine *verb* (**combines, combining, combined**) to join things or mix them together **combination** *noun*

combine harvester *noun* (*plural* **combine harvesters**) a machine that reaps and threshes grain

combustion *noun* what happens when something burns

come *verb* (**comes, coming, came, come**) 1 to move towards the person or place that is here ▶ *Are you coming to my party tomorrow?* 2 to arrive ▶ *A letter has come for you.* 3 to occur or happen ▶ *New Year comes a week after Christmas.* **come about** to happen **come to** to add up to ▶ *The bill came to £10.* **come true** to happen ▶ *Their holiday was a dream come true.*

comedian *noun* (*plural* **comedians**) someone who entertains people and makes them laugh

comedy *noun* (*plural* **comedies**) a play or film that makes people laugh

comet *noun* (*plural* **comets**) a distant object that moves across the sky with a bright tail of light

comfort *noun* (*plural* **comforts**) 1 a feeling of being warm and contented and in pleasant surroundings 2 a person or thing that makes you feel this
comfort *verb* (**comforts, comforting, comforted**) to make someone less upset or anxious

comfortable *adjective* 1 pleasant to use or wear 2 not having any pain or worries **comfortably** *adverb*

comic *noun* (*plural* **comics**) 1 a children's paper with illustrated stories 2 a comedian
comic or **comical** *adjective* funny, making people laugh

comic strip *noun* (*plural* **comic strips**) a series of drawings that tell a story

comma *noun* (*plural* **commas**) a punctuation mark (,) used to mark a pause in writing

command *noun* (*plural* **commands**) 1 an order to do something 2 authority or control 3 skill or ability in a subject ▶ *By the end of their stay the students had a good command of English.*
command *verb* (**commands, commanding, commanded**) 1 to tell someone to do something 2 to be in charge of a group of people

commander *noun* (*plural* **commanders**) a naval officer below captain

commandment *noun* (*plural* **commandments**) a sacred command, especially one of the Ten Commandments of Moses

commando *noun* (*plural* **commandos**) a soldier trained to make dangerous raids

commence *verb* (**commences, commencing, commenced**) (not an everyday word) to begin something **commencement** *noun* a beginning

commend *verb* (**commends, commending, commended**) (not an everyday word) to praise someone ▸ *One of the soldiers was commended for bravery.* **commendation** *noun*

comment *noun* (*plural* **comments**) a remark or opinion

comment *verb* (**comments, commenting, commented**) to make a comment

commentary *noun* (*plural* **commentaries**) a description of an event by someone who is watching it, especially for radio or television

commentator *noun* (*plural* **commentators**) a person who gives a commentary

commerce *noun* trade, buying and selling goods

commercial *adjective* to do with trade and making money

commercial *noun* (*plural* **commercials**) an advertisement on television or radio

commit *verb* (**commits, committing, committed**) to do something wrong, such as a crime **commit yourself** to promise to do something **commitment** *noun*

committee *noun* (*plural* **committees**) a group of people who meet to organize or discuss something

common *adjective* (**commoner, commonest**) 1 ordinary or usual 2 happening or used often 3 shared by several people ▸ *They became good friends, and shared a common interest in cooking.*

common *noun* (*plural* **commons**) an area of grass and trees that anyone can use

commonplace *adjective* ordinary, familiar

commonwealth *noun* (*plural* **commonwealths**) a group of countries that cooperate and help one another

commotion *noun* (*plural* **commotions**) a loud noise or din

commune *noun* (*plural* **communes**) a group of people sharing a home and way of life

communicate *verb* (**communicates, communicating, communicated**) to pass on news or information to other people **communicative** *adjective* keen to give information

communication *noun* (*plural* **communications**) 1 passing on information to people 2 a message or piece of information

Communion *noun* (*plural* **Communions**) a Christian ceremony in which people eat holy bread and drink wine to commemorate the death of Jesus Christ

communism *noun* a political system in which the state controls property and industry **communist** *noun*

community *noun* (*plural* **communities**) all the people living in a place

commuter *noun* (*plural* **commuters**) someone who travels to work every day by train or bus **commute** *verb* to travel to work

compact *adjective* small and neat

compact disc *noun* (*plural* **compact discs**) a small plastic disc which stores music or information as digital signals and is read by a laser beam; often called **CD**

companion *noun* (*plural* **companions**) someone you spend a lot of time with **companionship** *noun* friendship

company *noun* (*plural* **companies**) 1 a group of people, especially a business firm 2 having people with you ▸ *They enjoyed the food and the good company.* 3 a unit in the army

compare *verb* (**compares, comparing, compared**) 1 to see how alike or different several things are ▸ *Compare your answer with someone else's.* 2 to be as good as something else ▸ *Our track cannot compare with an Olympic stadium.*

comparison *noun* (*plural* **comparisons**) comparing different things

compartment *noun* (*plural* **compartments**) a separate part or division inside something

compass *noun* (*plural* **compasses**) an instrument with a magnetized needle that shows direction **compasses** or **pair of compasses** an instrument for drawing circles

compassion *noun* pity or mercy **compassionate** *adjective* sympathetic

compatible *adjective* able to exist or be used together

compel *verb* (**compels, compelling, compelled**) to force someone to do something

compensate *verb* (**compensates, compensating, compensated**) to make up for a loss or injury **compensation** *noun*

compete *verb* (**competes, competing, competed**) to take part in a competition

competent *adjective* able to do something well **competence** *noun*

competition *noun* (*plural* **competitions**) a game or race in which people try to do better than the others taking part **competitive** *adjective* liking to compete with other people **competitor** *noun* someone who competes in a game or race

compile *verb* (**compiles, compiling, compiled**) to collect and arrange information, stories, or poems in a book ▶ *She compiled a collection of children's poems.* **compilation** *noun* **compiler** *noun*

complacent *adjective* smug or too satisfied with the way things are

complain *verb* (**complains, complaining, complained**) 1 to say that you are not pleased about something 2 to say that you are ill or have a pain ▶ *She complained of cramp after her swim.*

complaint *noun* (*plural* **complaints**) 1 saying you are not pleased about something 2 a minor illness

complete *adjective* 1 having all its parts 2 finished, achieved ▶ *By evening the jigsaw puzzle was complete.* 3 utter, total ▶ *We heard the news in complete silence.*
complete *verb* (**completes, completing, completed**) to finish something or make it complete **completion** *noun*

completely *adverb* totally, utterly

complex *adjective* difficult and complicated **complexity** *noun*
complex *noun* (*plural* **complexes**) a large building with many parts, or a group of buildings ▶ *a shopping complex.*

complexion *noun* (*plural* **complexions**) the natural colour and appearance of your face

complicated *adjective* having many parts or details, so that it is difficult to understand or deal with

complication *noun* (*plural* **complications**) a new problem that makes something else more difficult

compliment *noun* (*plural* **compliments**) something you say to show you admire someone or something **complimentary** *adjective*

component *noun* (*plural* **components**) a part of a machine

compose *verb* (**composes, composing, composed**) to write a piece of music or poetry **be composed of** to have or contain ▶ *The estate is composed of several small farms.*

composer *noun* (*plural* **composers**) someone who writes music

composition *noun* (*plural* **compositions**) 1 composing or writing something 2 a piece of music or an essay

compost *noun* a mixture of decayed leaves, grass, and natural waste used to fertilize the ground

compound *noun* (*plural* **compounds**) 1 something made of several parts or ingredients ▶ *Water is a compound of hydrogen and oxygen.* 2 an area containing buildings and surrounded by a fence

comprehend *verb* (**comprehends, comprehending, comprehended**) to understand something

comprehensible *adjective* easy to understand

comprehension *noun* understanding

comprehensive *adjective* including everything that is wanted

comprehensive school *noun* (*plural* **comprehensive schools**) a ˈsecondary school for children of all abilities

compress *verb* (**compresses, compressing, compressed**) to press or squeeze something so that it becomes smaller or tighter **compression** *noun*

comprise *verb* (**comprises, comprising, comprised**) to include several people or things ▸ *The exhibition comprises forty paintings.*

compromise *noun* (*plural* **compromises**) an agreement to accept less than you really wanted, especially so as to settle a disagreement

compromise *verb* (**compromises, compromising, compromised**) to accept less than you really wanted

compulsory *adjective* having to be done because it is a rule ▸ *English and maths are compulsory subjects.*

computer *noun* (*plural* **computers**) an electronic machine that holds and sorts information (called **data**), does word processing and calculations, and can control other machines

comrade *noun* (*plural* **comrades**) a friend or companion **comradeship** *noun* friendship

concave *adjective* curved like the inside of a circle or ball

conceal *verb* (**conceals, concealing, concealed**) to hide something **concealment** *noun*

conceited *adjective* too proud of yourself or what you have done

conceive *verb* (**conceives, conceiving, conceived**) 1 to form an idea or plan in your mind 2 to become pregnant **conceivable** *adjective* able to be imagined

concentrate *verb* (**concentrates, concentrating, concentrated**) 1 to think hard about something 2 to bring people or things together in one place 3 to make a liquid denser and less watery

concentration *noun* thinking hard about something

concentric *adjective* having the same centre

concept *noun* (*plural* **concepts**) a new idea about something

conception *noun* (*plural* **conceptions**) 1 forming an idea 2 becoming pregnant

concern *verb* (**concerns, concerning, concerned**) 1 to be important or interesting to someone 2 to worry someone

concern *noun* (*plural* **concerns**) 1 something that matters to someone ▸ *I think that is my concern.* 2 a business

concerning *preposition* (not an everyday word) about, on the subject of ▸ *They wrote to us concerning our rubbish collection.*

concert *noun* (*plural* **concerts**) a performance of music

concertina *noun* (*plural* **concertinas**) a musical instrument with bellows that you squeeze

concise *adjective* saying all that is needed in a few words

conclude *verb* (**concludes, concluding, concluded**) 1 to end something 2 to reach a decision about something ▸ *The inquiry concluded that the crash was caused by a bomb.*

conclusion *noun* (*plural* **conclusions**) 1 an ending 2 a decision

concrete *noun* a strong building material made by mixing cement with water, sand, and small stones

concussion *noun* being unconscious for a short time from a hard knock on the head

condemn *verb* (**condemns, condemning, condemned**) 1 to say that something is wrong or that someone has done something wrong 2 to say that a building is not fit to be used **condemnation** *noun*

condensation *noun* drops of liquid formed from vapour that has touched a cold surface

condense *verb* (**condenses, condensing, condensed**) 1 to make a speech or piece of writing shorter 2 to change from a gas into a liquid

condition *noun* (*plural* **conditions**) 1 the state in which a person or thing is ▸ *For sale: mountain bike in good working condition.* 2 something that you must agree to for something to happen ▸ *Being able to swim is a condition of going sailing.*

condom *noun* (*plural* **condoms**) a rubber covering a man can wear on his penis during sexual intercourse, as a contraceptive and a protection against disease

conduct *verb* (**conducts, conducting, conducted**) (*pronounced* **kon-dukt**) 1 to organize something or carry it out ▸ *The council conducted a survey of rubbish collection in the area.* 2 to direct an orchestra or band when it plays a piece of music 3 to allow electricity or heat to pass along

conduct *noun* (*pronounced* **kon-dukt**) a person's behaviour

conductor *noun* (*plural* **conductors**) 1 someone who sells tickets on a bus or coach 2 someone who conducts an orchestra 3 something that conducts electricity or heat

cone *noun* (*plural* **cones**) 1 an object which is circular at its base and pointed at its top 2 the fruit of a pine, fir, or cedar

confer *verb* (**confers, conferring, conferred**) (not an everyday word) to have a discussion

conference *noun* (*plural* **conferences**) a meeting to discuss things

confess *verb* (**confesses, confessing, confessed**) to admit that you have done something wrong or embarrassing **confession** *noun*

confetti *plural noun* tiny pieces of coloured paper thrown over the bride and bridegroom after their wedding

confide *verb* (**confides, confiding, confided**) to tell someone something private or secret ▸ *It was good to have someone she could confide in.*

confidence *noun* trust or faith in what you or someone else can do **in confidence** as a secret ▸ *They told us in confidence that they were getting married.*

confident *adjective* having confidence

confidential *adjective* having to be kept secret ▸ *What you tell your doctor is confidential.* **confidentially** *adverb*

confine *verb* (**confines, confining, confined**) 1 to limit or restrict something ▸ *Fortunately the pain was confined to his right side.* 2 to shut a person or animal in a place **confinement** *noun*

confirm *verb* (**confirms, confirming, confirmed**) 1 to show that something is true 2 to make an arrangement definite **be confirmed** to become a full member of a Christian Church in a special ceremony **confirmation** *noun*

confiscate *verb* (**confiscates, confiscating, confiscated**) to take something away from someone as a punishment **confiscation** *noun*

conflict *noun* (*plural* **conflicts**) (*pronounced* kon-flikt) fighting or serious disagreement

conflict *verb* (**conflicts, conflicting, conflicted**) (*pronounced* kon-flikt) to disagree or be very different ▸ *Your version of what happened conflicts with hers.*

conform *verb* (**conforms, conforming, conformed**) to follow the normal rules or ideas **conformity** *noun*

confront *verb* (**confronts, confronting, confronted**) **1** to oppose someone face to face **2** to tackle a problem or difficulty bravely **confrontation** *noun*

confuse *verb* (**confuses, confusing, confused**) **1** to make someone puzzled or muddled **2** to mistake one thing for another **confusion** *noun*

congested *adjective* crowded with people or traffic **congestion** *noun*

congratulate *verb* (**congratulates, congratulating, congratulated**) to tell someone how pleased you are about something they have done **congratulations** *plural noun* what you say to congratulate someone

congregation *noun* (*plural* **congregations**) the people who take part in a church service

congress *noun* (*plural* **congresses**) a large meeting or conference **Congress** the parliament or government of the USA

conical *adjective* shaped like a cone

conifer *noun* (*plural* **conifers**) (*pronounced* kon-i-fer) a tree that produces cones **coniferous** *adjective*

conjunction *noun* (*plural* **conjunctions**) a joining word such as *and* or *but*

conjure *verb* (**conjures, conjuring, conjured**) to perform tricks that look like magic **conjurer** *noun*

conker *noun* (*plural* **conkers**) a hard shiny brown nut that grows on a horse chestnut tree

connect *verb* (**connects, connecting, connected**) to join one thing to another **connection** *noun*

conquer *verb* (**conquers, conquering, conquered**) to defeat an enemy or a country in war **conqueror** *noun*

conquest *noun* (*plural* **conquests**) conquering an enemy or country

conscience *noun* (*pronounced* kon-shens) a feeling you have about whether something is right or wrong

conscientious *adjective* (*pronounced* kon-shee-en-shus) careful and hard-working

conscious *adjective* (*pronounced* kon-shus) awake and knowing what is happening **consciousness** *noun*

consecutive *adjective* following one after another ▸ *The team has suffered three consecutive defeats now.*

consent *noun* permission or agreement for someone to do something

consent *verb* (**consents, consenting, consented**) to give permission

consequence *noun* (*plural* **consequences**) (not an everyday word) something which happens because of an event or action ▸ *Getting sore skin was a consequence of staying in the sun for too long.* **of no consequence** not very important **consequently** *adverb* as a result

conservation *noun* keeping buildings and natural surroundings in a good state

conservative *adjective* **1** wanting things to stay the same **2** cautious, prudent ▸ *£100 was a conservative estimate of how much the bike would cost.*

Conservative *noun* (*plural* **Conservatives**) someone who supports the Conservative Party, a British political party

conservatory *noun* (*plural* **conservatories**) a room with glass walls and a glass roof built on to a house

conserve *verb* (**conserves, conserving, conserved**) to keep something from being changed or spoilt

consider *verb* (**considers, considering, considered**) 1 to think carefully about something 2 to have an opinion about something ► *We consider that the criticism was fair.*

considerable *adjective* large or important **considerably** *adverb* very much

considerate *adjective* kind and thoughtful

consideration *noun* (*plural* **considerations**) 1 careful thought or attention 2 something you have to think about ► *Another very important consideration is money.*

consist *verb* (**consists, consisting, consisted**) to be made of something

consistent *adjective* 1 always the same, regular 2 agreeing with each other ► *The two explanations are not consistent.*

console *verb* (**consoles, consoling, consoled**) to give someone comfort or sympathy **consolation** *noun*

consonant *noun* (*plural* **consonants**) a letter that stands for any of the sounds that is made by stopping the flow of air through the front of your mouth
The consonants in the English alphabet are b, c, d, f, g, h, j, k, l, m, n, p, q, r, s, t, v, w, x, y, z. The letter y is a consonant in *yacht* and a vowel in *rhythm*.

conspicuous *adjective* noticeable, remarkable

conspiracy *noun* (*plural* **conspiracies**) a plot to do something wrong or illegal **conspirator** *noun*

conspire *verb* (**conspires, conspiring, conspired**) to plot together

constable *noun* (*plural* **constables**) an ordinary police officer

constant *adjective* 1 not changing; continual ► *There was a constant hum of traffic in the background.* 2 loyal and faithful ► *Her dog is her constant companion.* **constantly** *adverb* all the time

constellation *noun* (*plural* **constellations**) a group of stars forming a special shape

constipated *adjective* having difficulty in emptying your bowels **constipation** *noun*

constituency *noun* (*plural* **constituencies**) a district that elects a Member of Parliament

constitute *verb* (**constitutes, constituting, constituted**) (not an everyday word) to form something or be the parts of it ► *50 states constitute the USA.*

constitution *noun* (*plural* **constitutions**) 1 the set of principles or laws by which a country is governed 2 a person's state of health ► *I have a strong constitution.* **constitutional** *adjective*

construct *verb* (**constructs, constructing, constructed**) to make or build something **construction** *noun*

constructive *adjective* helpful and positive ► *My teacher made some constructive suggestions about my model.*

consul *noun* (*plural* **consuls**) an official who represents a country in a foreign country

consult *verb* (**consults, consulting, consulted**) to look for information or advice from a person or book **consultation** *noun*

consultant *noun* (*plural* **consultants**) an important hospital doctor

consume *verb* (**consumes, consuming, consumed**) 1 to eat food or take drink 2 to use something up or destroy it

consumer *noun* (*plural* **consumers**) someone who buys goods or services from shops

consumption *noun* using up food or fuel ► *Patients were asked to keep a record of their food consumption over a period of three days.*

contact *noun* (*plural* **contacts**) 1 touching someone or something 2 communication ► *John had lost contact with his brother.* 3 a person to communicate with ► *She got her job through a contact in the company.*

contact *verb* (**contacts, contacting, contacted**) to write to someone or telephone them

contact lens *noun* (*plural* **contact lenses**) a small plastic lens that you wear against your eyeball to improve your sight

contagious *adjective* (*pronounced* kon-tay-jus) (describing a disease) caught by contact with infected people

contain *verb* (**contains, containing, contained**) to have something inside

container *noun* (*plural* **containers**) something like a box or jar that is designed to hold things

contaminate *verb* (**contaminates, contaminating, contaminated**) to make something dirty, not pure, or diseased **contamination** *noun*

contemplate *verb* (**contemplates, contemplating, contemplated**) 1 to look hard at something or think about it 2 to plan or intend to do something **contemplation** *noun*

contemporary *adjective* 1 living at the same time 2 modern or up to date ▸ *The shop sells contemporary furniture.*

contempt *noun* a feeling of strong disapproval **contemptible** *adjective* deserving contempt **contemptuous** *adjective* showing contempt

contend *verb* (**contends, contending, contended**) (not an everyday word) 1 to struggle or compete 2 to claim or argue **contender** *noun*

content *adjective* (*pronounced* kon-tent) happy and willing ▸ *She had been content to stay in the house all day reading.* **contentment** *noun*

contented *adjective* happy and satisfied

contents *plural noun* (*pronounced* kon-tents) what something contains

contest *noun* (*plural* **contests**) (*pronounced* **kon**-test) a competition

contest *verb* (**contests, contesting, contested**) (*pronounced* kon-**test**) to argue or fight about something

contestant *noun* (*plural* **contestants**) (*pronounced* kon-**test**-ant) someone taking part in a contest

continent *noun* (*plural* **continents**) one of the main areas of land in the world The continents are Africa, Antarctica, Asia, Australia, Europe, North America, and South America. **the Continent** the mainland of Europe, not including the British Isles

continental *adjective* on the continent of Europe ▸ *I don't think we can afford a continental holiday this year.*

continual *adjective* happening repeatedly ▸ *She needs continual encouragement.* **continually** *adverb* repeatedly, often

continue *verb* (**continues, continuing, continued**) to go on doing something **continuation** *noun*

continuous *adjective* going on all the time; without a break ▸ *We could hear a continuous hum from the fridge.* **continuity** *noun* **continuously** *adverb* all the time

contour *noun* (*plural* **contours**) 1 an outline 2 a line on a map joining points that are the same height above sea level

contraceptive *noun* (*plural* **contraceptives**) something that is used to prevent a woman from becoming pregnant **contraception** *noun*

contract *noun* (*plural* **contracts**) (*pronounced* **kon**-trakt) a written legal agreement

contract *verb* (**contracts, contracting, contracted**) (*pronounced* kon-**trakt**) 1 to become smaller 2 to sign a contract to do something 3 to catch an illness **contraction** *noun*

contradict *verb* (**contradicts, contradicting, contradicted**) to say the opposite of what someone else has just said **contradiction** *noun* **contradictory** *adjective*

contraflow *noun* (*plural* **contraflows**) a special arrangement of traffic when a motorway is being repaired, with some traffic using the carriageway on the other side

contralto *noun* (*plural* **contraltos**) a female singer with a low voice

contraption *noun* (*plural* **contraptions**) a strange-looking device or machine

contrary *adjective* 1 (*pronounced* **kon-tra-ri**) opposite 2 (*pronounced* kon-**trair**-i) obstinate or awkward

contrast *verb* (**contrasts, contrasting, contrasted**) (*pronounced* kon-**trahst**) 1 to show that two things are different 2 to be clearly different from something else
contrast *noun* (*plural* **contrasts**) (*pronounced* **kon**-trahst) a clear difference between two things

contribute *verb* (**contributes, contributing, contributed**) 1 to give money or help for something along with other people 2 to help cause something ▸ *The bad weather contributed to the accident.* **contribution** *noun* **contributor** *noun*

control *verb* (**controls, controlling, controlled**) to have power over what someone or something does
control *noun* (*plural* **controls**) the power to control someone or something **controls** the switches and levers that make a machine work **in control** controlling things **controller** *noun*

controversy *noun* (*plural* **controversies**) (*pronounced* **kon**-tro-ver-si or kon-**trov**-er-si) argument or discussion about whether something is right or not **controversial** *adjective*

conundrum *noun* (*plural* **conundrums**) a riddle

convalescence *noun* a time when someone is recovering from an illness **convalescent** *adjective* recovering from an illness

convector *noun* (*plural* **convectors**) a heater that works by making warm air or liquid move around **convection** *noun*

convenient *adjective* easy to use or reach **convenience** *noun* **conveniently** *adverb*

convent *noun* (*plural* **convents**) a place where nuns live and work

conventional *adjective* 1 using the normal methods 2 following the normal way of life

converge *verb* (**converges, converging, converged**) to come together from different directions

conversation *noun* (*plural* **conversations**) talking between two or more people **conversational** *adjective*

conversion *noun* (*plural* **conversions**) changing or converting something

convert *verb* (**converts, converting, converted**) (*pronounced* kon-**vert**) 1 to change something to make it suitable for a new purpose 2 to persuade someone to change their beliefs
convert *noun* (*plural* **converts**) (*pronounced* **kon**-vert) someone who has changed their beliefs **convertible** *adjective*

convex *adjective* curved like the outside of a circle or ball

convey *verb* (**conveys, conveying, conveyed**) (not an everyday word) 1 to take someone or something to a place 2 to get someone to understand an idea or message

convict *noun* (*plural* **convicts**) (*pronounced* **kon**-vikt) a criminal who has been sent to prison
convict *verb* (**convicts, convicting, convicted**) (*pronounced* kon-**vikt**) to find someone guilty of a crime

conviction *noun* (*plural* **convictions**) 1 something you believe strongly 2 being convicted of a crime

convince *verb* (**convinces, convincing, convinced**) persuade someone that something is true or right

convoy *noun* (*plural* **convoys**) a group of ships or vehicles travelling together

cook *verb* (**cooks, cooking, cooked**) to make food ready to eat by heating it
cook *noun* (*plural* **cooks**) someone who cooks, especially as their job

cooker *noun* (*plural* **cookers**) an apparatus with an oven and hotplates for cooking food

cookery *noun* cooking food

cool *adjective* (**cooler, coolest**) 1 fairly cold 2 acting calmly in a difficult situation 3 rather unfriendly 4 (slang) good or fashionable **coolly** *adverb* **coolness** *noun*

cool *verb* (**cools, cooling, cooled**) 1 to make something cool 2 to become cool

coop *noun* (*plural* **coops**) a cage to keep poultry in

cooperate *verb* (**cooperates, cooperating, cooperated**) to work in a helpful and friendly way with other people **cooperation** *noun* **cooperative** *adjective* willing to cooperate

coordinate *verb* (**coordinates, coordinating, coordinated**) (*pronounced* koh-or-din-ayt) to organize people or things to work well together **coordination** *noun*

coot *noun* (*plural* **coots**) a black waterbird with a white patch on its head

cop (slang) *noun* (*plural* **cops**) a police officer **not much cop** not very good

cope *verb* (**copes, coping, coped**) to deal with something awkward or difficult ► *After her husband died, she found it difficult to cope by herself.*

copper *noun* (*plural* **coppers**) a reddish-brown metal used for making wire and pipes

copy *noun* (*plural* **copies**) 1 something made to be like something else 2 something written out again 3 one example of a newspaper, magazine, or book that is made in large numbers ► *Have you seen my copy of 'The BFG'?*

copy *verb* (**copies, copying, copied**) 1 to make a copy of something 2 to do the same as someone else

coral *noun* a hard substance on the sea bed, made from thousands of skeletons of tiny sea creatures

cord *noun* (*plural* **cords**) a piece of thin rope

cordial *adjective* warm and friendly ► *We got a cordial welcome.* **cordially** *adverb*

cordial *noun* (*plural* **cordials**) a sweet drink **cordiality** *noun*

corduroy *noun* (*pronounced* kor-der-oi) thick cotton cloth with ridges along it

core *noun* (*plural* **cores**) the middle part of something

corgi *noun* (*plural* **corgis**) a small dog with short legs and large upright ears

cork *noun* (*plural* **corks**) 1 the light tough bark of a kind of oak tree 2 a piece of this bark used to seal a bottle

corkscrew *noun* (*plural* **corkscrews**) a tool for taking corks out of bottles

corn *noun* (*plural* **corns**) 1 grain, the seeds of wheat, barley, oats, and rye 2 a painful piece of hard skin on your toe or foot

corner *noun* (*plural* **corners**) a place where two roads, walls, or lines meet

corner *verb* (**corners, cornering, cornered**) 1 to trap a person or animal you are trying to catch 2 to go round a corner

cornet *noun* (*plural* **cornets**) 1 a cone-shaped wafer open at the top for ice cream 2 a musical instrument like a trumpet

cornflakes *plural noun* a breakfast cereal of toasted maize flakes

cornflour *noun* a fine flour used for making puddings and sauces

corny *adjective* (**cornier, corniest**) (informal) not very good because people say it so often ► *What a corny joke.*

coronation *noun* (*plural* **coronations**) the ceremony of crowning a king or queen

coroner *noun* (*plural* **coroners**) an official who investigates when someone dies in an unnatural way

corporal *noun* (*plural* **corporals**) a soldier below sergeant in rank

corporal punishment *noun* punishment by hitting or beating someone

corps *noun* (*plural* **corps**) (*pronounced* kor) an army unit

corpse *noun* (*plural* **corpses**) a dead body

correct *adjective* true or accurate, without any mistakes ▸ *Please check that the address is correct.*

correct *verb* (**corrects, correcting, corrected**) **1** to mark the mistakes in a piece of work **2** to put mistakes right

correction *noun* (*plural* **corrections**) **1** correcting mistakes **2** a change done to make something right

correspond *verb* (**corresponds, corresponding, corresponded**) (not an everyday word) **1** to agree with something or match it ▸ *Your story corresponds to what I heard.* **2** to exchange letters with someone

correspondence *noun* **1** similarity or agreement **2** letters you write and receive

correspondent *noun* (*plural* **correspondents**) **1** someone who writes letters **2** a journalist who writes often for a newspaper ▸ *Julie is our Moscow correspondent.*

corridor *noun* (*plural* **corridors**) a long passage with doors which open into rooms or train compartments

corrode *verb* (**corrodes, corroding, corroded**) to wear away by rust or chemical action **corrosion** *noun* **corrosive** *adjective* likely to corrode something

corrugated iron *noun* sheets of metal that have been shaped into folds or ridges

corrupt *adjective* **1** morally wrong **2** likely to give or accept bribes **corruption** *noun*

corrupt *verb* (**corrupts, corrupting, corrupted**) to make someone corrupt

cosmetics *plural noun* substances like lipstick and eye shadow, for making the skin or hair look attractive

cosmic *adjective* (*pronounced* **koz**-mik) to do with the universe

cosmos *noun* the universe

cost *noun* (*plural* **costs**) what you have to spend to do or get something

cost *verb* (**costs, costing, cost**) **1** to have a certain amount as its price **2** to cause you to lose something ▸ *Losing his driving licence cost him his job.*

costly *adjective* (**costlier, costliest**) expensive

costume *noun* (*plural* **costumes**) clothes for a particular purpose or of a particular period

cosy *adjective* (**cosier, cosiest**) warm and comfortable **cosily** *adverb* **cosiness** *noun*

cot *noun* (*plural* **cots**) a baby's bed with high sides

cottage *noun* (*plural* **cottages**) a small house, usually in the country

cottage cheese *noun* soft white cheese made from skimmed milk

cotton *noun* **1** a soft white material covering the seeds of a tropical plant **2** thread or cloth made from cotton

couch *noun* (*plural* **couches**) a long soft seat or sofa

cough *verb* (**coughs, coughing, coughed**) (*pronounced* kof) to push air suddenly out of your lungs with a harsh noise

cough *noun* (*plural* **coughs**) **1** the action or sound of coughing **2** an illness which makes you cough a lot

could past tense of **can**[1] *verb*

couldn't short for *could not* ▸ *We couldn't find your letter.*

council *noun* (*plural* **councils**) a group of people chosen to run a town or city

councillor *noun* (*plural* **councillors**) a member of a council

counsellor *noun* (*plural* **counsellors**) someone who gives advice, especially as their job

count[1] *verb* (**counts, counting, counted**) 1 to use numbers to find out how many people or things there are in a place 2 to say numbers in their proper order 3 to include someone or something in a total ▸ *There were 20 in the bus, not counting the driver.* **count on** to rely on

count *noun* (*plural* **counts**) a total reached by counting ▸ *There is a high pollen count in the summer.*

count[2] *noun* (*plural* **counts**) a foreign nobleman

countdown *noun* (*plural* **countdowns**) a counting down to 0, especially before launching a rocket

countenance *noun* (*plural* **countenances**) your face or the expression on it

counter *noun* (*plural* **counters**) 1 a long table where customers are served in a shop or café 2 a small plastic disc used in board games

counterfeit *adjective* (*pronounced* **kown-ter-fit**) made as a copy of something real, to trick or cheat people ▸ *The £50 note was counterfeit.*

countess *noun* (*plural* **countesses**) the wife or widow of a count or earl; a female earl

countless *adjective* too many to count; very many

country *noun* (*plural* **countries**) 1 a part of the world where a particular nation of people lives 2 an area of open land, the countryside

countryside *noun* an area with fields, woods, and villages, away from towns

county *noun* (*plural* **counties**) one of the large areas that a country is divided into

couple *noun* (*plural* **couples**) 1 two people or things 2 a husband and wife, or two people having a romantic relationship

couple *verb* (**couples, coupling, coupled**) to join things together

coupling *noun* (*plural* **couplings**) a link or fastening, especially for vehicles

coupon *noun* (*plural* **coupons**) a piece of paper that gives you the right to receive or do something

courage *noun* the ability to be brave and overcome your fear

courageous *adjective* ready to face danger or pain **courageously** *adverb*

courgette *noun* (*plural* **courgettes**) (*pronounced* kor-**zhet**) a kind of vegetable like a small marrow

courier *noun* (*plural* **couriers**) (*pronounced* **koor**-i-er) 1 someone whose job is to guide and help groups of people on holiday 2 someone who carries a message

course *noun* (*plural* **courses**) 1 the direction in which something moves ▸ *The river follows a winding course.* 2 a series of lessons or exercises 3 each part of a meal 4 a piece of ground used for a sport, such as a golf course **of course** naturally; certainly

court *noun* (*plural* **courts**) 1 a place where legal trials take place, a lawcourt 2 an area marked out for ball games such as tennis or netball 3 the place where a king or queen lives together with their officials

court *verb* (**courts, courting, courted**) to try to win someone's love or support

courteous *adjective* (*pronounced* **ker**-ti-us) well-mannered and polite **courtesy** *noun* politeness

court martial *noun* (*plural* **courts martial**) a trial of a soldier who is accused of breaking a military law

courtyard *noun* (*plural* **courtyards**) a paved area surrounded by walls or buildings

cousin *noun* (*plural* **cousins**) a son or daughter of your uncle or aunt

cove *noun* (*plural* **coves**) a small bay

cover *verb* (**covers, covering, covered**) 1 to put something over another thing to hide or protect it 2 to deal with a subject or include it ▸ *The French course covers most of what you'll need on holiday.* 3 to be enough money for something ▸ *£2 should cover my fare.* **cover up** to make sure no one knows about something wrong or illegal

cover *noun* (*plural* **covers**) 1 something used for covering something else, such as a lid or wrapper 2 a place where someone can hide or take shelter ▸ *The soldiers found cover in an old house.*

covering *noun* (*plural* **coverings**) a layer that covers something

cow *noun* (*plural* **cows**) a female animal kept by farmers for its milk and beef

coward *noun* (*plural* **cowards**) someone who avoids difficulty or danger **cowardice** *noun* being a coward **cowardly** *adjective*

cowboy *noun* or **cowgirl** *noun* (*plural* **cowboys** or **cowgirls**) in the USA, a farm worker who rides round looking after cattle

cower *verb* (**cowers, cowering, cowered**) to crouch in fear

cox *noun* (*plural* **coxes**) a person who steers a racing boat

coy *adjective* (**coyer, coyest**) pretending to be shy or modest

crab *noun* (*plural* **crabs**) a shellfish with a pair of pincers and four pairs of legs

crack *noun* (*plural* **cracks**) 1 a line or narrow gap on the surface of something where it has broken but not come apart 2 a sudden sharp noise ▸ *They heard the crack of a pistol shot.* 3 a sudden sharp blow ▸ *They gave him a crack on his head and took his money.*

crack *verb* (**cracks, cracking, cracked**) 1 to make a crack in something 2 to split without breaking ▸ *The plate has cracked.* **crack a joke** to tell a joke

cracker *noun* (*plural* **crackers**) 1 a decorated paper tube which bangs when two people pull it apart, with a small gift inside it 2 a thin crisp biscuit

crackle *verb* (**crackles, crackling, crackled**) to make small cracking sounds, like a fire

crackling *noun* the hard skin of roast pork

cradle *noun* (*plural* **cradles**) a cot for a small baby

craft *noun* (*plural* **crafts**) 1 a job or activity which needs skill with the hands 2 a boat or aircraft

craftsman *noun* or **craftswoman** *noun* (*plural* **craftsmen** or **craftswomen**) someone who is good at making things with their hands **craftsmanship** *noun*

crafty *adjective* (**craftier, craftiest**) cunning and clever **craftily** *adverb* **craftiness** *noun*

crag *noun* (*plural* **crags**) a steep piece of rough rock **craggy** *adjective* steep and rocky

cram *verb* (**crams, cramming, crammed**) to force things into a small space

cramp *noun* (*plural* **cramps**) a sudden pain when your muscles become tight

cramped *adjective* tightly packed in a small space ▸ *Working conditions in those days were very cramped.*

crane *noun* (*plural* **cranes**) 1 a machine for lifting and moving heavy objects 2 a large bird with long legs and a long neck

crane *verb* (**cranes, craning, craned**) **crane your neck** to stretch your neck so that you can see something

crane-fly *noun* (*plural* **crane-flies**) an insect with wings and long thin legs, also called a **daddy-long-legs**

crank *noun* (*plural* **cranks**) 1 an L-shaped rod used to turn or control something 2 a person with weird or unusual ideas

crank *verb* (**cranks, cranking, cranked**) to turn an engine or machine with a crank

cranny *noun* (*plural* **crannies**) a narrow hole or space

crash *noun* (*plural* **crashes**) **1** the loud noise of something falling or breaking **2** a collision between road vehicles
crash *verb* (**crashes, crashing, crashed**) to collide or fall violently

crash helmet *noun* (*plural* **crash helmets**) a padded helmet worn by cyclists and motorcyclists

crate *noun* (*plural* **crates**) a large wooden container for transporting goods

crater *noun* (*plural* **craters**) **1** the mouth of a volcano **2** a hole in the ground made by a bomb

crave *verb* (**craves, craving, craved**) to have a strong wish for something

crawl *verb* (**crawls, crawling, crawled**) **1** to move along on your hands and knees **2** to move slowly ▸ *A slug was crawling across the path.* **3** to be full of something unpleasant ▸ *Her hair was crawling with insects.*
crawl *noun* **1** a crawling movement **2** a powerful swimming stroke in which you bring each arm over your head in turn

crayon *noun* (*plural* **crayons**) a coloured pencil or stick of wax for drawing or writing

craze *noun* (*plural* **crazes**) a brief fashion or enthusiasm ▸ *Yo-yos are the latest craze.*

crazy *adjective* (**crazier, craziest**) mad or foolish **crazily** *adverb* **craziness** *noun*

creak *verb* (**creaks, creaking, creaked**) to make a noise like a stiff door opening **creaky** *adjective* old and creaking
creak *noun* (*plural* **creaks**) a creaking noise

cream *noun* (*plural* **creams**) **1** the rich fatty part of milk **2** a yellowish-white colour **3** something that looks like cream, for example face cream **creamy** *adjective* smooth and thick like cream

crease *noun* (*plural* **creases**) a line made in cloth or paper by folding or pressing it
crease *verb* (**creases, creasing, creased**) to make a crease in cloth or paper

create *verb* (**creates, creating, created**) to bring something into existence **creation** *noun* **creator** *noun*

creative *adjective* showing imagination and thought ▸ *He had plenty of creative ideas to brighten up his bedroom.* **creativity** *noun*

creature *noun* (*plural* **creatures**) a living animal or person

crèche *noun* (*plural* **crèches**) (*pronounced* kresh) a place where babies and small children are looked after

credible *adjective* able to be believed; trustworthy **credibility** *noun* **credibly** *adverb*

credit *noun* **1** praise or approval ▸ *You have to give them credit for trying.* **2** a system of allowing someone to pay for something later ▸ *We bought our new television on credit.* **3** someone who brings honour or approval ▸ *They have a son and daughter who would be a credit to any family.*

credit card *noun* (*plural* **credit cards**) a plastic card that allows you to buy things and pay for them later

creed *noun* (*plural* **creeds**) a statement of what people believe in

creek *noun* (*plural* **creeks**) a narrow inlet on the coast

creep *verb* (**creeps, creeping, crept**) **1** to move along with the body close to the ground **2** to move quietly or secretly **creep up on** to go up to someone quietly from behind

creeper *noun* (*plural* **creepers**) a plant that grows close to the ground or up walls

cremate *verb* (**cremates, cremating, cremated**) to burn a dead body so that it becomes ashes **cremation** *noun*

crematorium *noun* (*plural* **crematoria**) (*pronounced* krem-a-**tor**-i-um) a place where dead bodies are cremated

crêpe *noun* (*plural* **crêpes**) (*pronounced* krayp) **1** cloth or paper with a wrinkled surface **2** a kind of thin French pancake

crept past tense and past participle of **creep**

crescent *noun* (*plural* **crescents**) **1** a narrow curved shape like a new moon **2** a street that curves round like a crescent

cress *noun* a green plant used in salads and sandwiches

crest *noun* (*plural* **crests**) **1** a tuft of hair, feathers, or skin on an animal's head **2** the top of a hill or wave **3** a badge or emblem

crevice *noun* (*plural* **crevices**) a deep crack in rock or in a wall

crew *noun* (*plural* **crews**) the people who work on a ship or aircraft

crib *noun* (*plural* **cribs**) **1** a baby's cot **2** a rack containing fodder for animals

cricket¹ *noun* a game played by two teams of eleven players with a hard ball, two bats, and two wickets **cricketer** *noun*

cricket² *noun* an insect like a grasshopper

cried past tense and past participle of **cry** *verb*

crime *noun* (*plural* **crimes**) an act that is against the law

criminal *noun* (*plural* **criminals**) someone who has committed a crime

crimson *noun* and *adjective* a deep red colour

cringe *verb* (**cringes**, **cringing**, **cringed**) to shrink back in fear or embarrassment

crinkle *noun* (*plural* **crinkles**) a small crease or wrinkle **crinkly** *adjective*

cripple *noun* (*plural* **cripples**) someone who cannot walk properly because they are ill or injured

crippled *adjective* being a cripple

crisis *noun* (*plural* **crises**) (*pronounced* **kry**-sis) a difficult or dangerous time or situation

crisp *adjective* (**crisper**, **crispest**) **1** hard and dry and easy to break **2** firm and fresh ▸ *He served a crisp salad to go with the fish.* **3** cold and frosty ▸ *It turned out to be a bright crisp day without rain.*

crisp *noun* (*plural* **crisps**) a thin fried slice of potato, sold in packets

criss-cross *adjective* and *adverb* with crossing lines

critic *noun* (*plural* **critics**) someone who criticizes or gives an opinion

critical *adjective* **1** criticizing **2** serious, reaching a crisis **critically** *adverb*

criticism *noun* (*plural* **criticisms**) (*pronounced* **krit**-i-si-zum) an opinion or judgement about something, usually pointing out its faults

criticize *verb* (**criticizes**, **criticizing**, **criticized**) (*pronounced* **krit**-i-syz) to give an opinion about someone or something, pointing out their faults

croak *verb* (**croaks**, **croaking**, **croaked**) to make a deep sound like a frog
croak *noun* (*plural* **croaks**) a croaking sound

crochet *noun* (*pronounced* **kroh**-shay) a kind of knitting done with a hooked needle

crockery *noun* dishes, plates, and cups and saucers

crocodile *noun* (*plural* **crocodiles**) a large reptile with a thick skin, long tail, and huge jaws

crocus *noun* (*plural* **crocuses**) a small spring flower

crook *noun* (*plural* **crooks**) **1** (informal) a criminal or dishonest person **2** a shepherd's or bishop's stick with a curved end

crooked *adjective* (*pronounced* **kruuk**-id) **1** bent or twisted **2** (informal) dishonest

crop *noun* (*plural* **crops**) **1** plants grown in a field for food ▸ *We're hoping for a good crop of potatoes this year.* **2** a kind of riding whip with a loop

crop *verb* (**crops, cropping, cropped**) to cut or bite the top off something ▸ *The goat had lowered its head and was cropping the grass.* **crop up** to happen or appear unexpectedly

cross *noun* (*plural* **crosses**) 1 a mark or shape like + or ✕ 2 an animal produced by mixing different breeds, such as a mule which is a cross between a donkey and a horse **the Cross** the cross-shaped gallows on which Christ was crucified, used as a symbol of Christianity

cross *verb* (**crosses, crossing, crossed**) 1 to go from one side of something to the other ▸ *He crossed the road carefully.* ▸ *A bit further on the road crossed a river.* 2 to put one of your fingers or legs over the other **cross out** to draw a line through something because it is wrong or not wanted

cross *adjective* (**crosser, crossest**) angry or bad-tempered

crossbar *noun* (*plural* **crossbars**) a horizontal bar between two upright bars

crossbow *noun* (*plural* **crossbows**) a powerful bow used for shooting arrows, fired by pulling a trigger

cross-country *adjective* (describing a race) run through fields and open country

cross-eyed *adjective* having eyes that appear to look in different directions

crossing *noun* (*plural* **crossings**) a place where people can cross a road or railway

crossroads *noun* (*plural* **crossroads**) a place where two or more roads cross one another

cross-section *noun* (*plural* **cross-sections**) a drawing of something as if it has been cut through

crossword *noun* (*plural* **crosswords**) a puzzle with blank squares in which you put the letters of words worked out from clues

crotchet *noun* (*plural* **crotchets**) (*pronounced* **kroch**-it) a musical note equal to half a minim, written ♩

crouch *verb* (**crouches, crouching, crouched**) to bend your arms and legs so that your body is close to the ground

crow *noun* (*plural* **crows**) a large black bird

crow *verb* (**crows, crowing, crowed**) 1 to make a noise like a cock 2 to boast loudly

crowbar *noun* (*plural* **crowbars**) an iron bar used as a lever

crowd *noun* (*plural* **crowds**) a large number of people in one place

crowd *verb* (**crowds, crowding, crowded**) to form a crowd

crowded *adjective* having too many people or things

crown *noun* (*plural* **crowns**) 1 the ornamental headdress worn by a king or queen 2 the king or queen of a country ▸ *The duke was a loyal servant of the crown.* 3 the top part of something, such as a hill or a person's head

crown *verb* (**crowns, crowning, crowned**) 1 to make someone king or queen 2 to form the top of something

crow's-nest *noun* (*plural* **crow's-nests**) a lookout position at the top of a ship's mast

crucial *adjective* (*pronounced* **kroo**-shal) extremely important

crucifix *noun* (*plural* **crucifixes**) a picture or model of Christ on the Cross

crucify *verb* (**crucifies, crucifying, crucified**) to execute someone by fixing their hands and feet to an upright cross **crucifixion** *noun*

crude *adjective* (**cruder, crudest**) 1 (describing oil) natural; not purified 2 rough and simple ▸ *It was a crude way of finding the answer, but it worked.* 3 rude or dirty

cruel *adjective* (**crueller, cruellest**) causing pain and suffering to others **cruelly** *adverb* **cruelty** *noun*

cruise *noun* (*plural* **cruises**) a holiday on a ship, visiting different places

cruise *verb* (**cruises, cruising, cruised**) 1 to sail or travel at a gentle speed 2 to go on a cruise on a ship

cruiser *noun* (*plural* **cruisers**) a fast warship or motor boat

crumb noun (*plural* **crumbs**) a tiny piece of bread or cake

crumble verb (**crumbles, crumbling, crumbled**) to break into small pieces **crumbly** adjective soft and likely to crumble

crumpet noun (*plural* **crumpets**) a soft flat cake that you toast

crumple verb (**crumples, crumpling, crumpled**) 1 to make something very creased 2 to become creased

crunch verb (**crunches, crunching, crunched**) to chew or crush something with a hard noise **crunchy** adjective

crunch noun (*plural* **crunches**) a crunching noise

crusade noun (*plural* **crusades**) 1 a campaign in support of something 2 a military expedition to Palestine made by Christians in the Middle Ages **crusader** noun

crush verb (**crushes, crushing, crushed**) 1 to press something so that it is damaged or broken 2 to defeat an enemy completely

crush noun (*plural* **crushes**) 1 a crowd or a crowded place 2 (informal) a sudden liking you have for someone

crust noun (*plural* **crusts**) the hard outside part or covering of something

crustacean noun (*plural* **crustaceans**) (*pronounced* krus-tay-shan) any kind of sea animal with a hard shell

crutch noun (*plural* **crutches**) a stick that fits under the arm, used as a support in walking

cry verb (**cries, crying, cried**) 1 to shout 2 to let tears fall from your eyes

cry noun (*plural* **cries**) 1 a loud shout 2 a spell of weeping

crypt noun (*plural* **crypts**) a large room underneath a church

crystal noun (*plural* **crystals**) 1 a hard clear mineral like glass 2 a small solid piece of snow or ice **crystalline** adjective made of crystals

crystallize verb (**crystallizes, crystallizing, crystallized**) to form into crystals

cub noun (*plural* **cubs**) a young animal, especially a lion, tiger, fox, or bear **Cub** a junior Scout

cube noun (*plural* **cubes**) 1 an object that has six square sides, like a box or dice 2 the result of multiplying something by itself twice. For example, the cube of 3 is $3 \times 3 \times 3 = 27$. **cubic** adjective

cubicle noun (*plural* **cubicles**) a small compartment in a room

cuckoo noun (*plural* **cuckoos**) a bird that lays its eggs in other birds' nests and makes a sound like 'cuck-oo'

cucumber noun (*plural* **cucumbers**) a long green vegetable that you eat raw in salads

cud noun half-digested food that cows bring up from their stomach to chew again

cuddle verb (**cuddles, cuddling, cuddled**) to hold someone in your arms and squeeze them lovingly **cuddly** adjective nice to cuddle

cudgel noun (*plural* **cudgels**) a short thick stick used as a weapon

cue noun (*plural* **cues**) 1 a word or signal that tells an actor when to start speaking or come on the stage 2 a long thin stick used to strike the ball in billiards or snooker

cuff noun (*plural* **cuffs**) the end part of a sleeve that goes round your wrist

cuff verb (**cuffs, cuffing, cuffed**) to hit someone with your hand

cul-de-sac noun (*plural* **cul-de-sacs**) a street that is closed at one end This word is French, and means 'bottom of a sack'.

cull verb (**culls, culling, culled**) to kill a number of animals in a larger herd or group in order to keep the numbers down

culprit noun (*plural* **culprits**) a person who is to blame for something

cult noun (*plural* **cults**) a religion, especially one with a small number of followers

cultivate verb (**cultivates, cultivating, cultivated**) to use the land for growing crops **cultivation** noun

cultivated *adjective* having good manners and education

culture *noun* (*plural* **cultures**) 1 the development of the mind by education and learning 2 the customs and traditions of a people **cultural** *adjective* to do with culture **cultured** *adjective* educated and having good manners

cunning *adjective* clever at deceiving people **cunningly** *adverb*

cup *noun* (*plural* **cups**) 1 a small container with a handle, for drinking from 2 a prize in the form of a silver cup or bowl

cupboard *noun* (*plural* **cupboards**) (*pronounced* **kub-erd**) a piece of furniture or part of a room with shelves and a door, for storing things

cupful *noun* (*plural* **cupfuls**) as much as a cup will hold

curator *noun* (*plural* **curators**) (*pronounced* **kewr-ay-ter**) someone in charge of a museum or art gallery

curb *verb* (**curbs**, **curbing**, **curbed**) to restrain a feeling ▶ *He tried hard to curb his anger.*

curd *noun* (*plural* **curds**) a thick soft substance formed when milk turns sour

curdle *verb* (**curdles**, **curdling**, **curdled**) to turn sour and form curds

cure *verb* (**cures**, **curing**, **cured**) 1 to make someone who is ill better 2 to put a stop to a problem or difficulty 3 to preserve meat, leather, tobacco, and some other substances by smoking them or treating them with salt

cure *noun* (*plural* **cures**) something that makes someone better or ends a difficulty

curfew *noun* (*plural* **curfews**) an order that people must be indoors each evening by a certain time
The word once meant an order for people to put out their fires in the evening. It comes from Old French words meaning 'to cover the fire'.

curiosity *noun* (*plural* **curiosities**) 1 being curious 2 something strange or interesting

curious *adjective* 1 wanting to find out about things 2 strange or unusual **curiously** *adverb*

curl *noun* (*plural* **curls**) a curve or coil, especially of hair

curl *verb* (**curls**, **curling**, **curled**) to form into a curl **curl up** to sit or lie with your knees drawn up

curly *adjective* (**curlier**, **curliest**) having a lot of curls

currant *noun* (*plural* **currants**) 1 a small black fruit made from dried grapes 2 a small juicy berry

currency *noun* (*plural* **currencies**) the money that is used in a country

current *noun* (*plural* **currents**) 1 a flow of water or air 2 a flow of electricity through a wire

current *adjective* happening or existing now **currently** *adverb*

curriculum *noun* (*plural* **curricula**) the subjects that you study in a school

curry *noun* (*plural* **curries**) a hot spicy food

curse *noun* (*plural* **curses**) 1 a call or prayer for someone to be harmed or killed 2 an angry word or words

curse *verb* (**curses**, **cursing**, **cursed**) to use a curse against someone

cursor *noun* (*plural* **cursors**) a flashing signal showing your position on a computer screen

curtain *noun* (*plural* **curtains**) a piece of material hung across a window or door, or at the front of a theatre stage

curtsy *noun* (*plural* **curtsies**) a movement that women and girls can make instead of a bow, by slightly bending the knees and lowering their body

curtsy *verb* (**curtsies**, **curtsying**, **curtsied**) to make a curtsy

curve noun (plural **curves**) a line that bends smoothly

curve verb (**curves, curving, curved**) to move or bend in the form of a curve

cushion noun (plural **cushions**) a fabric cover filled with soft material to sit or rest on

custard noun a sweet thick yellow liquid eaten with puddings

custody noun the right to take care of a child ▸ *My father was given custody of me when my parents were divorced.* **in custody** in prison waiting for a trial

custom noun (plural **customs**) something that people always do ▸ *There is the old English custom of dancing round the maypole.*

customary adjective usual

customer noun (plural **customers**) someone who uses a shop, bank, or business

customs noun the place at a port or airport where officials can check what people are bringing into the country

cut verb (**cuts, cutting, cut**) 1 to divide something or make a slit in it with a knife or scissors 2 to reduce prices or taxes 3 to divide a pack of playing cards **cut off** to interrupt someone ▸ *He cut me off before I could finish my sentence.*

cut noun (plural **cuts**) 1 a small wound caused by something sharp 2 an act of cutting; the result of cutting ▸ *I'll give your hair a quick cut.*

cute adjective (**cuter, cutest**) (informal) attractive, pretty, or charming

cutlass noun (plural **cutlasses**) a short sword with a wide curved blade

cutlery noun knives, forks, and spoons used for eating

cutlet noun (plural **cutlets**) a thick slice of meat still on the bone

cut-out noun (plural **cut-outs**) a design or shape cut out of paper or cardboard

cutting noun (plural **cuttings**) 1 something cut from a newspaper or magazine 2 a piece cut off a plant and put in the ground to grow 3 a deep passage cut through high ground for a railway or road

cycle noun (plural **cycles**) 1 a bicycle 2 a series of events that happen several times in the same order

cycle verb (**cycles, cycling, cycled**) to ride a bicycle **cyclist** noun someone who rides a bicycle

cyclone noun (plural **cyclones**) a strong wind circling round a calm central area

cygnet noun (plural **cygnets**) (pronounced **sig**-nit) a young swan

cylinder noun (plural **cylinders**) 1 an object with straight sides and round ends 2 part of an engine in which a piston moves **cylindrical** adjective shaped like a cylinder

cymbal noun (plural **cymbals**) a musical instrument like a round metal plate that you hit to make a ringing sound

cynical adjective (pronounced **sin**-ik-al) thinking that nothing is good or worthwhile

cypress noun (plural **cypresses**) a tall evergreen tree with dark leaves

Dd

dab verb (**dabs, dabbing, dabbed**) to touch something gently with something soft ▸ *She dabbed her skin with some hand cream.*

dabble verb (**dabbles, dabbling, dabbled**) 1 to splash something about in water 2 to do something occasionally but not very seriously ▸ *While they were on holiday they started to dabble in windsurfing.*

dachshund noun (plural **dachshunds**) (pronounced **daks**-huund or **daks**-huunt) a small dog with a long body and short legs

dad or **daddy** *noun* (*plural* **dads** or **daddies**) (informal) a name for your father

daddy-long-legs *noun* (*plural* **daddy-long-legs**) an insect with wings and long thin legs, also called a **crane-fly**

daffodil *noun* (*plural* **daffodils**) a yellow flower that grows from a bulb

daft *adjective* (**dafter, daftest**) silly or stupid

dagger *noun* (*plural* **daggers**) a short pointed knife with two edges, used as a weapon

dahlia *noun* (*plural* **dahlias**) (*pronounced* **day**-li-a) a garden plant with bright flowers

daily *adjective* and *adverb* happening once a day or every day

dainty *adjective* (**daintier, daintiest**) small and delicate **daintily** *adverb* **daintiness** *noun*

dairy *noun* (*plural* **dairies**) a place where milk, butter, cream, and cheese are made or sold

daisy *noun* (*plural* **daisies**) a small flower with white petals and a yellow centre

dale *noun* (*plural* **dales**) a valley

Dalmatian *noun* (*plural* **Dalmatians**) a large white dog with black or brown spots

dam *noun* (*plural* **dams**) a thick wall built across a river or lake to hold the water back

dam *verb* (**dams, damming, dammed**) to build a dam across water

damage *verb* (**damages, damaging, damaged**) to injure or harm something
damage *noun* injury or harm

damages *plural noun* money paid to someone to make up for something bad that has happened to them

damn *verb* (**damns, damning, damned**) to say that something is bad or wrong

damp *adjective* (**damper, dampest**) slightly wet; not quite dry

damp or **dampness** *noun* wetness in the air or on something

dampen *verb* (**dampens, dampening, dampened**) 1 to make something damp 2 to make a sound or noise softer

damson *noun* (*plural* **damsons**) a small purple plum

dance *verb* (**dances, dancing, danced**) to move about in time to music

dance *noun* (*plural* **dances**) 1 a set of steps and movements for dancing 2 a party where people dance **dancer** *noun*

dandelion *noun* (*plural* **dandelions**) a yellow wild flower with jagged leaves

dandruff *noun* small white flakes of dead skin in a person's hair

danger *noun* (*plural* **dangers**) something that may harm or injure you

dangerous *adjective* likely to harm or injure you **dangerously** *adverb*

dangle *verb* (**dangles, dangling, dangled**) to hang or swing loosely

dank *adjective* (**danker, dankest**) damp and cold

dappled *adjective* marked with light and dark patches

dare *verb* (**dares, daring, dared**) 1 to be brave or bold enough to do something 2 to challenge someone to do something bold or dangerous ▸ *Her friends were daring her to jump.*

daredevil *noun* (*plural* **daredevils**) someone who does bold or dangerous things for fun

daring *adjective* bold or brave

dark *adjective* (**darker, darkest**) 1 with little or no light 2 having a deep rich colour ▸ *She wore a dark green coat.*

dark or **darkness** *noun* a place or time with no light

darken verb (**darkens, darkening, darkened**) 1 to make something dark 2 to become dark

darling noun (plural **darlings**) someone you love very much

darn verb (**darns, darning, darned**) to mend a hole in cloth or wool by sewing across it

dart noun (plural **darts**) a small arrow that you throw at a target called a *dartboard* in the game of *darts*

dash verb (**dashes, dashing, dashed**) 1 to rush 2 to hurl something and smash it
▶ *In his anger he dashed the cup against the wall.*

dash noun (plural **dashes**) 1 a quick rush or a hurry ▶ *She made a dash for the door.* 2 a small amount of something 3 a short line (—) used in writing or printing

data noun (pronounced **day**-ta) items of information, especially in a computer

database noun (plural **databases**) a collection of information stored in a computer

date[1] noun (plural **dates**) 1 the day of the week, month, or year when something happens or happened 2 an appointment to meet someone

date verb (**dates, dating, dated**) to have existed from a certain date ▶ *The hospital buildings date from the nineteenth century.*

date[2] noun (plural **dates**) a sweet brown fruit that grows on a palm tree

daughter noun (plural **daughters**) a girl or woman who is someone's child

dawdle verb (**dawdles, dawdling, dawdled**) to go too slowly

dawn noun (plural **dawns**) the time when the sun rises

dawn verb (**dawns, dawning, dawned**) to become light in the morning **dawn on** to become clear or obvious to someone·

day noun (plural **days**) 1 the 24 hours between midnight and the next midnight 2 the part of the day when it is light 3 a period in time ▶ *Jamie's grandfather remarked that there were no computers in his day.*

daybreak noun the first light of day; dawn

daydream verb (**daydreams, daydreaming, daydreamed**) to have pleasant thoughts when you should be thinking of something else

daylight noun 1 the light of day 2 dawn

daze noun **in a daze** feeling stunned or unable to think clearly

daze verb (**dazes, dazing, dazed**) to make someone confused or unable to think clearly

dazzle verb (**dazzles, dazzling, dazzled**) to shine so brightly that it makes you unable to see for a time

dead adjective 1 no longer alive 2 not lively or active ▶ *The place is dead at weekends.*

deaden verb (**deadens, deadening, deadened**) to make noise or a pain weaker

dead end noun (plural **dead ends**) a road or passage that is closed at one end

deadline noun (plural **deadlines**) a time by which you have to do something
A **deadline** was once a real line drawn round a prison. Prisoners were shot if they stepped over it.

deadly adjective (**deadlier, deadliest**) likely to cause death

deaf adjective (**deafer, deafest**) unable to hear clearly **deafness** noun

deafen verb (**deafens, deafening, deafened**) to be so loud that you cannot hear anything else ▶ *There was a deafening roar from the engines.*

deal verb (**deals, dealing, dealt**) 1 to do business buying and selling things ▶ *He deals in scrap metal.* 2 to give playing cards to the players in a game **deal with** 1 to be concerned with something ▶ *There are a lot of good books that deal with this subject.* ▶ *The story deals with a day in the life of an orphan girl.* 2 to take action over someone or something ▶ *We have a few problems to deal with.* **dealer** noun

deal noun (plural **deals**) 1 an agreement or bargain 2 someone's turn to deal at cards **a good deal** or **a great deal** a large amount

dear adjective (**dearer, dearest**) 1 loved very much 2 the usual way of beginning a letter ▶ *Dear Mary.* 3 costing a lot of money, expensive **dearly** adverb

death *noun* (*plural* **deaths**) the end of life, when you die

deathly *adjective* like death; very quiet or spooky

debate *noun* (*plural* **debates**) a serious discussion in which people give their opinions about a subject

debate *verb* (**debates, debating, debated**) to discuss something seriously and carefully

debris *noun* (*pronounced* **deb-ree**) scattered fragments or wreckage

debt *noun* (*plural* **debts**) (*pronounced* det) an amount of money that a person owes someone else

début *noun* (*plural* **débuts**) (*pronounced* **day-bew** or **day-boo**) a first public appearance by someone

decade *noun* (*plural* **decades**) a period of ten years

decathlon *noun* (*plural* **decathlons**) an athletic competition that has ten events

decay *verb* (**decays, decaying, decayed**) to rot or go bad

decay *noun* the process of decaying

deceased *adjective* (*pronounced* di-**seest**) (not an everyday word) dead

deceit *noun* (*pronounced* di-**seet**) deceiving someone **deceitful** *adjective* **deceitfully** *adverb*

deceive *verb* (**deceives, deceiving, deceived**) (*pronounced* di-**seev**) to make someone believe something that is not true

December *noun* the last month of the year
The word **December** comes from the Latin word *decem* meaning 'ten', because it was the tenth month in the Roman calendar.

decent *adjective* **1** respectable and honest **2** proper or suitable ▸ *I'll go and put on a decent shirt for the party.* **decency** *noun*

deception *noun* (*plural* **deceptions**) an action or trick that deceives someone

deceptive *adjective* not what it seems to be ▸ *The bright sunshine was deceptive and it was cold outside.*

decibel *noun* (*plural* **decibels**) a unit for measuring the loudness of sound

decide *verb* (**decides, deciding, decided**) to make up your mind about something, to make a choice

deciduous *adjective* (describing a tree) losing its leaves in the autumn

decimal *adjective* using tens or tenths

decimal *noun* (*plural* **decimals**) a fraction with tenths shown as numbers after a dot ($\frac{3}{10}$ is 0.3; 1½ is 1.5)

decimal point *noun* (*plural* **decimal points**) the dot in a decimal fraction

decipher *verb* (**deciphers, deciphering, deciphered**) (*pronounced* di-**sy-fer**) to work out what a piece of writing means when it is in code or difficult to read

decision *noun* (*plural* **decisions**) what someone has decided

decisive *adjective* **1** ending or deciding something important ▸ *The decisive battle of the war was fought here.* **2** deciding things quickly and firmly

deck *noun* (*plural* **decks**) a floor on a ship or bus

deckchair *noun* (*plural* **deckchairs**) a folding chair with a seat of canvas or plastic material

declaration *noun* (*plural* **declarations**) an official or public statement

declare *verb* (**declares, declaring, declared**) **1** to say something clearly and openly **2** in cricket, to end a cricket innings before all the batsmen are out **declare war** to announce the start of a war with another country

decline *verb* (**declines, declining, declined**) **1** to become weaker or smaller **2** to refuse an offer politely

decode *verb* (**decodes, decoding, decoded**) to work out the meaning of something written in code

decompose *verb* (**decomposes, decomposing, decomposed**) to decay or rot **decomposition** *noun*

decorate *verb* (**decorates, decorating, decorated**) **1** to make something look more beautiful or colourful **2** to put new paint or wallpaper in a room

decoration *noun* (*plural* **decorations**) something that you use to make a place or thing look more attractive

decorative *adjective* pretty and colourful

decorator *noun* (*plural* **decorators**) a person whose job is to paint rooms and buildings and to put up wallpaper

decoy *noun* (*plural* **decoys**) something used to tempt a person or animal into a trap

decrease *verb* (**decreases, decreasing, decreased**) (*pronounced* di-**kreess**) 1 to make something smaller or less 2 to become smaller or less

decrease *noun* (*plural* **decreases**) (*pronounced* **dee**-kreess) the amount by which something is smaller or less

decree *noun* (*plural* **decrees**) an official order or decision

decree *verb* (**decrees, decreeing, decreed**) to make a decree about something

decrepit *adjective* (*pronounced* dik-**rep**-it) old and weak

dedicate *verb* (**dedicates, dedicating, dedicated**) 1 to spend all your time doing something ▸ *She dedicated her life to helping the poor.* 2 to name someone as a special honour at the beginning of a book you have written **dedication** *noun*

deduce *verb* (**deduces, deducing, deduced**) to work something out from what you know

deduct *verb* (**deducts, deducting, deducted**) to subtract an amount from a total ▸ *She deducted £5 from their money to pay for the broken window.*

deduction *noun* (*plural* **deductions**) 1 something worked out by reasoning 2 something taken off a total

deed *noun* (*plural* **deeds**) 1 something that someone has done 2 a legal document

deep *adjective* (**deeper, deepest**) 1 going down a long way 2 going back a long way from the front 3 having a strong colour ▸ *The house was painted a deep green.* 4 low in pitch ▸ *Henry had a deep voice for his age.* **deeply** *adverb* very, extremely

deepen *verb* (**deepens, deepening, deepened**) to become deeper

deer *noun* (*plural* **deer**) a fast and graceful animal. The male has horns called antlers.

deface *verb* (**defaces, defacing, defaced**) to spoil the appearance of something on purpose

defeat *verb* (**defeats, defeating, defeated**) to beat someone in a game or battle

defeat *noun* (*plural* **defeats**) 1 losing a game or battle 2 a lost game or battle

defect *noun* (*plural* **defects**) (*pronounced* **dee**-fekt) a fault or weakness

defect *verb* (**defects, defecting, defected**) (*pronounced* di-**fekt**) to leave one country or side and join the enemy **defection** *noun* **defector** *noun*

defective *adjective* not working properly, faulty

defence *noun* (*plural* **defences**) 1 defending something 2 something that defends or protects **defenceless** *adjective* unable to defend yourself

defend *verb* (**defends, defending, defended**) 1 to protect someone or something from an attack 2 to speak in support of someone or something **defender** *noun*

defendant *noun* (*plural* **defendants**) a person accused of a crime in a lawcourt

defensive *adjective* 1 used to defend something 2 anxious about being criticized

defer *verb* (**defers, deferring, deferred**) (not an everyday word) to put something off until later ▸ *She deferred her departure until Saturday.*

defiant *adjective* openly disobedient or defying someone **defiance** *noun* **defiantly** *adverb*

deficient *adjective* (not an everyday word) not being enough **deficiency** *noun*

define *verb* (**defines, defining, defined**) to explain what something means **definition** *noun* the meaning of a word

definite *adjective* fixed or certain

definite article *noun* (*plural* **definite articles**) the word *the*

definitely *adverb and interjection*
certainly, without doubt

deforestation *noun* cutting down a lot of
trees in an area

deformed *adjective* not having the right
shape **deformity** *noun*

defrost *verb* (**defrosts, defrosting,
defrosted**) 1 to remove the ice and frost
from something 2 to unfreeze frozen food

deft *adjective* (**defter, deftest**) skilful and
quick

defuse *verb* (**defuses, defusing, defused**)
1 to remove the fuse from a bomb so that it
cannot explode 2 to make a situation less
dangerous or tense

defy *verb* (**defies, defying, defied**) 1 to
refuse to obey someone 2 to challenge
someone to do something bold ▶ *I defy
you to walk on that wall.*

degree *noun* (*plural* **degrees**) 1 a unit for
measuring temperature ▶ *Water boils at
100 degrees centigrade, or 100°C.* 2 a unit
for measuring angles ▶ *There are 90
degrees (90°) in a right angle.* 3 a
qualification awarded to someone who has
successfully finished a college or
university course

dehydrated *adjective* dried out, with all
the water removed **dehydration** *noun*

de-ice *verb* (**de-ices, de-icing, de-iced**) to
remove ice from something

deity *noun* (*plural* **deities**) (*pronounced
dee-i-ti* or **day-i-ti**) a god or goddess

dejected *adjective* sad or depressed
dejection *noun*

delay *verb* (**delays, delaying, delayed**) 1 to
make someone or something late 2 to put
something off until later 3 to wait before
doing something
delay *noun* (*plural* **delays**) a period of
waiting ▶ *There was a further delay of 20
minutes.*

delete *verb* (**deletes, deleting, deleted**) to
cross out something written **deletion** *noun*

deliberate *adjective* (*pronounced* di-**lib**-er-
at) 1 done on purpose 2 slow and careful
▶ *She has a deliberate way of talking.*
deliberately *adverb*

delicacy *noun* (*plural* **delicacies**) 1 being
delicate 2 something small and tasty to eat

delicate *adjective* 1 easily broken or
damaged 2 soft and fine ▶ *Although it is a
delicate fabric it is also very strong.*
3 becoming ill easily, not strong in health
▶ *Laura was a delicate child.* 4 using or
needing great care ▶ *We realize that this
is a delicate situation.*

delicatessen *noun* (*plural* **delicatessens**)
a shop that sells unusual or foreign foods,
especially meats and cheeses

delicious *adjective* tasting or smelling very
good

delight *verb* (**delights, delighting,
delighted**) to give someone a lot of
pleasure
delight *noun* (*plural* **delights**) 1 great
pleasure 2 something that causes pleasure
▶ *Her singing was a delight.* **delighted**
adjective

delightful *adjective* causing great pleasure
delightfully *adverb*

delinquent *noun* (*plural* **delinquents**)
a young person who breaks the law
delinquency *noun*

delirious *adjective* 1 having a confused
mind after a fever or illness 2 wildly
excited about something

deliver *verb* (**delivers, delivering,
delivered**) 1 to take something to the place
it is meant to go to 2 to help with the birth
of a baby **delivery** *noun*

delta *noun* (*plural* **deltas**) 1 a triangular
area at the mouth of a river where it
spreads into branches 2 a triangular shape

delude *verb* (**deludes, deluding, deluded**) to deceive someone about something **delusion** *noun*

deluge *noun* (*plural* **deluges**) 1 a large flood 2 a heavy fall of rain

demand *verb* (**demands, demanding, demanded**) to ask for something forcefully
demand *noun* (*plural* **demands**) 1 what someone demands 2 a desire or need to have something ▸ *The demand for land increased when the new settlers arrived.* **in demand** wanted; popular

demerara *noun* (*pronounced* dem-er-**air**-a) a kind of light brown sugar

democracy *noun* (*plural* **democracies**) a system of government in which the leaders are elected by the people **democrat** *noun* someone who agrees with democracy **democratic** *adjective*

demolish *verb* (**demolishes, demolishing, demolished**) to knock down a building and break it up **demolition** *noun*

demon *noun* (*plural* **demons**) a devil or evil spirit
The word **demon** comes from a Greek word meaning 'a spirit'.

demonstrate *verb* (**demonstrates, demonstrating, demonstrated**) 1 to show or prove something 2 to take part in a demonstration or protest **demonstrator** *noun*

demonstration *noun* (*plural* **demonstrations**) 1 an action or display that shows how to do or work something 2 a march or meeting to support something or protest about something

den *noun* (*plural* **dens**) 1 the home or hiding-place of a wild animal 2 a person's private or secret place

denial *noun* (*plural* **denials**) a statement denying or refusing something

denim *noun* strong cotton cloth, used to make jeans

denote *verb* (**denotes, denoting, denoted**) (not an everyday word) to indicate or mean something ▸ *In road signs, P denotes 'parking'.*

denounce *verb* (**denounces, denouncing, denounced**) (not an everyday word) to say firmly or publicly that someone has done something wrong

dense *adjective* (**denser, densest**) 1 thick ▸ *The fog was becoming even more dense.* 2 packed close together ▸ *They lived on the edge of a dense forest.* 3 (informal) stupid **density** *noun* how heavy something is for its size

dent *noun* (*plural* **dents**) a hollow part made in a surface by hitting it or pressing it

dental *adjective* to do with teeth

dentist *noun* (*plural* **dentists**) a person who is trained to treat teeth, fill them or take them out, and fit false ones **dentistry** *noun* a dentist's work

dentures *plural noun* a set of false teeth

deny *verb* (**denies, denying, denied**) 1 to say that something is not true 2 to refuse a request

deodorant *noun* (*plural* **deodorants**) a powder or liquid put on the body to make it smell fresh

depart *verb* (**departs, departing, departed**) to go away or leave **departure** *noun*

department *noun* (*plural* **departments**) a part of a large organization or shop

department store *noun* (*plural* **department stores**) a large shop that sells many different kinds of goods

depend *verb* (**depends, depending, depended**) **depend on** 1 to rely on someone or something ▸ *The old man next door depends on me to do his shopping.* 2 to be decided by something ▸ *How you steer the boat depends on the strength of the wind.*

dependable *adjective* that you can depend on; reliable

dependant *noun* (*plural* **dependants**) a person who depends on someone else, especially for money

dependent *adjective* depending or relying on someone ▸ *He was dependent on his father for many years.* **dependence** *noun*

depict *verb* (**depicts, depicting, depicted**) to show something in a painting or drawing, or describe it in words

deplorable *adjective* extremely bad; shocking **deplorably** *adverb*

deplore *verb* (**deplores, deploring, deplored**) to be very angry or upset about something

deport *verb* (**deports, deporting, deported**) to send someone out of a country because they are not wanted there **deportation** *noun*

deposit *noun* (*plural* **deposits**) 1 an amount of money paid into a bank 2 a sum of money paid as a first instalment 3 a layer of something solid in or on the earth, such as rock or minerals
deposit *verb* (**deposits, depositing, deposited**) to pay money into a bank

depot *noun* (*plural* **depots**) (*pronounced* dep-oh) 1 a place where things are stored 2 a place where buses or trains are kept and repaired

depress *verb* (**depresses, depressing, depressed**) to make someone very sad

depression *noun* (*plural* **depressions**) 1 a feeling of great sadness and hopelessness 2 an area of low air pressure that might bring rain 3 a period when business is bad and many people have no work 4 a shallow dip in the ground

deprive *verb* (**deprives, depriving, deprived**) to take something away from someone ▸ *Prisoners are deprived of their freedom.* **deprivation** *noun* having something taken away from you

depth *noun* (*plural* **depths**) how deep something is ▸ *The river has a depth of 20 metres at this point.* **in depth** thoroughly

deputy *noun* (*plural* **deputies**) a substitute or chief assistant for someone

derail *verb* (**derails, derailing, derailed**) to cause a train to leave the track

derelict *adjective* (*pronounced* de-re-likt) left to fall into a state of ruin

derive *verb* (**derives, deriving, derived**) to get something from another person or thing ▸ *They derived a lot of pleasure from travelling.*

derrick *noun* (*plural* **derricks**) 1 a kind of large crane for lifting things 2 a tall framework that holds the machinery used for drilling an oil well

descant *noun* (*plural* **descants**) a tune sung or played above another tune

descend *verb* (**descends, descending, descended**) to go down **be descended from** to be in the same family as someone from an earlier time **descent** *noun*

descendant *noun* (*plural* **descendants**) a person who is descended from someone who lived at an earlier time

describe *verb* (**describes, describing, described**) to say what someone or something is like **description** *noun* **descriptive** *adjective* describing something

desert *noun* (*plural* **deserts**) (*pronounced* dez-ert) a large area of very dry sandy land
desert *verb* (**deserts, deserting, deserted**) (*pronounced* di-zert) to leave someone or something without intending to return **deserter** *noun* **desertion** *noun*

deserve *verb* (**deserves, deserving, deserved**) to have done something good enough for a reward or bad enough for a punishment ▸ *We all deserve a day off after our hard work.*

design *noun* (*plural* **designs**) 1 the way that something is made or arranged ▸ *The new building has a modern design.* 2 a plan or drawing that shows how something can be made 3 a pattern of lines and shapes
design *verb* (**designs, designing, designed**) to make a design or plan for something **designer** *noun*

desirable *adjective* worth having or worth doing

desire *verb* (**desires, desiring, desired**) to want something very much
desire *noun* (*plural* **desires**) a strong wish for something

desk *noun* (*plural* **desks**) a piece of furniture with a flat top and drawers, used for writing and reading

desolate *adjective* (not an everyday word) 1 (describing a person) lonely and unhappy 2 (describing a place) dreary and without any people in it **desolation** *noun*

despair *noun* a feeling of losing all hope

despair *verb* (**despairs, despairing, despaired**) to lose hope

desperate *adjective* 1 ready to do anything to get out of a difficulty ▶ *They lost their jobs and became desperate for money.* 2 extremely serious or hopeless ▶ *We were in desperate trouble.* **desperately** *adverb* **desperation** *noun*

despicable *adjective* deserving to be despised; bad or evil

despise *verb* (**despises, despising, despised**) to think that someone is inferior or worthless

despite *preposition* in spite of ▶ *He was able to cling to the branch despite being hit over the head.*

dessert *noun* (*plural* **desserts**) (*pronounced* di-**zert**) fruit or a sweet food eaten at the end of a meal

dessertspoon *noun* (*plural* **dessertspoons**) a medium-sized spoon used for eating puddings

destination *noun* (*plural* **destinations**) the place you are travelling to

destined *adjective* intended by fate ▶ *He felt sure he was destined to succeed.*

destiny *noun* (*plural* **destinies**) what is intended for someone; fate

destitute *adjective* having no money or home

destroy *verb* (**destroys, destroying, destroyed**) to ruin something or put an end to it **destruction** *noun* **destructive** *adjective* causing things to be destroyed

destroyer *noun* (*plural* **destroyers**) a kind of fast warship

detach *verb* (**detaches, detaching, detached**) to remove something that was fixed to something else

detached *adjective* not joined to something else

detail *noun* (*plural* **details**) 1 a small part of a design or picture 2 a small piece of information

detain *verb* (**detains, detaining, detained**) 1 to keep someone in a place against their will 2 to keep someone waiting ▶ *They promised not to detain us for too long.*

detect *verb* (**detects, detecting, detected**) to discover something **detection** *noun*

detective *noun* (*plural* **detectives**) a police officer who investigates crimes

detention *noun* (*plural* **detentions**) being made to stay in a place when you do not want to

deter *verb* (**deters, deterring, deterred**) to put someone off doing something

detergent *noun* (*plural* **detergents**) a kind of washing powder or washing liquid

deteriorate *verb* (**deteriorates, deteriorating, deteriorated**) (not an everyday word) to become worse ▶ *In the afternoon the weather began to deteriorate.* **deterioration** *noun*

determination *noun* a strong feeling that you will achieve something

determined *adjective* having your mind firmly made up

deterrent *noun* (*plural* **deterrents**) something used to put someone off doing something

detest *verb* (**detests, detesting, detested**) to dislike something very much

detonate *verb* (**detonates, detonating, detonated**) to make a bomb explode **detonation** *noun* **detonator** *noun* a device that makes a bomb explode

detour *noun* (*plural* **detours**) a less direct route used instead of the normal one

devastate *verb* (**devastates, devastating, devastated**) to ruin or destroy a place, making it impossible to live in **devastation** *noun*

develop *verb* (**develops, developing, developed**) 1 to make something bigger or better 2 to become bigger or better 3 to treat a photographic film with chemicals so that pictures appear on it **4** to get an illness ▸ *I got a cold and then developed a fever.*

development *noun* (*plural* **developments**) something interesting that has happened ▸ *There have been some important developments in the last two weeks.*

device *noun* (*plural* **devices**) a tool or instrument or machine for doing a particular thing

devil *noun* (*plural* **devils**) an evil spirit or person **devilish** *adjective*

devious *adjective* **1** doing things in unfair or dishonest ways **2** roundabout; not direct ▸ *The coach took a devious route to avoid the traffic jams.* **deviously** *adverb* **deviousness** *noun*

devise *verb* (**devises, devising, devised**) to invent or think up a plan or idea

devolution *noun* a system of allowing an area or region to run its own affairs

devoted *adjective* loving and loyal

devotion *noun* strong love or loyalty

devour *verb* (**devours, devouring, devoured**) (not an everyday word) to eat or swallow something greedily

devout *adjective* religious, sincere

dew *noun* tiny drops of water that form during the night on surfaces out of doors **dewy** *adjective*

diabetes *noun* (*pronounced* dy-a-**bee**-teez) a disease in which there is too much sugar in a person's blood **diabetic** *noun* and *adjective*

diabolical *adjective* like a devil; very wicked

diagnose *verb* (**diagnoses, diagnosing, diagnosed**) to find out what illness a person has and what treatment they need **diagnosis** *noun*

diagonal *noun* (*plural* **diagonals**) a straight line joining opposite corners of a square or rectangle **diagonally** *adverb*

diagram *noun* (*plural* **diagrams**) a drawing or picture that shows the parts of something or how it works

dial *noun* (*plural* **dials**) the round face of a clock or gauge

dial *verb* (**dials, dialling, dialled**) to choose numbers on a telephone by pressing numbered buttons or turning a dial

dialect *noun* (*plural* **dialects**) the form of a language used by people in one district but not in others

dialogue *noun* (*plural* **dialogues**) a conversation

diameter *noun* (*plural* **diameters**) a line drawn from one side of a circle through the centre to the other side

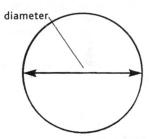

diameter

diamond *noun* (*plural* **diamonds**) **1** a very hard jewel that looks like clear glass **2** a shape which has four equal sides but no right angles **3** a playing card with red diamond shapes on it

diarrhoea *noun* (*pronounced* dy-a-**ree**-a) an illness that makes you need to go to the lavatory very often and makes the waste from your body go runny.

diary *noun* (*plural* **diaries**) a book giving the days of the year, in which you write what is happening each day

dice *noun* (*plural* **dice**) a small cube marked with one to six dots on each side, used in games

dictate *verb* (**dictates, dictating, dictated**) to speak or read something aloud for someone else to write down **dictation** *noun*

dictator *noun* (*plural* **dictators**) a ruler who has complete control **dictatorial** *adjective* like a dictator **dictatorship** *noun* a state ruled by a dictator

dictionary *noun* (*plural* **dictionaries**) a book with words listed in alphabetical order, telling you what they mean and how you spell them

did past tense of **do**

didn't short for *did not* ▶ *The postman didn't come.*

die *verb* (**dies, dying, died**) to stop living **die out** to disappear gradually ▶ *The tiger is beginning to die out.*

diesel *noun* (*plural* **diesels**) an engine that works by burning oil in compressed air

diet *noun* (*plural* **diets**) 1 the food that a person normally eats ▶ *They try to stick to a healthy diet.* 2 a choice of food that a person eats to be healthy or to lose weight

diet *verb* (**diets, dieting, dieted**) to have a special diet, usually because you are trying to lose weight

differ *verb* (**differs, differing, differed**) 1 to be not the same as something or someone else 2 to disagree

difference *noun* (*plural* **differences**) the way in which two or more people or things are different

different *adjective* not like something or someone else **differently** *adverb*

difficult *adjective* 1 needing a lot of effort or skill; not easy 2 hard to please ▶ *Our neighbour is a difficult person.*

difficulty *noun* (*plural* **difficulties**) something that is difficult; a problem

dig *verb* (**digs, digging, dug**) 1 to break up the ground or soil and move it 2 to make a hole or trench in the ground 3 to poke someone **digger** *noun* a machine used for digging

dig *noun* (*plural* **digs**) a sharp thrust or poke ▶ *My friend gave me a dig in the ribs.*

digest *verb* (**digests, digesting, digested**) to soften and change food in the stomach and intestine so that the body can absorb it **digestible** *adjective* easy to digest **digestion** *noun*

digestive *adjective* to do with digesting food

digit *noun* (*plural* **digits**) (*pronounced* **dij**-it) 1 any of the numbers from 0 to 9 2 a finger or toe

digital *adjective* 1 having a row of numbers instead of hands to show the time, speed, or other information ▶ *a digital watch* 2 using digits to record data ▶ *a digital computer*

dignified *adjective* having dignity, calm and serious

dignity *noun* a calm and serious manner

dike *noun* (*plural* **dikes**) 1 an earth wall made to hold back water and prevent flooding 2 a ditch for draining water from land

dilemma *noun* (*plural* **dilemmas**) a situation in which you have two choices, both of them bad in some way

dilute *verb* (**dilutes, diluting, diluted**) to make a liquid weaker or thinner by adding water to it **dilution** *noun*

dim *adjective* (**dimmer, dimmest**) only faintly lit and difficult to see **dimly** *adverb*

dimension *noun* (*plural* **dimensions**) a measurement such as length, width, area, or volume

diminish *verb* (**diminishes, diminishing, diminished**) 1 to make something smaller 2 to become smaller

dimple *noun* (*plural* **dimples**) a small hollow on the skin

din *noun* a loud noise

dine *verb* (**dines, dining, dined**) (not an everyday word) to have dinner **diner** *noun*

dinghy *noun* (*plural* **dinghies**) (*pronounced* **ding**-i) a kind of small boat

dingy *adjective* (**dingier, dingiest**) (*pronounced* **din**-ji) gloomy and dull

dinner *noun* (*plural* **dinners**) the main meal of the day

dinosaur *noun* (*plural* **dinosaurs**) a prehistoric animal, of many kinds and often enormous in size

dip *verb* (**dips, dipping, dipped**) 1 to put something into a liquid and take it out again 2 to go downwards ▶ *The road dips steeply after the bend.* 3 to lower the beam of a car's headlights

dip noun (plural **dips**) 1 a downward slope 2 a quick swim

diphtheria noun (pronounced dif-**theer**-i-a) a serious disease of the throat

diploma noun (plural **diplomas**) a certificate awarded to someone who has reached a certain standard in a subject

diplomacy noun keeping friendly with other countries or people

diplomat noun (plural **diplomats**) an official whose job is to keep friendly with other countries

diplomatic adjective 1 to do with diplomacy 2 tactful and courteous

dire adjective (**direr**, **direst**) dreadful or serious ▶ The refugees are in dire need of food and shelter.

direct adjective 1 as straight or quick as possible 2 frank and honest **directness** noun

direct verb (**directs**, **directing**, **directed**) 1 to show someone the way 2 to control or manage an activity or organization

direction noun (plural **directions**) 1 the way you go to get to a place 2 controlling an activity **directions** information on how to use or do something

directly adverb 1 by a direct route ▶ You can't go directly to Manchester but have to change trains at Crewe. 2 immediately ▶ Can you come directly?

director noun (plural **directors**) 1 a senior person who helps to manage a company 2 a person who directs a film or play

directory noun (plural **directories**) a list of people with their telephone numbers and addresses

dirt noun earth or soil, or anything that is not clean

dirty adjective (**dirtier**, **dirtiest**) 1 covered with dirt; not clean 2 rude or offensive 3 unfair or mean ▶ They keep playing dirty tricks. **dirtily** adverb **dirtiness** noun

disability noun (plural **disabilities**) something that prevents you from using your body in the usual way

disabled adjective having a disease or injury that prevents you from using your body properly

disadvantage noun (plural **disadvantages**) something that hinders you or makes things difficult

disagree verb (**disagrees**, **disagreeing**, **disagreed**) 1 to have a different opinion about something 2 to have a bad effect on someone ▶ Rich food often disagrees with me. **disagreement** noun

disagreeable adjective unpleasant

disappear verb (**disappears**, **disappearing**, **disappeared**) to stop being visible; to vanish **disappearance** noun

disappoint verb (**disappoints**, **disappointing**, **disappointed**) to let someone down because you do not do what they were hoping for **disappointing** adjective **disappointment** noun

disapprove verb (**disapproves**, **disapproving**, **disapproved**) to think that something or someone is bad or wrong **disapproval** noun

disaster noun (plural **disasters**) a serious accident or misfortune **disastrous** adjective

disc noun (plural **discs**) 1 a round flat object 2 a gramophone record or CD 3 a round flat piece of plastic on which sound or computer data is recorded This word is usually spelt **disk** when it has the computer meaning.

discard verb (**discards**, **discarding**, **discarded**) to throw something away because you no longer need it

disciple noun (plural **disciples**) (pronounced di-**sy**-pul) a follower of a political or religious leader

discipline noun (pronounced **dis**-i-plin) training and punishment that makes people behave well

disc jockey noun (plural **disc jockeys**) someone who introduces and plays records, especially on the radio

disclose verb (**discloses**, **disclosing**, **disclosed**) (not an everyday word) to tell someone about something secret **disclosure** noun

disco noun (plural **discos**) a place or party where people dance to records of pop music

discomfort noun a feeling of being uncomfortable or anxious

disconnect verb (**disconnects, disconnecting, disconnected**) to break an electrical connection by pulling out the plug **disconnection** noun

discontented adjective not contented; not satisfied

discord noun (plural **discords**) 1 loud disagreement 2 a harsh sound or noise

discount noun (plural **discounts**) an amount by which a price is reduced

discourage verb (**discourages, discouraging, discouraged**) 1 to take away someone's enthusiasm or confidence 2 to try to persuade someone not to do something **discouragement** noun

discover verb (**discovers, discovering, discovered**) to find something by chance or for the first time **discovery** noun

discreet adjective being careful in what you say and do

discriminate verb (**discriminates, discriminating, discriminated**) 1 to notice the differences between things, or to prefer one thing to another 2 to treat people differently or unfairly because of their race, sex, or religion **discrimination** noun

discus noun (plural **discuses**) (pronounced dis-kuss) a thick heavy disc thrown in an athletic contest

discuss verb (**discusses, discussing, discussed**) (pronounced dis-kuss) to talk with other people about something **discussion** noun

disease noun (plural **diseases**) an illness or sickness **diseased** adjective

disembark verb (**disembarks, disembarking, disembarked**) (not an everyday word) to get out of a boat or aircraft

disgrace noun 1 shame ▸ It's no disgrace to be poor. 2 something or someone that causes shame or disapproval ▸ The council have described our home as a disgrace.

disgrace verb (**disgraces, disgracing, disgraced**) to bring someone shame or disgrace

disgraceful adjective bringing shame or disgrace **disgracefully** adverb

disguise verb (**disguises, disguising, disguised**) to make someone or something look different so that people will not recognize them

disguise noun (plural **disguises**) something used for disguising a person or thing

disgust noun a strong feeling of dislike

disgust verb (**disgusts, disgusting, disgusted**) to cause someone disgust **disgusted** adjective **disgusting** adjective

dish noun (plural **dishes**) 1 a plate or bowl for serving food 2 one course or part of a meal 3 a television aerial shaped like a dish, for receiving satellite signals

dishevelled adjective having a rough untidy appearance

dishonest adjective not honest **dishonestly** adverb **dishonesty** noun

dishwasher noun (plural **dishwashers**) a machine for washing dishes

disinfect verb (**disinfects, disinfecting, disinfected**) to kill the germs in or on something

disinfectant noun (plural **disinfectants**) a liquid used to kill germs

disintegrate verb (**disintegrates, disintegrating, disintegrated**) to break up into small pieces **disintegration** noun

disinterested adjective not favouring one side more than the other; impartial
Disinterested does not mean the same as uninterested, which means 'not interested' or 'bored'.

disk noun (plural **disks**) (another spelling of **disc**) a round flat piece of plastic in a case, on which computer data is recorded

dislike *noun* (*plural* **dislikes**) a feeling of not liking someone or something
dislike *verb* (**dislikes, disliking, disliked**) not to like someone or something

dislocate *verb* (**dislocates, dislocating, dislocated**) to dislodge a bone in a part of your body **dislocation** *noun*

dislodge *verb* (**dislodges, dislodging, dislodged**) to move something from its right place by accident

disloyal *adjective* not loyal

dismal *adjective* gloomy or miserable **dismally** *adverb*

dismantle *verb* (**dismantles, dismantling, dismantled**) to take something to pieces

dismay *noun* a feeling of strong disappointment and shock
dismay *verb* (**dismays, dismaying, dismayed**) to make someone disappointed and shocked

dismiss *verb* (**dismisses, dismissing, dismissed**) 1 to send someone away 2 to tell someone who works for you to leave their job 3 to refuse to think about an idea or suggestion **dismissal** *noun* losing your job

dismount *verb* (**dismounts, dismounting, dismounted**) (not an everyday word) to get off a horse or bicycle

disobey *verb* (**disobeys, disobeying, disobeyed**) to do the opposite of what someone tells you to do **disobedience** *noun* **disobedient** *adjective*

disorder *noun* (*plural* **disorders**) 1 confusion or disturbance 2 an illness

disorderly *adjective* badly behaved

disorganized *adjective* not well organized; in a muddle

dispatch *verb* (**dispatches, dispatching, dispatched**) 1 to send something or someone off to a place 2 to kill someone
dispatch *noun* (*plural* **dispatches**) a report or message

dispense *verb* (**dispenses, dispensing, dispensed**) to prepare medicines for patients **dispense with** to do without something

disperse *verb* (**disperses, dispersing, dispersed**) 1 to send people away in various directions ▶ *The police managed to disperse the crowds.* 2 to go off in various directions **dispersal** *noun* being dispersed

display *verb* (**displays, displaying, displayed**) to arrange something so that people can look at it
display *noun* (*plural* **displays**) 1 a show or exhibition 2 pictures or information shown on a screen or panel

displease *verb* (**displeases, displeasing, displeased**) to annoy someone

disposable *adjective* made to be thrown away after it has been used

disposal *noun* getting rid of something you no longer need **at your disposal** ready for you to use

dispose *verb* (**disposes, disposing, disposed**) **be disposed** (not an everyday word) be ready and willing to do something ▶ *They were not at all disposed to help us.* **dispose of** to get rid of something you no longer need

disprove *verb* (**disproves, disproving, disproved**) to prove that something is not true

dispute *verb* (**disputes, disputing, disputed**) to have a quarrel or disagreement
dispute *noun* (*plural* **disputes**) a quarrel or disagreement

disqualify *verb* (**disqualifies, disqualifying, disqualified**) to remove someone from a race or competition because they have broken the rules **disqualification** *noun*

disregard *verb* (**disregards, disregarding, disregarded**) to take no notice of someone or something

disrespect *noun* lack of respect; rudeness **disrespectful** *adjective* showing disrespect **disrespectfully** *adverb* in a disrespectful way

disrupt *verb* (**disrupts, disrupting, disrupted**) to make something confused or disorganized ▶ *The bad weather has* *disrupted all our plans.* **disruption** *noun* confusion, disorder **disruptive** *adjective* causing confusion

dissatisfied *adjective* not satisfied **dissatisfaction** *noun*

dissect *verb* (**dissects, dissecting, dissected**) (*pronounced* di-**sekt**) to cut something into pieces so you can examine it **dissection** *noun*

dissolve *verb* (**dissolves, dissolving, dissolved**) 1 to mix something with a liquid so that it becomes part of the liquid 2 to melt or become liquid

dissuade *verb* (**dissuades, dissuading, dissuaded**) to persuade someone not to do something **dissuasion** *noun*

distance *noun* (*plural* **distances**) the amount of space between two places **in the distance** far away but able to be seen

distant *adjective* 1 far away 2 unfriendly

distil *verb* (**distils, distilling, distilled**) to purify a liquid by boiling it and then letting it cool so that it becomes liquid . again **distillation** *noun*

distillery *noun* (*plural* **distilleries**) a place where whisky and other alcoholic drinks are produced

distinct *adjective* easy to hear or see ▶ *There was a distinct tapping noise coming from the shed.* **distinctly** *adverb*

distinction *noun* (*plural* **distinctions**) 1 a difference 2 an achievement that brings honour or fame

distinctive *adjective* clearly distinguishing something from all the others ▶ *The letter had been written in a distinctive green ink.*

distinguish *verb* (**distinguishes, distinguishing, distinguished**) 1 to notice the differences between one thing and another 2 to see or hear something clearly

distinguished *adjective* famous and well respected

distort *verb* (**distorts, distorting, distorted**) to change something into a strange shape **distortion** *noun*

distract *verb* (**distracts, distracting, distracted**) to take someone's attention away from what they are doing **distraction** *noun*

distress *noun* great sorrow or trouble
distress *verb* (**distresses, distressing, distressed**) to cause someone distress

distribute *verb* (**distributes, distributing, distributed**) (not an everyday word) 1 to give things out to several people 2 to spread or scatter something around **distribution** *noun*

district *noun* (*plural* **districts**) an area of a town or country

distrust *verb* (**distrusts, distrusting, distrusted**) to not trust someone
distrust *noun* a lack of trust; suspicion **distrustful** *adjective* not trusting people

disturb *verb* (**disturbs, disturbing, disturbed**) 1 to interrupt someone while they are doing something 2 to make someone worried or upset 3 to move something from its right position **disturbance** *noun*

disused *adjective* no longer used ▶ *They rode their bikes across a piece of disused land.*

ditch *noun* (*plural* **ditches**) a narrow trench for carrying away water

dither *verb* (**dithers, dithering, dithered**) to make a fuss about what to do

ditto *noun* the same thing as the one before
Ditto marks (") are sometimes used in lists or bills to show where something is repeated.

divan *noun* (*plural* **divans**) a bed without a raised back or sides

dive *verb* (**dives, diving, dived**) 1 to go head first into water 2 to move downwards quickly

diver *noun* (*plural* **divers**) 1 a swimmer who dives 2 someone who works under water in a special suit called a *diving suit*

diverse *adjective* of several different kinds **diversity** *noun*

diversion *noun* (*plural* **diversions**) 1 a different way for traffic to go when the usual road is closed 2 something pleasant that takes your mind off something else

divert *verb* (**diverts, diverting, diverted**) 1 to change the direction that something is moving in 2 to take someone's mind off something by amusing them

divide *verb* (**divides, dividing, divided**) 1 to separate something into smaller parts or shares 2 to find out how many times one number is contained in another ▸ *Divide twelve by three and you get four* ($12 \div 3 = 4$).

divine *adjective* 1 belonging to God or coming from God 2 like a god **divinity** *noun* being divine

divine *verb* (**divines, divining, divined**) to find hidden water or metal by holding a Y-shaped stick called a *divining rod*

division *noun* (*plural* **divisions**) 1 dividing numbers or things 2 one of the parts into which something is divided **divisible** *adjective* able to be divided exactly ▸ *10 is divisible by 5.*

divorce *noun* (*plural* **divorces**) the legal ending of a marriage

divorce *verb* (**divorces, divorcing, divorced**) to end a marriage with someone

Diwali *noun* (*pronounced* di-**wah**-li) a festival of the Hindus, held in October or November

DIY short for *do-it-yourself*, doing house decorating and repairs yourself

dizzy *adjective* (**dizzier, dizziest**) giddy and feeling confused **dizziness** *noun*

DJ short for **disc jockey**

do *verb* (**does, doing, did, done**) 1 to perform something or deal with it ▸ *Have you done your work?* ▸ *There's one question I can't do.* 2 to be all right or suitable ▸ *There's not much food but perhaps an omelette will do.* 3 You also use **do** with other verbs in special ways. ▸ *Do you want this?* ▸ *He doesn't want it.* ▸ *I do like crisps.* ▸ *We work as hard as they do.* **do without** to manage without something

docile *adjective* gentle and obedient

dock *noun* (*plural* **docks**) 1 a part of a harbour where ships are loaded and unloaded or repaired 2 a place for the prisoner on trial in a lawcourt 3 a weed with broad leaves

dock *verb* (**docks, docking, docked**) 1 to come into a dock at a harbour 2 to join one spacecraft to another in orbit 3 to cut short an animal's tail

doctor *noun* (*plural* **doctors**) a person trained to heal sick or injured people

document *noun* (*plural* **documents**) a piece of paper with something important written or printed on it

documentary *noun* (*plural* **documentaries**) a film or television programme that gives information about real events or situations

doddery *adjective* unsteady or shaky because of being old

dodge *verb* (**dodges, dodging, dodged**) to move quickly to avoid something or someone

dodge *noun* (*plural* **dodges**) a trick or a clever way of doing something

dodgem *noun* (*plural* **dodgems**) a small open car that you drive round an enclosure at a funfair, dodging and bumping other cars

doe *noun* (*plural* **does**) a female deer, rabbit, or hare

does a form of **do**

doesn't short for *does not* ▸ *The toaster doesn't work.*

dog *noun* (*plural* **dogs**) a four-legged animal that barks

dogged *adjective* (*pronounced* **dog**-id) not giving up in spite of difficulties **doggedly** *adverb*

doldrums *plural noun* **in the doldrums** bored and unhappy

dole *noun* (informal) money paid by the government to people who are out of work

doll *noun* (*plural* **dolls**) a toy model of a child or person

dollar *noun* (*plural* **dollars**) a unit of money in the USA and some other countries

dolphin *noun* (*plural* **dolphins**) a sea animal like a small whale with a long snout

dome *noun* (*plural* **domes**) a tall rounded roof

domestic *adjective* to do with the home **domestic animal** an animal you can keep as a pet

domesticated *adjective* fitting in well with home life

dominant *adjective* most powerful or important **dominance** *noun*

dominate *verb* (**dominates, dominating, dominated**) to control people by being the most powerful **domination** *noun*

domino *noun* (*plural* **dominoes**) a small flat oblong piece of wood or plastic with dots (1 to 6) or a blank space at each end, used in the game of *dominoes*

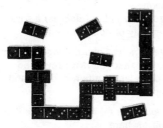

donate *verb* (**donates, donating, donated**) to give money to a charity or organization **donation** *noun* a gift of money to a charity or organization

done past participle of **do**

donkey *noun* (*plural* **donkeys**) an animal of the horse family with long ears

donor *noun* (*plural* **donors**) someone who gives something for a useful cause

don't short for *do not* ▸ *You don't have to come.*

doodle *noun* (*plural* **doodles**) a quick drawing or piece of writing done without thinking

doodle *verb* (**doodles, doodling, doodled**) to draw a doodle

doom *noun* a bad fate that you cannot avoid **doomed** *adjective*

door *noun* (*plural* **doors**) a panel of wood or glass that opens and closes the entrance to a room, building, or cupboard

doorway *noun* (*plural* **doorways**) the opening into which a door fits

dormitory *noun* (*plural* **dormitories**) a room for several people to sleep in

dormouse *noun* (*plural* **dormice**) a small animal that hibernates

dose *noun* (*plural* **doses**) an amount of medicine for taking at one time

dot *noun* (*plural* **dots**) a tiny spot

dotted *adjective* made of dots ▸ *Write on the dotted line.*

double *adjective* **1** twice as much or twice as many **2** having two of something ▸ *a double-barrelled shotgun* **3** suitable for two people ▸ *a double bed*

double *noun* (*plural* **doubles**) **1** twice the amount or cost **2** someone who looks exactly like someone else

double *verb* (**doubles, doubling, doubled**) **1** to make something twice as big or twice as many **2** to become twice as big **3** to fold something in two, so that one part lies on the other

double bass *noun* (*plural* **double basses**) a large musical instrument with strings, which you play standing up

double-cross *verb* (**double-crosses, double-crossing, double-crossed**) to cheat or betray someone when you are supposed to be helping them

double-decker *noun* (*plural* **double-deckers**) a bus with two floors, one above the other

doubly *adverb* twice as much ▸ *It's doubly important that you should go.*

doubt *verb* (**doubts, doubting, doubted**) to feel unsure about something ▸ *I doubt whether we'll get there in time.*

doubt *noun* (*plural* **doubts**) a feeling of not being sure

doubtful *adjective* **1** being unsure ▸ *The woman sounded doubtful, but let us in anyway.* **2** making you feel unsure ▸ *Their story was very doubtful.* **doubtfully** *adverb*

doubtless *adverb* without any doubt

dough *noun* a thick mixture of flour and water used for making bread or pastry **doughy** *adjective* like dough

doughnut *noun* (*plural* **doughnuts**) a round lump of sweetened dough that has been fried and covered with sugar

dove *noun* (*plural* **doves**) a kind of pigeon that makes a cooing sound

dovecote *noun* (*plural* **dovecotes**) a small building in which doves make their nests

dowdy *adjective* (**dowdier**, **dowdiest**) looking dull and uninteresting

down¹ *adverb* and *preposition* **1** from a higher point to a lower one ▸ *He fell down.* ▸ *Run down the hill.* **2** sad or dejected ▸ *I was feeling down.*

down² *noun* soft feathers or hair, such as ducks have **downy** *adjective* soft, like down

downcast *adjective* sad or dejected

downfall *noun* (*plural* **downfalls**) **1** ruin or fall from power **2** a heavy fall of rain or snow

downhill *adverb* down a hill or slope

downpour *noun* (*plural* **downpours**) a heavy fall of rain

downright *adjective* and *adverb* very, completely ▸ *She thought the idea was downright silly.*

downs *plural noun* grass-covered hills

downstairs *adverb* and *adjective* to or on a lower floor in a building

downstream *adverb* in the direction that a river or stream flows

downward or **downwards** *adverb* towards a lower place

doze *verb* (**dozes**, **dozing**, **dozed**) to sleep lightly **dozy** *adjective* sleepy
doze (*plural* **dozes**) *noun* a short light sleep

dozen *noun* (*plural* **dozens**) a set of twelve dozens (informal) lots

Dr short for **Doctor**

drab *adjective* (**drabber**, **drabbest**) dull and not colourful

draft *noun* (*plural* **drafts**) a rough sketch or plan of a design or piece of writing

drag *verb* (**drags**, **dragging**, **dragged**) **1** to pull something heavy along **2** to search a lake or river with nets and hooks

dragon *noun* (*plural* **dragons**) a monster in stories that breathes fire

dragonfly *noun* (*plural* **dragonflies**) a brightly coloured insect with a long body and transparent wings

drain *noun* (*plural* **drains**) a pipe or ditch for taking away water
drain *verb* (**drains**, **draining**, **drained**) **1** to take water away in drains **2** to flow or trickle away **3** to empty a glass or bottle of liquid **4** to exhaust someone

drainage *noun* a system of drains

drake *noun* (*plural* **drakes**) a male duck

drama *noun* (*plural* **dramas**) **1** writing or acting in plays **2** a play **3** a series of exciting events

dramatic *adjective* **1** to do with acting and the theatre **2** important and exciting ▸ *They have made some dramatic changes to the house.* **dramatically** *adverb*

dramatize *verb* (**dramatizes**, **dramatizing**, **dramatized**) **1** to make an ordinary story into a play **2** to exaggerate **dramatization** *noun*

drank past tense of **drink** *verb*

drape *verb* (**drapes**, **draping**, **draped**) to hang a cloth loosely over something

drastic *adjective* having a strong or extreme effect **drastically** *adverb*

draught *noun* (*plural* **draughts**) (*rhymes with* craft) a current of cold air indoors **draughty** *adjective*

draughts *noun* a game played with 24 round pieces on a chessboard

draw *verb* (**draws, drawing, drew, drawn**) 1 to make a picture or design with a pencil or pen 2 to pull something ▸ *She drew a handkerchief from her pocket.* ▸ *Shall I draw the curtains?* 3 to make people want to come ▸ *The circus will draw large crowds.* 4 to end a game or contest with equal scores on both sides **draw near** to approach, to come near

draw *noun* (*plural* **draws**) 1 a raffle or lottery in which the winner is found by picking numbers 2 a game that ends with equal scores on both sides 3 an attraction

drawback *noun* (*plural* **drawbacks**) a disadvantage

drawbridge *noun* (*plural* **drawbridges**) a bridge across a moat, hinged at one end so that it can be raised or lowered

drawer *noun* (*plural* **drawers**) a box-shaped container that slides in and out of a piece of furniture

drawing *noun* (*plural* **drawings**) something you draw with a pencil, pen, or crayon

drawing pin *noun* (*plural* **drawing pins**) a short pin with a large flat top, for fixing paper to a wall or board

dread *verb* (**dreads, dreading, dreaded**) to fear very much that something might happen

dread *noun* great fear

dreadful *adjective* very bad **dreadfully** *adverb*

dreadlocks *plural noun* hair twisted into long tight curls that hang around the head

dream *noun* (*plural* **dreams**) 1 things that you picture happening while you are asleep 2 something you would like to do or have very much **dreamy** *adjective* like a dream; not real

dream *verb* (**dreams, dreaming, dreamt** or **dreamed**) 1 to have a dream 2 to want something very much ▸ *He dreamed of becoming a pilot one day.*

dreary *adjective* (**drearier, dreariest**) 1 dull and uninteresting 2 gloomy **drearily** *adverb* **dreariness** *noun*

dredge *verb* (**dredges, dredging, dredged**) to clear away mud from the bottom of a river or harbour **dredger** *noun* a machine or boat used for dredging

drench *verb* (**drenches, drenching, drenched**) to make someone wet through

dress *noun* (*plural* **dresses**) 1 a piece of clothing worn by women and girls, covering the body from the shoulders to the legs 2 clothes or costume

dress *verb* (**dresses, dressing, dressed**) 1 to put clothes on 2 to clean a wound and put a bandage on it

dresser *noun* (*plural* **dressers**) a piece of furniture like a sideboard with shelves on top

dressing *noun* (*plural* **dressings**) 1 a thin sauce of oil or vinegar for a salad 2 a covering for a wound

dressing gown *noun* (*plural* **dressing gowns**) a loose indoor coat that you wear over pyjamas or a nightdress

drew past tense of **draw** *verb*

dribble *verb* (**dribbles, dribbling, dribbled**) 1 to let saliva trickle out of your mouth 2 in football or hockey, to kick the ball gently in front of you as you run forward

dried past tense and past participle of **dry** *verb*

drier *noun* (*plural* **driers**) a machine for drying washing

drift *verb* (**drifts, drifting, drifted**) 1 to be carried gently along by water or air ▸ *The little boat was drifting in the breeze.* 2 to

live without any real aims or plans

drift noun (plural **drifts**) a mass of snow or sand piled up by the wind

drill noun (plural **drills**) 1 a tool for making holes 2 exercises done by soldiers as part of their training 3 a practice for what to do in an emergency, such as a fire

drill verb (**drills, drilling, drilled**) 1 to make a hole with a drill 2 to do exercises or training

drink verb (**drinks, drinking, drank, drunk**) 1 to swallow liquid 2 to have a lot of alcohol ▸ Don't drink and drive.

drink noun (plural **drinks**) 1 a liquid that you drink 2 an alcoholic drink

drip noun (plural **drips**) a falling drop of liquid

drip verb (**drips, dripping, dripped**) 1 to fall in drops ▸ Water was dripping from the ceiling. 2 to let liquid fall in drops ▸ The tap was dripping.

drive verb (**drives, driving, drove, driven**) 1 to make a vehicle work and move along 2 to take someone along in a car ▸ Jem promised to drive her back home. 3 to force something in a certain direction ▸ The gales were driving ships on to the rocks. 4 to behave in a way that affects someone ▸ The noise was driving us crazy. 5 to make something work ▸ The washing machine is driven by an electric motor. **driver** noun someone who drives a vehicle

drive noun (plural **drives**) 1 a journey in a vehicle 2 energy and enthusiasm 3 a road leading up to a house 4 a powerful stroke of the ball in cricket, golf, and other games

drizzle noun light gentle rain

drizzle verb (**drizzles, drizzling, drizzled**) to rain gently

dromedary noun (plural **dromedaries**) a camel with one hump

drone verb (**drones, droning, droned**) 1 to make a low humming sound 2 to talk in a boring voice

drone noun (plural **drones**) 1 a low humming sound 2 a male bee

droop verb (**droops, drooping, drooped**) to hang down in a loose or limp way

drop noun (plural **drops**) 1 a small amount of liquid 2 a fall or decrease

drop verb (**drops, dropping, dropped**) 1 to fall 2 to let something fall **drop in** to visit someone casually

drought noun (plural **droughts**) (rhymes with out) a long period without any rain, so that there is not enough water

drove past tense of **drive** verb

drown verb (**drowns, drowning, drowned**) 1 to die from being under water and unable to breathe 2 to kill a person or animal by forcing them to stay under water 3 to make other sounds difficult to hear by making a lot of noise

drowsy adjective (**drowsier, drowsiest**) sleepy **drowsily** adverb **drowsiness** noun

drudgery noun hard dull work

drug noun (plural **drugs**) 1 a medicine 2 a substance that people swallow or smoke or inject into themselves that gives them special feelings, such as heroin

drug verb (**drugs, drugging, drugged**) to give drugs to someone

Druid noun (plural **Druids**) an ancient Celtic priest

drum noun (plural **drums**) 1 a round hollow musical instrument with a thin skin stretched over the end, which you beat with a stick or your hands 2 a container shaped like a drum

drum verb (**drums, drumming, drummed**) 1 to play a drum 2 to tap something repeatedly ▸ He drummed his fingers on the table. **drummer** noun

drumstick noun (plural **drumsticks**) 1 a stick used for hitting a drum 2 a cooked chicken's leg

drunk[1] *adjective* not able to control your behaviour because you have drunk too much alcohol

drunk or **drunkard** *noun* (*plural* **drunks** or **drunkards**) someone who is often drunk

drunk[2] past participle of **drink** *verb*

dry *adjective* (**drier, driest**) 1 not wet or damp 2 boring and dull **dryness** *noun*

dry *verb* (**dries, drying, dried**) 1 to become dry 2 to make something dry

dryer *noun* (*plural* **dryers**) another spelling of **drier**

dual *adjective* having two parts; double

dual carriageway *noun* (*plural* **dual carriageways**) a wide road with a central strip separating the two directions

dubious *adjective* doubtful, uncertain

duchess *noun* (*plural* **duchesses**) 1 a woman with the rank of a duke 2 the wife or widow of a duke

duck *noun* (*plural* **ducks**) 1 a waterbird with webbed feet and a flat beak 2 a batsman's score of nought at cricket

duck *verb* (**ducks, ducking, ducked**) 1 to bend down quickly to avoid something 2 to push someone under water quickly

duckling *noun* (*plural* **ducklings**) a young duck

due *adjective* 1 needing to be paid ► *Payment for the trip is now due.* 2 expected or about to happen ► *The bus is due shortly.* **due to** because of something or someone ► *Death had been due to drowning.*

due *adverb* directly ► *The camp is due north.*

duel *noun* (*plural* **duels**) a fight between two people, especially with pistols or swords

duet *noun* (*plural* **duets**) a piece of music for two players or singers

dug past tense and past participle of **dig** *verb*

dugout *noun* (*plural* **dugouts**) 1 an underground shelter 2 a canoe made by hollowing out a tree trunk

duke *noun* (*plural* **dukes**) a nobleman of the highest rank

dull *adjective* (**duller, dullest**) 1 not bright or clear; gloomy ► *It was a dull day.* 2 not sharp ► *I had a dull pain.* 3 boring or uninteresting ► *What a dull programme.* **dully** *adverb* **dullness** *noun*

duly *adverb* rightly, as it should be ► *The police duly returned with a warrant.*

dumb *adjective* (**dumber, dumbest**) unable to speak; silent

dumbfounded *adjective* so surprised that you are unable to say anything

dummy *noun* (*plural* **dummies**) 1 a large doll or model made to look like a human being 2 a rubber or plastic teat for a baby to suck

dump *noun* (*plural* **dumps**) a place where rubbish or unwanted things can be left or stored

dump *verb* (**dumps, dumping, dumped**) 1 to get rid of something when you don't want it 2 to put something down carelessly ► *Sheila rushed in and dumped her bags on the floor.*

dumpling *noun* (*plural* **dumplings**) a lump of boiled or baked dough, usually eaten with a stew

dune *noun* (*plural* **dunes**) a mound of loose sand formed by the wind

dung *noun* solid waste matter from an animal

dungarees *plural noun* trousers held up with shoulder straps and with a piece in front covering your chest

dungeon *noun* (*plural* **dungeons**) (*pronounced* **dun**-jon) an underground prison cell in a castle

duplicate *noun* (*plural* **duplicates**) (*pronounced* **dew**-pli-kat) an exact copy of something

duplicate *verb* (**duplicates, duplicating, duplicated**) (*pronounced* **dew**-pli-kayt) to make a copy of something **duplication** *noun*

durable *adjective* lasting and strong
durability *noun* how well something lasts

duration *noun* the time something lasts

during *preposition* 1 while something else is going on ▸ *Let's meet in the café during the interval.* 2 throughout ▸ *Charles didn't stop talking at all during lunch.*

dusk *noun* the time of fading light in the early evening

dust *noun* tiny particles of dry earth or dirt
dust *verb* (**dusts, dusting, dusted**) 1 to clean things of dust 2 to sprinkle something with a powder ▸ *Dust the cake with icing sugar.*

dustbin *noun* (*plural* **dustbins**) a bin kept outside a house for rubbish

duster *noun* (*plural* **dusters**) a cloth for dusting things

dustman *noun* (*plural* **dustmen**) a person whose job is to empty dustbins

dusty *adjective* (**dustier, dustiest**) covered with dust

dutiful *adjective* doing your duty; obedient
dutifully *adverb*

duty *noun* (*plural* **duties**) 1 what you have to do, because it is right or part of your job 2 a tax on things you buy

duvet *noun* (*plural* **duvets**) (*pronounced* doo-vay) a thick bed cover filled with soft material

dwarf *noun* (*plural* **dwarfs** or **dwarves**) a very small person or thing
dwarf *verb* (**dwarfs, dwarfing, dwarfed**) to make something nearby seem very small ▸ *The buildings are tall, dwarfing the trees in the park below.*

dwell *verb* (**dwells, dwelling, dwelt**) (not an everyday word) to live in a place

dwelling *noun* (*plural* **dwellings**) a place to live in

dwindle *verb* (**dwindles, dwindling, dwindled**) to get smaller gradually ▸ *His savings were starting to dwindle.*

dye *noun* (*plural* **dyes**) a liquid used to change the colour of material or hair
dye *verb* (**dyes, dyeing, dyed**) to colour something with a dye

dying present participle of **die** *verb*

dyke *noun* (*plural* **dykes**) another spelling of **dike**

dynamic *adjective* active and full of energy

dynamite *noun* a powerful explosive

dynamo *noun* (*plural* **dynamos**) a machine that produces electricity

dynasty *noun* (*plural* **dynasties**) (*pronounced* **din**-a-sti) a series of kings and queens from the same family

dyslexia *noun* (*pronounced* dis-**lek**-si-a) special difficulty in being able to read and spell words **dyslexic** *adjective* having dyslexia

Ee

each *adjective* and *pronoun* every; every one ▸ *Each city has its own postcode.* ▸ *I'll give each of you a new book.* ▸ *They were looking at each other.*

eager *adjective* wanting to do something very much

eagle *noun* (*plural* **eagles**) a large bird of prey

ear *noun* (*plural* **ears**) 1 the organ of the body that you use to hear 2 the spike of seeds at the top of a stalk of corn

earache *noun* a pain in the ear

earl *noun* (*plural* **earls**) a British nobleman

early *adverb* and *adjective* (**earlier, earliest**) 1 before the usual or expected time 2 near the beginning ▸ *The first murder comes early in the film.*

earn *verb* (**earns, earning, earned**) to get something by working for it or because you deserve it

earnest *adjective* serious; determined

earnings *plural noun* money that someone earns

earring *noun* (*plural* **earrings**) a piece of jewellery worn on the ear

earshot *noun* the distance in which you can hear something

earth *noun* (*plural* **earths**) **1** the planet that we live on **2** soil or the ground **3** the hole where a fox or badger lives

earthly *adjective* to do with life on earth

earthquake *noun* (*plural* **earthquakes**) a violent movement of part of the earth's surface

earwig *noun* (*plural* **earwigs**) a crawling insect with pincers at the end of its body

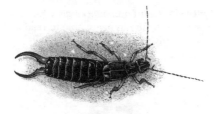

earthy *adjective* (**earthier, earthiest**) like earth or soil

ease *noun* freedom from difficulty or trouble

ease *verb* (**eases, easing, eased**) **1** to make something easier or less troublesome **2** to become less severe ▸ *The pain was beginning to ease.* **3** to move something gently into position

easel *noun* (*plural* **easels**) a stand for holding a blackboard or a painting

easily *adverb* **1** without difficulty; with ease **2** by far ▸ *This dress is easily the nicest.* **3** very likely ▸ *They could easily be lying.*

east *noun* the direction in which the sun rises

east *adjective* and *adverb* **1** towards the east or in the east **2** (describing the wind) coming from the east

Easter *noun* the day on which Christians remember the resurrection of Christ

easterly *adjective* **1** to the east or towards the east ▸ *We were travelling in an easterly direction.* **2** (describing the wind) blowing from the east

eastern *adjective* from or to do with the east

eastward or **eastwards** *adjective* and *adverb* towards the east

easy *adjective* (**easier, easiest**) able to be done or understood without trouble

eat *verb* (**eats, eating, ate, eaten**) to chew food and swallow it **eat up** or **eat into** to use something up or destroy it ▸ *The sea air has eaten into the woodwork.*

eatable *adjective* fit to be eaten

eaves *plural noun* the overhanging edges of a roof

eavesdrop *verb* (**eavesdrops, eavesdropping, eavesdropped**) to listen secretly to what someone else is saying

ebb *verb* (**ebbs, ebbing, ebbed**) **1** (used about the tide) to move away from the land **2** to become weaker or less ▸ *Towards the end of the day her strength began to ebb.*

ebb *noun* (*plural* **ebbs**) the movement of the tide when it is going out

ebony *noun* a hard black wood

eccentric *adjective* (*pronounced* ik-**sen**-trik) behaving strangely **eccentricity** *noun* strange behaviour

echo *verb* (**echoes, echoing, echoed**) **1** to make an echo **2** to repeat something someone has said

echo *noun* (*plural* **echoes**) a sound that is heard again as it bounces off something

éclair *noun* (*plural* **éclairs**) (*pronounced* ay-**klair**) a finger-shaped cake of pastry with a chocolate top and a cream filling

eclipse *noun* (*plural* **eclipses**) a time when the light from the sun is blocked by the moon or when light from the moon is blocked because the earth is between the moon and the sun

ecology *noun* (*pronounced* ee-**kol**-o-ji) the study of living things in their surroundings **ecological** *adjective* to do with ecology **ecologist** *noun*

economical *adjective* (*pronounced* eek-o-**nom**-ik-al) careful in using money and resources **economically** *adverb*

economics *noun* (*pronounced* eek-o-**nom**-iks or ek-o-**nom**-iks) the study of how money is used **economist** *noun*

economize verb (**economizes, economizing, economized**) (pronounced i-kon-o-myz) to use less money

economy noun (plural **economies**) (pronounced i-**kon**-o-mi) 1 the study of how money is earned and used 2 using your money wisely and carefully

ecstasy noun (plural **ecstasies**) a feeling of great delight or joy

eczema noun (pronounced eks-im-a) a skin disease that causes rough itching patches

edge noun (plural **edges**) 1 the part along the side or end of something 2 the sharp part of a knife or cutting tool **be on edge** to feel nervous and irritable

edge verb (**edges, edging, edged**) 1 to move gradually ▸ She edged back to her seat. 2 to form an edge or border on something ▸ The lawn was edged with a brick path.

edgeways adverb with the edge outwards or forwards

edgy adjective (**edgier, edgiest**) nervous and irritable

edible adjective suitable for eating; not poisonous ·

edit verb (**edits, editing, edited**) 1 to prepare a piece of writing, or a film or television progamme, by making changes and improvements to it 2 to prepare a newspaper or magazine for publication

edition noun (plural **editions**) all the copies of a newspaper, magazine, or book issued at the same time

editor noun (plural **editors**) someone who edits a book, newspaper, or magazine

educate verb (**educates, educating, educated**) to train someone or give them knowledge and skill

education noun the process of getting knowledge and learning skills **educational** adjective to do with learning or teaching ▸ Karen is allowed to watch television programmes that are educational.

eel noun (plural **eels**) a long snake-shaped fish

eerie adjective (**eerier, eeriest**) weird and frightening **eerily** adverb

effect noun (plural **effects**) 1 something that happens because of something else ▸ Unfortunately, their efforts with buckets of water had little effect on the fire. 2 a general impression ▸ The lights had a colourful effect.

effective adjective producing what you want; successful **effectively** adverb **effectiveness** noun

efficient adjective doing work well **efficiency** noun **efficiently** adverb

effort noun (plural **efforts**) 1 using energy or hard work 2 an attempt to do something **effortless** adjective not needing much effort; easy

e.g. for example ▸ The calendar had photos of large cities, e.g. London, Paris, New York.

egg noun (plural **eggs**) 1 an oval or round object with a thin shell, laid by birds, fish, reptiles, and insects, in which their young develop 2 a hen's or duck's egg used as food

egg verb (**eggs, egging, egged**) **egg on** to encourage someone

Eid noun (pronounced eed) a Muslim festival that marks the end of the fast of Ramadan

eiderdown noun (plural **eiderdowns**) (pronounced I-der-down) a bed covering stuffed with soft material

eight noun (plural **eights**) the number 8 **eighth** adjective and noun

eighteen noun (plural **eighteens**) the number 18 **eighteenth** adjective and noun

eighty noun (plural **eighties**) the number 80 **eightieth** adjective and noun

either adjective and pronoun 1 one of two ▸ Either side can win. ▸ I haven't seen either of them. ▸ Either come in or go out. 2 both of two ▸ There are fields on either side of the river.

either adverb also ▸ Kate doesn't like carrots, and I don't either.

eject verb (**ejects, ejecting, ejected**) 1 to send something out with force 2 to make someone leave **ejection** noun

elaborate adjective complicated or detailed **elaborately** adverb

elastic *noun* cord or material that can stretch and return to its original size

elated *adjective* very happy **elation** *noun* a feeling of being very happy

elbow *noun* (*plural* **elbows**) the joint at which your arm bends

elbow *verb* (**elbows, elbowing, elbowed**) to push someone with your elbow

elder[1] *adjective* older ▸ *Meet my elder sister.*

elder[2] *noun* (*plural* **elders**) a tree with white flowers and black berries **elderberry** *noun* a berry from an elder

elderly *adjective* rather old

eldest *adjective* oldest ▸ *Jack is my eldest brother.*

elect *verb* (**elects, electing, elected**) to choose someone by voting

election *noun* (*plural* **elections**) the process of voting for people to be the government or to run an organization

electric or **electrical** *adjective* to do with electricity, or worked by electricity **electrically** *adverb*

electrician *noun* (*plural* **electricians**) someone whose job is to fit and repair electrical equipment

electricity *noun* a kind of energy used for lighting, heating, and making machines work
The word **electricity** comes from a Greek word *elektron* meaning 'amber', because amber produces static electricity when you rub it.

electrocute *verb* (**electrocutes, electrocuting, electrocuted**) to kill someone by passing a high electric current through them **electrocution** *noun*

electron *noun* (*plural* **electrons**) a very small particle of matter that has a negative electric charge

electronic *adjective* using transistors and silicon chips which control electric currents, as computers, televisions, washing machines, and other devices do **electronically** *adverb*

electronics *plural noun* the use or study of electronic devices

elegant *adjective* graceful and smart **elegance** *noun* **elegantly** *adverb*

element *noun* (*plural* **elements**)
1 a substance that cannot be split up into simpler substances, for example copper and oxygen 2 a single part of something 3 a wire or coil that gives out heat in an electric heater or cooker **the elements** 1 the weather 2 the simplest parts of a subject, which you learn first

elementary *adjective* simple and basic

elephant *noun* (*plural* **elephants**) a large animal with a trunk and tusks

elevate *verb* (**elevates, elevating, elevated**) (not an everyday word) to lift something or raise it to a higher position **elevation** *noun*

eleven *noun* (*plural* **elevens**) 1 the number 11 2 a team of eleven people in cricket, football, and other sports **eleventh** *adjective* and *noun*

elf *noun* (*plural* **elves**) a small mischievous fairy in stories

eligible *adjective* qualified or suitable for something **eligibility** *noun*

eliminate *verb* (**eliminates, eliminating, eliminated**) to remove something or someone **elimination** *noun*

elk *noun* (*plural* **elk** or **elks**) a large kind of deer

ellipse *noun* (*plural* **ellipses**) an oval shape **elliptical** *adjective* shaped like an oval

elm *noun* (*plural* **elms**) a tall tree with a rough bark and broad leaves

elocution *noun* the art of speaking clearly and correctly

elongated *adjective* made long and thin **elongation** *noun*

eloquent *adjective* speaking well and expressing ideas clearly **eloquence** *noun* **eloquently** *adverb*

else *adverb* besides; instead ▸ *Does anyone else know?* **or else** otherwise ▸ *Run or else you'll be late.*

elsewhere *adverb* somewhere else

elude *verb* (**eludes, eluding, eluded**) to escape from someone or avoid being caught by them

elves plural of **elf**

e-mail short for *electronic mail*, a system of sending messages from one person to another, using computers

embankment *noun* (*plural* **embankments**) a wall or bank of earth built to hold back water or support a road or railway

embark *verb* (**embarks, embarking, embarked**) to go on board a ship **embark on** to begin something important **embarkation** *noun* going on board a ship

embarrass *verb* (**embarrasses, embarrassing, embarrassed**) to make someone feel awkward or self-conscious **embarrassment** *noun*

embassy *noun* (*plural* **embassies**) the home or office used by an ambassador

embedded *adjective* fixed firmly into something

embers *plural noun* small pieces of burning coal or wood in a dying fire

emblem *noun* (*plural* **emblems**) a symbol or badge

embrace *verb* (**embraces, embracing, embraced**) to hold someone closely in your arms

embroider *verb* (**embroiders, embroidering, embroidered**) to sew designs or pictures as decorations on cloth **embroidery** *noun*

embryo *noun* (*plural* **embryos**) a baby or young animal when it is first developing inside its mother or inside an egg

emerald *noun* (*plural* **emeralds**) a green jewel

emerge *verb* (**emerges, emerging, emerged**) to come out or appear **emergence** *noun* coming out

emergency *noun* (*plural* **emergencies**) a sudden dangerous or serious situation that needs quick action

emigrant *noun* (*plural* **emigrants**) someone who goes to live in another country

emigrate *verb* (**emigrates, emigrating, emigrated**) to go and live in another country **emigration** *noun*

eminent *adjective* famous and respected **eminence** *noun* fame, importance

emission *noun* (*plural* **emissions**) **1** the action of sending something out **2** something that is emitted, especially fumes or radiation

emit *verb* (**emits, emitting, emitted**) to send out something unpleasant such as smoke or fumes

emotion *noun* (*plural* **emotions**) a strong feeling in your mind, such as love, fear, or jealousy **emotional** *adjective* to do with emotion, or showing emotion **emotionally** *adverb*

emperor *noun* (*plural* **emperors**) a man who rules an empire

emphasis *noun* (*plural* **emphases**) special importance you give to something ▸ *The emphasis this term is on reading.* **emphatic** *adjective* using strong words or gestures to show that something is important **emphatically** *adverb*

emphasize *verb* (**emphasizes, emphasizing, emphasized**) to give something special importance, for example by saying it more loudly or by explaining it more fully

empire *noun* (*plural* **empires**) a group of countries governed by one ruler

employ *verb* (**employs, employing, employed**) 1 to pay someone to work for you 2 to use something

employee *noun* (*plural* **employees**) (*pronounced* im-**ploi**-ee) a person who works for someone else

employer *noun* (*plural* **employers**) a person or business that employs people

employment *noun* work for which you are paid

empress *noun* (*plural* **empresses**) a woman who rules an empire, or the wife of an emperor

empty *adjective* (**emptier, emptiest**) having nothing or no one inside **emptiness** *noun*

empty *verb* (**empties, emptying, emptied**) 1 to make something empty 2 to become empty

emu *noun* (*plural* **emus**) (*pronounced* **ee-mew**) a large Australian bird rather like an ostrich. Emus cannot fly.
The word **emu** comes from a Portuguese word *ema*.

enable *verb* (**enables, enabling, enabled**) to make it possible for someone to do something ▸ *The extra money enabled them to have a holiday.*

enamel *noun* (*plural* **enamels**) 1 a hard shiny coating on metal or pottery 2 a hard shiny paint 3 the hard white surface of your teeth

enchant *verb* (**enchants, enchanting, enchanted**) 1 to delight someone 2 in stories, to put a magic spell on someone **enchantment** *noun*

encircle *verb* (**encircles, encircling, encircled**) to surround someone or something

enclose *verb* (**encloses, enclosing, enclosed**) 1 to put something in a box or envelope 2 to put a fence or wall round a piece of land **enclosure** *noun* an enclosed piece of land

encore *noun* (*plural* **encores**) (*pronounced* **on**-kor) an extra item performed at the end of a concert or show

encounter *verb* (**encounters, encountering, encountered**) 1 to meet someone unexpectedly 2 to experience something ▸ *We have encountered a few problems.*

encounter *noun* (*plural* **encounters**) an unexpected meeting with someone

encourage *verb* (**encourages, encouraging, encouraged**) to give someone confidence or hope **encouragement** *noun*

encyclopedia *noun* (*plural* **encyclopedias**) a book or set of books containing information on many different subjects

end *noun* (*plural* **ends**) 1 the last part of something or the point where it stops ▸ *They reached the end of the path.* ▸ *This is the end of our journey.* 2 an aim or purpose **on end** continuously ▸ *She spoke for two hours on end.*

end *verb* (**ends, ending, ended**) to finish something

endanger *verb* (**endangers, endangering, endangered**) to cause someone or something danger **endangered** *adjective* in danger

endeavour *verb* (**endeavours, endeavouring, endeavoured**) (not an everyday word) to try hard to do something

ending *noun* (*plural* **endings**) the last part of something

endless *adjective* without an end **endlessly** *adverb*

endure *verb* (**endures, enduring, endured**) 1 to put up with something unpleasant such as pain or suffering 2 to continue or last **endurance** *noun*

enemy *noun* (*plural* **enemies**) 1 someone who is against you and wants to harm you 2 a nation or army that is fighting a war with another country

energetic *adjective* active and full of energy **energetically** *adverb*

energy *noun* (*plural* **energies**) the strength or power to do things

enforce *verb* (**enforces, enforcing, enforced**) to make people obey a law or rule **enforcement** *noun*

engage *verb* (**engages, engaging, engaged**) 1 to give someone a paid job 2 to involve someone ▶ *Rupert's mother engaged us in conversation.* **to become engaged** to agree to marry someone **engagement** *noun* getting engaged or being engaged

engine *noun* (*plural* **engines**) 1 a machine that turns energy into movement 2 a vehicle that pulls a railway train

engineer *noun* (*plural* **engineers**) a person who designs and builds machines, roads, bridges, and vehicles **engineering** *noun*

engrave *verb* (**engraves, engraving, engraved**) to cut a design of figures or words into a hard surface such as wood or metal **engraving** *noun* a print made by engraving a design

engrossed *adjective* having all your attention taken up ▶ *They were all engrossed in their work.*

engulfed *adjective* covered or swamped in something

enjoy *verb* (**enjoys, enjoying, enjoyed**) to get pleasure from something **enjoyable** *adjective* **enjoyment** *noun*

enlarge *verb* (**enlarges, enlarging, enlarged**) to make something larger **enlargement** *noun*

enormous *adjective* very large; huge **enormousness** *noun* **enormously** *adverb*

enough *adjective, noun,* and *adverb* as much as you need

enquire *verb* (**enquires, enquiring, enquired**) (not an everyday word) to ask for information ▶ *I enquired whether Chris would like a sandwich.* **enquiry** *noun*

enrage *verb* (**enrages, enraging, enraged**) to make a person or animal very angry

enrol *verb* (**enrols, enrolling, enrolled**) to put your name down to join something **enrolment** *noun*

ensure *verb* (**ensures, ensuring, ensured**) to make sure of something ▶ *We need to ensure that the doors are locked.*

entangle *verb* (**entangles, entangling, entangled**) to get something tangled up **entanglement** *noun*

enter *verb* (**enters, entering, entered**) 1 to come in or go in 2 to put a name or item in a list 3 to put data into a computer 4 to take part in a competition or exam

enterprise *noun* (*plural* **enterprises**) an adventurous or difficult task or project

enterprising *adjective* adventurous, bold, or imaginative

entertain *verb* (**entertains, entertaining, entertained**) 1 to amuse someone or give them pleasure 2 to have people as guests and give them food and drink **entertainer** *noun* **entertainment** *noun*

enthusiasm *noun* (*plural* **enthusiasms**) a strong liking or interest **enthusiast** *noun* someone with enthusiasm **enthusiastic** *adjective* full of enthusiasm

entire *adjective* whole or complete ▶ *The entire town turned out to watch the procession.* **entirely** *adverb* completely

entitle *verb* (**entitles, entitling, entitled**) to give you the right to do something or have something ▶ *A special pass entitles you to admission to five museums.* **entitlement** *noun* something you are entitled to

entrance[1] *noun* (*plural* **entrances**) (*pronounced* **en-transs**) 1 the way you go into a place 2 coming into a room or on to a stage or arena ▶ *Everybody laughed as the clowns made their entrance.*

entrance[2] *verb* (**entrances, entrancing, entranced**) (*pronounced* in-**trahnss**) to delight or enchant someone

entrant *noun* (*plural* **entrants**) someone who enters a competition or exam

entreat *verb* (**entreats, entreating, entreated**) to ask someone seriously for something **entreaty** *noun* a request for something important

entrust *verb* (**entrusts, entrusting, entrusted**) to give something to someone for them to look after ▸ *Can I entrust the plane tickets to you?*

entry *noun* (*plural* **entries**) 1 an entrance 2 something you do for a competition ▸ *Here is the winning entry.*

envelop *verb* (**envelops, enveloping, enveloped**) (*pronounced* in-vel-op) to cover or wrap something completely ▸ *The mountain was enveloped in mist.*

envelope *noun* (*plural* **envelopes**) (*pronounced* en-ve-lohp or on-ve-lohp) a paper wrapper for a letter

envious *adjective* feeling envy **enviously** *adverb*

environment *noun* (*plural* **environments**) 1 a person's or animal's natural surroundings 2 the natural world of the land and sea and air **environmental** *adjective*

envy *noun* an unhappy feeling you have when you want something that someone else has

envy *verb* (**envies, envying, envied**) to feel envy of someone

epic *noun* (*plural* **epics**) a long story or poem about heroes

epidemic *noun* (*plural* **epidemics**) a disease that affects a large number of people in an area

epilepsy *noun* a disease of the nervous system, which causes fits **epileptic** *adjective* and *noun*

episode *noun* (*plural* **episodes**) 1 one event in a series of happenings 2 one programme in a radio or television serial

epistle *noun* (*plural* **epistles**) a long or important letter

epitaph *noun* (*plural* **epitaphs**) words written on a tomb or describing a person who has died

equal *adjective* and *noun* (*plural* **equals**) the same in amount, size, or ability

equal *verb* (**equals, equalling, equalled**) to be the same in amount, size, or ability **equality** *noun*

equalize *verb* (**equalizes, equalizing, equalized**) 1 to make two things equal 2 to even the score in a game **equalizer** *noun* a goal that makes the score equal

equally *adverb* in the same way or to the same extent ▸ *They are all equally important.*

equation *noun* (*plural* **equations**) (*pronounced* i-**kway**-zhon) in mathematics, a formula stating that two amounts are equal, for example $6 + 4 = 8 + 2$

equator *noun* (*pronounced* i-**kway**-ter) an imaginary line round the earth halfway between the North and South Poles **equatorial** *adjective* near the equator

equilateral *adjective* (*pronounced* ee-kwi-**lat**-er-al) (describing a triangle) having all its sides equal

equilibrium *noun* (*plural* **equilibria**) (*pronounced* ee-kwi-**lib**-ri-um) a state of even balance

equinox *noun* (*plural* **equinoxes**) each of two days in the year, one in spring and the other in autumn, when day and night are equal in length

equip *verb* (**equips, equipping, equipped**) to give someone or something the things they need

equipment *noun* the things needed for a special purpose

equivalent *adjective* equal in value, importance, or meaning **equivalence** *noun*

era *noun* (*plural* **eras**) (*pronounced* **eer**-a) a long period of history

erase *verb* (**erases, erasing, erased**) to rub something out **eraser** *noun* a rubber

erect *adjective* standing upright

erect *verb* (**erects, erecting, erected**) to set something up or build it **erection** *noun* something set up; a building

erode *verb* (**erodes, eroding, eroded**) to wear something away ▸ *Powerful waves have eroded the cliffs.* **erosion** *noun* wearing something away

err *verb* (**errs, erring, erred**) to do wrong or make a mistake

errand *noun* (*plural* **errands**) a small job you are sent to do

erratic *adjective* (*pronounced* i-rat-ik) not reliable or regular **erratically** *adverb*

error *noun* (*plural* **errors**) a mistake **in error** by mistake

erupt *verb* (**erupts, erupting, erupted**) to burst out, as a volcano does when it sends out lava **eruption** *noun*

escalate *verb* (**escalates, escalating, escalated**) to become gradually greater or more serious ▸ *The argument escalated into violence.* **escalation** *noun*

escalator *noun* (*plural* **escalators**) a staircase with a moving band of steps

escape *verb* (**escapes, escaping, escaped**) 1 to become free or get away 2 to manage to avoid something ▸ *He ran into the road and narrowly escaped injury.*

escape *noun* (*plural* **escapes**) 1 an act of escaping 2 a way to escape

escort *noun* (*plural* **escorts**) (*pronounced* ess-kort) a person or a group of people or vehicles going with someone or something to give protection

escort *verb* (**escorts, escorting, escorted**) (*pronounced* i-skort) to act as an escort to someone or something

Eskimo *noun* (*plural* **Eskimos** or **Eskimo**) one of the people who live in very cold parts of North America, Greenland, and Siberia
The official name of the people who live in the far north of North America is **Inuit.**

especially *adverb* chiefly; more than anything else

espionage *noun* (*pronounced* ess-pi-on-ahzh) spying

esplanade *noun* (*plural* **esplanades**) a flat open area for walking by the sea

essay *noun* (*plural* **essays**) a short piece of writing on a subject

essence *noun* (*plural* **essences**) 1 the most important quality or part of something 2 a concentrated liquid used to flavour food or drink

essential *adjective* that you must have or do **essentially** *adverb*

essentials *plural noun* things that you must have or must do

establish *verb* (**establishes, establishing, established**) 1 to start something working, such as a business or a relationship with someone 2 to show that something is true ▸ *He established that he had not been there at the time.* **establishment** *noun*

estate *noun* (*plural* **estates**) 1 an area of land with houses or other buildings on it 2 a large area of land belonging to one person 3 the money and possessions that a person leaves in their will when they die

estate agent *noun* (*plural* **estate agents**) someone whose job is to sell buildings and land

estate car *noun* (*plural* **estate cars**) a long car with a door at the back, and extra space behind the rear seats

estimate *noun* (*plural* **estimates**) (*pronounced* ess-ti-mat) a rough calculation about what an amount or value is likely to be

estimate *verb* (**estimates, estimating, estimated**) (*pronounced* ess-ti-mayt) to make an estimate about something **estimation** *noun*

estuary *noun* (*plural* **estuaries**) (*pronounced* ess-tew-er-i) the wide part of a large river where it flows into the sea

etc. short for *et cetera*, which means 'and other similar things' ▸ *Please bring pens, pencils, etc.*

eternal *adjective* lasting for ever; not ending or changing **eternally** *adverb*

eternity *noun* a time that has no end

ethnic *adjective* belonging to a particular people or nation

EU short for *European Union*, a group of European countries that help each other

eucalyptus *noun* (*plural* **eucalyptuses**) (*pronounced* yoo-ka-lip-tus) an evergreen tree from which a special oil is obtained

euphemism *noun* (*plural* **euphemisms**) a word or phrase which is used instead of an impolite or less tactful one; 'pass away' is a euphemism for 'die' **euphemistic** *adjective* using words that won't upset people

euthanasia *noun* (*pronounced* yooth-an-ay-zi-a) allowing someone to die gently and without pain when they are suffering from a disease that can't be cured

evacuate *verb* (**evacuates, evacuating, evacuated**) to move people away from a place because it is dangerous **evacuation** *noun*

evade *verb* (**evades, evading, evaded**) to make an effort to avoid someone or something

evangelist *noun* (*plural* **evangelists**) someone who tells people about the Christian gospel

evaporate *verb* (**evaporates, evaporating, evaporated**) to change from liquid into steam or vapour **evaporation** *noun*

evasion *noun* (*plural* **evasions**) an answer that tries to avoid the question being asked

evasive *adjective* trying to avoid answering something

eve *noun* (*plural* **eves**) the day or evening before an important day, for example New Year's Eve

even *adjective* 1 level and smooth 2 calm and stable ▶ *He has a very even temper.* 3 equal ▶ *The scores were even.* **even number** a number that can be divided exactly by 2, for example 8 and 24 **evenly** *adverb* **evenness** *noun*

even *verb* (**evens, evening, evened**) 1 to make something even 2 to become even

even *adverb* a word you use to show that something is surprising or still more interesting ▶ *I'm afraid I haven't even started.* ▶ *You can do even better.*

evening *noun* (*plural* **evenings**) the time at the end of the afternoon before night time

event *noun* (*plural* **events**) 1 something important or interesting that happens 2 an item in an athletics contest

eventful *adjective* full of exciting or remarkable happenings ▶ *I told the other children about my eventful holiday.*

eventually *adverb* finally, in the end ▶ *He was a successful politician and eventually became president.*

ever *adverb* 1 at any time ▶ *It's the best present I've ever had.* 2 always ▶ *We are ever hopeful.* 3 used to express surprise or special interest ▶ *Why ever didn't you tell me?* ▶ *I'm ever so pleased.*

evergreen *noun* (*plural* **evergreens**) a tree that has green leaves all through the year

everlasting *adjective* lasting for ever or for a long time

every *adjective* each of the people or things mentioned ▶ *Every child should learn to swim.* **every other** every second one ▶ *Ann phoned her Mum every other day.*

everybody *pronoun* every person; all people

everyday *adjective* happening or used every day; ordinary ▶ *Everyday life has changed a lot in the last fifty years.*

everyone *pronoun* every person; all people

everything *pronoun* all things; all

everywhere *adverb* in all places

evict *verb* (**evicts, evicting, evicted**) to make someone move out of a house **eviction** *noun*

evidence *noun* facts or information that give people reason to believe something

evident *adjective* obvious; clearly seen **evidently** *adverb*

evil *adjective* wicked and harmful **evilly** *adverb*

evil *noun* (*plural* **evils**) something wicked or harmful

evolution noun (*pronounced* ee-vo-loo-shon) the development of animals and plants over many centuries from earlier or simpler forms of life **evolutionary** *adjective*

evolve verb (**evolves, evolving, evolved**) to develop gradually or naturally

ewe noun (*plural* **ewes**) (*pronounced* yoo) a female sheep

exact *adjective* completely correct or accurate **exactly** *adverb* **exactness** *noun*

exaggerate verb (**exaggerates, exaggerating, exaggerated**) to say that something is bigger or better or worse than it really is **exaggeration** *noun*

exam noun (*plural* **exams**) an examination or test

examination noun (*plural* **examinations**) 1 a test to find out how much you know about a subject 2 a close inspection of something

examine verb (**examines, examining, examined**) to look at something closely or in detail

example noun (*plural* **examples**) 1 a single thing or event that shows what others of the same kind are like ▸ *The play we are reading is a good example of a tragedy.* 2 a person or thing that you should copy or learn from **for example** as an example

exasperate verb (**exasperates, exasperating, exasperated**) to make someone very annoyed **exasperation** *noun*

excavate verb (**excavates, excavating, excavated**) to dig or find something by digging, especially in building or archaeology **excavation** *noun* **excavator** *noun* a machine that digs

exceed verb (**exceeds, exceeding, exceeded**) to be more than something else or go beyond it

exceedingly *adverb* extremely; very much

excel verb (**excels, excelling, excelled**) to be very good at something, or better than everyone else

excellent *adjective* very good; of the best kind **excellence** *noun* **excellently** *adverb*

except *preposition* not including; apart from

exception noun (*plural* **exceptions**) 1 something or someone that does not follow the normal rule 2 something that is not included

exceptional *adjective* unusual; very good ▸ *He was a man of exceptional generosity.* **exceptionally** *adverb*

excerpt noun (*plural* **excerpts**) a short piece taken from a book, story, or film

excess noun (*plural* **excesses**) too much of something

excessive *adjective* too much or too great **excessively** *adverb*

exchange verb (**exchanges, exchanging, exchanged**) to give something and get something else for it

exchange noun (*plural* **exchanges**) 1 changing one thing for another 2 a place where telephone lines are connected to each other when a call is made

excite verb (**excites, exciting, excited**) to make someone eager and enthusiastic about something **excitement** *noun*

exclaim verb (**exclaims, exclaiming, exclaimed**) to shout or cry out

exclamation noun (*plural* **exclamations**) a word or phrase you say out loud to show a strong feeling such as surprise, fear, or pain. Some exclamations are *oh!, good heavens!*, and *ouch!*

exclamation mark noun (*plural* **exclamation marks**) a punctuation mark (!) put after an exclamation

exclude verb (**excludes, excluding, excluded**) 1 to stop someone from taking part in something 2 to leave something out ▸ *There is a staff of 22, excluding the head.* **exclusion** *noun*

exclusive *adjective* not shared with other people ▸ *Today's newspaper has an exclusive story about the game.*

excruciating *adjective* very painful

excursion noun (*plural* **excursions**) a short journey made for pleasure

excuse noun (plural **excuses**) (pronounced iks-**kewss**) a reason you give to explain why you have done something wrong

excuse verb (**excuses, excusing, excused**) (pronounced iks-**kewz**) 1 to forgive someone for doing something wrong 2 to allow someone not to do something ▸ Peter was excused swimming because of his cold.

execute verb (**executes, executing, executed**) 1 to put someone to death as a legal punishment 2 to perform or produce something ▸ She executed a perfect somersault. **execution** noun putting someone to death **executioner** noun

executive noun (plural **executives**) a senior person in a business organization

exercise noun (plural **exercises**) 1 using your body to make it strong and healthy 2 a piece of work done for practice

exercise verb (**exercises, exercising, exercised**) to take exercise

exert verb (**exerts, exerting, exerted**) to make an effort to get something done **exertion** noun

exhale verb (**exhales, exhaling, exhaled**) to breathe out **exhalation** noun a puff of air

exhaust verb (**exhausts, exhausting, exhausted**) 1 to make someone very tired 2 to use something up completely **exhaustion** noun great tiredness

exhaust noun (plural **exhausts**) 1 the fumes and waste gases from an engine 2 the pipe these fumes and gases come out of

exhibit verb (**exhibits, exhibiting, exhibited**) to show something in public in a gallery or museum

exhibit noun (plural **exhibits**) something displayed in a gallery or museum

exhibition noun (plural **exhibitions**) a collection of things put on display for people to look at

exile verb (**exiles, exiling, exiled**) to make someone live away from their country as a punishment

exile noun (plural **exiles**) 1 having to live away from your own country ▸ He returned after 20 years in exile. 2 a person who is exiled

exist verb (**exists, existing, existed**) 1 to have life or be real ▸ Do ghosts exist? 2 to stay alive ▸ They existed on biscuits and water. **existence** noun

exit noun (plural **exits**) 1 the way out of a place 2 going out of a room or going off a stage or arena ▸ They decided it was time for a quick exit.

exit verb (**exits, exiting, exited**) to leave a stage or arena

exotic adjective unusual and colourful because it comes from another part of the world ▸ The rainforest was full of exotic plants.

expand verb (**expands, expanding, expanded**) 1 to become larger 2 to make something larger **expansion** noun

expanse noun (plural **expanses**) a wide area

expect verb (**expects, expecting, expected**) 1 to think that something will happen ▸ I expect it will rain. 2 to think that something ought to happen ▸ She expects us to be quiet. 3 to be waiting for someone to arrive ▸ Are you expecting visitors? **be expecting** to be pregnant

expectation noun (plural **expectations**) 1 hopeful that something will happen 2 something you hope to get **expectant** adjective expecting something

expedition noun (plural **expeditions**) a long journey made for a special purpose ▸ They are going on a climbing expedition.

expel verb (**expels, expelling, expelled**) 1 to send or force something out 2 to make someone leave a place ▸ He was expelled from school for bullying.

expenditure noun (not an everyday word) money that you spend ▸ We are trying to reduce our expenditure.

expense noun (plural **expenses**) the cost of doing something

expensive adjective costing a lot of money

experience noun (plural **experiences**)
1 what you learn from doing and seeing
things 2 something that has happened
to you
experience verb (**experiences,
experiencing, experienced**) to have
something happen to you

experienced adjective having skill or
knowledge from much experience

experiment noun (plural **experiments**)
a test made in order to study what
happens **experimental** adjective
experiment verb (**experiments,
experimenting, experimented**) to carry out
an experiment

expert noun (plural **experts**) someone
who has skill or special knowledge in a
subject
expert adjective having great knowledge or
skill

expire verb (**expires, expiring, expired**) 1 to
come to an end or to stop being usable
▶ The television licence has expired. 2 to die
expiry noun

explain verb (**explains, explaining,
explained**) 1 to make something clear to
someone else 2 to show why something
happens **explanation** noun

explode verb (**explodes, exploding,
exploded**) 1 to burst or suddenly release
energy with a loud bang 2 to set off a
bomb 3 to increase suddenly or quickly
▶ The city's population exploded to 3 million
in a year.

exploit noun (plural **exploits**)
(pronounced eks-ploit) a brave or exciting
deed
exploit verb (**exploits, exploiting,
exploited**) (pronounced iks-**ploit**) 1 to use
something well 2 to use someone unfairly
exploitation noun

explore verb (**explores, exploring,
explored**) 1 to travel through a place to
find out more about it 2 to study a subject
carefully **exploration** noun **explorer** noun

explosion noun (plural **explosions**) 1 the
exploding of a bomb or other weapon
2 a sudden or quick increase

explosive noun (plural **explosives**)
a substance that can explode
explosive adjective likely to explode or to
cause an explosion

export verb (**exports, exporting, exported**)
(pronounced iks-**port**) to send goods
abroad to be sold **exporter** noun
export noun (plural **exports**) (pronounced
eks-**port**) something that is exported

expose verb (**exposes, exposing, exposed**)
1 to reveal or uncover something 2 to show
publicly that someone is to blame for
something 3 to let light reach a film in a
camera when you take a photograph

exposure noun (plural **exposures**) 1 harm
done to you by the weather when you have
been in the open without enough
protection 2 a single photograph or frame
on a film

express noun (plural **expresses**) a fast
train stopping at only a few stations
express adjective going or sent quickly
express verb (**expresses, expressing,
expressed**) to show an idea or feeling by
using words or actions

expression noun (plural **expressions**)
1 the look on a person's face that shows
what they are thinking or feeling 2 a word
or phrase

expulsion noun (plural **expulsions**)
expelling someone or being expelled

exquisite adjective very delicate or
beautiful

extend verb (**extends, extending,
extended**) 1 to stretch out 2 to make
something longer or larger 3 to offer a
greeting or welcome

extension noun (plural **extensions**) 1 an
extra room or space added on to a building
2 an extra telephone in an office or house

extensive adjective (not an everyday
word) covering a large area ▶ From the
cliff top we had an extensive view of the sea.
extensively adverb

extent noun (plural **extents**) 1 the area or
length that something covers 2 the amount
or level of something

exterior *noun* (*plural* **exteriors**) the outside of something

exterminate *verb* (**exterminates, exterminating, exterminated**) to kill all the members of a people or breed of animal **extermination** *noun*

external *adjective* outside ▸ *The external walls of the house are painted pink.* **externally** *adverb*

extinct *adjective* 1 not existing any more ▸ *The dodo is an extinct bird.* 2 not burning or active ▸ *We saw an extinct volcano.* **extinction** *noun*

extinguish *verb* (**extinguishes, extinguishing, extinguished**) to put out a fire or light **extinguisher** *noun* a device for putting out fires

extra *adjective* more than usual; added
extra *noun* (*plural* **extras**) an extra person or thing

extract *verb* (**extracts, extracting, extracted**) (*pronounced* iks-**trakt**) to remove something or take it out of something else ▸ *She extracted her spare set of keys from the jar by the fireplace.* **extraction** *noun*
extract *noun* (*plural* **extracts**) (*pronounced* eks-**trakt**) a short piece taken from a book, play, or film

extraordinary *adjective* unusual or very strange **extraordinarily** *adverb*

extraterrestrial *adjective* existing in or coming from another planet

extravagant *adjective* spending or using too much **extravagance** *noun*

extreme *adjective* 1 very great or strong ▸ *He is suffering from extreme cold.* 2 farthest away ▸ *She lives in the extreme north of the country.*
extreme *noun* (*plural* **extremes**) 1 something very great, strong, or far away 2 either end of something

extremely *adverb* very, very much

exuberant *adjective* very cheerful or lively **exuberance** *noun*

exult *verb* (**exults, exulting, exulted**) to rejoice or be very pleased **exultant** *adjective* **exultation** *noun*

eye *noun* (*plural* **eyes**) 1 the organ of your body you use for seeing 2 the small hole in a needle 3 the centre of a storm
eye *verb* (**eyes, eyeing, eyed**) to look at someone or something closely

eyeball *noun* (*plural* **eyeballs**) the ball-shaped part of your eye, inside your eyelids

eyebrow *noun* (*plural* **eyebrows**) the curved line of hair growing above each eye

eyelash *noun* (*plural* **eyelashes**) one of the short hairs that grow on your eyelids

eyelid *noun* (*plural* **eyelids**) the upper or lower fold of skin that can close over your eyeball

eyepiece *noun* (*plural* **eyepieces**) the lens of a telescope or microscope that you put to your eye

eyesight *noun* the ability to see

eyesore *noun* (*plural* **eyesores**) something that is ugly to look at

eyewitness *noun* (*plural* **eyewitnesses**) someone who saw an accident or crime and can describe what happened

Ff

F is short for **Fahrenheit** and is used to show temperatures ▸ *The temperature is 61° F.* See the note at the entry for **Fahrenheit**.

fable *noun* (*plural* **fables**) a story about animals, which teaches a lesson about people and the way they behave
Examples of fables are the ones by Aesop, who lived about 2500 years ago. One of his fables was about a fox that saw a crow in a tree holding a piece of cheese in its beak. The fox wanted to get the cheese, and so it told the crow how beautiful it was and asked it to sing. When the crow opened its mouth to sing it dropped the cheese and the fox picked it up. The lesson of the fable, called the *moral*, is not to let yourself be fooled by flattery.

fabric *noun* (*plural* **fabrics**) cloth or material used for clothes, curtains, or furniture

fabulous *adjective* **1** (informal use) wonderful or marvellous ▸ *It was a fabulous view. You could see everything from there.* **2** belonging to stories and legends and not to real life

face *noun* (*plural* **faces**) **1** the front part of your head, with your eyes, nose, and mouth **2** the mood or feeling that you show in your face ▸ *The children had happy faces.* **3** one of the outside surfaces of something, for example the side of a mountain **face to face** looking directly at someone who is looking back at you

face *verb* (**faces, facing, faced**) **1** to have your face and eyes looking in a certain direction ▸ *The two boxers stood facing each other.* **2** to be pointing or have the front in a certain direction ▸ *The harbour faces south.* **3** to be ready to deal with a danger or problem bravely ▸ *The expedition had to face many dangers in the jungle.*

facility *noun* (*plural* **facilities**) (*pronounced* fa-sil-i-ti) (usually in the plural, **facilities**) buildings and equipment that help you to do special activities ▸ *We don't have the facilities for teaching tennis.*

fact *noun* (*plural* **facts**) something that is real or true or actually happened **in fact** used to show that something is rather surprising ▸ *The forecast said rain but in fact it was quite sunny.*

factor *noun* (*plural* **factors**) **1** one of the things that helps to make something happen ▸ *Slight changes in the earth's orbit are a major factor in altering the climate.* **2** in arithmetic, a number you can divide into a larger number exactly ▸ *4 and 5 are factors of 20.*

factory *noun* (*plural* **factories**) a large building with machinery for making things

fade *verb* (**fades, fading, faded**) **1** to lose colour or strength ▸ *The bedroom curtains were beginning to fade in the sunlight.* **2** to become weaker and more difficult to hear or see

Fahrenheit *adjective* (*pronounced* fa-ren-hyt) using the scale for measuring temperature that shows 32 degrees for freezing water and 212 degrees for boiling water

Fahrenheit is named after a German scientist called Daniel Fahrenheit, who lived around 1700. Other scales are **Celsius** and **centigrade**.

fail *verb* (**fails, failing, failed**) **1** to try to do something but not manage to do it **2** to do badly in a test or exam **3** to stop working properly ▸ *The lights in the house suddenly failed and they found themselves in darkness.* **4** to not do something you are supposed to do ▸ *When his wife failed to return from work the next day he rang the police.*

failing *noun* (*plural* **failings**) a fault or weakness that someone has

failure *noun* (*plural* **failures**) **1** being unable to do something you have been trying to do **2** someone or something that is unsuccessful

faint *adjective* (**fainter, faintest**) **1** not clear or easy to hear or see or smell **2** weak or ill and about to become unconscious ▸ *As Mary climbed up the stairs she began to feel faint.* **faintly** *adverb*

faint *verb* (**faints, fainting, fainted**) to be weak or ill and become unconscious

fair[1] *adjective* (**fairer, fairest**) **1** treating other people in a way that is right and just **2** light or pale in colour **3** fine and sunny **4** quite good, moderate **a fair number** or **a fair amount** quite a large number or amount but not a very large one **fairness** *noun*

fair[2] *noun* (*plural* **fairs**) **1** a place outdoors with rides and sideshows **2** an exhibition or market ▸ *My cousin makes jewellery and sells it at the Christmas fair.*

fairground *noun* (*plural* **fairgrounds**) a place where a fair is held

fairly *adverb* **1** a little but not very ▸ *I have brown hair, which is fairly curly.* **2** in a way that is honest and just ▸ *They believe in treating people fairly.*

fairy *noun* (*plural* **fairies**) in stories, a small creature with magic powers **Fairies** are usually kind creatures, and not mischievous like elves. In folklore, people have regarded them as living underground in a fairyland and as able to make themselves disappear when they do not want to be seen.

fairyland *noun* in stories, a place where fairies live, or a place lovely enough for fairies to live in

fairy story or **fairy tale** *noun* (*plural* **fairy stories** or **fairy tales**) a story or tale about fairies, or one that is not likely to be true

faith *noun* (*plural* **faiths**) 1 strong belief or trust 2 a religion that people belong to

faithful *adjective* reliable and trustworthy, and likely to support or help you **faithfully** *adverb*

fake *noun* (*plural* **fakes**) a copy of something that a person makes to fool people ▸ *The painting everyone thought was a genuine Picasso turned out to be a clever fake.*

fake *adjective* false, not real or genuine

fake *verb* (**fakes**, **faking**, **faked**) 1 to make something that is not genuine, and make it look real so as to fool people ▸ *Some people had faked a letter to the local newspaper.* 2 to pretend to be something that you are not really ▸ *He thought about faking an illness so as to miss the spelling test, but decided not to.*

falcon *noun* (*plural* **falcons**) a small kind of hawk that attacks other birds and animals

fall *verb* (**falls**, **falling**, **fell**, **fallen**) 1 to drop quickly towards the ground 2 to become lower or smaller ▸ *Prices of computers have fallen again this year.* 3 to be captured in a war ▸ *The city fell to the invading army.* 4 to die in a battle 5 to happen or become noticeable ▸ *When the dogs left the room silence fell at last.* 6 to happen on a particular day ▸ *Christmas falls on a Thursday this year.* 7 to be directed at someone or something ▸ *His glance fell on the pile of things on the table.* **fall out** to quarrel or disagree strongly **fall sick** or **ill** to become suddenly ill **fall through** to fail to happen

fall *noun* (*plural* **falls**) 1 the action of someone falling over and hurting themselves 2 becoming less or smaller ▸ *There has been a big fall in the number of road accidents this month.* 3 (in America) a name for autumn

fallacy *noun* (*plural* **fallacies**) (not an everyday word) a false idea or belief

fallout *noun* (technical word) dangerous radioactive material that is carried in the air after a nuclear explosion

falls *plural noun* a large and powerful waterfall **Falls** is used in the names of major waterfalls, for example **Niagara Falls**, **Victoria Falls**.

false *adjective* (**falser**, **falsest**) 1 untrue or incorrect 2 fake or not real 3 not able to be trusted; likely to trick you or let you down **falsely** *adverb*

falsehood *noun* (*plural* **falsehoods**) (not an everyday word) something that is not the truth; a lie

falter *verb* (**falters**, **faltering**, **faltered**) (not an everyday word) to hesitate or be unsteady when you move or speak

fame *noun* being famous or well known

familiar *adjective* 1 well known or often seen 2 knowing something very well ▸ *Are you familiar with this story?* 3 very friendly with someone ▸ *She was very familiar with me although we hadn't met before.* **familiarity** *noun*

family *noun* (*plural* **families**) 1 parents and their children, or a larger group who are closely related, including grandparents and aunts and uncles 2 a group of things that are alike or belong together, such as animals or plants ▸ *Tigers are members of the cat family.*

family planning *noun* using contraceptives to control how many children to have and when to have them
This is also called **birth control.**

family tree *noun* (*plural* **family trees**) a chart showing how people in a family are related
It is called a tree because it is drawn with lines like branches showing different parts of a family.

famine *noun* (*plural* **famines**) a severe shortage of food, so that many people starve

famished *adjective* (informal) extremely hungry

famous *adjective* well known to a lot of people

fan[1] *noun* (*plural* **fans**) something you use to make yourself cool. A fan can be a machine with a blade that goes round very fast, or a piece of hard folding material that you can spread out to form a half circle for waving in your face to disturb the air.

fan *verb* (**fans, fanning, fanned**) to make a draught of air so that you become cooler ▸ *It was so hot in the theatre she tried to fan her face with her programme.* **fan out** to spread out in the shape of a fan

fan[2] *noun* (*plural* **fans**) someone who supports a sports team or is keen on a famous person

fanatic *noun* (*plural* **fanatics**) (*pronounced* fa-**nat**-ik) someone who is so keen about something that they can hardly think of anything else **fanatical** *adjective*

fanciful *adjective* 1 unusual and showing imagination; not real ▸ *The story describes a fanciful scene in the year 3000.* 2 having a lot of ideas and imagination ▸ *She is a very fanciful person.*

fancy *adjective* (**fancier, fanciest**) decorated and pretty ▸ *They were all wearing fancy hats.*

fancy *verb* (**fancies, fancying, fancied**) 1 to want or like something or someone ▸ *James was looking for a holiday job but*

didn't fancy working in an office. 2 to imagine or think of something strange or unusual ▸ *Fancy having another baby at his age!*

fancy dress *noun* unusual clothes that you wear for fun at a party or dance, to make you look like someone else

fanfare *noun* (*plural* **fanfares**) a short burst of music played with trumpets to announce something important

fang *noun* (*plural* **fangs**) an animal's long sharp tooth

fantastic *adjective* 1 (informal) very good or enjoyable 2 very strange or unusual ▸ *He was tying the balloons into the most fantastic shapes.* **fantastically** *adverb*

fantasy *noun* (*plural* **fantasies**) something that you imagine, and that is more like a dream than real life

far *adverb* (**farther, farthest**) 1 a long way ▸ *We shan't go far.* 2 a lot ▸ *She's a far better singer than I am.*

far *adjective* (**farther, farthest**) 1 a long way away ▸ *They wanted to travel to far places.* 2 distant or opposite ▸ *Emma jumped in and swam to the far side of the river.*

far-away *adjective* a long way away

farce *noun* (*plural* **farces**) a far-fetched or very silly kind of comedy **farcical** *adjective* very silly, like a farce

fare *noun* (*plural* **fares**) the money you have to pay to travel on a bus, train, ship, or aeroplane

farewell *interjection* goodbye (usually in stories and poems)

far-fetched *adjective* difficult to believe

farm *noun* (*plural* **farms**) the land and buildings where someone grows crops and keeps animals for food

farm *verb* (**farms, farming, farmed**) to grow crops and raise animals for food

farmer *noun* (*plural* **farmers**) someone who owns or looks after a farm

farmhouse *noun* (*plural* **farmhouses**) the house where a farmer lives

farmyard *noun* (*plural* **farmyards**) the open area surrounded by farm buildings

farther *adverb* and *adjective* at a more distant place ▸ *She lives farther from the school than I do.*
You can also use **further**.

farthest *adverb* and *adjective* at the most distant place ▸ *Her cousin lives farthest from the school.*
You can also use **furthest**.

fascinate *verb* (**fascinates, fascinating, fascinated**) (*pronounced* **fas-in-ayt**) to attract or interest you very much
fascination *noun* a feeling of being fascinated

fascinating *adjective* unusual and very interesting

fashion *noun* (*plural* **fashions**) 1 the style of clothes or other things that most people like 2 a way of doing something ▸ *I wonder why they were behaving in such an odd fashion.*
fashion *verb* (**fashions, fashioning, fashioned**) (not an everyday word) to make something in a special shape or style ▸ *The local people fashioned tiny figures out of wood.*

fashionable *adjective* following the fashion of the time **fashionably** *adverb*

fast[1] *adjective* (**faster, fastest**) 1 moving quickly or doing something quickly 2 (describing a clock or watch) not showing the correct time, so you think it is later than it really is ▸ *I arrived at the cinema early because my watch was fast.*
3 (describing colours) not likely to fade
fast *adverb* 1 quickly, at a high speed 2 securely and firmly ▸ *A small white boat was tied fast to the jetty.* **fast asleep** sleeping deeply

fast[2] *verb* (**fasts, fasting, fasted**) to go without food

fasten *verb* (**fastens, fastening, fastened**) (*pronounced* **fah-sen**) to join or tie something firmly to something else

fastener or **fastening** *noun* (*plural* **fasteners** or **fastenings**) (*pronounced* **fah-sen-ing**) something you use to fasten a piece of clothing or a container

fat *noun* 1 the white greasy part of meat 2 the oily or greasy stuff used in cooking
fat *adjective* (**fatter, fattest**) 1 having a big round body 2 very thick ▸ *'Oliver Twist' is quite a fat book and takes a long time to read.*

fatal *adjective* causing death or disaster ▸ *She had a heart attack but it wasn't fatal.*
fatally *adverb* in a way that causes death ▸ *He was fatally injured in a car crash.*

fate *noun* (*plural* **fates**) 1 a power that seems to make things happen 2 what might happen to someone ▸ *Last time my grandmother came to stay she was ill, but she hopes to avoid the same fate this time.*

father *noun* (*plural* **fathers**) your male parent

father-in-law *noun* (*plural* **fathers-in-law**) the father of your husband or wife

fathom *noun* (*plural* **fathoms**) a unit for measuring the depth of water, equal to 1.83 metres or 6 feet

fatigue *noun* (*pronounced* **fa-teeg**) being very tired or weak

fatten *verb* (**fattens, fattening, fattened**) 1 to make something fat 2 to become fat

fatty *adjective* (**fattier, fattiest**) (describing food) having a lot of fat

fault *noun* (*plural* **faults**) something wrong; an error or mistake

faultless *adjective* having no faults; perfect **faultlessly** *adverb*

faulty *adjective* (**faultier, faultiest**) having a fault; not working properly

fauna *noun* (*pronounced* **faw-na**) the animals living in an area or in a particular period of time
See also **flora**, which refers to plants.

favour *noun* (*plural* **favours**) 1 something kind or helpful that you do for someone 2 approval or goodwill **be in favour of** to like or support something
favour *verb* (**favours, favouring, favoured**) to prefer someone or something to others

favourable *adjective* 1 helpful or advantageous 2 showing approval **favourably** *adverb*

favourite *adjective* that you like best
favourite *noun* (*plural* **favourites**)
a person or thing that you like best

favouritism *noun* unfairly liking one
person more than others

fawn *noun* (*plural* **fawns**) **1** a young deer
2 a light brown colour
fawn *adjective* having a light brown colour

fax *noun* (*plural* **faxes**) **1** a machine that
sends copies of written or printed pages
through a telephone line, and prints copies
of the ones it receives **2** a copy made by
this process
fax *verb* (**faxes**, **faxing**, **faxed**) to send a
copy of something using a fax machine
The word **fax** is a shortening of **facsimile**, which
means 'an exact copy'.

fear *noun* (*plural* **fears**) an unpleasant
feeling that something bad or unwelcome
may happen
fear *verb* (**fears**, **fearing**, **feared**) to be
afraid of someone or something

fearful *adjective* **1** frightened **2** (informal)
awful or horrid ▶ *There was a fearful din
coming from the classroom.* **fearfully** *adverb*

fearless *adjective* having no fear **fearlessly**
adverb

fearsome *adjective* frightening

feasible *adjective* able to be done; possible

feast *noun* (*plural* **feasts**) a special large
meal for a lot of people
feast *verb* (**feasts**, **feasting**, **feasted**) to
have a feast

feat *noun* (*plural* **feats**) something brave
or difficult that you do

feather *noun* (*plural* **feathers**) one of the
light coverings that grow from a bird's skin
feathery *adjective* soft and light

feature *noun* (*plural* **features**) **1** a part of
your face that people notice, such as the
eyes, nose, and chin **2** an important or
noticeable part of something **3** a special
film or television programme or
newspaper article
feature *verb* (**features**, **featuring**, **featured**)
to include something or someone as an
important part

February *noun* the second month of the
year
The word **February** comes from a Latin word
februum meaning 'purification', from a Roman
festival held about this time.

fed past tense and past participle of **feed**
verb

fed up *adjective* (informal) depressed or
unhappy

fee *noun* (*plural* **fees**) a payment or charge

feeble *adjective* (**feebler**, **feeblest**) not
having much strength or force **feebly**
adverb

feed *verb* (**feeds**, **feeding**, **fed**) **1** to give
food to a person or animal **2** to eat food
▶ *Sheep feed on grass.* **3** to put something
into a machine ▶ *You feed the information
into a computer program.*
feed *noun* (*plural* **feeds**) food for animals

feel *verb* (**feels**, **feeling**, **felt**) **1** to touch
something to find out what it is like **2** to
experience a feeling or emotion ▶ *I feel
very glad about it.* **feel like** to want
something ▶ *I feel like a drink.*
feel *noun* what something feels like ▶ *The
tablecloth has a funny feel.*

feeler *noun* (*plural* **feelers**) one of the two
long thin parts on the front of an insect's
body that are used for feeling

feeling *noun* (*plural* **feelings**) **1** the ability
to feel or touch things ▶ *She lost the
feeling in her right hand for a while.* **2** what
you have in your mind, such as love or fear
or an opinion about something

feet plural of **foot**

feline *adjective* to do with cats

fell¹ past tense of **fall** *verb*

fell² *verb* (**fells**, **felling**, **felled**) **1** to cut
down something tall such as a tree **2** to
knock down someone big and strong
fell *noun* (*plural* **fells**) a hill or area of wild
hilly country in the north of England

fellow *noun* (*plural* **fellows**) **1** someone
who belongs to the same group of people
as you **2** (informal) a man or boy
fellow *adjective* of the same group or kind
as you ▶ *The supermarket was crowded
and we kept crashing into fellow shoppers.*

fellowship *noun* (*plural* **fellowships**) a group of friends; a society

felt[1] past tense and past participle of **feel** *verb*

felt[2] *noun* thick woollen material

felt-tip pen or **felt-tipped pen** *noun* (*plural* **felt-tip pens** or **felt-tipped pens**) a pen with a tip made of stiff felt or fibre

female *adjective* of the sex that can produce babies or lay eggs

female *noun* (*plural* **females**) a female person or animal

feminine *adjective* to do with women; suitable for women

feminist *noun* (*plural* **feminists**) someone who believes that women should have the same rights as men **feminism** *noun* supporting women's rights

fen *noun* (*plural* **fens**) an area of low marshy land

fence *noun* (*plural* **fences**) a wooden or metal barrier round a piece of land

fence *verb* (**fences, fencing, fenced**) 1 to put a fence round something 2 to fight with long narrow swords called *foils*, as a sport **fencing** *noun* the sport of fighting with swords

fend *verb* (**fends, fending, fended**) **fend for yourself** to take care of yourself **fend off** to keep something or someone away from you

fender *noun* (*plural* **fenders**) a low guard placed round a fireplace to stop coal from falling into the room

ferment *verb* (**ferments, fermenting, fermented**) (used about bread or wine) to bubble and change chemically because it contains a substance such as yeast **fermentation** *noun*

fern *noun* (*plural* **ferns**) a plant with feathery green leaves

ferocious *adjective* fierce or savage **ferociously** *adverb* **ferocity** *noun* fierceness

ferret *noun* (*plural* **ferrets**) a small animal like a weasel, used for catching rabbits and rats

ferry *noun* (*plural* **ferries**) a ship or boat used for taking people or vehicles across a stretch of water

ferry *verb* (**ferries, ferrying, ferried**) 1 to take people or vehicles in a ferry 2 to take people by car ▶ *She had been ferrying the children around all day.*

fertile *adjective* 1 able to produce good crops 2 able to produce babies or young **fertility** *noun*

fertilize *verb* (**fertilizes, fertilizing, fertilized**) 1 to add chemicals or manure to the soil to make it more fertile 2 to put sperm into an egg or pollen into a plant so that it develops its young or seeds **fertilization** *noun*

fertilizer *noun* (*plural* **fertilizers**) chemicals or manure used to fertilize the soil

fervent *adjective* very keen or enthusiastic **fervently** *adverb* **fervour** *noun* enthusiasm or passion

festival *noun* (*plural* **festivals**) 1 a time when people celebrate a special event such as a religious holiday 2 a specially arranged series of events, such as films or concerts

festive *adjective* to do with a festival; joyful **festivity** *noun*

fetch *verb* (**fetches, fetching, fetched**) 1 to go and bring someone or something 2 to be sold for a price ▶ *My old bike fetched £10.*

fetching *adjective* attractive, pretty

fête *noun* (*plural* **fêtes**) (*pronounced* fayt) an outdoor event with stalls, games, and sideshows

feud *noun* (*plural* **feuds**) (*pronounced* fewd) a long-lasting quarrel between people or families

feudal *adjective* (*pronounced* **few**-dal) to do with the system used in the Middle Ages, in which people could farm land belonging to a lord if they worked and fought for him **feudalism** *noun* the feudal system

fever *noun* (*plural* **fevers**) an unusually high body temperature, usually with an illness **fevered** *adjective*

feverish *adjective* having a slight fever

few *adjective* (**fewer, fewest**) not many
few *noun* a small number of people or things **a good few** or **quite a few** a fairly large number

fiancé *noun* (*plural* **fiancés**) (*pronounced* fee-**ahn**-say) a man who is engaged to be married

fiancée *noun* (*plural* **fiancées**) (*pronounced* fee-**ahn**-say) a woman who is engaged to be married

fiasco *noun* (*plural* **fiascos**) (*pronounced* fi-**ass**-koh) a complete failure

fib *noun* (*plural* **fibs**) a lie about something unimportant
fib *verb* (**fibs, fibbing, fibbed**) to tell a small lie

fibre *noun* (*plural* **fibres**) (*pronounced* **fy**-ber) 1 a very thin thread 2 material made up of thin threads 3 a substance in food that helps you to digest it **fibrous** *adjective* like fibre, or containing fibre

fibreglass *noun* a kind of lightweight plastic containing glass fibres

fickle *adjective* often changing; not loyal to one person or group

fiction *noun* stories about made-up people and events **fictional** *adjective*

fictitious *adjective* not true; made up

fiddle *noun* (*plural* **fiddles**) a violin
fiddle *verb* (**fiddles, fiddling, fiddled**) 1 to play the violin 2 to play with something with your fingers 3 (informal) to be dishonest about something **fiddler** *noun* someone who plays the violin

fiddly *adjective* (informal) small and awkward to handle or use

fidelity *noun* (*pronounced* fi-**del**-i-ti) being faithful

fidget *verb* (**fidgets, fidgeting, fidgeted**) to keep moving with nervous and restless movements **fidgety** *adjective*

field *noun* (*plural* **fields**) 1 a piece of land with crops or grass growing on it, often surrounded by a hedge or fence 2 a piece of land for something special ▸ *The school has a games field.* 3 a subject that someone is studying or interested in ▸ *The book describes important developments in the field of science.* 4 the competitors in a race or hunt ▸ *She was well ahead of the field.*
field *verb* (**fields, fielding, fielded**) to stop or catch the ball in cricket and other ball games **fielder** *noun*

fiend *noun* (*plural* **fiends**) (*pronounced* feend) 1 a devil 2 a wicked or cruel person

fierce *adjective* (**fiercer, fiercest**) 1 angry and violent 2 strong or intense ▸ *They felt the fierce heat from the bonfire.*

fiery *adjective* (**fierier, fieriest**) 1 full of flames or heat 2 easily made angry ▸ *He had a fiery temper.*

fifteen *noun* (*plural* **fifteens**) 1 the number 15 2 a rugby team of 15 players **fifteenth** *adjective* and *noun*

fifth *adjective* and *noun* the next after the fourth **fifthly** *adverb*

fifty *noun* (*plural* **fifties**) the number 50 **fiftieth** *adjective* and *noun*

fifty-fifty *adjective* and *adverb* shared equally between two people or groups

fig *noun* (*plural* **figs**) a soft fruit full of small seeds

fight *noun* (*plural* **fights**) 1 a struggle against someone, using your hands or weapons 2 an attempt to achieve or overcome something ▸ *We are spending more money in the fight against crime.*
fight *verb* (**fights, fighting, fought**) 1 to have a fight with someone 2 to try to stop something ▸ *They fought the fire all night.* **fighter** *noun*

figure *noun* (*plural* **figures**) 1 one of the symbols that stand for numbers, such as 1, 2, and 53 2 the shape of a person's body

3 a diagram or illustration in a book
4 a pattern or shape ▸ *He made a figure of eight in the snow.*
figure *verb* (**figures, figuring, figured**) to work out ▸ *We figured that we had enough money for the holiday.*

file *noun* (*plural* **files**) 1 a box or folder for keeping papers in 2 a line of people one behind the other 3 a collection of data stored in a computer 4 a metal tool with a rough surface for making things smooth
file *verb* (**files, filing, filed**) 1 to smooth something with a file 2 to put papers in a box or folder 3 to walk one behind the other

fill *verb* (**fills, filling, filled**) 1 to make something full 2 to become full **fill in** to put information on a form

fillet *noun* (*plural* **fillets**) a piece of fish or meat with the bones taken out

filling *noun* (*plural* **fillings**) a piece of metal a dentist puts in a tooth to replace a decayed part

filling station *noun* (*plural* **filling stations**) a place where petrol is sold

film *noun* (*plural* **films**) 1 a moving picture that you see in a cinema or on television 2 a roll of plastic coated with a chemical that you use in a camera for taking photographs 3 a very thin layer ▸ *The table was covered with a film of grease.*
filmy *adjective* thin and transparent, like a film
film *verb* (**films, filming, filmed**) to make a film or video of something

filter *noun* (*plural* **filters**) a device that removes unwanted things from a liquid or gas which passes through it
filter *verb* (**filters, filtering, filtered**) 1 to pass a liquid or gas through a filter 2 to move round a corner into another line of traffic

filthy *adjective* (**filthier, filthiest**) very dirty

fin *noun* (*plural* **fins**) 1 a thin flat part on a fish's body that helps it to swim 2 a part like a fin on an aircraft or rocket that helps it to balance

final *adjective* coming at the end; last
finally *adverb* as the last thing
final *noun* (*plural* **finals**) the last game or match of a series, which decides the overall winner

finalist *noun* (*plural* **finalists**) a person or team taking part in a final

finance *noun* the business of using and looking after money
finance *verb* (**finances, financing, financed**) to provide money for something **financial** *adjective* to do with money

finch *noun* (*plural* **finches**) a small bird with a short thick beak

find *verb* (**finds, finding, found**) 1 to see or get something by chance or by looking for it 2 to learn something by experience ▸ *He found that digging is hard work.*
find out to get information about something

fine¹ *adjective* (**finer, finest**) 1 of good quality; excellent 2 dry and sunny 3 very thin; delicate ▸ *The curtains were made of a fine material.* 4 made of small particles ▸ *The sand on the beach was very fine.*
finely *adverb* into fine or small parts ▸ *Slice the tomato finely.*

fine² *noun* (*plural* **fines**) money which has to be paid as a punishment
fine *verb* (**fines, fining, fined**) to punish someone with a fine

finger *noun* (*plural* **fingers**) 1 one of the long thin parts of your hand 2 something with a shape like a finger
finger *verb* (**fingers, fingering, fingered**) to touch something with your fingers

fingernail *noun* (*plural* **fingernails**) the hard covering at the end of each finger

fingerprint *noun* (*plural* **fingerprints**) a mark made by the tip of your finger

finish *verb* (**finishes, finishing, finished**) 1 to bring something to an end 2 to come to an end
finish *noun* the end of something

fir *noun* (*plural* **firs**) an evergreen tree with cones and with leaves like needles

fire *noun* (*plural* **fires**) **1** the heat and bright light that come from burning things **2** a device that makes heat **3** the shooting of guns ▸ *Hold your fire!* **on** fire burning **set fire to** to make something burn

fire *verb* (**fires, firing, fired**) **1** to shoot a gun **2** to bake pottery or bricks in an oven **3** (informal) to dismiss someone from their job

firearm *noun* (*plural* **firearms**) a gun or rifle

fire engine *noun* (*plural* **fire engines**) a large vehicle that carries firefighters and their equipment to fight fires

fire extinguisher *noun* (*plural* **fire extinguishers**) a cylinder containing chemicals for putting out a fire

firefighter *noun* (*plural* **firefighters**) someone whose job is to put out fires

fireplace *noun* (*plural* **fireplaces**) an opening built into the wall of a room with a chimney, used for fires

fireproof *adjective* able to stand great heat without burning

firework *noun* (*plural* **fireworks**) a device containing chemicals that give off coloured sparks or make loud noises

firm *adjective* (**firmer, firmest**) **1** fixed or steady **2** definite; not likely to change ▸ *She has a firm belief in the power of fate.* **firmly** *adverb* **firmness** *noun*

firm *noun* (*plural* **firms**) a business organization

first *adjective* **1** coming before all the others **2** the most important ▸ *He plays in the First Eleven.*

first *adverb* before everything else ▸ *Finish your work first.* **at first** at the beginning; to start with

first aid *noun* emergency treatment given to an injured person before a doctor comes

first-class *adjective* **1** belonging to the best part of a service ▸ *I'll send the letter by first-class post.* **2** excellent

firstly *adverb* as the first thing ▸ *Firstly, let me tell you about our holiday.*

fish *noun* (*plural* **fish** or **fishes**) an animal that lives and breathes in water

fish *verb* (**fishes, fishing, fished**) to try to catch fish

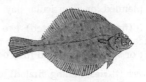

fisherman *noun* (*plural* **fishermen**) someone who tries to catch fish

fishmonger *noun* (*plural* **fishmongers**) a shopkeeper who sells fish

fishy *adjective* (**fishier, fishiest**) **1** smelling or tasting like a fish **2** (informal) suspicious ▸ *The excuse sounded fishy.*

fist *noun* (*plural* **fists**) your closed hand with the fingers bent tightly into the palm

fit[1] *adjective* (**fitter, fittest**) **1** suitable or good enough ▸ *The old house was no longer in a fit state to live in.* **2** healthy and strong ▸ *She looked remarkably fit for 62.* **3** ready or likely ▸ *They worked till they were fit to collapse.*

fit *verb* (**fits, fitting, fitted**) **1** to be the right size and shape for someone or something **2** to put something in place ▸ *A carpenter arrived to fit the new door.*

fit *noun* the way something fits ▸ *The jacket is a good fit.*

fit[2] *noun* (*plural* **fits**) a sudden illness that makes you unconscious with violent movements of your body

fitness *noun* being fit and healthy

fitting *adjective* suitable or proper ▸ *I tried hard to think of a fitting reply.*

fitting *noun* (*plural* **fittings**) something fixed or fitted in a room or building

five *noun* (*plural* **fives**) the number 5

fix *verb* (**fixes, fixing, fixed**) **1** to put something where it will not move, or join it firmly to something else **2** to decide or settle something ▸ *A date was fixed for the trial at the end of January.* **3** to mend something ▸ *We need to find someone to fix the broken window.* **fix up** to arrange or organize something

fix noun (*plural* **fixes**) (informal) an awkward situation ▶ *When Joe didn't turn up we were really in a fix.*

fixture noun (*plural* **fixtures**) a sports event planned for a particular day

fizz verb (**fizzes**, **fizzing**, fizzed) 1 to produce a lot of small bubbles 2 to make a hissing or spluttering sound **fizzy** *adjective*

fizzle verb (**fizzles**, **fizzling**, **fizzled**) to make a gentle hissing sound **fizzle out** to end in a feeble way

flabby *adjective* (**flabbier**, **flabbiest**) fat and soft; not firm

flag noun (*plural* **flags**) a piece of material with a coloured pattern or shape on it, used as the emblem of a country or organization

flag verb (**flags**, **flagging**, **flagged**) to become weak or tired

flagship noun (*plural* **flagships**) a ship that has the commander of the fleet on board and flies the commander's flag

flagstone noun (*plural* **flagstones**) a flat slab of stone used for paving

flake noun (*plural* **flakes**) 1 a light thin piece of something 2 a piece of falling snow **flaky** *adjective* like flakes, or breaking into flakes

flame noun (*plural* **flames**) a bright strip of fire

flame verb (**flames**, **flaming**, **flamed**) to produce flames

flamingo noun (*plural* **flamingos**) a pale pink wading bird with long thin legs and a long neck

flan noun (*plural* **flans**) a pie with an open top

flank noun (*plural* **flanks**) the side of a large animal's body

flannel noun (*plural* **flannels**) 1 a piece of soft cloth used for washing yourself 2 a soft woollen material

flap noun (*plural* **flaps**) a piece of material that hangs down to cover an opening

flap verb (**flaps**, **flapping**, **flapped**) 1 to move something up and down or from side to side ▶ *The bird flapped its wings.* 2 to wave about ▶ *Flags were flapping in the wind.*

flare noun (*plural* **flares**) 1 a sudden bright flame 2 a bright light fired into the sky as a signal 3 a gradual widening, especially in skirts or trousers

flare verb (**flares**, **flaring**, **flared**) 1 to burn with a sudden bright flame 2 to get gradually wider **flare up** to become suddenly angry

flash noun (*plural* **flashes**) a sudden burst of light **in a flash** very suddenly or quickly ▶ *She was gone in a flash.*

flash verb (**flashes**, **flashing**, **flashed**) 1 to give a sudden burst of light 2 to approach and go past very quickly ▶ *The bus flashed past without stopping.*

flashy *adjective* (**flashier**, **flashiest**) showy and bright

flask noun (*plural* **flasks**) a bottle for keeping liquid hot or cold

flat *adjective* (**flatter**, **flattest**) 1 smooth and level 2 spread out; lying at full length ▶ *Lie flat on the ground.* 3 dull or uninteresting ▶ *He always spoke in a flat voice.* 4 (describing a liquid) no longer fizzy 5 (describing a tyre) having lost its air 6 below the proper musical pitch

flat *adverb* exactly and no more ▶ *He did it in ten seconds flat.* **flat out** as fast as possible

flat noun (*plural* **flats**) 1 a set of rooms on one floor, for living in 2 a musical note that is slightly lower than the natural note; the sign (♭) that indicates this

flatten verb (**flattens**, **flattening**, **flattened**) 1 to make something flat 2 to become flat

flatter verb (**flatters**, **flattering**, **flattered**) to praise someone more than they deserve **flattery** noun too much praise

flavour noun (*plural* **flavours**) the taste of something

flavour verb (**flavours**, **flavouring**, **flavoured**) to give something a particular taste **flavouring** noun a substance that gives a flavour to food or drink

flaw noun (plural **flaws**) a fault or weakness **flawed** adjective having a fault

flax noun a plant that produces fibres for cloth and seeds for oil

flea noun (plural **fleas**) a small jumping insect that sucks blood

fledgling noun (plural **fledglings**) a young bird that is ready to start flying

flee verb (**flees, fleeing, fled**) to run away in fear

fleece noun (plural **fleeces**) 1 the wool that covers a sheep's body 2 a jacket made from a soft warm material **fleecy** adjective

fleet noun (plural **fleets**) a group of ships, aircraft, or vehicles

flesh noun the soft substance of people and animals, between the bones and skin **fleshy** adjective

flew past tense of **fly** verb

flex noun (plural **flexes**) insulated wire for electric current

flexible adjective bending or changing easily **flexibility** noun

flick verb (**flicks, flicking, flicked**) to hit or move something with a light movement

flicker verb (**flickers, flickering, flickered**) to burn or shine unsteadily

flight noun (plural **flights**) 1 flying 2 a journey in an aircraft or rocket 3 escaping or running away 4 a set of stairs

flimsy adjective (**flimsier, flimsiest**) light and easily broken

flinch verb (**flinches, flinching, flinched**) to make a movement showing fear

fling verb (**flings, flinging, flung**) to throw something carelessly or hard

flint noun (plural **flints**) a very hard kind of stone

flip verb (**flips, flipping, flipped**) to turn something over quickly

flipper noun (plural **flippers**) 1 a limb that water animals use for swimming 2 a flat rubber shoe shaped like a duck's foot, for swimming underwater

flit verb (**flits, flitting, flitted**) to move lightly and quickly

float verb (**floats, floating, floated**) 1 to stay on the surface of a liquid or in the air 2 to make something float
float noun (plural **floats**) 1 a light object that is designed to float on water 2 a vehicle with a platform used for delivering milk or for carrying a display in a parade

flock noun (plural **flocks**) a group of sheep, goats, or birds
flock verb (**flocks, flocking, flocked**) to move in a large group

flog verb (**flogs, flogging, flogged**) 1 to beat someone violently with a whip or stick 2 (slang) to sell something

flood noun (plural **floods**) 1 a large amount of water spreading over land that is usually dry 2 a large amount of something ▶ After their concert the band got a flood of letters.
flood verb (**floods, flooding, flooded**) 1 to cover something with a large amount of water 2 to arrive in large amounts ▶ Money flooded in after the appeal.

floodlight noun (plural **floodlights**) an outdoor lamp that gives a broad bright beam **floodlit** adjective

floor noun (plural **floors**) 1 the part of a room that people walk on 2 all the rooms on the same level in a building ▶ They live on the top floor.

flop verb (**flops, flopping, flopped**) 1 to fall or sit down heavily or carelessly 2 (informal) To flop is to be a failure.
flop noun (plural **flops**) (informal) a failure or disappointment ▶ His latest film was a complete flop.

floppy *adjective* (**floppier, floppiest**) hanging loosely or heavily

floppy disk *noun* (*plural* **floppy disks**) a flexible disc in a hard case, used for storing data in a computer

flora *noun* (*pronounced* flor-a) the plants growing in an area or at a particular period of time
See also **fauna**, which refers to animals.

floral *adjective* made of flowers

florist *noun* (*plural* **florists**) a shopkeeper who sells flowers

flounder *verb* (**flounders, floundering, floundered**) to move or behave awkwardly or clumsily when in difficulty

flour *noun* a fine powder made from corn and used for making bread, cakes, and pastry **floury** *adjective* powdery like flour

flourish *verb* (**flourishes, flourishing, flourished**) 1 to grow or develop strongly; to be successful 2 to wave something about proudly

flow *verb* (**flows, flowing, flowed**) 1 to move along smoothly 2 to hang loosely ► *She was tall with long flowing hair.*

flow *noun* (*plural* **flows**) a flowing movement

flower *noun* (*plural* **flowers**) 1 the colourful part of a plant from which the seed or fruit develops 2 a plant with a flower

flower *verb* (**flowers, flowering, flowered**) to produce flowers

flown past participle of **fly** *verb*

flu *noun* (short for **influenza**) an illness that gives you a heavy cold and a headache

fluent *adjective* able to speak quickly and easily **fluency** *noun* **fluently** *adverb*

fluff *noun* small pieces of soft stuff that come off wool or cloth **fluffiness** *noun* **fluffy** *adjective*

fluid *noun* (*plural* **fluids**) a liquid or gas that flows easily

fluke *noun* (*plural* **flukes**) something you do well by luck

flung past tense and past participle of **fling**

fluorescent *adjective* very bright when light shines on it

fluorescent light *noun* (*plural* **fluorescent lights**) a very bright light in the shape of a tube

fluoride *noun* a chemical that is added to water and toothpaste to help prevent tooth decay

flush *verb* (**flushes, flushing, flushed**) 1 to blush slightly 2 to clean something with a fast flow of liquid

flush *noun* (*plural* **flushes**) 1 a slight blush 2 a fast flow of water

flustered *adjective* nervous and confused

flute *noun* (*plural* **flutes**) a musical instrument made of a long pipe with holes that are covered by fingers or keys

flutter *verb* (**flutters, fluttering, fluttered**) to make quick flapping movements

fly *verb* (**flies, flying, flew, flown**) 1 to move through the air 2 to wave in the air ► *A flag was flying from the roof.* 3 to make something move through the air ► *They were flying model aircraft.* 4 to move or pass quickly

fly *noun* (*plural* **flies**) a small flying insect

flyover *noun* (*plural* **flyovers**) a bridge that carries one road over another

foal *noun* (*plural* **foals**) a young horse

foam *noun* 1 a mass of tiny bubbles on a liquid 2 a spongy kind of rubber or plastic

foam *verb* (**foams, foaming, foamed**) to form frothy bubbles

focus *verb* (**focuses, focusing, focused**) 1 to adjust your eye or the lens of a camera so that objects appear clearly 2 to concentrate on something

focus *noun* (*plural* **focuses** or **foci**) the distance at which an object appears most clearly to your eye or in a lens

fodder *noun* food for horses and farm animals

foe *noun* (*plural* **foes**) (old use) an enemy

foetus *noun* (*plural* **foetuses**) (*pronounced* **fee**-tus) an unborn animal or human baby in the womb

fog *noun* (*plural* **fogs**) a thick mist that makes it difficult to see **foggy** *adjective*

foil[1] *noun* (*plural* **foils**) **1** a very thin sheet of metal **2** a long narrow sword used in fencing

foil[2] *verb* (**foils, foiling, foiled**) to prevent someone from doing something

fold *verb* (**folds, folding, folded**) to bend something so that one part lies on another part

fold *noun* (*plural* **folds**) a line where something is folded

folder *noun* (*plural* **folders**) a cover to keep loose papers in

foliage *noun* the leaves of plants and trees

folk *plural noun* ordinary people

folklore *noun* old beliefs and legends

follow *verb* (**follows, following, followed**) **1** to go or come after someone **2** to take someone as a guide or example **3** to take an interest in a team or a famous group of people **4** to understand something or someone ▸ *I'm afraid I didn't follow what you said.* **5** to happen afterwards **follower** *noun*

folly *noun* (*plural* **follies**) something foolish or silly

fond *adjective* (**fonder, fondest**) **1** loving ▸ *She gave him a fond goodbye kiss.* **2** unwisely hopeful ▸ *They have fond hopes of being friends again.* **be fond of** to like someone or something **fondly** *adverb* **fondness** *noun*

fondle *verb* (**fondles, fondling, fondled**) to touch or stroke someone gently

font *noun* (*plural* **fonts**) a stone basin in a church, to hold water for baptism

food *noun* (*plural* **foods**) anything that a plant or animal takes into its body to make it grow and give it energy

fool *noun* (*plural* **fools**) **1** a silly person **2** a jester or clown ▸ *Ian was playing the fool.*

fool *verb* (**fools, fooling, fooled**) **1** to behave like a fool **2** to trick someone **fool about** or **fool around** to behave stupidly

foolish *adjective* stupid or unwise **foolishly** *adverb* **foolishness** *noun*

foolproof *adjective* easy to use or do correctly

foot *noun* (*plural* **feet**) **1** the part of your leg that you stand on **2** the lowest part of something ▸ *The little house stood at the foot of a hill.* **3** a measure of length, 12 inches or about 30 centimetres

football *noun* (*plural* **footballs**) **1** a game played by two teams which try to score goals with a large ball **2** the ball used in this game **footballer** *noun*

footing *noun* a secure position to stand on ▸ *He lost his footing and slipped.*

footlights *plural noun* a row of lights along the front of the stage in a theatre

footnote *noun* (*plural* **footnotes**) a note printed at the bottom of a page

footpath *noun* (*plural* **footpaths**) a path for walking along

footprint *noun* (*plural* **footprints**) a mark made in the ground by a foot or shoe

footsteps *plural noun* the sounds or marks made by someone walking

for *preposition* used to show **1** who something belong to ▸ *This letter is for you.* **2** an amount of time or distance ▸ *We've been waiting for hours.* ▸ *They walked for three miles.* **3** what something costs ▶ *She bought it for £2.* **4** something given in exchange ▶ *Can I swap this for a bigger one?* **5** a cause or reason ▶ *He was rewarded for bravery.* ▶ *I only did it for the money.* **6** someone or something you support ▶ *Are you for us or against us?* **for ever** always

for *conjunction* because ▶ *They paused, for they heard a noise.*

forbid *verb* (**forbids, forbidding, forbade, forbidden**) **1** to tell someone not to do something **2** to say that something is not allowed ▶ *They have forbidden smoking in the shopping centre.*

force *noun* (*plural* **forces**) **1** strength or power **2** an organized group of soldiers or police

force *verb* (**forces, forcing, forced**) **1** to use your power or strength to make someone do something **2** to break something open using force ▶ *The burglars had forced the kitchen window.*

forceps *plural noun* (*pronounced* **for**-seps) special pincers or tongs used by a dentist or surgeon

forcible *adjective* done by force **forcibly** *adverb* with force

ford *noun* (*plural* **fords**) a shallow place where you can wade or drive across a river

forecast *verb* (**forecasts, forecasting, forecast** or **forecasted**) to say what is likely to happen in the future

forecast *noun* (*plural* **forecasts**) a statement about what is likely to happen

foregone conclusion *noun* a result or ending that you know will happen

foreground *noun* (*plural* **foregrounds**) the part of a picture or view that is nearest to you

forehead *noun* (*plural* **foreheads**) (*pronounced* **for**-hed or **fo**-rid) the part of your face above your eyebrows

foreign *adjective* belonging to or coming from another country

foreigner *noun* (*plural* **foreigners**) a person from another country

foremost *adjective* most important

forename *noun* (*plural* **forenames**) a person's first name

foresee *verb* (**foresees, foreseeing, foresaw, foreseen**) to realize that something is likely to happen **foreseeable** *adjective* able to be thought about before it happens

foresight *noun* the ability to realize that certain things are likely to happen

forest *noun* (*plural* **forests**) a large area of land with trees growing close together **forester** *noun* a worker in a forest

forestry *noun* the science of planting forests and looking after them

forfeit *noun* (*plural* **forfeits**) (*pronounced* **faw**-fit) something that you lose or have to pay as a penalty

forfeit *verb* (**forfeits, forfeiting, forfeited**) to lose something as a penalty

forgave past tense of **forgive**

forge[1] *noun* (*plural* **forges**) a blacksmith's workshop

forge *verb* (**forges, forging, forged**) **1** to shape metal by heating and hammering it **2** to make a copy of something in order to deceive people

forgery *noun* (*plural* **forgeries**) a copy of something, made in order to deceive people

forget *verb* (**forgets, forgetting, forgot, forgotten**) **1** not to remember something **2** to stop thinking about something

forgetful *adjective* often forgetting things

forget-me-not *noun* (*plural* **forget-me-nots**) a plant with small blue flowers
The flower got its name because lovers used to wear it as a token of their love.

forgive *verb* (**forgives, forgiving, forgave, forgiven**) to stop being angry with someone for something they have done **forgiveness** *noun*

fork *noun* (*plural* **forks**) **1** a small tool with prongs for lifting food to your mouth **2** a large tool with prongs used for digging or lifting things **3** a place where a road or river divides into two or more parts

fork *verb* (**forks, forking, forked**) 1 to dig or lift something with a fork 2 to divide into two or more branches

forlorn *adjective* alone and unhappy

form *noun* (*plural* **forms**) 1 the shape and general appearance of something ▸ *The dark form of a tree stood out on the brow of the hill.* 2 a kind of thing ▸ *Ice is a form of water.* 3 a class in a school 4 a piece of paper with printed questions and spaces for the answers
form *verb* (**forms, forming, formed**) 1 to shape or make something 2 to develop or start to exist ▸ *Icicles formed on the window sill.*

formal *adjective* 1 following the accepted rules or customs ▸ *I'll send you a formal invitation.* 2 suitable for important occasions ▸ *We will have to wear formal dress.* **formally** *adverb*

formality *noun* (*plural* **formalities**) 1 formal behaviour 2 something you do to obey a rule or custom

formation *noun* (*plural* **formations**) 1 the process of forming or making something 2 a special pattern or arrangement

former *adjective* earlier; of past times ▸ *a former president* **the former** the first of two people or things just mentioned ▸ *I've been to Paris and Rome but I prefer the former.* See also **latter**.

formerly *adverb* once; in the past

formula *noun* (*plural* **formulas** or **formulae**) 1 a set of chemical symbols showing what something consists of ▸ *H_2O is the formula for water.* 2 a recipe or list of ingredients 3 a rule or statement expressed in symbols or numbers

forsake *verb* (**forsakes, forsaking, forsook, forsaken**) (not an everyday word) to abandon someone

fort *noun* (*plural* **forts**) a building with strong walls and defences against attack

forth *adverb* (not an everyday word) forwards or onwards ▸ *From that day forth they never fought again.*

fortify *verb* (**fortifies, fortifying, fortified**) 1 to make a place strong against attack 2 to make someone strong and fit

fortnight *noun* (*plural* **fortnights**) a period of two weeks **fortnightly** *adverb* and *adjective* every two weeks

fortress *noun* (*plural* **fortresses**) a large fort or fortified town

fortunate *adjective* lucky **fortunately** *adverb* luckily

fortune *noun* (*plural* **fortunes**) 1 luck or chance 2 a large amount of money

fortune-teller *noun* (*plural* **fortune-tellers**) someone who tells you what will happen to you in the future

forty *noun* (*plural* **forties**) the number 40 **fortieth** *adjective* and *noun*

forward *adjective* 1 facing the front 2 too eager or bold
forward *noun* (*plural* **forwards**) a player in the front line of a team at football, hockey, and other games

forwards *adverb* towards the front; in the direction you are facing

fossil *noun* (*plural* **fossils**) the remains of a prehistoric animal or plant that has become hardened in rock **fossilized** *adjective* formed into a fossil

foster *verb* (**fosters, fostering, fostered**) 1 to bring up someone else's child as part of your own family 2 to encourage something ▸ *We are trying to foster good relations with other schools in the area.*

foster child *noun* (*plural* **foster children**) a child brought up by foster parents

foster parent *noun* (*plural* **foster parents**) a parent who is fostering a child

fought past tense and past participle of **fight** *verb*

foul *adjective* (**fouler, foulest**) 1 dirty or disgusting 2 unfair; breaking the rules of a game **foully** *adverb*
foul *noun* (*plural* **fouls**) something a player does that breaks the rules of a sport
foul *verb* (**fouls, fouling, fouled**) to commit a foul against another player in a sport

found[1] *verb* (**founds, founding, founded**) to start or establish something ▸ *The college had been founded in the eighteenth century.* **founder** *noun* someone who founds something

found[2] past tense and past participle of **find**

foundation *noun* (*plural* **foundations**) 1 the solid base on which a building stands 2 the process of founding something

founder *verb* (**founders, foundering, foundered**) 1 (used about a ship) to fill with water and sink 2 to fail completely ▸ *Their plans have foundered from lack of money.*

foundry *noun* (*plural* **foundries**) a place where metal or glass is made

fountain *noun* (*plural* **fountains**) an outdoor structure which sends jets of water into the air

fountain pen *noun* (*plural* **fountain pens**) a pen that has a nib and holds its own supply of ink

four *noun* (*plural* **fours**) the number 4 **on all fours** on your hands and knees **fourth** *adjective* and *noun*

fourteen *noun* (*plural* **fourteens**) the number 14 **fourteenth** *adjective* and *noun*

fowl *noun* (*plural* **fowl** or **fowls**) a bird that is kept for its eggs or meat

fox *noun* (*plural* **foxes**) a wild animal with a red-brown coat and a long furry tail **fox** *verb* (**foxes, foxing, foxed**) to puzzle or confuse someone

foxglove *noun* (*plural* **foxgloves**) a tall plant with bell-shaped flowers

foyer *noun* (*plural* **foyers**) (*pronounced* **foi-ay**) the entrance hall of a cinema or other large building

fraction *noun* (*plural* **fractions**) 1 a number that is not a whole number, for example ½ and 0.5 2 a small part of something

fracture *verb* (**fractures, fracturing, fractured**) to break or crack one of your bones **fracture** *noun* (*plural* **fractures**) a break or crack in a bone

fragile *adjective* (*pronounced* **fra-jyl**) easy to break or damage **fragility** *noun*

fragment *noun* (*plural* **fragments**) a small piece broken off something

fragrant *adjective* (*pronounced* **fray-grant**) having a sweet or pleasant smell **fragrance** *noun* a sweet smell

frail *adjective* (**frailer, frailest**) weak or fragile **frailty** *noun* being frail

frame *noun* (*plural* **frames**) 1 a set of wooden or metal strips that fit round the outside of a picture to hold it 2 a rigid structure that supports something **frame of mind** the way you think or feel for a while **frame** *verb* (**frames, framing, framed**) to put a frame round a picture

framework *noun* (*plural* **frameworks**) a structure that supports something

franc *noun* (*plural* **francs**) a unit of money in France and some other countries

frank *adjective* (**franker, frankest**) making your thoughts and feelings clear to people **frankly** *adverb*

frantic *adjective* wildly agitated or excited **frantically** *adverb*

fraud *noun* (*plural* **frauds**) 1 the crime of getting money by deceiving people 2 someone who is not what they pretend to be **fraudulent** *adjective* dishonest

fraught *adjective* tense and upset

frayed *adjective* worn and ragged at the edge

freak *noun* (*plural* **freaks**) someone or something very strange or unusual

freckle *noun* (*plural* **freckles**) a small brown spot on the skin **freckled** *adjective*

free *adjective* (**freer, freest**) **1** able to do what you want to do or go where you want to go ▸ *They were now free to leave.* **2** not costing anything ▸ *You get a free book with every £20 you spend.* **3** not being used or occupied ▸ *Our afternoons are free.* **4** generous ▸ *She is very free with her money.* **be free of** not to have something or be affected by it ▸ *The roads are free of ice.* **freely** *adverb*

free *verb* (**frees, freeing, freed**) to make someone free

freedom *noun* being free; independence

free-range *adjective* (describing hens) allowed to move freely in the open without being caged

freewheel *verb* (**freewheels, freewheeling, freewheeled**) to ride a bicycle without pedalling

freeze *verb* (**freezes, freezing, froze, frozen**) **1** to turn into ice or become covered with ice ▸ *The pond froze last night.* **2** to be very cold ▸ *My hands are freezing.* **3** to store food at a low temperature to preserve it **4** to stand still with fright

freezer *noun* (*plural* **freezers**) a large container for keeping food frozen

freezing point *noun* (*plural* **freezing points**) the temperature at which a liquid freezes

freight *noun* (*pronounced* frayt) cargo carried by goods vehicles

French window *noun* (*plural* **French windows**) a long window that reaches down to the ground and opens like a door

frenzy *noun* (*plural* **frenzies**) wild excitement; madness **frenzied** *adjective*

frequency *noun* (*plural* **frequencies**) **1** how often something happens **2** the rate at which a wave of sound or light vibrates

frequent *adjective* happening often **frequently** *adverb*

fresh *adjective* (**fresher, freshest**) **1** newly made or produced ▸ *We need fresh bread.* **2** not tinned or preserved ▸ *Would you like some fresh fruit?* **3** cool and clean ▸ *It's nice to be in the fresh air.* **freshly** *adverb* **freshness** *noun*

freshen *verb* (**freshens, freshening, freshened**) **1** to make something fresh **2** to become fresh

freshwater *adjective* (describing a fish) living in rivers or lakes and not the sea

fret *verb* (**frets, fretting, fretted**) to worry or be upset about something **fretful** *adjective* worried or upset

fretsaw *noun* (*plural* **fretsaws**) a narrow saw used for making decorative patterns in wood

friar *noun* (*plural* **friars**) a man belonging to a religious group that has taken an oath to live a life of poverty

friction *noun* **1** the resistance caused when one thing rubs against another **2** argument or quarrelling

Friday *noun* (*plural* **Fridays**) the sixth day of the week
Friday is named after the Norse goddess Frigg, the wife of Odin.

fridge *noun* (*plural* **fridges**) (*informal*) a refrigerator

friend *noun* (*plural* **friends**) **1** someone you know well and like **2** a helpful or kind person

friendly *adjective* (**friendlier, friendliest**) kind and helpful **friendliness** *noun*

friendship *noun* (*plural* **friendships**) being friends

frieze *noun* (*plural* **friezes**) (*pronounced* freez) a decorated strip along the top of a wall

frigate *noun* (*plural* **frigates**) a small fast warship

fright *noun* (*plural* **frights**) sudden fear

frighten *verb* (**frightens, frightening, frightened**) to make someone afraid

frightful *adjective* awful; very great or bad **frightfully** *adverb* awfully; very

frill *noun* (*plural* **frills**) a decorative edging on a dress or curtain **frilled** *adjective* **frilly** *adjective*

fringe *noun* (*plural* **fringes**) 1 a decorative edging with threads hanging down loosely 2 a straight line of short hair hanging down over the forehead 3 the edge of something ▸ *There is a picnic area at the fringe of the wood.* **fringed** *adjective*

frisk *verb* (**frisks, frisking, frisked**) 1 to jump or run around playfully 2 (informal) to search someone by moving your hands over their body

frisky *adjective* (**friskier, friskiest**) playful or lively **friskily** *adverb* **friskiness** *noun*

fritter *noun* (*plural* **fritters**) a slice of meat, potato, or fruit fried in batter

fritter *verb* (**fritters, frittering, frittered**) to waste something gradually

frivolous *adjective* silly or playful

fro *adverb* **to and fro** backwards and forwards

frock *noun* (*plural* **frocks**) a dress

frog *noun* (*plural* **frogs**) a small jumping animal that can live both in water and on land

frogman *noun* (*plural* **frogmen**) an underwater swimmer wearing a rubber suit and breathing apparatus

frolic *verb* (**frolics, frolicking, frolicked**) to play about cheerfully

from *preposition* used to show 1 where someone or something starts ▸ *She comes from London.* ▸ *Buses run from 8 o'clock.* 2 how far something is ▸ *We are a mile from home.* 3 where you get something ▸ *Buy some milk from the supermarket.* 4 how things are different ▸ *Can you tell margarine from butter?*

front *noun* (*plural* **fronts**) 1 the part of something that faces forwards ▸ *I stood at the front of the house.* 2 the part of a thing that is furthest forward ▸ *We'd*

better go to the front of the queue. 3 a wide road or path along the seashore 4 the place where fighting is happening in a war

frontier *noun* (*plural* **frontiers**) the boundary between two countries or regions

frost *noun* (*plural* **frosts**) 1 powdery ice that covers the ground in freezing weather 2 freezing weather **frosty** *adjective*

frostbite *noun* harm done to the body by very cold weather **frostbitten** *adjective*

froth *noun* a mass of tiny bubbles on top of a liquid **frothy** *adjective*

froth *verb* (**froths, frothing, frothed**) to form a froth

frown *verb* (**frowns, frowning, frowned**) to wrinkle your forehead when you are angry or concentrating

frown *noun* (*plural* **frowns**) the wrinkling of your forehead when you frown

froze past tense of **freeze**

frozen past participle of **freeze**

fruit *noun* (*plural* **fruit** or **fruits**) 1 the part of a tree or plant that contains the seeds and is often used as food, such as apples, oranges, and bananas 2 the good result of doing something ▸ *I'll show you the fruits of our efforts.*

fruitful *adjective* 1 successful; having good results 2 producing fruit

fruitless *adjective* unsuccessful; having no results

fruity *adjective* (**fruitier, fruitiest**) tasting like fruit

frustrate *verb* (**frustrates, frustrating, frustrated**) to make someone feel disappointed by preventing them from doing something **frustration** *noun*

fry *verb* (**fries, frying, fried**) to cook food in hot fat

fudge *noun* a soft brown sweet made with milk, sugar, and butter

fuel *noun* (*plural* **fuels**) something that is burned to make heat or power, such as coal and oil

fugitive noun (plural **fugitives**)
(pronounced **few**-ji-tiv) someone who is
running away from the police

fulfil verb (**fulfils, fulfilling, fulfilled**) to
complete a task or promise **fulfilment** noun
fulfilling something

full adjective (**fuller, fullest**) 1 containing all
it can ▸ There is a full bottle in the fridge.
2 having many people or things ▸ The bus
is full. 3 complete ▸ Let's hear the full
story. 4 the greatest possible ▸ He drove
at full speed. 5 fitting loosely; having many
folds ▸ She was wearing a full skirt. **in full**
not leaving anything out **fully** adverb
completely

full moon noun (plural **full moons**) the
moon when you can see the whole of it as
a bright disc

full stop noun (plural **full stops**) a dot (.)
used as a punctuation mark at the end of a
sentence or to show that a word has been
shortened

fumble verb (**fumbles, fumbling, fumbled**)
to hold or handle something clumsily

fumes plural noun strong-smelling smoke
or gas

fuming adjective very angry

fun noun amusement or enjoyment **make
fun of** to make someone or something look
silly or funny

function noun (plural **functions**) 1 what
someone or something is supposed to do
▸ The function of a doctor is to cure sick
people. 2 an important event or party
function verb (**functions, functioning,
functioned**) to work properly

fund noun (plural **funds**) a collection of
money for a special purpose ▸ We are
starting a holiday fund.

fundamental adjective basic, important
fundamentally adverb

funeral noun (plural **funerals**) the
ceremony at which a dead person is buried
or cremated

fungus noun (plural **fungi**) a soft spongy
growth such as a mushroom or toadstool

funnel noun (plural **funnels**) 1 a chimney
on a ship 2 a tube that is wide at the top
and narrow at the bottom, for pouring
something into a narrow opening

funny adjective (**funnier, funniest**) 1 making
you laugh or smile 2 strange or odd
▸ There's a funny smell in here. **funnily**
adverb

funny bone noun (plural **funny bones**)
the part of your elbow which gives you a
strange tingling feeling if you knock it

fur noun (plural **furs**) the soft hairy
covering that some animals have **furry**
adjective

furious adjective very angry **furiously**
adverb

furnace noun (plural **furnaces**) an oven for
producing great heat

furnish verb (**furnishes, furnishing,
furnished**) to provide a room or building
with furniture or equipment

furniture noun tables, chairs, beds,
cupboards, and other things you need
inside a building

furrow noun (plural **furrows**) 1 a long cut
in the ground made by a plough 2 a deep
wrinkle on the skin

further adverb and adjective 1 to a greater
distance ▸ I can't walk any further. 2 more
▸ The idea needed further thought.

furthermore adverb also; moreover

furthest adverb and adjective to the
greatest distance; most distant

furtive adjective cautious and sly, trying
not to be seen **furtively** adverb **furtiveness**
noun

fury noun wild anger or rage

fuse noun (plural **fuses**) 1 a safety device
in an electric circuit 2 a device for setting
off an explosive
fuse verb (**fuses, fusing, fused**) 1 to stop
working because a fuse has melted ▸ The
lights have fused. 2 to blend things
together by melting them

fuselage noun (plural **fuselages**)
(pronounced **few**-ze-lahzh) the body of an
aircraft

fuss *noun* (*plural* **fusses**) unnecessary excitement or worry about something unimportant

fuss *verb* (**fusses, fussing, fussed**) to be excited or worried about something unimportant

fussy *adjective* (**fussier, fussiest**) wanting things to be exactly right; choosy **fussily** *adverb*

futile *adjective* (*pronounced* few-tyl) useless; having no good purpose **futility** *noun* uselessness

futon *noun* (*plural* **futons**) (*pronounced* foo-ton) a seat with a mattress that rolls out to form a bed
Futon is a Japanese word.

future *noun* the time that is still to come **in future** from now on

fuzzy *adjective* (**fuzzier, fuzziest**) 1 blurred; not clear 2 covered in something soft and hairy **fuzziness** *noun*

Gg

gabble *verb* (**gabbles, gabbling, gabbled**) to talk quickly and not clearly

gable *noun* (*plural* **gables**) the part of a wall between two sloping roofs, shaped like a triangle

gadget *noun* (*plural* **gadgets**) a useful device or tool

Gaelic *noun* a Celtic language spoken in Ireland and (in a different form) in the Highlands of Scotland

gag *noun* (*plural* **gags**) 1 something put over someone's mouth to stop them speaking 2 a joke
gag *verb* (**gags, gagging, gagged**) to put a gag over someone's mouth

gaiety *noun* fun or light-heartedness

gain *verb* (**gains, gaining, gained**) to get something you did not have before **gain on** to come closer to someone when you are following them
gain *noun* (*plural* **gains**) something you have gained; a profit

gala *noun* (*plural* **galas**) (*pronounced* gah-la) 1 a festival 2 a series of swimming or other sports contests

galaxy *noun* (*plural* **galaxies**) (*pronounced* gal-ak-si) a large group of stars **galactic** *adjective*

gale *noun* (*plural* **gales**) a very strong and dangerous wind

gallant *adjective* brave or courteous **gallantly** *adverb* **gallantry** *noun*

galleon *noun* (*plural* **galleons**) in older times, a large Spanish sailing ship

gallery *noun* (*plural* **galleries**) 1 a long room or passage 2 a building or room where people can see works of art displayed 3 a platform built on to the inside wall of a building 4 the highest set of seats in a cinema or theatre

galley *noun* (*plural* **galleys**) 1 in older times, a type of long ship driven by oars 2 the kitchen on a ship or aircraft

gallon *noun* (*plural* **gallons**) a measure of liquid, 8 pints or about 4.5 litres

gallop *noun* the fastest pace that a horse can go
gallop *verb* (**gallops, galloping, galloped**) to ride fast on a horse

gallows *plural noun* in older times, a framework with a noose for hanging criminals

galore *adjective* in large amounts ► *There was food galore at the party.*

gamble *verb* (**gambles, gambling, gambled**) 1 to bet money in a game or at a race 2 to take great risks ► *The bullfighter was gambling with his life.* **gambler** *noun*
gamble *noun* (*plural* **gambles**) a risk

game *noun* (*plural* **games**) 1 something that you play according to rules 2 wild animals or birds hunted for sport or food **give the game away** to reveal a secret

gammon *noun* a kind of ham or thick bacon

gander *noun* (*plural* **ganders**) a male goose

gang noun (plural **gangs**) 1 a group of people who do things together 2 a group of criminals

gang verb (**gangs, ganging, ganged**) gang up on to form a group to bully someone

gangplank noun (plural **gangplanks**) a plank for walking on or off a ship

gangster noun (plural **gangsters**) a member of a gang of violent criminals

gangway noun (plural **gangways**) 1 a gap between rows of seats 2 a movable bridge for walking on or off a ship

gaol noun and verb another spelling of **jail**

gaoler noun another spelling of **jailer**

gap noun (plural **gaps**) 1 an opening or space between two things 2 an interval

gape verb (**gapes, gaping, gaped**) 1 to stare in amazement with your mouth open 2 to be wide open ▸ *There was a gaping hole in the road.*

garage noun (plural **garages**) (*pronounced* ga-rah*z*h or ga-rij) 1 a building for keeping vehicles in 2 a place where vehicles are serviced and repaired and where petrol is sold

garbage noun household rubbish

garbled adjective confused and difficult to understand ▸ *He gave us a garbled account of what the film had been about.*

garden noun (plural **gardens**) a piece of ground where flowers, fruit, or vegetables are grown

gardener noun (plural **gardeners**) someone who looks after a garden, especially as a job

gardening noun looking after a garden

gargle verb (**gargles, gargling, gargled**) to wash your throat by breathing through liquid at the back of your mouth without swallowing it

gargoyle noun (plural **gargoyles**) an ugly or comical carving of a face near the roof of a building, used as a spout for rainwater

garland noun (plural **garlands**) a wreath of flowers worn as a decoration

garlic noun a plant with a strong-tasting bulb divided into sections (called cloves), used in cooking

garment noun (plural **garments**) (not an everyday word) a piece of clothing

garnish verb (**garnishes, garnishing, garnished**) to decorate food with extra items such as salad

garrison noun (plural **garrisons**) troops put in a town or fort to defend it

gas noun (plural **gases**) 1 a freely moving substance such as oxygen 2 a gas that burns and is used for heating or cooking
gaseous adjective like gas, or containing gas

gas verb (**gasses, gassing, gassed**) to kill or injure people or animals with a poisonous gas
Gas is an invented word based on the Greek word *chaos*.

gash noun (plural **gashes**) a long deep cut

gasp verb (**gasps, gasping, gasped**) 1 to breathe in suddenly when you are shocked or surprised 2 to struggle to breathe when you are ill or tired

gastric adjective to do with the stomach

gate noun (plural **gates**) 1 a movable barrier on hinges, used as a door in a wall or fence 2 the number of people attending a sports event

gateau noun (plural **gateaux**) (*pronounced* gat-oh) a rich cake, usually with cream in it
Gateau is a French word, and this is why the plural ends in x and not s.

gateway *noun* (*plural* **gateways**) an opening or entrance with a gate

gather *verb* (**gathers, gathering, gathered**) 1 to come together 2 to bring people or things together 3 to learn or discover a piece of information ► *I gather you've been on holiday.* **gather speed** to move faster

gathering *noun* (*plural* **gatherings**) the people attending a meeting or party

gaudy *adjective* (**gaudier, gaudiest**) bright and showy

gauge *noun* (*plural* **gauges**) (*pronounced* gayj) 1 an instrument for measuring something, such as a fuel gauge 2 the distance between a pair of railway lines
gauge *verb* (**gauges, gauging, gauged**) to measure or estimate something ► *I tried to gauge how high the building was.*

gauntlet *noun* (*plural* **gauntlets**) a glove with a wide covering for the wrist

gauze *noun* thin transparent material

gave past tense of **give**

gay *adjective* (**gayer, gayest**) 1 homosexual 2 bright and cheerful **gaily** *adverb*

gaze *verb* (**gazes, gazing, gazed**) to look hard at something or someone
gaze *noun* (*plural* **gazes**) a long steady look

gear *noun* (*plural* **gears**) 1 one of a set of wheels with teeth, which work together to connect the engine and wheels of a vehicle 2 equipment or clothes ► *We'll need our rain gear.*

geese plural of **goose**

Geiger counter *noun* (*plural* **Geiger counters**) a device that detects and measures radioactivity
The **Geiger counter** is named after a German scientist called Hans Geiger, who helped invent it.

gel *noun* (*plural* **gels**) (*pronounced* jel) a substance like runny jelly

gem *noun* (*plural* **gems**) a precious stone or jewel

gender *noun* (*plural* **genders**) (*pronounced* jen-der) the sex of a person

gene *noun* (*plural* **genes**) the part of a living cell that controls what is passed from parents to children, for example the colour of their hair

general *adjective* 1 to do with most people or things ► *The general feeling is that we should leave after lunch.* 2 not detailed or special ► *Just give a general description of the town.* **in general** usually; to do with most people
general *noun* (*plural* **generals**) an army officer of high rank

generally *adverb* usually; to do with most people

generate *verb* (**generates, generating, generated**) to produce or create something

generation *noun* (*plural* **generations**) 1 all the people born at about the same time 2 a single stage in a family ► *There were four generations of people at the party.* 3 generating something

generator *noun* (*plural* **generators**) a machine for producing electricity

generous *adjective* ready to give or share what you have **generosity** *noun* **generously** *adverb*

genetic *adjective* (*pronounced* ji-**net**-ik) to do with genes and with characteristics inherited from parents **genetically** *adverb*

genetics *plural noun* the study of the way characteristics are passed from one generation to the next by means of genes

genial *adjective* kind and pleasant **geniality** *noun* **genially** *adverb*

genie *noun* (*plural* **genies**) a magical being in stories who can grant wishes

genitals *plural noun* the parts of the body used for sexual intercourse

genius *noun* (*plural* **geniuses**) 1 an unusually clever person 2 a special talent that someone has

gentle *adjective* (**gentler, gentlest**) 1 kind and quiet; not rough or severe 2 gradual ► *The ball rolled down a gentle slope.* **gentleness** *noun* **gently** *adverb*

gentleman *noun* (*plural* **gentlemen**)
1 a polite word for a man
2 a well-mannered or honest man

genuine *adjective* real; not faked or pretending **genuinely** *adverb*

geography *noun* the study of the world and its climate, peoples, and produce **geographer** *noun* someone who studies geography **geographical** *adjective*

geology *noun* the study of the earth's crust and its layers **geological** *adjective* **geologist** *noun* someone who studies geology

geometry *noun* the study in mathematics of lines, angles, surfaces, and solids **geometric** or **geometrical** *adjective*

geranium *noun* (*plural* **geraniums**) (*pronounced* je-**ray**-ni-um) a plant with red, pink, or white flowers

gerbil *noun* (*plural* **gerbils**) (*pronounced* **jer**-bil) a small brown animal with long back legs

geriatric *adjective* to do with old people

germ *noun* (*plural* **germs**) a tiny living thing that can cause disease

germinate *verb* (**germinates, germinating, germinated**) (used about a seed) to start growing and developing **germination** *noun*

gesture *noun* (*plural* **gestures**) a movement or action which expresses what you feel

get *verb* (**gets, getting, got**) This word has many meanings, depending on the words that go with it. 1 to obtain or receive something ▸ *Jane got a letter from her cousin.* 2 to become something ▸ *It began to get cold in the New Year.* 3 to reach a place ▸ *We'll get to York after dark.* 4 to do something to a thing ▸ *I can't get my shoe on.* 5 to make something ready ▸ *Molly's mother went indoors to get the dinner.* 6 to move somewhere ▸ *Let's get on the next bus.* 7 to catch an illness ▸ *I'm afraid I've got a cold.* 8 to persuade or order someone to do something ▸ *See if you can get him to play the banjo.* 9 (informal) to understand something ▸ *I didn't quite get what he meant.* **get away with** to escape being punished for something you have

done **get by** to manage **get on** to make progress, or to be friendly with someone **get out of** to avoid having to do something **get over** to recover from something unpleasant **get your own back** to have your revenge **have got to** must

getaway *noun* (*plural* **getaways**) an escape

geyser *noun* (*plural* **geysers**) (*pronounced* **gee**-zer or **gy**-zer) a natural spring that shoots up hot water and steam

ghastly *adjective* (**ghastlier, ghastliest**) horrible; awful

ghetto *noun* (*plural* **ghettos**) (*pronounced* **get**-oh) an area of a city where poor people or people from another country live apart from other people

ghost *noun* (*plural* **ghosts**) the spirit of a dead person that appears to a living person **ghostly** *adjective*

giant *noun* (*plural* **giants**) a huge person in stories

giant *adjective* very large

gibberish *noun* words or speech that are nonsense

giddy *adjective* (**giddier, giddiest**) unsteady or dizzy **giddiness** *noun*

gift *noun* (*plural* **gifts**) 1 something you give to someone; a present 2 an ability or talent ▸ *Jenny has a gift for music.*

gifted *adjective* having a special ability

gigantic *adjective* huge

giggle *verb* (**giggles, giggling, giggled**) to laugh in a silly way

giggle *noun* (*plural* **giggles**) a silly laugh

gild *verb* (**gilds, gilding, gilded**) to cover something with a thin layer of gold paint or gold

gills *plural noun* the part of a fish's body used for breathing

gimmick *noun* (*plural* **gimmicks**) something unusual done as a way of attracting attention

gin *noun* a colourless alcoholic drink

ginger *noun* 1 a hot-tasting root of a plant, used as a flavouring for food 2 a reddish-yellow colour **gingery** *adjective*

gingerbread *noun* a cake or biscuit flavoured with ginger

gingerly *adverb* very cautiously

gipsy *noun* (*plural* **gipsies**) another spelling of **gypsy**

giraffe *noun* (*plural* **giraffes**) a tall African wild animal with a long neck and long legs

girder *noun* (*plural* **girders**) a strong metal beam supporting part of a building or bridge

girl *noun* (*plural* **girls**) 1 a female child 2 a young woman **girlhood** *noun* the time of being a girl **girlish** *adjective* like a girl

girlfriend *noun* (*plural* **girlfriends**) a female friend or lover

girth *noun* (*plural* **girths**) the measurement round something

gist *noun* (*pronounced* jist) the main points or general meaning of a speech or conversation

give *verb* (**gives, giving, gave, given**) 1 to let someone have something to use or keep ▶ *She gave me a small box of chocolates.* ▶ *Let me give you some advice.* 2 to pay ▶ *I'll give £20 for it.* 3 to make a sudden sound or movement ▶ *He gave a loud gasp.* 4 to present or perform something ▶ *They are giving a concert to raise money.* **give away** to betray someone or something **give in** to surrender **give up** to stop doing or trying something **give way** to break or collapse **giver** *noun*

glacier *noun* (*plural* **glaciers**) (*pronounced* **glas-i-er**) a mass of ice that moves slowly down a high valley

glad *adjective* (**gladder, gladdest**) pleased; happy **be glad of** to be grateful for something **gladly** *adverb* **gladness** *noun*

gladden *verb* (**gladdens, gladdening, gladdened**) to make someone glad

gladiator *noun* (*plural* **gladiators**) in ancient Rome, a man who fought with a sword or other weapons at public shows

glamour *noun* beauty or attractiveness that is exciting **glamorous** *adjective*

glance *verb* (**glances, glancing, glanced**) 1 to look at something quickly 2 to hit something and slide off it ▶ *The ball glanced off his bat.*

glance *noun* (*plural* **glances**) a quick look

gland *noun* (*plural* **glands**) an organ that separates substances from the blood, so that the body can use them or get rid of them

glare *verb* (**glares, glaring, glared**) 1 to shine with a bright light 2 to look angrily at someone

glare *noun* (*plural* **glares**) 1 a strong light 2 an angry look

glass *noun* (*plural* **glasses**) 1 a hard brittle substance that lets light through 2 a container made of glass, for drinking out of 3 a mirror or lens **glassy** *adjective* like glass

glasses *plural noun* a frame with lenses that you wear over your eyes to improve your sight

glaze *verb* (**glazes, glazing, glazed**) 1 to put glass into a window 2 to give pottery a shiny surface

glaze *noun* (*plural* **glazes**) a shiny surface

glazier *noun* (*plural* **glaziers**) someone who fits glass into windows and doors

gleam *noun* (*plural* **gleams**) a beam of soft light

gleam *verb* (**gleams, gleaming, gleamed**) to shine softly

glee *noun* delight; joy **gleeful** *adjective*

glen *noun* (*plural* **glens**) a narrow valley

glide *verb* (**glides, gliding, glided**) 1 to fly or move smoothly 2 to fly without using an engine

glider *noun* (*plural* **gliders**) a light aircraft that has no engine and floats on air currents

glimmer *noun* (*plural* **glimmers**) a faint light

glimmer *verb* (**glimmers, glimmering, glimmered**) to shine with a faint light

glimpse *verb* (**glimpses, glimpsing, glimpsed**) to see something briefly

glimpse *noun* (*plural* **glimpses**) a brief view of something

glint *verb* (**glints, glinting, glinted**) to shine with a flash of light

glint *noun* (*plural* **glints**) a brief flash of light

glisten *verb* (**glistens, glistening, glistened**) (*pronounced* **gliss**-en) to shine like something wet

glitter *verb* (**glitters, glittering, glittered**) to shine with tiny flashes of light

glitter *noun* something that glitters

gloat *verb* (**gloats, gloating, gloated**) to be pleased in an unkind way that you have done better than someone else

global *adjective* to do with the whole world **globally** *adverb*

globe *noun* (*plural* **globes**) 1 something shaped like a ball 2 a map of the world on the surface of a globe

gloomy *adjective* (**gloomier, gloomiest**) 1 dark and unpleasant 2 sad or depressed **gloomily** *adverb* **gloominess** *noun*

glorious *adjective* splendid or magnificent

glory *noun* (*plural* **glories**) 1 fame and honour; praise 2 splendour or beauty

gloss *noun* the shine on a smooth surface **glossy** *adjective* shiny

glove *noun* (*plural* **gloves**) a covering for the hand

glow *noun* 1 a brightness and warmth without flames 2 a warm or cheerful feeling ▶ *We felt a glow of pride when our vegetables won a prize at the show.*

glow *verb* (**glows, glowing, glowed**) to shine with a soft light

glower *verb* (**glowers, glowering, glowered**) (*rhymes with* tower) to stare with an angry look

glow-worm *noun* (*plural* **glow-worms**) an insect with a tail that shines green in the dark

glucose *noun* a type of sugar found in fruits and honey

glue *noun* (*plural* **glues**) a thick liquid for sticking things together

glue *verb* (**glues, gluing, glued**) to stick something with glue

glum *adjective* (**glummer, glummest**) sad or depressed

glutton *noun* (*plural* **gluttons**) someone who eats too much **gluttonous** *adjective* **gluttony** *noun* greed

gnat *noun* (*plural* **gnats**) (*pronounced* nat) a tiny fly that bites

gnaw *verb* (**gnaws, gnawing, gnawed**) (*pronounced* naw) to keep biting something

gnome *noun* (*plural* **gnomes**) (*pronounced* nohm) a kind of dwarf in fairy tales that lives underground

go *verb* (**goes, going, went, gone**) 1 to move from one place to another ▶ *Where are you going?* ▶ *We'll have to go soon.* 2 to lead somewhere ▶ *The road on the left goes to the village.* 3 to become ▶ *The fruit has gone mouldy.* 4 to work ▶ *My watch isn't going.* 5 to belong ▶ *The box goes on the top shelf.* 6 to disappear ▶ *My money has gone.* 7 to make a sound ▶ *The gun went bang.* **be going to** to be ready to do something **go in for** to take part in a competition or race **go off** to explode **go on** to happen or continue ▶ *What's going on?*

go *noun* (*plural* **goes**) 1 a turn or try ▶ *James wanted to have a go.* 2 (informal) energy or liveliness ▶ *He is always full of go.*

goal *noun* (*plural* **goals**) 1 the two posts that the ball must go between to score a point in football, hockey, and other games 2 a point scored by doing this 3 something that you try to do or to achieve

goalkeeper *noun* (*plural* **goalkeepers**) the player who guards the goal in football and hockey

goalpost *noun* (*plural* **goalposts**) each of the upright posts of a goal in sports

goat *noun* (*plural* **goats**) a farm animal with horns

gobble *verb* (**gobbles**, **gobbling**, **gobbled**) to eat something quickly and greedily

goblin *noun* (*plural* **goblins**) an ugly and mischievous creature in stories

God *noun* the creator of the universe in some religions

god *noun* (*plural* **gods**) a male being that is worshipped

godchild *noun* (*plural* **godchildren**) a child who has a godparent. A boy is a **godson** and a girl is a **god-daughter**.

goddess *noun* (*plural* **goddesses**) a female being that is worshipped

godparent *noun* (*plural* **godparents**) a person who promises to see that a child is brought up as a Christian. A man is a **godfather** and a woman is a **godmother**.

goggles *plural noun* large glasses that you wear to protect your eyes from wind, water, or dust, or from chemicals in laboratories

gold *noun* **1** a precious yellow metal used to make jewellery **2** a bright yellow colour **golden** *adjective*

goldfinch *noun* (*plural* **goldfinches**) a small brightly-coloured bird with yellow wing feathers

goldfish *noun* (*plural* **goldfish**) a small red or orange fish kept as a pet

golf *noun* an outdoor game played on a course by hitting a small ball into a series of small holes, using a club **golfer** *noun*

gondola *noun* (*plural* **gondolas**) (*pronounced* **gon**-do-la) a long narrow boat with high pointed ends, used on the canals in Venice

gondolier *noun* (*plural* **gondoliers**) a person who moves a gondola through the water with a pole

gone past participle of **go** *verb*

gong *noun* (*plural* **gongs**) a large metal disc that makes a deep sound when it is hit with a hammer

good *adjective* (**better**, **best**) **1** of the kind that people like, want, or praise ▸ *I read a good book last night.* **2** honest or well-behaved ▸ *They are very good people.* ▸ *Be a good boy.* **3** kind ▸ *It was good of you to come.* **4** healthy; giving benefit ▸ *Exercise is good for you.* **5** thorough ▸ *Give it a good clean.*

good *noun* **1** something that is good or right ▸ *Do good to others.* **2** benefit or advantage ▸ *I'm telling you for your own good.* **for good** for ever **goodness** *noun*

goodbye *interjection* a word you use when you are leaving someone

Good Friday *noun* the Friday before Easter

goods *plural noun* **1** things that are bought and sold **2** things that are carried on trains or lorries

goose *noun* (*plural* **geese**) a large waterbird with webbed feet

gooseberry *noun* (*plural* **gooseberries**) (*pronounced* **guuz**-be-ri) a small green fruit that grows on a prickly bush

goose pimples *plural noun* small bumps that you get on your skin when you are cold or afraid

gore *verb* (**gores, goring, gored**) (used about an animal) to wound someone with a horn or tusk

gorge *noun* (*plural* **gorges**) a narrow valley with steep sides

gorge *verb* (**gorges, gorging, gorged**) to eat greedily

gorgeous *adjective* magnificent; beautiful

gorilla *noun* (*plural* **gorillas**) a large strong African ape

gorse *noun* a prickly bush with small yellow flowers

gory *adjective* (**gorier, goriest**) having a lot of blood and violence

gosling *noun* (*plural* **goslings**) a young goose

gospel *noun* (*plural* **gospels**) the teaching of Jesus Christ **the Gospels** the first four books of the New Testament, telling of the life of Christ

gossip *noun* unkind talk about other people

gossip *verb* (**gossips, gossiping, gossiped**) to talk unkindly about other people

got past tense and past participle of **get**

govern *verb* (**governs, governing, governed**) to be in charge of a country **governor** *noun* someone who governs a country, or helps to run a school

government *noun* (*plural* **governments**) the group of people who are in charge of a country

gown *noun* (*plural* **gowns**) 1 a loose flowing piece of clothing 2 a long dress worn by a woman

grab *verb* (**grabs, grabbing, grabbed**) to take hold of something suddenly or roughly

grace *noun* (*plural* **graces**) 1 beautiful movement 2 a short prayer before or after a meal

graceful *adjective* beautiful and elegant in movement or shape **gracefully** *adverb* **gracefulness** *noun*

gracious *adjective* 1 kind and pleasant to other people 2 merciful **graciously** *adverb* **graciousness** *noun*

grade *noun* (*plural* **grades**) 1 a step in a scale of quality or size 2 a standard achieved in an exam or piece of work

grade *verb* (**grades, grading, graded**) to sort things into grades

gradient *noun* (*plural* **gradients**) 1 a slope 2 the amount that a road or railway slopes

gradual *adjective* happening slowly but steadily **gradually** *adverb*

graduate *noun* (*plural* **graduates**) someone who has a degree from a university or college

graffiti *plural noun* (*pronounced* gra-fee-tee) words or drawings scribbled on a wall Graffiti is an Italian word meaning 'scratches'.

grain *noun* (*plural* **grains**) 1 the hard seed of a cereal such as wheat or rice 2 cereals when they are growing or after they have been harvested 3 a small amount of something ▸ *Grains of sand had got into my sandwich.* 4 the pattern of lines going through wood

gram *noun* (*plural* **grams**) a unit of weight in the metric system, a thousandth of a kilogram

grammar *noun* the rules for speaking and writing language **grammatical** *adjective* to do with grammar, or following the rules of grammar

granary *noun noun* (*plural* **granaries**) a building used for storing grain

grand *adjective* (**grander, grandest**) splendid or important **grandly** *adverb*

grandad *noun* (*plural* **grandads**) (informal) a name for your grandfather

grandchild *noun* (*plural* **grandchildren**) a child of your son or daughter. A girl is a **granddaughter**, and a boy is a **grandson**.

grandfather *noun* (*plural* **grandfathers**) the father of your mother or father

grandfather clock *noun* (*plural* **grandfather clocks**) a clock in a tall wooden case

grandma *noun* (*plural* **grandmas**) (informal) a name for your grandmother

grandmother *noun* (*plural* **grandmothers**) the mother of your mother or father

grandpa *noun* (*plural* **grandpas**) (informal) a name for your grandfather

grandparent *noun* (*plural* **grandparents**) a grandmother or grandfather

grandstand *noun* (*plural* **grandstands**) a building at a racecourse or sports ground, with an open front for spectators

granite *noun* a hard grey kind of rock used in building

granny *noun* (*plural* **grannies**) (informal) a name for your grandmother

grant *verb* (**grants, granting, granted**) to allow someone to have what they have asked for **take for granted** to assume that something is true or will happen
grant *noun* (*plural* **grants**) a sum of money given for a special purpose

grape *noun* (*plural* **grapes**) a small green or purple fruit that grows in bunches on a vine

grapefruit *noun* (*plural* **grapefruit**) a round yellow fruit like a large orange

graph *noun* (*plural* **graphs**) a diagram with lines drawn across squares, used to show information about numbers and amounts

graphic *adjective* **1** short and lively ► *He gave a graphic description of what happened.* **2** to do with drawing or painting ► *She wants to be a graphic artist.* **graphically** *adverb* in a graphic way

graphics *plural noun* diagrams, lettering, and drawings

grapple *verb* (**grapples, grappling, grappled**) **1** to fight with someone **2** to hold something tightly **3** to try to deal with a problem

grasp *verb* (**grasps, grasping, grasped**) **1** to hold something tightly **2** to understand something
grasp *noun* **1** a firm hold **2** the power to understand things ► *She has a good grasp of geometry.*

grass *noun* (*plural* **grasses**) **1** a green plant with thin stalks **2** a piece of ground covered with grass **grassy** *adjective*

grasshopper *noun* (*plural* **grasshoppers**) a small jumping insect that makes a shrill noise

grate[1] *noun* (*plural* **grates**) a metal frame that keeps coal or wood in a fireplace

grate[2] *verb* (**grates, grating, grated**) **1** to shred something into small pieces **2** to make an unpleasant noise by rubbing something

grateful *adjective* feeling glad that someone has helped you **gratefully** *adverb*

grating *noun* (*plural* **gratings**) a grid of metal bars across an opening

gratitude *noun* being grateful

grave *noun* (*plural* **graves**) the place where a dead body is buried
grave *adjective* (**graver, gravest**) serious or solemn ► *We have had some grave news.*

gravel *noun* small stones and sand, used to make paths **gravelled** *adjective*

gravestone *noun* (*plural* **gravestones**) a stone monument over a grave

graveyard *noun* (*plural* **graveyards**) a place where dead bodies are buried

gravity *noun* **1** the force that pulls everything towards the earth **2** seriousness

gravy *noun* a hot brown sauce made from meat juices

graze *verb* (**grazes, grazing, grazed**) 1 (used about animals) to feed on growing grass 2 to scrape your skin slightly against something rough

graze *noun* (*plural* **grazes**) a sore place where your skin has been scraped

grease *noun* thick fat or oil **greasiness** *noun* **greasy** *adjective*

grease *verb* (**greases, greasing, greased**) to cover or wipe something with grease

great *adjective* (**greater, greatest**) 1 very large 2 very important or distinguished ▶ *He was a great writer.* 3 (informal) very good or enjoyable ▶ *It's great to see you again.* 4 older or younger by one generation, as in *great-grandmother* and *great-grandson* **greatly** *adverb* **greatness** *noun*

greed *noun* being greedy

greedy *adjective* (**greedier, greediest**) wanting more food or money than you need **greedily** *adverb* **greediness** *noun*

Greek *noun* (*plural* **Greeks**) 1 a member of a people living in ancient or modern Greece 2 the language of the Greeks

Greek *adjective* to do with the Greeks or their language

green *adjective* (**greener, greenest**) 1 having the colour of grass and leaves 2 concerned with protecting the natural environment

green *noun* (*plural* **greens**) 1 the colour of grass and leaves 2 an open area covered with grass

greenery *noun* green leaves or plants

greengage *noun* (*plural* **greengages**) a green kind of plum

greengrocer *noun* (*plural* **greengrocers**) a shopkeeper who sells fruit and vegetables

greenhouse *noun* (*plural* **greenhouses**) a glass building that is kept warm inside for growing plants

greenhouse effect *noun* the warming of the earth's surface by gases which trap heat in the earth's atmosphere

greens *plural noun* green vegetables such as cabbage and spinach

greet *verb* (**greets, greeting, greeted**) to welcome someone when they arrive

greeting *noun* (*plural* **greetings**) the words you use to welcome someone **greetings** good wishes

grenade *noun* (*plural* **grenades**) a small bomb thrown by hand

grew past tense of **grow**

grey *adjective* (**greyer, greyest**) having a colour between black and white, like ashes or dark clouds

grey *noun* the colour of ashes or dark clouds

greyhound *noun* (*plural* **greyhounds**) a slim dog with long legs, used in racing

grid *noun* (*plural* **grids**) a pattern of lines crossing each other to form squares

grief *noun* great sadness or sorrow when someone has died

grievance *noun* (*plural* **grievances**) something that you want to complain about

grieve *verb* (**grieves, grieving, grieved**) to feel sad or sorrowful when someone has died

grill *noun* (*plural* **grills**) part of a cooker that sends heat downwards

grill *verb* (**grills, grilling, grilled**) to cook food under a grill

grille *noun* (*plural* **grilles**) a grating

grim *adjective* (**grimmer, grimmest**) 1 stern or severe 2 frightening or unpleasant ▶ *Being lost on the moors was a grim experience.*

grimace *noun* (*plural* **grimaces**) a strange or twisted expression on your face

grime *noun* a layer of dirt on a surface **grimy** *adjective*

grin *noun* (*plural* **grins**) a broad smile

grin *verb* (**grins, grinning, grinned**) to smile broadly

grind *verb* (**grinds, grinding, ground**) 1 to crush something hard into a powder 2 to sharpen or polish something by rubbing it on a rough surface **grinder** *noun*

grip *verb* (**grips, gripping, gripped**) to hold something tightly
grip *noun* (*plural* **grips**) 1 a firm hold on something 2 a handle

gripping *adjective* holding your attention because it is interesting or exciting

grisly *adjective* (**grislier, grisliest**) (*pronounced* griz-li) disgusting or horrible ▸ *They came across the grisly remains of a dead sheep.*

gristle *noun* (*pronounced* gris-el) the tough rubbery part of meat **gristly** *adjective*

grit *noun* 1 tiny pieces of stone or sand 2 courage or determination **gritty** *adjective*
grit *verb* (**grits, gritting, gritted**) 1 to clench your teeth tightly 2 to put grit on a road

grizzly bear *noun* (*plural* **grizzly bears**) a large bear of North America

groan *verb* (**groans, groaning, groaned**) to make a long deep sound when in pain or distress
groan *noun* (*plural* **groans**) a sound of groaning

grocer *noun* (*plural* **grocers**) a shopkeeper who sells food and other household goods

groceries *plural noun* things you buy in a grocer's shop

groin *noun* (*plural* **groins**) the flat part where your thighs join the rest of your body

groom *noun* (*plural* **grooms**) 1 someone who looks after horses 2 a bridegroom
groom *verb* (**grooms, grooming, groomed**) to clean and brush a horse's coat

groove *noun* (*plural* **grooves**) a long narrow channel cut in a surface

grope *verb* (**gropes, groping, groped**) to feel about for something you cannot see

gross *adjective* (**grosser, grossest**) 1 fat and ugly 2 having bad manners; crude or vulgar 3 very bad or shocking ▸ *Leaving the baby alone in the house was gross stupidity.* 4 total; without anything taken off ▸ *What is your gross income?*
gross *noun* (*plural* **gross**) twelve dozen or 144

grotesque *adjective* (*pronounced* groh-tesk) strange and ugly

grotto *noun* (*plural* **grottos**) a small attractive cave

ground[1] *noun* (*plural* **grounds**) 1 the surface of the earth 2 a sports field

ground[2] past tense and past participle of **grind**

groundless *adjective* without a reason or motive

grounds *plural noun* 1 the gardens of a large house 2 reasons ▸ *There are good grounds for suspecting their story.* 3 bits of coffee or dregs at the bottom of a cup

groundsheet *noun* (*plural* **groundsheets**) a waterproof sheet for spreading on the ground to put a tent over

group *noun* (*plural* **groups**) 1 a number of people, animals, or things that belong together 2 several musicians who play or sing together
group *verb* (**groups, grouping, grouped**) to make things into a group

grouse *noun* (*plural* **grouse**) a large bird that some people shoot as a sport
grouse *verb* (**grouses, grousing, groused**) to grumble or complain

grove *noun* (*plural* **groves**) a small wood

grovel *verb* (**grovels, grovelling, grovelled**) 1 to crawl along the ground 2 to be extremely humble and obedient towards someone when you want something from them

grow *verb* (**grows, growing, grew, grown**) 1 to become bigger or taller 2 (used about seeds and plants) to develop in the ground 3 to plant something in the ground and look after it ▸ *She grows lovely roses.* 4 to become something ▸ *He quickly grew angry.* **grow up** to become an adult

growl *verb* (**growls, growling, growled**) to make a deep rough sound in the throat
growl *noun* (*plural* **growls**) a deep rough sound

grown-up *noun* (*plural* **grown-ups**) an adult

growth noun (plural **growths**) 1 the process of growing or developing 2 something unwanted that has grown in the body

grub noun (plural **grubs**) 1 a tiny creature that will become an insect; a larva 2 (slang) food

grubby adjective (**grubbier**, **grubbiest**) rather dirty

grudge noun (plural **grudges**) a feeling of dislike or anger for someone because of something they have done
grudge verb (**grudges**, **grudging**, **grudged**) to feel angry that someone has something **grudging** adjective

gruelling adjective difficult and tiring
▶ They looked tired after their gruelling journey.

gruesome adjective horrible or disgusting

gruff adjective (**gruffer**, **gruffest**) having a rough unfriendly voice or manner **gruffly** adverb **gruffness** noun

grumble verb (**grumbles**, **grumbling**, **grumbled**) to complain in a bad-tempered way

grumpy adjective (**grumpier**, **grumpiest**) bad-tempered **grumpily** adverb

grunt verb (**grunts**, **grunting**, **grunted**) to make a snorting sound like a pig
grunt noun (plural **grunts**) a snorting sound

guarantee noun (plural **guarantees**) a promise to repair or replace something if it goes wrong after you have bought it
guarantee verb (**guarantees**, **guaranteeing**, **guaranteed**) to promise to do something

guard verb (**guards**, **guarding**, **guarded**) 1 to keep someone or something safe 2 to watch someone to prevent them from escaping
guard noun (plural **guards**) 1 protecting or guarding ▶ Keep the prisoners under close guard. 2 someone who watches or protects a person or place 3 an official in charge of a railway train 4 a shield or device protecting people from a danger ▶ We need a guard for the coal fire.

guardian noun (plural **guardians**) someone who is legally in charge of a child instead of the child's parents

guerrilla noun (plural **guerrillas**) (pronounced ge-ril-a) a member of a small army or band that fights by means of surprise attacks
This word comes from the Spanish word guerra meaning 'war'.

guess noun (plural **guesses**) an opinion or answer that you give without being sure
guess verb (**guesses**, **guessing**, **guessed**) to make a guess

guesswork noun something you do by guessing

guest noun (plural **guests**) (pronounced gest) someone who is staying at another person's house or at a hotel

guidance noun guiding or giving help

guide noun (plural **guides**) someone who shows people the way or helps them **Guide** a member of the Girl Guides Association, an organization for girls
guide verb (**guides**, **guiding**, **guided**) to show someone the way or help them do something

guidebook noun (plural **guidebooks**) a book with information for visitors to a place

guide dog noun (plural **guide dogs**) a dog that is trained to lead a blind person

guided missile noun (plural **guided missiles**) an explosive rocket that is guided to its target from the ground

guillotine noun (plural **guillotines**) (pronounced gil-o-teen) 1 a machine once used in France for beheading people 2 a device with a sharp blade for cutting paper
The word **guillotine** is named after a French doctor named Joseph Guillotin, who suggested using it in France, although he did not invent it.

guilt noun (pronounced gilt) the fact that you have done something wrong, or the bad feeling you have about it

guilty adjective (**guiltier**, **guiltiest**) (pronounced gil-ti) having done something wrong **guiltily** adverb

guinea pig *noun* (*plural* **guinea pigs**)
1 a small furry animal without a tail, kept as a pet 2 a person who is used in an experiment

guitar *noun* (*plural* **guitars**) a musical instrument played by plucking its strings **guitarist** *noun*

gulf *noun* (*plural* **gulfs**) a large area of sea partly surrounded by land

gull *noun* (*plural* **gulls**) a large seabird

gullet *noun* (*plural* **gullets**) the tube leading from the throat to the stomach

gully *noun* (*plural* **gullies**) a narrow channel that carries water

gulp *verb* (**gulps, gulping, gulped**) to swallow something quickly or greedily
gulp *noun* (*plural* **gulps**) a loud swallowing noise

gum *noun* (*plural* **gums**) 1 the firm fleshy part of your mouth that holds your teeth 2 thick glue 3 chewing gum

gun *noun* (*plural* **guns**) a weapon that fires bullets or shells from a metal tube
gun *verb* (**guns, gunning, gunned**) **gun down** to kill someone with a gun

gunboat *noun* (*plural* **gunboats**) a small warship

gunfire *noun* the firing of guns

gunman *noun* (*plural* **gunmen**) a man armed with a gun

gunpowder *noun* a type of explosive

gurgle *verb* (**gurgles, gurgling, gurgled**) to make a bubbling sound

guru *noun* (*plural* **gurus**) a Hindu religious teacher

gush *verb* (**gushes, gushing, gushed**) to flow fast and strongly

gust *noun* (*plural* **gusts**) a sudden rush of wind or rain **gusty** *adjective*

gut *verb* (**guts, gutting, gutted**) to remove the insides from a dead fish before cooking it

gutted *adjective* (describing a building) destroyed by fire

guts *plural noun* 1 the insides of a person or animal 2 (informal) courage

gutter *noun* (*plural* **gutters**) a narrow channel for carrying away rainwater

guy *noun* (*plural* **guys**) 1 a figure of Guy Fawkes, burnt on or near 5 November in memory of the Gunpowder Plot to blow up Parliament in 1605 2 (informal) a man

guy rope *noun* (*plural* **guy ropes**) a rope used to hold a tent in place

guzzle *verb* (**guzzles, guzzling, guzzled**) to eat or drink greedily

gym *noun* (*plural* **gyms**) (*pronounced* jim) (informal) 1 a gymnasium 2 gymnastics

gymkhana *noun* (*plural* **gymkhanas**) (*pronounced* jim-kah-na) a competition for horses and riders

gymnasium *noun* (*plural* **gymnasiums**) a place equipped for gymnastics

gymnast *noun* (*plural* **gymnasts**) someone who does gymnastics

gymnastics *plural noun* exercises and movements to strengthen your body and show how agile you are

gypsy *noun* (*plural* **gypsies**) a member of a community of people, also called **travellers**, who live in caravans and travel from place to place

Hh

habit *noun* (*plural* **habits**) something you do so often that you no longer think about it **habitual** *adjective* done often or as a habit **habitually** *adverb*

habitat *noun* (*plural* **habitats**) the natural home of an animal or plant

hack *verb* (**hacks, hacking, hacked**) to chop or cut something roughly

hacker *noun* (*plural* **hackers**) someone who gets access to a computer system without permission

hacksaw *noun* (*plural* **hacksaws**) a saw for cutting metal

had past tense and past participle of **have**

haddock *noun* (*plural* **haddock**) a sea fish used for food

hadn't short for *had not* ▸ *They hadn't seen us.*

hag *noun* (*plural* **hags**) an ugly old woman

haggard *adjective* looking very tired or unwell

haggis *noun* (*plural* **haggises**) a Scottish food made from parts of a sheep and oatmeal

haggle *verb* (**haggles, haggling, haggled**) to argue about the price of something

hail *noun* frozen drops of rain
hail *verb* (**hails, hailing, hailed**) 1 to fall as hail 2 to call out to someone

hair *noun* (*plural* **hairs**) 1 the soft covering that grows on the heads and bodies of people and animals 2 one of the strands that form this covering

hairbrush *noun* (*plural* **hairbrushes**) a brush for tidying your hair

haircut *noun* (*plural* **haircuts**) the cutting of a person's hair, or the style in which it is cut

hairdresser *noun* (*plural* **hairdressers**) someone who cuts and arranges people's hair

hair-raising *adjective* terrifying or dangerous

hairy *adjective* (**hairier, hairiest**) having a lot of hair **hairiness** *noun*

halal *noun* meat prepared according to Muslim law

half *noun* (*plural* **halves**) each of two equal parts of something
half *adverb* partly; not completely ▸ *The potatoes are only half cooked.*

half-hearted *adjective* not very enthusiastic **half-heartedly** *adverb*

half-mast *noun* the position of a flag halfway down its flagpole, as a sign that someone important has died

half-term *noun* (*plural* **half-terms**) a short holiday in the middle of a school term

half-time *noun* an interval halfway through a game

halfway *adverb* and *adjective* at a point half the distance between two places

hall *noun* (*plural* **halls**) 1 a large room for meetings, concerts, or other large gatherings of people 2 a large building or house 3 an area or passage inside the front door of a house

hallo *interjection* another spelling of **hello**

Hallowe'en *noun* the evening of 31 October, when people used to think that ghosts and witches might appear

hallucination *noun* (*plural* **hallucinations**) something you think you can see or hear when it is not really there

halo *noun* (*plural* **haloes**) a circle of light shown round the head of a saint in a picture

halt *verb* (**halts, halting, halted**) to stop or make something stop

halter *noun* (*plural* **halters**) a rope or strap put round a horse's head to control it

halve *verb* (**halves, halving, halved**) (*pronounced* harv) 1 to divide something into halves 2 to reduce something to half its size

halves plural of **half** *noun*

ham *noun* (*plural* **hams**) meat from a pig's leg

hamburger *noun* (*plural* **hamburgers**) a round flat cake of fried minced beef in a bread roll

hamlet *noun* (*plural* **hamlets**) a small village of a few houses

hammer *noun* (*plural* **hammers**) a tool with a heavy metal head, used for hitting nails

hammer *verb* (**hammers, hammering, hammered**) 1 to hit something with a hammer 2 to knock loudly ▶ *Someone was hammering on the door.* 3 (informal) to defeat an opponent by a wide margin

hammock *noun* (*plural* **hammocks**) a long piece of cloth or net hung up above the ground and used to lie or sleep on

hamper *noun* (*plural* **hampers**) a large basket with a lid

hamper *verb* (**hampers, hampering, hampered**) to get in someone's way or make it difficult for them to do something ▶ *Thick foliage outside the prison walls hampered the escape.*

hamster *noun* (*plural* **hamsters**) a small furry animal with cheek pouches, kept as a pet

hand *noun* (*plural* **hands**) 1 the part of your body at the end of your arm 2 a pointer on a clock or dial 3 a member of a ship's crew 4 the cards held by one player in a card game **at hand** near or close by **give a hand** to help someone **out of hand** out of control

hand *verb* (**hands, handing, handed**) to pass something to someone with your hands

handbag *noun* (*plural* **handbags**) a small bag for holding money and personal items

handcuffs *plural noun* a pair of metal rings joined by a short chain, used for locking a prisoner's wrists together

handful *noun* (*plural* **handfuls**) 1 as much as you can carry in one hand 2 a small number of people or things 3 (informal) someone who is difficult to control

handicap *noun* (*plural* **handicaps**) 1 something that makes it difficult to do things 2 a disability affecting a person **handicapped** *adjective*

handicraft *noun* (*plural* **handicrafts**) artistic work done with your hands, such as woodwork and pottery

handiwork *noun* something done or made with your hands

handkerchief *noun* (*plural* **handkerchiefs**) (*pronounced* **hang-ker-cheef**) a square piece of cloth for wiping your nose

handle *noun* (*plural* **handles**) the part of a thing you use to hold or control it

handle *verb* (**handles, handling, handled**) 1 to touch or feel something with your hands 2 to deal with a problem

handlebars *plural noun* a bar with handles at the front of a bicycle or motorcycle, used by the rider for steering

handsome *adjective* (**handsomer, handsomest**) 1 attractive or good-looking 2 generous ▶ *After a few years the company made a handsome profit.*

handstand *noun* (*plural* **handstands**) an exercise in which you balance on your hands with your feet in the air

handwriting *noun* writing done by hand **handwritten** *adjective*

handy *adjective* (**handier, handiest**) 1 useful or easy to use ▶ *A tin-opener would be handy.* 2 in a convenient place ▶ *The house is handy for the station.* 3 clever at doing practical things ▶ *She's handy at putting up pictures.*

hang *verb* (**hangs, hanging, hung**) 1 to fix the top part of something so that the lower part is free 2 to paste wallpaper in strips on to a wall 3 (in this meaning, the past tense and past participle are **hanged**) to execute someone by hanging them from a rope that tightens around the neck **hang about** or **hang around** to wait around with nothing to do **hang on** (informal) to wait ▶ *Could you hang on a moment?* **hang on to** to hold something tightly **hang up** to end a telephone call by putting down the receiver

hangar *noun* (*plural* **hangars**) a large shed used for keeping aircraft

hanger *noun* (*plural* **hangers**) a device with a hook, for hanging clothes on

hang-glider *noun* (*plural* **hang-gliders**) a device like a large kite on which a person can glide through the air for sport **hang-gliding** *noun*

hanker *verb* (**hankers, hankering, hankered**) to want something badly ▸ *Even now, she still hankered to go back.*

hanky *noun* (*plural* **hankies**) (*informal*) a handkerchief

Hanukkah *noun* (*pronounced* **han-ook-a**) a Jewish festival held in December

haphazard *adjective* (*pronounced* **hap-haz-erd**) done or chosen by chance, without planning

happen *verb* (**happens, happening, happened**) to take place or occur **happen to** to do something by chance without planning it ▸ *I happened to be at the bus stop when they drove past.*

happening *noun* (*plural* **happenings**) something that happens; an event

happy *adjective* (**happier, happiest**) 1 pleased or contented 2 lucky, fortunate ▸ *By a happy chance they were still at home when we called.* **happily** *adverb* **happiness** *noun*

harass *verb* (**harass, harassing, harassed**) (*pronounced* **ha-ras**) to keep annoying or troubling someone **harassment** *noun*

harbour *noun* (*plural* **harbours**) a place where ships can shelter or unload

harbour *verb* (**harbours, harbouring, harboured**) to give someone shelter or a place to hide

hard *adjective* (**harder, hardest**) 1 firm or solid; not soft ▸ *There had been a frost and the ground was hard.* 2 difficult ▸ *She asks hard questions.* 3 severe or harsh ▸ *It was a hard frost.* 4 energetic; using great effort ▸ *Jackie is a hard worker.* **hard up** short of money

hard *adverb* (**harder, hardest**) with great effort ▸ *We try to work hard.*

hardboard *noun* stiff board made from squashed wood pulp

hard disk *noun* (*plural* **hard disks**) a disk fitted inside a computer, able to store large amounts of data

harden *verb* (**hardens, hardening, hardened**) 1 to make something hard 2 to become hard

hard-hearted *adjective* uncaring; not having much sympathy

hardly *adverb* only just; only with difficulty ▸ *He was hardly able to speak, he was so nervous.*

hardship *noun* (*plural* **hardships**) 1 suffering or difficulty 2 something that causes suffering

hardware *noun* 1 household tools and implements 2 the machinery of a computer

hardy *adjective* (**hardier, hardiest**) able to endure cold or difficult conditions

hare *noun* (*plural* **hares**) a fast-running animal like a large rabbit

harm *verb* (**harms, harming, harmed**) to hurt or damage someone or something

harm *noun* injury or damage

harmful *adjective* causing harm or damage

harmless *adjective* safe; not causing harm

harmonica *noun* (*plural* **harmonicas**) a mouth organ

harmonize *verb* (**harmonizes, harmonizing, harmonized**) to combine together in an effective or pleasing way

harmony *noun* (*plural* **harmonies**) 1 a pleasing combination of musical notes 2 agreement; friendship **harmonious** *adjective*

harness *noun* (*plural* **harnesses**) a set of straps put over a horse's head and neck to control it

harness *verb* (**harnesses, harnessing, harnessed**) 1 to put a harness on a horse 2 to make use of something ▸ *We can harness the winds to make energy.*

harp *noun* (*plural* **harps**) a musical instrument made of strings stretched across a frame and plucked with the fingers **harpist** *noun* someone who plays the harp

harp *verb* (**harps, harping, harped**) **harp on** to go on talking about something in a tiresome way ▸ *He keeps harping on about his new bike.*

harpoon *noun* (*plural* **harpoons**) a spear attached to a rope, fired from a gun to catch whales

harpsichord *noun* (*plural* **harpsichords**) a musical instrument like a piano but with the strings plucked and not struck

harrow *noun* (*plural* **harrows**) a heavy device pulled over the ground to break up the soil

harsh *adjective* (**harsher, harshest**) **1** cruel or severe **2** rough and unpleasant **harshly** *adverb* **harshness** *noun*

harvest *noun* (*plural* **harvests**) **1** the time for cutting and gathering in corn, fruit, or vegetables **2** the crop that is gathered in **harvest** *verb* (**harvests, harvesting, harvested**) to gather in crops

has a form of **have**

hasn't short for *has not* ▸ *It hasn't rained at all today.*

hassle *noun* (*plural* **hassles**) (*informal*) something that is difficult or troublesome

haste *noun* doing things too quickly

hasten *verb* (**hastens, hastening, hastened**) (*pronounced* **hay**-sen) to hurry

hasty *adjective* (**hastier, hastiest**) (*pronounced* **hay**-sti) done too quickly **hastily** *adverb*

hat *noun* (*plural* **hats**) a covering for the head

hatch *noun* (*plural* **hatches**) an opening in a floor or wall

hatch *verb* (**hatches, hatching, hatched**) **1** (used about a bird or reptile) to break out of an egg **2** to keep an egg warm until a young bird hatches from it **3** to form a plan

hatchback *noun* (*plural* **hatchbacks**) a car with a rear door hinged at the top

hatchet *noun* (*plural* **hatchets**) a small axe

hate *verb* (**hates, hating, hated**) to dislike someone or something very much **hate** *noun* (*plural* **hates**) a strong dislike

hateful *adjective* hated; very unpleasant

hatred *noun* (*pronounced* **hay**-trid) a feeling of strong dislike

hat trick *noun* (*plural* **hat tricks**) three successes or victories in a row

haughty *adjective* (**haughtier, haughtiest**) (*pronounced* **haw**-ti) proud of yourself and looking down on other people **haughtily** *adverb* **haughtiness** *noun*

haul *verb* (**hauls, hauling, hauled**) to pull something using a lot of power or strength **haul** *noun* (*plural* **hauls**) an amount of something won or taken ▸ *The trawler brought home a large haul of fish.*

haunt *verb* (**haunts, haunting, haunted**) (used about a ghost) to visit a place often

have *verb* (**has, having, had**) **1** to own or possess something ▸ *We have a dog and a hamster.* **2** to contain something ▸ *Their new house has two bathrooms and a study.* **3** to organize an event ▸ *Next week we're having a party.* **4** to experience something ▸ *I'm afraid she has had an accident.* **5** to get something done ▸ *I'm having my watch mended.* **6** to receive something ▸ *I've had a letter from my cousin.* **have to** to be obliged or forced to do something ▸ *We have to go now.*

The verb **have** can also be used to help make other verbs. ▶ *They have gone.* ▶ *Has he seen my book?* ▶ *We had eaten them..*

haven *noun* (*plural* **havens**) (*pronounced* hay-ven) a safe place

haven't short for *have not* ▶ *I haven't been to Germany.*

havoc *noun* great confusion or destruction

hawk *noun* (*plural* **hawks**) a bird of prey with strong eyesight

hawthorn *noun* (*plural* **hawthorns**) a thorny tree with small red berries

hay *noun* dried grass used as food for animals

hay fever *noun* an allergy to pollen, causing irritation of the nose, throat, and eyes

haystack *noun* (*plural* **haystacks**) a pile of stored hay made into a neat stack

hazard *noun* (*plural* **hazards**) a risk or danger **hazardous** *adjective* risky

haze *noun* a thin mist

hazel *noun* (*plural* **hazels**) 1 a type of small nut tree 2 a nut from this tree 3 a light brown colour
hazel *adjective* having a light brown colour

hazy *adjective* (**hazier, haziest**) 1 misty 2 uncertain or unclear ▶ *He has only a hazy memory of what happened.* **hazily** *adverb* **haziness** *noun*

he *pronoun* used as the subject of a verb to talk about a male person or animal already mentioned

head¹ *noun* (*plural* **heads**) 1 the top part of the body, containing the brain, eyes, and mouth 2 the top or front part of something ▶ *The dog waited at the head of the stairs.* 3 the broad top part of something, such as a pin or nail 4 the person in charge ▶ *His uncle was the head of a large building firm.* **keep your head** to stay calm
head *verb* (**heads, heading, headed**) 1 to be in charge of something ▶ *She heads a research team.* 2 in some ball games, to hit the ball with the head 3 to start going in a certain direction ▶ *After a while they headed for home.*

headache *noun* (*plural* **headaches**) a pain in your head

headdress *noun* (*plural* **headdresses**) a covering or band worn as a decoration for the head

heading *noun* (*plural* **headings**) words at the top of a piece of printing or writing

headlight *noun* (*plural* **headlights**) a strong light at the front of a vehicle

headline *noun* (*plural* **headlines**) a heading in large print in a newspaper or magazine

headlong *adverb* and *adjective* 1 falling with the head forward 2 in a hasty or thoughtless way

head-on *adverb* and *adjective* with the front parts hitting each other ▶ *Two lorries collided head-on at the crossroads.*

headphones *plural noun* a device that fits over your head so that you can listen privately to speech or music

headquarters *noun* (*plural* **headquarters**) the central office from which an organization is controlled

headteacher *noun* (*plural* **headteachers**) the person in charge of a school

heal *verb* (**heals, healing, healed**) 1 to make someone healthy again 2 to become healthy **healer** *noun*

health *noun* how well or ill a person is ▶ *His health is good for his age.*

healthy *adjective* (**healthier, healthiest**) 1 free from illness; having good health 2 leading to good health ▶ *Fresh air is healthy.* **healthily** *adverb* **healthiness** *noun*

heap *noun* (*plural* **heaps**) an untidy pile **heaps** (*informal*) a large amount ▶ *We've got heaps of time.*
heap *verb* (**heaps, heaping, heaped**) to put things in a heap

hear *verb* (**hears, hearing, heard**) 1 to take in sounds through your ears 2 to receive news or information

hearing *noun* (*plural* **hearings**) 1 the ability to hear 2 a chance to be heard 3 a trial in court

hearing aid *noun* (*plural* **hearing aids**) a small device that a deaf person puts into their ear to make them hear better

hearse *noun* (*plural* **hearses**) a large black car that takes a coffin to a funeral

heart *noun* (*plural* **hearts**) 1 the organ that pumps blood round the body 2 the middle or most important part of something 3 a person's feelings or emotions; sympathy 4 courage or enthusiasm ► *We could tell that the team had lost heart.* 5 a playing card with the shape of a heart printed on it **break someone's heart** to make someone very unhappy **by heart** by using your memory

heart attack *noun* (*plural* **heart attacks**) a sudden failure of the heart to work properly, causing pain and sometimes death

hearth *noun* (*plural* **hearths**) (*pronounced* hahth) the floor of a fireplace

heartless *adjective* showing no feeling or pity **heartlessly** *adverb* **heartlessness** *noun*

hearty *adjective* (**heartier, heartiest**) 1 strong and vigorous ► *Jim always had a hearty appetite.* 2 enthusiastic; sincere ► *They gave us a hearty welcome.* **heartily** *adverb* **heartiness** *noun*

heat *noun* (*plural* **heats**) 1 being hot; great warmth 2 a first stage in a sports competition to decide who will take part in the finals
heat *verb* (**heats, heating, heated**) 1 to make something hot 2 to become hot

heater *noun* (*plural* **heaters**) a device for making a room or car warmer

heath *noun* (*plural* **heaths**) a piece of wild flat land covered with heather or bushes

heather *noun* (*pronounced* he-ther) a low-growing bush with small purple, pink, or white flowers

heatwave *noun* (*plural* **heatwaves**) a long period of hot weather

heave *verb* (**heaves, heaving, heaved** or, in the ship meaning, **hove**) to lift or move something with great effort **heave a sigh** to sigh deeply **heave to** (used about a ship) to stop without anchoring or mooring

heaven *noun* 1 the place where God and the angels are thought to live 2 a very pleasant place or condition **the heavens** the sky

heavenly *adjective* 1 to do with the sky or in the sky 2 (informal) very pleasing or delicious

heavy *adjective* (**heavier, heaviest**) 1 weighing a lot; hard to lift or carry 2 strong or severe ► *Heavy rain was falling.* 3 hard or difficult ► *It was heavy work digging the garden.* **heavily** *adverb* **heaviness** *noun*

heavyweight *noun* (*plural* **heavyweights**) a boxer or wrestler of the heaviest weight

Hebrew *noun* the language of the ancient Jews, or a modern form used in Israel

hectare *noun* (*plural* **hectares**) (*pronounced* hek-tar) a unit of area equal to 10,000 square metres or about 2 ½ acres

hectic *adjective* very active or busy

hedge *noun* (*plural* **hedges**) a row of bushes forming a boundary round a garden or field

hedgehog *noun* (*plural* **hedgehogs**) a small animal covered with prickles, which rolls into a ball when threatened

hedgerow *noun* (*plural* **hedgerows**) a row of bushes forming a hedge by the side of a road

heed *verb* (**heeds, heeding, heeded**) to pay attention to something ► *You should have heeded my warning.*
heed *noun* care or attention ► *We shouted, but they took no heed.*

heedless *adjective* taking no notice

heel *noun* (*plural* **heels**) 1 the back part of your foot 2 the part of a sock or shoe that fits the heel

hefty *adjective* (**heftier, heftiest**) big and strong

heifer *noun* (*plural* **heifers**) (*pronounced* hef-er) a young cow

height *noun* (*plural* **heights**) **1** how high someone or something is **2** the highest or most important part of something ▸ *Our holiday will be at the height of the summer season.*

heir *noun* (*plural* **heirs**) (*pronounced* air) a person who will inherit somebody's property or title

heiress *noun* (*plural* **heiresses**) (*pronounced* air-ess) a girl or woman who will inherit somebody's property or title

held past tense and past participle of **hold** *verb*

helicopter *noun* (*plural* **helicopters**) a kind of aircraft without wings, lifted by a large horizontal propeller on top

helium *noun* (*pronounced* hee-li-um) a light gas used in balloons and airships

hell *noun* **1** in some religions, a place where wicked people are thought to be punished after they die **2** a very unpleasant place or situation ▸ *The town centre can be hell on Saturday mornings.*

hello *interjection* a word used to greet someone or to attract their attention

helm *noun* (*plural* **helms**) the handle or wheel used to steer a ship

helmet *noun* (*plural* **helmets**) a strong hard hat that you wear to protect your head

help *verb* (**helps, helping, helped**) **1** to do something useful for someone **2** to avoid doing something ▸ *I couldn't help sneezing.* **helper** *noun*

help *noun* (*plural* **helps**) **1** something useful you do for someone ▸ *Do you need any help?* **2** someone who does something useful ▸ *They were a great help at the party.*

helpful *adjective* giving help; useful **helpfully** *adverb* **helpfulness** *noun*

helping *noun* (*plural* **helpings**) a portion of food at a meal

helpless *adjective* not able to do things or look after yourself **helplessly** *adverb* **helplessness** *noun*

helter-skelter *noun* (*plural* **helter-skelters**) a spiral slide at a fair

hem *noun* (*plural* **hems**) the edge of a piece of cloth that is folded over and sewn down

hem *verb* (**hems, hemming, hemmed**) hem in to surround someone and stop them moving

hemisphere *noun* (*plural* **hemispheres**) each half of the earth, the northern hemisphere and the southern hemisphere

hen *noun* (*plural* **hens**) a female chicken or other bird

hence *adverb* **1** from this time on **2** therefore

her *pronoun* a word used for **she** when it is the object of a verb, or when it comes after a preposition ▸ *I can see her.* ▸ *He took the books from her.*

her *adjective* belonging to her ▸ *That is her pen.*

herald *noun* (*plural* **heralds**) in earlier times, an official who made announcements or carried important messages

heraldry *noun* the study of family badges and coats of arms **heraldic** *adjective* to do with heraldry

herb *noun* (*plural* **herbs**) a plant used for flavouring food or making medicines **herbal** *adjective* made from herbs

herd *noun* (*plural* **herds**) a group of cattle or other animals that feed together

herd *verb* (**herds, herding, herded**) to gather animals together or move them in a large group

here *adverb* in or to this place **here and there** in various places or directions

hereditary *adjective* able to be passed on from parents to their children **heredity** *noun* the process of passing characteristics from parents to children through the genes

heritage *noun* things that have come down to us from the past, such as music, literature, and ancient buildings

hermit *noun* (*plural* **hermits**) someone who decides to live completely alone

hero *noun* (*plural* **heroes**) 1 a person who has done something very brave 2 the most important man or boy in a story or play **heroic** *adjective* like a hero **heroism** *noun* being a hero
The word **hero** comes from a Greek word *heros*, meaning a brave fighter like the ones who fought in the Trojan War.

heroin *noun* a strong drug that people can become addicted to

heroine *noun* (*plural* **heroines**) 1 a woman or girl who has done something very brave 2 the most important woman or girl in a story or play

heron *noun* (*plural* **herons**) a wading bird with long legs and a long neck

herring *noun* (*plural* **herring** or **herrings**) a sea fish used for food

hers *pronoun* belonging to her ▸ *The pen is hers.*

herself *pronoun* used to refer to the person already mentioned as 'she' ▸ *She has hurt herself.* **by herself** on her own; alone ▸ *She did the work all by herself.*

hesitate *verb* (**hesitates, hesitating, hesitated**) to stop for a moment before you say or do something **hesitant** *adjective* hesitating **hesitation** *noun*

hexagon *noun* (*plural* **hexagons**) a shape with six sides **hexagonal** *adjective*

hibernate *verb* (**hibernates, hibernating, hibernated**) (*pronounced* **hy-ber-nayt**) to pass the winter in a deep sleep, as some animals do **hibernation** *noun*

hiccup *noun* (*plural* **hiccups**) a sudden gasp of breath caused by your diaphragm tightening suddenly, making you let out a sharp noise

hide[1] *verb* (**hides, hiding,** *past tense* **hidden** or **hid,** *past participle* **hidden**) 1 to go somewhere where you cannot be seen ▸ *She hid in the garden until everyone had gone.* 2 to put something in a place where no one can see it ▸ *He hid the book hurriedly under a towel.*

hide[2] *noun* an animal's skin

hide-and-seek *noun* a game in which one person looks for others who are hiding

hideous *adjective* very ugly or unpleasant **hideously** *adverb*

hideout *noun* (*plural* **hideouts**) a place in which to hide

hieroglyphics *plural noun* (*pronounced* **hyr-o-glif-iks**) in ancient Egypt, a system of writing using pictures or symbols to stand for words

higgledy-piggledy *adverb* and *adjective* in a muddle; completely mixed up

high *adjective* (**higher, highest**) 1 reaching up a long way ▸ *The city has many high buildings.* 2 far above the ground or above sea level ▸ *High clouds were passing overhead.* 3 measuring from top to bottom ▸ *The post is two metres high.* 4 more than the normal amount or importance ▸ *His father had a high position in one of the big banks.* ▸ *House prices are higher than last year.* 5 strong ▸ *The bridge had to be closed for a while when the wind was high.* 6 at the top end of a musical scale ▸ *I can't manage the high notes.*

highlands *plural noun* mountainous country, especially in Scotland **highlander** *noun* someone who lives in the highlands

highlight *noun* (*plural* **highlights**) the most interesting part of something
highlight *verb* (**highlights, highlighting, highlighted**) to make something especially clear or prominent

highly *adverb* 1 very, extremely ▸ *He was highly amused.* 2 favourably ▸ *She thinks highly of him.*

highly-strung *adjective* very sensitive or nervous

Highness noun (plural **Highnesses**) a title of a prince or princess ► His Royal Highness, the Prince of Wales.

highway noun (plural **highways**) a main road or route

highwayman noun (plural **highwaymen**) in earlier times, a man on horseback who robbed travellers

hijack verb (**hijacks, hijacking, hijacked**) to seize control of an aircraft or vehicle during a journey **hijacker** noun

hike noun (plural **hikes**) a long walk in the country
hike verb (**hikes, hiking, hiked**) to go for a hike **hiker** noun

hilarious adjective very funny **hilariously** adverb **hilarity** noun great amusement

hill noun (plural **hills**) a piece of high ground with sloping sides **hillside** noun **hilly** adjective

hilt noun (plural **hilts**) the handle of a sword or dagger **up to the hilt** completely

him pronoun a word used for **he** when it is the object of a verb, or when it comes after a preposition ► I like him. ► I gave it to him.

himself pronoun used to refer to the person already mentioned as 'he' ► He has hurt himself. **by himself** on his own; alone ► He did the work all by himself.

hind adjective (pronounced hynd) at the back ► The dog scratched its head with a hind foot.

hinder verb (**hinders, hindering, hindered**) (pronounced hin-der) to get in someone's way or make it difficult for them to do something **hindrance** noun something that gets in your way or makes things difficult

Hindi noun a language spoken in northern India

Hindu noun (plural **Hindus**) someone who believes in **Hinduism**, which is one of the religions of India

hinge noun (plural **hinges**) a joining device on which a door, gate, or lid swings when it opens

hint noun (plural **hints**) a slight indication or suggestion ► Give me a hint of what you want.
hint verb (**hints, hinting, hinted**) to give a hint

hip noun (plural **hips**) the bony part on each side of your body between your waist and the tops of your legs

hippo noun (plural **hippos**) (informal) a hippopotamus

hippopotamus noun (plural **hippopotamuses**) a very large African animal that lives near water
The word **hippopotamus** comes from Greek words meaning 'river horse'.

hire verb (**hires, hiring, hired**) to pay to use something for a time

his adjective belonging to him ► That is his book.

hiss verb (**hisses, hissing, hissed**) to make a sound like a long s, as some snakes do
hiss noun (plural **hisses**) a sound of hissing

historian noun (plural **historians**) someone who writes or studies history

historic adjective famous or important in history ► A historic battle was fought near here.

historical adjective to do with history ► The story is based on historical events.

history noun (plural **histories**) the study of important events that happened in the past

hit verb (**hits, hitting, hit**) 1 to come up against someone or something with force, or to give them a blow ► The car hit a post. ► I saw you hit your dog. 2 to have a bad effect on a place ► A hurricane hit central America. 3 to send something somewhere by hitting it ► They hit the ball into the neighbours' garden. 4 to have a bad effect on someone ► Putting up the cost of swimming would hit lots of families. **hit on** to think of an idea suddenly ► I've hit on the answer.
hit noun (plural **hits**) 1 a knock or stroke 2 a shot that hits the target 3 a successful song or show

hitch *verb* (**hitches, hitching, hitched**) 1 to fasten something with a loop or hook 2 (informal) to get a ride by hitch-hiking **hitch up** to pull something up quickly or with a jerk ▸ *He hitched up his trousers.*

hitch *noun* (*plural* **hitches**) 1 a slight difficulty or delay 2 a knot

hitch-hike *verb* (**hitch-hikes, hitch-hiking, hitch-hiked**) to travel by getting a ride in someone else's car **hitch-hiker** *noun*

hither *adverb* (not an everyday word) to or towards this place

hitherto *adverb* (not an everyday word) up to now

HIV short for *human immunodeficiency virus*, a virus that can cause Aids

hive *noun* (*plural* **hives**) 1 a beehive 2 a very busy place ▸ *The room was a hive of activity.*

hoard *noun* (*plural* **hoards**) a secret store of something valuable

hoard *verb* (**hoards, hoarding, hoarded**) to store lots of things away **hoarder** *noun*

hoarding *noun* (*plural* **hoardings**) a tall fence covered with advertisements

hoarse *adjective* (**hoarser, hoarsest**) having a rough or croaking voice **hoarsely** *adverb*

hoax *noun* (*plural* **hoaxes**) a trick you play to deceive someone

hoax *verb* (**hoaxes, hoaxing, hoaxed**) to deceive someone with a trick

hobble *verb* (**hobbles, hobbling, hobbled**) to walk with short awkward steps because your feet are hurt

hobby *noun* (*plural* **hobbies**) something you like to do in your spare time

hockey *noun* an outdoor team-game played with curved sticks and a small hard ball

hoe *noun* (*plural* **hoes**) a tool used for scraping up weeds

hog *noun* (*plural* **hogs**) 1 a male pig 2 (informal) a greedy person

hog *verb* (**hogs, hogging, hogged**) (informal) to take more than your fair share of something

Hogmanay *noun* New Year's Eve in Scotland

hoist *verb* (**hoists, hoisting, hoisted**) to lift something heavy using ropes or pulleys

hold *verb* (**holds, holding, held**) 1 to have something in your hands ▸ *He came in holding a large torch.* 2 to restrain someone or stop them getting away ▸ *I couldn't hold her and she struggled free.* 3 to be the owner or winner of something ▸ *Do you hold a driving licence?* ▸ *She holds the world high jump record.* 4 to organize something or make something happen ▸ *They decided to hold a meeting in the village hall.* 5 to contain an amount of something ▸ *I'm not sure my suitcase will hold all my things.* 6 to support someone or something ▸ *This plank won't hold my weight.* 7 to stay good or favourable ▸ *The good weather should hold until the weekend.* 8 to believe an opinion ▸ *She holds some strange views.* **hold on** (informal) to wait ▸ *Hold on while I see who's at the door.* **hold out** to last or continue **hold up** 1 to rob someone with threats of force 2 to delay someone or something ▸ *They arrived late, complaining that they had been held up by the traffic.* **holder** *noun* someone who holds something, or a device for holding something

hold *noun* (*plural* **holds**) 1 a way of holding something; a grasp 2 something to hold on to 3 the part of a ship or aircraft where cargo is stored

holdall *noun* (*plural* **holdalls**) a large bag for travelling with

hold-up *noun* (*plural* **hold-ups**) 1 a delay 2 a robbery with threats or force

hole *noun* (*plural* **holes**) 1 a gap or opening made in something 2 an animal's burrow

Holi *noun* a Hindu festival held in the spring

holiday *noun* (*plural* **holidays**) 1 a day or time when you do not go to work or school 2 a time when you go away to enjoy yourself
The word **holiday** comes from *holy day*, because holidays were originally religious festivals.

hollow *adjective* having an empty space inside; not solid

hollow *noun* (*plural* **hollows**) 1 a hollow or sunken place 2 a small valley

hollow *verb* (**hollows, hollowing, hollowed**) to make something hollow

hollow *adverb* (informal) by a lot; completely ▶ *They beat us hollow.*

holly *noun* an evergreen bush with shiny prickly leaves and red berries

hologram *noun* (*plural* **holograms**) a type of photograph made by laser beams, which appears to have depth as well as height and width

holster *noun* (*plural* **holsters**) a leather case for a pistol, worn on a belt

holy *adjective* (**holier, holiest**) 1 to do with God and treated with religious respect 2 (describing a person) devoted to God or a religion **holiness** *noun*

home *noun* (*plural* **homes**) 1 the place where you live 2 the place where you were born or where you feel you belong 3 a place where people live together and are looked after ▶ *She went to a home for the elderly.* **feel at home** to feel comfortable and happy

home *adverb* to or at the place where you live ▶ *I'd better go home now.* ▶ *Is she home yet?* **bring something home to someone** to make someone realize something

home *verb* (**homes, homing, homed**) **home in on** to aim for something

homeless *adjective* having nowhere to live **homelessness** *noun*

homely *adjective* simple or ordinary

home-made *adjective* made at home and not bought from a shop

homesick *adjective* sad or upset because you are away from home **homesickness** *noun*

homework *noun* school work that you do at home

homosexual *adjective* sexually attracted to people of the same sex

homosexual *noun* (*plural* **homosexuals**) a homosexual person **homosexuality** *noun* being homosexual

honest *adjective* (*pronounced* **on-ist**) truthful and just; not stealing, cheating, or telling lies **honestly** *adverb* **honesty** *noun* being honest

honey *noun* a sweet sticky food made by bees

honeycomb *noun* (*plural* **honeycombs**) a wax structure made by bees to store their honey and eggs

honeymoon *noun* (*plural* **honeymoons**) a holiday spent together by a couple who have just got married

honeysuckle *noun* a climbing plant with sweet-smelling yellow or pink flowers

honour *noun* (*plural* **honours**) (*pronounced* **on-er**) 1 great respect or reputation 2 something given to a deserving person, such as an award 3 something a person is proud to do ▶ *They were offered the honour of taking part in the Lord Mayor's show.*

honour *verb* (**honours, honouring, honoured**) 1 to feel or show honour for someone 2 to keep a promise or agreement

honourable *adjective* honest or loyal **honourably** *adverb*

hood *noun* (*plural* **hoods**) 1 a part of a coat or anorak that covers your head and neck 2 the folding roof of a car or covering of a pram **hooded** *adjective* having a hood

hoodwink *verb* (**hoodwinks, hoodwinking, hoodwinked**) to deceive or trick someone

hoof *noun* (*plural* **hoofs** or **hooves**) the hard part of the feet of horses, cattle, or deer

hook *noun* (*plural* **hooks**) a piece of curved metal, wood, or plastic used for hanging things on or for catching hold of something **hooked** *adjective* having a shape like a hook

hook *verb* (**hooks, hooking, hooked**) 1 to fasten something with a hook or on a hook 2 to catch a fish with a hook

hooligan *noun* (*plural* **hooligans**) a noisy or violent person, especially someone in a gang

hoop *noun* (*plural* **hoops**) a large ring made of metal, wood, or plastic

hoot *verb* (**hoots, hooting, hooted**) to make a sound like the cry of an owl or the sound of a car horn

hoot *noun* (*plural* **hoots**) **1** a hooting sound **2** a jeer

hooter *noun* (*plural* **hooters**) a horn or other device that makes a hooting sound

hop *verb* (**hops, hopping, hopped**) **1** to jump on one foot **2** (used about a bird) to move in jumps on both feet at once

hop *noun* (*plural* **hops**) **1** a jump made on one foot **2** a climbing plant used to make beer

hope *noun* (*plural* **hopes**) **1** the feeling that something you want will happen **2** a person or thing that makes you feel like this ▸ *Mary was their last hope for raising the money.*

hope *verb* (**hopes, hoping, hoped**) to want something and expect it to happen

hopeful *adjective* **1** having hope **2** likely to be good or successful ▸ *There is some hopeful news about the hostages.* **hopefully** *adverb*

hopeless *adjective* **1** without hope **2** very bad at something ▸ *I'm hopeless at cricket.* **hopelessly** *adverb* **hopelessness** *noun*

hopscotch *noun* a game in which you hop into squares marked on the ground

horde *noun* (*plural* **hordes**) a large group or crowd

horizon *noun* (*plural* **horizons**) (*pronounced* ho-**ry**-zon) the line where the sky appears to meet the land or sea

horizontal *adjective* going across from left to right, like the horizon **horizontally** *adverb*

hormone *noun* (*plural* **hormones**) a chemical made in glands in your body and sent round with your blood to make other organs work in special ways

horn *noun* (*plural* **horns**) **1** a hard pointed bone that grows on the head of some animals **2** a brass musical instrument that you blow **3** a device on a vehicle for making a warning sound

hornet *noun* (*plural* **hornets**) a large kind of wasp

horoscope *noun* (*plural* **horoscopes**) a forecast made about someone's future from the positions of stars and planets when they were born

horrible *adjective* very unpleasant or nasty **horribly** *adverb*

horrid *adjective* horrible

horrific *adjective* terrifyingly bad **horrifically** *adverb*

horrify *verb* (**horrifies, horrifying, horrified**) to make someone feel afraid or disgusted

horror *noun* (*plural* **horrors**) **1** a feeling of great fear or disgust **2** a horrifying person or thing

horse *noun* (*plural* **horses**) **1** a four-legged animal used for riding on or pulling carts **2** a tall box or frame for jumping over in gymnastics

horseback *noun* **on horseback** riding on a horse

horse chestnut *noun* (*plural* **horse chestnuts**) a large tree that produces dark brown nuts called conkers

horsepower *noun* (*plural* **horsepower**) a unit for measuring the power of an engine It was called **horsepower** because it was based on the amount of work a horse could do.

horseshoe *noun* (*plural* **horseshoes**) a U-shaped piece of metal nailed as a shoe to a horse's hoof

hose *noun* (*plural* **hoses**) a long flexible tube that liquids or gases can pass through

hospitable *adjective* friendly and welcoming **hospitably** *adverb*

hospital *noun* (*plural* **hospitals**) a place where sick or injured people are given medical treatment

hospitality *noun* welcoming people and giving them food and entertainment

host *noun* (*plural* **hosts**) 1 someone who has guests and looks after them 2 someone who introduces a television show 3 a large number of people or things

hostage *noun* (*plural* **hostages**) someone who is held prisoner by a person or organization as a way of getting what they want

hostel *noun* (*plural* **hostels**) a building where students or other people can live

hostile *adjective* 1 unfriendly, behaving like an enemy ▸ *She stared back at him in a hostile way.* 2 opposed to someone or something ▸ *They are hostile to the idea.* **hostility** *noun*

hot *adjective* (**hotter**, **hottest**) 1 having a high temperature; very warm 2 having a burning taste like pepper or mustard 3 excited or angry ▸ *He has a hot temper.*

hot dog *noun* (*plural* **hot dogs**) a hot sausage in a bread roll

hotel *noun* (*plural* **hotels**) a building where you can pay to have meals and stay for the night

hotpot *noun* (*plural* **hotpots**) a kind of stew

hound *noun* (*plural* **hounds**) a dog used in hunting or racing
hound *verb* (**hounds**, **hounding**, **hounded**) to chase or harass someone ▸ *The family was hounded by reporters.*

hour *noun* (*plural* **hours**) 1 a unit of time equal to 60 minutes, one of the 24 into which a day is divided 2 a particular time ▸ *Why are you up at this hour?*

hourly *adjective* and *adverb* every hour; done once an hour

house *noun* (*plural* **houses**) (*pronounced* howss) 1 a building where people live, usually designed for one family 2 a building used for a special purpose ▸ *We visited the Houses of Parliament.* 3 one of the divisions in some schools for sports competitions and other events
house *verb* (**houses**, **housing**, **housed**) (*pronounced* howz) to provide a house or room for someone or a building for something

household *noun* (*plural* **households**) the people who live together in a house

housekeeper *noun* (*plural* **housekeepers**) a person whose job is to look after a house

housekeeping *noun* 1 looking after a household 2 the money for food and other things used in a house

housework *noun* the work of looking after a house and keeping it clean

hover *verb* (**hovers**, **hovering**, **hovered**) (*pronounced* hov-er) 1 to stay in one place in the air 2 to wait near someone or something

hovercraft *noun* (*plural* **hovercraft**) (*pronounced* hov-er-krahft) a vehicle that travels just above the surface of water or land, supported on a cushion of air made by its engines

how *adverb* 1 in what way ▸ *Tell me how you did it.* 2 to what extent ▸ *How much sugar do you take?* 3 in what condition ▸ *How are you?*

however *adverb* 1 in whatever way; to whatever extent ▸ *You will never find them, however hard you try.* 2 nevertheless ▸ *It's snowing; however, we can go out if we wrap up well.*
however *conjunction* in any way ▸ *You can do it however you like.*

howl *verb* (**howls**, **howling**, **howled**) to make a long loud cry like an animal in pain
howl *noun* (*plural* **howls**) a howling sound

hub *noun* (*plural* **hubs**) the centre of a wheel

hubbub *noun* a confused noise

huddle verb (**huddles, huddling, huddled**) to crowd together with other people for warmth or comfort

hue noun (*plural* **hues**) a colour or tint

huff noun **in a huff** in a cross mood

hug verb (**hugs, hugging, hugged**) 1 to clasp someone tightly in your arms 2 to keep close to something while moving ▶ *The little boat was hugging the shore.*

hug noun (*plural* **hugs**) a tight or loving clasp

huge adjective (**huger, hugest**) extremely large **hugely** adverb

hulk noun (*plural* **hulks**) 1 the remains of an old decaying ship 2 a large clumsy person or thing **hulking** adjective

hull noun (*plural* **hulls**) the body or framework of a ship

hullo interjection another spelling of **hello**

hum verb (**hums, humming, hummed**) 1 to make a low buzzing sound like bees 2 to sing a tune with your lips closed

hum noun (*plural* **hums**) a humming sound

human or **human being** noun (*plural* **humans** or **human beings**) a living person; a man, woman, or child

human adjective to do with humans

humane adjective (*pronounced* hew-**mayn**) kind or merciful **humanely** adverb

humanity noun 1 all the people in the world 2 being human

humble adjective (**humbler, humblest**) modest; not proud **humbly** adverb

humid adjective (*pronounced* hew-mid) damp or moist in the air **humidity** noun

humiliate verb (**humiliates, humiliating, humiliated**) to make someone feel ashamed or disgraced **humiliation** noun

humility noun being humble

humorous adjective amusing or funny **humorously** adverb

humour noun 1 the ability to be funny or amusing, or to enjoy amusing things ▶ *He has a good sense of humour.* 2 a person's mood ▶ *They came back in a good humour.*

humour verb (**humours, humouring, humoured**) to keep someone happy by doing what they want

hump noun (*plural* **humps**) a rounded lump or mound

hump verb (**humps, humping, humped**) to carry something heavy on your back

hunch noun (*plural* **hunches**) an idea based on what you feel rather than what you know ▶ *His suggestion had been no more than a hunch.*

hunch verb (**hunches, hunching, hunched**) to bend your shoulders upward so that your back is rounded

hunchback noun (*plural* **hunchbacks**) someone with a hump on their back

hundred noun (*plural* **hundreds**) the number 100 **hundredth** adjective and noun

hung past tense and past participle of **hang**

hunger noun the feeling that you need food

hungry adjective (**hungrier, hungriest**) feeling that you need food **hungrily** adverb

hunk noun (*plural* **hunks**) a large piece or chunk of something

hunt verb (**hunts, hunting, hunted**) 1 to chase and kill animals for food or sport 2 to look hard for something **hunter** noun

hunt noun (*plural* **hunts**) 1 the sport of hunting animals 2 a group of people who go hunting 3 a search

hurdle noun (*plural* **hurdles**) 1 an upright frame that runners jump over in an athletics race 2 a problem or difficulty

hurl verb (**hurls, hurling, hurled**) to throw something as far as you can

hurrah or **hurray** interjection a shout of joy or approval

hurricane noun (*plural* **hurricanes**) a violent storm with a strong wind

hurry verb (**hurries, hurrying, hurried**) 1 to move or act quickly 2 to try to make someone be quick **hurriedly** adverb quickly, in a hurry

hurry noun moving or doing something quickly **in a hurry** hurrying or impatient

hurt verb (**hurts, hurting, hurt**) **1** to harm a person or animal or cause them pain **2** to upset or offend someone

hurtle verb (**hurtles, hurtling, hurtled**) to move very quickly or dangerously ▸ *The car hurtled round the corner.*

husband noun (*plural* **husbands**) the man that a woman has married

hush verb (**hushes, hushing, hushed**) to make someone be quiet **hush something up** to prevent people knowing about something

hush noun quiet or silence ▸ *Let's have a bit of hush.*

husk noun (*plural* **husks**) the dry outer covering of a seed

husky adjective (**huskier, huskiest**) **1** hoarse ▸ *He spoke in a low husky voice.* **2** big and strong **huskily** adverb

husky noun (*plural* **huskies**) a large strong dog used in the Arctic for pulling sledges

hustle verb (**hustles, hustling, hustled**) **1** to hurry busily **2** to push someone rudely

hut noun (*plural* **huts**) a small roughly made house or shelter

hutch noun (*plural* **hutches**) a box or cage for a rabbit or other pet animal

hyacinth noun (*plural* **hyacinths**) a sweet-smelling flower that grows from a bulb
The word **hyacinth** comes from the name *Hyacinthus*, a Greek youth in a legend who was accidentally killed by Apollo and turned into the flower.

hybrid noun (*plural* **hybrids**) an animal or plant that is produced from two different species

hydrant noun (*plural* **hydrants**) an outdoor water tap for fixing a hose to

hydraulic adjective worked by forcing water or other liquid through thin pipes

hydroelectric adjective using water power to make electricity

hydrofoil noun (*plural* **hydrofoils**) a boat that skims over the surface of the water, resting on supports that lift it above the surface

hydrogen noun a very light gas which burns well. With oxygen it makes water.

hyena noun (*plural* **hyenas**) (*pronounced* hy-**ee**-na) a wild animal like a wolf that makes a shrieking howl

hygiene noun keeping clean and healthy **hygienic** adjective **hygienically** adverb

hymn noun (*plural* **hymns**) (*pronounced* him) a religious song praising God

hypermarket noun (*plural* **hypermarkets**) a very large supermarket, usually outside a town

hyphen noun (*plural* **hyphens**) a short dash (-) used to join words or parts of words, for example in *house-proud*

hypnosis noun (*pronounced* hip-**noh**-sis) putting someone into a kind of deep sleep so that you can make them do certain things

hypnotize verb (**hypnotizes, hypnotizing, hypnotized**) to put someone to sleep by hypnosis **hypnotism** noun using hypnosis **hypnotist** noun someone who hypnotizes people

hypocrite noun (*plural* **hypocrites**) (*pronounced* **hip**-o-krit) someone who pretends to be a better person than they really are **hypocrisy** noun being a hypocrite **hypocritical** adjective

hypodermic syringe noun (*plural* **hypodermic syringes**) a medical device for injecting drugs under the skin

hypotenuse noun (*plural* **hypotenuses**) (*pronounced* hy-**pot**-i-newz) the side opposite the right angle in a right-angled triangle

hypothermia noun a dangerous condition when your body temperature is well below normal

hysteria noun excitement or emotion that you can't control **hysterical** adjective extremely excited or emotional **hysterics** *plural* noun a state of being excited or emotional

Ii

I *pronoun* a word you use use when you are speaking about yourself

ice *noun* (*plural* **ices**) 1 frozen water 2 an ice cream

ice *verb* (**ices, icing, iced**) 1 to become covered in ice 2 to put icing on a cake

iceberg *noun* (*plural* **icebergs**) a large mass of ice floating in the sea

ice cream *noun* (*plural* **ice creams**) a sweet creamy frozen food

ice hockey *noun* a game like hockey played on ice by players who wear skates

ice rink *noun* (*plural* **ice rinks**) a building that has a floor of ice for skating on

icicle *noun* (*plural* **icicles**) a pointed piece of hanging ice formed from dripping water

icing *noun* a sugary covering for cakes

icon *noun* (*plural* **icons**) 1 a small picture or symbol on a computer screen 2 a painting of a holy person

icy *adjective* (**icier, iciest**) 1 very cold, like ice 2 covered in ice **icily** *adverb* **iciness** *noun*

idea *noun* (*plural* **ideas**) something that you think of; a thought or plan

ideal *adjective* exactly what you want; perfect ▶ *This would be an ideal time to work in the garden.* **ideally** *adverb*

ideal *noun* (*plural* **ideals**) something or someone that is perfect or the best to have

identical *adjective* exactly the same **identically** *adverb*

identify *verb* (**identifies, identifying, identified**) to discover who or what someone or something is ▶ *The police have identified the person seen in the video.* **identification** *noun*

identity *noun* (*plural* **identities**) who someone is or what something is ▶ *They had no way of proving their identity.*

idiom *noun* (*plural* **idioms**) a phrase or group of words that together have a special meaning that is not obvious from the words themselves, for example *to be in hot water* means to be in trouble or difficulty

idiot *noun* (*plural* **idiots**) a stupid or foolish person **idiotic** *adjective* **idiocy** *noun* foolish behaviour ➡ Rachel

idle *adjective* (**idler, idlest**) 1 (describing a person) lazy or doing nothing 2 (describing a machine) not being used 3 not really serious ▶ *They were only idle threats.*
idle *verb* (**idles, idling, idled**) (used about an engine) to run slowly **idly** *adverb* in an idle way ▶ *He idly wondered if anyone had made the tea yet.*

idol *noun* (*plural* **idols**) 1 a statue or image that people worship as a god 2 a famous person who is admired by many people

idolize *verb* (**idolizes, idolizing, idolized**) to admire or love someone very much

i.e. short for Latin *id est*, which means 'that is'. It is used to explain something. ▶ *Adults, i.e. people who are 18 or over, have to pay the full fare.*

if *conjunction* 1 on condition that ▶ *I'll tell you if you promise to keep it secret.* 2 although; even though ▶ *Sarah was going to finish the job if it was the last thing she did.* 3 whether ▶ *Do you know if Jane has arrived?*

igloo *noun* (*plural* **igloos**) a round house made of blocks of hard snow, built by the Inuit people of the Arctic

ignite *verb* (**ignites, igniting, ignited**) 1 to set fire to something 2 to catch fire

ignition *noun* the system in a motor engine that ignites the fuel

ignorant *adjective* 1 not knowing about something ▸ *He was ignorant of the fact that his mother was right behind him.* 2 not knowing much about anything ▸ *My older cousins always make me feel ignorant.* **ignorance** *noun*

ignore *verb* (**ignores, ignoring, ignored**) to take no notice of someone or something

ill *adjective* 1 not well; in bad health 2 bad or harmful ▸ *There were no ill effects.*

illegal *adjective* not legal; against the law **illegally** *adverb*

illegible *adjective* (*pronounced* i-**lej**-i-bul) not clear enough to read **illegibly** *adverb*

illegitimate *adjective* born of parents who are not married to each other

illiterate *adjective* unable to read or write **illiteracy** *noun*

illness *noun* (*plural* **illnesses**) 1 something that makes you ill 2 the state of being ill

illogical *adjective* not logical or having any good reason **illogically** *adverb*

ill-treat *verb* (**ill-treats, ill-treating, ill-treated**) to treat someone or something badly

illuminate *verb* (**illuminates, illuminating, illuminated**) to light up a place or decorate it with lights **illumination** *noun*

illusion *noun* (*plural* **illusions**) something that looks or seems real but is not

illustrate *verb* (**illustrates, illustrating, illustrated**) to show or explain something with pictures or examples

illustration *noun* (*plural* **illustrations**) a picture in a book or magazine

image *noun* (*plural* **images**) 1 a picture or statue of a person or thing 2 what you see in a mirror or through a lens ▸ *The little girl could see an image of herself in the glass.* 3 a picture you have in your mind 4 the way you seem to other people ▸ *Local businesses are keen to put across a friendly image.*

imaginary *adjective* existing only in your mind; not real

imagination *noun* (*plural* **imaginations**) the ability to imagine things

imaginative *adjective* having good ideas ▸ *Kevin wrote an imaginative story about a long journey.* **imaginatively** *adverb*

imagine *verb* (**imagines, imagining, imagined**) to form a picture of something in your mind **imaginable** *adjective* that you can imagine

imam *noun* (*plural* **imams**) a Muslim religious leader

imbecile *noun* (*plural* **imbeciles**) (informal) a very stupid person

imitate *verb* (**imitates, imitating, imitated**) to do the same as someone or something else **imitation** *noun* **imitator** *noun*

immature *adjective* not fully grown or developed **immaturity** *noun*

immediate *adjective* 1 happening or done without any delay ▸ *We'd like an immediate answer to our question.* 2 nearest; with nothing or no one between ▸ *Their immediate neighbours had lived in the street for years.*

immediately *adverb* now; at once

immense *adjective* very large **immensely** *adverb* **immensity** *noun*

immerse *verb* (**immerses, immersing, immersed**) to put something completely in liquid **be immersed in** to be very interested in something **immersion** *noun* immersing something or being immersed

immigrant *noun* (*plural* **immigrants**) someone who has come into a country to live there

immigrate *verb* (**immigrates, immigrating, immigrated**) to come into a country to live there **immigration** *noun*

immobile *adjective* not moving or not able to move **immobility** *noun*

immobilize *verb* (**immobilizes, immobilizing, immobilized**) to make something unable to move or work ▸ *The car had been immobilized with a clamp.*

immoral *adjective* not following the usual standards of right and wrong **immorality** *noun* being immoral

immortal *adjective* living for ever
immortality *noun*

immune *adjective* protected from the
danger of catching a disease **immunity**
noun protection against a disease

immunize *verb* (**immunizes, immunizing,
immunized**) to make someone immune
from a disease, usually by giving them an
injection **immunization** *noun*

imp *noun* (*plural* **imps**) in stories, a small
mischievous devil **impish** *adjective*
mischievous

impact *noun* (*plural* **impacts**) 1 the force
of one thing hitting another 2 a strong
influence or effect ▸ *The advertising
campaign has had a major impact on the
company's sales.*

impair *verb* (**impairs, impairing, impaired**)
to harm or weaken something ▸ *Her
vision was impaired by the fog.*

impartial *adjective* fair, not favouring one
side more than the other **impartiality** *noun*
fairness **impartially** *adverb*

impassable *adjective* (describing a road)
not able to be travelled along

impatient *adjective* not patient; in a hurry
impatience *noun* **impatiently** *adverb*

impede *verb* (**impedes, impeding,
impeded**) to hinder someone or get in their
way

imperative *adjective* important or urgent
▸ *It is imperative that you all stay together
in the cave.*

imperceptible *adjective* too small or
gradual to be noticed ▸ *He said no with
an almost imperceptible shake of his head.*
imperceptibly *adverb*

imperfect *adjective* not perfect; not
complete **imperfection** *noun*

imperial *adjective* belonging to an empire
or its rulers

impersonal *adjective* not showing any
emotions or personal feelings **impersonally**
adverb

impersonate *verb* (**impersonates,
impersonating, impersonated**) to pretend
to be someone else **impersonation** *noun*
impersonator *noun*

impertinent *adjective* not showing
respect; rude **impertinence** *noun*
impertinently *adverb*

impetuous *adjective* acting too quickly,
without thinking **impetuosity** *noun*
impetuously *adverb*

implement *noun* (*plural* **implements**)
a tool or utensil

implication *noun* (*plural* **implications**)
something that someone implies or
suggests

implore *verb* (**implores, imploring,
implored**) to beg someone to do something

imply *verb* (**implies, implying, implied**) to
suggest something without actually saying
it ▸ *The games teacher implied that I
would be in the netball team.*

impolite *adjective* not polite; rude
impolitely *adverb*

import *verb* (**imports, importing,
imported**) (*pronounced* im-**port**) to bring
in goods from another country to sell them
import *noun* (*plural* **imports**) (*pronounced*
im-port) something that is imported

important *adjective* 1 needing to be taken
seriously ▸ *Choosing a school is an
important decision.* 2 powerful or
influential ▸ *Many important people came
to the meeting.* **importance** *noun*
importantly *adverb*

impose *verb* (**imposes, imposing, imposed**)
to force someone to accept something
▸ *A speed limit of 20 miles per hour has
been imposed on the road through the
village.* **imposition** *noun* imposing
something, or a thing that has been imposed

imposing *adjective* looking grand or
important

impossible *adjective* 1 not possible
2 (informal) very annoying ▸ *He is
impossible!* **impossibility** *noun* something
that is impossible **impossibly** *adverb*

impostor *noun* (*plural* **impostors**)
someone who pretends to be someone else

impracticable *adjective* not able to be done or used

impractical *adjective* not likely to work or be useful

impress *verb* (**impresses, impressing, impressed**) 1 to give someone reason to admire you ▸ *Kerry impressed everyone with her singing.* 2 to make someone realize or remember something ▸ *We must impress on them that this is urgent.* **impressive** *adjective*

impression *noun* (*plural* **impressions**) 1 a vague idea or feeling ▸ *I had the impression that they were writers.* 2 an effect on someone's mind or feelings ▸ *The book left a strong impression on me.* 3 an imitation of a person or a sound ▸ *She does a good impression of the Prime Minister.*

imprison *verb* (**imprisons, imprisoning, imprisoned**) to put someone in prison **imprisonment** *noun*

improbable *adjective* unlikely **improbability** *noun*

improper *adjective* 1 not proper; wrong 2 rude, indecent

improve *verb* (**improves, improving, improved**) 1 to make something better 2 to become better **improvement** *noun*

improvise *verb* (**improvises, improvising, improvised**) 1 to do something without any rehearsal or preparation 2 to make something quickly with whatever materials are available **improvisation** *noun*

impudent *adjective* not respectful; rude **impudence** *noun* rudeness **impudently** *adverb*

impulse *noun* (*plural* **impulses**) a sudden wish to do something **impulsive** *adjective*

impure *adjective* not pure **impurity** *noun*

in *preposition* and *adverb* 1 at or inside something ▸ *The house is in London.* ▸ *Please come in.* 2 into ▸ *She fell in the river.* 3 during ▸ *We came in April.* 4 consisting of ▸ *The serial was in four parts.* **in all** including everything ▸ *The bill came to £500 in all.*

inability *noun* being unable to do something

inaccessible *adjective* not able to be reached

inaccurate *adjective* not accurate **inaccuracy** *noun*

inactive *adjective* not working or doing anything **inactivity** *noun*

inadequate *adjective* not enough

inanimate *adjective* not living or moving

inappropriate *adjective* not appropriate or suitable **inappropriately** *adverb*

inattentive *adjective* not listening or paying attention **inattention** *noun*

inaudible *adjective* not able to be heard **inaudibly** *adverb*

incapable *adjective* unable to do something ▸ *They are incapable of understanding the problem.*

incapacity *noun* not being able to do something

incense *noun* (*pronounced* **in-senss**) a substance that makes a sweet pleasant smell when it burns

incense *verb* (**incenses, incensing, incensed**) (*pronounced* **in-senss**) to make someone very angry

incentive *noun* (*plural* **incentives**) a thing that encourages a person to do something

inch *noun* (*plural* **inches**) a measure of length, one-twelfth of a foot or 2.54 centimetres

incident *noun* (*plural* **incidents**) something unusual or interesting that happens

incidental *adjective* happening along with something else; not so important **incidentally** *adverb*

incinerator *noun* (*plural* **incinerators**) a bin or container for burning rubbish

incite *verb* (**incites, inciting, incited**) to encourage someone to do something wrong

inclination *noun* (*plural* **inclinations**) a tendency or wish to do something

incline *verb* (**inclines, inclining, inclined**) (*pronounced* in-**klyn**) to lean or bend **be inclined to 1** to feel like doing something ► *They were inclined to accept the invitation.* **2** to do something a lot ► *The door is inclined to creak.*

incline *noun* (*plural* **inclines**) (*pronounced* in-klyn) a slope

include *verb* (**includes, including, included**) to contain something as part of the whole ► *Does the price include VAT?* **inclusion** *noun*

inclusive *adjective* including everything mentioned ► *We want to stay from Monday to Thursday inclusive.*

income *noun* (*plural* **incomes**) the money that a person earns regularly for their work

incompatible *adjective* not able to exist or be used together ► *The computer game is incompatible with your PC.*

incompetent *adjective* unable to do something properly **incompetence** *noun*

incomplete *adjective* not complete

incomprehensible *adjective* not able to be understood

incongruous *adjective* (*pronounced* in-kon-groo-us) not suitable; out of place

inconsiderate *adjective* not thinking of other people **inconsiderately** *adverb*

inconsistent *adjective* not consistent; contradicting yourself **inconsistency** *noun* **inconsistently** *adverb*

inconspicuous *adjective* not easy to see or notice

inconvenient *adjective* not convenient; awkward **inconvenience** *noun* **inconveniently** *adverb*

incorporate *verb* (**incorporates, incorporating, incorporated**) to include something as a part of something else

incorrect *adjective* not correct; wrong **incorrectly** *adverb*

increase *verb* (**increases, increasing, increased**) (*pronounced* in-**kreess**) **1** to make something bigger **2** to become bigger

increase *noun* (*plural* **increases**) (*pronounced* in-**kreess**) the amount by which something gets bigger

incredible *adjective* hard to believe **incredibly** *adverb*

incredulous *adjective* finding it difficult to believe someone

incubate *verb* (**incubates, incubating, incubated**) to hatch eggs by keeping them warm **incubation** *noun*

incubator *noun* (*plural* **incubators**) **1** a specially heated container for keeping newly born babies warm **2** a container for hatching eggs

indecent *adjective* not decent; improper **indecency** *noun* **indecently** *adverb*

indeed *adverb* used to emphasize something ► *It was very cold indeed.*

indefinite *adjective* not definite; vague

indefinite article *noun* (*plural* **indefinite articles**) the word *a* or *an*

indefinitely *adverb* for an uncertain or unlimited time ► *I'm staying at my aunt's indefinitely.*

indelible *adjective* hard to rub out or remove **indelibly** *adverb*

independent *adjective* not controlled by another person or country **independence** *noun* **independently** *adverb*

index *noun* (*plural* **indexes**) a list of names or topics in alphabetical order at the end of a book

index finger *noun* (*plural* **index fingers**) the finger next to your thumb

indicate *verb* (**indicates, indicating, indicated**) to point something out or show that it is there **indication** *noun* a sign of something **indicator** *noun*

indifferent *adjective* 1 not caring about something; not interested 2 not very good; ordinary ▸ *He is an indifferent cook.* **indifference** *noun*

indigestible *adjective* not easy to digest

indigestion *noun* a pain that you get when food is hard to digest

indignant *adjective* angry at something that seems wrong or unjust **indignantly** *adverb* **indignation** *noun* a feeling of being indignant

indigo *noun* a deep blue colour
indigo *adjective* having a deep blue colour

indirect *adjective* not direct or straight **indirectly** *adverb*

indispensable *adjective* essential; that you have to have

indistinct *adjective* not clear **indistinctly** *adverb*

indistinguishable *adjective* impossible to tell apart from something else

individual *adjective* 1 of or for one person 2 single or separate **individually** *adverb*
individual *noun* (*plural* **individuals**) a person

indoctrinate *verb* (**indoctrinates, indoctrinating, indoctrinated**) to make someone have particular ideas or beliefs **indoctrination** *noun*

indoor *adjective* done inside a building ▸ *We enjoy indoor sports.*

indoors *adverb* inside a building ▸ *We'd better go indoors.*

induce *verb* (**induces, inducing, induced**) to persuade someone to do something **inducement** *noun* something that is used to persuade someone

indulge *verb* (**indulges, indulging, indulged**) to let someone have or do what they want **indulge in** to have or do something that you like

indulgent *adjective* kind and allowing people to do what they want **indulgence** *noun*

industrial *adjective* to do with industry

industrious *adjective* working hard **industriously** *adverb*

industry *noun* (*plural* **industries**) 1 the work of making or producing goods to sell, especially in factories 2 a trade or business

ineffective *adjective* not effective; not working well **ineffectively** *adverb*

inefficient *adjective* not doing work well; wasting energy **inefficiency** *noun* **inefficiently** *adverb*

inequality *noun* (*plural* **inequalities**) not being equal

inevitable *adjective* unavoidable **inevitability** *noun* **inevitably** *adverb*

inexhaustible *adjective* that you cannot use up completely

inexpensive *adjective* not expensive

inexperienced *adjective* not having much experience of something

inexplicable *adjective* impossible to explain **inexplicably** *adverb*

infallible *adjective* always right; never making a mistake **infallibility** *noun* **infallibly** *adverb*

infamous *adjective* (*pronounced* in-fa-mus) well known for being bad or wicked **infamy** *noun* being infamous

infant *noun* (*plural* **infants**) a baby or young child **infancy** *noun* the time when someone is an infant
The word **infant** comes from a Latin word meaning 'unable to speak'.

infantile *adjective* childish and silly

infantry *noun* soldiers who fight on foot

infect *verb* (**infects, infecting, infected**) to pass on a disease to someone

infection *noun* (*plural* **infections**) a disease caused by germs

infectious *adjective* (describing a disease) passed from one person to another

infer *verb* (**infers, inferring, inferred**) to work something out from what someone says or does ▸ *I inferred that he did not want to come with us.* **inference** *noun* something that you infer

inferior *adjective* less good or less important **inferiority** *noun*

inferno *noun* (*plural* **infernos**) a fierce fire

infested *adjective* full of pests such as insects or rats

infinite *adjective* endless; too large to be measured or imagined **infinitely** *adverb*

infinitive *noun* (*plural* **infinitives**) the basic form of a verb, for example *to go* and *to hit*

infinity *noun* an infinite number or distance

infirm *adjective* weak from illness or old age **infirmity** *noun*

infirmary *noun* (*plural* **infirmaries**) a hospital

inflamed *adjective* 1 made sore and red 2 angry

inflammable *adjective* that can easily be set alight
The opposite of **inflammable**, meaning 'not easily set alight', is **non-flammable**. **Flammable** means the same as **inflammable**.

inflammation *noun* (*plural* **inflammations**) a painful swelling on the body

inflate *verb* (**inflates, inflating, inflated**) to fill something with air or gas **inflatable** *adjective*

inflation *noun* a general rise in prices

inflexible *adjective* not easy to bend or change

inflict *verb* (**inflicts, inflicting, inflicted**) to make someone suffer something ▸ *The knife inflicted a nasty wound on him.*

influence *noun* (*plural* **influences**) the power to affect someone or something
influence *verb* (**influences, influencing, influenced**) to have an effect on someone or something ▸ *The tides are influenced by the moon.*

influential *adjective* having a big influence; important

influenza *noun* (*pronounced* in-floo-en-za) an illness that causes fever, catarrh, and headaches. It is more usually called **flu**.

inform *verb* (**informs, informing, informed**) 1 to tell someone about something 2 to give information about someone to the police ▸ *He denied that he had ever informed on his friends.*

informal *adjective* not formal; relaxed **informally** *adverb*

informant *noun* (*plural* **informants**) a person who gives information

information *noun* facts or knowledge about something

information technology *noun* the use of computers and telecommunications to store and pass on information

informative *adjective* providing helpful information

infrequent *adjective* not frequent **infrequency** *noun* **infrequently** *adverb*

infuriate *verb* (**infuriates, infuriating, infuriated**) to make someone very angry

ingenious *adjective* 1 clever at doing things 2 cleverly made or done **ingeniously** *adverb*

ingenuity *noun* (*pronounced* in-ji-**nyoo**-i-ti) cleverness or skill in doing things

ingot *noun* (*plural* **ingots**) a lump of gold or silver

ingredient *noun* (*plural* **ingredients**) (*pronounced* in-**greed**-i-ent) one of the parts that make a mixture, especially in cooking

inhabit *verb* (**inhabits, inhabiting, inhabited**) to live in a place

inhabitant *noun* (*plural* **inhabitants**) one of the people who live in a place

inhale *verb* (**inhales, inhaling, inhaled**) to breathe in

inherit *verb* (**inherits, inheriting, inherited**) 1 to receive money, property, or a title when someone dies 2 to get qualities or characteristics from your parents or ancestors ▸ *He has inherited his mother's sense of humour.* **inheritance** *noun* something that someone inherits

inhospitable *adjective* (*pronounced* in-hos-pit-a-bul) **1** unfriendly to visitors **2** giving no shelter ► *They reached an inhospitable rocky island.*

inhuman *adjective* cruel; without pity or kindness **inhumanity** *noun*

initial *noun* (*plural* **initials**) the first letter of someone's name
initial *adjective* first; of the beginning ► *Their initial response was encouraging.* **initially** *adverb* at first

initiate *verb* (**initiates, initiating, initiated**) (*pronounced* in-**ish**-i-ayt) (not an everyday word) to start something working or happening **initiation** *noun* making someone a new member of a group

initiative *noun* (*plural* **initiatives**) the ability or power to start things or to get them done on your own

inject *verb* (**injects, injecting, injected**) to put a medicine or drug through someone's skin using a hollow needle **injection** *noun*

injure *verb* (**injures, injuring, injured**) to harm or hurt someone

injury *noun* (*plural* **injuries**) harm or damage done to someone

injustice *noun* (*plural* **injustices**) unfairness in the way someone is treated

ink *noun* (*plural* **inks**) a coloured liquid used for writing and drawing **inky** *adjective*

inkling *noun* (*plural* **inklings**) a slight idea or suspicion ► *Jim had an inkling that something strange was about to happen.*

inland *adjective* and *adverb* away from the sea ► *Vienna is an inland city.*

inlet *noun* (*plural* **inlets**) a strip of water reaching into the land from a sea or lake

inn *noun* (*plural* **inns**) a small hotel or pub

inner *adjective* inside; nearer the centre **innermost** *adjective*

innings *noun* (*plural* **innings**) in cricket, a team's or player's turn to bat

innocent *adjective* **1** not guilty of doing something wrong **2** harmless **innocence** *noun* **innocently** *adverb*

innovation *noun* (*plural* **innovations**) something new that someone has just invented or started using **innovative** *adjective* new or original

innumerable *adjective* too many to be counted

inoculate *verb* (**inoculates, inoculating, inoculated**) to inject someone with a vaccine to stop them getting a disease **inoculation** *noun*

input *noun* (*plural* **inputs**) what you put into something, especially data put into a computer

inquest *noun* (*plural* **inquests**) an official investigation after someone's death, to decide why they died

inquire *verb* (**inquires, inquiring, inquired**) **1** to ask about something **2** to make an official investigation about something

inquiry *noun* (*plural* **inquiries**) an official investigation

inquisitive *adjective* curious about other people **inquisitively** *adverb*

insane *adjective* not sane; mad **insanely** *adverb* **insanity** *noun* madness

insanitary *adjective* dirty and unhealthy

inscribe *verb* (**inscribes, inscribing, inscribed**) to write or carve words on a surface ► *The watch was inscribed with the words 'For Dorothy'.* **inscription** *noun*

insect *noun* (*plural* **insects**) a small animal with six legs and no backbone, for example a fly or an ant

insecticide *noun* (*plural* **insecticides**) a chemical used for killing insects

insecure *adjective* **1** not secure or safe **2** (describing a person) not feeling confident; anxious **insecurity** *noun* being insecure

insensitive *adjective* not thinking about the feelings of others **insensitivity** *noun*

inseparable *adjective* 1 not able to be separated 2 always together ▶ *The friends are inseparable.* **inseparably** *adverb*

insert *verb* (**inserts, inserting, inserted**) to put one thing into another ▶ *You have to insert a coin in the slot.* **insertion** *noun*

inside *noun* (*plural* **insides**) the middle or centre of something **insides** your stomach or abdomen

inside *adjective* placed on the inside of something ▶ *Stick the picture on an inside page.*

inside *adverb* and *preposition* in or to the inside of something ▶ *Come inside.* ▶ *Look inside the box.*

insignificant *adjective* not important **insignificance** *noun*

insincere *adjective* not sincere **insincerity** *noun* not being sincere

insist *verb* (**insists, insisting, insisted**) to say something very firmly ▶ *He insisted that he was innocent.* **insist on** to demand something ▶ *We insist on seeing the manager.*

insistent *adjective* insisting on doing or having something **insistence** *noun*

insolent *adjective* very rude and insulting **insolence** *noun* **insolently** *adverb*

insoluble *adjective* 1 impossible to solve ▶ *This is an insoluble problem.* 2 impossible to dissolve ▶ *Some chemicals are insoluble.* **insolubility** *noun*

insomnia *noun* (*pronounced* in-**som**-ni-a) being unable to sleep

inspect *verb* (**inspects, inspecting, inspected**) to look carefully at someone or something, especially to check them **inspection** *noun*

inspector *noun* (*plural* **inspectors**) 1 someone whose job is to inspect things or people 2 a police officer above a sergeant

inspire *verb* (**inspires, inspiring, inspired**) to fill someone with ideas or enthusiasm **inspiration** *noun*

install *verb* (**installs, installing, installed**) to put equipment or a device in its proper place ready for use ▶ *We want to install central heating.* **installation** *noun*

instalment *noun* (*plural* **instalments**) 1 one of several payments made over a period of time 2 an episode in a story

instance *noun* (*plural* **instances**) an example **for instance** for example

instant *adjective* happening immediately or very quickly ▶ *The show was an instant success.*

instant *noun* a moment ▶ *They had gone in an instant.* **instantly** *adverb* immediately

instantaneous *adjective* (*pronounced* in-stun-**tay**-ni-us) done or happening straight away

instead *adverb* in place of something else; as a substitute ▶ *There were no potatoes, so we had rice instead.*

instep *noun* (*plural* **insteps**) the top of your foot between your toes and your ankle

instinct *noun* (*plural* **instincts**) an ability to do something naturally, without having to learn it ▶ *The bandit had an animal's instinct for survival.* **instinctive** *adjective* done by insitinct **instinctively** *adverb*

institute *noun* (*plural* **institutes**) a society or organization set up for a special purpose

institution *noun* (*plural* **institutions**) 1 an organization where people can live or work together, such as a bank or a university 2 something that is an established habit or custom ▶ *The Sunday swim was a family institution.*

instruct *verb* (**instructs, instructing, instructed**) 1 to teach someone a subject or skill 2 to give someone orders **instruction** *noun* **instructor** *noun*

instrument *noun* (*plural* **instruments**) 1 a device played to make musical sounds 2 a tool used for delicate or scientific work

insufficient *adjective* not enough

insulate *verb* (**insulates, insulating, insulated**) to cover something so that heat or electricity cannot passing through it **insulation** *noun*

insult *verb* (**insults, insulting, insulted**) (*pronounced* in-**sult**) to hurt someone's feelings by being very rude to them

insult *noun* (*plural* **insults**) (*pronounced* **in**-sult) a remark or action that insults someone

insurance *noun* an agreement with a company that they will pay you money if you suffer a loss or injury, in return for a regular payment called a premium

insure *verb* (**insures, insuring, insured**) to protect yourself or your property with insurance

intact *adjective* whole and undamaged ▸ *Despite the storm our tent was still intact.*

integer *noun* (*plural* **integers**) (*pronounced* **in**-ti-jer) a whole number, such as 0, 1, 24, and not a fraction

integrate *verb* (**integrates, integrating, integrated**) to combine different things or parts into a whole or into one group **integration** *noun*

integrity *noun* (*pronounced* in-**teg**-ri-ti) honesty

intellect *noun* (*plural* **intellects**) the ability to think and work things out

intellectual *adjective* **1** involving the mind and thinking ▸ *He enjoys chess and other intellectual activities.* **2** able to think effectively; keen to study and learn

intelligent *adjective* able to think and learn well **intelligence** *noun* **intelligently** *adverb*

intelligible *adjective* able to be understood ▸ *The message was barely intelligible.* **intelligibility** *noun* **intelligibly** *adverb*

intend *verb* (**intends, intending, intended**) to have something in mind that you want to do ▸ *We intend to find out who it was.*

intense *adjective* very strong or great ▸ *In the sun the heat was intense.* **intensity** *noun* how intense something is

intensive *adjective* using a lot of effort; thorough ▸ *We didn't find her, despite an intensive search.*

intent *adjective* very eager or interested ▸ *They were intent on finishing the work in the garden before it grew dark.* **intently** *adverb*

intention *noun* (*plural* **intentions**) what you intend to do; a plan

intentional *adjective* done on purpose **intentionally** *adverb*

interactive *adjective* allowing communication in two directions, especially between a computer system and its user

intercept *verb* (**intercepts, intercepting, intercepted**) to stop someone or something that is going from one place to another **interception** *noun*

interchange *noun* (*plural* **interchanges**) a place where traffic moves from one main road or motorway to another

interchangeable *adjective* able to be changed or swapped round ▸ *My pen has interchangeable nibs.*

intercom *noun* (*plural* **intercoms**) a device by which people in different rooms or places can communicate with one another

intercourse *noun* **1** communication or dealings between people **2** sexual intercourse

interest *verb* (**interests, interesting, interested**) to make someone want to know about something or take part in something

interest *noun* (*plural* **interests**) **1** wanting to know more about something **2** a thing that interests you ▸ *Jane's main interest is music.* **3** extra money that the borrower of a loan has to pay to the lender

interfere *verb* (**interferes, interfering, interfered**) **1** to become involved in something that has nothing to do with you **2** to get in the way of something happening ▸ *I hope the weather won't interfere with our picnic.*

interference *noun* 1 interfering in something 2 a crackling or distorting of a radio or television signal

interior *noun* (*plural* **interiors**) the inside of something

interjection *noun* (*plural* **interjections**) another word for **exclamation**

interlude *noun* (*plural* **interludes**) an interval

intermediate *adjective* coming between two things in place, order, or time

interminable *adjective* (*pronounced* in-ter-min-a-bul) seeming to go on for ever **interminably** *adverb*

intern *verb* (**interns, interning, interned**) to keep someone in a special camp or building, usually during a war **internment** *noun*

internal *adjective* on the inside of something **internally** *adverb*

internal-combustion engine *noun* (*plural* **internal-combustion engines**) an engine that produces power by burning fuel

international *adjective* to do with more than one country ► *Interpol is an international police organization.* **internationally** *adverb*

internet *noun* a computer network that allows people all over the world to share information and send messages

interpret *verb* (**interprets, interpreting, interpreted**) 1 to work out what something means ► *The ancient writing was hard to interpret.* ► *We interpreted their signal as meaning we should walk towards them.* 2 to translate what a speaker is saying into another language **interpretation** *noun* an explanation or translation **interpreter** *noun*

interrogate *verb* (**interrogates, interrogating, interrogated**) to question someone carefully **interrogation** *noun*

interrupt *verb* (**interrupts, interrupting, interrupted**) 1 to stop someone while they are talking or doing something 2 to stop something for a time **interruption** *noun*

intersect *verb* (**intersects, intersecting, intersected**) to divide something by going across it ► *The tablecloth had a design of intersecting lines.*

intersection *noun* (*plural* **intersections**) a place where lines or roads cross each other

interval *noun* (*plural* **intervals**) 1 a time between two events or between two parts of a play, film, or concert 2 a space between two things

intervene *verb* (**intervenes, intervening, intervened**) 1 to come between two events ► *During the intervening years they went abroad.* 2 to interrupt an argument or fight and try to stop it **intervention** *noun*

interview *noun* (*plural* **interviews**) a meeting with someone to ask them questions or discuss something

interview *verb* (**interviews, interviewing, interviewed**) to ask someone questions at an interview **interviewer** *noun*

intestines *plural noun* the long tube which food passes along after leaving your stomach

intimate *adjective* 1 very friendly ► *The two girls have been intimate since nursery school.* 2 private or personal ► *I'm not telling you my intimate thoughts.* **intimacy** *noun* closeness or friendship **intimately** *adverb*

intimidate *verb* (**intimidates, intimidating, intimidated**) to frighten someone into doing what you want **intimidation** *noun*

into *preposition* 1 to the inside of something ► *Go into the house.* 2 so as to become ► *The frog changed into a prince.*

intolerable *adjective* unbearable ► *The noise was intolerable.* **intolerably** *adverb*

intolerant *adjective* not able to accept people or ideas that are different in some way **intolerance** *noun*

intonation *noun* the way your voice gets higher and lower when you speak

intoxicate *verb* (**intoxicates, intoxicating, intoxicated**) to make someone drunk **intoxication** *noun*

intrepid *adjective* brave or fearless **intrepidly** *adverb*

intricate *adjective* complicated **intricacy** *noun* **intricately** *adverb*

intrigue *verb* (**intrigues, intriguing, intrigued**) (*pronounced* in-**treeg**) to make someone very interested

intrigue *noun* (*plural* **intrigues**) a mysterious plan or plot

introduce *verb* (**introduces, introducing, introduced**) 1 to make someone known to other people 2 to get something into general use 3 to say a few words to explain a radio or television programme

introduction *noun* (*plural* **introductions**) 1 introducing someone or something 2 a piece at the beginning of a book, explaining what it is about **introductory** *adjective* as a way of introducing something

intrude *verb* (**intrudes, intruding, intruded**) to come in or join in when you are not wanted **intruder** *noun* someone who goes into a place to commit a crime **intrusion** *noun*

intuition *noun* (*pronounced* in-tew-**ish**-on) the power to know or understand things without having to think about them

invade *verb* (**invades, invading, invaded**) to take an army into another country in order to take it over **invader** *noun*

invalid[1] *noun* (*plural* **invalids**) (*pronounced* **in**-va-lid) someone who is ill or disabled

invalid[2] *adjective* (*pronounced* in-**val**-id) not valid ▶ *My passport is invalid.*

invaluable *adjective* very valuable or useful

invariable *adjective* never changing; always the same **invariably** *adverb*

invasion *noun* (*plural* **invasions**) the act of attacking another country with an army

invent *verb* (**invents, inventing, invented**) 1 to be the first person to make something or think of it 2 to make up a story or excuse **invention** *noun* **inventor** *noun*

invertebrate *noun* (*plural* **invertebrates**) an animal without a backbone, such as a worm or an amoeba

inverted commas *plural noun* punctuation marks (" " or ' ') put round spoken words and quotations

invest *verb* (**invests, investing, invested**) to use money to earn interest or make a profit **investment** *noun* money you invest **investor** *noun* someone who invests money

investigate *verb* (**investigates, investigating, investigated**) to find out as much as you can about something or someone **investigation** *noun* **investigator** *noun*

invincible *adjective* not able to be defeated

invisible *adjective* not able to be seen **invisibility** *noun* **invisibly** *adverb*

invite *verb* (**invites, inviting, invited**) to ask someone to come to a party or to do something special **invitation** *noun*

invoice *noun* (*plural* **invoices**) a bill that you get when someone has sold you something or done a job for you

involuntary *adjective* done without thinking

involve *verb* (**involves, involving, involved**) to include something as a necessary part or result ▶ *The job involved a lot of travelling.* **be involved in** to take part in something ▶ *One of his friends had been involved in a bank robbery.* **involvement** *noun* being involved in something

involved *adjective* complicated ▶ *The story was a long and involved one.*

inward *adjective* on the inside, or facing the inside **inwardly** *adverb*

inward or **inwards** *adverb* towards the inside

IQ *noun* a measure of a person's intelligence **IQ** stands for 'intelligence quotient'.

irate *adjective* very angry

iris *noun* (*plural* **irises**) 1 the coloured part of your eyeball 2 a flower with long pointed leaves

iron *noun* (*plural* **irons**) 1 a strong heavy metal 2 a flat-bottomed device that heats up and is used for smoothing clothes

iron *verb* (**irons, ironing, ironed**) to smooth clothes with an iron

irony *noun* saying the opposite of what you mean, so that you emphasize it. For example, it is irony to say 'What a lovely day' when it is pouring with rain.

irregular *adjective* 1 not regular or usual 2 against the rules

irrelevant *adjective* not having anything to do with what is being considered **irrelevance** *noun*

irresistible *adjective* too good or tempting to resist

irresponsible *adjective* not trustworthy; not sensible **irresponsibility** *noun* behaving in an irresponsible way **irresponsibly** *adverb*

irreverent *adjective* not respectful **irreverence** *noun* lack of respect

irrigate *verb* (**irrigates, irrigating, irrigated**) to supply land with water so that crops can grow **irrigation** *noun*

irritable *adjective* easily annoyed **irritability** *noun* crossness; bad temper **irritably** *adverb*

irritate *verb* (**irritates, irritating, irritated**) 1 to annoy someone 2 to make a part of your body itch or feel sore **irritation** *noun* something that irritates you, or a feeling of being irritated

is see **be**

Islam *noun* the religion of Muslims, following the teachings of Muhammad **Islamic** *adjective*

island *noun* (*plural* **islands**) (*sounds like* eye land) a piece of land surrounded by water

isle *noun* (*plural* **isles**) (*rhymes with* mile) an island

isn't short for *is not* ▶ *It really isn't fair.*

isolate *verb* (**isolates, isolating, isolated**) to separate someone or something so that they are alone **isolation** *noun*

issue *verb* (**issues, issuing, issued**) 1 to send something or give it out to people ▶ *They issue blankets to the homeless.* 2 to publish a book or piece of information 3 to come out of something ▶ *Smoke was issuing from the chimney.*

issue *noun* (*plural* **issues**) 1 a subject for discussion or thought ▶ *Traffic problems were a major issue in the local elections.* 2 an edition of a magazine or newspaper sold on one day ▶ *The January issue is out now.*

it *pronoun* 1 used as the subject of a verb to refer to a thing already mentioned ▶ *When the tree fell it hit the greenhouse.* 2 used to say things about the weather or the time ▶ *It's raining.* ▶ *Is it lunch time yet?*

italics *plural noun* letters printed so that they slope, *like this*

itch *noun* (*plural* **itches**) a tickling feeling in your skin that makes you want to scratch it **itchy** *adjective*

itch *verb* (**itches, itching, itched**) to have an itch

item *noun* (*plural* **items**) one thing in a list or group of things

itinerary *noun* (*plural* **itineraries**) a list of places to be visited on a journey

its *pronoun* of it; belonging to it ▶ *The cat hurt its paw.*

it's short for *it is* and (before a verb in the past tense) *it has* ▶ *It's snowing.* ▶ *It's been snowing.*

itself *pronoun* used to refer to the thing already mentioned as 'it' ▶ *The cat has hurt itself.* **by itself** on its own, alone ▶ *The house stood by itself at the end of a lane.*

ivory *noun* the hard creamy-white substance that elephants' tusks are made of

ivy *noun* a climbing evergreen plant with shiny leaves

Jj

jab *verb* (**jabs, jabbing, jabbed**) 1 to poke someone or something with a hard or pointed object 2 to push something roughly into something else

jabber *verb* (jabbers, jabbering, jabbered) to speak very quickly and not clearly

jack *noun* (*plural* jacks) 1 a device for lifting something heavy off the ground 2 a playing card with a picture of a young man
jack *verb* (jacks, jacking, jacked) jack up to lift something heavy with a jack

jackal *noun* (*plural* jackals) a kind of wild dog

jackdaw *noun* (*plural* jackdaws) a bird like a small crow

jacket *noun* (*plural* jackets) 1 a short coat covering the top half of the body 2 a paper cover for a book

jackpot *noun* (*plural* jackpots) the highest prize in a game or lottery

jade *noun* a precious green stone used to make jewellery and ornaments

jagged *adjective* (*pronounced* jag-id) having an uneven edge with sharp points

jaguar *noun* (*plural* jaguars) a large fierce South American animal like a leopard

jail *noun* (*plural* jails) a prison
jail *verb* (jails, jailing, jailed) to put someone in prison

jailer *noun* (*plural* jailers) someone who is in charge of prisoners in a jail

jam¹ *noun* (*plural* jams) 1 a sweet food made of fruit boiled with sugar 2 a lot of people or vehicles crowded together so that they cannot move **in a jam** (informal) in a difficult situation

jam² *verb* (jams, jamming, jammed) to wedge something so that it is tight or stuck, or to become stuck ▶ *I jammed my things in a bag.* ▶ *The window has jammed.*

jamboree *noun* (*plural* jamborees) 1 a large party or celebration 2 a rally of Scouts

jangle *verb* (jangles, jangling, jangled) to make a harsh ringing sound

January *noun* the first month of the year
The word **January** comes from the name of the Roman god Janus, who was the patron of doors and beginnings.

jar¹ *noun* (*plural* jars) a container made of glass or pottery

jar² *verb* (jars, jarring, jarred) 1 to cause a nasty shock or jolt ▶ *The crash jarred my neck.* 2 to sound harsh or unpleasant ▶ *His voice jarred terribly.*

jaundice *noun* a disease that makes your skin yellow

jaunt *noun* (*plural* jaunts) (old use) a short trip or outing

jaunty *adjective* (jauntier, jauntiest) lively and cheerful **jauntily** *adverb*

javelin *noun* (*plural* javelins) a light spear used for throwing in athletics

jaw *noun* (*plural* jaws) 1 one of the two bones that hold your teeth 2 the lower part of your face

jay *noun* (*plural* jays) a noisy brightly-coloured bird

jazz *noun* a kind of music with strong rhythms, first played by black Americans

jealous *adjective* (*pronounced* jel-us) unhappy because you feel that someone is better or luckier than you, or because someone you love seems to love someone else more **jealously** *adverb* **jealousy** *noun* the feeling of being jealous

jeans *plural noun* trousers made of denim

Jeep *noun* (*plural* Jeeps) a small strong vehicle used on rough ground

jeer *verb* (jeers, jeering, jeered) to laugh or shout at someone rudely or unkindly

jelly *noun* (*plural* jellies) 1 a sweet wobbly food with a fruit flavour 2 any soft slippery substance

jellyfish *noun* (*plural* jellyfish) a sea animal with a body like jelly

jerk *verb* (jerks, jerking, jerked) 1 to make a sudden sharp movement 2 to pull something suddenly

jerk *noun* (*plural* **jerks**) a sudden sharp movement **jerky** *adjective* with sudden quick movements **jerkily** *adverb*

jersey *noun* (*plural* **jerseys**) a piece of knitted clothing with sleeves that you wear on the top half of your body; a jumper
The word **jersey** comes from Jersey in the Channel Islands, where a special kind of woollen cloth is made.

jest *noun* (*plural* **jests**) a joke
jest *verb* (**jests, jesting, jested**) to make jokes

jester *noun* (*plural* **jesters**) an entertainer at a royal court in the Middle Ages

jet *noun* (*plural* **jets**) 1 a fast stream of liquid, gas, or flame 2 a narrow opening from which a jet comes out 3 an aircraft driven by engines that send out a powerful jet of hot gas at the back

jet black *noun* a deep black colour
jet black *adjective* having a deep black colour

jetty *noun* (*plural* **jetties**) a small pier or landing stage

Jew *noun* (*plural* **Jews**) 1 a member of the race of people descended from the ancient tribes of Israel 2 someone who believes in the religion of Judaism **Jewish** *adjective*

jewel *noun* (*plural* **jewels**) a precious stone such as a diamond or ruby

jeweller *noun* (*plural* **jewellers**) someone who sells or makes jewellery

jewellery *noun* jewels and ornaments that you wear, such as rings and necklaces

jig *noun* (*plural* **jigs**) a fast lively dance
jig *verb* (**jigs, jigging, jigged**) 1 to dance a jig 2 to move up and down with quick jerks

jigsaw *noun* (*plural* **jigsaws**) 1 a puzzle made of shapes that you fit together to make a picture 2 a saw that can cut curved shapes

jingle *verb* (**jingles, jingling, jingled**) to make a tinkling or clinking sound
jingle *noun* (*plural* **jingles**) 1 a jingling sound 2 a simple tune or song used in a television or radio advertisement

job *noun* (*plural* **jobs**) 1 work that someone does to make money 2 a piece of work to be done

jockey *noun* (*plural* **jockeys**) someone who rides horses in races

jodhpurs *plural noun* (*pronounced* jodperz) trousers that fit closely from the knee to the ankle, worn by horse riders
The word **jodhpurs** comes from the name Jodhpur, a city in India where trousers like these are worn.

jog *verb* (**jogs, jogging, jogged**) 1 to run at a slow pace for exercise 2 to give someone a slight knock or push **jog someone's memory** to help someone remember something **jogger** *noun* someone who jogs for exercise

join *verb* (**joins, joining, joined**) 1 to put things together, or fix one thing to another 2 to become a member of a group or organization ▸ *When he was eighteen he joined the army.* **join in** to take part in something
join *noun* (*plural* **joins**) a place where things are joined

joiner *noun* (*plural* **joiners**) someone who makes furniture and other things out of wood **joinery** *noun* the work that a joiner does

joint *noun* (*plural* **joints**) 1 a place where two things are fixed together 2 the place where two bones fit together 3 a large piece of meat
joint *adjective* shared or done by several people **jointly** *adverb*

joist *noun* (*plural* **joists**) a long beam supporting a floor or ceiling

joke *noun* (*plural* **jokes**) something that you say or do to make people laugh
joke *verb* (**jokes, joking, joked**) to make jokes, or to talk in a way that is not serious

joker *noun* (*plural* **jokers**) 1 someone who makes jokes 2 an extra playing card with a picture of a jester on it

jolly *adjective* (**jollier, jolliest**) happy and cheerful
jolly *adverb* (informal) very ▶ *It's jolly cold.*

jolt *verb* (**jolts, jolting, jolted**) 1 to bump someone or something with a jerk 2 to move along unsteadily
jolt *noun* (*plural* **jolts**) 1 a sudden sharp movement 2 a surprise or shock

jostle *verb* (**jostles, jostling, jostled**) to push someone roughly

jot *verb* (**jots, jotting, jotted**) jot down to write something quickly ▶ *The man jotted down a few details.*

journal *noun* (*plural* **journals**) 1 a newspaper or magazine 2 a diary

journalist *noun* (*plural* **journalists**) someone who writes regularly for a newspaper or magazine **journalism** *noun* collecting and writing news and articles

journey *noun* (*plural* **journeys**) travelling from one place to another

joust *verb* (**jousts, jousting, jousted**) to fight on horseback with lances, as knights did in the Middle Ages

jovial *adjective* cheerful and jolly **joviality** *noun* cheerfulness **jovially** *adverb*

joy *noun* (*plural* **joys**) 1 great happiness or pleasure 2 something that gives happiness

joyful *adjective* feeling or causing great joy **joyfully** *adverb*

joyride *verb* (**joyrides, joyriding**) (informal) to ride in a stolen car for fun **joyrider** *noun*
This word is normally used in the form **joyriding**.

joystick *noun* (*plural* **joysticks**) a control lever that can be moved in several directions, used in computer games

jubilee *noun* (*plural* **jubilees**) a special anniversary celebrating an important event
A **silver jubilee** is the 25th anniversary, a **golden jubilee** is the 50th anniversary, and a **diamond jubilee** is the 60th anniversary.

Judaism *noun* (*pronounced* **joo-day-izm**) the religion of the Jewish people

judge *noun* (*plural* **judges**) 1 someone who listens to cases in a lawcourt and decides what should be done 2 someone who decides the winner of a contest or competition 3 someone who knows enough to make a decision or give an opinion about something ▶ *She's a good judge of character.*
judge *verb* (**judges, judging, judged**) 1 to be a judge in a law case or a competition 2 to estimate or guess an amount ▶ *It's hard to judge the distance from here.*

judgement *noun* (*plural* **judgements**) 1 the ability to make decisions wisely ▶ *You showed good judgement.* 2 a ruling or opinion about something

judo *noun* a Japanese form of wrestling in which you try to bring your opponent to the ground

jug *noun* (*plural* **jugs**) a container for liquids, with a handle and lip

juggernaut *noun* (*plural* **juggernauts**) a large articulated lorry
The word **juggernaut** comes from the name of a Hindu god whose image was carried in a procession on a huge vehicle.

juggle *verb* (**juggles, juggling, juggled**) to keep throwing a number of objects into the air and catch them again without dropping any **juggler** *noun*

juice *noun* (*plural* **juices**) the liquid from fruit, vegetables, or other food **juicy** *adjective*

jukebox *noun* (*plural* **jukeboxes**) a machine that plays music of your choice when you put a coin in

July *noun* the seventh month of the year
The word **July** comes from the Roman month *Julius*, named after Julius Caesar.

jumble *verb* (**jumbles, jumbling, jumbled**) to mix things up in a confused way
jumble *noun* a confused mixture of things

jumble sale *noun* (*plural* **jumble sales**) a sale of second-hand clothes and other things to raise money

jumbo jet *noun* (*plural* **jumbo jets**) a large jet aircraft

jump *verb* (**jumps, jumping, jumped**) **1** to move suddenly from the ground into the air **2** to go over something by jumping **3** to move quickly or suddenly ▸ *He jumped into a passing taxi.* **jump at** (*informal*) to take something eagerly ▸ *When they invited her to visit, she jumped at the chance.*

jump *noun* (*plural* **jumps**) a sudden movement into the air

jumper *noun* (*plural* **jumpers**) a jersey

junction *noun* (*plural* **junctions**) a place where roads or railway lines join

June *noun* the sixth month of the year
The word **June** comes from the Roman month *Junius*, named in honour of the goddess Juno.

jungle *noun* (*plural* **jungles**) a thick tangled forest in a hot country

junior *adjective* **1** younger **2** for young children ▸ *She goes to a junior school.* **3** lower in rank or importance

junior *noun* (*plural* **juniors**) a child at a junior school

junk *noun* rubbish or worthless things

junk food *noun* food that contains a lot of sugar and starch and is not good for you

jury *noun* (*plural* **juries**) a group of twelve people who listen to what people say in a lawcourt and decide whether an accused person is guilty or not guilty

just *adjective* **1** fair and right ▸ *The judges listened to all the arguments so they could reach a just decision.* **2** deserved ▸ *He got his just reward after years of hard work.*

just *adverb* **1** exactly ▸ *It's just what I need.* **2** only; simply ▸ *I just wanted another drink.* **3** by a small amount ▸ *The ball hit* her just below the knee. **4** a short time ago ▸ *They had just gone.* **5** now, immediately ▸ *I'm just leaving.*

justice *noun* just or fair treatment of people

justify *verb* (**justifies, justifying, justified**) to show that something is fair or reasonable ▸ *I justified giving Martin more money by saying that he was older.* **justifiable** *adjective* easy to justify **justification** *noun* a good reason for something

jut *verb* (**juts, jutting, jutted**) to stick out

juvenile *adjective* **1** to do with young people **2** childish

juvenile delinquent *noun* (*plural* **juvenile delinquents**) a young person who keeps breaking the law

Kk

kaleidoscope *noun* (*plural* **kaleidoscopes**) (*pronounced* kal-I-dos-kohp) a tube that you look through and turn to see changing brightly-coloured patterns

kangaroo *noun* (*plural* **kangaroos**) an Australian animal with strong hind legs for jumping

karaoke *noun* (*pronounced* ka-ri-oh-ki) a party entertainment in which people sing along to recorded background music
The word **karaoke** comes from Japanese words meaning 'empty orchestra'.

karate noun (*pronounced* ka-**rah**-ti) a Japanese method of self-defence using your hands, arms, and feet
The word **karate** comes from Japanese words meaning 'empty hand'.

kayak noun (*plural* **kayaks**) (*pronounced* ky-ak) a small canoe with a covering that fits round your waist

kebab noun (*plural* **kebabs**) small pieces of meat, vegetables, or other food cooked on a skewer

keel noun (*plural* **keels**) a long piece of wood or metal running along the middle of the bottom of a boat

keel verb (**keels, keeling, keeled**) keel over to overturn or fall sideways

keen adjective (**keener, keenest**) 1 eager or enthusiastic ▸ *They are keen swimmers.* ▸ *She is keen on dancing.* ▸ *We are very keen to go.* 2 strong or sharp ▸ *Cats have keen eyesight.* **keenly** adverb **keenness** noun

keep verb (**keeps, keeping, kept**) 1 to have something and not get rid of it 2 to let something or someone continue in a certain way ▸ *I'll try to keep my room clean.* 3 to continue to do something or feel something ▸ *You'll need a coat to keep warm.* 4 to do something repeatedly ▸ *They kept laughing at us.* 5 to fulfil a promise ▸ *I hope you'll keep your word.* 6 to have animals or pets and look after them ▸ *He has a nephew who keeps chickens.* 7 to stay in good condition ▸ *The milk should keep for a few days.* **keep up** to continue doing something **keep up with** to go as fast as someone

keep noun (*plural* **keeps**) 1 the food or money someone needs to live ▸ *They have to earn their keep.* 2 a strong tower in a castle

keeper noun (*plural* **keepers**) 1 someone who looks after animals 2 a goalkeeper

keeping noun good care or protection ▸ *Give me your tickets for safe keeping.*

keg noun (*plural* **kegs**) a small barrel

kennel noun (*plural* **kennels**) a shelter for a dog

kept past tense and past participle of **keep** verb

kerb noun (*plural* **kerbs**) the row of stones at the edge of a pavement

kernel noun (*plural* **kernels**) the part inside the shell of a nut

kestrel noun (*plural* **kestrels**) a kind of small falcon

ketchup noun a thick tomato sauce

kettle noun (*plural* **kettles**) a container with a spout and handle, used for boiling water in

key noun (*plural* **keys**) 1 a piece of metal made to fit and open a lock or to wind up clockwork 2 each of the small levers on a piano or keyboard that you press to work it 3 a scale of musical notes ▸ *The song is in the key of C major.* 4 something that solves a problem or mystery

keyboard noun (*plural* **keyboards**) 1 a set of keys on a piano, typewriter, or computer 2 an electronic musical instrument with keys like a small piano

keyhole noun (*plural* **keyholes**) the hole in a lock where the key goes

khaki noun (*pronounced* **kah**-ki) a dull yellowish-brown colour

kick verb (**kicks, kicking, kicked**) 1 to hit someone or something sharply with your foot 2 to move your legs about vigorously **kick off** to start a football match with the first kick of the ball

kick noun (*plural* **kicks**) a kicking movement

kick-off noun (*plural* **kick-offs**) the start of a football match

kid noun (*plural* **kids**) 1 a young goat 2 (informal) a child

kid verb (**kids, kidding, kidded**) (informal) to fool or tease someone

kidnap verb (**kidnaps, kidnapping, kidnapped**) to capture someone by force, usually to get ransom **kidnapper** noun

kidney *noun* (*plural* **kidneys**) each of two organs in your body that remove waste products from your blood and produce urine

kill *verb* (**kills, killing, killed**) to cause the death of a person or animal **killer** *noun*

kiln *noun* (*plural* **kilns**) an oven for baking pottery or bricks to make them hard

kilo *noun* (*plural* **kilos**) a kilogram
Words beginning **kilo-** come from a Greek word *chilioi* meaning 'thousand'.

kilogram *noun* (*plural* **kilograms**) a unit of weight equal to 1,000 grams or about 2.2 pounds

kilometre *noun* (*plural* **kilometres**) a unit of length equal to 1,000 metres or about 0.62 of a mile

kilowatt *noun* (*plural* **kilowatts**) a unit of electrical power equal to 1,000 watts

kilt *noun* (*plural* **kilts**) 1 a kind of pleated tartan skirt. Kilts are worn as traditional dress by Scottish men. 2 a skirt like a kilt, worn by girls and women

kimono *noun* (*plural* **kimonos**) (*pronounced* ki-**moh**-noh) a loose robe with large sleeves, worn as traditional dress by Japanese women

kin *noun* your family or relatives **next of kin** your closest relative

kind *noun* (*plural* **kinds**) a type or sort of something ▶ *What kind of food do you like?*

kind *adjective* (**kinder, kindest**) helpful and friendly **kindness** *noun*

kindergarten *noun* (*plural* **kindergartens**) (*pronounced* kin-der-gah-ten) a school for very young children

kind-hearted *adjective* kind and generous **kind-heartedness** *noun*

kindle *verb* (**kindles, kindling, kindled**) 1 to make something start burning 2 to start burning

kindly *adverb* 1 in a kind way ▶ *He spoke kindly to the little boy.* 2 please ▶ *Kindly close the door.*

kindly *adjective* (**kindlier, kindliest**) kind ▶ *He gave a kindly smile.* **kindliness** *noun*

king *noun* (*plural* **kings**) 1 a man who has been crowned as the ruler of a country 2 a piece in chess that has to be captured to win the game 3 a playing card with a picture of a king on it

kingdom *noun* (*plural* **kingdoms**) a country that is ruled by a king or queen

kingfisher *noun* (*plural* **kingfishers**) a brightly-coloured bird that lives near water and feeds on fish

kink *noun* (*plural* **kinks**) a short twist in a rope or wire

kiosk *noun* (*plural* **kiosks**) 1 a small hut or stall where you can buy newspapers, sweets, and other things 2 a telephone box
The word **kiosk** comes from a Turkish word meaning 'pavilion'.

kipper *noun* (*plural* **kippers**) a smoked herring

kiss *verb* (**kisses, kissing, kissed**) to touch someone with your lips as a sign of affection or greeting

kiss *noun* (*plural* **kisses**) an act of kissing someone

kit *noun* (*plural* **kits**) 1 a set of equipment or clothes for a special purpose 2 a set of parts that you buy to make something

kitchen *noun* (*plural* **kitchens**) a room where you prepare and cook food

kite *noun* (*plural* **kites**) a light frame covered with cloth or paper, which you fly in the wind at the end of a long string

kitten *noun* (*plural* **kittens**) a young cat

kitty *noun* (*plural* **kitties**) an amount of money for a special purpose

kiwi *noun* (*plural* **kiwis**) a New Zealand bird that cannot fly

kiwi fruit *noun* (*plural* **kiwi fruits**) a fruit with a hairy skin and soft green flesh

knack *noun* a special skill or ability to do something

knapsack *noun* (*plural* **knapsacks**) a bag carried on the back by hikers or soldiers

knave *noun* (*plural* **knaves**) (old use) 1 a dishonest man 2 a jack in a pack of playing cards

knead *verb* (**kneads, kneading, kneaded**) to press and stretch dough with your hands, to make it ready for baking

knee *noun* (*plural* **knees**) the joint where your leg bends

kneecap *noun* (*plural* **kneecaps**) the bone at the front of your knee

kneel *verb* (**kneels, kneeling, knelt**) to go down on your knees

knew past tense of **know**

knickers *plural noun* underpants worn by women or girls

knife *noun* (*plural* **knives**) a cutting tool made of a blade set in a handle

knife *verb* (**knifes, knifing, knifed**) to stab someone with a knife

knight *noun* (*plural* **knights**) 1 a man who has been given the title 'Sir' by a king or queen 2 in the Middle Ages, a nobleman who fought on horseback for a king or lord 3 a piece in chess, with a horse's head **knighthood** *noun* the honour of being made a knight

knit *verb* (**knits, knitting, knitted**) to make clothes from threads of wool by using long needles or a machine

knob *noun* (*plural* **knobs**) a thick round handle or control button **knobbly** *adjective* having a lumpy or bumpy surface

knock *verb* (**knocks, knocking, knocked**) to hit something hard so as to make a noise **knock out** to hit someone so that they become unconscious

knock *noun* (*plural* **knocks**) the act or sound of knocking something

knocker *noun* (*plural* **knockers**) a device for knocking on a door

knockout *noun* (*plural* **knockouts**) 1 knocking someone out 2 a game or contest in which the loser in each round has to drop out

knot *noun* (*plural* **knots**) 1 a join made by tying string, rope, or ribbon 2 a tangle; a lump 3 a round spot on a piece of wood where a branch once joined it 4 a cluster of people or things 5 a unit for measuring the speed of ships and aircraft, 1.85 kilometres or 2,025 yards per hour

knot *verb* (**knots, knotting, knotted**) to tie something with a knot

know *verb* (**knows, knowing, knew, known**) 1 to have something in your mind that you have learned or discovered ▸ *Do you know the answer?* ▸ *Jenny knows several languages.* 2 to recognize or remember a person or place ▸ *I've known these people for years.* ▸ *I don't know the way home.*

knowledge *noun* (*pronounced* **nol**-ij) the facts or information that someone knows

knowledgeable *adjective* (*pronounced* **nol**-ij-a-bul) knowing a lot **knowledgeably** *adverb*

knuckle *noun* (*plural* **knuckles**) a joint in your finger

koala *noun* (*plural* **koalas**) (*pronounced* koh-**ah**-la) a furry Australian animal that lives in trees

Koran *noun* (*pronounced* kor-**ahn**) the holy book of Islam
The word **Koran** comes from an Arabic word meaning 'reading'.

kosher *adjective* (describing food) prepared according to Jewish religious law

Ll

label *noun* (*plural* **labels**) a piece of paper, cloth, metal, or plastic with writing on it, fixed to something to provide information about it

label *verb* (**labels, labelling, labelled**) to put a label on something

laboratory *noun* (*plural* **laboratories**) a room or building equipped for scientific work

laborious *adjective* needing a lot of effort; very hard **laboriously** *adverb* **laboriousness** *noun*

labour *noun* 1 hard work 2 the work a woman does when she is giving birth to a baby

labourer *noun* (*plural* **labourers**) someone who does hard work with their hands, especially outdoors

Labour Party *noun* one of the main British political parties

Labrador *noun* (*plural* **Labradors**) a large black or light-brown dog

labyrinth *noun* (*plural* **labyrinths**) a complicated set of passages or paths
The word **labyrinth** comes from a Greek word that originally referred to the maze in Greek mythology where the Minotaur lived.

lace *noun* (*plural* **laces**) 1 a fine thin material with patterns of small holes in it 2 a piece of thin cord used to tie up a shoe or boot
lace *verb* (**laces, lacing, laced**) to tie a shoe or boot with a lace

lack *noun* being without something
▸ *There is a lack of water every summer.*
lack *verb* (**lacks, lacking, lacked**) to be without something ▸ *She lacked enthusiasm for the task.*

lacquer *noun* a kind of varnish that dries hard

lad *noun* (*plural* **lads**) a boy

ladder *noun* (*plural* **ladders**) 1 something you can climb up, made of upright pieces of wood, metal, or rope, with crosspieces called rungs 2 a tear in tights or stockings

laden *adjective* (not an everyday word) carrying a heavy load

ladle *noun* (*plural* **ladles**) a large deep spoon with a long handle

lady *noun* (*plural* **ladies**) 1 a polite word for a woman 2 a well-mannered woman, or a woman who is high up in society **Lady** the title of a noblewoman or the wife of a knight

ladybird *noun* (*plural* **ladybirds**) a small flying beetle, usually red with black spots

lag *verb* (**lags, lagging, lagged**) 1 to go too slowly and not keep up with others 2 to wrap pipes with insulating material to keep in the heat

lager *noun* (*plural* **lagers**) (*pronounced* **lah-ger**) a pale-coloured beer

lagoon *noun* (*plural* **lagoons**) a lake separated from the sea by sandbanks or reefs

laid past tense and past participle of **lay** *verb*

lain past participle of **lie**[1] *verb*

lair *noun* (*plural* **lairs**) the place where a wild animal lives

lake *noun* (*plural* **lakes**) a large area of water surrounded by land

lama *noun* (*plural* **lamas**) a Buddhist priest or monk in Tibet

lamb *noun* (*plural* **lambs**) 1 a young sheep 2 meat from a young sheep

lame *adjective* (**lamer, lamest**) 1 unable to walk normally 2 feeble or weak ▸ *a lame excuse* **lameness** *noun*

lamp *noun* (*plural* **lamps**) a device for producing light from electricity, gas, or oil

lamp-post *noun* (*plural* **lamp-posts**) a tall post in a street or public place, with a lamp at the top

lance *noun* (*plural* **lances**) a long spear once used by soldiers on horseback

land *noun* (*plural* **lands**) 1 the dry parts of the world's surface 2 the ground or soil 3 a country or nation
land *verb* (**lands, landing, landed**) 1 to arrive on land after a journey in a ship or

aircraft **2** to reach the ground after jumping or falling **3** to bring someone to a place in a ship or aircraft

landing *noun* (*plural* **landings**) a flat area at the top of a flight of stairs

landlady *noun* (*plural* **landladies**) **1** a woman who owns a house or rooms that people can rent **2** a woman who looks after a pub

landlord *noun* (*plural* **landlords**) **1** a person who owns a house or rooms that people can rent **2** a person who looks after a pub

landmark *noun* (*plural* **landmarks**) an object on land that you can easily see from a distance

landowner *noun* (*plural* **landowners**) a person who owns a large amount of land

landscape *noun* (*plural* **landscapes**) **1** what you can see when you look across an area of land **2** a picture of the countryside

landslide *noun* (*plural* **landslides**) a fall of earth or rocks down the side of a mountain or hill

lane *noun* (*plural* **lanes**) **1** a narrow road, usually in the country **2** a strip of road for a single line of traffic **3** a strip of track or water for one runner or swimmer in a race

language *noun* (*plural* **languages**) **1** the words people use to speak and write **2** a system of signs or symbols giving information, especially in computing

lanky *adjective* (**lankier, lankiest**) extremely tall and thin

lantern *noun* (*plural* **lanterns**) a frame with transparent sides for holding a light and shielding it from the wind

lap *noun* (*plural* **laps**) **1** the top part of your legs when you are sitting down **2** one circuit of a racetrack

lap *verb* (**laps, lapping, lapped**) **1** to drink liquid with the tongue, as a cat or dog does **2** to make a gentle splash on rocks or the shore, as waves do **3** to be so far ahead of other runners going round a track that you pass them from behind

lapel *noun* (*plural* **lapels**) (*pronounced* la-**pel**) the flap folded back at each front edge of a coat or jacket

lapse *noun* (*plural* **lapses**) **1** a slight mistake or fault **2** the passing of time ► *After a lapse of three months work began again.*

lapse *verb* (**lapses, lapsing, lapsed**) to be no longer valid ► *My passport has lapsed.*

laptop *noun* (*plural* **laptops**) a small portable computer

larch *noun* (*plural* **larches**) a tall tree that has small cones

lard *noun* white greasy fat from pigs, used in cooking

larder *noun* (*plural* **larders**) a cupboard or small room for keeping food cool

large *adjective* (**larger, largest**) more than the ordinary or average size; big **at large** free and dangerous ► *A lion from the zoo may be at large.*

largely *adverb* mainly; mostly ► *We are largely to blame for the mistake.*

lark *noun* (*plural* **larks**) a small sandy-brown bird

larva *noun* (*plural* **larvae**) an insect in the first stage of its life, after it comes out of the egg

lasagne *noun* (*pronounced* la-**zan**-ya) a dish made of strips of pasta with minced meat and a cheese sauce
The word **lasagne** is Italian, and comes from a Latin word meaning 'cooking pot'.

laser *noun* (*plural* **lasers**) a device that makes a strong narrow beam of light

lash *noun* (*plural* **lashes**) **1** a whip **2** an eyelash

lash *verb* (**lashes, lashing, lashed**) **1** to hit something like a whip ► *Rain lashed the* *window.* **2** to tie something tightly with a rope or cord **lash out** to speak or hit out angrily

lass *noun* (*plural* **lasses**) a girl or young woman

lasso *noun* (*plural* **lassos**) (*pronounced* la-soo) a rope with a loop at the end which tightens when you pull on it, used for catching cattle

last *adjective* and *adverb* **1** coming at the end ▶ *Try not to miss the last bus.* **2** most recent or latest ▶ *Where were you last night?*

last *noun* a person or thing that is last ▶ *You are the last to arrive.* **at last** finally; at the end

last *verb* (**lasts, lasting, lasted**) **1** to continue ▶ *The journey lasts for two hours.* **2** to go on without being used up ▶ *Our supplies won't last much longer.*

lastly *adverb* in the last place; finally

latch *noun* (*plural* **latches**) a small bar for fastening a gate or door

late *adjective* and *adverb* (**later, latest**) **1** after the proper or expected time ▶ *We were late because of a bus strike.* **2** near the end of a period of time ▶ *They came late in the afternoon.* **3** recent ▶ *Have you heard the latest news?* **4** no longer alive ▶ *A statue was put up in honour of the late king.*

lately *adverb* recently ▶ *She has been very tired lately.*

lathe *noun* (*plural* **lathes**) (*pronounced* laythh) a machine for holding and turning pieces of wood or metal while you shape them

lather *noun* (*plural* **lathers**) a thick froth of soap bubbles

Latin *noun* the language of the ancient Romans

latitude *noun* (*plural* **latitudes**) the distance of a place north or south of the equator, measured in degrees on a map

latter *adjective* towards the end ▶ *November is in the latter part of the year.* **the latter** the second of two people or things just mentioned ▶ *If it's a choice*

between a picnic or a swim I prefer the latter.
See also **former**.

laugh *verb* (**laughs, laughing, laughed**) to make sounds that show you are happy or that you think something is funny

laugh *noun* (*plural* **laughs**) an act or sound of laughing

laughter *noun* laughing or the sound of laughing

launch *verb* (**launches, launching, launched**) **1** to send a ship into the water for the first time **2** to send a rocket into space **3** to start a project or business

launch *noun* (*plural* **launches**) **1** the launching of a ship or spacecraft **2** a large motor boat

launderette *noun* (*plural* **launderettes**) a shop with washing machines that people pay to use

laundry *noun* (*plural* **laundries**) **1** clothes to be washed **2** a place where clothes are sent or taken to be washed

laurel *noun* (*plural* **laurels**) an evergreen bush with smooth shiny leaves

lava *noun* liquid rock that flows from a volcano

lavatory *noun* (*plural* **lavatories**) a toilet

lavender *noun* **1** a sweet-smelling shrub with pale purple flowers **2** a pale purple colour

lavender *adjective* having a pale purple colour

lavish *adjective* generous or plentiful **lavishly** *adverb*

law *noun* (*plural* **laws**) **1** a rule or set of rules that everyone must keep **2** a rule in science, such as the law of gravity

lawcourt *noun* (*plural* **lawcourts**) a room or building where a judge and jury or a magistrate decide whether someone has broken the law

lawful *adjective* allowed by the law **lawfully** *adverb*

lawn *noun* (*plural* **lawns**) an area of short grass in a garden

lawnmower *noun* (*plural* **lawnmowers**) a machine you use for cutting grass

lawyer *noun* (*plural* **lawyers**) someone who is an expert in the law and helps people with legal matters

lax *adjective* not strict; tolerant

lay¹ *verb* (**lays, laying, laid**) 1 to put something down carefully or in a special way 2 to arrange things on a table or other surface, especially for a meal 3 (used about a bird) to produce an egg **lay on** to provide something ▸ *The company lays on a dinner for the workers each year.*

lay² past tense of **lie**¹ *verb*

layby *noun* (*plural* **laybys**) a space by the side of a road where vehicles can stop for a while

layer *noun* (*plural* **layers**) something flat that covers the surface of something else ▸ *A layer of snow covered the ground.*

layout *noun* (*plural* **layouts**) the arrangement or design of something

laze *verb* (**lazes, lazing, lazed**) to spend time in a lazy way

lazy *adjective* (**lazier, laziest**) not wanting to work; doing little work **lazily** *adverb* **laziness** *noun*

lead¹ *verb* (**leads, leading, led**) (*pronounced* leed) 1 to guide a person or animal by going in front 2 to be in charge of an activity 3 to be winning in a race or competition 4 to go in a particular direction ▸ *This road leads to the beach.* **lead to** to cause something ▸ *Carelessness led to the accident.*

lead *noun* (*plural* **leads**) (*pronounced* leed) 1 leading or guidance ▸ *Give us a lead.* 2 a leading place or position ▸ *She took the lead.* 3 a strap or cord for leading a dog 4 an electric wire

lead² *noun* (*plural* **leads**) (*pronounced* led) 1 a soft heavy grey metal 2 the part running through the middle of a pencil that makes marks

leader *noun* (*plural* **leaders**) someone who leads or is in charge **leadership** *noun* the ability to be a good leader

leaf *noun* (*plural* **leaves**) 1 one of the flat and usually green parts that grow on a tree or plant 2 a page of a book 3 a thin sheet of something **leafy** *adjective* having a lot of leaves or trees

leaflet *noun* (*plural* **leaflets**) a piece of paper printed with information about something

league *noun* (*plural* **leagues**) (*pronounced* leeg) 1 a group of sports teams that play matches against each other 2 a group of countries that have agreed to help each other

leak *noun* (*plural* **leaks**) a hole or crack that liquid or gas can escape through **leaky** *adjective*

leak *verb* (**leaks, leaking, leaked**) 1 to let liquid or gas escape through a hole or crack ▸ *The sink is leaking.* 2 to escape through a hole or crack ▸ *Oil was leaking from one of the pipes.* **leakage** *noun* an escape of liquid or gas

lean¹ *verb* (**leans, leaning, leaned** or **leant**) 1 to bend your body towards something or over it 2 to put something in a sloping position against a surface ▸ *She leaned her bicycle against the wall.* 3 to rest against something

lean² *adjective* (**leaner, leanest**) 1 (describing meat) having little fat 2 (describing a person) thin **leanness** *noun*

leap *verb* (**leaps, leaping, leapt** or **leaped**) to jump high in the air, or a long way

leap *noun* (*plural* **leaps**) a big jump

leapfrog *noun* a game in which you jump with your legs apart over another player who is bending down

leapfrog *verb* (**leapfrogs, leapfrogging, leapfrogged**) to jump over someone in a game of leapfrog

leap year *noun* (*plural* **leap years**) a year with an extra day in it, on 29 February
A year is a leap year when you can divide it by 4, as you can with 2000 and 2004. It is probably called leap year because the dates from March onwards 'leap' one day forward after the extra day.

learn *verb* (**learns, learning, learnt** or **learned**) to get knowledge or skill about something

learned *adjective* (*pronounced* **ler**-nid) knowing a lot

learner *noun* (*plural* **learners**) someone who is learning something, especially how to drive a car

lease *noun* (*plural* **leases**) an agreement that lets you use a building or land in return for payment

leash *noun* (*plural* **leashes**) a strap or cord for leading a dog

least *adjective* and *adverb* smallest in amount or size ▸ *Cycling is my least favourite sport.*

least *noun* the smallest amount ▸ *The least she could do was offer him a lift.* **at least** not less than and probably more than ▸ *We'll need at least two people to move the bookcase.*

leather *noun* a strong material made from the skins of animals **leathery** *adjective* tough, like leather

leave *verb* (**leaves, leaving, left**) **1** to go away from a person, place, or group **2** to let something stay where it is or remain as it is ▸ *I've left my sandwiches at home.* **3** to give something to someone in a will ▸ *My uncle left me his watch.*

leave *noun* permission to be away from work

leaves plural of **leaf**

lecture *noun* (*plural* **lectures**) a talk about a subject to an audience or a class

lecture *verb* (**lectures, lecturing, lectured**) to give a lecture **lecturer** *noun*

led past tense and past participle of **lead** *verb*

ledge *noun* (*plural* **ledges**) a narrow shelf or flat surface

leek *noun* (*plural* **leeks**) a long white vegetable with broad green leaves at one end

leer *verb* (**leers, leering, leered**) to look unpleasantly at someone

leeward *adjective* facing away from the wind

left[1] *adjective* and *adverb* on the side that faces west if you think of yourself as facing north

left *noun* the left side

left[2] past tense and past participle of **leave** *verb*

left-handed *adjective* using your left hand more than your right hand

leg *noun* (*plural* **legs**) **1** one of the parts of a human's or animal's body on which they stand or move **2** the part of a piece of clothing that covers your leg **3** each of the supports of a table or chair **4** each of a pair of matches between the same teams in a competition

legacy *noun* (*plural* **legacies**) (*pronounced* **leg**-a-si) an amount of money or property that someone receives in a will

legal *adjective* **1** allowed by the law **2** to do with the law or lawyers **legality** *noun* **legally** *adverb*

legalize *verb* (**legalizes, legalizing, legalized**) to make something legal

legend *noun* (*plural* **legends**) (*pronounced* **lej**-und) an old story handed down from the past **legendary** *adjective* to do with legends

legible *adjective* (*pronounced* **lej**-i-bul) clear enough to read ▸ *I hope my writing is legible.* **legibility** *noun* how easily you can read something **legibly** *adverb*

legion *noun* (*plural* **legions**) **1** a division of the ancient Roman army **2** a group of soldiers

legislation *noun* the process of making laws

legitimate *adjective* allowed by a law or custom; valid ▸ *We need a legitimate reason for being late.* **legitimacy** *noun* whether something is allowed **legitimately** *adverb*

leisure *noun* free time, when you can do what you like

leisurely *adjective* done with plenty of time; not hurried ▸ *We went for a leisurely stroll.*

lemon *noun* (*plural* **lemons**) **1** a yellow citrus fruit with a sharp sour taste **2** a pale yellow colour

lemon *adjective* having a pale yellow colour

lemonade *noun* (*plural* **lemonades**) a drink with a lemon flavour

lend *verb* (**lends, lending, lent**) to let someone have something of yours for a time, after which they must give it back

length *noun* (*plural* **lengths**) **1** the distance a thing is from one end to the other **2** a piece of something cut from a longer piece, for example string or cloth

lengthen *verb* (**lengthens, lengthening, lengthened**) **1** to make something longer **2** to become longer

lengthy *adjective* (**lengthier, lengthiest**) going on for a long time ▶ *a lengthy speech.*

lenient *adjective* kind; not strict **lenience** *noun* or **leniency** *noun* **leniently** *adverb*

lens *noun* (*plural* **lenses**) **1** a curved piece of glass or plastic used to focus the light in a camera or a pair of glasses **2** the part of your eye that focuses the light

Lent *noun* the six weeks before Easter, during which Christians fast

lent past tense and past participle of **lend**

lentil *noun* (*plural* **lentils**) a small green, orange, yellow, or brown seed that can be dried and then cooked

leopard *noun* (*plural* **leopards**) (*pronounced* **lep**-erd) a large fierce African and Asian cat with a yellow-brown coat and black spots

leotard *noun* (*plural* **leotards**) (*pronounced* **lee**-o-tard) a close-fitting piece of clothing worn by acrobats and dancers
The word **leotard** is named after a French trapeze artist called Jules Léotard, who invented it.

less *adjective* and *adverb* smaller; not so much ▶ *Make less noise.* ▶ *It is less important.*

less *noun* a smaller amount ▶ *I have less than you.*

lessen *verb* (**lessens, lessening, lessened**) **1** to make something smaller or not so much **2** to become smaller or not so much

lesson *noun* (*plural* **lessons**) **1** the time when someone is being taught **2** something that you have to learn **3** a passage from the Bible read in church

let *verb* (**lets, letting, let**) **1** to allow someone to do something ▶ *Do let them stay.* **2** to cause something to happen ▶ *Don't let your bike slide into the ditch.* **3** to allow someone to use a house or room in return for payment **4** to allow someone to go in or out ▶ *Please let me in.* **let down** to disappoint someone **let off** to excuse someone from a punishment or duty

lethal *adjective* (*pronounced* **lee**-thal) causing death **lethally** *adverb*

letter *noun* (*plural* **letters**) **1** one of the symbols used for writing words, such as a, b, or c **2** a written message sent to another person

letter box *noun* (*plural* **letter boxes**) **1** a slot in a door for delivering letters **2** a postbox

lettuce *noun* (*plural* **lettuces**) a green vegetable with crisp leaves used in salads

leukaemia *noun* (*pronounced* **lew**-kee-mi-a) a serious blood disease

level *adjective* **1** flat and even or horizontal ▶ *The ground is level near the house.* **2** equal or even ▶ *After half an hour the scores were still level.*

level *verb* (**levels, levelling, levelled**) **1** to make something flat or horizontal **2** to become horizontal

level *noun* (*plural* **levels**) **1** a height or position ▶ *The shelf is at eye level.* ▶ *The village is thousands of metres above sea level.* **2** a device that shows if something is horizontal **3** a standard or grade of achievement

level crossing noun (plural **level crossings**) a place where a road crosses a railway at the same level

lever noun (plural **levers**) 1 a bar that you push or pull to lift something heavy or force something open 2 a handle you use to make a machine work

liable adjective 1 likely to do or get something ▸ *They are liable to forget things.* 2 responsible for something ▸ *If there is any damage you will be liable.*

liar noun (plural **liars**) someone who tells lies

liberal adjective 1 generous ▸ *Put a liberal amount of sun cream on your skin.* 2 not strict; tolerant **liberally** adverb

Liberal Democrats plural noun members of a British political party

liberate verb (**liberates, liberating, liberated**) to set someone free **liberation** noun

liberty noun (plural **liberties**) freedom

librarian noun (plural **librarians**) someone who looks after a library or works in one

library noun (plural **libraries**) a place where you can go to read or borrow books

lice plural of **louse**

licence noun (plural **licences**) an official document allowing someone to do or use something ▸ *a television licence.*

license verb (**licenses, licensing, licensed**) to give someone a licence to do something

lichen noun (plural **lichens**) (pronounced **ly-ken**) a dry-looking plant that grows on rocks and trees

lick verb (**licks, licking, licked**) to move your tongue over something
lick noun (plural **licks**) the action of licking something

lid noun (plural **lids**) 1 a cover for a box or jar 2 an eyelid

lie¹ verb (**lies, lying, lay, lain**) 1 to be in or get into a flat position ▸ *People were sitting in chairs or lying on the floor.* 2 to be or remain a certain way ▸ *The castle was*

lying in ruins.
You must say ▸ *She was lying down* and not ▸ *She was laying down..*

lie² verb (**lies, lying, lied**) to say something that you know is not true
lie noun (plural **lies**) something you say that you know is not true

lieutenant noun (plural **lieutenants**) (pronounced **lef-ten-ant**) an officer in the army or navy

life noun (plural **lives**) 1 the time when a person or animal is alive and able to grow and move 2 all living things ▸ *There is unlikely to be life on Mars.* 3 energy or liveliness ▸ *She is full of life.*

lifeboat noun (plural **lifeboats**) a boat for rescuing people at sea

life cycle noun (plural **life cycles**) the series of changes in the life of a living thing

lifeguard noun (plural **lifeguards**) someone who rescues swimmers in difficulty

life jacket noun (plural **life jackets**) a special safety jacket that will help a person to float in water

lifeless adjective 1 without life 2 unconscious

lifelike adjective looking exactly like a real person or thing

life-size adjective (describing a statue or model) having the size of the person or thing it represents

lifetime noun (plural **lifetimes**) the time when someone is alive

lift verb (**lifts, lifting, lifted**) 1 to pick something up or raise it to a higher level 2 to rise or go upwards ▸ *The fog was beginning to lift.*
lift noun (plural **lifts**) 1 a device like a small moving room for taking people or goods from one floor to another in a building 2 a ride in someone else's car or other vehicle

light¹ noun (plural **lights**) 1 the form of energy that takes away darkness and makes it possible to see things ▸ *The climbers found their way back by the light of*

the moon. **2** something that gives out light
▶ *Switch on the light.*

light *adjective* (**lighter**, **lightest**) **1** full of
light; not dark **2** pale ▶ *light blue.*

light *verb* (**lights**, **lighting**, **lit** or **lighted**) **1** to
start something burning **2** to begin to burn
▶ *The fire won't light.* **3** to provide a place
with light ▶ *The streets were lit by
gaslamps.*

light² *adjective* (**lighter**, **lightest**) **1** not
weighing very much **2** not large or strong
▶ *A light wind began to blow.* **3** not needing
much effort ▶ *I can do a little light work.*
4 lively and pleasant rather than serious
▶ *She was listening to light music on the car
radio.* **lightly** *adverb* **lightness** *noun*

lighten *verb* (**lightens**, **lightening**,
lightened) **1** to make something lighter or
brighter **2** to become lighter

lighter *noun* (*plural* **lighters**) a device for
lighting a cigarette or a fire

light-hearted *adjective* **1** cheerful and
having nothing to worry about **2** not
serious **light-heartedly** *adverb* **light-
heartedness** *noun*

lighthouse *noun* (*plural* **lighthouses**)
a tower with a bright light at the top to
guide ships and warn them of danger

lightning *noun* a flash of bright light in the
sky during a thunderstorm

light year *noun* (*plural* **light years**) the
distance that light travels in one year
(about 9.5 million million km or 6 million
million miles)

like¹ *verb* (**likes**, **liking**, **liked**) to think that
someone or something is pleasant or
enjoyable **should like** or **would like** to want
▶ *I should like a holiday.* **likeable** *adjective*
easy to like

like² *preposition* **1** similar to ▶ *She looks
like her mother.* **2** in the same way as ▶ *He
fought like a bear.* **3** such as ▶ *We need
things like knives and forks.* **4** typical of
▶ *It was like her to forgive him.*

like *adjective* similar ▶ *They are as like as
two peas.*

likely *adjective* (**likelier**, **likeliest**) probable;
expected to happen or to be true

likeness *noun* (*plural* **likenesses**)
a similarity or resemblance

likewise *adverb* in the same way

liking *noun* a feeling that you like
something or someone ▶ *a liking for
chocolate.*

lilac *noun* (*plural* **lilacs**) a bush with sweet-
smelling purple or white flowers

lily *noun* (*plural* **lilies**) a tall garden flower
grown from a bulb

limb *noun* (*plural* **limbs**) (*pronounced* lim)
a leg or an arm

lime *noun* (*plural* **limes**) **1** a green fruit like
a small round lemon **2** a tree with yellow
blossom **3** a white chalky powder used to
make cement or as a fertilizer

limelight *noun* in the limelight getting a lot
of attention

limerick *noun* (*plural* **limericks**)
(*pronounced* **lim-er-ik**) an amusing poem
with five lines and a strong rhythm

limestone *noun* a kind of rock used for
building and for making lime (the chalky
powder)

limit *noun* (*plural* **limits**) a line or point
that you cannot or should not pass ▶ *You
must obey the speed limit.*

limit *verb* (**limits**, **limiting**, **limited**) to keep
someone or something within a limit
limitation *noun* something that limits what
you can do

limp[1] *verb* (**limps, limping, limped**) to walk with difficulty because you have hurt or damaged your leg or foot
limp *noun* (*plural* **limps**) a limping movement

limp[2] *adjective* (**limper, limpest**) not stiff; without much strength ▸ *He gave her a limp handshake.* **limply** *adverb* **limpness** *noun*

limpet *noun* (*plural* **limpets**) a small shellfish that clings firmly to rocks

line[1] *noun* (*plural* **lines**) 1 a long thin mark 2 a row or series of people or things 3 a length of something long and thin like rope, string, or wire 4 a railway or a length of railway track
line *verb* (**lines, lining, lined**) 1 to mark something with lines 2 to form an edge or border along something ▸ *The streets are lined with trees.* 3 to put a lining in a piece of clothing **line up** to form lines or rows ▸ *The children lined up in the playground.*

linen *noun* 1 a heavy cloth made from flax, used to make things such as shirts, sheets, and tablecloths 2 things made of this cloth

liner *noun* (*plural* **liners**) a large passenger ship or aircraft

linesman *noun* (*plural* **linesmen**) an official in football, tennis, and other games who decides whether the ball has crossed the line

linger *verb* (**lingers, lingering, lingered**) to stay around or be slow to leave

linguist *noun* (*plural* **linguists**) someone who studies languages or can speak several languages well **linguistic** *adjective* to do with languages

lining *noun* (*plural* **linings**) a layer of material covering the inside of a piece of clothing

link *noun* (*plural* **links**) 1 one of the rings in a chain 2 a connection
link *verb* (**links, linking, linked**) to join things together

lino or **linoleum** *noun* a stiff shiny floor covering

lion *noun* (*plural* **lions**) a large powerful wild animal found in Africa and Asia

lioness *noun* (*plural* **lionesses**) a female lion

lip *noun* (*plural* **lips**) 1 each of the two fleshy edges of your mouth 2 the edge of something hollow such as a cup or a crater 3 the pointed part at the top of a jug or saucepan, for pouring from

lipstick *noun* (*plural* **lipsticks**) a waxy form of make-up used for colouring the lips

liquid *noun* (*plural* **liquids**) a substance such as water or oil that is wet and can flow
liquid *adjective* flowing freely

liquidizer *noun* (*plural* **liquidizers**) a machine for turning food into a liquid or pulp

liquor *noun* (*plural* **liquors**) (*pronounced* **lik-er**) any strong alcoholic drink

liquorice *noun* (*pronounced* **lik-er-iss** or **lik-er-ish**) a soft black sweet with a strong taste, made from the root of a plant

lisp *noun* (*plural* **lisps**) a way of speaking, in which *s* and *z* are pronounced like *th*
lisp *verb* (**lisps, lisping, lisped**) to speak with a lisp

list[1] *noun* (*plural* **lists**) a group of names or items written or said one after another
list *verb* (**lists, listing, listed**) to make a list of things

list[2] *verb* (**lists, listing, listed**) (used about a ship) to lean over to one side in the water

listen *verb* (**listens, listening, listened**) (*pronounced* **liss-en**) to try to hear someone or something **listener** *noun*

listless *adjective* tired and unable to do very much **listlessly** *adverb* **listlessness** *noun*

lit past tense and past participle of **light** *verb*

literacy *noun* the ability to read and write

literally *adverb* really; meaning exactly what the words say ▸ *The noise made me literally jump out of my seat.*

literate *adjective* (*pronounced* **lit-er-at**) able to read and write

literature *noun* great or famous works of fiction such as poems, plays, and novels

litmus *noun* a blue substance used to show whether something is an acid or an alkali

litre *noun* (*plural* **litres**) (*pronounced* lee-ter) a measure of liquid, 1,000 cubic centimetres or about 1.75 pints

litter *noun* (*plural* **litters**) **1** an untidy mass of unwanted paper or rubbish **2** a number of young animals born to one mother at one time

little *adjective* (**less** or **littler**, **least** or **littlest**) **1** small; not great or not much ▸ *She had a little dog.* ▸ *We have very little time.* **2** a small amount of something ▸ *Have a little sugar.*
little *adverb* not much ▸ *They go swimming very little now.*

live¹ *verb* (**lives**, **living**, **lived**) (*rhymes with* give) **1** to be alive **2** to have your home in a place ▸ *She is living in Rome now.* **3** to spend your life in a certain way ▸ *He lived as a hermit.* **live on** to use something as food ▸ *The islanders live mainly on fish.*

live² *adjective* (*rhymes with* hive) **1** alive **2** carrying electricity ▸ *One of the wires is live.* **3** seen or heard on television or radio while it is actually happening

livelihood *noun* (*plural* **livelihoods**) the way in which you earn a living

lively *adjective* (**livelier**, **liveliest**) full of life and energy; cheerful **liveliness** *noun* being lively

liver *noun* (*plural* **livers**) **1** an organ in your body that cleans your blood **2** an animal's liver, used for food

livery *noun* (*plural* **liveries**) the special colours used by a company on its vehicles, or worn as a uniform

lives plural of **life**

livestock *noun* farm animals

livid *adjective* **1** very angry **2** having a strong bluish-grey colour, like a bruise

living *noun* (*plural* **livings**) something you do to earn money ▸ *She makes a living selling jewellery.*

living room *noun* (*plural* **living rooms**) a room for general use during the day

lizard *noun* (*plural* **lizards**) a small four-legged reptile with scaly skin and a long tail

llama *noun* (*plural* **llamas**) (*pronounced* lah-ma) a South American woolly animal like a small camel without a hump

load *noun* (*plural* **loads**) something large or heavy that has to be carried
load *verb* (**loads**, **loading**, **loaded**) **1** to put a load into a vehicle that will carry it ▸ *We've loaded the crates into the van.* **2** to put a bullet or shell into a gun, ready for firing **3** to put something into a machine, such as a film in a camera or a cassette in a tape recorder **4** to enter programs or data on a computer

loaf *noun* (*plural* **loaves**) a mass of bread baked in one piece
loaf *verb* (**loafs**, **loafing**, **loafed**) to loiter or waste time

loan *noun* (*plural* **loans**) something that has been lent to someone, especially money
loan *verb* (**loans**, **loaning**, **loaned**) to lend something

loathe *verb* (**loathes**, **loathing**, **loathed**) (*rhymes with* clothe) to dislike something or someone very much

loathsome *adjective* disgusting; horrible

lob *verb* (**lobs**, **lobbing**, **lobbed**) to throw or hit something high into the air

lobby *noun* (*plural* **lobbies**) an entrance hall

lobe *noun* (*plural* **lobes**) the thick rounded part at the bottom of your ear

lobster *noun* (*plural* **lobsters**) a shellfish with a hard shell and two large claws

local *adjective* belonging to a particular place or area ▸ *the local shops* **locally** *adverb*

locality *noun* (*plural* **localities**) an area or district

locate *verb* (**locates, locating, located**) (not an everyday word) to discover where something is ▸ *I have located the fault.* **be located** to be situated ▸ *The Post Office is located in the High Street.*

location *noun* (*plural* **locations**) the place where something is **on location** filmed in natural surroundings, not in a studio

loch *noun* (*plural* **lochs**) (*pronounced* lok) a lake in Scotland

lock *noun* (*plural* **locks**) 1 a device for fastening a door or window or container, needing a key to open it 2 a section of a canal or river with gates at each end, allowing the water and the boats on it to be changed to different levels 3 a few strands of hair formed into a loop
lock *verb* (**locks, locking, locked**) 1 to fasten something with a lock 2 to become fixed in one position

locker *noun* (*plural* **lockers**) a small cupboard for keeping things safe

locket *noun* (*plural* **lockets**) a small case holding a photograph or lock of hair, worn on a chain round the neck

locomotive *noun* (*plural* **locomotives**) a railway engine

locust *noun* (*plural* **locusts**) an insect like a large grasshopper. Locusts fly in swarms that eat all the plants in an area.

lodge *noun* (*plural* **lodges**) a small house, often at the entrance to a large house or building
lodge *verb* (**lodges, lodging, lodged**) 1 to stay at a place as a lodger 2 to become fixed ▸ *The ball lodged in the branches.*

lodger *noun* (*plural* **lodgers**) someone who pays to live in a room in someone else's house

loft *noun* (*plural* **lofts**) a room or space under the roof of a house

lofty *adjective* (**loftier, loftiest**) tall, high

log *noun* (*plural* **logs**) 1 a large piece cut from a tree that has fallen or been cut down 2 a detailed record of a journey by a ship or aircraft

log *verb* (**logs, logging, logged**) **log in** or **log on** to start using a computer **log out** or **log off** to finish using a computer

logic *noun* correct thinking and working out of ideas **logical** *adjective* **logically** *adverb*

logo *noun* (*plural* **logos**) (*pronounced* loh-goh) a printed symbol used by a business company or other organization

loiter *verb* (**loiters, loitering, loitered**) to stand about doing nothing

lollipop *noun* (*plural* **lollipops**) a hard sticky sweet on the end of a stick

lolly *noun* (*plural* **lollies**) a piece of flavoured ice on a stick

lonely *adjective* (**lonelier, loneliest**) 1 unhappy because you are on your own 2 far from other inhabited places ▸ *a lonely village* **loneliness** *noun*

long[1] *adjective* (**longer, longest**) 1 measuring a lot from one end to the other ▸ *a long path* 2 taking a lot of time ▸ *a long holiday* 3 measured from one end to the other ▸ *A cricket pitch is 22 yards long.*
long *adverb* (**longer, longest**) 1 for a long time ▸ *Have you been waiting long?* 2 a long time before or after ▸ *They left long ago.* **as long as** or **so long as** provided that; on condition that ▸ *I'll come as long as I can bring my dog.*
long *verb* (**longs, longing, longed**) **long for** to want something very much

longitude *noun* (*plural* **longitudes**) the distance of a place east or west of an imaginary line passing through Greenwich in London, measured in degrees on a map

loo *noun* (*plural* **loos**) (informal) a lavatory

look *verb* (**looks, looking, looked**) 1 to use your eyes to see 2 to appear a certain way ▸ *You look happy.* **look after** to take care of something or someone **look for** to try to find something or someone **look forward to** to be waiting eagerly for something to happen **look out** to be careful **look up** to look for something in a book
look *noun* (*plural* **looks**) 1 the act of looking ▸ *Can you have a look for my shoes?* ▸ *His look changed when he heard*

the news. **2** the appearance of someone or something, or what they seem to be ▸ *The house had a deserted look.*

lookout *noun* (*plural* **lookouts**) **1** a place where you watch for something **2** someone who keeps watch

loom[1] *noun* (*plural* **looms**) a machine for weaving cloth

loom[2] *verb* (**looms, looming, loomed**) to appear large and threatening ▸ *An iceberg loomed out of the fog.*

loop *noun* (*plural* **loops**) the shape made by something that bends round and crosses over itself, such as a piece of string or wire
loop *verb* (**loops, looping, looped**) to make something into a loop

loophole *noun* (*plural* **loopholes**) a way of getting round a law or rule without quite breaking it

loose *adjective* (**looser, loosest**) **1** not tight or firm ▸ *The door handle had become loose.* **2** not tied up or shut in ▸ *The dog got loose.*

loosen *verb* (**loosens, loosening, loosened**) **1** to make something loose **2** to become loose

loot *noun* things that have been stolen
loot *verb* (**loots, looting, looted**) to rob a place during a riot, especially in a time of rioting or war **looter** *noun*

lopsided *adjective* with one side lower than the other; uneven **lopsidedly** *adverb*

lord *noun* (*plural* **lords**) a nobleman, especially one who is allowed to use the title 'Lord' in front of his name **Lord** a name used by Christians for God or Christ

lordly *adjective* grand or proud

lorry *noun* (*plural* **lorries**) a large motor vehicle for carrying goods

lose *verb* (**loses, losing, lost**) (*pronounced* looz) **1** to no longer have something, especially because you cannot find it ▸ *I've lost my pen.* **2** to be beaten in a game or competition ▸ *The local team lost on*

Saturday. **3** (used about a clock or watch) to show a time that is later than the correct time **lose your way** not to know where you are **loser** *noun* someone who loses a game, or who often loses or fails at things

loss *noun* (*plural* **losses**) **1** losing something **2** something you have lost **at a loss** puzzled or confused

lost *adjective* **1** not knowing where you are or where to go **2** not able to be found

lot *noun* (*plural* **lots**) a large number of people or things **the lot** or **the whole lot** everything **draw lots** to choose one person or thing from a group by a method that depends on chance

lotion *noun* (*plural* **lotions**) a liquid that you put on your skin to clean or soothe it

lottery *noun* (*plural* **lotteries**) a game in which prizes are given to people who have winning tickets that are chosen by a draw

loud *adjective* (**louder, loudest**) **1** noisy; easily heard **2** bright or gaudy ▸ *loud colours* **loudly** *adverb* **loudness** *noun*

loudspeaker *noun* (*plural* **loudspeakers**) the part of a radio or music system that produces the sound

lounge *noun* (*plural* **lounges**) a sitting room
lounge *verb* (**lounges, lounging, lounged**) to sit about lazily

louse *noun* (*plural* **lice**) a small insect that sucks the blood of humans or animals

lousy *adjective* (**lousier, lousiest**) (*pronounced* **low-zi**) **1** full of lice **2** (informal) very bad or unpleasant

lout *noun* (*plural* **louts**) a bad-mannered person

love *noun* **1** a strong feeling of liking someone or something very much **2** in games, a score of nothing **be in love with** to love someone very much
love *verb* (**loves, loving, loved**) to like someone or something very much **lovable** *adjective* easy to love; attractive **lover** *noun* someone who is in love with another person

lovely *adjective* (**lovelier, loveliest**) 1 fine or beautiful 2 (*informal*) very pleasant or enjoyable **loveliness** *noun*

low[1] *adjective* (**lower, lowest**) 1 only reaching a short way up; not high ▸ *She sat on a low wall.* 2 below average in amount or importance ▸ *They are soldiers of a low rank.* ▸ *Prices are low.* 3 unhappy ▸ *I'm feeling low.* 4 at the bottom end of a musical scale

low[2] *verb* (**lows, lowing, lowed**) to make a sound like a cow

lower *verb* (**lowers, lowering, lowered**) 1 to make something less high 2 to move something down 3 to make a sound less loud ▸ *Please lower your voices.*

lowly *adjective* (**lowlier, lowliest**) humble and unimportant **lowliness** *noun*

loyal *adjective* faithful to your friends or country **loyally** *adverb* **loyalty** *noun* being loyal

lozenge *noun* (*plural* **lozenges**) a small sweet tablet containing medicine

Ltd. in names of companies, short for *limited*, which means that the people who own shares in the company do not have to pay all the company's debts

lubricate *verb* (**lubricates, lubricating, lubricated**) to put oil or grease on machinery so that it moves smoothly **lubrication** *noun*

lucid *adjective* clear and easy to understand **lucidity** *noun* how clear something is

luck *noun* 1 the way things happen by chance, without being planned 2 a good thing that happens by chance

lucky *adjective* (**luckier, luckiest**) 1 having good luck 2 bringing good luck **luckily** *adverb*

ludicrous *adjective* (*pronounced* **loo-di-krus**) very silly or absurd

lug *verb* (**lugs, lugging, lugged**) to carry or drag something heavy

luggage *noun* suitcases and bags that you take on a journey

lukewarm *adjective* slightly warm

lull *verb* (**lulls, lulling, lulled**) to soothe or calm someone

lull *noun* (*plural* **lulls**) a short period of quiet or rest

lullaby *noun* (*plural* **lullabies**) a song that is sung to send a baby to sleep

lumber *noun* 1 junk or unwanted things 2 rough timber

lumber *verb* (**lumbers, lumbering, lumbered**) to move along clumsily or noisily

lumberjack *noun* (*plural* **lumberjacks**) someone who cuts down trees and transports them

luminous *adjective* shining or glowing in the dark

lump *noun* (*plural* **lumps**) 1 a solid piece of something 2 a swelling **lumpy** *adjective*

lunacy *noun* madness

lunar *adjective* to do with the moon

lunatic *noun* (*plural* **lunatics**) an insane person

lunch *noun* (*plural* **lunches**) a meal eaten in the middle of the day
The word **lunch** is a short form of **luncheon**, which is no longer an everyday word.

lung *noun* (*plural* **lungs**) each of the two organs in your chest that you use for breathing

lunge *verb* (**lunges, lunging, lunged**) to move forward suddenly

lupin *noun* (*plural* **lupins**) a garden plant with tall spikes of flowers

lurch *verb* (**lurches, lurching, lurched**) to stagger or lean suddenly ▸ *The drunken man lurched clumsily from one lamp-post to the next.*

lurch *noun* (*plural* **lurches**) a sudden staggering or leaning movement **to leave someone in the lurch** to desert someone when they are in difficulty

lure *verb* (**lures, luring, lured**) to tempt a person or animal into a trap or difficulty

lurid *adjective* **1** extremely bright or glowing ▸ *His tie was a lurid orange.* **2** unpleasant or shocking ▸ *The newspapers had lurid details of the accident.*

lurk *verb* (**lurks, lurking, lurked**) to wait threateningly where you cannot be seen

luscious *adjective* tasting or smelling delicious

lush *adjective* (**lusher, lushest**) **1** growing abundantly **2** luxurious

lust *noun* (*plural* **lusts**) a strong or greedy desire

lustre *noun* brightness or brilliance **lustrous** *adjective* shining brightly

lute *noun* (*plural* **lutes**) an old musical instrument like a guitar but with a deeper and rounder body

luxury *noun* (*plural* **luxuries**) **1** something expensive that you enjoy but do not need ▸ *New curtains would be a luxury.* **2** having many expensive things ▸ *They lead a life of luxury.* **luxurious** *adjective*

lying present participle of **lie**[1] *verb* and **lie**[2] *verb*

lynch *verb* (**lynches, lynching, lynched**) (used about a mob of people) to put someone to death without a proper trial
The word **lynch** is named after an American judge called William Lynch, who allowed this kind of punishment in the 18th century.

lyre *noun* (*plural* **lyres**) an ancient musical instrument like a small harp

lyrical *adjective* like a song

lyrics *plural noun* the words of a popular song

Mm

macaroni *noun* a kind of pasta in the shape of short tubes

machine *noun* (*plural* **machines**) a device with moving parts that work together to do something

machine-gun *noun* (*plural* **machine-guns**) a gun that can keep firing bullets quickly one after another

machinery *noun* machines, or the moving parts of a machine

mackerel *noun* (*plural* **mackerel**) a sea fish used as food

mackintosh *noun* (*plural* **mackintoshes**) a type of waterproof coat
Mackintosh is named after a Scotsman who invented the material it is made from. He was called Charles Macintosh, and he spelt his name without a *k*.

mad *adjective* (**madder, maddest**) **1** having something wrong with your mind; not sane **2** (informal) very excited or annoyed **3** (informal) silly or foolish ▸ *I've had a mad idea about that.* **like mad** (informal) with great speed, energy, or enthusiasm **mad about** liking or interested in something or someone very much **madly** *adverb* **madness** *noun*

madam *noun* a word used when speaking politely to a woman, instead of her name ▸ *Will you step this way, madam?*

madden *verb* (**maddens, maddening, maddened**) to make someone angry or mad

made past tense and past participle of **make** *verb*

madman *noun* (*plural* **madmen**) a mad person

magazine *noun* (*plural* **magazines**) **1** a kind of newspaper with articles, stories, and pictures, which comes out every week or month **2** the part of a gun that holds the cartridges **3** a store for

weapons, ammunition, or explosives
4 a device that holds film for a camera
or slides for a projector

maggot *noun* (*plural* **maggots**) the larva
of some kinds of fly. Maggots look like
short fat worms.

magic *noun* 1 in stories, the power to do
wonderful or supernatural things that
people cannot usually do 2 clever tricks
that seems like magic

magical *adjective* 1 done by magic or as if
by magic 2 wonderful; marvellous
magically *adverb*

magician *noun* (*plural* **magicians**)
someone who does magic tricks

magistrate *noun* (*plural* **magistrates**)
a judge in a local court who deals with
crimes that are not very serious

magnet *noun* (*plural* **magnets**) a piece of
metal that can attract iron or steel
magnetic *adjective* **magnetism** *noun*

magnetize *verb* (**magnetizes, magnetizing,
magnetized**) to make something into a
magnet

magnificent *adjective* extremely fine or
splendid **magnificence** *noun* **magnificently**
adverb

magnify *verb* (**magnifies, magnifying,
magnified**) to make something look bigger
than it really is **magnification** *noun*
magnifying something, or the amount that
something is magnified

magnitude *noun* (*plural* **magnitudes**)
how large or important something is

magpie *noun* (*plural* **magpies**) a black and
white bird with a long tail, which likes to
collect bright objects

mahogany *noun* a hard reddish-brown
wood

maid *noun* (*plural* **maids**) 1 a female
servant in a hotel or private house 2 (old
use) a girl

maiden *noun* (*plural* **maidens**) (old use)
a girl

maiden voyage *noun* (*plural* **maiden
voyages**) a ship's first voyage

mail *noun* 1 letters and parcels sent by post
2 armour made of metal rings joined
together

mail *verb* (**mails, mailing, mailed**) to send
something by post

maim *verb* (**maims, maiming, maimed**) to
injure someone so that they are disabled

main *adjective* largest or most important

main or **mains** *noun* the pipes or cables
carrying water, gas, or electricity to a
building

mainland *noun* the main part of a country
or continent, not the islands around it

mainly *adverb* mostly or chiefly

maintain *verb* (**maintains, maintaining,
maintained**) 1 to keep something in good
condition ▶ *The farmer has several
tractors to maintain.* 2 to have an opinion
or belief ▶ *I maintain that travelling by
train is best.* 3 to provide money for
someone to live ▶ *They have a family to
maintain.*

maintenance *noun* keeping something in
good condition

maize *noun* a tall kind of corn with large
seeds

majestic *adjective* stately and dignified
majestically *adverb*

majesty *noun* being stately and dignified
Your majesty a title used to address a king
or queen

major *adjective* more important; main
▶ *The major roads are shown in red on the
map.*

major *noun* (*plural* **majors**) an army
officer higher than a captain

majority *noun* (*plural* **majorities**) (*pronounced* ma-jo-ri-ti) the greatest part of a group of people or things

make *verb* (**makes, making, made**) 1 to build or produce something ▸ *The factory down the road makes furniture.* 2 to cause something to happen ▸ *The noise made us jump.* 3 to earn or achieve something ▸ *She makes money selling jewellery.* 4 to reach somewhere in time ▸ *Do you think we can make the 7 o'clock train?* 5 to estimate or judge something ▸ *What do you make the time?* 6 to add up to a total ▸ *5 and 7 make 12.* 7 to give someone a promise 8 to tidy or arrange a bed for someone to use **make do** to manage with something that is not what you really want **make for** to go towards a place ▸ *They are making for Glasgow.* **make out** to manage to see or hear something ▸ *Can you make out what's going on?* **make up** to invent a story or excuse **make up for something** to give or do something in return for something disappointing that has happened **make up your mind** to decide **maker** *noun*

make *noun* (*plural* **makes**) a type of goods made by a particular manufacturer

make-believe *noun* pretending or imagining things

makeshift *adjective* used because you have nothing better ▸ *When visitors come we use the sofa as a makeshift bed.*

make-up *noun* coloured powders and creams that women and actors use on their faces

malaria *noun* a disease with a fever, spread by mosquito bites

male *adjective* of the sex that produces young by fertilizing the female's egg cells
male *noun* (*plural* **males**) a male person or animal

malevolent *adjective* (*pronounced* ma-lev-o-lent) wanting to harm other people **malevolence** *noun*

malice *noun* a desire to harm other people

malicious *adjective* intending to do harm **maliciously** *adverb*

mallet *noun* (*plural* **mallets**) a large wooden hammer

malnutrition *noun* bad health caused by not having enough food

malt *noun* dried barley used in brewing and making vinegar

mammal *noun* (*plural* **mammals**) an animal that is born alive, rather than in an egg, and feeds on its mother's milk

mammoth *noun* (*plural* **mammoths**) an extinct kind of hairy elephant with long curved tusks
mammoth *adjective* huge

man *noun* (*plural* **men**) 1 a grown-up male human being 2 all the people in the world ▸ *Look what harm man is doing to the environment.* 3 one of the pieces used in a board game
man *verb* (**mans, manning, manned**) to supply something with the people needed to work it ▸ *Three astronauts will man the spacecraft.*

manage *verb* (**manages, managing, managed**) 1 to be able to do something although it is difficult ▸ *Did you manage to tell them the news?* 2 to be in charge of a business or group of people **manageable** *adjective* that you can manage easily **management** *noun* **manager** *noun*

mane *noun* (*plural* **manes**) the long hair along the back of the neck of a horse or lion

manger *noun* (*plural* **mangers**) a box or trough in a stable for animals to feed from

mangle *verb* (**mangles, mangling, mangled**) to crush something or cut it up roughly

mango *noun* (*plural* **mangoes**) a juicy tropical fruit with yellow flesh

manhandle *verb* (**manhandles, manhandling, manhandled**) to handle someone or something roughly

manhole *noun* (*plural* **manholes**) a hole with a cover, through which a person can reach a sewer or boiler to inspect or repair it

mania *noun* (*plural* **manias**) 1 violent madness 2 a strong enthusiasm ▸ *They have a mania for board games.*

maniac *noun* (*plural* **maniacs**) a mad or violent person

manic *adjective* mad or wildly excited

manipulate *verb* (**manipulates, manipulating, manipulated**) 1 to handle something skilfully or carefully 2 to get someone to do what you want by treating them cleverly **manipulation** *noun* **manipulator** *noun*

mankind *noun* all the people in the world

manly *adjective* (**manlier, manliest**) 1 strong or brave 2 suitable for a man or like a man ▸ *He has a manly voice.* **manliness** *noun*

manner *noun* (*plural* **manners**) 1 the way that something happens or is done ▸ *He looked at me in a suspicious manner.* 2 the way someone behaves or speaks ▸ *He has a very gentle manner.*

manners *plural noun* polite or courteous behaviour

manoeuvre *noun* (*plural* **manoeuvres**) (*pronounced* ma-**noo**-ver) a skilful or clever action

manoeuvre *verb* (**manoeuvres, manoeuvring, manoeuvred**) 1 to move skilfully or cleverly 2 to move something skilfully into position

manor *noun* (*plural* **manors**) a large important country house with an estate

mansion *noun* (*plural* **mansions**) a grand house

manslaughter *noun* (*pronounced* **man-slaw-ter**) the crime of killing someone without intending to

mantelpiece *noun* (*plural* **mantelpieces**) a shelf above a fireplace

manual *adjective* done with the hands ▸ *manual work* **manually** *adverb*

manual *noun* (*plural* **manuals**) a book of instructions

manufacture *verb* (**manufactures, manufacturing, manufactured**) to make things with machines in a factory **manufacturer** *noun*

manure *noun* animal dung added to the soil to make it more fertile

manuscript *noun* (*plural* **manuscripts**) something written or typed but not printed

many *adjective* (**more, most**) large in number ▸ *Tania's sweatshirt had many holes in it.*

many *noun* a large number of people or things ▸ *Many of them wanted to stay.*

Maori *noun* (*plural* **Maoris**) (*pronounced* **mow-ri**) 1 a member of the aboriginal people of New Zealand 2 the language of the Maoris

map *noun* (*plural* **maps**) a diagram of part or all of the earth's surface, showing features such as towns, mountains, and rivers

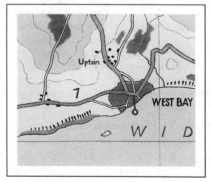

map *verb* (**maps, mapping, mapped**) to make a map of an area **map out** to plan something in a general way

maple *noun* (*plural* **maples**) a tree with broad leaves

mar *verb* (**mars, marring, marred**) to spoil something

marathon *noun* (*plural* **marathons**) a race for runners, usually 26 miles (42 kilometres) long
The word **marathon** comes from the name of a place near Athens in Greece. The ancient Greeks fought the Persians in a battle in 490 BC, and a runner is said to have run to Athens with news of the Greek victory.

marble *noun* (*plural* **marbles**) **1** a small glass ball used in games **2** a hard kind of stone that is polished and used for building or sculpture

March *noun* the third month of the year
The word **March** comes from the Roman month *Martius*, named in honour of the god Mars.

march *verb* (**marches, marching, marched**) **1** to walk with regular steps **2** to make someone walk somewhere ▶ *His mother marched him round to the doctor.*

march *noun* (*plural* **marches**) **1** a walk done by marching **2** a piece of music suitable for marching to

mare *noun* (*plural* **mares**) a female horse or donkey

margarine *noun* a soft creamy food like butter, made from animal or vegetable fats

margin *noun* (*plural* **margins**) **1** the blank space round the writing or pictures on the page of a book **2** the difference between two scores or prices ▶ *We won by a narrow margin.*

marigold *noun* (*plural* **marigolds**) a garden plant with yellow or orange flowers

marijuana *noun* (*pronounced* ma-ri-**wah**-na) a drug made from hemp

marina *noun* (*plural* **marinas**) (*pronounced* ma-**ree**-na) a harbour for yachts and motor boats

marine *adjective* (*pronounced* ma-**reen**) to do with the sea
marine *noun* (*plural* **marines**) a soldier trained to serve on land and sea
The word **marine** comes from the Latin word *maris* meaning 'of the sea'.

mariner *noun* (*plural* **mariners**) (*pronounced* ma-ri-ner) (old use) a sailor

mark[1] *noun* (*plural* **marks**) **1** a spot, line, or stain on something **2** a number or letter put on a piece of work to show how good it is **3** a special feature or sign of something ▶ *He raised his hat as a mark of respect.*
mark *verb* (**marks, marking, marked**) **1** to put a mark on something **2** to give a number or letter to a piece of work to show how good it is **3** to keep close to an opposing player in football, netball, and other games

mark[2] *noun* (*plural* **marks**) a unit of money in Germany

market *noun* (*plural* **markets**) a place where people buy and sell things, usually from stalls in the open air

marksman *noun* (*plural* **marksmen**) an expert in shooting at a target

marmalade *noun* jam made from oranges or lemons

maroon[1] *verb* (**maroons, marooning, marooned**) to abandon someone in a place far away from other people

maroon[1] *adjective* dark red
maroon *noun* a dark red colour

marquee *noun* (*plural* **marquees**) (*pronounced* mar-**kee**) a large tent used for a party or exhibition

marriage *noun* (*plural* **marriages**) **1** the state of being married **2** a wedding ceremony

marrow *noun* (*plural* **marrows**) **1** the soft substance inside bones **2** a large green or yellow vegetable with a hard skin

marry *verb* (**marries, marrying, married**) **1** to become someone's husband or wife **2** to declare that two people are husband and wife at a special ceremony

marsh *noun* (*plural* **marshes**) a low-lying area of wet ground **marshy** *adjective*

marshal *noun* (*plural* **marshals**) **1** an official who supervises a contest or ceremony **2** a law officer in the USA

marshmallow *noun* (*plural* **marshmallows**) a soft spongy sweet

marsupial *noun* (*plural* **marsupials**) an animal such as a kangaroo or wallaby. The female has a pouch for carrying its young.

martial *adjective* to do with war or fighting

martial arts *plural noun* fighting sports such as karate and judo

martyr *noun* (*plural* **martyrs**) (*pronounced* **mar-ter**) someone who is killed or suffers because of their beliefs **martyrdom** *noun* being a martyr

marvel *noun* (*plural* **marvels**) a wonderful thing

marvel *verb* (**marvels, marvelling, marvelled**) to be filled with wonder or astonishment by something

marvellous *adjective* wonderful; very good **marvellously** *adverb*

marzipan *noun* a soft sweet food made from almonds and sugar

mascot *noun* (*plural* **mascots**) a person, animal, or object that people think will bring them good luck

masculine *adjective* to do with men; suitable for men

mash *verb* (**mashes, mashing, mashed**) to crush something into a soft mass

mask *noun* (*plural* **masks**) a covering worn over your face to disguise or protect it

mask *verb* (**masks, masking, masked**) 1 to cover your face with a mask 2 to cover or conceal something

mason *noun* (*plural* **masons**) someone who builds or works with stone

masonry *noun* the stone parts of a building

Mass *noun* (*plural* **Masses**) the Communion service in a Roman Catholic church

mass *noun* (*plural* **masses**) 1 a large amount of something; a lump or heap 2 in science, how much matter there is in an object

massacre *verb* (**massacres, massacring, massacred**) (*pronounced* **mas-a-ker**) to kill a large number of people

massacre *noun* (*plural* **massacres**) the killing of a large number of people

massage *verb* (**massages, massaging, massaged**) (*pronounced* **mas-ahzh**) to rub and press someone's body to make it less stiff or less painful

massage *noun* (*plural* **massages**) massaging the body

massive *adjective* very large and heavy

mast *noun* (*plural* **masts**) a tall pole that supports a ship's sails

master *noun* (*plural* **masters**) 1 a man who is in charge of something 2 a male owner of a dog, horse, or other animal 3 a man who teaches in a school 4 a great artist or composer 5 something from which copies are made

master *verb* (**masters, mastering, mastered**) 1 to learn a subject completely 2 to control a fear or difficulty ▶ *He found it hard to master all his feelings.*

masterly *adjective* very clever or skilful

masterpiece *noun* (*plural* **masterpieces**) a very fine piece of work

mat *noun* (*plural* **mats**) 1 a small piece of material that covers part of a floor 2 a small piece of material put on a table to protect the surface

match *noun* (*plural* **matches**) 1 a game or contest between two teams or players 2 one person or thing that is equal or similar to another 3 a small stick with a chemical at one end that gives a flame when you rub it on something rough

match *verb* (**matches, matching, matched**) 1 to be equal to someone or something else 2 to go well with something ▶ *The jacket and trousers don't match.*

mate *noun* (*plural* **mates**) 1 a friend or companion 2 one of a pair of animals that have come together to have offspring 3 one of the officers on a ship 4 checkmate in chess

mate *verb* (**mates, mating, mated**) (used about animals) to come together to have offspring

material *noun* (*plural* **materials**) 1 cloth or fabric 2 a substance used for making something

maternal *adjective* to do with a mother, or like a mother

maternity *noun* having a baby

mathematics *noun* the study of numbers, measurements, and shapes **mathematical** *adjective* **mathematician** *noun* someone who studies mathematics

maths *noun* mathematics

matinée *noun* (*plural* **matinées**) (*pronounced* mat-i-nay) an afternoon performance at a theatre or cinema

matrimony *noun* marriage **matrimonial** *adjective*

matt *adjective* not shiny ▸ *matt paint*

matted *adjective* tangled

matter *noun* (*plural* **matters**) 1 a substance ▸ *Peat consists mainly of vegetable matter.* 2 something you need to think about or do ▸ *It is a serious matter.* **what's the matter?** what is wrong?
matter *verb* (**matters, mattering, mattered**) to be important

mattress *noun* (*plural* **mattresses**) a thick layer of soft material covered in cloth and used on a bed

mature *adjective* fully grown or developed; grown-up **maturity** *noun*

maul *verb* (**mauls, mauling, mauled**) to injure someone badly by treating them very roughly

mauve *adjective* pale purple
mauve *noun* a pale purple colour

maximum *noun* the greatest number or amount ▸ *The temperature reaches a maximum in July.*
maximum *adjective* greatest ▸ *The maximum number allowed in the lift is 6.*

May *noun* the fifth month of the year
The word **May** comes from the Roman month *Maius*, named in honour of the goddess Maia.

may *verb* (*past tense* **might**) 1 to be allowed to ▸ *May I come too?* 2 to be possible ▸ *It may rain soon.* ▸ *He might have missed the train.*

maybe *adverb* perhaps

mayonnaise *noun* (*pronounced* may-on-ayz) a thick creamy sauce made from eggs, oil, and vinegar, and used on salads

mayor *noun* (*plural* **mayors**) the person in charge of the council in a town or city

maze *noun* (*plural* **mazes**) a complicated arrangement of paths that you try to find your way through for fun

me *pronoun* a word used for *I* when it is the object of a verb or when it comes after a preposition ▸ *She saw me.* ▸ *They gave it to me.*

meadow *noun* (*plural* **meadows**) (*pronounced* med-oh) a field of grass

meagre *adjective* very little; barely enough

meal *noun* (*plural* **meals**) food eaten at one time, such as at breakfast or lunch or dinner

mean[1] *verb* (**means, meaning, meant**) 1 (used about a word, sign, or idea) to have as its explanation or equivalent ▸ *'Maybe' means 'perhaps'.* 2 to intend to do something ▸ *Kate had meant to pick some flowers, but there was no time.*

mean[2] *adjective* (**meaner, meanest**) 1 not generous; selfish ▸ *a mean person* 2 unkind; spiteful ▸ *a mean trick* **meanly** *adverb* **meanness** *noun* being mean

meaning *noun* (*plural* **meanings**) what something means **meaningless** *adjective* having no meaning

means *noun* a way of doing something; a method ▸ *Which means of transport do you use?* **by all means** certainly
means *plural noun* money or other resources for doing things ▸ *The princess had no means of escaping from the tower.*

meantime *noun* **in the meantime** meanwhile

meanwhile *adverb* while something else is happening

measles *plural noun* an infectious disease that causes small red spots on the skin

measure *verb* (**measures, measuring, measured**) 1 to find out how large something is 2 to be a certain size ▸ *The window measures eight feet.*

measure *noun* (*plural* **measures**) 1 a unit used for measuring 2 a device used for measuring 3 the size of something 4 something done for a particular purpose; a law or rule ▸ *We are bringing in new measures to deal with bullies.*

measurement *noun* (*plural* **measurements**) the size or length of something

meat *noun* (*plural* **meats**) animal flesh used as food **meaty** *adjective* full of meat or like meat

mechanic *noun* (*plural* **mechanics**) (*pronounced* me-kan-ik) someone who repairs and looks after machinery

mechanical *adjective* 1 to do with machines 2 automatic; done without thought **mechanically** *adverb*

mechanism *noun* (*plural* **mechanisms**) (*pronounced* mek-an-izm) a machine or the moving parts of a machine

medal *noun* (*plural* **medals**) a piece of metal shaped like a coin, star, or cross, given to someone for bravery or for achieving something

medallist *noun* (*plural* **medallists**) a winner of a medal

meddle *verb* (**meddles, meddling, meddled**) to interfere in something **meddlesome** *adjective* always interfering

media *plural noun* the media newspapers and radio and television, which give people information about things that are happening in the world
Media is the plural form of the noun **medium**.

medical *adjective* to do with the treatment of disease **medically** *adverb*

medicine *noun* (*plural* **medicines**) 1 a liquid or tablet that you swallow to treat an illness 2 the treatment of illness **medicinal** *adjective*

medieval *adjective* to do with the Middle Ages

mediocre *adjective* (*pronounced* meed-i-oh-ker) only fairly good **mediocrity** *noun*

meditate *verb* (**meditates, meditating, meditated**) to think deeply and seriously about something **meditation** *noun*

medium *adjective* average; of middle size

medium *noun* (*plural* **media** or **mediums**) 1 a way of showing or telling people something ▸ *Local radio is a good medium for traffic information.* 2 someone who claims to be able to communicate with the dead
The plural is **media** in the first meaning and **mediums** in the second meaning.

meek *adjective* (**meeker, meekest**) quiet and obedient **meekly** *adverb*

meet *verb* (**meets, meeting, met**) 1 to come face to face with someone, by accident or on purpose ▸ *I met my friend in the park.* ▸ *Let's meet on Friday.* 2 to go to a place to greet someone who is arriving there ▸ *Is anyone coming to the airport to meet you?* 3 to come together ▸ *There is a statue where the two roads meet.* ▸ *The reading group will meet this evening.*

meeting *noun* (*plural* **meetings**) a time when people come together for a special purpose

melancholy *adjective* sad and gloomy

mellow *adjective* (**mellower, mellowest**) (describing sounds or colours) having a soft rich quality

melody *noun* (*plural* **melodies**) a tune **melodic** *adjective*

melon *noun* (*plural* **melons**) a large juicy fruit with yellow or green skin

melt *verb* (**melts, melting, melted**) 1 to turn something into liquid by heating it 2 to become liquid; to dissolve 3 to go away or disappear gradually ▸ *The crowd slowly melted away.*

member *noun* (*plural* **members**) someone who belongs to a society or group **membership** *noun* being a member; all the members of a group

memorable *adjective* 1 worth remembering ▸ *a memorable holiday.* 2 easy to remember ▸ *a memorable face.* **memorably** *adverb*

memorial *noun* (*plural* **memorials**) something set up to remind people of an important person or event ▸ *They passed a war memorial in the High Street.*

memorize *verb* (**memorizes, memorizing, memorized**) to learn something so that you can remember it

memory *noun* (*plural* **memories**) 1 the ability to remember things 2 something interesting or special that you remember 3 the part of a computer where information is stored

men plural of **man** *noun*

menace *noun* (*plural* **menaces**) something dangerous or threatening

menace *verb* (**menaces, menacing, menaced**) to threaten someone with harm or danger

mend *verb* (**mends, mending, mended**) to make something that is broken or damaged whole again or able to work again

menstruation *noun* the natural flow of blood from a woman's womb, normally happening every 28 days

mental *adjective* to do with your mind **mentally** *adverb*

mention *verb* (**mentions, mentioning, mentioned**) to speak briefly about something or someone

menu *noun* (*plural* **menus**) 1 a list of the food you can choose in a restaurant 2 a list of possible actions shown on a computer screen

mercenary *noun* (*plural* **mercenaries**) a soldier paid to fight in a foreign country

merchandise *noun* goods for buying or selling

merchant *noun* (*plural* **merchants**) someone who buys and sells things

merciful *adjective* showing mercy **mercifully** *adverb*

merciless *adjective* showing no mercy; cruel **mercilessly** *adverb*

mercury *noun* a heavy silvery metal used in thermometers

mercy *noun* kindness or pity shown towards someone you have the power to punish

mere *adjective* not more than ▸ *She's a mere child.*

merely *adverb* only; simply ▸ *I was merely repeating what he told me.*

merge *verb* (**merges, merging, merged**) 1 to combine things or blend them 2 to come together

meridian *noun* (*plural* **meridians**) a line on a map or globe from the North Pole to the South Pole

meringue *noun* (*plural* **meringues**) (*pronounced* mer-**rang**) a crisp white cake made from the whites of eggs mixed with sugar

merit *noun* (*plural* **merits**) something that deserves praise

mermaid *noun* (*plural* **mermaids**) in stories, a sea creature with a woman's body and a fish's tail

merry *adjective* (**merrier, merriest**) happy and cheerful **merrily** *adverb* **merriment** *noun* enjoyment, fun

merry-go-round *noun* (*plural* **merry-go-rounds**) a roundabout at a fair, with horses and other things to ride on

mesh *noun* (*plural* **meshes**) a net, or material made like a net

mess *noun* (*plural* **messes**) 1 an untidy or dirty state 2 a difficult or confused situation 3 a place where soldiers or sailors eat their meals

mess *verb* (**messes, messing, messed**) **mess about** to behave stupidly or lazily **mess up** to do something badly

message *noun* (*plural* **messages**) a piece of information sent from one person to another

messenger *noun* (*plural* **messengers**) someone who carries a message

messy *adjective* (**messier, messiest**) 1 untidy or dirty 2 difficult or complicated **messily** *adverb* in a messy way **messiness** *noun* being messy

met past tense and past participle of **meet**

metal *noun* (*plural* **metals**) a hard substance such as gold, silver, copper, and iron **metallic** *adjective* like metal, especially sounding like it or shining like it

meteor *noun* (*plural* **meteors**) a piece of rock or metal that moves through space and burns up as it enters the earth's atmosphere

meteorite *noun* (*plural* **meteorites**) a piece of a meteor that has landed on the earth

meteorology *noun* the study of the weather **meteorological** *adjective* **meteorologist** *noun*

meter *noun* (*plural* **meters**) a device for measuring amounts, especially how much of something has been used

method *noun* (*plural* **methods**) a way of doing something

methodical *adjective* (*pronounced* mi-thod-i-kal) done carefully; well organized **methodically** *adverb*

methylated spirit or **spirits** *noun* a liquid fuel made from alcohol

meticulous *adjective* very careful and precise **meticulously** *adverb* **meticulousness** *noun*

metre *noun* (*plural* **metres**) 1 the main unit of length in the metric system, equal to 100 centimetres or about 39.5 inches 2 a particular type of rhythm in poetry

metric system *noun* a measuring system based on decimal units (the metre, litre, and gram)

miaow *verb* (**miaows, miaowing, miaowed**) (*pronounced* mee-ow) to make the sound of a cat

mice plural of **mouse**

microbe *noun* (*plural* **microbes**) a tiny organism that you need a microscope to see

microchip *noun* (*plural* **microchips**) a very small piece of silicon working as an electric circuit in electronic equipment

microcomputer *noun* (*plural* **microcomputers**) a small computer that uses microchips

microphone *noun* (*plural* **microphones**) an electrical device that picks up sound waves for amplifying, broadcasting, or recording

microscope *noun* (*plural* **microscopes**) a device with lenses that make tiny objects appear larger so that you can study them

microscopic *adjective* (*pronounced* my-kro-**skop**-ik) too small to be seen without a microscope; tiny

microwave *noun* (*plural* **microwaves**) a type of oven which heats things rapidly by using energy in very short waves

microwave *verb* (**microwaves, microwaving, microwaved**) to cook food in a microwave

mid *adjective* in the middle of ▶ *The holidays start in mid-July.*

midday *noun* the middle of the day; twelve o'clock noon

middle *noun* (*plural* **middles**) 1 the part of something that is at the same distance from all its sides or edges or from both its ends 2 your waist

middle *adjective* placed in the middle

middle-aged *adjective* aged between about forty and sixty

Middle Ages *noun* the period in history from about AD 1100 to 1500

Middle East *noun* the countries to the east of the Mediterranean Sea, from Egypt to Iran

midge *noun* (*plural* **midges**) a small insect like a gnat

midget *noun* (*plural* **midgets**) an unusually short person

midnight *noun* twelve o'clock at night

midsummer *noun* the middle of summer, when the days are longest

midway *adverb* halfway

midwife *noun* (*plural* **midwives**) a person trained to look after a woman who is giving birth to a baby

might[1] past tense of **may** *verb*

might[2] *noun* great power or strength

mighty *adjective* (**mightier, mightiest**) very strong or powerful **mightily** *adverb*

migraine *noun* (*plural* **migraines**) (*pronounced* **mee-grayn** or **my-grayn**) a very bad headache that can make you feel sick

migrate *verb* (**migrates, migrating, migrated**) 1 to go to live in another country 2 (used about birds) to fly to a warmer region for the winter **migrant** *noun* someone who migrates **migration** *noun*

mild *adjective* (**milder, mildest**) gentle; not harsh or severe **mildly** *adverb* **mildness** *noun*

mildew *noun* (*pronounced* **mil-dyew**) a white coating of fungus that forms on warm damp surfaces

mile *noun* (*plural* **miles**) a measure of distance, equal to 1,760 yards or about 1.6 kilometres

mileage *noun* (*plural* **mileages**) the number of miles that you have travelled

militant *adjective* eager to fight **militancy** *noun*

military *adjective* to do with soldiers or fighting

milk *noun* a white liquid that female mammals produce in their bodies to feed to their young
milk *verb* (**milks, milking, milked**) to get milk from a cow or other female animal

milkman *noun* (*plural* **milkmen**) a person who delivers milk to people's houses

milky *adjective* (**milkier, milkiest**) 1 white and smooth like milk 2 made with a lot of milk **milkiness** *noun*

mill *noun* (*plural* **mills**) 1 a building where corn is ground to make flour 2 a factory for processing materials, such as a paper mill
mill *verb* (**mills, milling, milled**) to grind or crush something in a mill

millennium *noun* (*plural* **millenniums** or **millennia**) a period of 1,000 years
The word **millennium** comes from Latin words meaning 'a thousand years'.

milligram *noun* (*plural* **milligrams**) one thousandth of a gram

millilitre *noun* (*plural* **millilitres**) one thousandth of a litre

millimetre *noun* (*plural* **millimetres**) one thousandth of a metre

million *noun* (*plural* **millions**) a thousand thousands (1,000,000) **millionth** *adjective* and *noun*

millionaire *noun* (*plural* **millionaires**) a rich person who has more than a million pounds or dollars

millipede *noun* (*plural* **millipedes**) a small creature with a long body and many legs

mime *verb* (**mimes, miming, mimed**) to describe something or tell a story using movements and gestures but no words
mime *noun* (*plural* **mimes**) a performance using movements instead of words

mimic *verb* (**mimics, mimicking, mimicked**) to imitate someone, especially to amuse people
mimic *noun* (*plural* **mimics**) a person who mimics someone

minaret *noun* (*plural* **minarets**) a tall thin tower attached to a mosque
The word **minaret** comes from an Arabic word meaning 'lighthouse'.

mince *verb* (**minces, mincing, minced**) to cut meat or other food into very small pieces **mincer** *noun* a machine for mincing meat
mince *noun* minced meat

mincemeat *noun* a sweet mixture of currants, raisins, and chopped fruit, used in pies

mind *noun* (*plural* **minds**) the ability of your brain to think and remember; your thoughts and feelings **change your mind** to have a new opinion or make a different decision about something
mind *verb* (**minds, minding, minded**) 1 to look after someone or something for a time ▶ *Will you mind my suitcase for a while?* 2 to be bothered about something ▶ *I don't mind where we go.* 3 to be careful or watch out for something ▶ *Mind you don't trip on the step.*

minder *noun* someone who looks after an old or unwell person

mine¹ *adjective* and *pronoun* belonging to me ▶ *One of these books is mine.*

mine² *noun* (*plural* **mines**) 1 a large deep hole in the ground from where coal, metal, or precious stones are dug out 2 an explosive hidden under the ground or in the sea that explodes when anything comes close to it
mine *verb* (**mines, mining, mined**) 1 to dig something from a mine 2 to lay explosives in the ground or in the sea

minefield *noun* (*plural* **minefields**) an area where explosive mines have been laid

miner *noun* (*plural* **miners**) someone who works in a mine

mineral *noun* (*plural* **minerals**) 1 a hard substance that can be dug out of the ground, such as coal and iron ore 2 a cold fizzy drink

mingle *verb* (**mingles, mingling, mingled**) to mix or blend together

miniature *adjective* (*pronounced* **min-i-cher**) very small, made in a smaller size than usual

minibus *noun* (*plural* **minibuses**) a small bus

minim *noun* (*plural* **minims**) a musical note equal to two crotchets, written ♩

minimum *noun* the smallest number or amount ▶ *I'll need a minimum of 20 minutes in the library.*
minimum *adjective* least or smallest ▶ *The minimum charge is £5.*

minister *noun* (*plural* **ministers**) 1 a member of the government who is in charge of a department ▶ *The education minister visited our school.* 2 a member of the clergy

ministry *noun* (*plural* **ministries**) 1 a department of the government 2 the work of a minister in the church

mink *noun* (*plural* **minks**) 1 a small animal rather like a stoat 2 the soft brown fur of this animal

minnow *noun* (*plural* **minnows**) a tiny freshwater fish

minor *adjective* not very important, especially when compared to something else

minority *noun* (*plural* **minorities**) (*pronounced* **myn-o-ri-ti**) 1 the smaller part of a group of people or things ▶ *Only a minority of people bothered to vote.* 2 a small group that is different from others, especially because they speak a different language or belong to a different race or religion

minstrel noun (plural **minstrels**) a travelling musician in the Middle Ages

mint noun 1 a green plant with strong-smelling leaves used in cooking 2 a sweet flavoured with peppermint 3 a place where coins are made

minus preposition less; with the next number taken away ▸ Twelve minus four equals eight (12 − 4 = 8).

minute[1] noun (plural **minutes**) (pronounced **min**-it) 1 a unit of time equal to one-sixtieth of an hour 2 (informal) a short time ▸ We'll be there in a minute.

minute[2] adjective (pronounced my-**newt**) 1 tiny ▸ The cover is fixed on with three minute screws. 2 very detailed ▸ a minute examination

miracle noun (plural **miracles**) a wonderful or magical happening that cannot be explained **miraculous** adjective

mirage noun (plural **mirages**) (pronounced mi-**rahzh**) something that seems to be visible but is not really there, like a film of water on a hot road

mirror noun (plural **mirrors**) a sheet of glass painted with silver on the back so that it reflects things clearly

misbehave verb (**misbehaves**, **misbehaving**, **misbehaved**) to behave badly **misbehaviour** noun

miscarriage noun (plural **miscarriages**) the birth of a baby before it has developed enough to survive

miscellaneous adjective (pronounced mis-el-**ay**-ni-us) of various kinds; mixed

mischief noun naughty or troublesome behaviour **mischievous** adjective full of mischief **mischievously** adverb

miser noun (plural **misers**) (pronounced **my**-zer) someone who stores money away and is mean about spending it **miserly** adjective

miserable adjective very unhappy ▸ She went home feeling tired and miserable. **miserably** adverb

misery noun (plural **miseries**) great unhappiness or suffering

misfire verb (**misfires**, **misfiring**, **misfired**) to go wrong or fail to work ▸ Their plan misfired.

misfit noun (plural **misfits**) someone who does not fit in well with other people

misfortune noun (plural **misfortunes**) 1 bad luck 2 an unlucky event or accident

mishap noun (plural **mishaps**) (pronounced **mis**-hap) an unfortunate accident

misjudge verb (**misjudges**, **misjudging**, **misjudged**) to form a wrong idea or opinion about someone or something

mislay verb (**mislays**, **mislaying**, **mislaid**) to lose something for a short time

mislead verb (**misleads**, **misleading**, **misled**) to give someone a wrong idea or impression deliberately

misprint noun (plural **misprints**) a mistake in printing

Miss noun (plural **Misses**) a title put before the name of a girl or unmarried woman

miss verb (**misses**, **missing**, **missed**) 1 to fail to hit, reach, or catch something ▸ The bullet missed him by inches. ▸ Kate had missed a few things from her list. 2 to fail to see, hear, or find something ▸ I missed my favourite programme because I got home late. 3 to be sad about someone because they are not with you ▸ I'll miss them when they go home. 4 to notice that something has gone ▸ I lost my bag but I didn't miss it till this morning.

miss noun (plural **misses**) a failure to hit or reach something

missile noun (plural **missiles**) a weapon or object fired or thrown through the air

missing adjective lost, or not in the right place

mission noun (plural **missions**) 1 an important job that someone is sent somewhere to do 2 a place or building where missionaries work

missionary noun (plural **missionaries**) someone who goes to another country to teach a religious faith

misspell *verb* (**misspells, misspelling, misspelt** or **misspelled**) to spell a word wrongly

mist *noun* (*plural* **mists**) a thin fog of damp cloudy air **misty** *adjective*

mistake *noun* (*plural* **mistakes**) something done or said wrongly
mistake *verb* (**mistakes, mistaking, mistook, mistaken**) to confuse one person or thing for another ▸ *It was easy to mistake our cat for the one across the road.*

mistaken *adjective* incorrect; wrong

mistletoe *noun* (*pronounced* **miss**-el-toh) a green plant that has white berries in winter

mistreat *verb* (**mistreats, mistreating, mistreated**) to treat someone badly or unfairly **mistreatment** *noun*

mistress *noun* (*plural* **mistresses**) 1 the girlfriend of a man who is married to someone else 2 a woman who teaches in a school 3 the woman owner of a dog or other animal

mistrust *verb* (**mistrusts, mistrusting, mistrusted**) not to trust someone

misunderstand *verb* (**misunderstands, misunderstanding, misunderstood**) to get a wrong idea or impression about something **misunderstanding** *noun* a wrong idea or impression

misuse *verb* (**misuses, misusing, misused**) to use something wrongly or treat it badly

mite *noun* (*plural* **mites**) 1 a tiny insect found in food 2 a small child

mitten *noun* (*plural* **mittens**) a kind of glove without separate parts for the fingers

mix *verb* (**mixes, mixing, mixed**) 1 to stir or shake different things together to make one thing 2 to come together in a group **mix up** to confuse people or things

mixture *noun* (*plural* **mixtures**) something made by mixing various things together

moan *verb* (**moans, moaning, moaned**) 1 to make a long low sound of pain or sadness 2 to grumble
moan *noun* (*plural* **moans**) a sound of moaning

moat *noun* (*plural* **moats**) a deep ditch round a castle

mob *noun* (*plural* **mobs**) 1 a large crowd of people who are hard to control 2 a gang
mob *verb* (**mobs, mobbing, mobbed**) to crowd round someone

mobile *adjective* able to be moved or carried about ▸ *a mobile phone* **mobility** *noun* the ability to move
mobile *noun* (*plural* **mobiles**) a decoration made to be hung up so that it moves about in the air

mock *adjective* not real; imitation ▸ *The shoes are made of mock leather.*
mock *verb* (**mocks, mocking, mocked**) to make fun of someone or something **mockery** *noun* making fun of someone or something

mode *noun* (*plural* **modes**) the way that something is done ▸ *Flying is the fastest mode of transport.*

model *noun* (*plural* **models**) 1 a small copy of something larger 2 a particular version or design of something ▸ *Our car is an older model than yours.* 3 someone who poses for an artist or photographer or displays clothes by wearing them 4 someone or something worth copying or imitating
model *verb* (**models, modelling, modelled**) 1 to make something out of a material such as clay 2 to work as an artist's model or a fashion model **model yourself on someone** to try to be like someone ▸ *You should model yourself on your sister.*

modem *noun* (*plural* **modems**) (*pronounced* **moh**-dem) a device that sends information from a computer along a telephone line

moderate *adjective* average; not too little and not too much

modern *adjective* belonging to the present day or recent times

modernize *verb* (**modernizes, modernizing, modernized**) to make something more modern **modernization** *noun*

modest *adjective* **1** not thinking or saying how good you are **2** average; not extreme ▸ *The cost was fairly modest.* **modestly** *adverb* **modesty** *noun* being modest

modify *verb* (**modifies, modifying, modified**) to change something slightly **modification** *noun* a slight change

module *noun* (*plural* **modules**) (*pronounced* **mod**-yool) a part that can be attached to other parts of something, such as a spacecraft or building

moist *adjective* slightly damp **moistness** *noun* being moist **moisture** *noun* tiny drops of water

moisten *verb* (**moistens, moistening, moistened**) (*pronounced* **moi**-sen) to make something moist

mole *noun* (*plural* **moles**) **1** a small furry animal that lives in holes it digs under the ground **2** a small dark spot on your skin

molecule *noun* (*plural* **molecules**) (*pronounced* **mol**-i-kewl) a very small particle of matter, the smallest part that a substance can be divided into without changing its nature

molehill *noun* (*plural* **molehills**) a small pile of earth thrown up by a mole **make a mountain out of a molehill** to make something seem too important

molest *verb* (**molests, molesting, molested**) (*pronounced* mo-**lest**) to annoy or pester someone in an unfriendly way

mollusc *noun* (*plural* **molluscs**) an animal with a soft body and usually with a hard shell, such as a snail or an oyster

molten *adjective* melted; made into liquid by great heat

moment *noun* (*plural* **moments**) **1** a very short period of time ▸ *It will only take a moment.* **2** a particular time ▸ *They arrived at the last moment.* **at the moment** now

momentary *adjective* (*pronounced* **moh**-men-ter-i) lasting for only a moment **momentarily** *adverb* for a moment

momentous *adjective* (*pronounced* moh-**ment**-us) very important **momentousness** *noun*

momentum *noun* (*pronounced* moh-**ment**-um) a force developed by something moving ▸ *The car gained momentum as it rolled down the hill.*

monarch *noun* (*plural* **monarchs**) (*pronounced* **mon**-uk) a king, queen, emperor, or empress **monarchy** *noun* a country that has a monarch

monastery *noun* (*plural* **monasteries**) (*pronounced* **mon**-a-ster-i) a building where monks live and work **monastic** *adjective* to do with monks or monasteries

Monday *noun* (*plural* **Mondays**) the second day of the week
Monday is an Old English name meaning 'day of the moon'.

money *noun* coins and notes that people use to buy things

mongrel *noun* (*plural* **mongrels**) (*pronounced* **mung**-rel) a dog of mixed breeds

monitor *noun* (*plural* **monitors**) **1** the screen of a computer **2** a device with a screen or display, used for checking how something is working ▸ *a heart monitor*

monitor *verb* (**monitors, monitoring, monitored**) to watch or test something to see how it is working

monk *noun* (*plural* **monks**) a member of a religious group of men living in a monastery

monkey *noun* (*plural* **monkeys**) an animal with long arms, hands with thumbs, and a tail

monopoly *noun* (*plural* **monopolies**) (*pronounced* mo-**nop**-o-li) a situation where one person or company is the only one to sell something that people need **monopolize** *verb* to keep something to yourself without letting other people use it

monorail *noun* (*plural* **monorails**) a railway that runs on a single rail

monotonous *adjective* dull because it does not change ▸ *a monotonous song* **monotony** *noun* dullness

monsoon *noun* (*plural* **monsoons**) a strong wind that blows in the Indian Ocean, bringing heavy rain in summer

monster *noun* (*plural* **monsters**) a huge and frightening creature

monstrous *adjective* 1 huge, like a monster 2 very shocking or wrong ▸ *a monstrous crime* **monstrosity** *noun*   a huge and ugly thing

month *noun* (*plural* **months**) one of the twelve parts into which a year is divided The word **month** is an Old English word related to **moon**, because time was measured by the phases of the moon.

monthly *adjective* and *adverb* happening once a month or every month

monument *noun* (*plural* **monuments**) a statue or building put up to remember a person or an event

moo *verb* (**moos, mooing, mooed**) to make the sound of a cow

mood *noun* (*plural* **moods**) the way that you feel ▸ *She seems to be in a good mood.*

moody *adjective* (**moodier, moodiest**) 1 gloomy or bad-tempered 2 likely to have sudden changes of mood **moodily** *adverb* **moodiness** *noun*

moon *noun* (*plural* **moons**) 1 the natural satellite which orbits the earth and shines in the sky at night 2 a natural satellite of another planet

moonlight *noun* the light reflected from the moon **moonlit** *adjective*

moor[1] *noun* (*plural* **moors**) an area of rough land covered with bracken and bushes

moor[2] *verb* (**moors, mooring, moored**) to tie up a boat at a quay

moorhen *noun* (*plural* **moorhens**) a small black waterbird

mooring *noun* (*plural* **moorings**) a place where a boat can be moored

moose *noun* (*plural* **moose**) a North American brown elk

mop *noun* (*plural* **mops**) a piece of soft material on a long handle, used for cleaning floors
mop *verb* (**mops, mopping, mopped**) to clean something with a mop

mope *verb* (**mopes, moping, moped**) to be sad and moody

moped *noun* (*plural* **mopeds**) (*pronounced* moh-ped) a kind of small motorcycle with pedals

moral *adjective* 1 to do with right and wrong behaviour 2 being or doing good **morality** *noun* how moral someone or something is **morally** *adverb*
moral *noun* (*plural* **morals**) a lesson taught by a story **morals** rules and standards of behaviour

morale *noun* (*pronounced* mo-**rahl**) confidence or courage

morbid *adjective* thinking too much about sad or unpleasant things

more *adjective* and *adverb* a larger number or amount ▸ *Can we have more bread?* ▸ *This chair is more comfortable.* ▸ *I want more.* ▸ *You must work more.* **more or less** almost; approximately ▸ *We've more or less finished.*

morning *noun* (*plural* **mornings**) the early part of the day before noon

morose *adjective* gloomy and bad-tempered

morphine *noun* a drug made from opium, given by doctors to people who are in great pain

morris dance *noun* (*plural* **morris dances**) a traditional English dance performed by people in costume with ribbons and bells
It was originally called **Moorish dance**, because people thought the dance came from the Moors, a Muslim people of North Africa.

Morse code *noun* a code for sending messages by radio, using dots and dashes to represent letters and numbers
Morse code is named after an American called S.F.B. Morse, who invented it.

morsel *noun* (*plural* **morsels**) a small piece of food

mortal *adjective* **1** certain to die ▸ *We are all mortal beings.* **2** causing death ▸ *He received a mortal wound in the battle.*
mortality *noun* being certain to die
mortally *adverb*

mortar *noun* **1** a mixture of sand, cement, and water used to hold bricks together **2** a small kind of cannon

mortgage *noun* (*plural* **mortgages**) (*pronounced* **mor**-gij) a loan of money from a bank or building society to buy a house

mortuary *noun* (*plural* **mortuaries**) a place where dead bodies are kept before they are buried or cremated

mosaic *noun* (*plural* **mosaics**) (*pronounced* moh-**zay**-ik) a picture or design made from small coloured pieces of glass or stone

mosque *noun* (*plural* **mosques**) (*pronounced* mosk) a building where Muslims worship

mosquito *noun* (*plural* **mosquitoes**) (*pronounced* mos-**kee**-toh) an insect that sucks blood and carries disease

moss *noun* (*plural* **mosses**) a plant that grows close to the ground in damp places and forms a soft green surface **mossy** *adjective*

most *adjective* and *adverb* greatest in number or amount ▸ *Most people go by car.* ▸ *We've eaten most of the food.* ▸ *It was most amusing.*

mostly *adverb* mainly, usually

motel *noun* (*plural* **motels**) a hotel for people travelling by road, with parking near the rooms

moth *noun* (*plural* **moths**) an insect like a butterfly, which usually flies around at night and is attracted by light

mother *noun* (*plural* **mothers**) your female parent

mother-in-law *noun* (*plural* **mothers-in-law**) the mother of your husband or wife

motion *noun* (*plural* **motions**) moving, movement **motionless** *adjective* not moving

motive *noun* (*plural* **motives**) what makes you want to do something

motor *noun* (*plural* **motors**) a machine that provides power to drive machinery

motorbike *noun* (*plural* **motorbikes**) (informal) a motorcycle

motor car *noun* (*plural* **motor cars**) an engine-driven vehicle able to carry several people

motorcycle *noun* (*plural* **motorcycles**) a two-wheeled vehicle with a petrol engine **motorcyclist** *noun*

motorist *noun* (*plural* **motorists**) someone who drives a car

motorway *noun* (*plural* **motorways**) a wide road with two or more lanes for fast traffic

mottled *adjective* marked with coloured spots or patches

motto *noun* (*plural* **mottoes**) a short saying or slogan

mould *noun* (*plural* **moulds**) (*rhymes with* sold) **1** a container for making liquid things like jelly or plaster form a special shape when they harden **2** a furry growth that appears on damp surfaces or stale food

mould *verb* (**moulds, moulding, moulded**) to give something a special shape

mouldy *adjective* (**mouldier, mouldiest**) having mould on it; decaying

moult *verb* (**moults, moulting, moulted**) (*rhymes with* bolt) to lose feathers or hair, as some animals do

mound *noun* (*plural* **mounds**) a pile or small hill

mount *verb* (**mounts, mounting, mounted**) 1 to climb on a horse or bicycle so that you can ride it 2 to rise or increase ▸ *The excitement was mounting.* 3 to put a picture or photograph in a frame or album

mount *noun* (*plural* **mounts**) a mountain, especially in names such as *Mount Everest*

mountain *noun* (*plural* **mountains**) 1 a very high hill 2 a large amount ▸ *a mountain of work* **mountainous** *adjective* having a lot of mountains

mountaineer *noun* (*plural* **mountaineers**) someone who climbs mountains **mountaineering** *noun*

mourn *verb* (**mourns, mourning, mourned**) to be very sad because someone has died **mourner** *noun* someone who is mourning at a funeral

mouse *noun* (*plural* **mice**) 1 a small furry animal with a long tail and a pointed nose 2 a device that you move around with your hand to control the movement of a cursor on a computer screen

mousse *noun* (*plural* **mousses**) (*pronounced* **mooss**) 1 a creamy pudding flavoured with chocolate or fruit 2 a light frothy substance that you use to style your hair

moustache *noun* (*plural* **moustaches**) (*pronounced* mus-**tahsh**) hair left to grow above a man's upper lip

mouth *noun* (*plural* **mouths**) 1 the part of your face that opens for eating and speaking 2 an opening or outlet, for example where you enter a cave or where a river flows into the sea

mouthful *noun* (*plural* **mouthfuls**) an amount of food you put in your mouth

mouth organ *noun* (*plural* **mouth organs**) a small musical instrument. You play it by holding it to your mouth and blowing and sucking through it.

mouthpiece *noun* (*plural* **mouthpieces**) the part of a musical instrument or other device that you put to your mouth

move *verb* (**moves, moving, moved**) 1 to take something from one place to another 2 to go from one place to another 3 to affect someone's feelings ▸ *I was moved by your story.* **movable** *adjective*

move *noun* (*plural* **moves**) 1 a movement 2 a turn in a game ▸ *It's your move.*

movement *noun* (*plural* **movements**) 1 moving or being moved 2 a group of people working together to achieve something ▸ *They supported the civil rights movement.* 3 one of the main parts of a long piece of classical music

movie *noun* (*plural* **movies**) a cinema film

moving *adjective* affecting your emotions or feelings ▸ *It was a moving story about a family separated during a war.*

mow *verb* (**mows, mowing, mowed, mown**) to cut grass with a machine **mow down** to knock people down and kill them **mower** *noun* a machine for cutting grass

MP short for *Member of Parliament* Members of Parliament meet to make laws and make decisions that affect how we live.

Mr *noun* (*pronounced* **mis**-ter) a title put before a man's name

Mrs *noun* (*pronounced* **mis**-iz) a title put before a married woman's name

Ms *noun* (*pronounced* **miz**) a title put before a woman's name, whether or not she is married

much *adjective* and *adverb* a large amount ▸ *There is much work to do.* ▸ *£5 is not very much.* ▸ *That's much better.*

muck *noun* 1 manure in a farmyard 2 (informal) dirt or filth **mucky** *adjective*

muck *verb* (**mucks, mucking, mucked**) (informal) **muck about** or **muck around** to behave stupidly or lazily **muck up** to do something badly

mud *noun* wet soft earth **muddy** *adjective*

muddle *verb* (**muddles, muddling, muddled**) 1 to mix things up 2 to confuse someone

muddle *noun* (*plural* **muddles**) a confusion or mess

mudguard *noun* (*plural* **mudguards**) a curved cover fitted over a bicycle wheel to stop mud and water being thrown up on to the rider

muesli *noun* (*pronounced* **mooz**-li or **myooz**-li) a food made of cereals, nuts, and dried fruit

muffle *verb* (**muffles, muffling, muffled**) 1 to cover or wrap something to protect it or keep it warm 2 to make a sound quieter by covering the place that it is coming from

mug *noun* (*plural* **mugs**) a kind of large cup with straight sides and no saucer

mug *verb* (**mugs, mugging, mugged**) to attack and rob someone in the street **mugger** *noun*

muggy *adjective* (**muggier, muggiest**) (describing the weather) unpleasantly warm and damp

mule *noun* (*plural* **mules**) an animal produced from a male donkey and a female horse

multi-coloured *adjective* having many colours

multiple *adjective* having many parts
multiple (*plural* **multiples**) *noun* a number that you can divide another number into without having a remainder ▸ *20 is a multiple of 5.*

multiply *verb* (**multiplies, multiplying, multiplied**) 1 to add a number to itself a certain number of times ▸ *Five multiplied by four equals twenty* ($5 \times 4 = 20$). 2 to increase in number **multiplication** *noun* multiplying

multiracial *adjective* having people of different races

multi-storey *adjective* (describing a building) having many floors ▸ *We can use the multi-storey car park.*

multitude *noun* (*plural* **multitudes**) a large number of people or things

mum *noun* (*plural* **mums**) (informal) a name for your mother

mumble *verb* (**mumbles, mumbling, mumbled**) to speak softly and unclearly

mummy *noun* (*plural* **mummies**) 1 (informal) a name for your mother 2 in ancient Egypt, a dead body wrapped in cloth and treated with oils for burial

mumps *noun* an infectious disease that makes your neck swell painfully

munch *verb* (**munches, munching, munched**) to chew food noisily

mural *noun* (*plural* **murals**) a picture painted on a wall

murder *verb* (**murders, murdering, murdered**) to kill someone deliberately **murderer** *noun*
murder *noun* (*plural* **murders**) a deliberate killing

murky *adjective* (**murkier, murkiest**) dark and gloomy

murmur *noun* (*plural* **murmurs**) a continuous low or soft sound, especially of voices
murmur *verb* (**murmurs, murmuring, murmured**) to make a continuous low or soft sound

muscle *noun* (*plural* **muscles**) (*pronounced* **muss**-el) a part of your body that can stretch or tighten to make you move

muscular *adjective* having strong muscles

museum *noun* (*plural* **museums**) a place where interesting old or valuable objects are displayed for people to see

mushroom *noun* (*plural* **mushrooms**) a fungus with a flat or rounded top, especially the kind that you can eat

music *noun* pleasant or interesting sounds made by instruments or voices

musical *adjective* 1 to do with music 2 good at music or interested in it **musically** *adverb*
musical *noun* (*plural* **musicals**) a play or film with music and songs

musician *noun* (*plural* **musicians**) someone who plays music

musket *noun* (*plural* **muskets**) an old type of rifle used by soldiers

Muslim *noun* (*plural* **Muslims**) someone who believes in the religious teachings of Muhammad, as set out in the Koran

muslin *noun* fine cotton cloth

mussel *noun* (*plural* **mussels**) a black shellfish, often found clinging to rocks

must *verb* a word used with another verb to show **1** that you have to do something ▶ *I must do my clarinet practice.* **2** that something is certain ▶ *It must be raining.*

mustard *noun* a hot-tasting yellow paste that some people eat with meat

mustard and cress *plural noun* small green plants eaten in salads

muster *verb* (**musters, mustering, mustered**) to assemble or gather something together ▶ *They mustered all their strength to move the rock.*

musty *adjective* (**mustier, mustiest**) smelling or tasting mouldy or stale **mustiness** *noun*

mute *adjective* not able to speak

mutilate *verb* (**mutilates, mutilating, mutilated**) to damage something by breaking or cutting off part of it **mutilation** *noun*

mutiny *noun* (*plural* **mutinies**) a decision by soldiers or sailors not to obey the people in charge of them **mutinous** *adjective* having a mutiny

mutiny *verb* (**mutinies, mutinying, mutinied**) to take part in a mutiny

mutter *verb* (**mutters, muttering, muttered**) to speak in a low quiet voice that is difficult to understand

mutton *noun* meat from a sheep

mutual *adjective* given or done to each other ▶ *mutual help* **mutually** *adverb*

muzzle *noun* (*plural* **muzzles**) **1** an animal's nose and mouth **2** a cover put over an animal's nose and mouth so that it cannot bite **3** the open end of a gun

muzzle *verb* (**muzzles, muzzling, muzzled**) to put a muzzle on an animal

my *adjective* belonging to me ▶ *This is my book.*

myself *pronoun* used to refer to the person who is speaking ▶ *I have hurt myself.* **by myself** on my own; alone ▶ *I did the work all by myself.*

mystery *noun* (*plural* **mysteries**) something strange or puzzling **mysterious** *adjective* strange, or hard to explain **mysteriously** *adverb*

mystify *verb* (**mystifies, mystifying, mystified**) to puzzle someone very much

myth *noun* (*plural* **myths**) an old story about gods and heroes in ancient times **mythical** *adjective* in myths

mythology *noun* a collection of myths, or the study of myths **mythological** *adjective* to do with myths

Nn

nag *verb* (**nags, nagging, nagged**) to keep criticizing someone or complaining to them

nail *noun* (*plural* **nails**) **1** the hard covering on the end of your finger or toe **2** a small pointed piece of metal used to fix pieces of wood together

nail *verb* (**nails, nailing, nailed**) to fasten something with nails

naked *adjective* without any clothes or coverings on **with the naked eye** without the help of a telescope or microscope **nakedness** *noun*

name *noun* (*plural* **names**) what a person or thing is called

name *verb* (**names, naming, named**) **1** to give someone a name **2** to say what something is called

nameless *adjective* not having a name

namely *adverb* that is to say ▶ *She lived in a city, namely Paris.*

nanny *noun* (*plural* **nannies**) a woman who looks after small children

nanny goat *noun* (*plural* **nanny goats**) a female goat

nap *noun* (*plural* **naps**) a short sleep

napkin *noun* (*plural* **napkins**) a piece of cloth or paper to wipe your lips and hands at meals

nappy *noun* (*plural* **nappies**) a piece of cloth or a paper pad put round a baby's bottom

narcotic *noun* (*plural* **narcotics**) a drug that makes you sleepy or unconscious

narrate *verb* (**narrates, narrating, narrated**) to tell a story or your experiences **narration** *noun* **narrator** *noun*

narrative *noun* (*plural* **narratives**) a story or account that someone tells

narrow *adjective* (**narrower, narrowest**) 1 not wide 2 only just achieved ▶ *a narrow escape* **narrowly** *adverb*

narrow-minded *adjective* not liking or understanding other people's ideas or beliefs

nasal *adjective* (*pronounced* **nay-zal**) to do with the nose

nasty *adjective* (**nastier, nastiest**) 1 not pleasant, not nice 2 unkind or cruel **nastily** *adverb* **nastiness** *noun*

nation *noun* (*plural* **nations**) 1 a country and the people who live there 2 a large number of people who have the same history, language, and customs

national *adjective* belonging to a nation or country **nationally** *adverb*

nationalist *noun* someone who supports their country and wants it to be independent **nationalism** *noun*

nationality *noun* (*plural* **nationalities**) belonging to a nation ▶ *They are of German nationality.*

nationalize *verb* (**nationalizes, nationalizing, nationalized**) to bring an industry or organization under government control **nationalization** *noun*

nationwide *adjective and adverb* over the whole of a nation or country

native *noun* (*plural* **natives**) a person born in a particular place ▶ *a native of Italy*

native *adjective* 1 of the country where you were born ▶ *my native language* 2 belonging to someone from birth ▶ *native ability*

Nativity *noun* the birth of Jesus Christ

natural *adjective* 1 made or done by nature, not by people or machines 2 normal; not surprising ▶ *Anger was a natural reaction to the news.* **naturally** *adverb*

natural *noun* (*plural* **naturals**) a musical note that is neither sharp nor flat; the sign (♮) showing this

nature *noun* (*plural* **natures**) 1 everything in the world that was not made by people, such as animals, trees and plants, and the earth and sea 2 what a person or thing is like ▶ *Everyone admired William's friendly nature.*

naughty *adjective* (**naughtier, naughtiest**) badly behaved or disobedient **naughtily** *adverb* **naughtiness** *noun*

nausea *noun* (*pronounced* **naw-zi-a**) a feeling of sickness or disgust **nauseous** *adjective* feeling sick

nautical *adjective* to do with ships or sailors

naval *adjective* to do with a navy

nave *noun* (*plural* **naves**) the main central part of a church

navel *noun* (*plural* **navels**) the small hollow at the front of your stomach

navigate *verb* (**navigates, navigating, navigated**) to use maps or instruments to guide a ship or aircraft **navigation** *noun* **navigator** *noun*

navy *noun* (*plural* **navies**) a fleet of ships and their crews

navy blue *noun and adjective* dark blue

Nazi *noun* (*plural* **Nazis**) (*pronounced* **nah-tsi**) a member of the German National Socialist Party in Hitler's time **Nazism** *noun*

near *adverb and adjective* (**nearer, nearest**) not far away

near *preposition* not far away from something ▶ *We live near the sea.*

near *verb* (**nears, nearing, neared**) to come close to a place ▶ *The ships were nearing the harbour.*

nearby *adjective* not far away ▶ *a nearby town.*

nearly *adverb* almost ► *It was nearly midnight.* **not nearly** not at all ► *There is not nearly enough for everyone.*

neat *adjective* (**neater, neatest**) 1 tidy; simple and pleasant to look at 2 skilfully done **neatly** *adverb* **neatness** *noun*

necessary *adjective* needed very much; essential **necessarily** *adverb*

necessity *noun* (*plural* **necessities**) something that is needed

neck *noun* (*plural* **necks**) 1 the part of your body that joins your head to your shoulders 2 a narrow part of something, especially of a bottle

necklace *noun* (*plural* **necklaces**) a piece of jewellery that you wear round your neck

nectar *noun* a sweet liquid that bees collect from flowers

nectarine *noun* (*plural* **nectarines**) a kind of peach with a smooth skin

need *verb* (**needs, needing, needed**) 1 to be without something when you should have it ► *I need something to eat.* 2 to have to do something ► *You need to practise your clarinet.*

need *noun* (*plural* **needs**) 1 something that you need 2 a situation in which something is necessary ► *There was no need for them to stay.* **in need** needing money or help **needless** *adjective* unnecessary

needle *noun* (*plural* **needles**) 1 a thin pointed piece of metal used for sewing 2 something long, thin, and sharp, such as a knitting needle or a pine needle 3 the pointer of a meter or compass

needlework *noun* sewing or embroidery

needy *adjective* (**needier, neediest**) very poor

negative *adjective* saying or meaning 'no' **negative number** a number less than nought

negative *noun* (*plural* **negatives**) 1 something that means 'no' 2 a photograph or film with the dark parts light and the light parts dark

neglect *verb* (**neglects, neglecting, neglected**) 1 to fail to look after someone or something 2 to fail to do something

neglect *noun* failing to look after someone or do something **neglectful** *noun*

negotiate *verb* (**negotiates, negotiating, negotiated**) (*pronounced* nig-oh-shi-ayt) 1 to try to reach agreement about something by discussing it ► *The school council negotiated a new policy on homework.* 2 to get past an obstacle or difficulty ► *On my way up the stairs I had to negotiate several shoes and a roller skate.* **negotiation** *noun* **negotiator** *noun*

neigh *verb* (**neighs, neighing, neighed**) (*rhymes with* say) to make the sound of a horse

neighbour *noun* (*plural* **neighbours**) someone who lives near you

neighbourhood *noun* (*plural* **neighbourhoods**) the area you live in

neighbourly *adjective* friendly and helpful to people who live near you

neither *adjective* and *pronoun* not one or the other ► *Neither light was working.* ► *Neither of them saw you.*
neither *conjunction* **neither ... nor ...** not one thing and not the other ► *I neither know nor care.*

neon light *noun* a kind of street light using a gas that glows when electricity passes through it

nephew *noun* (*plural* **nephews**) the son of your brother or sister

nerve *noun* (*plural* **nerves**) 1 one of the fibres inside your body that carry messages between your brain and parts of the body 2 courage and calmness ► *Don't lose your nerve.* 3 (informal) cheek or rudeness ► *He had the nerve to ask for more.* **get on someone's nerves** to irritate someone **nerves** nervousness ► *I was suffering from nerves before my exam.*

nervous *adjective* 1 easily upset or agitated; timid 2 to do with the nerves **nervously** *adverb* **nervousness** *noun*

nest *noun* (*plural* **nests**) a home that a bird or animal makes to have its young and feed them

nest *verb* (**nests, nesting, nested**) (used about birds) to make a nest and live in it

nestle *verb* (**nestles, nestling, nestled**) (*pronounced* **ness**-el) to curl up comfortably

net *noun* (*plural* **nets**) 1 material made of pieces of thread, cord, or wire joined together in a criss-cross pattern with holes between 2 something made from this material ▸ *a fishing-net*

netball *noun* a team game in which you throw a ball through a high net on a ring

nettle *noun* (*plural* **nettles**) a wild plant with leaves that sting when you touch them

network *noun* (*plural* **networks**) 1 a criss-cross arrangement 2 a system with many connections or parts, such as a railway or computer system

neuter *adjective* neither male nor female

neuter *verb* (**neuters, neutering, neutered**) to remove the sexual organs from an animal so that it cannot breed

neutral *adjective* 1 not supporting either side in a war or quarrel 2 (describing a colour) not bright or strong 3 (describing a gear) not connected to the driving parts of an engine

neutron *noun* (*plural* **neutrons**) a particle of matter with no electric charge

never *adverb* at no time; not ever

nevertheless *conjunction* and *adverb* in spite of that; nonetheless .

new *adjective* (**newer, newest**) 1 not existing before ▸ *That is a new idea.* 2 just bought or received ▸ *Do you like my new*

shoes? 3 different or unfamiliar ▸ *They've moved to a new area.* **newly** *adverb* **newness** *noun* being new

newcomer *noun* (*plural* **newcomers**) someone who has recently arrived in a place

news *noun* information about people or recent events

newsagent *noun* (*plural* **newsagents**) a shopkeeper who sells newspapers and magazines

newspaper *noun* (*plural* **newspapers**) large sheets of printed paper folded together, containing news reports and articles

newt *noun* (*plural* **newts**) a small animal like a lizard, which lives near or in water

next *adjective* and *adverb* nearest; coming immediately after

nib *noun* (*plural* **nibs**) the pointed metal part of a pen

nibble *verb* (**nibbles, nibbling, nibbled**) to eat something with small bites

nice *adjective* (**nicer, nicest**) pleasant or kind **nicely** *adverb*

nick *noun* (*plural* **nicks**) a small cut or notch **in the nick of time** only just in time

nick *verb* (**nicks, nicking, nicked**) 1 to make a small cut in something 2 (slang) to steal something

nickel *noun* (*plural* **nickels**) a silvery-white metal

nickname *noun* (*plural* **nicknames**) a name that you call a friend instead of their real name

nicotine *noun* a poisonous substance found in tobacco

niece *noun* (*plural* **nieces**) the daughter of your brother or sister

night *noun* (*plural* **nights**) the time when it is dark, between sunset and sunrise

nightdress *noun* (*plural* **nightdresses**) a loose light dress that girls and women wear in bed

nightfall *noun* the time when it becomes dark just after sunset

nightingale *noun* (*plural* **nightingales**) a small brown bird that sings sweetly

nightly *adjective* happening once a night or every night

nightmare *noun* (*plural* **nightmares**) a frightening or unpleasant dream **nightmarish** *adjective* terrifying
The word **nightmare** comes from *night* and *mare*, an evil spirit that was thought to cause bad dreams.

nil *noun* nothing, nought

nimble *adjective* (**nimbler, nimblest**) moving quickly or easily **nimbly** *adverb*

nine *noun* (*plural* **nines**) the number 9 **ninth** *adjective* and *noun*

nineteen *noun* (*plural* **nineteens**) the number 19 **nineteenth** *adjective* and *noun*

ninety *noun* (*plural* **nineties**) the number 90 **ninetieth** *adjective* and *noun*

nip *verb* (**nips, nipping, nipped**) 1 to pinch or bite someone sharply 2 (informal) to go somewhere quickly ▸ *I'll just nip into the paper shop.*

nip *noun* (*plural* **nips**) 1 a quick pinch or bite 2 a cold feeling ▸ *There's a nip in the air.*

nipple *noun* (*plural* **nipples**) the small pink part in the middle of a person's breast

nit *noun* (*plural* **nits**) a louse or the egg of a louse

nitrogen *noun* a gas that makes up about four-fifths of the air we breathe

no *adjective* and *adverb* not any ▸ *We have no money.* ▸ *She is no better.*

no *interjection* a word used to deny or refuse something

noble *adjective* (**nobler, noblest**) 1 coming from the highest class in society; aristocratic 2 having a good and generous nature ▸ *a noble emperor* 3 grand or handsome ▸ *a noble building* **nobility** *noun* being noble; the highest class in soicety **nobly** *adverb*

noble *noun* (*plural* **nobles**) a person who comes from a noble family, for example a duke or an earl

nobleman or **noblewoman** *noun* (*plural* **noblemen** or **noblewomen**) a man or woman from the highest class in society

nobody *pronoun* no person; not anyone ▸ *Nobody knows his name.*

nocturnal *adjective* happening or active at night ▸ *Badgers are nocturnal animals.*

nod *verb* (**nods, nodding, nodded**) to move your head up and down as a way of agreeing with someone or saying 'yes'

noise *noun* (*plural* **noises**) a loud sound, especially an unpleasant one

noisy *adjective* (**noisier, noisiest**) making a lot of noise **noisily** *adverb* **noisiness** *noun*

nomad *noun* (*plural* **nomads**) a member of a tribe that moves from place to place **nomadic** *adjective*

no man's land *noun* the land between two armies in a war

nominate *verb* (**nominates, nominating, nominated**) to suggest that someone would be a good person to do a job **nomination** *noun*

none *pronoun* not any; not one ▸ *None of us went.*

none *adverb* not at all ▸ *He's none too pleased.*

nonetheless *adverb* in spite of that; nevertheless

non-existent *adjective* not existing

non-fiction *noun* books about real things and true events, not stories

nonsense *noun* 1 words that do not make any sense 2 silly ideas or behaviour **nonsensical** *adjective*

non-stop *adverb* and *adjective* not stopping ▸ *Sara talks non-stop.* ▸ *A non-stop flight to Cape Town.*

noodles *plural noun* thin strips of pasta, used in soups and stir-fries

noon *noun* twelve o'clock midday

no one *pronoun* no person; not anyone

noose *noun* (*plural* **nooses**) a loop of rope that gets smaller when it is pulled

nor *conjunction* and not ▸ *He can't hear you; nor can I.*

normal *adjective* usual or ordinary ▸ *It's normal to want a holiday.* **normality** *noun* a situation where things are normal **normally** *adverb*

north *noun* the direction to the left of a person facing east

north *adjective* and *adverb* 1 towards the north or in the north 2 (describing the wind) coming from the north

north-east *noun* and *adjective* and *adverb* midway between north and east

northerly *adjective* 1 to the north or towards the north ▸ *We were travelling in a northerly direction.* 2 (describing the wind) blowing from the north

northern *adjective* from or to do with the north

northerner *noun* (*plural* **northerners**) someone who lives in the north of a country

northward or **northwards** *adjective* and *adverb* towards the north

north-west *noun* and *adjective* and *adverb* midway between north and west

nose *noun* (*plural* **noses**) 1 the part of your face that you use for breathing and smelling 2 the front part of a vehicle or aircraft

nose *verb* (**noses, nosing, nosed**) to move slowly forward ▸ *The car nosed through the crowds.*

nosedive *noun* (*plural* **nosedives**) a steep dive in an aircraft

nostalgia *noun* (*pronounced* nos-**tal**-ja) a longing for the past **nostalgic** *adjective* The word **nostalgia** comes from a Greek word *nostos* meaning 'a return home', like the heroes returning home after the Trojan War.

nostril *noun* (*plural* **nostrils**) each of the two openings in your nose

nosy *adjective* (**nosier, nosiest**) prying into other people's business **nosily** *adverb* **nosiness** *adjective*

not *adverb* a word used to change the meaning of something to its opposite

notable *adjective* remarkable or famous **notably** *adverb*

notch *noun* (*plural* **notches**) a small V-shaped cut or mark

note *noun* (*plural* **notes**) 1 words written down to help you remember something 2 a short letter or message 3 a single sound in music 4 a sound or tone that indicates something ▸ *There was a note of anger in his voice.* 5 a piece of paper money ▸ *a five-pound note* **take note of** to listen to something said and understand it

note *verb* (**notes, noting, noted**) to pay attention to something or write it down as a reminder

notebook *noun* (*plural* **notebooks**) a book for writing things down

notepaper *noun* paper for writing letters

nothing *noun* not anything

notice *noun* (*plural* **notices**) 1 something written and displayed for people to see 2 a person's attention ▸ *It escaped my notice.* 3 a warning that something is going to happen ▸ *We weren't given any notice of the fire practice.*

notice *verb* (**notices, noticing, noticed**) to see something or become aware of it

noticeboard *noun* (*plural* **noticeboards**) a board on which notices can be displayed

notify *verb* (**notifies, notifying, notified**) to tell someone about something officially ▸ *This letter is to notify you that you have been successful in applying for the job.*

notion *noun* (*plural* **notions**) a vague idea or belief ▸ *The notion that the earth might be flat seemed to amuse him.*

notorious *adjective* well-known for doing something bad **notoriously** *adverb*

nougat *noun* (*pronounced* **noo**-gah) a chewy sweet made from nuts and sugar or honey

nought *noun* (*plural* **noughts**) the figure 0

noun *noun* (*plural* **nouns**) a word that stands for a person, place, or thing GRAMMAR Nouns are called **common nouns** when they stand for many different people or things, for example *girl, horse, town, table.* They are called **abstract nouns** when they stand for things you can't feel or touch, for example *happiness, sport.*

They are called **proper nouns** when they are the name of one person or thing, for example *Jane, Paris, Concorde.*

nourish *verb* (**nourishes, nourishing, nourished**) to give someone the food they need to keep them alive and well **nourishment** *noun*

nourishing *adjective* (describing food) full of things your body needs to stay healthy

novel *adjective* unusual ▶ *What a novel idea.*

novel *noun* (*plural* **novels**) a book that contains one long story

novelist *noun* (*plural* **novelists**) someone who writes novels

novelty *noun* (*plural* **novelties**) something new and unusual

November *noun* the eleventh month of the year
The word **November** comes from the Latin word *novem* meaning 'nine', because it was the ninth month in the Roman calendar.

novice *noun* (*plural* **novices**) a beginner

now *adverb* at this time ▶ *We live in France now.* **now and then** occasionally; sometimes

now *conjunction* since or as ▶ *Now I think of it, I saw her recently.*

now *noun* this moment ▶ *They should be home by now.*

nowadays *adverb* at the present time

nowhere *adverb* not anywhere; in no place or to no place

nozzle *noun* (*plural* **nozzles**) the part at the end of a hose or pipe that liquid flows from

nuclear *adjective* 1 to do with a nucleus, especially of an atom 2 using the energy that is created by splitting the nuclei of atoms ▶ *nuclear weapons*

nucleus *noun* (*plural* **nuclei**) (*pronounced* **nyoo**-klee-us) 1 the part in the centre of something, round which other things are grouped 2 the central part of an atom or cell

nude *adjective* not wearing any clothes; naked **nudity** *noun* nakedness

nudge *verb* (**nudges, nudging, nudged**) to touch or push someone gently with your elbow

nugget *noun* (*plural* **nuggets**) a lump of gold from the ground

nuisance *noun* (*plural* **nuisances**) (*pronounced* **nyoo**-sans) an annoying person or thing

numb *adjective* unable to feel or move **numbness** *noun* being numb

number *noun* (*plural* **numbers**) 1 a symbol or word that tells you how many of something there are 2 a quantity of people or things ▶ *A large number of people were still waiting.* 3 one issue of a magazine or newspaper 4 a song or piece of music

number *verb* (**numbers, numbering, numbered**) 1 to count things or mark them with numbers ▶ *Please number the pages of your essay.* 2 to reach an amount ▶ *The crowd numbered 10,000.*

numeral *noun* (*plural* **numerals**) a symbol or figure that stands for a number

numerous *adjective* many ▶ *There are numerous kinds of cat.*

nun *noun* (*plural* **nuns**) a member of a religious group of women living in a convent

nurse *noun* (*plural* **nurses**) a person trained to look after people who are ill or injured

nurse *verb* (**nurses, nursing, nursed**) to look after someone who is ill or injured

nursery *noun* (*plural* **nurseries**) 1 a place where young children are looked after and play 2 a place where young plants are grown and sold

nursery rhyme *noun* (*plural* **nursery rhymes**) a simple poem or song for young children

nursery school *noun* (*plural* **nursery schools**) a school for very young children

nut *noun* (*plural* **nuts**) 1 a fruit with a hard shell containing a softer part that you can sometimes eat 2 a hollow piece of metal for screwing on to a bolt

nutcrackers *plural noun* pincers for cracking the shells of nuts

nutmeg *noun* (*plural* **nutmegs**) a hard seed that is made into a powder and used as a spice

nutritious *adjective* (describing food) good for you; nourishing **nutrition** *noun* giving you the food your body needs to stay healthy

nutty *adjective* (**nuttier, nuttiest**) 1 full of nuts, or tasting of nuts 2 (slang) crazy, mad

nuzzle *verb* (**nuzzles, nuzzling, nuzzled**) to rub gently against someone with the nose, as some animals do

nylon *noun* a lightweight synthetic cloth or fibre

nymph *noun* (*plural* **nymphs**) in myths, a young goddess who lives in trees or water

Oo

oak *noun* (*plural* **oaks**) a large tree with seeds called acorns

OAP *noun* (*plural* **OAPs**) an elderly person who has retired and receives money called a pension
OAP stands for 'old-age pensioner'.

oar *noun* (*plural* **oars**) a pole with a flat blade, used for rowing a boat

oasis *noun* (*plural* **oases**) (*pronounced* oh-ay-sis) a fertile place in a desert, with water and trees

oath *noun* (*plural* **oaths**) 1 a solemn promise 2 a swear word

oatmeal *noun* oats ground into powder

oats *plural noun* a cereal used to make food for humans and animals

obedient *adjective* doing as you are told; obeying **obedience** *noun* **obediently** *adverb*

obey *verb* (**obeys, obeying, obeyed**) to do what you are told to do

object *noun* (*plural* **objects**) (*pronounced* ob-jekt) 1 something that can be seen or touched 2 the purpose of something
▶ *One object of the meeting was to tell people about the summer camps.* 3 in language, the word naming the person or thing that the action of a verb affects, for example *her* in the sentence *Jim saw her.*

object *verb* (**objects, objecting, objected**) (*pronounced* ob-jekt) to say that you do not like something or do not agree with it
▶ *I object to people smoking in buses.*
objection *noun* saying that you do not like something or do not agree with it

objectionable *adjective* unpleasant or nasty

objective *noun* (*plural* **objectives**) something you are trying to do ▶ *Our objective is to raise £100 for new sports equipment.*

obligation *noun* (*plural* **obligations**) something you have to do

obligatory *adjective* (*pronounced* ob-lig-at-ri) having to be done; compulsory

oblige *verb* (**obliges, obliging, obliged**) 1 to force someone to do something ▶ *We were obliged to leave.* 2 (not an everyday word) to help and please someone ▶ *Will you oblige me by closing the window?*

oblong *noun* (*plural* **oblongs**) a four-sided shape with right angles that is longer than it is wide

obnoxious *adjective* nasty or unpleasant

oboe *noun* (*plural* **oboes**) (*pronounced* oh-boh) a high-pitched woodwind instrument **oboist** *noun*

obscene *adjective* (*pronounced* ob-seen) offending people's feelings, especially because of being rude in a sexual way **obscenity** *noun* obscene language or behaviour

obscure *adjective* 1 difficult to see or understand; not clear 2 not well-known **obscurity** *noun* being hardly known

observant *adjective* quick at observing or noticing things

observation *noun* (*plural* **observations**) 1 observing or watching 2 a comment or remark

observatory *noun* (*plural* **observatories**) (*pronounced* ob-zerv-a-ter-i) a building with large telescopes for looking at the stars or the weather

observe *verb* (**observes, observing, observed**) 1 to watch someone or something carefully 2 to obey a law or follow a custom 3 to state a fact ▸ *She observed that it was starting to snow.* **observer** *noun*

obsessed *adjective* always thinking about something ▸ *He is obsessed with food.* **obsession** *noun* something that you think about all the time

obsolete *adjective* not used any more; out of date

obstacle *noun* (*plural* **obstacles**) something that gets in the way or makes it difficult to move forward

obstinate *adjective* not willing to change your ideas or ways **obstinacy** *noun* being obstinate **obstinately** *adverb*

obstruct *verb* (**obstructs, obstructing, obstructed**) to block or hinder someone or something ▸ *There was a large sign obstructing the pavement.* **obstruction** *noun* something causing a blockage

obtain *verb* (**obtains, obtaining, obtained**) (not an everyday word) to get something or be given it **obtainable** *adjective*

obtuse *adjective* slow to understand; stupid **obtuse angle** an angle of between 90 and 180 degrees

obvious *adjective* easy to see or understand **obviously** *adverb*

occasion *noun* (*plural* **occasions**) 1 a particular time that something happens ▸ *On this occasion, the train was early.* 2 a special event ▸ *The coronation was a grand occasion.*

occasional *adjective* happening from time to time **occasionally** *adverb*

occupant *noun* (*plural* **occupants**) someone who is living in a building or using a room

occupation *noun* (*plural* **occupations**) 1 a person's job or profession 2 the capturing of a country by an invading army

occupy *verb* (**occupies, occupying, occupied**) 1 to live in a place or building 2 to fill a space or position 3 to capture a place in a war and keep an army in it 4 to keep someone busy or interested

occur *verb* (**occurs, occurring, occurred**) to happen or take place **occur to** to come into someone's mind ▸ *An idea has occurred to me.* **occurrence** *noun* something that happens

ocean *noun* (*plural* **oceans**) each of the areas of salt water that surround the continents

o'clock *adverb* used with numbers to show an exact hour ▸ *8 o'clock*
The word **o'clock** is a shortened form of the phrase *of the clock.*

octagon *noun* (*plural* **octagons**) a flat shape with eight sides **octagonal** *adjective*

octave *noun* (*plural* **octaves**) in music, a range between one note and the next note of the same name above or below it, or these two notes played together

October *noun* the tenth month of the year
The word **October** comes from the Latin word *octo* meaning 'eight', because it was the eighth month in the Roman calendar.

octopus *noun* (*plural* **octopuses**) a sea creature with eight arms (called *tentacles*)

odd *adjective* (**odder, oddest**) 1 strange or unusual ▸ *It was odd that nobody saw us.* ▸ *We heard an odd noise outside.* 2 left over or spare ▸ *I found an odd sock under the bed.* 3 of various kinds; occasional ▸ *She has a few odd jobs to do.* **odd number** a number that cannot be divided by 2, such as 3 or 21 **oddity** *noun* something that is odd or strange

oddments *plural noun* small things of various kinds

odious *adjective* hateful, horrible

odds *plural noun* the chances that something will happen ▸ *The odds are they won't come.* **odds and ends** small things of various kinds

odour *noun* (*plural* **odours**) an unpleasant smell

of *preposition* 1 belonging to ▸ *the father of the child* 2 about; concerning ▸ *Is there any news of your mother?* 3 from; out of ▸ *The house is built of stone.* 4 coming from ▸ *a native of Spain*

off *adverb* and *preposition* 1 away; not on ▸ *Her hat blew off.* ▸ *They ran off.* ▸ *He fell off his chair.* 2 not working or happening ▸ *Turn the television off.* ▸ *The match is off.* 3 beginning to go bad ▸ *I think the milk is off.* 4 not taking or wanting ▸ *They are off their food.* 5 taken away ▸ *£5 off*

offence *noun* (*plural* **offences**) 1 something that is a crime or breaks a rule 2 a feeling of being annoyed or hurt **cause offence** to hurt someone's feelings

offend *verb* (**offends, offending, offended**) 1 to hurt someone's feelings or be unpleasant to them 2 to break a law or do wrong **offender** *noun*

offensive *adjective* 1 insulting or causing offence ▸ *Some people found his remarks offensive.* 2 used for attacking; aggressive ▸ *offensive weapons*

offer *verb* (**offers, offering, offered**) 1 to say that someone can have something if they want it ▸ *Offer them a chocolate.* 2 to say that you are willing to do something ▸ *I offered to collect her from the station.* 3 to say how much you are willing to pay for something ▸ *He offered me £50.*
offer *noun* (*plural* **offers**) the action of offering something, or something you offer

offering *noun* (*plural* **offerings**) something you offer or give to someone, especially a gift or a sacrifice to a god

office *noun* (*plural* **offices**) 1 a room or building with desks and equipment, where people do business work 2 an important job or position ▸ *the office of President*

officer *noun* (*plural* **officers**) 1 a senior person in the army, navy, or air force 2 a policeman or policewoman 3 an official

official *adjective* 1 done or said by the government, or by someone in charge ▸ *an official statement* 2 to do with an important job ▸ *official responsibilities* **officially** *adverb*
official *noun* (*plural* **officials**) someone who has power or makes decisions as part of their job

officious *adjective* (*pronounced* o-fish-us) wanting to order people about; bossy and unpleasant

off-licence *noun* (*plural* **off-licences**) a shop with a licence to sell alcoholic drinks for people to take away

offside *adjective* and *adverb* in sports, in a position which is not allowed by the rules

offspring *noun* (*plural* **offspring**) a person's child or an animal's young

often *adverb* many times; in many cases

ogre *noun* (*plural* **ogres**) (*pronounced* oh-ger) a cruel giant in stories

oh *interjection* a cry of surprise, pain, or delight

oil *noun* (*plural* **oils**) a thick slippery liquid that does not mix with water. Different kinds of oil are used in cooking, as a fuel, to make paints, and to keep machinery working smoothly.
oil *verb* (**oils, oiling, oiled**) to put oil on something to make it work smoothly

oil painting *noun* (*plural* **oil paintings**) a painting done using paints made with oil

oil rig *noun* (*plural* **oil rigs**) a tall frame used to drill for oil

oily *adjective* (**oilier, oiliest**) like oil or covered in oil **oiliness** *noun*

ointment *noun* (*plural* **ointments**) a cream you put on your skin to treat sore places and cuts

OK *adverb* and *adjective* (informal) all right
The letters **OK** probably come from *orl korrect*, a joking way of writing 'all correct' in America in the 19th century.

old *adjective* (**older**, **oldest**) **1** not new; born or made a long time ago ► *An old woman came to the door.* ► *An old car was parked outside.* **2** of a particular age ► *The cat is ten years old today.* **3** former or original ► *I went back to my old school for a visit.* **4** belonging to the past ► *They miss the old days.*

old-fashioned *adjective* of a kind that is no longer usual; out of date

olive *noun* (*plural* **olives**) **1** a small black or green fruit with a stone and a bitter taste, which you can eat or make into olive oil **2** the evergreen tree on which olives grow

Olympic Games or **Olympics** *plural noun* international sports contests held every four years in different countries
The name comes from *Olympia* in Greece, where games were held in ancient times.

omelette *noun* (*plural* **omelettes**) (*pronounced* **om**-lit) a food made by beating eggs together and frying them

omen *noun* (*plural* **omens**) (*pronounced* **oh**-men) an event taken as a sign that something is going to happen

ominous *adjective* giving a warning that trouble is coming **ominously** *adverb*

omit *verb* (**omits**, **omitting**, **omitted**) (not an everyday word) **1** to leave something out ► *Several names had been omitted from the list.* **2** to fail to do something ► *I omitted to lock the door.* **omission** *noun*

omnivore *noun* (*plural* **omnivores**) an animal that eats plants as well as meat **omnivorous** *adjective* eating plants and meat

on *adverb* and *preposition* **1** over the top of something ► *Put your hat on.* ► *Sit on the floor.* **2** at the time of ► *Come on Monday.* **3** about; concerning ► *a book on snakes* **4** forwards ► *Move on.* **5** working; in action ► *Put the heater on.*

once *adverb* **1** at one time ► *I once lived near here.* **2** ever ► *They never once offered to pay.*

once *conjunction* as soon as ► *We can leave once I've finished my work.*

one *noun* (*plural* **ones**) the smallest whole number, 1

one *pronoun* a person or thing on their own ► *I've bought some apples and wondered if you'd like one.* **one another** each other

one *adjective* single ► *I have one packet left.*

oneself *pronoun* used to refer to the person speaking or to people in general ► *One should not always think of oneself.*

onion *noun* (*plural* **onions**) a round vegetable with a strong flavour

online *adjective* connected to a computer

only *adjective* being the one person or thing ► *He's the only person we can trust.*

only *adverb* no more than ► *There are only three cakes left.*

only *conjunction* but then; however ► *I'd like to come, only I'm busy.*

onward or **onwards** *adverb* forward

ooze *verb* (**oozes**, **oozing**, **oozed**) to flow out slowly ► *A thick black liquid was oozing out of the crack.*

opaque *adjective* (*pronounced* oh-**payk**) not able to be seen through

open *adjective* **1** allowing people or things to pass through; not shut ► *Someone had left the door open.* **2** not enclosed ► *There is a lot of open space behind the houses.* **3** not folded; spread out ► *She greeted us with open arms.* **4** honest, not hiding anything ► *They were quite open about what they had done.* **5** not settled or finished ► *Who would be in charge was still an open question.* **in the open air** outdoors; not inside a house or building

open *verb* (**opens, opening, opened**) **1** to make something open; to become open **2** to begin ▸ *The sale opens at 2 o'clock.*

opener *noun* (*plural* **openers**) a device for opening a bottle or can

opening *noun* (*plural* **openings**) **1** a space or gap **2** the beginning of something

openly *adverb* not secretly; publicly

open-minded *adjective* ready to listen to other people's ideas

opera *noun* (*plural* **operas**) a play where the words are sung, not spoken **operatic** *adjective*

operate *verb* (**operates, operating, operated**) **1** to use or work something ▸ *Can you operate the tape recorder?* **2** to work or be in action ▸ *The lifts are not operating.* **3** to perform a surgical operation on someone

operation *noun* (*plural* **operations**) **1** something done to a patient's body by a surgeon to remove or repair a part of it **2** a big activity that you plan ▸ *Moving house is a difficult operation.* **3** making something work; working **in operation** working

operator *noun* (*plural* **operators**) **1** someone who works a machine **2** someone who works a telephone switchboard or exchange

opinion *noun* (*plural* **opinions**) what you think about something

opponent *noun* (*plural* **opponents**) someone who is against you in a game or contest

opportunity *noun* (*plural* **opportunities**) a good time or chance to do something

oppose *verb* (**opposes, opposing, opposed**) to speak or act against someone or something **be opposed to** to disagree with something ▸ *We are opposed to building on this land.* **opposition** *noun* opposing someone or something, or the people who do this

opposite *adjective* and *adverb* **1** on the other side; facing ▸ *The sisters lived on opposite sides of the road.* ▸ *I'll sit opposite.* **2** completely different ▸ *They have opposite opinions about many things.*

opposite *noun* (*plural* **opposites**) something that is opposite to something else ▸ *'Large' is the opposite of 'small'.*

oppress *verb* (**oppresses, oppressing, oppressed**) **1** to govern or treat people cruelly or unjustly **2** to trouble someone with worry or sadness **oppression** *noun* oppressing people, or being oppressed **oppressor** *noun* someone who treats people cruelly

oppressive *adjective* **1** harsh and cruel ▸ *an oppressive ruler* **2** hot and tiring ▸ *oppressive weather*

opt *verb* (**opts, opting, opted**) to choose something ▸ *I opted for the cash prize.* ▸ *We opted to go abroad.* **opt out** to decide not to join in

optical *adjective* to do with sight or your eyes **optically** *adverb*

optician *noun* (*plural* **opticians**) someone who tests your eyesight and sells glasses

optimist *noun* (*plural* **optimists**) someone who usually expects things to turn out well **optimism** *noun*

optimistic *adjective* expecting things to turn out well **optimistically** *adverb*

option *noun* (*plural* **options**) a choice or the right to choose

optional *adjective* that you can choose if you want to ▸ *You have to study French, but Spanish is optional.*

or *conjunction* used to show that there is a choice ▸ *Do you want to stay here or come with us?*

oral *adjective* **1** spoken, not written **2** to do with your mouth or using your mouth ▸ *Oral hygiene is important.* **orally** *adverb*

orange *noun* (*plural* **oranges**) **1** a round juicy fruit with a thick reddish-yellow skin **2** a reddish-yellow colour
orange *adjective* reddish-yellow

orang-utan *noun* (*plural* **orang-utans**)
(*pronounced* o-rang-u-**tan**) a large kind of
ape found in Indonesia
The word **orang-utan** comes from Malay words
meaning 'man of the forest'.

orbit *noun* (*plural* **orbits**) the curved path
that a moving object takes round a planet
or another body in space
orbit *verb* (**orbits, orbiting, orbited**) to
move round a planet or another body
▸ *The spacecraft will orbit Mars.*

orchard *noun* (*plural* **orchards**) a piece of
ground with fruit trees

orchestra *noun* (*plural* **orchestras**)
(*pronounced* or-kis-tra) a group of
musicians playing together **orchestral**
adjective to do with an orchestra

orchid *noun* (*plural* **orchids**) (*pronounced*
or-kid) a plant with bright flowers that
have unusual shapes

ordeal *noun* (*plural* **ordeals**) a difficult or
unpleasant experience

order *noun* (*plural* **orders**) **1** a command
▸ *The general gave the order to attack.*
2 a request for something to be supplied
▸ *The waiter took our order.* **3** obedience or
good behaviour ▸ *After all the fun it was
difficult to restore order.* **4** the way things
are arranged ▸ *I'll put these cards in the
right order.* **5** a group of religious monks,
priests, or nuns **in order that** or **in order to**
for the purpose of **out of order** not working
▸ *The drinks machine is out of order.*
order *verb* (**orders, ordering, ordered**) **1** to
tell someone do something **2** to ask for
something to be supplied to you ▸ *I've
ordered a drink.*

orderly *adjective* **1** arranged tidily or well
2 well-behaved; obedient

ordinary *adjective* normal or usual; not
special **ordinarily** *adverb*

ore *noun* (*plural* **ores**) rock with metal in
it, such as iron ore

organ *noun* (*plural* **organs**) **1** a musical
instrument with a keyboard and pedals,
making sounds by air forced through pipes
2 a part of your body that does a particular
job, for example the liver which cleans the
blood

organic *adjective* **1** to do with living things
2 (describing plants or food) grown or
produced without using artificial
fertilizers or pesticides **organically** *adverb*

organism *noun* (*plural* **organisms**) a living
animal or plant

organist *noun* (*plural* **organists**) someone
who plays the organ

organization *noun* (*plural* **organizations**)
1 a group of people working together for a
purpose **2** the organizing of something

organize *verb* (**organizes, organizing,
organized**) **1** to plan or arrange something
▸ *It's our job to organize the parade.* **2** to
put things in order ▸ *Someone needs to
organize the books.* **organizer** *noun*

oriental *adjective* to do with eastern
countries, such as China and Japan

orienteering *noun* the sport of finding
your way across rough country with a map
and compass

origin *noun* (*plural* **origins**) the point
where something began

original *adjective* **1** existing from the start;
earliest ▸ *The original idea was to go by
train.* **2** new; not a copy or an imitation
▸ *The furniture has an original design.*
3 producing new ideas; inventive
▸ *Natasha is an original thinker.* **originality**
noun **originally** *adverb*

originate *verb* (**originates, originating,
originated**) to start in a certain way
▸ *Supermarkets originated in America.*

ornament *noun* (*plural* **ornaments**) an object used as a decoration **ornamental** *adjective*

ornithology *noun* the study of birds **ornithologist** *noun*

orphan *noun* (*plural* **orphans**) a child whose parents are dead **orphaned** *adjective*

orphanage *noun* (*plural* **orphanages**) a home for orphans

orthodox *adjective* 1 having beliefs that are generally accepted 2 following the old, traditional form of a religion

ostrich *noun* (*plural* **ostriches**) a large long-legged bird that can run fast but cannot fly
People talk about 'burying your head in the sand' or being 'ostrich-like' when they think you are fooling yourself by what you do or say. These expressions come from an old story that the ostrich buried its head in the sand when it was trying to escape from hunters, thinking that if it couldn't see them they couldn't see it.

other *adjective* and *pronoun* not the same as one just mentioned ▶ *Play some other tune.* ▶ *I can't find my other glove.* ▶ *Where are the others?* **every other day** every second day, for example Monday, Wednesday, and Friday **the other day** a few days ago

otherwise *adverb* and *conjunction* 1 if not; if things happen differently ▶ *We'd better hurry, otherwise we'll miss the bus.* 2 in other ways ▶ *It rained a lot but otherwise the holiday was good.*

otter *noun* (*plural* **otters**) an animal with thick fur and a flat tail, which lives near water

ouch *interjection* a cry of pain

ought *verb* used with other words to show 1 what you should or must do ▶ *I ought to write some letters.* 2 what is likely to happen ▶ *The bus ought to be here soon.*

ounce *noun* (*plural* **ounces**) a unit of weight equal to 1/16 of a pound or about 28 grams

our *adjective* belonging to us ▶ *This is our house.*

ours *pronoun* belonging to us ▶ *This house is ours.*

ourselves *pronoun* used to refer to the people already mentioned as 'we' ▶ *We have hurt ourselves.* **by ourselves** on our own; alone ▶ *We did the work all by ourselves.*

out *adverb* 1 away from a place or not in it; not at home ▶ *They must be out.* 2 into the open or outdoors ▶ *Shall we go out today?* 3 away from its position inside something ▶ *Take the key out of the lock.* 4 not burning or working ▶ *The lights have gone out.* 5 strongly or fully ▶ *He cried out.* ▶ *Stretch your hand out.* **be out of** to have no more of something left ▶ *The shop was out of cat food.* **out of date** old-fashioned; not used any more **out of doors** in the open air **out of the way** remote or distant

outback *noun* the remote inland areas of Australia

outbreak *noun* (*plural* **outbreaks**) the sudden start of something unpleasant, such as war or a disease

outburst *noun* (*plural* **outbursts**) the sudden showing of anger or another strong feeling

outcast *noun* (*plural* **outcasts**) someone who has been rejected by their family and friends

outcome *noun* (*plural* **outcomes**) a result of what has happened

outcry *noun* (*plural* **outcries**) a strong protest from many people

outdo *verb* (**outdoes, outdoing, outdid, outdone**) to do better than someone else

outdoor *adjective* done or used outdoors ▶ *outdoor clothes*

outdoors *adverb* in the open air ▶ *It is cold outdoors*

outer *adjective* nearer the outside; external

outer space *noun* space beyond the earth's atmosphere

outfit *noun* (*plural* **outfits**) 1 a set of clothes worn together 2 a set of things needed for doing something

outgrow *verb* (**outgrows, outgrowing, outgrew, outgrown**) 1 to grow too big or too old for something 2 to grow faster or taller than someone

outing *noun* (*plural* **outings**) a trip or short journey for enjoyment

outlaw *noun* (*plural* **outlaws**) (old use) a robber or bandit

outlaw *verb* (**outlaws, outlawing, outlawed**) to make something illegal

outlet *noun* (*plural* **outlets**) 1 a way for something to get out ▶ *The tank has an outlet at the side.* 2 a shop selling goods made by a particular company

outline *noun* (*plural* **outlines**) 1 a line that shows the edge or shape of something 2 a simple drawing showing only the main features of something 3 a summary

outline *verb* (**outlines, outlining, outlined**) 1 to draw a line round something to show its shape 2 to describe something briefly

outlive *verb* (**outlives, outliving, outlived**) to live longer than someone

outlook *noun* (*plural* **outlooks**) 1 the way that someone thinks about things 2 what seems likely to happen ▶ *The outlook is bright.* 3 a view that you see when you look out of a window

outlying *adjective* far from a town or city; distant ▶ *outlying districts*

outnumber *verb* (**outnumbers, outnumbering, outnumbered**) to be greater in number than something

outpatient *noun* (*plural* **outpatients**) a patient who visits a hospital for treatment but does not stay there overnight

output *noun* (*plural* **outputs**) 1 the amount produced by a factory or business 2 information produced by a computer

output *verb* (**outputs, outputting, output**) to get information from a computer

outrage *noun* (*plural* **outrages**) something very shocking or cruel

outrageous *adjective* causing shock or outrage; dreadful **outrageously** *adverb* **outrageousness** *noun*

outright *adverb* and *adjective* completely; all at once

outside *noun* (*plural* **outsides**) the outer side or surface of a thing

outside *adjective* 1 on or coming from the outside 2 slight or remote ▶ *There is an outside chance of snow.*

outside *adverb* and *preposition* on or to the outside of something ▶ *They are waiting outside.* ▶ *It's outside the house.*

outsider *noun* (*plural* **outsiders**) 1 someone who is not a member of a particular group of people 2 a horse or person thought to have no chance of winning a race or contest

outskirts *plural noun* the suburbs or edges of a town

outspoken *adjective* plainly saying what you think

outstanding *adjective* 1 extremely good or distinguished ▶ *an outstanding athlete* 2 not yet settled or dealt with ▶ *outstanding debts*

outward *adjective* 1 going outwards 2 on the outside

outwardly *adverb* on the outside; for people to see ▶ *They were outwardly calm.*

outwards *adverb* towards the outside

outwit *verb* (**outwits, outwitting, outwitted**) to deceive or defeat someone by being clever

oval *adjective* shaped like an egg or a number 0

oval *noun* (*plural* **ovals**) an oval shape

oven *noun* (*plural* **ovens**) a closed space, often part of a cooker, in which things are cooked or heated

over *adverb* 1 down or sideways; out and down from the top or edge ▶ *He fell over.* 2 across to a place ▶ *We walked over to the house.* 3 so that a different side shows ▶ *Turn the sheet over.* 4 finished ▶ *The lesson is over.* 5 left or remaining ▶ *There are a few apples over.* **over and over** repeatedly; many times

over *preposition* 1 above or on top of ▶ *There's a light over the door.* ▶ *I'll put a cover over the birdcage.* 2 more than ▶ *The house is over a mile away.* 3 concerning;

about   ▶ *The dogs fought over a bone.*

over *noun* (*plural* **overs**) in cricket, a series of six balls bowled by one person

overall *adjective* and *adverb* including everything; total   ▶ *What is the overall cost?*

overalls *plural noun* clothes that you wear over other clothes to protect them, usually trousers and a top joined together

overboard *adverb* over the side of a boat into the water   ▶ *He nearly fell overboard.*

overcast *adjective* covered with cloud ▶ *an overcast sky.*

overcome *verb* (**overcomes, overcoming, overcame, overcome**) 1 to control or defeat a difficulty   ▶ *I am trying to overcome my fear of heights.* 2 to make someone weak or helpless   ▶ *She was overcome by the fumes.* 3 to gain a victory over someone

overcrowded *adjective* having too many people

overdose *noun* (*plural* **overdoses**) a dangerously large dose of a drug or medicine

overdue *adjective* later than it should be ▶ *The train is overdue.*

overflow *verb* (**overflows, overflowing, overflowed**) to flow over the edges of something

overgrown *adjective* covered with weeds or unwanted plants

overhaul *verb* (**overhauls, overhauling, overhauled**) to check a machine or vehicle thoroughly and repair it if necessary

overhead *adjective* and *adverb* over your head; above

overhear *verb* (**overhears, overhearing, overheard**) to hear what someone is saying to another person

overjoyed *adjective* very pleased

overlap *verb* (**overlaps, overlapping, overlapped**) to lie across part of something ▶ *Each piece of the fence overlaps the next.*

overleaf *adverb* on the other side of the page or piece of paper

overload *verb* (**overloads, overloading, overloaded**) to put too big a load on something

overlook *verb* (**overlooks, overlooking, overlooked**) 1 to fail to notice something ▶ *They have completely overlooked the problems caused by the extra traffic.* 2 to decide not to punish someone   ▶ *I'll overlook your mistake this time.* 3 to have a view over something   ▶ *The house overlooks the sea.*

overnight *adverb* and *adjective* for or during a night   ▶ *We stayed overnight in a hotel.*   ▶ *There will be an overnight stop in Paris.*

overpower *verb* (**overpowers, overpowering, overpowered**) to overcome someone by force

overrun *verb* (**overruns, overrunning, overran, overrun**) 1 (used about something harmful) to spread over an area   ▶ *The garden was overrun with worms.* 2 to go on for longer than it should   ▶ *The programme overran by ten minutes.*

overseas *adverb* abroad   ▶ *They travelled overseas.*

overseas *adjective* from abroad; foreign ▶ *We met some overseas students.*

oversight *noun* (*plural* **oversights**) a mistake made by not noticing something

oversleep *verb* (**oversleeps, oversleeping, overslept**) to sleep longer than you meant to

overtake *verb* (**overtakes, overtaking, overtook, overtaken**) to pass a vehicle that is travelling in the same direction, and go in front of it

overthrow *verb* (**overthrows, overthrowing, overthrew, overthrown**) to defeat someone or force them out of power

overtime *noun* time spent working outside the normal hours

overture *noun* (*plural* **overtures**) a piece of music played at the start of a concert, opera, or ballet

overturn verb (**overturns, overturning, overturned**) 1 to make something turn over or fall over 2 to turn over

overwhelm verb (**overwhelms, overwhelming, overwhelmed**) 1 to bury or submerge someone under a huge mass ▸ *During the gales the sea overwhelmed several coastal villages.* 2 to overcome someone completely ▸ *She was overwhelmed with grief.*

owe verb (**owes, owing, owed**) 1 to have to pay something back or give it to someone ▸ *I owe you a pound.* 2 to have something because of what someone else has done ▸ *They owed their lives to their rescuers.*

owing to preposition because of

owl noun (*plural* **owls**) a bird of prey with large eyes, which flies at night

own adjective belonging to you ▸ *We've brought our own food.* **on your own** by yourself; alone

own verb (**owns, owning, owned**) to have something as your property **own up to** (informal) to admit that you did something

owner noun (*plural* **owners**) the person who owns something **ownership** noun owning something

ox noun (*plural* **oxen**) a male animal of the cow family, used for pulling loads

oxygen noun one of the gases in the air that people need to stay alive

oyster noun (*plural* **oysters**) a kind of shellfish, with a shell that sometimes contains a pearl

ozone noun a gas that is a form of oxygen

ozone layer noun a layer of ozone in the atmosphere, which protects the earth from the sun's radiation

Pp

pace noun (*plural* **paces**) 1 one step in walking or running 2 speed ▸ *The leaders set a fast pace.*

pace verb (**paces, pacing, paced**) to walk with slow or regular steps ▸ *He paced round the room.*

pacifist noun (*plural* **pacifists**) someone who believes that wars and fighting are wrong **pacifism** noun

pacify verb (**pacifies, pacifying, pacified**) to calm someone who is angry or upset

pack noun (*plural* **packs**) 1 a collection of things wrapped or tied together 2 a set of playing cards 3 a bag or rucksack 4 a group of hounds, wolves, or other animals 5 a group of Brownies or Cub Scouts

pack verb (**packs, packing, packed**) 1 to put things into a suitcase or bag before travelling 2 to fill a room or building with people

package noun (*plural* **packages**) 1 a parcel or packet 2 a number of things offered or taken together

package holiday noun (*plural* **package holidays**) a holiday with all travel and accommodation organized in advance and included in the price

packet noun (*plural* **packets**) a small parcel

pact noun (*plural* **pacts**) a formal agreement

pad[1] noun (*plural* **pads**) 1 a piece of soft material used to protect or shape something 2 a number of sheets of blank or lined paper joined together along one edge 3 a flat surface from which helicopters take off or rockets are launched

pad verb (**pads, padding, padded**) 1 to put a piece of soft material into something to protect or shape it 2 to walk softly

padding *noun* soft material used to protect something or make it more comfortable

paddle *verb* (**paddles, paddling, paddled**) 1 to walk about with bare feet in shallow water 2 to move a boat along with a short oar

paddle *noun* (*plural* **paddles**) 1 a time spent paddling in water 2 a short oar with a broad blade

paddock *noun* (*plural* **paddocks**) a small field for keeping horses

paddy field *noun* (*plural* **paddy fields**) a wet field where rice is grown

padlock *noun* (*plural* **padlocks**) a lock with a metal loop that you open with a key

pagan *noun* (*plural* **pagans**) someone who does not have a religion
This word is normally used about people in the past.

page *noun* (*plural* **pages**) 1 a piece of paper, or one side of a piece of paper that is part of a book or newspaper 2 a boy who acts as an attendant or runs errands

pageant *noun* (*plural* **pageants**) (*pronounced* **paj-ent**) a show or procession of people in costume acting out scenes from history

pagoda *noun* (*plural* **pagodas**) (*pronounced* pa-**goh**-da) an Asian temple in the form of a tower

paid past tense and past participle of **pay** *verb*

pail *noun* (*plural* **pails**) a bucket

pain *noun* (*plural* **pains**) an unpleasant feeling in your body, caused by injury or disease **take pains** to make a careful effort over something

painful *adjective* causing pain **painfully** *adverb*

paint *noun* (*plural* **paints**) a liquid substance put on something to colour or cover it

paint *verb* (**paints, painting, painted**) to use paint to colour something or to make a picture **painter** *noun*

painting *noun* (*plural* **paintings**) 1 using paints to make a picture ▸ *She's good at painting.* 2 a painted picture

pair *noun* (*plural* **pairs**) 1 two things that go together ▸ *a pair of shoes* 2 something made of two parts joined together ▸ *a pair of scissors*

pal *noun* (*plural* **pals**) (informal) a friend

palace *noun* (*plural* **palaces**) a grand house where a king or queen or other important person lives

palate *noun* (*plural* **palates**) (*pronounced* **pal**-it) the roof of your mouth

pale *adjective* (**paler, palest**) 1 having a light colour ▸ *He had a pale face.* 2 not bright; faint ▸ *The sky was a pale blue.* **paleness** *noun*

palette *noun* (*plural* **palettes**) a board that an artist uses to mix colours

pallid *adjective* (describing a person's face) pale from illness

palm *noun* (*plural* **palms**) (*rhymes with* harm) 1 the inner side of your hand, between your fingers and wrist 2 a tree that grows in hot countries, with large leaves at the top and no branches

pamper *verb* (**pampers, pampering, pampered**) to treat someone too kindly and let them have whatever they want

pamphlet *noun* (*plural* **pamphlets**) a thin book with a paper cover

pan *noun* (*plural* **pans**) 1 a flat metal dish used for cooking 2 something shaped like an open dish

pancake *noun* (*plural* **pancakes**) a thin flat cake of batter fried in a pan

panda *noun* (*plural* **pandas**) a large black-and-white animal like a bear, found in China

pandemonium *noun* a loud noise or disturbance

pane *noun* (*plural* **panes**) a sheet of glass in a window

panel *noun* (*plural* **panels**) 1 a long flat piece of wood, metal, or other material that is part of a door, wall, or other surface 2 a group of people chosen to judge a competition or take part in a television quiz

pang *noun* (*plural* **pangs**) a sudden feeling of pain or strong emotion

panic *noun* a sudden feeling of fear that spreads rapidly **panicky** *adjective*
panic *verb* (**panics, panicking, panicked**) to be overcome with fear or anxiety and behave wildly

panorama *noun* (*plural* **panoramas**) a view or picture of a wide area

pansy *noun* (*plural* **pansies**) a garden plant with bright flowers

pant *verb* (**pants, panting, panted**) to take short quick breaths after running or working hard

panther *noun* (*plural* **panthers**) a leopard

pantomime *noun* (*plural* **pantomimes**) a Christmas show with dancing and songs, based on a fairy tale

pantry *noun* (*plural* **pantries**) a cupboard or small room for storing food

pants *plural noun* 1 underpants or knickers 2 (in America) a word for trousers

paper *noun* (*plural* **papers**) 1 a thin material made in sheets and used for writing or printing or drawing on, or for wrapping things 2 a newspaper
paper *verb* (**papers, papering, papered**) to cover a wall with wallpaper

paperback *noun* (*plural* **paperbacks**) a book with a paper cover

papier mâché *noun* (*pronounced* pap-yay mash-ay) paper made into pulp and used to make models or ornaments

papyrus *noun* (*plural* **papyri**) (*pronounced* pa-py-rus) a kind of paper made in ancient Egypt from reeds

parable *noun* (*plural* **parables**) a story told to teach people something

parachute *noun* (*plural* **parachutes**) an umbrella-shaped device used for floating slowly to the ground from an aircraft

parade *noun* (*plural* **parades**) 1 a procession of people and vehicles 2 soldiers assembled for an inspection or drill
parade *verb* (**parades, parading, paraded**) 1 to move in a public procession 2 to assemble for a parade

paradise *noun* 1 heaven; a heavenly place 2 in the Bible, the Garden of Eden
The word **paradise** comes from an old Persian word meaning 'garden'.

paraffin *noun* a kind of oil used as fuel

paragraph *noun* (*plural* **paragraphs**) a section of a piece of writing, beginning on a new line

parallel *adjective* (describing lines) the same distance apart for their whole length, like railway lines

parallelogram *noun* (*plural* **parallelograms**) a four-sided figure with opposite sides that are parallel to each other and equal in length

paralyse *verb* (**paralyses, paralysing, paralysed**) to make someone unable to feel anything or to move

paralysis *noun* (*pronounced* pa-ral-i-sis) being unable to move or feel anything

parapet *noun* (*plural* **parapets**) a low wall along the edge of a bridge or balcony

paraphernalia *noun* (*pronounced* pa-ra-fer-nay-li-a) various pieces of equipment or small possessions

paraplegic *adjective* (*pronounced* pa-ra-plee-jik) paralysed by injury or disease in the lower part of your body

parasite *noun* (*plural* **parasites**) an animal or plant that gets its food from another living thing by living on or inside it

parasol *noun* (*plural* **parasols**) a light umbrella used to shade yourself from the sun

paratroops *plural noun* troops trained to be dropped from aircraft by parachute **paratrooper** *noun* a soldier who does this

parcel *noun* (*plural* **parcels**) something wrapped up in paper for sending in the post

parched *adjective* very dry or thirsty

parchment *noun* a kind of heavy writing material made from animal skins, used before paper was invented
The word **parchment** comes from the name of Pergamum, an ancient city in Asia Minor (now Turkey), where parchment was first made.

pardon *verb* (**pardons, pardoning, pardoned**) to forgive or excuse someone
pardon *noun* forgiving someone

parent *noun* (*plural* **parents**) a father or mother **parental** *adjective* to do with parents

parish *noun* (*plural* **parishes**) a district that has its own church

park *noun* (*plural* **parks**) a large area with grass and trees for people to use
park *verb* (**parks, parking, parked**) to leave a vehicle in a place for a time

parliament *noun* (*plural* **parliaments**) the group of people who make a country's laws **parliamentary** *adjective*

parole *noun* letting someone out of prison before they have finished their sentence, on condition that they behave well ▸ *He was on parole.*

parrot *noun* (*plural* **parrots**) a brightly-coloured bird with a hooked beak. Parrots can learn to imitate sounds.

parsley *noun* a herb with crinkled green leaves

parsnip *noun* (*plural* **parsnips**) a pale yellow root vegetable

parson *noun* (*plural* **parsons**) a member of the Christian clergy, especially a vicar

part *noun* (*plural* **parts**) 1 some but not all of a thing or a number of things ▸ *I've read part of the book.* 2 a share in something ▸ *We had no part in this adventure.* 3 the character played by an actor or actress 4 the words spoken by a character in a play
part *verb* (**parts, parting, parted**) 1 to separate or divide people or things 2 to become separated **part with** to give something away or get rid of it

partial *adjective* 1 not complete or total ▸ *We only got a partial answer to our question.* 2 favouring one person or side more than another; unfair **partial to** fond of something **partially** *adverb*

participate *verb* (**participates, participating, participated**) to take part in something or have a share in it **participant** *noun* someone who takes part in something **participation** *noun* taking part

participle *noun* (*plural* **participles**) a word formed from a verb and used as part of the verb or as an adjective, for example 'going', 'gone', 'sailed', 'sailing'

particle *noun* (*plural* **particles**) a very small piece of something

particular *adjective* 1 one and no other; special ▸ *Is there a particular day you'd like me to come?* 2 fussy; hard to please **in particular** especially; chiefly **particularly** *adverb*

particulars *plural noun* information or details about something

parting *noun* (*plural* **partings**) 1 leaving or separation 2 the line where hair is combed in different directions

partition *noun* (*plural* **partitions**) a thin wall that divides a space into separate areas

partly *adverb* not completely

partner *noun* (*plural* **partners**) **1** one of a pair of people who do something together ▸ *a business partner* **2** someone who is married to someone else or living with them **partnership** *noun* being partners

part of speech *noun* (*plural* **parts of speech**) each of the groups into which words can be divided in grammar: noun, adjective, verb, pronoun, adverb, preposition, conjunction, and interjection

partridge *noun* (*plural* **partridges**) a bird with brown feathers that some people shoot as a sport

part-time *adjective* and *adverb* working for only some of the normal hours

party *noun* (*plural* **parties**) **1** a time when people get together to enjoy themselves ▸ *a birthday party* **2** a group of people working or travelling together ▸ *a search party* **3** an organized group of people with similar political beliefs ▸ *the Labour Party*

pass *verb* (**passes, passing, passed**) **1** to go past something or someone ▸ *On the way we passed some dancers.* **2** to give something to someone with your hand ▸ *Can I pass you anything?* **3** to do well in an examination ▸ *If you work hard you should pass.* **4** to make use of something ▸ *How shall we pass the time?* **5** to finish or no longer be there ▸ *After a while the feeling of fear began to pass.* **6** to make a law or rule **7** in a ball game, to kick or throw the ball to another player in your team **pass away** to die

pass *noun* (*plural* **passes**) **1** a permit to go in or out of a place **2** a success in an examination **3** a narrow way between hills **4** in ball games, a throw or kick of the ball to another player in your team

passable *adjective* just about acceptable or all right

passage *noun* (*plural* **passages**) **1** a corridor or narrow street **2** a journey by sea or air ▸ *He worked as a cabin boy to pay for his passage.* **3** a section of a piece of writing or music **4** passing ▸ *The house became run down with the passage of time.*

passenger *noun* (*plural* **passengers**) someone who is driven in a car or travels by public transport

passer-by *noun* (*plural* **passers-by**) someone who happens to be going past

passion *noun* (*plural* **passions**) strong feeling or enthusiasm

passionate *adjective* full of passion or strong feeling **passionately** *adverb*

passive *adjective* not active; not resisting or fighting against something **passively** *adverb*

Passover *noun* a Jewish religious festival, celebrating the escape of the ancient Jews from slavery in Egypt

passport *noun* (*plural* **passports**) an official document that you carry when you travel abroad to show who you are

password *noun* (*plural* **passwords**) a secret word or phrase that allows you to go into a place or use a computer system

past *noun* **1** the time that has gone by ▸ *stories about the past* **2** the form of a verb that describes something that has happened, for example *came* in the sentence *My uncle came to visit us*

past *adjective* of the time gone by ▸ *the past few days*

past *adverb* and *preposition* **1** beyond ▸ *The bus went past.* ▸ *Go past the school and turn right.* **2** later than ▸ *It is past midnight.*

pasta *noun* a food made from flour and eggs and formed into shapes such as shells or bows

paste *noun* a thick glue for sticking things

paste *verb* (**pastes, pasting, pasted**) to stick something to a surface with paste

pastel *noun* (*plural* **pastels**) a chalk crayon

pastel *adjective* pale ▸ *The room was painted in pastel colours.*

pasteurize *verb* (**pasteurizes, pasteurizing, pasteurized**) to purify milk by heating and then cooling it
This process is named after Louis Pasteur, a 19th-century French scientist who invented it.

pastime *noun* (*plural* **pastimes**) something you do for enjoyment

past participle *noun* (*plural* **past participles**) a form of a verb used after *has, have, had, was,* or *were* to describe something that has happened, for example *been* and *written*

pastry *noun* (*plural* **pastries**) 1 a dough made from flour, fat, and water for baking 2 a cake made with pastry

pasture *noun* (*plural* **pastures**) land covered with grass where cattle, sheep, or horses can feed

pasty[1] *noun* (*plural* **pasties**) (*pronounced* **pas-ti**) a small meat or vegetable pie

pasty[2] *adjective* (**pastier, pastiest**) (*pronounced* **pay-sti**) (describing someone's skin) pale or white like paste

pat *verb* (**pats, patting, patted**) to tap something gently with your open hand
pat *noun* (*plural* **pats**) a patting movement or sound

patch *noun* (*plural* **patches**) 1 a piece of material put over a hole 2 an area that is different from the rest ▸ *a black cat with a white patch on its chest* 3 a small area of land 4 a small piece of something ▸ *There were patches of oil on the floor.*
patch *verb* (**patches, patching, patched**) to repair something with a patch **patch up to** repair something roughly

patchwork *noun* small pieces of different material sewn together

patchy *adjective* (**patchier, patchiest**) 1 occurring in some areas but not others ▸ *There was patchy fog.* 2 uneven; not complete ▸ *Gina's understanding of decimals is patchy.*

pâté *noun* (*pronounced* **pat-ay**) a meat or fish paste with a strong taste

paternal *adjective* to do with a father, or like a father

path *noun* (*plural* **paths**) 1 a narrow way to walk or ride along 2 the line along which something moves ▸ *the path of the meteor*

pathetic *adjective* 1 sad and causing pity 2 weak or useless ▸ *He made a pathetic attempt to climb the tree.* **pathetically** *adverb*

patience *noun* 1 the ability to be patient 2 a game of cards that you play by yourself

patient *adjective* able to wait for a long time or put up with a difficulty without getting anxious or angry **patiently** *adverb*
patient *noun* (*plural* **patients**) a person who is being treated by a doctor or dentist

patio *noun* (*plural* **patios**) (*pronounced* **pat-ee-oh**) a paved area beside a house

patriot *noun* (*plural* **patriots**) (*pronounced* **pat-ree-ot** or **pay-tree-ot**) someone who loves and supports their country **patriotic** *adjective* **patriotism** *noun*

patrol *verb* (**patrols, patrolling, patrolled**) (*pronounced* **pa-trohl**) to go round a place to guard it and make sure that all is well
patrol *noun* (*plural* **patrols**) 1 a group of people or vehicles patrolling a place 2 a group of Scouts or Guides

patron *noun* (*plural* **patrons**) (*pronounced* **pay-tron**) 1 someone who supports a charity or group with money or other help 2 a regular customer of a shop or pub

patron saint *noun* (*plural* **patron saints**) a saint who is thought of as protecting a place or activity

patter *verb* (**patters, pattering, pattered**) to make light tapping sounds ▸ *Rain pattered on the glass roof.*

pattern *noun* (*plural* **patterns**) 1 an arrangement of lines or shapes 2 a thing that you copy to make something ▸ *a dress pattern*

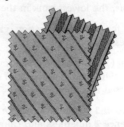

pauper *noun* (*plural* **paupers**) a very poor person

pause *verb* (**pauses, pausing, paused**) to stop for a short while
pause *noun* (*plural* **pauses**) a short stop

pave *verb* (**paves, paving, paved**) to put a hard surface on a road or path

pavement *noun* (*plural* **pavements**) a hard path at the side of a road

pavilion *noun* (*plural* **pavilions**) a building at a sports ground for players and spectators to use

paw *noun* (*plural* **paws**) an animal's foot
paw *verb* (**paws, pawing, pawed**) to touch something clumsily with a hand or foot

pawn *noun* (*plural* **pawns**) one of the small chess pieces that are at the front on each side
pawn *verb* (**pawns, pawning, pawned**) to leave something with a pawnbroker in exchange for money

pawnbroker *noun* (*plural* **pawnbrokers**) someone who lends money in return for objects which are later sold if the money is not paid back

pay *verb* (**pays, paying, paid**) 1 to give money in return for something ▸ *I'd better pay for these books.* 2 to be profitable or worthwhile ▸ *It pays to be honest.* 3 to suffer for something you have done wrong ▸ *You will pay for your laziness.* **pay attention** to listen carefully **pay back** to pay money that you owe
pay *noun* money that you earn

payment *noun* (*plural* **payments**) 1 paying for something 2 money that you pay

PC short for **personal computer**, and *police constable*, the lowest rank in the police

PE short for *physical education*, games and exercises you do at school

pea *noun* (*plural* **peas**) a small round green seed growing inside a pod on a climbing plant, used as a vegetable

peace *noun* 1 a time when there is no war or violence 2 quietness and calm

peaceful *adjective* quiet and calm **peacefully** *adverb*

peach *noun* (*plural* **peaches**) a soft juicy fruit with a slightly furry skin and a large stone

peacock *noun* (*plural* **peacocks**) a male bird with a long brightly coloured tail that it can spread out like a fan. The female is called a **peahen**.

peak *noun* (*plural* **peaks**) 1 the top of a mountain 2 the highest or best point of something 3 the part of a cap that sticks out in front

peal *verb* (**peals, pealing, pealed**) (used about bells) to make a loud ringing sound
peal *noun* (*plural* **peals**) a sound of bells

peanut *noun* (*plural* **peanuts**) a nut that grows in a pod in the ground

pear *noun* (*plural* **pears**) a juicy round fruit that is narrower near the stalk

pearl *noun* (*plural* **pearls**) a small shiny white stone found in some oysters and used as a jewel

peasant *noun* (*plural* **peasants**) (*pronounced* **pez-ant**) a person who works on the land, especially in poor countries or in the Middle Ages

peat *noun* rotted plant material dug out of the ground and used as fuel or fertilizer

pebble *noun* (*plural* **pebbles**) a small round stone **pebbly** *adjective*

peck *verb* (**pecks, pecking, pecked**) (used about birds) to bite or eat something with the beak

peckish *adjective* slightly hungry

peculiar *adjective* strange or unusual **peculiar to** belonging to a particular place or people ▸ *The custom is peculiar to Ireland.*

pedal *noun* (*plural* **pedals**) a lever that you press with your foot to make something work
pedal *verb* (**pedals, pedalling, pedalled**) to push or turn the pedals of a bicycle

pedestrian *noun* (*plural* **pedestrians**) someone who is walking in the street

pedigree *noun* (*plural* **pedigrees**) a list of an animal's ancestors, showing how well it has been bred

pedlar *noun* (*plural* **pedlars**) (old use) someone who goes from house to house selling small things

peel *noun* (*plural* **peels**) the skin of a fruit or vegetable

peel *verb* (**peels, peeling, peeled**) 1 to remove the peel from a vegetable or piece of fruit 2 to lose a covering or skin ▸ *The paint started to peel.*

peep *verb* (**peeps, peeping, peeped**) to look quickly or through a narrow opening

peep *noun* (*plural* **peeps**) a quick look

peer¹ *verb* (**peers, peering, peered**) to look hard or with difficulty at someone or something

peer² *noun* (*plural* **peers**) a nobleman or noblewoman

peg *noun* (*plural* **pegs**) 1 a pin or small rod that sticks out, for hanging things on 2 a clip for fixing things in place

peg *verb* (**pegs, pegging, pegged**) to fix something with pegs

Pekingese *noun* (*plural* **Pekingese**) a breed of small dog with short legs and long silky hair

pelican *noun* (*plural* **pelicans**) a large bird with a pouch in its long beak for storing fish

pellet *noun* (*plural* **pellets**) a small round lump of something

pelt *verb* (**pelts, pelting, pelted**) 1 to throw a lot of things at someone ▸ *We pelted him with snowballs.* 2 to run fast 3 to rain hard

pen *noun* (*plural* **pens**) 1 a device with a metal point for writing with ink 2 an enclosure for cattle or other animals

penalize *verb* (**penalizes, penalizing, penalized**) 1 to punish someone 2 to award a penalty against a side in a game

penalty *noun* (*plural* **penalties**) 1 a punishment 2 an advantage given to one side in a game when the other side breaks a rule

pence *plural noun* pennies

pencil *noun* (*plural* **pencils**) a device for drawing or writing, made of a length of lead (called graphite) or coloured chalk with a wood or metal casing

pendant *noun* (*plural* **pendants**) an ornament hung round the neck on a long chain or string

pendulum *noun* (*plural* **pendulums**) a swinging rod with a weight at the end, used in some clocks

penetrate *verb* (**penetrates, penetrating, penetrated**) to find a way into something or through it **penetration** *noun*

penfriend *noun* (*plural* **penfriends**) someone in another country you write to, usually without meeting them

penguin *noun* (*plural* **penguins**) an Antarctic seabird with short flippers, which cannot fly

penicillin *noun* a drug that kills bacteria, used to cure infections

peninsula *noun* (*plural* **peninsulas**) a piece of land that is almost surrounded by water

penis *noun* (*plural* **penises**) the part of the body with which a male person or animal urinates and has sexual intercourse

penknife *noun* (*plural* **penknives**) a small folding knife

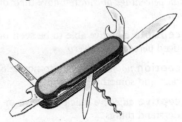

penniless *adjective* having no money; very poor

penny *noun* (*plural* **pennies** or **pence**) a British coin. There are a hundred pennies in one pound.

pension *noun* (*plural* **pensions**) a regular payment made to someone who has retired **pensioner** *noun* someone who is receiving a pension

pensive *adjective* thinking hard and quietly about something

pentagon *noun* (*plural* **pentagons**) a flat shape with five sides

pentathlon noun (plural **pentathlons**) an athletic competition that has five events

people plural noun human beings

people noun (plural **peoples**) the people of a particular country ▸ *The country was inhabited by a peaceful people.*

pepper noun (plural **peppers**) 1 a hot-tasting powder used to flavour food 2 a bright green, red, orange, or yellow vegetable **peppery** adjective

peppermint noun (plural **peppermints**) 1 a kind of mint used for flavouring 2 a sweet flavoured with peppermint

per preposition for each ▸ *The charge is £2 per person.*

perceive verb (**perceives, perceiving, perceived**) (not an everyday word) to see or notice something

per cent adverb for every hundred ▸ *The interest on the loan is 5 per cent (5%).* ▸ *Fifty per cent of the pupils walk to school.*

percentage noun (plural **percentages**) an amount or rate in each 100 ▸ *Out of £300 he spent £60, a percentage of 20.* ▸ *Only a small percentage of children have their own computer.*

perceptible adjective able to be seen or noticed **perceptibly** adverb

perception noun the ability to notice or understand something

perceptive adjective quick to notice or understand things

perch[1] noun (plural **perches**) a place where a bird sits or rests

perch verb (**perches, perching, perched**) to sit or stand on a small surface

perch[2] noun (plural **perch**) a freshwater fish used for food

percussion instrument noun (plural **percussion instruments**) a musical instrument that you play by striking or shaking it, such as a drum, cymbal, or tambourine

perennial adjective lasting for many years ▸ *a perennial plant*

perfect adjective (pronounced **per-fikt**) 1 so good that it cannot be made any better 2 complete ▸ *The man was a perfect stranger.* **perfection** noun

perfect verb (**perfects, perfecting, perfected**) (pronounced **per-fekt**) to make something perfect

perforate verb (**perforates, perforating, perforated**) to make small holes in something

perform verb (**performs, performing, performed**) 1 to carry something out or complete it ▸ *The surgeon performed the operation on Tuesday.* 2 to present something in front of an audience ▸ *They performed a play in the school hall.* **performance** noun **performer** noun

perfume noun (plural **perfumes**) 1 a sweet or pleasant smell 2 a sweet-smelling liquid that you put on your skin

perhaps adverb it may be; possibly

peril noun (plural **perils**) danger ▸ *We were in great peril.* **perilous** adjective dangerous **perilously** adverb

perimeter noun (plural **perimeters**) (pronounced **per-im-it-er**) the outside edge of something

period noun (plural **periods**) 1 a length of time 2 the time every month when a woman or girl bleeds from her womb

periodical noun (plural **periodicals**) a magazine that is published regularly

periscope noun (plural **periscopes**) a device with a tube and mirrors that lets you see things at a higher level. Periscopes are used in submarines.

perish verb (**perishes, perishing, perished**) 1 to die or be destroyed 2 to rot ▸ *The tyres on the old bike had perished.* 3 (informal) to feel extremely cold ▸ *We felt perished in the wind.* **perishable** adjective likely to go bad quickly

perm noun (plural **perms**) a special treatment of hair with chemicals to make it curly or wavy
Perm is short for 'permanent wave'.

permanent adjective lasting for ever or for a long time **permanently** adverb

permissible *adjective* allowable; permitted

permission *noun* being allowed to do something ▸ *We need permission to take photographs in the museum.*

permissive *adjective* letting people do what they want

permit *verb* (**permits, permitting, permitted**) (*pronounced* per-**mit**) to allow someone to do something

permit *noun* (*plural* **permits**) (*pronounced* **per**-mit) a written or printed statement allowing someone to do something

perpendicular *adjective* standing upright or at a right angle to a surface

perpetual *adjective* lasting for a long time; permanent **perpetually** *adverb*

perplex *verb* (**perplexes, perplexing, perplexed**) to puzzle someone very much

persecute *verb* (**persecutes, persecuting, persecuted**) to be continually cruel to someone, especially because you disagree with their beliefs **persecution** *noun* **persecutor** *noun*

persevere *verb* (**perseveres, persevering, persevered**) to keep trying in spite of difficulties **perseverance** *noun*

persist *verb* (**persists, persisting, persisted**) to keep on doing something in spite of objections or difficulties ▸ *They persist in arriving late.* **persistent** *adjective* keeping on doing something

person *noun* (*plural* **people** or **persons**) a man, woman, or child

personal *adjective* **1** belonging to a particular person ▸ *The house is her personal property.* **2** done by a particular person ▸ *The President made a personal appeal to the nation.* **3** private ▸ *We have personal business to discuss.* **personally** *adverb*

personal computer *noun* (*plural* **personal computers**) a small computer designed to be used by one person

personality *noun* (*plural* **personalities**) **1** a person's nature and character ▸ *She has a cheerful personality.* **2** a well-known person ▸ *a TV personality*

personnel *noun* (*pronounced* per-so-**nel**) the people employed by a business or in a particular place

perspective *noun* (*plural* **perspectives**) the impression of space and distance in a picture or scene **in perspective** giving a balanced view of things

perspire *verb* (**perspires, perspiring, perspired**) (not an everyday word) to sweat **perspiration** *noun* sweat

persuade *verb* (**persuades, persuading, persuaded**) to make someone agree about something or do something, by giving them reasons **persuasion** *noun* persuading someone **persuasive** *adjective* able to persuade people

perverse *adjective* obstinate or unreasonable **perversity** *noun* being unreasonable

pervert *verb* (**perverts, perverting, perverted**) to make someone behave wickedly or abnormally

pessimist *noun* (*plural* **pessimists**) someone who usually expects things to turn out badly **pessimism** *noun*

pessimistic *adjective* expecting things to turn out badly **pessimistically** *adverb*

pest *noun* (*plural* **pests**) **1** an insect or animal that destroys things, such as a locust or a mouse **2** an annoying person

pester *verb* (**pesters, pestering, pestered**) to keep annoying or bothering someone

pet *noun* (*plural* **pets**) **1** a tame animal that you keep at home **2** a person treated as a favourite

petal *noun* (*plural* **petals**) each of the separate coloured outer parts of a flower

petition *noun* (*plural* **petitions**) a written request for someone in authority to do something, usually signed by a large number of people

petrify *verb* (**petrifies, petrifying, petrified**) to make someone so frightened that they cannot act or move
This word used to mean 'to turn something into stone', and it comes from a Greek word meaning 'stone'.

petrol *noun* a liquid fuel made from oil and used in vehicle engines

petticoat *noun* (*plural* **petticoats**) a piece of women's clothing worn under a skirt or dress

petty *adjective* (**pettier, pettiest**) **1** minor and unimportant ▶ *They were fed up with all the petty rules.* **2** mean and selfish about small things **pettiness** *noun*

pew *noun* (*plural* **pews**) a long wooden bench in a church

pewter *noun* a grey alloy of tin and lead

pH *noun* a measure of how much acid or alkali a solution contains. Acids have a pH between 0 and 7, and alkalis have a pH between 7 and 14.

phantom *noun* (*plural* **phantoms**) a ghost

pharaoh *noun* (*plural* **pharaohs**) (*pronounced* **fair-**oh) a king of ancient Egypt

pharmacy *noun* (*plural* **pharmacies**) a shop that sells medicines

phase *noun* (*plural* **phases**) a stage in the progress or development of something

pheasant *noun* (*plural* **pheasants**) (*pronounced* **fez-**ant) a bird with a long tail. Some people like to shoot pheasants for sport.

phenomenal *adjective* amazing or remarkable **phenomenally** *adverb*

phenomenon *noun* (*plural* **phenomena**) a remarkable fact or event

philosophical *adjective* **1** to do with philosophy **2** calmly accepting suffering or difficulty ▶ *He tried to be philosophical about his illness.* **philosophically** *adverb*

philosophy *noun* (*plural* **philosophies**) (*pronounced* fil-**os**-o-fi) **1** the study of what life and human behaviour is all about

2 a particular way of thinking or a system of beliefs **philosopher** *noun* someone who studies philosophy

phobia *noun* (*plural* **phobias**) an unusual fear of something

phone *noun* (*plural* **phones**) a telephone
phone *verb* (**phones, phoning, phoned**) to telephone someone

phoney *adjective* (informal) false; not genuine ▶ *He spoke with a phoney Australian accent.*

phosphorescent *adjective* shining or glowing in the dark **phosphorescence** *noun*

phosphorus *noun* a yellowish substance that glows in the dark **phosphoric** *adjective* like phosphorus

photo *noun* (*plural* **photos**) (informal) a photograph

photocopier *noun* (*plural* **photocopiers**) a machine that makes copies of documents **photocopy** *verb* to make a copy with a photocopier

photograph *noun* (*plural* **photographs**) a picture made on film with a camera and then printed on special paper
photograph *verb* (**photographs, photographing, photographed**) to take a photograph of someone or something

photography *noun* taking photographs with a camera **photographer** *noun* someone who takes photographs **photographic** *adjective* to do with photography

phrase *noun* (*plural* **phrases**) **1** a group of words that do not make a complete sentence **2** a short section of a tune

physical *adjective* **1** to do with the body ▶ *physical fitness* **2** to do with things you can touch or see ▶ *physical science* **physically** *adverb* in a physical way

physician *noun* (*plural* **physicians**) a doctor

physics *noun* the study of physical matter and energy, including movement, heat, light, and sound **physicist** *noun* someone who studies physics

pianist *noun* (*plural* **pianists**) someone who plays the piano

piano *noun* (*plural* **pianos**) a large keyboard instrument with strings that are struck with hammers

piccolo *noun* (*plural* **piccolos**) a small high-pitched flute

pick[1] *verb* (**picks, picking, picked**) **1** to choose something or someone ▸ *Go and pick another book to read.* **2** to cut or pull off flowers or fruit **3** to steal from someone's pocket **4** to open a lock without using a key **5** to pull pieces off or out of something **pick on** to keep criticizing or bothering someone **pick up 1** to take something from the ground or a surface **2** to collect someone or something in a vehicle

pick *noun* **1** a choice ▸ *Take your pick.* **2** the best part of something ▸ *The pick of the second-hand books had already been sold.*

pickaxe *noun* (*plural* **pickaxes**) a heavy tool with a long handle for breaking up hard ground

picket *noun* (*plural* **pickets**) a group of workers on strike who try to persuade other people not to go into the place where they work

pickle *noun* (*plural* **pickles**) a strong-tasting food made of vegetables preserved in vinegar

pickle *verb* (**pickles, pickling, pickled**) to preserve food in vinegar or salt water

pickpocket *noun* (*plural* **pickpockets**) a thief who steals from people's pockets or bags

picnic *noun* (*plural* **picnics**) a meal eaten in the open air

picnic *verb* (**picnics, picnicking, picnicked**) to have a picnic **picnicker** *noun*

pictorial *adjective* with or using pictures **pictorially** *adverb*

picture *noun* (*plural* **pictures**) a painting, drawing, or photograph **in the picture** having the information about something

picture *verb* (**pictures, picturing, pictured**) **1** to show something or someone in a picture **2** to imagine something or someone

picturesque *adjective* (*pronounced* pik-cher-**esk**) attractive or charming ▸ *a picturesque village*

pie *noun* (*plural* **pies**) a baked dish of meat or fruit covered with pastry

piece *noun* (*plural* **pieces**) **1** a part or bit of something ▸ *a piece of cheese* **2** a work of art or writing or music ▸ *a piece of piano music* **3** one of the objects used in a board game ▸ *a chess piece*

pier *noun* (*plural* **piers**) **1** a long structure built out into the sea for people to walk on **2** a pillar supporting a bridge or arch

pierce *verb* (**pierces, piercing, pierced**) to make a hole through something

piercing *adjective* very strong or loud ▸ *She gave a piercing shriek.* ▸ *There was a piercing wind.*

pig *noun* (*plural* **pigs**) **1** a farm animal with short legs and a blunt snout, kept for its meat **2** (informal) someone who is greedy, dirty, or unpleasant

pigeon *noun* (*plural* **pigeons**) (*pronounced* **pij-en**) a fairly large grey bird with a small head and large chest

piggy bank *noun* (*plural* **piggy banks**) a money box in the shape of a pig

piglet *noun* (*plural* **piglets**) a young pig

pigment *noun* (*plural* **pigments**) a substance that colours something

pigsty *noun* (*plural* **pigsties**) a building for keeping pigs

pigtail *noun* (*plural* **pigtails**) a plait of hair

pike[1] *noun* (*plural* **pike**) a large fish that lives in rivers and lakes

pike[2] *noun* (*plural* **pikes**) a heavy spear

pilchard *noun* (*plural* **pilchards**) a small sea fish

pile *noun* (*plural* **piles**) a number of things on top of one another

pile *verb* (**piles, piling, piled**) to put things into a pile

pilfer *verb* (**pilfers, pilfering, pilfered**) to steal small or unimportant things

pilgrim *noun* (*plural* **pilgrims**) someone who goes on a journey to a holy place

pilgrimage *noun* (*plural* **pilgrimages**) a journey made by pilgrims

pill *noun* (*plural* **pills**) a small piece of medicine for swallowing **the pill** a special kind of pill taken regularly by a woman so that she doesn't get pregnant

pillar *noun* (*plural* **pillars**) a tall stone post supporting part of a building

pillar box *noun* (*plural* **pillar boxes**) a postbox standing in a street

pillion *noun* (*plural* **pillions**) a seat for a passenger behind the driver's seat on a motorcycle
The word **pillion** comes from a Scottish Gaelic word meaning 'cushion'.

pillow *noun* (*plural* **pillows**) a cushion on a bed, for resting your head on

pillowcase *noun* (*plural* **pillowcases**) a cloth cover for a pillow

pilot *noun* (*plural* **pilots**) 1 someone who flies an aircraft 2 someone who helps to steer a ship in and out of a port
pilot *verb* (**pilots, piloting, piloted**) to be the pilot of an aircraft or ship

pilot light *noun* (*plural* **pilot lights**) a small flame in a boiler or cooker, which lights the main flames

pimple *noun* (*plural* **pimples**) a small round swelling on the skin **pimply** *adjective*

pin *noun* (*plural* **pins**) a short piece of metal with a sharp point and a rounded head, used to fasten things **pins and needles** a tingling feeling in your skin
pin *verb* (**pins, pinning, pinned**) to fasten something with a pin

pinafore *noun* (*plural* **pinafores**) a large apron

pincer *noun* (*plural* **pincers**) the claw of a shellfish such as a lobster

pincers *plural noun* a tool for gripping and pulling things

pinch *verb* (**pinches, pinching, pinched**) 1 to squeeze something tightly between your finger and thumb 2 (informal) to steal something
pinch *noun* (*plural* **pinches**) 1 a firm squeezing movement 2 a small amount of something ▸ *a pinch of salt*

pine *noun* (*plural* **pines**) an evergreen tree with leaves shaped like needles
pine *verb* (**pines, pining, pined**) to feel a sad longing for someone or something

pineapple *noun* (*plural* **pineapples**) a large tropical fruit with yellow flesh and a prickly skin

ping-pong *noun* table tennis

pink *adjective* (**pinker, pinkest**) pale red
pink *noun* (*plural* **pinks**) 1 a sweet-smelling garden flower 2 a pale red colour

pinnacle *noun* (*plural* **pinnacles**) the very top of something tall

pint *noun* (*plural* **pints**) a measure of liquid, an eighth of a gallon or about 568 millilitres

pioneer *noun* (*plural* **pioneers**) one of the first people to go to a place or do something new

pious *adjective* very religious or devout

pip *noun* (*plural* **pips**) the small hard seed of a fruit

pipe *noun* (*plural* **pipes**) 1 a tube for carrying liquid or gas 2 a short tube with a small bowl at one end, used to smoke tobacco 3 a musical instrument in the shape of a small tube
pipe *verb* (**pipes, piping, piped**) 1 to send liquid or gas along pipes 2 to play music on a pipe or the bagpipes

pipeline *noun* (*plural* **pipelines**) a pipe for carrying oil, water, or gas over a long distance

piper *noun* (*plural* **pipers**) someone who plays a pipe or the bagpipes

piping *adjective* **piping hot** (describing food) very hot and ready to eat

pirate *noun* (*plural* **pirates**) a sailor who attacks and robs other ships **piracy** *noun* robbing ships

pistol noun (plural **pistols**) a small gun held in one hand

piston noun (plural **pistons**) the part of an engine that moves up and down inside a cylinder

pit noun (plural **pits**) 1 a deep hole in the ground 2 a coal mine 3 the part of a race circuit where cars are refuelled and serviced during a race

pitch noun (plural **pitches**) 1 a piece of ground marked out for a game 2 how high or low a voice or musical note is 3 strength or intensity ▸ *The excitement reached a high pitch.* 4 a black sticky substance like tar

pitch verb (**pitches, pitching, pitched**) 1 to throw something 2 to put up a tent 3 to fall heavily ▸ *He tripped over the doorstep and pitched forward.* 4 (used about a ship) to move up and down in a rough sea

pitcher noun (plural **pitchers**) a large jug with two handles

pitchfork noun (plural **pitchforks**) a large fork with two prongs for lifting hay

pitfall noun (plural **pitfalls**) an unexpected danger or difficulty

pitiful adjective 1 making you feel pity ▸ *a pitiful sight* 2 feeble ▸ *a pitiful attempt* **pitifully** adverb

pitiless adjective showing no pity

pity noun 1 a feeling of sorrow for someone who is suffering or in difficulty 2 something that you regret ▸ *It's a pity they can't come.* **take pity on** to help someone in trouble

pity verb (**pities, pitying, pitied**) to feel pity for someone

pivot noun (plural **pivots**) a point on which something turns or balances

pixie or **pixy** noun (plural **pixies**) a small fairy or elf

pizza noun (plural **pizzas**) (*pronounced* **peet-sa**) a layer of dough that is covered with toppings such as cheese, vegetables, and herbs and baked

placard noun (plural **placards**) (*pronounced* **plak-ahd**) a large poster or notice

place noun (plural **places**) 1 a particular position or area 2 a seat ▸ *Are there any places left?* **in place of** instead of **take place** to happen

place verb (**places, placing, placed**) to put something in a particular place

placid adjective (*pronounced* **plass**-id) calm and peaceful **placidly** adverb

plague noun (plural **plagues**) 1 a dangerous illness that spreads very quickly 2 a large number of something harmful ▸ *a plague of locusts*

plague verb (**plagues, plaguing, plagued**) to pester or annoy someone

plaice noun (plural **plaice**) a flat sea fish used for food

plain adjective (**plainer, plainest**) 1 simple; not decorated ▸ *The room had plain wallpaper.* 2 not pretty ▸ *I wished I wasn't so plain.* 3 easy to understand or see ▸ *It was plain that they wanted to come.* 4 frank; straightforward ▸ *This is the plain truth.* **plainly** adverb **plainness** noun

plain noun (plural **plains**) a large flat area of country

plain clothes plural noun ordinary clothes worn instead of a uniform

plaintive adjective sounding sad ▸ *a plaintive cry*

plait noun (plural **plaits**) (*pronounced* plat) a length of hair or rope made by twisting several strands together

plait verb (**plaits, plaiting, plaited**) to make hair or rope into a plait

plan noun (plural **plans**) 1 a way of doing something that you think out in advance 2 a drawing showing the parts of something 3 a map of a town or district

plan verb (**plans, planning, planned**) to make a plan to do something

plane noun (plural **planes**) 1 an aeroplane 2 a tool for making wood smooth 3 a flat or level surface 4 a tall tree with broad leaves

plane verb (**planes, planing, planed**) to smooth wood with a plane

planet noun (plural **planets**) one of the bodies in space that move in an orbit round the sun

The main planets of the solar system are Mercury, Venus, Earth, Mars, Jupiter, Saturn, Uranus, Neptune, and Pluto.

plank *noun* (*plural* **planks**) a long flat piece of wood

plankton *noun* tiny creatures that float in the sea and lakes

plant *noun* (*plural* **plants**) 1 a living thing that grows out of the ground, including flowers, bushes, trees, and vegetables 2 the buildings and equipment of a factory

plant *verb* (**plants, planting, planted**) 1 to put a plant or tree in the ground to grow 2 to put something down firmly ▶ *He planted his feet on the ground.* 3 to put something where you want it to be ▶ *A bomb was planted on the train.*

plantation *noun* (*plural* **plantations**) an area of land where a crop such as tobacco, tea, or rubber is planted

plaque *noun* (*plural* **plaques**) (*pronounced* plahk) 1 a flat piece of metal or porcelain fixed on a wall as a memorial or an ornament 2 a substance that forms a thin layer on teeth, allowing bacteria to develop

plaster *noun* (*plural* **plasters**) 1 a dressing put over a wound to protect it 2 a mixture of lime, sand, and water, used to cover walls and ceilings

plaster *verb* (**plasters, plastering, plastered**) 1 to cover a wall or ceiling with plaster 2 to cover a surface with something thick or sticky **plasterer** *noun* someone who puts plaster on walls and ceilings

plastic *noun* (*plural* **plastics**) a strong light substance that is made from chemicals and can be moulded into different shapes

plastic *adjective* made of plastic
▶ *a plastic bag*

plasticine *noun* a soft and easily shaped substance used for making models

plastic surgery *noun* an operation done by a surgeon to change the look of someone's body

plate *noun* (*plural* **plates**) 1 a flat or nearly flat dish used for eating 2 a thin flat sheet of a hard material 3 a special illustration on a separate page in a book

plate *verb* (**plates, plating, plated**) to cover metal with a thin layer of gold, silver, or other soft metal

plateau *noun* (*plural* **plateaux**) (*pronounced* **plat**-oh) a flat area of high land
Plateau is a French word, and this is why the plural ends in x and not s.

platform *noun* (*plural* **platforms**) 1 a flat raised area along the side of the line at a railway station 2 a raised area for speakers or performers in a hall

platinum *noun* a valuable silver-coloured metal

platoon *noun* (*plural* **platoons**) a small unit of soldiers

platypus *noun* (*plural* **platypuses**) an Australian furry animal with a beak and webbed feet. The female lays eggs but feeds its young with milk.

plausible *adjective* seeming to be true or convincing

play *verb* (**plays, playing, played**) 1 to take part in a game 2 to do something for fun 3 to make music with an instrument 4 to perform a part in a film or play **play up** to behave badly **player** *noun*

play *noun* (*plural* **plays**) 1 a story presented by actors 2 a spell of playing or having fun

playful *adjective* 1 wanting to play; full of fun 2 not serious **playfully** *adverb*

playground *noun* (*plural* **playgrounds**) an outdoor area where children can play

playgroup *noun* (*plural* **playgroups**) a place where young children can play together and are looked after by parents and other helpers

playing card *noun* (*plural* **playing cards**) one of a set of cards used in card games

playing field *noun* (*plural* **playing fields**) a field for playing games

playwright *noun* (*plural* **playwrights**) someone who writes plays

plc short for *public limited company*, which means that people can buy shares in the company

plea *noun* (*plural* **pleas**) 1 a request or appeal 2 an accused person's answer of 'guilty' or 'not guilty' when they are charged with a crime in a lawcourt

plead *verb* (**pleads, pleading, pleaded**) to beg someone to do something **plead guilty** or **not guilty** to say in a lawcourt that you are guilty or not guilty of a crime

pleasant *adjective* (**pleasanter, pleasantest**) (*pronounced* **plez**-ant) pleasing; nice **pleasantly** *adverb*

please *verb* (**pleases, pleasing, pleased**) 1 to make someone happy or satisfied 2 a word you use when you want to ask something politely ▸ *Please shut the door.*

pleasure *noun* (*plural* **pleasures**) (*pronounced* **plezh**-er) 1 a feeling of being pleased 2 something that pleases you

pleat *noun* (*plural* **pleats**) a fold made in cloth by pressing or sewing it

pledge *noun* (*plural* **pledges**) a solemn promise

pledge *verb* (**pledges, pledging, pledged**) to promise something

plentiful *adjective* large in amount **plentifully** *adverb*

plenty *noun* a large amount or number of something ▸ *We have plenty of chairs.*

pliable *adjective* easy to bend; flexible

pliers *plural noun* a tool with strong jaws for gripping things

plight *noun* a difficult or dangerous situation ▸ *They were stranded for several days before anyone knew of their plight.*

plod *verb* (**plods, plodding, plodded**) to walk slowly and heavily

plop *noun* (*plural* **plops**) the sound of something dropping into water

plot *noun* (*plural* **plots**) 1 a secret plan to do something illegal or bad 2 the main story of a book, film, or play 3 a small piece of land

plot *verb* (**plots, plotting, plotted**) 1 to make a secret plan 2 to draw a chart or graph **plotter** *noun* someone who plots something bad

plough *noun* (*plural* **ploughs**) (*pronounced* plow) a large farm tool pulled by a tractor or animal, used for turning over the soil **ploughman** *noun*

plough *verb* (**ploughs, ploughing, ploughed**) to turn soil over with a plough

pluck *verb* (**plucks, plucking, plucked**) 1 to pick a flower or fruit 2 to pull something hard ▸ *She plucked out a splinter from my finger.* 3 to pull out the feathers of a bird you are going to cook 4 to pull a string of a musical instrument and let it go **pluck up courage** to be brave

pluck *noun* courage or bravery **plucky** *adjective* brave

plug *noun* (*plural* **plugs**) 1 something that fits in a hole, especially a stopper in a bath or basin 2 a device for connecting electrical equipment to an electric socket

plug *verb* (**plugs, plugging, plugged**) 1 to put a plug in a hole 2 (*informal*) to publicize something ▸ *He's only on the show to plug his new film.* **plug in** to connect something to an electric socket with a plug

plum *noun* (*plural* **plums**) a soft juicy red or purple fruit with a stone in the middle

plumage *noun* (*pronounced* **ploo**-mij) a bird's feathers

plumber *noun* (*plural* **plumbers**) (*pronounced* **plumm**-er) someone who fits and mends water pipes, tanks, and heating

plumbing *noun* the set of water pipes and tanks in a building

plume *noun* (*plural* **plumes**) a large feather

plump *adjective* (**plumper, plumpest**) rounded or slightly fat **plumpness** *noun*

plunder *verb* (**plunders, plundering, plundered**) to rob a place, especially during a war **plunderer** *noun*

plunder *noun* things taken by plundering

plunge *verb* (**plunges, plunging, plunged**)
1 to jump or dive into water with force 2 to push something firmly into a liquid or something soft

plunge *noun* (*plural* **plunges**) a sudden fall or dive

plural *noun* (*plural* **plurals**) the form of a word when it means more than one thing or person, such as *houses* and *children*

plus *preposition* added to ► *2 plus 2 equals 4 (2 + 2 = 4).*

p.m. short for Latin *post meridiem*, which means 'after midday'. You use it to show the time in the afternoon. ► *The programme starts at 6.30 p.m.*

pneumatic *adjective* (*pronounced* new-mat-ik) 1 worked by compressed air ► *a pneumatic drill* 2 filled with air ► *a pneumatic tyre*

pneumonia *noun* (*pronounced* new-moh-ni-a) a serious disease of the lungs

poach *verb* (**poaches, poaching, poached**)
1 to cook food, such as eggs or fish, in boiling water 2 to catch animals illegally on someone else's land **poacher** *noun* someone who poaches animals

pocket *noun* (*plural* **pockets**) a small bag sewn into a piece of clothing, for keeping things in
pocket *verb* (**pockets, pocketing, pocketed**) to put something in your pocket

pocket money *noun* an amount of money given regularly to a child

pod *noun* (*plural* **pods**) a long seed-container on a pea or bean plant

podgy *adjective* (**podgier, podgiest**) short and fat

poem *noun* (*plural* **poems**) a piece of writing with a special rhythm and usually written in short lines

poet *noun* (*plural* **poets**) someone who writes poems

poetry *noun* poems, or writing poems

point *noun* (*plural* **points**) 1 the narrow or sharp end of a knife or tool 2 a dot or mark ► *a decimal point* 3 a particular place or time ► *They gave up at this point.* ► *We*

meet at this point on the map. 4 a unit for scoring in games ► *A correct answer wins three points.* 5 reason or purpose ► *The point of the game is to finish with no cards.*
point *verb* (**points, pointing, pointed**) 1 to show where something is, usually by holding out your finger towards it 2 to aim or direct something ► *She pointed a gun at us.* **points** a movable part of a railway line that allows trains to change from one track to another **point out** to show or explain something

point-blank *adjective* and *adverb* 1 close to the target 2 directly and completely ► *He refused point-blank.*

pointed *adjective* having a point at the end

pointer *noun* (*plural* **pointers**) a stick or device used to point at something

pointless *adjective* having no purpose or meaning **pointlessly** *adverb* **pointlessness** *noun*

poise *noun* 1 a dignified and self-confident manner 2 a state of balance

poised *adjective* ready to do something ► *They were poised to attack.*

poison *noun* (*plural* **poisons**) a substance that can kill or harm living things if they eat or absorb it **poisonous** *adjective*
poison *verb* (**poisons, poisoning, poisoned**) 1 to kill or harm a living thing with poison 2 to put poison in something ► *She wondered if someone had poisoned the blancmange.*

poke *verb* (**pokes, poking, poked**) to push or jab something with a finger or pointed object

poker *noun* (*plural* **pokers**) 1 a metal rod for poking a fire 2 a card game where you bet on who has the best cards

polar *adjective* to do with the North or South Pole, or near one of them

polar bear *noun* (*plural* **polar bears**) a powerful white bear living near the North Pole

pole noun (*plural* **poles**) 1 a long thin piece of wood or metal 2 each of the two points on the earth that are furthest from the equator, the **North Pole** and the **South Pole** 3 each end of a magnet

pole vault noun an athletic sport in which you jump over a high bar using a long springy pole

police noun the people whose job is to catch criminals and make sure the law is obeyed **policeman** noun **policewoman** noun

police officer noun (*plural* **police officers**) a member of the police

policy noun (*plural* **policies**) a set of plans or aims

polish verb (**polishes, polishing, polished**) to make the surface of something shiny or smooth

polish noun (*plural* **polishes**) 1 something you use for polishing 2 a shine you get by polishing

polite adjective (**politer, politest**) having good manners **politely** adverb **politeness** noun being polite

political adjective to do with the governing of a country **politically** adverb

politician noun (*plural* **politicians**) someone who is involved in politics

politics noun the business of governing a country

poll noun (*plural* **polls**) 1 a political election 2 a survey of what people think about something
The word **poll** once meant 'head'. It came to mean 'voting' because votes were sometimes counted by counting people's heads.

pollen noun a powder found inside flowers. Pollen contains seeds that fertilize other flowers.

pollinate verb (**pollinates, pollinating, pollinated**) to fertilize a flower with pollen

pollute verb (**pollutes, polluting, polluted**) to make a place or thing dirty or impure **pollution** noun

polo noun a game like hockey, with players on horseback using long mallets

poltergeist noun (*plural* **poltergeists**) (*pronounced* **pol-ter-gyst**) a ghost that is thought to move things or throw them about

polygon noun (*plural* **polygons**) a figure or shape with many sides

polythene noun a light kind of plastic used to make bags and wrappings

pomp noun the dignified and solemn way in which an important ceremony is conducted

pompous adjective speaking or behaving grandly, thinking too much of your own importance **pomposity** noun being pompous **pompously** adverb

pond noun (*plural* **ponds**) a small lake

ponder verb (**ponders, pondering, pondered**) to think seriously about something

pony noun (*plural* **ponies**) a small horse

ponytail noun (*plural* **ponytails**) a bunch of long hair tied at the back of the head

poodle noun (*plural* **poodles**) a dog with curly hair

pool noun (*plural* **pools**) 1 a small area of water or another liquid 2 a swimming pool 3 an amount of money 4 a group of things shared by several people ▶ *The firm has a pool of cars that people can use.* **the pools** a gambling game based on the results of football matches

poor adjective (**poorer, poorest**) 1 having very little money ▶ *a poor family* 2 not good or adequate ▶ *poor work* 3 unfortunate ▶ *Poor Jill's got flu.*

poorly adjective unwell ▶ *I'm feeling poorly today.*
poorly adverb badly ▶ *My Mum did poorly in her driving test.*

pop noun (*plural* **pops**) 1 a small sharp bang 2 a fizzy drink 3 modern popular music
pop verb (**pops, popping, popped**) 1 to make a small sharp bang 2 (informal) to move somewhere or put something somewhere quickly ▶ *I'd better pop the milk in the fridge.*

popcorn *noun* a snack made from grains of maize that have been heated until they burst

Pope *noun* (*plural* **Popes**) the head of the Roman Catholic Church

poplar *noun* (*plural* **poplars**) a tall straight tree

poppy *noun* (*plural* **poppies**) a plant with large red flowers

popular *adjective* liked by a lot of people
popularity *noun* how popular something or someone is

populated *adjective* having people living there ▶ *a heavily populated country*

population *noun* (*plural* **populations**) the people living in a place

porcelain *noun* (*pronounced* por-se-lin) a fine kind of china

porch *noun* (*plural* **porches**) a covered area in front of the door of a building

porcupine *noun* (*plural* **porcupines**) a small animal covered with long sharp spines

pore *noun* (*plural* **pores**) a tiny hole in the skin, through which moisture passes

pork *noun* meat from a pig

porous *adjective* allowing liquid or air to pass through

porpoise *noun* (*plural* **porpoises**) (*pronounced* por-pus) a sea animal like a dolphin or small whale

porridge *noun* a food made by boiling oatmeal in water or milk

port *noun* (*plural* **ports**) 1 a harbour, or a town with a harbour 2 the left-hand side of a ship or aircraft when you are facing forward 3 a rich sweet red wine

portable *adjective* light enough to carry around

portcullis *noun* (*plural* **portcullises**) a heavy grating that can be lowered over the entrance to a castle

porter *noun* (*plural* **porters**) someone whose job is to carry things around at a railway station or in a hotel or hospital

porthole *noun* (*plural* **portholes**) a small round window in the side of a ship

portion *noun* (*plural* **portions**) 1 a part or share given to someone 2 an amount of food for one person

portrait *noun* (*plural* **portraits**) a picture of a person

portray *verb* (**portrays, portraying, portrayed**) to describe someone or something ▶ *The article portrayed her as a selfish and uncaring woman.*

pose *verb* (**poses, posing, posed**) 1 to stand or sit in a special position 2 to pretend to be someone else ▶ *The man was posing as a police officer.* 3 to put a question or problem

posh *adjective* (**posher, poshest**) (informal) very smart or high-class ▶ *Gemma's friend lived in a posh house.*

position *noun* (*plural* **positions**) 1 the place where something is or should be 2 the way in which someone or something is placed or arranged ▶ *He was in a sitting position.* 3 a regular job

positive *adjective* 1 sure or definite ▶ *I am positive I saw them.* ▶ *Do you have positive proof?* 2 agreeing or saying 'yes' ▶ *a positive answer* **positive number** a number greater than nought **positively** *adverb*

posse *noun* (*plural* **posses**) (*pronounced* poss-i) a group of people who help a sheriff

possess *verb* (**possesses, possessing, possessed**) to own something

possessed *adjective* behaving as if you are controlled by an outside force

possession *noun* (*plural* **possessions**) something that you own

possessive *adjective* wanting to keep things for yourself **possessiveness** *noun*

possible *adjective* able to exist, happen, be done, or be used **possibility** *noun* something that can be done **possibly** *adverb*

post *noun* (*plural* **posts**) 1 an upright piece of wood, concrete, or metal standing in the ground 2 a system of sending letters and parcels from one place to another 3 the letters and parcels sent by post 4 a person's job 5 a place where a sentry stands
post *verb* (**posts, posting, posted**) to send a letter or parcel by post

postage *noun* what you pay for sending something by post

postal *adjective* to do with the post; by post

postbox *noun* (*plural* **postboxes**) a box for posting letters

postcard *noun* (*plural* **postcards**) a card that you write a message on and post without an envelope

postcode *noun* (*plural* **postcodes**) a group of letters and numbers at the end of an address. They make it easier for machines to sort letters and parcels.

poster *noun* (*plural* **posters**) a large picture or notice for putting on a wall

postman *noun* (*plural* **postmen**) someone who collects and delivers letters and parcels

postmark *noun* (*plural* **postmarks**) an mark stamped on a letter or parcel showing when and where it was posted

post office *noun* (*plural* **post offices**) a place where you can buy stamps and post letters and parcels

postpone *verb* (**postpones, postponing, postponed**) to arrange for something to take place later than originally planned
▶ *The meeting has been postponed for two weeks.* **postponement** *noun*

posture *noun* (*plural* **postures**) the way that you stand or sit

posy *noun* (*plural* **posies**) a small bunch of flowers

pot *noun* (*plural* **pots**) 1 a deep round container 2 a flowerpot

potassium *noun* a soft silvery-white metallic substance that living things need

potato *noun* (*plural* **potatoes**) a root vegetable that grows underground

potent *adjective* powerful **potency** *noun* power

potential *adjective* possible or capable of happening in the future ▶ *a potential disaster* **potentially** *adverb*

pothole *noun* (*plural* **potholes**) a large hole in a road, or a deep natural hole in the ground

potion *noun* (*plural* **potions**) a drink containing medicine or poison

potter *noun* (*plural* **potters**) someone who makes pottery

pottery *noun* pots, cups, plates, and other things made of baked clay

pouch *noun* (*plural* **pouches**) 1 a small bag or pocket 2 a fold of skin in which a kangaroo keeps its young

poultry *noun* chickens, geese, turkeys, and other birds kept for their eggs and meat

pounce *verb* (**pounces, pouncing, pounced**) to jump on someone or attack them suddenly

pound¹ noun (*plural* **pounds**) **1** a unit of money in Britain and some other countries. A British pound is equal to 100 pence. **2** a unit of weight equal to 16 ounces or about 454 grams

pound² verb (**pounds, pounding, pounded**) **1** to hit something again and again to crush it **2** to make a dull thumping sound, or to beat heavily ▸ *His heart was pounding with the excitement.*

pour verb (**pours, pouring, poured**) **1** to make a liquid flow out of a container **2** to flow in a large amount ▸ *After the storm water was pouring from the broken gutters.* **3** to rain heavily **4** to come or go in large numbers or amounts ▸ *People poured off the train.*

pout verb (**pouts, pouting, pouted**) to stick out your lips when you are annoyed or sulking

poverty noun being poor

powder noun (*plural* **powders**) something in the form of tiny pieces of dry stuff, like flour or dust **powdery** adjective

power noun (*plural* **powers**) **1** strength or great energy **2** the ability to do something ▸ *the power of speech* **3** the right to do something ▸ *the power of arrest* **4** a powerful country **5** electricity or another form of energy ▸ *nuclear power* **6** in mathematics, the result obtained by multiplying a number by itself one or more times ▸ *27 is the third power of 3* ($3 \times 3 \times 3 = 27$).

powerful adjective **1** strong ▸ *The lion was crunching a bone in its powerful jaws.* **2** having a lot of power or influence ▸ *He had friends who were now powerful people.* **powerfully** adverb

powerless adjective not having the power or strength to do something **powerlessness** noun

power station noun (*plural* **power stations**) a building where electricity is produced

practical adjective **1** good at doing or making things ▸ *Any reasonably practical person could make this in a weekend.* **2** sensible and likely to be useful ▸ *The*

boys tried to offer some practical help. **3** concerned with doing or making things ▸ *He has had practical experience.*

practical joke noun (*plural* **practical jokes**) a trick played on someone

practically adverb **1** almost ▸ *In her job she met famous people practically every day.* **2** in a practical way

practice noun (*plural* **practices**) **1** doing something regularly to become better at it ▸ *I must do my piano practice.* **2** actually doing something rather than thinking or talking about it ▸ *It was a good idea but it didn't work out in practice.* **3** the business of a doctor or lawyer

practise verb (**practises, practising, practised**) **1** to do something regularly to become better at it **2** to do something regularly **3** to work as a doctor, lawyer, or other professional person

prairie noun (*plural* **prairies**) a large grassy area of land in North America

praise verb (**praises, praising, praised**) to say that someone or something is good or has done well

praise noun (*plural* **praises**) words that praise someone or something

pram noun (*plural* **prams**) a small open carriage for a baby, pushed by a person walking

prance verb (**prances, prancing, pranced**) to jump about in a lively way

prank noun (*plural* **pranks**) a trick played on someone for fun

prawn noun (*plural* **prawns**) a shellfish like a large shrimp, used for food

pray verb (**prays, praying, prayed**) **1** to talk to God **2** to ask seriously for something

prayer noun (*plural* **prayers**) words that you say when you pray

preach verb (**preaches, preaching, preached**) to give a talk about religion or about right and wrong **preacher** noun

precarious adjective not very safe or secure **precariously** adverb

precaution *noun* (*plural* **precautions**) something you do to prevent possible trouble or danger ▸ *I took the precaution of bringing my umbrella.*

precede *verb* (**precedes, preceding, preceded**) to come or go in front of something or someone

precinct *noun* (*plural* **precincts**) 1 a part of a town where traffic is not allowed ▸ *a shopping precinct* 2 the area round a cathedral

precious *adjective* very valuable or loved

precipice *noun* (*plural* **precipices**) the steep face of a mountain or cliff

precise *adjective* 1 exact, correct ▸ *The measurements are precise.* 2 clearly stated ▸ *I gave them precise instructions.* **precisely** *adverb* **precision** *noun* being precise

predator *noun* (*plural* **predators**) an animal that hunts other animals **predatory** *adjective* hunting other animals

predecessor *noun* (*plural* **predecessors**) someone who did something before you did it

predict *verb* (**predicts, predicting, predicted**) to say that something will happen in the future **prediction** *noun*

predictable *adjective* likely or expected ▸ *His angry reaction was predictable.* ▸ *Gloria was very predictable and always chose the biggest.*

preen *verb* (used about birds) to clean their feathers with their beak

preface *noun* (*plural* **prefaces**) (*pronounced* **pref**-iss) an introduction at the beginning of a book

prefect *noun* (*plural* **prefects**) an older pupil in some schools who has special duties

prefer *verb* (**prefers, preferring, preferred**) to like one person or thing more than another **preference** *noun* the thing you prefer

preferable *adjective* (*pronounced* **pref**-er-a-bul) better or liked more than something else **preferably** *adverb*

prefix *noun* (*plural* **prefixes**) a group of letters joined to the beginning of a word to change its meaning, as in *re*play, *over*flow, and *un*happy

pregnant *adjective* having a baby growing inside the womb **pregnancy** *noun* a time of being pregnant

prehistoric *adjective* belonging to a time long ago, before people wrote things down **prehistory** *noun* prehistoric times

prejudice *noun* (*plural* **prejudices**) an unfair opinion you have about someone before you have thought about them **prejudiced** *adjective* having a prejudice

preliminary *adjective* coming before something or preparing for it

prelude *noun* (*plural* **preludes**) (*pronounced* **prel**-yood) an introduction to a play, poem, or event

premature *adjective* happening or coming too soon ▸ *a premature baby*

première *noun* (*plural* **premières**) (*pronounced* **prem**-yair) the first public performance of a play or film

premises *plural noun* a building and the land that belongs to it

premium *noun* (*plural* **premiums**) an amount you pay regularly for an insurance policy

preoccupied *adjective* thinking hard about something and not noticing other things **preoccupation** *noun*

prepare *verb* (**prepares, preparing, prepared**) to get something ready **be prepared** to be willing to do something ▸ *They are prepared to help us.* **preparation** *noun* preparing for something

preposition *noun* (*plural* **prepositions**) (*pronounced* **prep**-o-zish-on) a word put in front of a noun or pronoun to show how it is connected with other words, for example *on* in the sentence *Put the book on the shelf* and *to* in the sentence *Give the book to me.*

preposterous *adjective* absurd, ridiculous

prescribe *verb* (**prescribes, prescribing, prescribed**) to say which medicine a patient should take

prescription *noun* (*plural* **prescriptions**) a written order from a doctor for a chemist to prepare a medicine for a patient

presence *noun* being at a place ▸ *Your presence is requested at the wedding.*

present *adjective* (*pronounced* **prez**-ent) 1 in a place; here ▸ *At least one adult has to be present.* 2 existing or happening now ▸ *It is difficult to be sure in the present circumstances.*

present *noun* (*plural* **presents**) (*pronounced* **prez**-ent) 1 something you give someone or receive from them 2 the time now ▸ *Let's leave it for the present.* 3 the form of a verb that describes something happening now, for example *sits* in the sentence *The old man sits in his chair.*

present *verb* (**presents, presenting, presented**) (*pronounced* pri-**zent**) 1 to give something to someone in public ▸ *A famous guest will present the prizes.* 2 to perform a play or other entertainment 3 to introduce a radio or television programme 4 to show people something you have done or made **presenter** *noun*

presentation *noun* (*plural* **presentations**) a talk showing or explaining something

presently *adverb* soon; in a while ▸ *They will be here presently.*

present participle *noun* (*plural* **present participles**) a form of a verb that ends in -*ing* and describes something that is or was happening, for example *watching* in the sentences *I am watching television* and *They were watching television.*

preserve *verb* (**preserves, preserving, preserved**) to keep something safe or in good condition **preservation** *noun* preserving something

president *noun* (*plural* **presidents**) 1 the head of a country that is a republic 2 the person in charge of a society, business, or club **presidency** *noun* **presidential** *adjective*

press *verb* (**presses, pressing, pressed**) 1 to push something firmly 2 to make clothes or soft material flat and smooth 3 to urge someone to do or give something ▸ *We must press them for more money.*

press *noun* (*plural* **presses**) a printing machine **the press** newspapers and journalists

pressing *adjective* urgent

pressure *noun* (*plural* **pressures**) 1 the force with which one thing pushes against another or squeezes it 2 a strong feeling that you have to do something, because someone is persuading you ▸ *They put pressure on us to agree.*

prestige *noun* (*pronounced* pres-**teezh**) respect or importance that someone or something has because they are good or successful

presume *verb* (**presumes, presuming, presumed**) 1 to suppose that something is true ▸ *I presume they are coming.* 2 to dare to do something ▸ *We would not presume to contradict you.*

presumptuous *adjective* too bold or confident

pretend *verb* (**pretends, pretending, pretended**) 1 to behave as if something untrue or imaginary is true ▸ *Let's pretend we're on holiday.* 2 to claim to be something you are not ▸ *They pretended to be policemen.* **pretence** *noun*

pretty *adjective* (**prettier, prettiest**) pleasant to look at or hear; attractive **prettily** *adverb* **prettiness** *noun*

pretty *adverb* (*informal*) quite; moderately ▸ *It's pretty cold outside.*

prevent *verb* (**prevents, preventing, prevented**) 1 to stop something from happening or make it impossible 2 to stop someone from doing something **prevention** *noun* preventing something

preview *noun* (*plural* **previews**) a showing of a film or play before it is shown to most people

previous *adjective* coming before this ▸ *I had seen them the previous week.* **previously** *adverb* before; earlier

prey *noun* (*pronounced* pray) an animal that is hunted by another animal for food

prey *verb* (**preys, preying, preyed**) (*pronounced* pray) **prey on** (used about an animal) to hunt and kill other animals for food

price *noun* (*plural* **prices**) the amount of money you have to pay for something

priceless *adjective* very valuable

prick *verb* (**pricks, pricking, pricked**) 1 to make a tiny hole in something using a sharp point 2 to hurt someone with something sharp or pointed **prick up your ears** to start listening closely

prickle *noun* (*plural* **prickles**) a sharp point on a plant or animal **prickly** *adjective*

pride *noun* (*plural* **prides**) 1 a feeling of being proud 2 a group of lions

priest *noun* (*plural* **priests**) someone who performs religious ceremonies **priesthood** *noun* the job of being a priest

prim *adjective* (**primmer, primmest**) liking things to be correct **primly** *adverb*

primary *adjective* first; most important **primarily** *adverb*

primary colours *plural noun* the colours red, yellow, and blue, which can be mixed to make other colours

primary school *noun* (*plural* **primary schools**) a first school for children from the age of 5 onwards

prime *adjective* chief or most important ▶ *Fog was the prime cause of the accident.*

prime minister *noun* (*plural* **prime ministers**) the leader of a government

prime number *noun* (*plural* **prime numbers**) a number that cannot be divided exactly except by itself and the number one, for example 2, 3, 5, 7, and 11

primitive *adjective* 1 belonging to early times ▶ *Primitive humans were hunters rather than farmers.* 2 basic or simple ▶ *You can make a primitive sledge from an old tray.*

primrose *noun* (*plural* **primroses**) a pale yellow flower that comes out in spring

prince *noun* (*plural* **princes**) a man or boy in a royal family, especially the son of a king or queen **princely** *adjective* like a prince, or suitable for a prince

princess *noun* (*plural* **princesses**) a woman or girl in a royal family, especially the daughter of a king or queen, or the wife of a prince

principal *adjective* chief or most important **principally** *adverb*

principal *noun* (*plural* **principals**) the head of a college or school

principle *noun* (*plural* **principles**) a general belief or rule **in principle** in general, not in details

print *verb* (**prints, printing, printed**) 1 to put words or pictures on paper with a machine 2 to write the letters of words separately and not joined together 3 to make a photograph on special paper from a negative

print *noun* (*plural* **prints**) 1 printed words or pictures 2 a mark made by something pressing on a surface ▶ *His thumb left a print on the glass.* 3 a photograph made from a negative

printer *noun* (*plural* **printers**) 1 someone who prints books or newspapers 2 a machine that prints on paper

printout *noun* (*plural* **printouts**) a printed copy of information from data in a computer

prior *adjective* (not an everyday word) earlier ▶ *We cannot go without prior permission.* **prior to** before ▶ *They lived apart prior to their marriage.*

priority *noun* (*plural* **priorities**) (*pronounced* pry-o-ri-ti) 1 something that is more urgent or important than other things ▶ *Our priority must be to finish the building on time.* 2 the right to be first ▶ *Trains have priority at crossings.*

prise *verb* (**prises, prising, prised**) to force something open

prism *noun* (*plural* **prisms**) a piece of glass that breaks up light into the colours of the rainbow

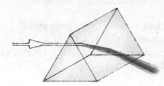

prison *noun* (*plural* **prisons**) a place where people are locked up as a punishment for crimes

prisoner *noun* (*plural* **prisoners**) someone who is kept in a prison or who is a captive

privacy *noun* (*pronounced* **priv-a-si**) being private or away from other people

private *adjective* 1 belonging to a particular person or group of people ► *a private road* 2 meant to be kept secret ► *These letters are private.* 3 away from other people ► *Is there a private place to swim?* 4 not controlled by the government ► *a private hospital* **in private** where only particular people can see or hear; not in public **privately** *adverb* separately; not with other people

private *noun* (*plural* **privates**) a soldier of the lowest rank

privatize *verb* (**privatizes, privatizing, privatized**) to sell a public business or organization to private owners to run **privatization** *noun*

privilege *noun* (*plural* **privileges**) a special right or advantage given to some people but not others **privileged** *adjective* lucky because you have something special

prize *noun* (*plural* **prizes**) something you get for winning a game or competition

prize *verb* (**prizes, prizing, prized**) to value something very highly

probable *adjective* likely to be true or to happen **probability** *noun* how likely something is to happen **probably** *adverb*

probation *noun* a period of time used for testing a person's character or behaviour, or for making sure they are suitable for a job

probation officer *noun* (*plural* **probation officers**) an official who supervises the behaviour of someone who is convicted of a crime but not sent to prison

probe *verb* (**probes, probing, probed**) to look at something closely

probe *noun* (*plural* **probes**) a long thin instrument used to look closely at something

problem *noun* (*plural* **problems**) something that is difficult to answer or deal with

procedure *noun* (*plural* **procedures**) a fixed or special way of doing something

proceed *verb* (**proceeds, proceeding, proceeded**) (*pronounced* **pro-seed**) to go on with something or continue forwards

proceedings *plural noun* things that happen; activities

proceeds *plural noun* (*pronounced* **proh-seedz**) the money made from a sale or event

process *noun* (*plural* **processes**) a series of actions for making or doing something

process *verb* (**processes, processing, processed**) to deal with something in a special way

procession *noun* (*plural* **processions**) a line of people or vehicles moving slowly forwards

proclaim *verb* (**proclaims, proclaiming, proclaimed**) to announce something publicly **proclamation** *noun* a grand announcement

prod *verb* (**prods, prodding, prodded**) to poke or jab something or someone

produce *verb* (**produces, producing, produced**) (*pronounced* **pro-dewss**) 1 to make or create something 2 to bring something out so that people can see it ► *Martin suddenly produced a letter.* 3 to organize the performance of a play or film **producer** *noun* **production** *noun*

produce *noun* (*pronounced* **prod-yewss**) food grown by farmers or gardeners

product *noun* (*plural* **products**)
1 something made to be sold 2 the result of multiplying two numbers ▸ *12 is the product of 4 and 3.*

productive *adjective* producing a lot of things **productivity** *noun*

profession *noun* (*plural* **professions**)
a type of work that needs special knowledge and training, for example medicine or law

professional *adjective* 1 to do with a profession 2 doing a certain type of work to earn money ▸ *a professional golfer* 3 expertly done **professionally** *adverb*

professional *noun* (*plural* **professionals**)
someone doing a certain type of work to earn money

professor *noun* (*plural* **professors**)
a teacher of the highest rank in a university

proficient *adjective* (*pronounced* pro-**fish**-ent) skilled; doing something well **proficiency** *noun*

profile *noun* (*plural* **profiles**) 1 a side view of a person's face 2 a short description of a person's life or character

profit *noun* (*plural* **profits**) 1 the extra money earned by selling something for more than it cost 2 an advantage or benefit

profit *verb* (**profits, profiting, profited**) to gain a profit or advantage from something **profitable** *adjective* making a profit, or useful

profound *adjective* very deep or intense ▸ *profound knowledge* **profoundly** *adverb*

program *noun* (*plural* **programs**) a series of instructions for a computer to carry out

program *verb* (**programs, programming, programmed**) to control a computer by means of a program
This is the American spelling of the word **programme**, and we use it for computers.

programme *noun* (*plural* **programmes**)
1 a show, play, or talk on radio or television 2 a list of planned events 3 a leaflet giving details of a concert or show

progress *noun* (*pronounced* **proh**-gress)
1 forward movement ▸ *The procession made slow progress.* 2 development or improvement ▸ *Jamila has made progress this term.*

progress *verb* (**progresses, progressing, progressed**) (*pronounced* pro-**gress**) 1 to move forward 2 to develop or improve **progression** *noun* **progressive** *adjective* modern; wanting to move forward

prohibit *verb* (**prohibits, prohibiting, prohibited**) to forbid something ▸ *Smoking is prohibited.* **prohibition** *noun* forbidding something

project *noun* (*plural* **projects**) (*pronounced* **proj**-ekt) 1 a task of getting information on a topic and writing about it 2 a plan or scheme

project *verb* (**projects, projecting, projected**) (*pronounced* pro-**jekt**) 1 to stick out 2 to show a picture or film with a projector on a screen **projection** *noun* something that sticks out; showing a picture or film on a screen

projector *noun* (*plural* **projectors**)
a machine for showing films or photographs on a screen

prologue *noun* (*plural* **prologues**) (*pronounced* **proh**-log) an introduction to a poem or play

prolong *verb* (**prolongs, prolonging, prolonged**) to make something last longer

promenade *noun* (*plural* **promenades**) (*pronounced* prom-en-**ahd**) a wide path for walking beside the sea

prominent *adjective* 1 easily seen; standing out 2 important **prominence** *noun* being prominent **prominently** *adverb*

promise *verb* (**promises, promising, promised**) to say that you will definitely do something, or not do something

promise *noun* (*plural* **promises**)
1 a statement promising something 2 a hope of future success ▸ *They show strong promise.*

promising *adjective* likely to be good or successful ▸ *a promising pupil*

promote *verb* (**promotes, promoting, promoted**) 1 to give someone a more senior or more important job or rank ▸ *Miss Hudson had been promoted to Head of Maths.* 2 to give a lot of publicity to a product ▸ *She is visiting bookshops to promote her latest novel.* 3 to do things to make something successful ▸ *They want to promote the cause of peace.* **promotion** *noun* promoting someone or something

prompt *adjective* (**prompter, promptest**) happening soon or without delay ▸ *I'd like a prompt answer.* **promptly** *adverb*

prompt *verb* (**prompts, prompting, prompted**) 1 to encourage someone to do something ▸ *The computer program prompts you to save your work every 10 minutes.* 2 to remind an actor what words to say next in a play

prone *adjective* **be prone to** to be likely to do something ▸ *He is prone to lose his temper.*

prong *noun* (*plural* **prongs**) one of the pointed pieces of a fork

pronoun *noun* (*plural* **pronouns**) a word used instead of a noun, such as *she, him, it, them,* and *these*

pronounce *verb* (**pronounces, pronouncing, pronounced**) 1 to say a word in a particular way ▸ *You pronounce 'pair' and 'pear' the same way.* 2 to declare something formally ▸ *After a short rest he pronounced himself fit again.*

pronounced *adjective* noticeable; definite ▸ *The pitch has a pronounced slope.*

pronouncement *noun* (*plural* **pronouncements**) something said formally; a declaration

pronunciation *noun* (*plural* **pronunciations**) the way a word is pronounced

proof *noun* (*plural* **proofs**) evidence which shows that something is true

proof *adjective* giving protection against something ▸ *He was wearing a bullet-proof jacket.*

prop *noun* (*plural* **props**) 1 a support 2 an object used on stage in a theatre

prop *verb* (**props, propping, propped**) to support something by leaning it on something else ▸ *You can prop your bicycle against the wall.*

propaganda *noun* ideas and information spread by an organization to make people believe something

propel *verb* (**propels, propelling, propelled**) to send something rapidly forward

propeller *noun* (*plural* **propellers**) a set of blades on a hub that spin round to drive a ship or aircraft

proper *adjective* 1 suitable or right ▸ *Show me the proper way to hold the bat.* 2 respectable ▸ *We tried to behave in a proper fashion.* 3 (informal) real, complete ▸ *I haven't had a proper meal for days.* **properly** *adverb*

proper noun *noun* (*plural* **proper nouns**) the name given to one person or thing and written with a capital letter, such as *Ben* and *New York*

property *noun* (*plural* **properties**) 1 something that belongs to you 2 buildings or land belonging to someone 3 a quality or characteristic ▸ *People thought the berries had healing properties.*

prophecy *noun* (*plural* **prophecies**) (*pronounced* **prof**-i-si) a statement that something will happen in the future

prophesy *verb* (**prophesies, prophesying, prophesied**) (*pronounced* **prof**-i-sy) to make a prophecy

prophet *noun* (*plural* **prophets**) 1 someone who makes prophecies 2 a religious teacher who is believed to speak the word of God **the Prophet** a name for Muhammad

proportion *noun* (*plural* **proportions**) 1 a part of something ▸ *A large proportion of our income is spent on rent.* 2 the number or amount of one thing compared to another ▸ *The proportion of women to men is roughly 3 to 1.* **proportional** *adjective*

propose *verb* (**proposes, proposing, proposed**) 1 to suggest an idea or plan 2 to ask someone to marry you ▸ *Craig proposed to his girlfriend last night.* **proposal** *noun* a plan, or an offer of marriage

proprietor *noun* (*plural* **proprietors**) (*pronounced* pro-**pry**-et-er) the owner of a shop or business

propulsion *noun* the action of propelling something or driving it forward

prose *noun* writing that is like ordinary speech, not verse

prosecute *verb* (**prosecutes, prosecuting, prosecuted**) to accuse someone of a crime and have them tried in a lawcourt **prosecution** *noun* **prosecutor** *noun*

prospect *noun* (*plural* **prospects**) (*pronounced* **pros**-pekt) a possibility or hope ▸ *We have good prospects of winning.*

prosper *verb* (**prospers, prospering, prospered**) to be successful or do well

prosperous *adjective* rich and successful **prosperity** *noun* wealth, success

prostitute *noun* (*plural* **prostitutes**) someone who has sexual intercourse for payment

protect *verb* (**protects, protecting, protected**) to keep someone or something safe **protection** *noun* **protector** *noun*

protective *adjective* wanting to protect someone or something

protein *noun* (*plural* **proteins**) (*pronounced* **proh**-teen) a substance in food that you need to keep you healthy and make you grow

protest *noun* (*plural* **protests**) (*pronounced* **proh**-test) something you say or do because you disapprove of someone or something
protest *verb* (**protests, protesting, protested**) (*pronounced* pro-**test**) to make a protest ▸ *A crowd stood protesting about the plan for a new bypass.* **protester** *noun*

Protestant *noun* (*plural* **Protestants**) (*pronounced* **prot**-is-tant) a member of a western Christian Church other than the Roman Catholic Church

proton *noun* (*plural* **protons**) a particle of matter carrying a positive electric charge

protractor *noun* (*plural* **protractors**) an instrument for measuring and drawing angles

protrude *verb* (**protrudes, protruding, protruded**) to stick out **protrusion** *noun* something that sticks out

proud *adjective* (**prouder, proudest**) **1** pleased with yourself or with someone else who has done well ▸ *Fiona was proud of her daughter's singing ability.* **2** too satisfied because of who you are or what you have done ▸ *They were too proud to ask for help.* **proudly** *adverb*

prove *verb* (**proves, proving, proved**) **1** to show that something is true ▸ *Can you prove that Gary took your ruler?* **2** to happen in a certain way ▸ *The weather forecast proved to be correct.*

proverb *noun* (*plural* **proverbs**) a short well-known saying that gives advice or says something about life, for example 'Too many cooks spoil the broth.' **proverbial** *adjective* well known

provide *verb* (**provides, providing, provided**) **1** to supply or give something that someone needs ▸ *Can you provide your own sheets and towels?* **2** to prepare for something unwelcome ▸ *They have provided for all possible disasters.* **provided** or **providing** on condition; on condition that ▸ *You can come providing you bring some food.*

province *noun* (*plural* **provinces**) a part of a country

provision *noun* providing something ▸ *the provision of good bus services* **provisions** supplies of food and drink

provisional *adjective* arranged for the time being, but likely to be changed ▸ *10 July is the provisional date for the summer fair.*

provocative *adjective* likely to make someone angry ▸ *a provocative answer*

provoke *verb* (**provokes, provoking, provoked**) **1** to try to make someone angry **2** to arouse or cause a feeling ▸ *Her remarks provoked a lot of criticism.* **provocation** *noun* provoking someone, or something that provokes you

prow *noun* (*plural* **prows**) (*rhymes with* cow) the front end of a ship

prowl *verb* (**prowls, prowling, prowled**) to move about quietly or cautiously, as if about to attack **prowler** *noun*

prudent *adjective* wise and careful
prudence *noun* **prudently** *adverb*

prune[1] *noun* (*plural* **prunes**) a dried plum

prune[2] *verb* (**prunes, pruning, pruned**) to
cut off unwanted parts from a tree or plant

pry *verb* (**pries, prying, pried**) to be nosy or
inquisitive about someone else's business

PS something you write at the end of a
letter when you want to add something
else to it
PS is short for *postscript*, which means 'something
written after'.

psalm *noun* (*plural* **psalms**) (*pronounced*
sahm) a religious song from the Bible

pseudonym *noun* (*plural* **pseudonyms**)
(*pronounced* s'**yoo**-do-nim) a name used
by an author instead of their real name

psychiatrist *noun* (*plural* **psychiatrists**)
(*pronounced* sy-**ky**-a-trist) a doctor who
treats mental illness **psychiatric** *adjective*
psychiatry *noun*

psychic *adjective* (*pronounced* **sy**-kik)
knowing about the future or what other
people are thinking

psychologist *noun* (*plural* **psychologists**)
(*pronounced* sy-**kol**-o-jist) someone who
studies how the mind works **psychological**
adjective **psychology** *noun*

PTO short for *please turn over*, which you
write at the bottom of a page when there is
more on the next page

pub *noun* (*plural* **pubs**) (informal) a place
where people can buy and drink alcoholic
drinks
Pub is short for *public house*.

puberty *noun* (*pronounced* **pew**-ber-ti) the
time when a young person starts to
develop into an adult

public *adjective* belonging to everyone, or
used or known by everyone **in public**
where everyone can see or take part **the
public** all the people; everyone **publicly**
adverb in public

publication *noun* (*plural* **publications**)
1 publishing books or magazines 2 a book
or magazine that is printed and sold

publicity *noun* something you say or do to
make people know about someone or
something

public school *noun* (*plural* **public
schools**) a secondary school that charges
fees

publish *verb* (**publishes, publishing,
published**) 1 to print and sell books or
magazines 2 to make information known
publicly **publisher** *noun*

pudding *noun* (*plural* **puddings**) 1 a hot
sweet cooked food ▸ *rice pudding*
2 a savoury food made with flour or suet
▸ *Yorkshire pudding* 3 the sweet course of
a meal ▸ *What's for pudding?*

puddle *noun* (*plural* **puddles**) a small pool
of water on the ground

puff *noun* (*plural* **puffs**) a small amount of
breath, wind, smoke, or steam

puff *verb* (**puffs, puffing, puffed**) 1 to blow
out smoke or steam 2 to breathe hard and
quickly 3 to swell or inflate something
▸ *Pigeons seem to puff out their chests.*

puffin *noun* (*plural* **puffins**) a seabird with
a large beak

pull *verb* (**pulls, pulling, pulled**) to get hold
of something and make it come towards
you or follow behind you **pull a face** to
make a strange face **pull out** to stop taking
part in something ▸ *Half the competitors
pulled out just before the race.* **pull
someone's leg** to tease someone **pull
through** to recover from an illness **pull up**
to stop ▸ *A car pulled up beside them.* **pull
yourself together** to calm down after being
upset

pull *noun* (*plural* **pulls**) an action of pulling
▸ *I had to give the window a sharp pull.*

pulley *noun* (*plural* **pulleys**) a wheel with
a rope round it, for lifting heavy things

pullover *noun* (*plural* **pullovers**) a knitted
piece of clothing that you pull on over
your head

pulp *noun* (*plural* **pulps**) a soft wet mass of
something
pulp *verb* (**pulps, pulping, pulped**) to make
something into a pulp

pulpit *noun* (*plural* **pulpits**) a raised platform in a church, where the priest or minister speaks to the congregation

pulse *noun* (*plural* **pulses**) 1 the movement of blood in your arteries, which shows how fast your heart is beating 2 a regular vibration or movement ▸ *The music had a throbbing pulse.*

puma *noun* (*plural* **pumas**) a large wild cat of North America

pumice *noun* (*pronounced* **pum-iss**) a kind of soft stone used to clean or polish hard surfaces

pump *noun* (*plural* **pumps**) 1 a device that forces air or liquid into or out of something, or along pipes 2 a light flat shoe
pump *verb* (**pumps, pumping, pumped**) to force air or liquid along with a pump **pump up** to fill a balloon or tyre with air or gas

pumpkin *noun* (*plural* **pumpkins**) a large round fruit with a hard yellow skin

pun *noun* (*plural* **puns**) a clever use of a word with two different meanings, or two words that sound the same, as in *Choosing where to bury him was a grave decision.*

punch *verb* (**punches, punching, punched**) 1 to hit someone with your fist 2 to make a hole in something ▸ *The guard will punch your tickets.*
punch *noun* (*plural* **punches**) 1 a blow or hit with the fist 2 a tool for making holes 3 a hot alcoholic drink

punctual *adjective* exactly on time; not arriving late **punctuality** *noun* how punctual someone is **punctually** *adverb*

punctuate *verb* (**punctuates, punctuating, punctuated**) to put the commas, full stops, and other punctuation in writing

punctuation *noun* a set of marks such as commas, full stops, and brackets put into a piece of writing to make it easier to understand
These are punctuation marks: apostrophe '
brackets ( ) [ ]   colon :   comma ,   dash —
exclamation mark !   full stop .   hyphen -
question mark ?   quotation marks ' ' " "
semicolon ;

puncture *noun* (*plural* **punctures**) a small hole made in a tyre by a sharp object
puncture *verb* (**punctures, puncturing, punctured**) to make a hole in something

punish *verb* (**punishes, punishing, punished**) to make someone suffer because they have done wrong **punishment** *noun*

puny *adjective* (**punier, puniest**) (*pronounced* **pew-ni**) small and weak

pupa *noun* (*plural* **pupae**) (*pronounced* **pew-pa**) a chrysalis

pupil *noun* (*plural* **pupils**) 1 someone who is being taught by a teacher 2 the opening in the centre of your eye

puppet *noun* (*plural* **puppets**) a doll that you can move by putting your fingers in it or by pulling strings attached to it

puppy *noun* (*plural* **puppies**) a young dog

purchase *verb* (**purchases, purchasing, purchased**) (not an everyday word) to buy something **purchaser** *noun*
purchase *noun* (*plural* **purchases**) 1 something you have bought ▸ *I was pleased with my purchases.* 2 the fact of buying something ▸ *A receipt is proof of purchase.*

pure *adjective* (**purer, purest**) clean and clear, not mixed with something else ▸ *Use pure olive oil.* **purity** *noun* how pure something is

purely *adverb* only, simply ▸ *They did it purely for fun.*

purify *verb* (**purifies, purifying, purified**) to make something pure

purple *adjective* deep reddish-blue
purple *noun* a deep reddish-blue colour

purpose *noun* (*plural* **purposes**) 1 what you intend to do 2 what something is used for **on purpose** deliberately

purposely *adverb* on purpose

purr *verb* (**purrs, purring, purred**) to make a gentle murmuring sound like a cat when it is pleased

purse *noun* (*plural* **purses**) a small bag for holding money

pursue *verb* (**pursues, pursuing, pursued**)
1 to chase someone or something ▶ *He ran down the road, pursued by an angry neighbour.* 2 to work continuously at something ▶ *She would like to pursue a career as a journalist.* **pursuer** *noun* someone who is chasing you

pursuit *noun* (*plural* **pursuits**) 1 chasing someone ▶ *The police were in hot pursuit.* 2 something you spend a lot of time doing

pus *noun* a thick yellow substance produced in sore places on the body

push *verb* (**pushes, pushing, pushed**) 1 to move something away from you by applying pressure to it ▶ *The man was pushing a shopping trolley.* 2 to press something in ▶ *Try pushing the button.*
push *noun* (*plural* **pushes**) a pushing movement

pushchair *noun* (*plural* **pushchairs**) a small chair with wheels, in which a child can be pushed along

pussy *noun* (*plural* **pussies**) (informal) a cat

put *verb* (**puts, putting, put**) 1 to place or move something somewhere ▶ *Put the shopping down here.* 2 to say something in a certain way ▶ *He tried to put the idea as simply as he could.* **put off** 1 to make someone less keen to do something ▶ *The hot sun began to put us off our swim.* 2 to postpone something ▶ *We'll put off the party for a week.* **put on** 1 to switch on a light or other electrical device 2 to start wearing a piece of clothing ▶ *I'll just put on my coat.* **put out** to stop a fire or light from burning or shining **put up** 1 to give someone a place to sleep ▶ *We could put you up for a few nights.* 2 to build something or make it stand up ▶ *Let's put the tent up here.* **put up with** to be willing to accept something although you do not like it

putty *noun* a soft paste that hardens when it sets, used to fit windows in their frames

puzzle *noun* (*plural* **puzzles**) 1 a tricky game that you have to solve 2 a difficult question; a problem
puzzle *verb* (**puzzles, puzzling, puzzled**) 1 to give someone a problem that is hard to understand 2 to think hard about something

pygmy *noun* (*plural* **pygmies**) (*pronounced* **pig**-mi) an unusually small person or animal

pyjamas *plural noun* a loose set of jacket and trousers that you wear in bed

pylon *noun* (*plural* **pylons**) a metal tower for supporting electric cables

pyramid *noun* (*plural* **pyramids**) 1 a solid shape that has a square base and four sides coming to a point 2 a large ancient Egyptian monument shaped like this

python *noun* (*plural* **pythons**) a large snake that crushes its prey

Qq

quack *verb* (**quacks, quacking, quacked**) to make a noise like a duck
quack *noun* (*plural* **quacks**) a quacking noise

quad *noun* (*plural* **quads**) (informal) 1 a quadruplet 2 a quadrangle

quadrangle *noun* (*plural* **quadrangles**) a square courtyard with buildings round it

quadrant *noun* (*plural* **quadrants**) a quarter of a circle

quadrilateral *noun* (*plural* **quadrilaterals**) a flat shape with four sides

quadruple *adjective* four times as much or as many

quadruplet *noun* (*plural* **quadruplets**) one of four babies born to the same mother at one time

quail *noun* (*plural* **quails**) a bird like a small partridge

quaint *adjective* (**quainter, quaintest**) unusual in an attractive or old-fashioned way ▶ *The choir sang quaint old English folk songs.* **quaintly** *adverb* **quaintness** *noun*

quake *verb* (**quakes, quaking, quaked**) to tremble or shake

Quaker *noun* (*plural* **Quakers**) a member of a Christian religious group called the Society of Friends

qualification *noun* (*plural* **qualifications**) a skill or ability to do a job

qualify *verb* (**qualifies, qualifying, qualified**) to be suitable for a job or reach the standard needed for something, for example by passing an exam

quality *noun* (*plural* **qualities**) 1 how good or bad something is 2 what something is like ▶ *The paper had a shiny quality.*

quantity *noun* (*plural* **quantities**) the number or amount of something ▶ *A large quantity of letters came through the door.*

quarantine *noun* a period when a person or animal is kept apart from others in case they have a disease
The word **quarantine** comes from the Italian word *quaranta* meaning 'forty', because the period used to last for forty days.

quarrel *noun* (*plural* **quarrels**) a strong or angry argument
quarrel *verb* (**quarrels, quarrelling, quarrelled**) to have a quarrel with someone

quarrelsome *adjective* often quarrelling

quarry *noun* (*plural* **quarries**) 1 a place where stone for building is dug out of the ground 2 an animal that is being hunted

quart *noun* (*plural* **quarts**) a measure of liquid, a quarter of a gallon

quarter *noun* (*plural* **quarters**) 1 each of four equal parts into which something can be divided 2 a period of three months ▶ *We get a phone bill every quarter.* **quarters** an official place to stay **at close quarters** close together ▶ *They fought at close quarters.*

quartet *noun* (*plural* **quartets**) a group of four musicians or singers

quartz *noun* (*pronounced* kworts) a hard mineral found as crystals in rocks and used in clocks and watches

quaver *verb* (**quavers, quavering, quavered**) to tremble
quaver *noun* (*plural* **quavers**) 1 a trembling sound 2 a musical note equal to half a crotchet, written ♪

quay *noun* (*plural* **quays**) (*pronounced* kee) a harbour wall or pier where ships can load and unload

queasy *adjective* (**queasier, queasiest**) feeling slightly sick **queasiness** *noun*

queen *noun* (*plural* **queens**) 1 a woman who has been crowned as the ruler of a country 2 a king's wife 3 a female bee or ant that produces eggs 4 a piece in chess, the most powerful on the board 5 a playing card with a picture of a queen on it

queen mother *noun* the mother of the present king or queen

queer *adjective* (**queerer, queerest**) 1 strange or odd ▶ *The juice had a queer taste.* 2 ill or unwell ▶ *I feel a bit queer.*

quench *verb* (**quenches, quenching, quenched**) 1 to make your thirst go away by drinking 2 to put out a fire

query *noun* (*plural* **queries**) (*pronounced* kweer-i) a small or quick question
query *verb* (**queries, querying, queried**) to ask whether something is true or correct ▶ *The bill seemed rather large so Maggie queried it.*

quest *noun* (*plural* **quests**) a long search for something important

question *noun* (*plural* **questions**) 1 something you ask when you want to find out something 2 a problem or subject for discussion **out of the question** impossible; not allowed
question *verb* (**questions, questioning, questioned**) 1 to ask someone questions ▶ *The police questioned me about the accident.* 2 to say that you are doubtful about something ▶ *Nobody questioned my right to speak at the meeting.* **questioner** *noun*

question mark *noun* (*plural* **question marks**) a punctuation mark (?) put at the end of a question

questionnaire *noun* (*plural* **questionnaires**) (*pronounced* kwes-chon-air*) a list of questions that you ask several people when you are doing a survey

queue *noun* (*plural* **queues**) (*pronounced* kew) a line of people or vehicles waiting for something

queue *verb* (**queues, queueing, queued**) (*pronounced* kew) to wait in a queue

quiche *noun* (*plural* **quiches**) (*pronounced* keesh) an open tart with a savoury filling

quick *adjective* (**quicker, quickest**) 1 taking only a short time ▸ *We had a quick trip back because there wasn't much traffic.* 2 done in a short time ▸ *I expect you would like a quick answer.* 3 able to learn easily; intelligent **quickly** *adverb*

quicken *verb* (**quickens, quickening, quickened**) to become quicker

quicksand *noun* (*plural* **quicksands**) loose wet sand that sucks in anything that falls into it

quid *noun* (*plural* **quid**) (slang) a pound (£1)

quiet *adjective* (**quieter, quietest**) 1 silent, or not loud ▸ *Shaun spoke in a quiet voice that you could hardly hear.* 2 calm and peaceful ▸ *All they asked for was a quiet life.* **quietly** *adverb*

quieten *verb* (**quietens, quietening, quietened**) 1 to make something or someone quiet 2 to become quiet

quill *noun* (*plural* **quills**) a large feather, used as a pen

quilt *noun* (*plural* **quilts**) a thick soft cover for a bed

quintet *noun* (*plural* **quintets**) a group of five musicians or singers

quit *verb* (**quits, quitting, quitted** or **quit**) 1 to leave a place 2 (informal) to stop doing something ▸ *He wants to quit smoking.*

quite *adverb* 1 completely; truly ▸ *I haven't quite finished.* 2 somewhat; rather ▸ *The news was quite bad, though not as bad as we feared.*

quiver[1] *verb* (**quivers, quivering, quivered**) to tremble ▸ *She was quivering with excitement.*

quiver[2] *noun* (*plural* **quivers**) a long container for arrows

quiz *noun* (*plural* **quizzes**) a competition or game in which you have to answer a lot of questions

quoits *plural noun* (*pronounced* koits) a game in which you try to throw rings over a peg

quota *noun* (*plural* **quotas**) (*pronounced* kwoh-ta) a fixed share or amount

quotation *noun* (*plural* **quotations**) an interesting sentence or set of words taken from a book or from what someone else has said

quotation marks *plural noun* inverted commas, used to show a quotation

quote *verb* (**quotes, quoting, quoted**) to use words that someone else has already said or written

quotient *noun* (*plural* **quotients**) (*pronounced* kwoh-shent) what you get when you divide one number by another ▸ *The quotient of 12 divided by 3 is 4.*

Rr

rabbi *noun* (*plural* **rabbis**) (*pronounced* rab-I) a Jewish religious leader

rabbit *noun* (*plural* **rabbits**) a small furry animal with long ears and a short tail, which lives in a burrow

rabble *noun* a loud or badly behaved crowd of people

rabies *noun* (*pronounced* ray-beez) a fatal disease which causes madness in dogs and cats and can be passed to humans

raccoon *noun* (*plural* **raccoons**) a small North American furry animal with a bushy striped tail

race *noun* (*plural* **races**) 1 a competition to be the first to reach a particular place or to do something 2 a large group of people with the same ancestors and the same physical features, such as colour of skin

race *verb* (**races, racing, raced**) 1 to have a race against someone 2 to move very fast

racecourse *noun* (*plural* **racecourses**) a place where horse races are run

racial *adjective* to do with race **racially** *adverb*

racist *adjective* believing that some races of people are superior, and treating members of other races badly **racism** *noun*

racist *noun* someone who has racist views

rack *noun* (*plural* **racks**) 1 a framework for holding things 2 a device for torturing people by stretching their joints, used in the past

rack *verb* (**racks, racking, racked**) to **rack your brains** to think hard to remember something or solve a problem

racket *noun* (*plural* **rackets**) 1 a bat with strings stretched across a frame, used in tennis and similar games 2 a loud noise 3 a dishonest way of making money
The word **racket** meaning 'a bat' comes from an Arabic word meaning 'the palm of the hand'.

radar *noun* a system that uses radio waves to show the position of objects by bouncing back off them
The word **radar** comes from 'radio detection and ranging'.

radiant *adjective* 1 radiating light or heat 2 looking bright and happy **radiance** *noun* **radiantly** *adverb*

radiate *verb* (**radiates, radiating, radiated**) 1 to send out rays of heat, light, or other energy 2 to spread out from a centre

radiation *noun* heat, light, or radioactive energy given out by something

radiator *noun* (*plural* **radiators**) 1 a metal container through which steam or hot water flows, used to heat a room 2 a device that cools a car's engine

radical *adjective* thorough or drastic
▶ *The new manager has made radical changes.* **radically** *adverb*

radii plural of **radius**

radio *noun* (*plural* **radios**) a device for sending or receiving sound by means of electrical waves

radioactive *adjective* giving out dangerous radiation **radioactivity** *noun*

radiography *noun* photography of the body using X-rays **radiographer** *noun*

radish *noun* (*plural* **radishes**) a small hard red vegetable, eaten raw in salads

radius *noun* (*plural* **radii**) a straight line from the centre of a circle to the edge (circumference)

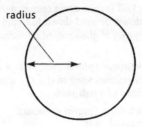

radius

raffle *noun* (*plural* **raffles**) a way of raising money by selling numbered tickets. If you have the right ticket, you win a prize.

raffle *verb* (**raffles, raffling, raffled**) to give something as a prize in a raffle

raft *noun* (*plural* **rafts**) a floating platform of logs or barrels tied together

rafter *noun* (*plural* **rafters**) one of the long sloping pieces of wood that hold up a roof

rag *noun* (*plural* **rags**) an old or torn piece of cloth

rage *noun* (*plural* **rages**) great or violent anger

rage *verb* (**rages, raging, raged**) 1 to be very angry 2 to be violent or noisy ▶ *A storm was raging.*

ragged *adjective* (*pronounced* **rag**-id) 1 torn or frayed 2 wearing torn or old clothes

raid *noun* (*plural* **raids**) 1 a sudden attack 2 a surprise visit by the police to search a place or arrest people

raid *verb* (**raids, raiding, raided**) to make a raid on a place **raider** *noun*

rail *noun* (*plural* **rails**) **1** a bar or rod for hanging things on **2** a bar that is part of a fence or banisters **3** a long metal strip forming part of a railway track **by rail** by train

railings *plural noun* a fence made of metal rails

railway *noun* (*plural* **railways**) **1** a system of transport with trains running on rails **2** the track that trains run on

rain *noun* drops of water that fall from the sky

rain *verb* (**rains, raining, rained**) **1** to fall as rain ▸ *It was still raining when they went out.* ▸ *Will it rain again tomorrow?* **2** to come down or send down like rain ▸ *Fragments of glass rained on them from above.*

rainbow *noun* (*plural* **rainbows**) a curved band of colours seen in the sky when the sun shines through rain

raincoat *noun* (*plural* **raincoats**) a waterproof coat

raindrop *noun* (*plural* **raindrops**) a single drop of rain

rainfall *noun* the amount of rain that falls in a particular place

rainforest *noun* (*plural* **rainforests**) a tropical forest in an area where there is a lot of rain

raise *verb* (**raises, raising, raised**) **1** to move something to a higher position ▸ *They were going to need a crane to raise such a large block.* **2** to succeed in collecting a sum of money ▸ *We are trying to raise £5,000.* **3** to mention a subject or idea for people to think about **4** to bring up and educate children **5** to breed animals or grow plants

raisin *noun* (*plural* **raisins**) a dried grape

rake *noun* (*plural* **rakes**) a gardening tool with a row of short spikes fixed to a long handle

rake *verb* (**rakes, raking, raked**) to move something or smooth it with a rake

rally *noun* (*plural* **rallies**) **1** a large meeting for a special purpose **2** a competition to test skill in driving **3** a series of strokes and return strokes of the ball in tennis

rally *verb* (**rallies, rallying, rallied**) **1** to bring people together for a special effort **2** to come together to support someone **3** to recover after an illness or setback

ram *noun* (*plural* **rams**) a male sheep

ram *verb* (**rams, ramming, rammed**) to push one thing hard against another

Ramadan *noun* (*pronounced* ram-a-dan) the ninth month of the Muslim year, when Muslims do not eat or drink during the daytime

ramble *verb* (**rambles, rambling, rambled**) **1** to go for a long walk in the country **2** to go on talking in a confused way **rambler** *noun* a walker

ramp *noun* (*plural* **ramps**) a slope leading from one level to another

rampage *verb* (**rampages, rampaging, rampaged**) to rush about wildly or violently

rampart *noun* (*plural* **ramparts**) a thick wall defending a place

ramshackle *adjective* (describing a building) in a very bad state

ran past tense of **run** *verb*

ranch *noun* (*plural* **ranches**) a large cattle-farm in America

random *noun* **at random** by chance; without any purpose or plan

random *adjective* done or taken at random ▸ *The police were making random checks on passing cars.* **randomly** *adverb*

rang past tense of **ring**[2] *verb*

range *noun* (*plural* **ranges**) **1** a line of mountains **2** a variety or collection of things ▸ *The newsagent sells a wide range of magazines.* **3** the distance that a gun can shoot, or an aircraft can fly, or a sound can be heard **4** a place with targets for shooting practice **5** a kitchen fireplace with ovens

range *verb* (**ranges, ranging, ranged**) **1** to reach from one limit to another ▸ *Ages ranged from 5 to 25.* **2** to arrange people or things in a line ▸ *Crowds were ranged along the streets.* **3** (used about animals) to wander in the open

ranger *noun* (*plural* **rangers**) someone who looks after a park or forest

rank *noun* (*plural* **ranks**) 1 a position that shows a person's level or importance ▸ *He had the rank of captain.* 2 a line of people or things ▸ *a rank of soldiers* ▸ *a taxi rank*

rank *verb* (**ranks, ranking, ranked**) to have a certain rank or position ▸ *She ranks among the greatest writers of the century.*

ransack *verb* (**ransacks, ransacking, ransacked**) to search a place thoroughly, leaving it untidy

ransom *noun* (*plural* **ransoms**) money that someone must pay so that a prisoner can be set free **hold to ransom** to keep someone prisoner and demand a ransom

ransom *verb* (**ransoms, ransoming, ransomed**) to pay a ransom for a prisoner

rap *verb* (**raps, rapping, rapped**) to knock quickly and loudly

rap *noun* (*plural* **raps**) 1 a rapping movement or sound 2 a kind of music in which the words are spoken to the rhythm

rape *verb* (**rapes, raping, raped**) to force someone to have sexual intercourse

rapid *adjective* moving or working at speed **rapidity** *noun* **rapidly** *adverb*

rapids *plural noun* part of a river where the water flows fast over rocks

rapier *noun* (*plural* **rapiers**) a narrow lightweight sword

rapture *noun* (*plural* **raptures**) great joy or delight

rare *adjective* (**rarer, rarest**) unusual; not often happening ▸ *She died of a rare disease.* **rarely** *adverb* **rarity** *noun* something that is rare

rascal *noun* (*plural* **rascals**) a dishonest or mischievous person

rash *adjective* (**rasher, rashest**) acting too quickly or without proper thought **rashly** *adverb*

rash *noun* (*plural* **rashes**) a series of red spots or patches on the skin

rasher *noun* (*plural* **rashers**) a slice of bacon

raspberry *noun* (*plural* **raspberries**) a small soft red fruit

Rastafarian *noun* (*plural* **Rastafarians**) (*pronounced* ras-ta-**fair**-i-an) a member of a religious group that started in Jamaica The word **Rastafarian** comes from *Ras Tafari*, a king of Ethiopia who is the group's hero.

rat *noun* (*plural* **rats**) an animal like a large mouse

rate *noun* (*plural* **rates**) 1 the speed at which someone does something ▸ *Everyone was working at a furious rate.* 2 the number of something in a particular period ▸ *The birth rate is rising.* 3 a quality or standard ▸ *Their work is first-rate.* 4 a cost or charge ▸ *What is the rate for a letter to Europe?* **at any rate** anyway

rate *verb* (**rates, rating, rated**) to estimate or value something or someone ▸ *She is rated very highly as an actor.*

rather *adverb* 1 slightly; somewhat ▸ *It was rather late.* 2 preferably; more willingly ▸ *We would rather stay here.* 3 really; more truly ▸ *He lay down, or rather fell, on the bed.*

ratio *noun* (*plural* **ratios**) (*pronounced* **ray**-shi-oh) the way one number or amount relates to another ▸ *In a group of 2 girls and 10 boys, the ratio of girls to boys is 1 to 5.*

ration *noun* (*plural* **rations**) (*pronounced* **rash**-on) an amount of something that each person is allowed when there is a shortage

ration *verb* (**rations, rationing, rationed**) (*pronounced* **rash**-on) to share something out when there is a shortage

rational *adjective* (*pronounced* **rash**-o-nal) reasonable or sensible ▸ *It was not easy to find a rational explanation for what happened.* **rationally** *adverb*

rattle *verb* (**rattles, rattling, rattled**) to make a series of short sharp hard sounds

rattle *noun* (*plural* **rattles**) 1 a rattling sound 2 a baby's toy that rattles when you shake it

rattlesnake *noun* (*plural* **rattlesnakes**) a poisonous snake that makes rattling sounds with its tail

rave verb (**raves, raving, raved**) **1** to talk wildly, like a mad person **2** to be very keen or excited about something

rave noun (plural **raves**) a big party with loud music and bright lights

raven noun (plural **ravens**) a large black bird like a crow

ravenous adjective (pronounced rav-e-nus) very hungry **ravenously** adverb

ravine noun (plural **ravines**) (pronounced ra-**veen**) a deep narrow valley

raw adjective **1** not cooked **2** in the natural state; not yet processed ▸ What raw materials do you need? **3** without experience ▸ They are just raw beginners. **4** cold and damp ▸ There was a raw wind blowing. **5** sore and tender ▸ Andrea's shoe had rubbed a raw patch on her heel. **rawness** noun

ray noun (plural **rays**) **1** a thin line of light, heat, or other energy **2** a large sea fish with a flat body and a long tail

razor noun (plural **razors**) a device with a sharp blade used for shaving the skin

reach verb (**reaches, reaching, reached**) **1** to go as far as a place and arrive there **2** to stretch out your hand to get or touch something ▸ Diane reached for the milk. **3** to be long enough to touch something ▸ The carpet won't reach the wall.

reach noun (plural **reaches**) **1** the distance you can reach with your hand **2** a distance that you can easily travel ▸ I'd like to live within reach of the sea.

react verb (**reacts, reacting, reacted**) to act in response to another person or thing

reaction noun (plural **reactions**) what you feel or say or do when something happens, or when someone does something

reactor noun (plural **reactors**) an apparatus for producing nuclear power

read verb (**reads, reading, read**) **1** to look at something written or printed and understand it or say it aloud **2** to have a measurement or figure that you can read ▸ The thermometer reads 20°.

reader noun (plural **readers**) **1** someone who reads **2** a book that helps you learn to read

readily adverb (pronounced **red**-i-li) **1** willingly or eagerly ▸ We readily agreed to help. **2** easily; without difficulty ▸ Spare parts are readily available.

ready adjective (**readier, readiest**) **1** able or willing to do something ▸ I'm ready to help you. **2** prepared for use ▸ Is dinner ready? **readiness** noun

real adjective **1** true or existing; not imaginary ▸ The story is based on real events. **2** genuine; not a copy ▸ Are those pearls real?

realistic adjective true to life; seeing things as they really are **realistically** adverb

reality noun (plural **realities**) what is real

realize verb (**realizes, realizing, realized**) to understand that something is true **realization** noun realizing something

really adverb truly; certainly; in fact

realm noun (plural **realms**) (pronounced relm) a kingdom

reap verb (**reaps, reaping, reaped**) to cut down corn and gather it in when it is ripe **reaper** noun

reappear verb (**reappears, reappearing, reappeared**) to appear again after going away **reappearance** noun a time when someone or something reappears

rear[1] noun (plural **rears**) the back part of something

rear adjective placed or found at the back ▸ A child was looking out of the rear window.

rear[2] verb (**rears, rearing, reared**) **1** to bring up young children or animals or help them grow **2** (used about an animal) to rise up on the hind legs

reason noun (plural **reasons**) **1** a cause or explanation for something **2** reasoning or common sense ▸ Please listen to reason.

reason verb (**reasons, reasoning, reasoned**) to think or argue in a logical way

reasonable *adjective* **1** sensible or logical **2** fair or moderate ▸ *She earns a reasonable income now.* **reasonably** *adverb*

reassure *verb* (**reassures, reassuring, reassured**) to take away someone's doubts or fears ▸ *Juliet saw that he was upset and tried to reassure him.* ▸ *I reassured Dominic that the spider had gone.* **reassurance** *noun* something you say that reassures someone

rebel *verb* (**rebels, rebelling, rebelled**) (*pronounced* ri-**bel**) to refuse to obey someone in authority, especially the government

rebel *noun* (*plural* **rebels**) (*pronounced* **reb**-el) someone who refuses to obey people who are in charge, and behaves differently from other people **rebellion** *noun* a time when people rebel **rebellious** *adjective* unwilling to obey people in charge

rebound *verb* (**rebounds, rebounding, rebounded**) to bounce back after hitting something

rebuild *verb* (**rebuilds, rebuilding, rebuilt**) to build something again after it has been destroyed

rebuke *verb* (**rebukes, rebuking, rebuked**) to tell someone off for doing something wrong

recall *verb* (**recalls, recalling, recalled**) **1** to tell someone to come back, or to bring something back **2** to remember something

recap *verb* (**recaps, recapping, recapped**) (informal) to summarize what has been said

recapture *verb* (**recaptures, recapturing, recaptured**) to capture someone again after they have escaped

recede *verb* (**recedes, receding, receded**) to go back ▸ *The floods have receded.*

receipt *noun* (*plural* **receipts**) (*pronounced* ri-**seet**) a piece of paper showing that you have paid money for something

receive *verb* (**receives, receiving, received**) **1** to get something when it is given or sent to you **2** to greet a guest or visitor

receiver *noun* (*plural* **receivers**) **1** a radio or television set **2** the part of a telephone that you hold to your ear

recent *adjective* made or happening a short time ago **recently** *adverb*

receptacle *noun* (*plural* **receptacles**) (not an everyday word) a container used for holding something

reception *noun* (*plural* **receptions**) **1** the sort of welcome that someone gets ▸ *They were given a friendly reception.* **2** a formal party to receive guests ▸ *We are going to a wedding reception.* **3** a place in a hotel or office where visitors report or check in

receptionist *noun* (*plural* **receptionists**) someone in an office or hotel who deals with visitors and answers the telephone

recession *noun* (*plural* **recessions**) a time when a country is not trading well and a lot of people can't find jobs

recipe *noun* (*plural* **recipes**) (*pronounced* **ress**-i-pi) a set of instructions for preparing or cooking food

recital *noun* (*plural* **recitals**) (*pronounced* ri-**sy**-tal) a performance of music by a small number of players

recite *verb* (**recites, reciting, recited**) to say something such as a poem aloud

reckless *adjective* doing things without thinking or caring about what might happen **recklessly** *adverb* **recklessness** *noun*

reckon *verb* (**reckons, reckoning, reckoned**) **1** to think something or have an opinion about it ▸ *I reckon it's going to snow.* **2** to calculate something

reclaim *verb* (**reclaims, reclaiming, reclaimed**) **1** to make land usable again **2** to get something back by claiming it **reclamation** *noun* reclaiming land

recline *verb* (**reclines, reclining, reclined**) to lean or lie back

recognize *verb* (**recognizes, recognizing, recognized**) **1** to know who someone is or what something is because you have seen them before **2** to admit a fault or mistake ▸ *We recognize that we may have acted* *unfairly.* **recognition** *noun* recognizing someone or something **recognizable** *adjective* able to be recognized

recoil *verb* (**recoils, recoiling, recoiled**) to move backwards suddenly ▸ *He recoiled in fear.*

recollect *verb* (**recollects, recollecting, recollected**) to remember something **recollection** *noun* a memory of something

recommend *verb* (**recommends, recommending, recommended**) to suggest someone or something because you think they are good or suitable ▸ *I recommend that you wear your boots.* **recommendation** *noun*

reconcile *verb* (**reconciles, reconciling, reconciled**) to make people or countries friendly again after they have quarrelled **reconciliation** *noun* becoming friendly again

reconsider *verb* (**reconsiders, reconsidering, reconsidered**) to think again about something and perhaps change your mind

reconstruction *noun* (*plural* **reconstructions**) 1 building something up again 2 acting out an event that took place in the past ▸ *The police organized a reconstruction of the bank robbery.*

record *verb* (**records, recording, recorded**) (*pronounced* ri-kord) 1 to put sounds or pictures on tape or a disc so they can be heard or seen again 2 to put something down in writing

record *noun* (*plural* **records**) (*pronounced* rek-ord) 1 a disc with recorded sound on it 2 the best performance in a sport or some other activity ▸ *She has broken the world long-jump record.* 3 a set of information or facts about something or someone

recorder *noun* (*plural* **recorders**) 1 a musical instrument played by blowing into one end and covering holes with your fingers 2 a tape recorder

recording *noun* (*plural* **recordings**) sound or pictures on a record or tape

record player *noun* (*plural* **record players**) a machine for playing records

recover *verb* (**recovers, recovering, recovered**) 1 to get better after being ill 2 to get something back after losing it **recovery** *noun* getting better, or getting something back

recreation *noun* (*plural* **recreations**) something you do for fun or enjoyment

recruit *noun* (*plural* **recruits**) someone who has just joined the armed forces or a business or club

recruit *verb* (**recruits, recruiting, recruited**) to bring someone in as a recruit

rectangle *noun* (*plural* **rectangles**) a shape with four straight sides and four right angles **rectangular** *adjective*

rectify *verb* (**rectifies, rectifying, rectified**) to put something right

recuperate *verb* (**recuperates, recuperating, recuperated**) to get better after an illness **recuperation** *noun*

recur *verb* (**recurs, recurring, recurred**) to happen again **recurrence** *noun* another time when something happens **recurrent** *adjective* happening over and over again

recycle *verb* (**recycles, recycling, recycled**) to treat used paper or other material so that it can be used again

red *adjective* (**redder, reddest**) having the colour of blood

red *noun* the colour of blood **see red** to become very angry **redness** *noun*

redden *verb* (**reddens, reddening, reddened**) 1 to make something red 2 to become red

red-handed *adjective* in the act of doing something wrong ▸ *We were caught red-handed.*

reduce *verb* (**reduces, reducing, reduced**) 1 to make something smaller or less 2 to be forced to do something ▸ *He was reduced to asking for more money.*

reduction *noun* (*plural* **reductions**) 1 when something gets smaller or fewer ▸ *There has been a reduction in the number of children having school dinners.* 2 an amount by which something is reduced ▸ *They gave us a reduction of £5.*

redundant *adjective* not needed any more to do a particular job **redundancy** *noun* being redundant

reed *noun* (*plural* **reeds**) 1 a plant that grows in or near water 2 a thin strip in a wind instrument such as a clarinet, which vibrates to make the sound

reef *noun* (*plural* **reefs**) a line of rocks just below the surface of the sea

reef knot *noun* (*plural* **reef knots**) a double knot for tying two cords together

reek *verb* (**reeks, reeking, reeked**) to have a strong unpleasant smell

reel *noun* (*plural* **reels**) 1 a round device on which a thread, film, or fishing-line is wound 2 a lively Scottish dance

reel *verb* (**reels, reeling, reeled**) 1 to stagger 2 to feel dizzy

refer *verb* (**refers, referring, referred**) 1 to mention something ▸ *I won't refer to the matter again.* 2 to go to a book or a person for information ▸ *You'll need to refer to an encyclopedia for the answer.* 3 to send someone to an expert for help ▸ *The doctor referred him to an ear specialist.*

referee *noun* (*plural* **referees**) an official in a game who makes sure that the players keep to the rules

referee *verb* (**referees, refereeing, refereed**) to act as the referee in a game

reference *noun* (*plural* **references**) 1 a mention of something 2 a place in a book or file where information can be found 3 a letter or note about how well someone has done a job

reference book *noun* (*plural* **reference books**) a book, such as an encyclopedia or a dictionary, which gives information

referendum *noun* (*plural* **referendums**) (*pronounced* ref-er-en-dum) a vote on an important matter by the people of a country

refill *verb* (**refills, refilling, refilled**) to fill something again

refill *noun* (*plural* **refills**) a replacement for something that has been used up ▸ *My pen needs a refill.*

refine *verb* (**refines, refining, refined**) to purify or improve something

refined *adjective* having good manners **refinement** *noun* elegance and politeness

refinery *noun* (*plural* **refineries**) a factory for refining a product, such as oil or sugar

reflect *verb* (**reflects, reflecting, reflected**) 1 to send back light, heat, or sound from a surface 2 to form an image ▸ *Their faces were reflected in the mirror.* 3 to think seriously about something ▸ *They reflected on what had happened that morning.* **reflection** *noun* an image in a mirror or in water **reflector** *noun* a coloured piece of glass that reflects light

reflex *noun* (*plural* **reflexes**) (*pronounced* ree-fleks) a movement or action you make without thinking about it

reform *verb* (**reforms, reforming, reformed**) to improve something by changing it

reform *noun* (*plural* **reforms**) 1 changing something to improve it 2 a change in a system or law **reformer** *noun* someone who tries to change a system

refrain *verb* (**refrains, refraining, refrained**) (not an everyday word) to keep yourself from doing something ▸ *Please refrain from eating in the library.*

refrain *noun* (*plural* **refrains**) the chorus of a song

refresh *verb* (**refreshes, refreshing, refreshed**) to make someone feel fresher or less tired

refreshments *plural noun* food and drink

refrigerator *noun* (*plural* **refrigerators**) a cabinet for keeping food at a low temperature

refuel *verb* (**refuels, refuelling, refuelled**) to supply a ship or aircraft with more fuel

refuge *noun* (*plural* **refuges**) a place where someone goes to escape danger

refugee *noun* (*plural* **refugees**) (*pronounced* ref-yoo-jee) someone who has had to leave their home or country because of a war or other disaster

refund *verb* (**refunds, refunding, refunded**) (*pronounced* ri-**fund**) to pay back money

refund *noun* (*plural* **refunds**) (*pronounced* **ree**-fund) money someone pays back to you

refuse *verb* (**refuses, refusing, refused**) (*pronounced* ri-**fewz**) to say that you will not do something ▸ *They refuse to help.* **refusal** *noun*

refuse *noun* (*pronounced* **ref**-yooss) rubbish or waste material

regain *verb* (**regains, regaining, regained**) to get something back

regal *adjective* royal **regally** *adverb*

regard *verb* (**regards, regarding, regarded**) 1 to think of someone or something in a certain way ▸ *I regard her as a friend.* 2 to look hard at someone or something ▸ *The policeman regarded us closely.*

regarding *preposition* to do with ▸ *The notice has rules regarding use of the library.*

regardless *adjective* and *adverb* without caring about something ▸ *Buy it, regardless of the cost.* ▸ *We asked her to stop, but she carried on regardless.*

regards *plural noun* kind wishes sent in a message

regatta *noun* (*plural* **regattas**) (*pronounced* ri-**gat**-a) a meeting for boat or yacht races

regent *noun* (*plural* **regents**) (*pronounced* **ree**-jent) a person who rules a country when the king or queen is too young or is unable to rule

reggae *noun* (*pronounced* **reg**-ay) a West Indian style of music with a strong beat

regiment *noun* (*plural* **regiments**) a large army unit **regimental** *adjective*

region *noun* (*plural* **regions**) a part of a country or of the world **regional** *adjective*

register *noun* (*plural* **registers**) an official list of people's names with information about them, such as when and where they were born

register *verb* (**registers, registering, registered**) 1 to put information on a register or list 2 to show a measurement ▸ *The thermometer registered 25°.* 3 to have a letter or parcel officially recorded for sending with special care **registration** *noun* registering something

regret *verb* (**regrets, regretting, regretted**) to feel sorry or sad about something

regret *noun* (*plural* **regrets**) the feeling of being sorry or sad about something

regretful *adjective* feeling regret

regrettable *adjective* likely to be regretted; unfortunate

regular *adjective* 1 happening often at the right times ▸ *You need regular meals.* 2 normal or correct ▸ *The bus followed its regular route.* **regularity** *noun* being regular **regularly** *adverb*
The word **regular** comes from a Latin word *regula* meaning 'a rule'.

regulate *verb* (**regulates, regulating, regulated**) 1 to control something 2 to adjust a machine so that it works properly

regulation *noun* (*plural* **regulations**) a rule or law

rehearse *verb* (**rehearses, rehearsing, rehearsed**) to practise something before you perform it in public **rehearsal** *noun* a practice for a performance

reign *verb* (**reigns, reigning, reigned**) (*pronounced like* rain) to rule as a king or queen

reign *noun* (*plural* **reigns**) the time when someone is king or queen

rein *noun* (*plural* **reins**) a strap used by a rider to guide a horse

reindeer *noun* (*plural* **reindeer**) a kind of deer that lives in Arctic regions

reinforce *verb* (**reinforces, reinforcing, reinforced**) to strengthen something

reinforcements *plural noun* extra troops sent to strengthen a military force

reject *verb* (**rejects, rejecting, rejected**) (*pronounced* ri-**jekt**) **1** to refuse to accept something or someone ▸ *They rejected our offer of help.* **2** to get rid of something **rejection** *noun* being rejected

rejoice *verb* (**rejoices, rejoicing, rejoiced**) to be very happy or pleased

relate *verb* (**relates, relating, related**) **1** to compare or connect one thing with another **2** to tell a story

related *adjective* belonging to the same family ▸ *John and Nancy are related.*

relation *noun* (*plural* **relations**) someone who belongs to the same family as you

relationship *noun* (*plural* **relationships**) **1** the way people or things are connected with each other **2** the way people get on with one another ▸ *Emily has a good relationship with her sister.*

relative *noun* (*plural* **relatives**) someone who is related to you

relative *adjective* compared with something else ▸ *They live in relative comfort.* **relatively** *adverb*

relax *verb* (**relaxes, relaxing, relaxed**) **1** to become less anxious or worried **2** to rest or stop working **3** to make a part of your body less stiff or tense ▸ *Try to relax your arm.* **relaxation** *noun*

relay *verb* (**relays, relaying, relayed**) to receive a message and pass it on

relay *noun* (*plural* **relays**) a fresh group taking the place of another ▸ *The firemen worked in relays.*

relay race *noun* (*plural* **relay races**) a race between two teams in which each competitor covers part of the distance

release *verb* (**releases, releasing, released**) **1** to set a person or animal free **2** to let something go **3** to make a film or record available to the public

release *noun* (*plural* **releases**) **1** the act of releasing a person or animal **2** a new film or record

relegate *verb* (**relegates, relegating, relegated**) **1** to put something into a lower group or position than before **2** to put a sports team into a lower division of a league **relegation** *noun*

relent *verb* (**relents, relenting, relented**) to be less angry or severe than you were going to be

relentless *adjective* going on in an unpleasant way ▸ *They faced relentless criticism.* **relentlessly** *adverb*

relevant *adjective* connected with what is being discussed or dealt with **relevance** *noun* how relevant something is

reliable *adjective* able to be relied on; trustworthy **reliability** *noun* how reliable something is **reliably** *adverb*

relic *noun* (*plural* **relics**) something that has survived from an ancient time

relief *noun* (*plural* **reliefs**) **1** the ending or lessening of suffering or worry ▸ *It was a relief to reach home.* **2** help for people in need ▸ *famine relief*

relief map *noun* (*plural* **relief maps**) a map that uses shading to show hills and valleys

relieve *verb* (**relieves, relieving, relieved**) to end or lessen suffering or worry ▸ *The medicine started to relieve his pain.*

religion *noun* (*plural* **religions**) the worship of God or gods, and what people believe about them **religious** *adjective* to do with religion, or believing in a religion

relieved *adjective* happy and thankful because you no longer have to worry about something

relish *verb* (**relishes, relishing, relished**) to enjoy something very much

reluctant *adjective* not wanting to do something **reluctance** *noun* **reluctantly** *adverb*

rely *verb* (**relies, relying, relied**) rely on to trust someone or something and need them to help you

remain *verb* (**remains, remaining, remained**) 1 to continue in the same way or the same place ▸ *Your mother will have to remain in hospital for a few more days.* 2 to be left over ▸ *A lot of food remained after the party.*

remainder *noun* (*plural* **remainders**) something that remains or is left over

remains *plural noun* 1 something left over 2 ruins or relics 3 a dead body

remark *verb* (**remarks, remarking, remarked**) to say something that you have thought or noticed
remark *noun* (*plural* **remarks**) something you say

remarkable *adjective* so good or interesting that you notice or remember it **remarkably** *adverb*

remedy *noun* (*plural* **remedies**) a cure for an illness or for something wrong

remember *verb* (**remembers, remembering, remembered**) to keep something in your mind, or bring it into your mind when you need to **remembrance** *noun* remembering something or someone

remind *verb* (**reminds, reminding, reminded**) to help or make someone remember something **reminder** *noun*

remnant *noun* (*plural* **remnants**) a small piece or amount left over

remorse *noun* deep regret that you feel when you have done something wrong **remorseful** *adjective*

remote *adjective* (**remoter, remotest**) far away **remotely** *adverb*

remote control *noun* (*plural* **remote controls**) 1 controlling a device from a distance using radio or electricity 2 a device you use for this

remove *verb* (**removes, removing, removed**) 1 to take something or someone away 2 to take something off ▸ *Please remove your shoes before going in.* **removal** *noun*

render *verb* (**renders, rendering, rendered**) (not an everyday word) 1 to leave someone or something in a particular state ▸ *The illness rendered him unfit for work.* 2 to provide help or a service

rendezvous *noun* (*plural* **rendezvous**) (*pronounced* **ron-day-voo**) an arrangement to meet someone

renew *verb* (**renews, renewing, renewed**) 1 to make something as it was before or replace it with something new 2 to have something made valid for a further period ▸ *I must renew my passport before next summer.* **renewal** *noun*

renewable *adjective* able to be renewed or replaced; never completely used up ▸ *Wind is a renewable source of energy.*

renounce *verb* (**renounces, renouncing, renounced**) to say you are giving something up

renovate *verb* (**renovates, renovating, renovated**) to make something like new again ▸ *The new owners of the big house are planning to renovate it.*

renowned *adjective* famous

rent *noun* (*plural* **rents**) a regular payment for using a house or part of a house that someone else owns
rent *verb* (**rents, renting, rented**) to pay money to use something

rental *noun* money you pay as rent

repair *verb* (**repairs, repairing, repaired**) to mend something
repair *noun* (*plural* **repairs**) something you do to mend something that is broken, torn, or damaged ▸ *The car is in for repair.* in good repair in good condition

repay *verb* (**repays, repaying, repaid**) to pay something back **repayment** *noun*

repeat *verb* (**repeats, repeating, repeated**) to say or do something again
repeat *noun* (*plural* **repeats**) something that is repeated

repeatedly *adverb* several times

repel *verb* (**repels, repelling, repelled**) 1 to drive or force someone or something away 2 to make someone feel disgusted **repellent** *adjective* disgusting

repent *verb* (**repents, repenting, repented**) to be sorry for what you have done **repentance** *noun* **repentant** *adjective*

repetition *noun* (*plural* **repetitions**) happening again or doing something again

repetitive *adjective* happening or being done too many times

replace *verb* (**replaces, replacing, replaced**) **1** to put something back in its place **2** to take the place of someone or something **3** to provide a new thing in the place of something ▶ *I promise I'll replace the book I lost.* **replacement** *noun*

replay *noun* (*plural* **replays**) **1** a game played again after a draw **2** the playing or showing again of a recording

replica *noun* (*plural* **replicas**) an exact copy of something

reply *noun* (*plural* **replies**) an answer
reply *verb* (**replies, replying, replied**) to give an answer

report *verb* (**reports, reporting, reported**) **1** to describe something that has happened **2** to complain about someone to a person in authority **3** to tell someone you have arrived or are available ▶ *When you arrive, report to the reception desk.*
report *noun* (*plural* **reports**) **1** a description or account of something **2** an explosive sound

reporter *noun* (*plural* **reporters**) someone who writes news articles for a newspaper or reports on the news for radio or television

represent *verb* (**represents, representing, represented**) **1** to stand for something or someone ▶ *The dotted lines represent state boundaries.* **2** to act or speak on behalf of other people ▶ *Tina was chosen to represent her school in the competition.* **representation** *noun*

representative *noun* a person who acts or speaks for other people

reprieve *verb* (**reprieves, reprieving, reprieved**) to cancel or postpone someone's punishment

reprieve *noun* (*plural* **reprieves**) cancelling or putting off a punishment

reprimand *verb* (**reprimands, reprimanding, reprimanded**) to scold someone or tell them off

reprisal *noun* (*plural* **reprisals**) an act of revenge

reproach *verb* (**reproaches, reproaching, reproached**) to tell someone that they have done something wrong, in a way that shows how sad or disappointed you are

reproduce *verb* (**reproduces, reproducing, reproduced**) **1** to cause something to be heard or seen again ▶ *CDs can reproduce sound.* **2** to make a copy of something **3** to have offspring **reproduction** *noun* reproducing something; a copy of something

reptile *noun* (*plural* **reptiles**) an animal with scaly skin and often with short legs or no legs at all, for example a snake, lizard or tortoise

republic *noun* (*plural* **republics**) a country that is governed by an elected president and does not have a king or queen

repulsive *adjective* disgusting; revolting

reputation *noun* (*plural* **reputations**) what people think about a person or thing ▶ *The local garage has a reputation for reliability.*

request *verb* (**requests, requesting, requested**) to ask politely or formally for something
request *noun* (*plural* **requests**) what you ask someone

require *verb* (**requires, requiring, required**) **1** to need or want something **2** to make someone do something ▶ *Pedestrians are required to walk on the pavements.* **requirement** *noun* something that you need

rescue *verb* (**rescues, rescuing, rescued**) to save someone from danger or capture
rescue *noun* (*plural* **rescues**) the action of rescuing someone **rescuer** *noun*

research *noun* careful study of a subject to get more information about it **researcher** *noun*

resemblance *noun* (*plural* **resemblances**) being similar ► *There is a strong resemblance between Kirsty and her sister.*

resemble *verb* (**resembles, resembling, resembled**) to look or sound like something or someone else

resent *verb* (**resents, resenting, resented**) to feel angry about something that you think is unfair **resentful** *adjective* **resentment** *noun*

reservation *noun* (*plural* **reservations**) 1 reserving something 2 something that has been reserved 3 an area of land kept for a special purpose 4 a doubt or feeling of unease ► *I had reservations about the excuses he made.*

reserve *verb* (**reserves, reserving, reserved**) to keep something or ask for it to be kept so that you can use it later

reserve *noun* (*plural* **reserves**) 1 a person or thing kept ready to be used if necessary 2 an area of land kept for a special purpose ► *a nature reserve*

reserved *adjective* shy and not wanting to say much

reservoir *noun* (*plural* **reservoirs**) (*pronounced* **rez-er-vwar**) an artificial lake where water is stored

reside *verb* (**resides, residing, resided**) (not an everyday word) to live in a place

residence *noun* (*plural* **residences**) (*pronounced* **rez-id-ens**) a place where someone lives, especially when it is large or grand

resident *noun* (*plural* **residents**) someone who lives in a particular place

resign *verb* (**resigns, resigning, resigned**) to give up your job or position **resign yourself** to accept something although you are not happy about it ► *In the end we resigned ourselves to staying at home.* **resignation** *noun* saying that you are giving up your job

resin *noun* (*plural* **resins**) (*pronounced* **rez-in**) a sticky substance that comes from plants or is made artificially

resist *verb* (**resists, resisting, resisted**) 1 to oppose someone or something and try to stop them 2 to stop yourself doing something ► *I can't resist telling her what happened.* **resistance** *noun*

resolute *adjective* (*pronounced* **rez-o-loot**) with your mind made up; determined or firm **resolutely** *adverb* in a resolute way

resolution *noun* (*plural* **resolutions**) something that you have made up your mind to do

resolve *verb* (**resolves, resolving, resolved**) 1 to decide firmly to do something ► *We resolved to do better next time.* 2 to overcome a difficulty ► *The problem was not an easy one to resolve.*

resort *noun* (*plural* **resorts**) a place where people like to go on holiday **the last resort** the only thing you can do when everything else has failed

resort *verb* (**resorts, resorting, resorted**) **resort to** to do something because it is the only way to get what you want ► *Jill was afraid they might resort to cheating.*

resound *verb* (**resounds, resounding, resounded**) (*pronounced* ri-**zownd**) to echo or fill a place with sound

resources *plural noun* things that people need and can use ► *The land is rich in natural resources.*

respect *noun* (*plural* **respects**) 1 a good opinion of someone's qualities or achievements 2 serious consideration or concern ► *Have respect for people's feelings.* 3 a particular detail or aspect ► *In some respects, he is like his sister.*

respect *verb* (**respects, respecting, respected**) 1 to have a good opinion of someone ► *I respect her for her honesty.* 2 to treat something with consideration ► *They will try to respect our wishes.*

respectable *adjective* 1 having good manners and character 2 of a good size or standard ► *Neil got respectable marks in the exam.* **respectability** *noun* being respectable **respectably** *adverb*

respectful *adjective* showing respect; polite **respectfully** *adverb*

respectively *adverb* in the same order as the people or things already mentioned ► *Thomas and his mother are 10 and 35 respectively.*

respiration *noun* the action of breathing **respiratory** *adjective* to do with breathing

respond *verb* (**responds, responding, responded**) to reply or react to someone or something

response *noun* (*plural* **responses**) a reply or reaction

responsible *adjective* **1** having the duty to do something and likely to take the blame if anything goes wrong ► *She is responsible for locking up at night.* **2** causing something ► *His carelessness was responsible for their deaths.* **3** able to be trusted ► *We need a responsible babysitter.* **4** important and needing trust ► *She has a responsible job.* **responsibility** *noun* being responsible, or something that you are responsible for **responsibly** *adverb*

rest¹ *noun* (*plural* **rests**) **1** a time when you can sleep or relax **2** a support for something ► *a book-rest* **the rest** what is left; the others

rest *verb* (**rests, resting, rested**) **1** to sleep or relax **2** to lean on or against something ► *The ladder is resting against the wall.* **3** to place something so that it is leaning or supported ► *Rest the ladder on the roof.*

restaurant *noun* (*plural* **restaurants**) a place where you can buy a meal and eat it

restless *adjective* unable to rest or keep still **restlessly** *adverb* **restlessness** *noun*

restore *verb* (**restores, restoring, restored**) to put something back as it was or make it new again **restoration** *noun* restoring something

restrain *verb* (**restrains, restraining, restrained**) to hold someone or something or keep them tightly controlled **restraint** *noun* keeping someone or something controlled; something that controls what you can do

restrict *verb* (**restricts, restricting, restricted**) to keep someone or something within certain limits ► *After the accident*

his life became restricted to sitting in a wheelchair. **restriction** *noun* something that restricts you

result *noun* (*plural* **results**) **1** a thing that happens because something else has happened **2** the score or situation at the end of a game, competition, or race **3** the answer to a calculation

result *verb* (**results, resulting, resulted**) to happen because something else has happened **result in** to have something as a result ► *The election resulted in a new government.*

resume *verb* (**resumes, resuming, resumed**) to start again after stopping

resurrection *noun* coming back to life after being dead

retail *verb* (**retails, retailing, retailed**) to sell goods to people in ordinary shops **retail** *noun* the business of retailing

retain *verb* (**retains, retaining, retained**) (not an everyday word) **1** to keep something ► *Retain your tickets for inspection.* **2** to hold something in position

retaliate *verb* (**retaliates, retaliating, retaliated**) to do harm to someone in return for harm they have done to you

retina *noun* (*plural* **retinas**) (*pronounced* ret-i-na) the part at the back of your eyeball that receives light signals and sends information about them to your brain

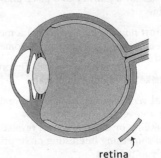

retina

retire *verb* (**retires, retiring, retired**) **1** to give up regular work when you reach a certain age ► *Frank is 64 and will retire next year.* **2** to go somewhere quiet ► *I'll retire to my room now.* **retirement** *noun*

retiring *adjective* shy; avoiding company

retort *verb* (**retorts, retorting, retorted**) to reply quickly or angrily

retrace *verb* (**retraces, retracing, retraced**) to go back over something ▸ *Daisy retraced her steps to look for her lost coin.*

retreat *verb* (**retreats, retreating, retreated**) to move back when you are attacked or defeated

retreat *noun* (*plural* **retreats**) 1 moving back 2 a safe or quiet place to go to

retrieve *verb* (**retrieves, retrieving, retrieved**) to get something back or find it again ▸ *Before he could leave James had to retrieve his coat.* **retrieval** *noun*

retriever *noun* (*plural* **retrievers**) a large dog used by people shooting to bring back dead birds

return *verb* (**returns, returning, returned**) 1 to come or go back to a place 2 to give or send something back

return *noun* (*plural* **returns**) the act of returning something ▸ *I'm waiting for the return of my book.*

return match *noun* (*plural* **return matches**) a second match between two teams who have recently played each other

return ticket *noun* (*plural* **return tickets**) a ticket for a journey to a place and back again

reunion *noun* (*plural* **reunions**) a meeting of people who have not met for some time

rev *verb* (**revs, revving, revved**) (informal) to make an engine run quickly

reveal *verb* (**reveals, revealing, revealed**) (not an everyday word) to show something or make it known **revelation** *noun* something interesting or surprising that you find out

revel *verb* (**revels, revelling, revelled**) to have a merry or lively time **revelry** *noun* enjoyment or celebration

revenge *noun* the act of harming someone because they have done harm to you

revenue *noun* (*plural* **revenues**) (*pronounced* rev-e-nyoo) income that a government gets from taxes

revere *verb* (**reveres, revering, revered**) (*pronounced* ri-veer) to respect someone or something deeply or religiously

Reverend *noun* the title of a member of the clergy ▸ *This is the Reverend John Smith.*

reverent *adjective* feeling or showing awe or respect **reverence** *noun* a feeling of awe and respect **reverently** *adverb*

reverse *noun* 1 the opposite ▸ *They seem to do the reverse of what I say.* 2 the back of something, such as a picture or a coin 3 a gear used to drive a vehicle backwards in **reverse** going in the opposite direction

reverse *verb* (**reverses, reversing, reversed**) 1 to turn something round 2 to go backwards in a vehicle 3 to change or cancel a decision **reversal** *noun* **reversible** *adjective*

review *noun* (*plural* **reviews**) 1 an inspection or survey 2 a published report about a book, film, play, or concert

review *verb* (**reviews, reviewing, reviewed**) 1 to inspect or survey something 2 to write a review about a book, film, play, or concert **reviewer** *noun* someone who writes a review

revise *verb* (**revises, revising, revised**) 1 to study work that you have already done 2 to correct or change something **revision** *noun* revising work; a change or correction

revive *verb* (**revives, reviving, revived**) 1 to start using or doing something again ▸ *The village wants to revive its traditional pancake race.* 2 to become conscious again after fainting 3 to make someone conscious again or give them energy ▸ *A hot meal will revive us.* **revival** *noun*

revolt *verb* (**revolts, revolting, revolted**) 1 to rebel ▸ *People in the cities began to revolt against the government.* 2 to disgust or horrify someone ▸ *All the bloodshed revolted them.*

revolt *noun* (*plural* **revolts**) a rebellion

revolting *adjective* horrid and disgusting

revolution *noun* (*plural* **revolutions**)
1 a rebellion to get rid of the government of a country 2 a complete change 3 one turn of a wheel or engine

revolutionary *adjective* 1 completely new or original 2 to do with a revolution

revolutionize *verb* (**revolutionizes, revolutionizing, revolutionized**) to change something completely

revolve *verb* (**revolves, revolving, revolved**) to turn round in a circle

revolver *noun* (*plural* **revolvers**) a small gun with a revolving cylinder that holds the bullets

reward *noun* (*plural* **rewards**) a gift given to someone in return for something good they have done

reward *verb* (**rewards, rewarding, rewarded**) to give someone a reward

rewarding *adjective* satisfying and worth doing

rewrite *verb* (**rewrites, rewriting, rewrote, rewritten**) to write something again or in a different way

rheumatism *noun* (*pronounced* **roo-ma-tizm**) a disease that causes pain and stiffness in your joints

rhinoceros *noun* (*plural* **rhinoceroses** or **rhinoceros**) (*pronounced* ry-**noss**-er-os) a large heavy animal with a thick skin and a horn or two horns on its nose

rhombus *noun* (*plural* **rhombuses**) a shape with four equal sides and no right angles, like a diamond on a playing card

rhubarb *noun* a plant with pink or green stalks that you can cook and eat

rhyme *noun* (*plural* **rhymes**) 1 similar sounds in the endings of words, as in *house* and *mouse, battle* and *cattle* 2 a short rhyming poem

rhyme *verb* (**rhymes, rhyming, rhymed**) 1 to form a rhyme with another word ▸ *House rhymes with mouse.* 2 (used about a poem) to have rhymes at the ends of lines

rhythm *noun* (*plural* **rhythms**) (*pronounced* rithm) a regular pattern of beats, sounds, or movements in music and poetry **rhythmic** *adjective* or **rhythmical** *adjective* having a regular pattern or beat **rhythmically** *adverb*

rib *noun* (*plural* **ribs**) one of the curved bones in your chest

ribbon *noun* (*plural* **ribbons**) a strip of soft material, used for tying things or for decoration

rice *noun* white seeds from a cereal plant, which you can cook and eat

rich *adjective* (**richer, richest**) 1 having a lot of money or possessions 2 full of goodness, quality, or strength ▸ *fruit that is rich in vitamins* 3 costly or luxurious ▸ *The house has rich furnishings.* **richness** *noun*

riches *plural noun* wealth

richly *adverb* 1 in a rich or luxurious way ▸ *The hall was richly decorated.* 2 thoroughly, completely ▸ *The punishments were richly deserved.*

rickety *adjective* unsteady; likely to break or fall down

rickshaw *noun* (*plural* **rickshaws**) a two-wheeled carriage pulled by one or more people, used in some Asian countries
The word **rickshaw** is from Japanese, and is a shorter form of *jinriksha* which means 'person-power vehicle'.

ricochet *verb* (**ricochets, ricocheting, ricocheted**) (*pronounced* rik-o-shay) to hit something hard and bounce sharply off it

rid *verb* (**rids, ridding, rid**) to free a person or place of something unwanted ▸ *We have to rid the house of mice.* **get rid of** to make something or someone go away

riddance *noun* **good riddance** used to show that you are glad that something or someone has gone

riddle *noun* (*plural* **riddles**) a puzzling question with a clever answer

ride *verb* (**rides, riding, rode, ridden**) **1** to sit on a horse or bicycle and be carried along on it **2** to travel in a car **rider** *noun* someone riding a horse or a bicycle

ride *noun* (*plural* **rides**) a journey on a horse or bicycle, or in a car

ridge *noun* (*plural* **ridges**) a long narrow part at the top of something with sloping sides, such as a hill or a mountain

ridicule *verb* (**ridicules, ridiculing, ridiculed**) to make fun of someone or something

ridiculous *adjective* extremely silly or absurd **ridiculously** *adverb*

rifle *noun* (*plural* **rifles**) a long gun that you hold against your shoulder when you fire it

rift *noun* (*plural* **rifts**) **1** a crack or split **2** a disagreement between friends

rig *verb* (**rigs, rigging, rigged**) to provide a ship with rigging, sails, and other equipment **rig up** to make something quickly

rig *noun* (*plural* **rigs**) a large framework used in engineering, for example an oil rig

rigging *noun* the ropes that support a ship's masts and sails

right *adjective* **1** on the side that faces east if you think of yourself as facing north **2** correct ▸ *Is the answer right?* **3** fair or honest ▸ *It's not right to cheat.* **rightly** *adverb*

right *adverb* **1** on or towards the right ▸ *Turn right.* **2** completely ▸ *Move right round.* **3** exactly ▸ *She stood right in the middle.* **4** straight; directly ▸ *Go right ahead.* **right away** immediately

right *noun* (*plural* **rights**) **1** the right side **2** what is fair or just, or what you are allowed to do ▸ *You have the right to vote when you are 18.* ▸ *He had no right to talk to you like that.*

right *verb* (**rights, righting, righted**) to make something right again ▸ *The fault might right itself.*

right angle *noun* (*plural* **right angles**) an angle of 90 degrees, like angles in a rectangle

rightful *adjective* deserved or proper ▸ *Give the money back to its rightful owner.*

right-handed *adjective* using your right hand more than your left hand

rights *plural noun* the freedom and benefits that people should have

rigid *adjective* (*pronounced* rij-id) **1** firm or stiff **2** strict or harsh ▸ *rigid rules* **rigidity** *noun* how rigid something is **rigidly** *adverb*

rim *noun* (*plural* **rims**) the outer edge of a cup or wheel or other round object

rind *noun* (*plural* **rinds**) (*rhymes with* kind) the tough skin on bacon, cheese, or some types of fruit

ring¹ *noun* (*plural* **rings**) **1** a circle **2** a thin circular piece of metal worn on a finger **3** the space where a circus performs **4** the place where a boxing match or other contest is held

ring *verb* (**rings, ringing, ringed**) to put a ring round something ▸ *Please ring the correct answer.*

ring² *verb* (**rings, ringing, rang, rung**) **1** to strike or shake a bell so that it makes a sound **2** to make a clear musical sound like a bell **3** to telephone someone

ring *noun* (*plural* **rings**) **1** a ringing sound like a bell **2** a call on the telephone ▸ *Give me a ring later.*

ringleader *noun* (*plural* **ringleaders**) someone who leads a group of people in doing wrong

ringlet *noun* (*plural* **ringlets**) a long curled piece of hair

ring road *noun* (*plural* **ring roads**) a road that take traffic round a town

rink *noun* (*plural* **rinks**) a hard area for roller-skating, or an area of ice for ice-skating

rinse *verb* (**rinses, rinsing, rinsed**) to wash something in clean water without soap

riot *noun* (*plural* **riots**) a wild or violent protest by a crowd of people

riot *verb* (**riots, rioting, rioted**) to run wild and behave violently **riotous** *adjective* noisy or out of control

rip *verb* (**rips, ripping, ripped**) to tear something roughly **rip off** (slang) to cheat someone or charge them too much

rip *noun* (*plural* **rips**) a torn place

ripe *adjective* (**riper, ripest**) (describing fruit or crops) ready to be harvested or eaten **ripeness** *noun*

ripen *verb* (**ripens, ripening, ripened**) to become ripe, or to make something ripe ▶ *Leave the pears by the window to ripen.*

ripple *noun* (*plural* **ripples**) a small wave on the surface of water

ripple *verb* (**ripples, rippling, rippled**) to form small waves

rise *verb* (**rises, rising, rose, risen**) 1 to go upwards ▶ *Smoke was rising from the fire.* 2 to get larger or more ▶ *Prices have risen again this year.* 3 to get up from sleeping or sitting

rise *noun* (*plural* **rises**) 1 an increase, especially in prices or wages 2 an upward slope

risk *verb* (**risks, risking, risked**) to take a chance of damaging or losing something ▶ *They risked their lives during the rescue.*

risk *noun* (*plural* **risks**) a chance of danger or loss **risky** *adjective* dangerous, or uncertain

rite *noun* (*plural* **rites**) a ceremony or ritual

ritual *noun* (*plural* **rituals**) a ceremony or series of actions carried out at a special time

rival *noun* (*plural* **rivals**) someone who does the same thing as someone else and competes with them **rivalry** *noun* competition between people

rival *verb* (**rivals, rivalling, rivalled**) to be a rival of someone
The word **rival** comes from a Latin word for someone who shared the same river (for water) as someone else and was therefore their 'rival'.

river *noun* (*plural* **rivers**) a large natural stream of water that flows into the sea or into a lake

road *noun* (*plural* **roads**) a level way with a hard surface made for traffic to go along

roam *verb* (**roams, roaming, roamed**) to wander about

roar *verb* (**roars, roaring, roared**) to make a loud deep sound of the kind that a lion makes

roar *noun* (*plural* **roars**) a roaring sound

roast *verb* (**roasts, roasting, roasted**) to cook food in an oven or over a fire

rob *verb* (**robs, robbing, robbed**) to steal something from someone or from a place ▶ *He robbed me of my watch.* ▶ *They are going to rob the local shop.* **robber** *noun* **robbery** *noun*

robe *noun* (*plural* **robes**) a long loose piece of clothing

robin *noun* (*plural* **robins**) a small bird with a red breast

robot *noun* (*plural* **robots**) a machine that can move and do things like a person

robust *adjective* tough and strong

rock *noun* (*plural* **rocks**) 1 a large stone, or a mass of stone 2 a hard sweet in the form of a stick 3 a type of music with a heavy beat

rock *verb* (**rocks, rocking, rocked**) 1 to move gently backwards and forwards or from side to side 2 to make something rock

rockery *noun* (*plural* **rockeries**) a part of a garden where flowers grow between large stones

rocket *noun* (*plural* **rockets**) 1 a firework that shoots high into the air 2 a pointed tube propelled into the air by hot gases and carrying a spacecraft or weapon

rocky *adjective* (**rockier, rockiest**) 1 having a lot of rocks 2 unsteady **rockiness** *noun*

rod *noun* (*plural* **rods**) a long thin stick or bar

rode past tense of **ride** *verb*

rodent *noun* (*plural* **rodents**) an animal that has large front teeth for gnawing things. Rats, mice, and squirrels are rodents.
The word **rodent** comes from a Latin word meaning 'gnawing'.

rodeo *noun* (*plural* **rodeos**) (*pronounced* roh-**day**-oh or **roh**-di-oh) a contest in which cowboys show their skills in riding and in controlling cattle

roe *noun* (*plural* **roes**) a fish's eggs in a lump

rogue *noun* (*plural* **rogues**) a dishonest or mischievous person **roguish** *adjective* mischievous

role *noun* (*plural* **roles**) 1 a performer's part in a play, film, or story 2 the purpose something has ▸ *Computers have a role in language learning.*

roll *verb* (**rolls, rolling, rolled**) 1 to move along by turning over and over, like a ball or wheel 2 to form something into the shape of a cylinder or ball 3 to flatten something soft by moving a round heavy object over it 4 to sway from side to side, as a ship does 5 to make a long rumbling sound, as a drum does

roll *noun* (*plural* **rolls**) 1 a cylinder made by rolling something up 2 a small loaf of bread shaped like a bun 3 a list of names 4 the rumbling sound of drums or thunder

roller *noun* (*plural* **rollers**) 1 a cylinder-shaped object, especially one that is used for flattening things 2 a small cylinder that you wrap your hair round to make it curl

roller skates *plural noun* a pair of boots with wheels under them, for skating on hard surfaces **roller skating** *noun*

rolling pin *noun* (*plural* **rolling pins**) a heavy cylinder that you roll over pastry to flatten it

Roman Catholic *noun* (*plural* **Roman Catholics**) a member of the Christian Church that has the Pope in Rome as its leader

romance *noun* (*plural* **romances**) 1 the feelings and experiences of people who are in love 2 a love affair or love story

Roman numerals *plural noun* the letters used by the ancient Romans to represent numbers
I = 1, V = 5, X = 10, L = 50, C = 100, D = 500, and M = 1000.

romantic *adjective* to do with love or romance **romantically** *adverb*

romp *verb* (**romps, romping, romped**) to play and jump about in a rough or lively way

roof *noun* (*plural* **roofs**) 1 the part that covers the top of a building or vehicle 2 the upper part of your mouth

rook *noun* (*plural* **rooks**) 1 a large black bird that looks like a crow 2 a piece in chess, also called a *castle*

room *noun* (*plural* **rooms**) 1 a part of a building with its own walls, floor, and ceiling 2 space for someone or something ▸ *Is there room for me?*

roomy *adjective* (**roomier, roomiest**) having plenty of space

roost *noun* (*plural* **roosts**) the place where a bird rests

root *noun* (*plural* **roots**) 1 the part of a plant that grows under the ground 2 the part from which something grows, such as a tooth or a hair 3 the cause or origin of something ▸ *Lack of money is the root of our problem.* 4 a number that gives another number when multiplied by itself ▸ *4 is the square root of 16.* **take root** to grow roots or to become established

root *verb* (**roots, rooting, rooted**) 1 to grow roots in the ground 2 to fix someone firmly ▸ *Fear rooted him to the spot.*

rope *noun* (*plural* **ropes**) a strong thick cord made of strands twisted together **show someone the ropes** to show someone how to do something

rose[1] *noun* (*plural* **roses**) a scented flower with a long thorny stem

rose[2] past tense of **rise** *verb*

rosy *adjective* (**rosier, rosiest**) 1 pink 2 hopeful or cheerful ▸ *The future looks rosy.* **rosiness** *noun*

rot *verb* (**rots, rotting, rotted**) to go soft or bad so that it is useless ▸ *The fruit was beginning to rot.*
rot *noun* decay

rota *noun* (*plural* **rotas**) a list of tasks to be done and the people who have to do them

rotary *adjective* turning round like a wheel

rotate *verb* (**rotates, rotating, rotated**) 1 to turn round like a wheel 2 to take turns at something **rotation** *noun* a rotating movement or pattern

rotor *noun* (*plural* **rotors**) the large rotating blade on top of a helicopter

rotten *adjective* 1 rotted and not fit for use ▸ *I'll throw away that rotten tomato.* 2 (informal) nasty or very bad ▸ *We had rotten weather.*

rough *adjective* (**rougher, roughest**) 1 not smooth; uneven ▸ *His skin was rough and covered in bristles.* 2 violent; not gentle ▸ *The wind was rough.* 3 not exact; done quickly ▸ *I can make a rough guess.*
roughly *adverb* approximately; not exactly **roughness** *noun*

roughen *verb* (**roughens, roughening, roughened**) 1 to make something rough 2 to become rougher

round *adjective* (**rounder, roundest**) 1 shaped like a circle or ball or cylinder 2 returning to the start ▸ *You will need a week for the round trip.*
round *adverb* 1 in a circle or curve ▸ *The wheel was spinning round.* ▸ *Go round to the back of the house.* 2 in every direction or to every person ▸ *Hand the cakes round.* 3 in a new direction ▸ *Della looked round at us.* 4 to someone's house or place of work ▸ *I'll come round tomorrow.*
round *preposition* 1 on all sides of something ▸ *There is a tall fence round the field.* 2 in a curve or circle about something ▸ *The earth moves round the sun.* 3 to every part of something ▸ *We showed our visitors round the garden.*
round *noun* (*plural* **rounds**) 1 each stage in a competition ▸ *The winners go on to the next round.* 2 a series of visits or calls made by a doctor, postman, or other person 3 a shot or series of shots from a gun; a piece of ammunition 4 a round shape or object ▸ *Cut the pastry into rounds.* 5 a whole slice of bread, or a sandwich made from two whole slices of bread 6 a number of drinks someone buys for several people ▸ *It must be my round.* 7 a song in which people sing the same words but start at different times
round *verb* (**rounds, rounding, rounded**) 1 to make something round 2 to travel round something ▸ *A huge lorry rounded the corner.* **round off** to finish something **round up** to gather people or things together

roundabout *noun* (*plural* **roundabouts**) 1 a road junction at which traffic moves round a circular island 2 a merry-go-round
roundabout *adjective* not using the shortest or most direct way ▸ *We went by a roundabout route.*

rounders *noun* a game in which players try to hit a ball and run round a circuit

roundly *adverb* thoroughly or severely ▸ *We were roundly told off for being late.*

round number *noun* (*plural* **round numbers**) an easy number such as 5, 10, 20, 100, and so on, which is not exact ▸ *We paid £49.99, or in round numbers £50.*

rouse *verb* (**rouses, rousing, roused**) 1 to wake someone up 2 to stir up someone's interest ▸ *The newspaper article roused my curiosity.*

rout *verb* (**routs, routing, routed**) (*pronounced* rowt) to defeat an enemy and chase them away

route *noun* (*plural* **routes**) (*pronounced* root) the way you go to reach a place

routine *noun* (*plural* **routines**) (*pronounced* roo-**teen**) a regular way of doing things

rove *verb* (**roves, roving, roved**) to roam or wander

row[1] *noun* (*plural* **rows**) (*rhymes with* go) a line of people or things

row[2] *verb* (**rows, rowing, rowed**) (*rhymes with* go) to use oars to make a boat move through the water **rower** *noun*

row[3] *noun* (*plural* **rows**) (*rhymes with* cow) 1 a noisy quarrel 2 a loud disturbing noise

rowdy *adjective* (**rowdier, rowdiest**) noisy and rough **rowdiness** *noun*

rowing boat *noun* (*plural* **rowing boats**) a small boat that you move using oars

royal *adjective* to do with a king or queen **royalty** *noun* the members of a royal family

rub *verb* (**rubs, rubbing, rubbed**) to move something backwards and forwards against something else ▸ *He rubbed his hands together.* **rub out** to make something disappear by rubbing it

rubber *noun* (*plural* **rubbers**) 1 a strong elastic substance made from the sap of a special tree or made artificially. Rubber is used for making tyres, balls, hoses, and other things. 2 a piece of rubber or soft plastic for rubbing out pencil marks **rubbery** *adjective* soft and easy to stretch

rubbish *noun* 1 things that are not wanted or needed 2 nonsense

rubble *noun* broken pieces of brick or stone

ruby *noun* (*plural* **rubies**) a red jewel

rucksack *noun* (*plural* **rucksacks**) a bag with straps for carrying on your back

rudder *noun* (*plural* **rudders**) a flat hinged upright part at the back of a ship or aircraft, used for steering it

ruddy *adjective* (**ruddier, ruddiest**) red and healthy-looking

rude *adjective* (**ruder, rudest**) 1 not polite; having bad manners 2 not decent or proper ▸ *Mark was telling us a rude joke.* **rudely** *adverb* **rudeness** *noun* being rude

ruffian *noun* (*plural* **ruffians**) a rough violent person

ruffle *verb* (**ruffles, ruffling, ruffled**) 1 to make something untidy or less smooth ▸ *The bird ruffled its feathers.* 2 to annoy or upset someone ▸ *The bad news had ruffled him.*

rug *noun* (*plural* **rugs**) 1 a thick piece of material that partly covers a floor 2 a thick blanket

Rugby or **Rugby football** *noun* a kind of football game using an oval ball that players may kick or carry and pass to other players
Rugby is named after Rugby School in England, where it was first played.

rugged *adjective* (*pronounced* rug-id) having a rough or uneven surface or outline

ruin *verb* (**ruins, ruining, ruined**) to spoil something or destroy it completely

ruin *noun* (*plural* **ruins**) 1 a building that has almost all fallen down 2 the loss of all your money or hopes ▸ *They were facing financial ruin.* **ruinous** *adjective* leading to ruin

rule *noun* (*plural* **rules**) 1 something that people have to obey 2 ruling or governing ▸ *The country used to be under Spanish rule.* **as a rule** usually; normally

rule *verb* (**rules, ruling, ruled**) 1 to govern a country or people 2 to make a decision ▸ *The judge ruled that the evidence was unreliable.* 3 to draw a straight line with a ruler or other guide

ruler *noun* (*plural* **rulers**) 1 someone who governs 2 a strip of wood, plastic, or metal with straight edges, used for measuring and for drawing lines

ruling *noun* (*plural* **rulings**) a judgement or decision

rum *noun* (*plural* **rums**) a strong alcoholic drink made from sugar cane

rumble *verb* (**rumbles, rumbling, rumbled**) to make a deep heavy sound like thunder

rumble *noun* (*plural* **rumbles**) a rumbling sound

rummage *verb* (**rummages, rummaging, rummaged**) to turn things over or move them about while you are looking for something

rummy *noun* a card game in which players try to make sets of cards

rumour *noun* (*plural* **rumours**) something that a lot of people are saying, although it may not be true

rump *noun* (*plural* **rumps**) the hind part of an animal

rumple *verb* (**rumples, rumpling, rumpled**) to crease or crumple something

run *verb* (**runs, running, ran, run**) 1 to move with quick steps ▸ *We had to run to catch the bus.* 2 to move or go or travel ▸ *Trains run every hour.* 3 to flow, as liquid does ▸ *Water was running from the tap.* 4 to work or function ▸ *The engine was running smoothly.* 5 to organize or manage something ▸ *She runs a corner shop.* 6 to give someone a lift somewhere ▸ *I'll just run you to the station.* **run a risk** to take a chance **run away** to leave a place quickly or secretly **run out of** to have no more left of something **run over** to knock someone down with a car or bicycle

run *noun* (*plural* **runs**) 1 a spell of running ▸ *Nita came back sweating after her run.* 2 a point scored in cricket or baseball 3 a series of damaged stitches in a pair of tights or other piece of clothing 4 a continuous series of events ▸ *We had a run of bad luck.* 5 a place with a fence round it for keeping animals **on the run** running away, especially from the police

runaway *noun* (*plural* **runaways**) someone who has run away

rung[1] *noun* (*plural* **rungs**) each of the short crossbars on a ladder

rung[2] past participle of **ring**[2] *verb*

runner *noun* (*plural* **runners**) 1 a person or animal that runs in a race 2 the part of a sledge that slides along the ground

runner bean *noun* (*plural* **runner beans**) a kind of climbing bean

runner-up *noun* (*plural* **runners-up**) someone who comes second in a race or competition

runny *adjective* (**runnier, runniest**) watery; like liquid **runniness** *noun*

runway *noun* (*plural* **runways**) a long hard strip for aircraft to take off and land

rural *adjective* to do with the countryside; in the country

ruse *noun* (*plural* **ruses**) a cunning scheme or trick

rush[1] *verb* (**rushes, rushing, rushed**) 1 to move or go very quickly ▸ *When the doorbell rang I rushed to see who it was.* ▸ *We had to rush Linda to hospital.* 2 to make someone hurry ▸ *I'm trying not to rush you.* 3 to attack or capture someone by surprise

rush *noun* 1 a hurry ▸ *I can't stop, I'm in a rush.* 2 a time of great activity ▸ *There was a rush to get tickets for the concert.*

rush[2] *noun* (*plural* **rushes**) a plant with a thin stem that grows in wet or marshy places

rush hour *noun* the time of day when traffic is busiest

rusk *noun* (*plural* **rusks**) a kind of hard dry biscuit for babies to chew

rust *noun* a red or brown substance formed on metal when it becomes wet

rust *verb* (**rusts, rusting, rusted**) to become covered in rust

rustic *adjective* to do with the country

rustle *verb* (**rustles, rustling, rustled**) 1 to make a gentle sound like dry leaves being blown by the wind 2 to steal horses or cattle

rusty *adjective* (**rustier, rustiest**) 1 covered with rust 2 weak from lack of practice ▸ *My French is a bit rusty.*

rut *noun* (*plural* **ruts**) a deep groove made by wheels in soft ground **in a rut** having a dull life with no changes

ruthless *adjective* cruel and having no pity **ruthlessly** *adverb* **ruthlessness** *noun*

rye *noun* a cereal used to make bread and biscuits

Ss

sabbath *noun* (*plural* **sabbaths**) the day of the week used for rest and religious worship
The word **sabbath** comes from a Hebrew word *shabat*, meaning 'rest'.

sabotage *noun* (*pronounced* **sab-o-tah***z*h) deliberate damage done to machinery or equipment

sabotage *verb* (**sabotages, sabotaging, sabotaged**) to damage something deliberately

sabre *noun* (*plural* **sabres**) a sword with a curved blade

sachet *noun* (*plural* **sachets**) (*pronounced* **sash**-ay) a small sealed packet of a liquid or a powder, for example shampoo

sack *noun* (*plural* **sacks**) a large bag made of strong material **get the sack** (informal) to be dismissed from a job

sack *verb* (**sacks, sacking, sacked**) (informal) to dismiss someone from their job

sacred *adjective* holy or religious

sacrifice *verb* (**sacrifices, sacrificing, sacrificed**) 1 to kill an animal or make some other offering to please a god 2 to give up something valuable or important so that someone else can have something

sacrifice *noun* (*plural* **sacrifices**) 1 something offered to a god 2 giving up something that you like or value highly **sacrificial** *adjective* to do with a sacrifice

sad *adjective* (**sadder, saddest**) unhappy, or showing sorrow **sadly** *adverb* **sadness** *noun* being sad

sadden *verb* (**saddens, saddening, saddened**) to make someone sad or unhappy

saddle *noun* (*plural* **saddles**) a seat for the rider of a horse or bicycle

saddle *verb* (**saddles, saddling, saddled**) to put a saddle on a horse's back

sadist *noun* (*plural* **sadists**) (*pronounced* **say**-dist) someone who enjoys hurting other people **sadism** *noun* **sadistic** *adjective*

safari *noun* (*plural* **safaris**) (*pronounced* sa-**far**-i) an expedition to see wild animals or hunt them

safari park *noun* (*plural* **safari parks**) a park where wild animals live and roam around. You can drive through the park to see the animals.

safe *adjective* (**safer, safest**) 1 free from danger; protected 2 not causing danger
▸ *It is important to drive at a safe speed.*
safely *adverb*

safe *noun* (*plural* **safes**) a strong cupboard or box in which valuable things can be locked to keep them safe

safeguard *verb* (**safeguards, safeguarding, safeguarded**) to protect something

safety *noun* being safe; protection

safety belt *noun* (*plural* **safety belts**) a belt to hold someone securely in a seat

safety pin *noun* (*plural* **safety pins**) a curved pin with a clip that covers the point when it is closed

sag verb (**sags, sagging, sagged**) to sink in the middle because something heavy is pressing on it

saga noun (plural **sagas**) a long story with many adventures

sage noun a herb used in cooking

said past tense and past participle of **say** verb

sail noun (plural **sails**) 1 a large piece of strong cloth that the wind blows into to make a ship or boat move through the water 2 an arm of a windmill **set sail** to start on a voyage in a ship

sail verb (**sails, sailing, sailed**) 1 to travel in a ship 2 to control a ship or boat 3 to be moved along by a sail or sails ▶ *The boat sails beautifully.*

sailor noun (plural **sailors**) 1 a member of a ship's crew 2 someone who sails

saint noun (plural **saints**) a holy or very good person **saintly** adjective holy, like a saint

sake noun **for the sake of** in order to get something ▶ *He'll do anything for the sake of money.* **for someone's sake** in order to help or please someone ▶ *She went to a lot of trouble for my sake.*

salad noun (plural **salads**) a mixture of cold or raw vegetables

salami noun (plural **salamis**) (pronounced sa-lah-mi) a kind of strong spicy sausage

salary noun (plural **salaries**) an amount of money paid to someone every month for the work they do

sale noun (plural **sales**) 1 the selling of something 2 a time when a shop sells things at reduced prices **for sale** or **on sale** able to be bought

salesperson noun (plural **salespersons** or **salespeople**) someone whose job is to sell things **salesman** noun **saleswoman** noun

saliva noun (pronounced sa-ly-va) the natural liquid that collects in your mouth

salmon noun (plural **salmon**) a large fish with pink flesh, used for food

salon noun (plural **salons**) a shop where a hairdresser works

salt noun a white substance found in sea water, used for flavouring food **salty** adjective tasting of salt

salt verb (**salts, salting, salted**) to use salt in food to flavour or preserve it

salute verb (**salutes, saluting, saluted**) to raise your hand to your forehead as a sign of respect or greeting

salute noun (plural **salutes**) the act of saluting

salvage verb (**salvages, salvaging, salvaged**) to save something damaged, especially a ship, or rescue parts of it

salvation noun saving someone or something

same adjective not different; exactly equal or alike ▶ *We are the same age.* ▶ *He's the same person we saw yesterday.*

samosa noun (plural **samosas**) (pronounced sa-**moh**-za) a case of crisp pastry filled with spicy meat or vegetables

sample noun (plural **samples**) a small amount of something to show what it is like ▶ *We borrowed some carpet samples from the shop.*

sample verb (**samples, sampling, sampled**) 1 to take a sample of something ▶ *Scientists sampled the lake water.* 2 to try a small part of something ▶ *Would you like to sample my cake?*

sanctuary noun (plural **sanctuaries**) a place where people or animals are protected ▶ *There is a bird sanctuary near the lake.*

sand noun tiny pieces of rock on the ground on beaches and in deserts

sandal noun (plural **sandals**) a light open shoe with straps that go round your foot

sandpaper *noun* strong paper coated with hard grains, used to smooth wood or other hard surfaces

sands *plural noun* a beach or sandy area

sandwich *noun* (*plural* **sandwiches**) slices of bread with a filling such as cheese or meat between them

sandy *adjective* (**sandier, sandiest**) covered with sand

sane *adjective* (**saner, sanest**) having a healthy mind; not mad **sanity** *noun* being sane

sang past tense of **sing**

sanitary *adjective* free from germs and dirt; hygienic

sanitary towel *noun* (*plural* **sanitary towels**) a soft pad used by a woman to soak up blood during her period

sanitation *noun* arrangements for drainage and getting rid of sewage

sank past tense of **sink** *verb*

Sanskrit *noun* an ancient language of India

sap *noun* the juice inside a tree or plant

sap *verb* (**saps, sapping, sapped**) to use up someone's strength or energy

sapling *noun* (*plural* **saplings**) a young tree

sapphire *noun* (*plural* **sapphires**) a bright blue jewel

sarcasm *noun* using words that mean the opposite of what they say, to tease or criticize someone ▸ *'Thank you for all your help,' she said with sarcasm when she found them watching television.* **sarcastic** *adjective* **sarcastically** *adverb*

sardine *noun* (*plural* **sardines**) a small sea fish, sold packed tightly in tins

sari *noun* (*plural* **saris**) (*pronounced* **sar**-i) a long length of cotton or silk worn by Indian women

sash *noun* (*plural* **sashes**) a band of cloth worn round the waist or over one shoulder

sat past tense and past participle of **sit**

satchel *noun* (*plural* **satchels**) a bag for school books, with a long strap worn over your shoulder
The word **satchel** comes from a Latin word *sacellus* meaning 'little sack'.

satellite *noun* (*plural* **satellites**) 1 a moon that moves in an orbit round a planet 2 an object sent into space to orbit the earth or another planet

satellite dish *noun* (*plural* **satellite dishes**) an aerial shaped like a dish, for receiving television signals sent by satellite

satin *noun* a silky material that is shiny on one side

satire *noun* (*plural* **satires**) a type of comedy that uses humour or exaggeration to show what is bad or weak about a person or thing, especially the government **satirical** *adjective*

satisfactory *adjective* good enough; sufficient **satisfactorily** *adverb*

satisfy *verb* (**satisfies, satisfying, satisfied**) to give someone what they need or want **be satisfied** to be convinced or sure about something ▸ *We are satisfied that they are telling the truth.* **satisfaction** *noun* a feeling of pleasure when you have what you want

saturate *verb* (**saturates, saturating, saturated**) to soak something with liquid ▸ *My clothes are saturated with rain.* **saturation** *noun* being saturated

Saturday *noun* (*plural* **Saturdays**) the seventh day of the week
Saturday is named after the Roman god Saturn.

sauce *noun* (*plural* **sauces**) a thick liquid served with food to add flavour

saucepan *noun* (*plural* **saucepans**) a metal cooking pan with a long handle and a lid

saucer *noun* (*plural* **saucers**) a small curved plate for resting a cup on

saucy *adjective* (**saucier, sauciest**) rude or cheeky **saucily** *adverb* **sauciness** *noun*

sauna noun (plural **saunas**) (pronounced saw-na) a room filled with steam, used as a kind of bath

saunter verb (**saunters, sauntering, sauntered**) to walk about in a leisurely way

sausage noun (plural **sausages**) a tube of edible skin or plastic stuffed with minced meat

sausage roll noun (plural **sausage rolls**) a short roll of pastry filled with sausage meat

savage adjective 1 wild and fierce 2 cruel or violent ▸ a savage assault **savagely** adverb **savagery** noun cruel or violent behaviour

savage verb (**savages, savaging, savaged**) to attack someone fiercely

savannah noun (plural **savannahs**) (pronounced sa-van-a) a grassy plain in a hot country, with few trees

save verb (**saves, saving, saved**) 1 to free someone or something from danger or harm 2 to keep money or something else so that you can use it later 3 to instruct a computer to keep data on its hard disk 4 in football, to stop the ball going into your goal

savings plural noun money that you save

saviour noun (plural **saviours**) a person who saves someone

savoury adjective tasting spicy or salty rather than sweet

saw¹ noun (plural **saws**) a tool with sharp teeth for cutting wood

saw verb (**saws, sawing, sawed, sawn** or **sawed**) to cut something with a saw

saw² past tense of **see**

sawdust noun powder that comes from wood when you cut it with a saw

saxophone noun (plural **saxophones**) a wind instrument with a tube that curves upward with a wider opening

say verb (**says, saying, said**) 1 to make words with your voice 2 to show information ▸ What does the clock say?

saying noun (plural **sayings**) a well-known phrase or proverb

scab noun (plural **scabs**) a hard covering that forms over a cut or graze while it is healing

scabbard noun (plural **scabbards**) a cover for a sword or dagger

scaffold noun (plural **scaffolds**) a platform on which criminals were executed in the past

scaffolding noun a structure of poles and planks for workers to stand on when they are building a house or repairing it

scald verb (**scalds, scalding, scalded**) to burn your skin with hot liquid or steam

scale¹ noun (plural **scales**) 1 a series of units or marks for measuring something ▸ The ruler has a scale in centimetres. 2 a series of musical notes going up or down in a fixed pattern 3 the size of a map in relation to real life ▸ The map has a scale of one centimetre to the kilometre.

scale verb (**scales, scaling, scaled**) to climb up something tall or upright
This word **scale** comes from a Latin word scala meaning 'ladder'.

scale² noun (plural **scales**) one of the thin overlapping parts on the outside of fish, snakes, and other animals **scaly** adjective

scales plural noun a device for weighing things

scalp noun (plural **scalps**) the skin on top of your head

scalpel noun (plural **scalpels**) a small knife that a surgeon uses

scampi noun large shrimps that you eat

scamper verb (**scampers, scampering, scampered**) to run quickly or playfully

scan verb (**scans, scanning, scanned**) 1 to look at something in detail 2 to look quickly through something in order to find what you want ▸ She scanned the book for a picture of the village. 3 (used about poetry) to have the right rhythm

scandal noun (plural **scandals**) something that people think is disgraceful or shocking **scandalous** adjective disgraceful or shocking

scanner *noun* (*plural* **scanners**)
1 a machine used to examine part of the body, using an electronic beam 2 a machine that converts print and pictures into data that can be read by a computer

scanty *adjective* (**scantier, scantiest**) hardly enough; small **scantily** *adverb* barely; just sufficiently

scapegoat *noun* (*plural* **scapegoats**) someone who is blamed or punished for other people's mistakes

scar *noun* (*plural* **scars**) a mark left on your skin by a cut or burn after it has healed
scar *verb* (**scars, scarring, scarred**) to make a scar on your skin

scarce *adjective* (**scarcer, scarcest**) not enough to supply people ▸ *Fresh fruit was scarce because of the war.* **scarcity** *noun* a shortage

scarcely *adverb* hardly; only just ▸ *She could scarcely walk.*

scare *verb* (**scares, scaring, scared**) to frighten someone
scare *noun* (*plural* **scares**) a fright ▸ *You gave me quite a scare.*

scarecrow *noun* (*plural* **scarecrows**) a figure of a person dressed in old clothes, set up to frighten birds away from crops

scarf *noun* (*plural* **scarves**) a strip of material that you wear round your head or neck

scarlet *adjective* bright red
scarlet *noun* a bright red colour

scary *adjective* (**scarier, scariest**) (*informal*) frightening

scatter *verb* (**scatters, scattering, scattered**) 1 to throw things in all directions 2 to move quickly in different directions ▸ *The crowd scattered when the police arrived.*

scavenge *verb* (**scavenges, scavenging, scavenged**) to look through rubbish to find something useful **scavenger** *noun*

scene *noun* (*plural* **scenes**) 1 the place where something happens ▸ *This is the scene of the incident.* 2 a part of a play or film ▸ *The prince dies in the last scene.* 3 a view you can see ▸ *The house looked out on a rural scene.* 4 an embarrassing show of temper ▸ *They made a scene when they were kept waiting.*

scenery *noun* 1 the natural features of an area ▸ *The local scenery includes hills and woods.* 2 painted panels and other things put on a stage to make it look like a place

scenic *adjective* having beautiful scenery

scent *noun* (*plural* **scents**) (*pronounced* sent) 1 a pleasant smell 2 a liquid that has a pleasant smell 3 the smell of a person or animal, leaving a trail which other animals can follow **scented** *adjective* having a pleasant smell

sceptic *noun* (*plural* **sceptics**) (*pronounced* **skep**-tik) someone who does not believe things easily **sceptical** *adjective* **scepticism** *noun* doubt or suspicion

schedule *noun* (*plural* **schedules**) (*pronounced* **shed**-yool) a timetable of things to be done **on schedule** on time; not late

scheme *noun* (*plural* **schemes**) a plan of what to do
scheme *verb* (**schemes, scheming, schemed**) to make secret plans

scholar *noun* (*plural* **scholars**) 1 someone who studies a subject in detail 2 someone who has been given a scholarship

scholarly *adjective* showing knowledge and learning

scholarship *noun* (*plural* **scholarships**) a grant of money given to someone for their education

school *noun* (*plural* **schools**) 1 a place where children go to be taught 2 a place where you can learn a skill ▸ *a driving school* 3 a group of whales or fish swimming together

schooner *noun* (*plural* **schooners**) (*pronounced* **skoo**-ner) a large fast sailing ship

science *noun* the study of things in the world that people can observe, or a branch of this study such as physics, chemistry, and biology **scientific** *adjective* to do with science

science fiction *noun* stories about imaginary worlds, especially in space and in the future

scientist *noun* (*plural* **scientists**) someone who studies science

scissors *plural noun* a tool for cutting, made of two blades joined together

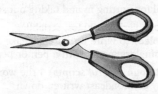

scoff *verb* (**scoffs, scoffing, scoffed**) 1 to make fun of someone or something 2 (*informal*) to eat quickly and greedily

scold *verb* (**scolds, scolding, scolded**) to tell someone off harshly

scone *noun* (*plural* **scones**) (*pronounced* skon) a small plain cake, usually eaten with butter and jam

scoop *noun* (*plural* **scoops**) 1 a deep spoon for serving soft food 2 a deep shovel 3 an important piece of news that one newspaper prints before all the others
scoop *verb* (**scoops, scooping, scooped**) to take something out with a scoop

scooter *noun* (*plural* **scooters**) 1 a toy with two wheels and a narrow platform for riding on 2 a kind of small motorcycle

scope *noun* 1 an opportunity or possibility for something ▸ *We like to give you plenty of scope for trying out your own ideas.* 2 what something deals with or includes ▸ *That question doesn't come within the scope of this book.*

scorch *verb* (**scorches, scorching, scorched**) to make something go brown by slightly burning it

score *noun* (*plural* **scores**) 1 the number of points or goals that you get in a game 2 (*old use*) twenty
score *verb* (**scores, scoring, scored**) 1 to get a goal or a point in a game 2 to keep a count of the score in a game 3 to scratch the surface of something **scorer** *noun* someone who scores in a game

scorn *noun* a strong feeling that someone or something is bad or not good enough for you
scorn *verb* (**scorns, scorning, scorned**) to show scorn for someone or something **scornful** *adjective* full of scorn **scornfully** *adverb*

scorpion *noun* (*plural* **scorpions**) an animal related to the spider, with pincers and a curved tail that has a poisonous sting at its end

scoundrel *noun* (*plural* **scoundrels**) a wicked or dishonest person

scour *verb* (**scours, scouring, scoured**) 1 to rub a surface with something hard to clean it 2 to search an area thoroughly

Scout *noun* (*plural* **Scouts**) a member of the Scout Association

scout *noun* (*plural* **scouts**) someone sent out to collect information, especially a soldier sent to find out where enemies are

scowl *verb* (**scowls, scowling, scowled**) to look angry or bad-tempered

scramble *verb* (**scrambles, scrambling, scrambled**) 1 to move quickly and awkwardly ▸ *We scrambled up the steep slope.* 2 to cook eggs by mixing them and heating them in a pan 3 to struggle to get hold of something ▸ *Everyone scrambled for the ball.*
scramble *noun* (*plural* **scrambles**) 1 a climb or walk over rough ground 2 a struggle to get something ▸ *There was a scramble for the best seats.* 3 a motorcycle race across rough country

scrap *noun* (*plural* **scraps**) 1 a small piece of something 2 metal things that have been thrown away 3 a fight or quarrel
scrap *verb* (**scraps, scrapping, scrapped**) 1 to get rid of something when you do not want it 2 to fight or quarrel

scrapbook *noun* (*plural* **scrapbooks**) a book of blank pages for sticking cuttings into

scrape *verb* (**scrapes, scraping, scraped**) to rub a surface against something rough, hard, or sharp **scrape through** to achieve something only with great difficulty ▸ *He scraped through his driving test at the third*

try. **scrape together** to collect enough of something with difficulty ▸ *They scraped together enough money for a holiday.*
scraper *noun* a device for scraping something clean

scrape *noun* (*plural* **scrapes**) 1 a scraping movement or sound 2 a mark made by scraping something 3 (informal) an awkward situation ▸ *They were in a bit of a scrape.*

scrappy *adjective* (**scrappier, scrappiest**) 1 made of scraps or bits 2 done carelessly or untidily **scrappily** *adverb*

scratch *verb* (**scratches, scratching, scratched**) 1 to damage a surface by rubbing something sharp over it 2 to rub your skin with your fingers when it itches
scratch *noun* (*plural* **scratches**) 1 a mark made by scratching ▸ *You've got a scratch on your cheek.* 2 the action of scratching ▸ *The dog was having a good scratch.* **be up to scratch** to be good enough **start from scratch** to begin at the very beginning

scrawl *verb* (**scrawls, scrawling, scrawled**) to write something untidily or carelessly
scrawl *noun* (*plural* **scrawls**) a piece of untidy writing

scream *verb* (**screams, screaming, screamed**) to give a loud shrill cry of pain or fear or anger
scream *noun* (*plural* **screams**) a loud shrill cry

screech *verb* (**screeches, screeching, screeched**) to give a harsh high-pitched sound of fear or surprise
screech *noun* (*plural* **screeches**) a harsh high-pitched sound

screen *noun* (*plural* **screens**) 1 a flat surface on which cinema films are projected 2 a glass panel on which television pictures or computer images appear 3 a movable panel used to hide or protect something 4 a vehicle's windscreen
screen *verb* (**screens, screening, screened**) 1 to hide or protect something with a screen ▸ *A tall fence screened the tennis courts from the park.* 2 to test people to find out if they have a disease 3 to show a film or television programme

screw *noun* (*plural* **screws**) 1 a metal pin with a spiral groove (or *thread*) round it, which holds things by being twisted into them 2 a propeller
screw *verb* (**screws, screwing, screwed**) 1 to fix something in position with a screw 2 to put a lid on something by twisting it

screwdriver *noun* (*plural* **screwdrivers**) a tool for putting in and taking out screws

scribble *verb* (**scribbles, scribbling, scribbled**) to write untidily or make meaningless marks with a pen or pencil

script *noun* (*plural* **scripts**) 1 the words of a play or broadcast written down 2 handwriting or something handwritten

scripture *noun* (*plural* **scriptures**) the sacred writings of a religion

scroll *noun* (*plural* **scrolls**) a roll of paper or parchment with writing on it

scrounge *verb* (**scrounges, scrounging, scrounged**) (informal) to get something by begging someone for it ▸ *He scrounged a meal from us.* **scrounger** *noun*

scrub[1] *verb* (**scrubs, scrubbing, scrubbed**) to rub something with a hard brush to clean it

scrub[2] *noun* an area of land covered with low trees and bushes

scruffy *adjective* (**scruffier, scruffiest**) shabby and untidy **scruffily** *adverb*

scrum or **scrummage** *noun* (*plural* **scrums** or **scrummages**) in rugby football, a group of players from each side who push against each other to get the ball with their feet

scrutinize *verb* (**scrutinizes, scrutinizing, scrutinized**) to look at something very carefully **scrutiny** *noun* looking carefully at something

scuba diving *noun* swimming underwater with an air supply carried on your back
The word **scuba** comes from the first letters of the words 'self-contained underwater breathing apparatus'.

scuffle *verb* (**scuffles, scuffling, scuffled**) to fight in a confused way
scuffle *noun* (*plural* **scuffles**) a confused struggle or fight

sculptor *noun* (*plural* **sculptors**) someone who makes sculptures or carvings

sculpture *noun* (*plural* **sculptures**) **1** an object or figure made out of stone or some other hard material **2** the art or work of making sculptures

scum *noun* froth or dirt on the top of a liquid

scurry *verb* (**scurries, scurrying, scurried**) to run or hurry with short steps

scurvy *noun* a disease that people get if they don't eat enough fresh fruit and vegetables

scuttle *verb* (**scuttles, scuttling, scuttled**) **1** to run with quick short steps **2** to sink a ship deliberately

scythe *noun* (*plural* **scythes**) (*pronounced syth*) a tool with a long curved blade for cutting grass or corn

sea *noun* (*plural* **seas**) **1** an area of salt water covering part of the earth's surface **2** a large area of something ▶ *I looked down from the stage at the sea of faces in the audience.*

seafarer *noun* someone who travels or works at sea **seafaring** *noun* travelling on the sea

seafood *noun* fish or shellfish from the sea, eaten as food

seagull *noun* (*plural* **seagulls**) a white or grey seabird with long wings

sea horse *noun* (*plural* **sea horses**) a small fish that swims upright, with a head like a horse's head

seal[1] *noun* (*plural* **seals**) a furry sea animal that breeds on land

seal[2] *noun* (*plural* **seals**) **1** a piece of wax stamped with a design and fixed to a document to show it is genuine **2** something that closes an opening tightly **seal** *verb* (**seals, sealing, sealed**) to close something by sticking two parts together ▶ *I've sealed the envelope.*

sea lion *noun* (*plural* **sea lions**) a large kind of seal

seam *noun* (*plural* **seams**) the line where two pieces of material are joined together

search *verb* (**searches, searching, searched**) to look carefully to try to find someone or something

search *noun* (*plural* **searches**) a careful look for someone or something

searchlight *noun* (*plural* **searchlights**) a light with a strong beam that can be turned in any direction

seashore *noun* the land close to the sea

seasick *adjective* feeling sick from the movement of a ship **seasickness** *noun*

seaside *noun* a place by the sea

season *noun* (*plural* **seasons**) **1** one of the four parts that a year is divided into: spring, summer, autumn, and winter **2** the time of year when something happens ▶ *the football season.* ▶ *the rainy season* **seasonal** *adjective* happening in one particular season

season *verb* (**seasons, seasoning, seasoned**) to add salt, pepper, or other flavourings to food **seasoning** *noun* salt, pepper, and other flavourings

season ticket *noun* (*plural* **season tickets**) a ticket that can be used as often as you like for a certain period

seat *noun* (*plural* **seats**) **1** something used for sitting on **2** a place in parliament or on a council

seat *verb* (**seats, seating, seated**) to have seats for people ▶ *The stadium seats 50,000.*

seat belt *noun* (*plural* **seat belts**) a strap to hold you securely in the seat of a vehicle or aircraft

seaweed *noun* (*plural* **seaweeds**) a plant that grows in the sea

secateurs *plural noun* (*pronounced sek-a-terz*) a garden tool used for pruning plants

secluded *adjective* quiet and in a place away from large numbers of people ▶ *They found a secluded beach for their picnic.* **seclusion** *noun* being away from other people

second *adjective* and *noun* the next after the first **have second thoughts** to wonder whether your decision was right **secondly** *adverb*

second   segment

second *noun* (*plural* **seconds**) **1** a very short period of time, one-sixtieth of a minute **2** a person or thing that is second **3** someone who helps a fighter in a boxing match or duel

second *verb* (**seconds, seconding, seconded**) to support an idea or proposal at a meeting

secondary school *noun* (*plural* **secondary schools**) a school for children after they have left primary school

second-hand *adjective* bought or used after someone else has used it ▸ *I can only afford a second-hand car.*

secrecy *noun* being secret

secret *adjective* **1** hidden, or not known by many people ▸ *The house had a secret passage.* **2** not meant to be told or shown to other people ▸ *What I told you is secret.* **secretly** *adverb*

secret *noun* (*plural* **secrets**) a piece of information that is secret **in secret** secretly

secretary *noun* (*plural* **secretaries**) (*pronounced* **sek-re-tri**) someone who types letters, answers the telephone, and does other general tasks in an office

secrete *verb* (**secretes, secreting, secreted**) (*pronounced* si-**kreet**) to release a substance in the body ▸ *Saliva is secreted in the mouth.* **secretion** *noun*

secretive *adjective* wanting to keep things secret

sect *noun* (*plural* **sects**) a group of people who have special or unusual religious opinions or beliefs

section *noun* (*plural* **sections**) a part of something

sector *noun* (*plural* **sectors**) part of an area or organization

secure *adjective* **1** firmly fixed **2** made safe or protected from attack ▸ *Check that all the doors and windows are secure.* **securely** *adverb*

secure *verb* (**secures, securing, secured**) to make something safe or firmly fastened

security *noun* being secure or safe

sedate *adjective* (*pronounced* si-**dayt**) calm and dignified **sedately** *adverb*

sediment *noun* solid matter that floats in liquid or sinks to the bottom of it

see *verb* (**sees, seeing, saw, seen**) **1** to use your eyes to notice something or someone or be aware of them **2** to meet or visit someone ▸ *I went to see my Mum in her office.* **3** to understand something ▸ *She saw what I meant.* **4** to imagine someone being something ▸ *Can you see yourself as a singer?* **5** to make sure that something is done ▸ *See that the door is locked when you leave.* **6** to escort or lead someone somewhere ▸ *I'll see you to the gate.* **see through** not to be deceived by someone or something ▸ *We soon saw through her disguise.* **see to** to deal with something ▸ *Can you see to the lunch?*

seed *noun* (*plural* **seeds**) a part of a plant that can grow in the ground to make a new plant

seedling *noun* (*plural* **seedlings**) a young plant that has just started to grow

seek *verb* (**seeks, seeking, sought**) to try to find or get or do something ▸ *You need to seek medical advice.* ▸ *All we seek is a little peace.*

seem *verb* (**seems, seeming, seemed**) to give the appearance or impression of something ▸ *They seem happy in their new house.*

seen past participle of **see**

seep *verb* (**seeps, seeping, seeped**) to flow slowly through or into or out of something ▸ *Water was seeping into the basement.*

see-saw *noun* (*plural* **see-saws**) a plank balanced in the middle so that a person can sit at each end and make it go up and down
The word **see-saw** comes from an old rhyme or chant that people used when sawing wood.

seethe *verb* (**seethes, seething, seethed**) **1** to boil or bubble **2** to be very angry or excited

segment *noun* (*plural* **segments**) a part that can be separated from something ▸ *He ate a few segments of an orange.*

segregate *verb* (**segregates, segregating, segregated**) (*pronounced* **seg-ri-gayt**) to make one group of people stay apart from another **segregation** *noun*

seize *verb* (**seizes, seizing, seized**) (*pronounced* **seez**) **1** to take hold of something or someone suddenly or eagerly **2** to capture something using force **seize up** to become jammed or stuck

seizure *noun* (*plural* **seizures**) **1** the act of seizing something **2** a sudden attack of an illness

seldom *adverb* rarely; not often

select *verb* (**selects, selecting, selected**) to choose a person or thing carefully
select *adjective* small and carefully chosen
▸ *They have a select group of friends.*

self *noun* (*plural* **selves**) a person's own nature or interests ▸ *After a while Kieran was back to his usual self.*

self-centred *adjective* selfish; thinking about yourself too much

self-confident *adjective* confident about what you can do **self-confidence** *noun*

self-conscious *adjective* embarrassed or shy about what people are thinking about you **self-consciousness** *noun*

self-defence *noun* defending yourself against attack

self-employed *adjective* working for yourself, or in your own business, and not for an employer

selfish *adjective* doing what you want without thinking of other people **selfishly** *adverb* **selfishness** *noun*

self-service *adjective* where customers serve themselves ▸ *a self-service garage*

sell *verb* (**sells, selling, sold**) to offer goods or services in exchange for money **sell out** to sell all you have of something

semaphore *noun* a system of signalling by holding flags out in positions that stand for letters of the alphabet

semen *noun* (*pronounced* **see-men**) a white liquid containing male sperm

semibreve *noun* (*plural* **semibreves**) (*pronounced* **sem-i-breev**) a note in music, the longest normally used, written ○

semicircle *noun* (*plural* **semicircles**) half a circle **semicircular** *adjective*

semicolon *noun* (*plural* **semicolons**) a punctuation mark (;) used to mark a more definite break in a sentence than a comma does

semi-detached *adjective* (describing a house) joined to another house on one side

semi-final *noun* (*plural* **semi-finals**) a match played to decide who will take part in the final

senate *noun* (*pronounced* **sen-at**) a group of people forming part of the government in some countries **senator** *noun* a member of a senate

send *verb* (**sends, sending, sent**) to make something or someone go somewhere or be taken there **send for** to ask for someone to come to you ▸ *We'd better send for the doctor.*

senile *adjective* weak or sick because of old age

senior *adjective* **1** older than someone else **2** higher in rank or position ▸ *He is a senior officer in the navy.* **seniority** *noun* being older or more experienced than other people

senior citizen *noun* (*plural* **senior citizens**) an elderly person

sensation *noun* (*plural* **sensations**) **1** a feeling ▸ *There's an itching sensation in my leg.* **2** a very exciting event or the excitement caused by it ▸ *The news caused quite a sensation.*

sensational *adjective* causing great excitement or shock

sense *noun* (*plural* **senses**) **1** one of the ways in which you know about things around you: seeing, hearing, smelling, touching, or tasting **2** the ability to feel or appreciate something ▸ *a good sense of rhythm* **3** the power to think or make good judgements ▸ *Fortunately she had the sense to keep quiet.* **4** meaning ▸ *The word* *'set' has many senses.* **make sense** to have a meaning you can understand

sense *verb* (**senses, sensing, sensed**) **1** to feel something or be aware of it ▸ *I sensed that she did not like me.* **2** to detect something ▸ *The device senses radioactivity.*

senseless *adjective* **1** stupid; not sensible ▸ *The war was a senseless conflict that could have been avoided.* **2** unconscious ▸ *The wounded man lay senseless on the ground.*

sensible *adjective* wise; having or showing good sense **sensibly** *adverb*

sensitive *adjective* **1** affected by the sun or chemicals or something else physical ▸ *You should use sun cream if you have sensitive skin.* **2** easily offended ▸ *He's quite sensitive about being criticized.* **sensitivity** *noun* being sensitive

sensor *noun* (*plural* **sensors**) a device that detects something physical such as heat or light

sent past tense and past participle of **send**

sentence *noun* (*plural* **sentences**) **1** a group of words that express a complete thought. A sentence can be a statement or a question or a command. **2** the punishment given to a convicted person in a lawcourt

sentence *verb* (**sentences, sentencing, sentenced**) to give someone a sentence in a lawcourt ▸ *The judge sentenced him to six months in prison.*

sentimental *adjective* arousing or showing too much emotion ▸ *The film is a sentimental love story.*

sentry *noun* (*plural* **sentries**) a soldier standing outside a building to guard it

separate *adjective* (*pronounced* **sep**-er-at) not joined to anything; on its own **separately** *adverb*

separate *verb* (**separates, separating, separated**) (*pronounced* **sep**-er-ayt) **1** to take things or people away from others **2** to stop being together or living together **3** to go in different directions **separation** *noun*

September *noun* the ninth month of the year

The word **September** comes from the Latin word *septem* meaning 'seven', because it was the seventh month in the Roman calendar.

septic *adjective* (describing a wound) infected with harmful bacteria

sequel *noun* (*plural* **sequels**) (*pronounced* **see**-kwel) a book or film that continues the story of an earlier one

sequence *noun* (*plural* **sequences**) (*pronounced* **see**-kwenss) a series of things coming in a particular order

serene *adjective* calm and peaceful **serenity** *noun* being serene

sergeant *noun* (*plural* **sergeants**) (*pronounced* **sar**-jent) a soldier or police officer who is in charge of others

serial *noun* (*plural* **serials**) a story that is shown on television in several separate parts

series *noun* (*plural* **series**) a number of similar things following each other ▸ *A series of disasters followed.*

serious *adjective* **1** not funny; important ▸ *We have to discuss some serious business.* **2** thoughtful; solemn ▸ *When she heard the news her expression became serious.* **3** very bad ▸ *He's had a serious car accident.* **seriously** *adverb* **seriousness** *noun*

sermon *noun* (*plural* **sermons**) a serious talk a preacher gives during a religious service

serpent *noun* (*plural* **serpents**) a snake

servant *noun* (*plural* **servants**) a person who works in someone else's house

serve *verb* (**serves, serving, served**) **1** to work for a person or organization **2** to sell things to people in a shop **3** to give people food at a meal **4** to be suitable for a purpose **5** in tennis, to start play by hitting the ball to your opponent ▸ *it serves you right* you deserve it

service *noun* (*plural* **services**) **1** working for a person or organization ▸ *He retired after forty years' service.* **2** something that helps people or supplies what they want ▸ *There is a good bus service into town.* **3** a religious ceremony in a church **4** the servicing of a vehicle or machine **5** in tennis, the action of serving **the services** the armed forces of a country

service *verb* (**services, servicing, serviced**) to check a car or machine and repair it if necessary

service station *noun* (*plural* **service stations**) a place beside the road where petrol is sold

serviette *noun* (*plural* **serviettes**) a cloth or paper napkin that you can wipe your hands and mouth on

session *noun* (*plural* **sessions**) **1** a time spent doing a particular thing **2** a meeting or series of meetings ▸ *The Queen will open the next session of Parliament.*

set *verb* (**sets, setting, set**) **1** to put something in a particular place ▸ *He set the basket down on the table.* **2** to make a device ready to work ▸ *She closed the oven door and set the timer for ten minutes.* **3** to become solid or hard ▸ *By the time we returned the cement had set hard.* **4** (used about the sun) to go down towards the horizon at the end of the day **5** to start someone doing something ▸ *Jake's mother set him peeling some potatoes.* **6** to prepare a table for a meal **7** to give someone a task to do or a problem to solve ▸ *I'd better set you some more work.* **set off** or **set out** to begin a journey **set up** to get something started ▸ *The bank has set up a new branch in Edinburgh.*

set *noun* (*plural* **sets**) **1** a group of people or things that belong together **2** a radio or television receiver **3** a group of games in a tennis match **4** the scenery or furniture on a stage or in a film

setback *noun* (*plural* **setbacks**) something that causes a difficulty for a while

set square *noun* (*plural* **set squares**) a drawing instrument in the shape of a triangle with one right angle

settee *noun* (*plural* **settees**) a sofa

setting *noun* (*plural* **settings**) the things that are around a place or building ▸ *The house stood in a rural setting.*

settle *verb* (**settles, settling, settled**) **1** to become relaxed and comfortable ▸ *She settled down in an armchair.* **2** to go and live in a place ▸ *The family wants to settle in Australia.* **3** to solve a problem or difficulty or decide about it **4** (used about something light such as dust or snow) to come to rest on something **5** to pay a bill or debt

settlement *noun* (*plural* **settlements**) **1** an agreement about something **2** a group of people or houses in a new area

settler *noun* (*plural* **settlers**) one of the first people to live in a new area

set-up *noun* (*plural* **set-ups**) the way that something is organized or arranged

seven *noun* (*plural* **sevens**) the number 7 **seventh** *adjective* and *noun*

seventeen *noun* (*plural* **seventeens**) the number 17 **seventeenth** *adjective* and *noun*

seventy *noun* (*plural* **seventies**) the number 70 **seventieth** *adjective* and *noun*

sever *verb* (**severs, severing, severed**) to cut or break something off

several *adjective* more than two but not many

severe *adjective* (**severer, severest**) **1** strict; not gentle or kind **2** very bad; violent ▸ *He was suffering from a severe cold.* **severely** *adverb* **severity** *noun* being severe, or how severe something is

sew *verb* (**sews, sewing, sewed, sewn** or **sewed**) (*pronounced* so) to use a needle and thread to make cloth or other soft material into clothes

sewage *noun* (*pronounced* soo-ij) waste matter carried away in drains

sewer *noun* (*plural* **sewers**) (*pronounced* soo-er) an underground drain that carries away sewage

sewing machine *noun* (*plural* **sewing machines**) a machine used for sewing things

sex *noun* (*plural* **sexes**) 1 one the two groups, male or female, that people and animals belong to 2 sexual intercourse

sexism *noun* unfair treatment of people of a particular sex **sexist** *adjective* and *noun*

sexual *adjective* to do with sex or the sexes **sexuality** *noun* being sexual **sexually** *adverb* in a sexual way

sexual intercourse *noun* the act in which a man puts his penis into a woman's vagina and ejects seed into it

sexy *adjective* (**sexier**, **sexiest**) 1 attractive in a sexual way ▶ *a sexy pop singer* 2 to do with sex ▶ *a sexy film* **sexily** *adverb* **sexiness** *noun*

shabby *adjective* (**shabbier**, **shabbiest**) 1 old and worn ▶ *The young woman was wearing a shabby straw hat.* 2 mean or unfair ▶ *Charles had treated his first wife in a very shabby way.* **shabbily** *adverb* **shabbiness** *noun*

shack *noun* (*plural* **shacks**) a roughly-built hut

shade *noun* (*plural* **shades**) 1 an area sheltered from strong light 2 a device that reduces or shuts out strong light 3 how light or dark a colour is ▶ *The sea looked a dark shade of green.*
shade *verb* (**shades**, **shading**, **shaded**) 1 to shelter something or someone from strong light 2 to make parts of a drawing darker than the rest

shadow *noun* (*plural* **shadows**) 1 a dark shape that falls on a surface when something is blocking the light 2 an area of shade **shadowy** *adjective* dark or hard to see
shadow *verb* (**shadows**, **shadowing**, **shadowed**) to follow someone secretly

shady *adjective* (**shadier**, **shadiest**) 1 in the shade ▶ *The hotel is located in a shady avenue near the beach.* 2 dishonest or suspect ▶ *He's always making shady deals on his mobile phone.*

shaft *noun* (*plural* **shafts**) 1 a long thin rod, or the straight part of something 2 a deep narrow hole leading underground 3 a ray of light

shaggy *adjective* (**shaggier**, **shaggiest**) (describing hair or fur) long and untidy

shake *verb* (**shakes**, **shaking**, **shook**, **shaken**) 1 to tremble or move in a quick jerky way ▶ *Her grandmother's hand was shaking a little.* 2 to move something quickly up and down or from side to side ▶ *Claire picked up the rug and shook it out of the window.* ▶ *He took her hand and shook it.* 3 to shock or upset someone ▶ *I think the news shook him pretty badly.*
shaky *adjective* unsteady or weak

shall *verb* used with *I* and *we* to talk about the future ▶ *I shall take Mary with me.*

shallow *adjective* (**shallower**, **shallowest**) not deep

sham *noun* (*plural* **shams**) a person or thing that is not genuine

shamble *verb* (**shambles**, **shambling**, **shambled**) to walk or run in a lazy or awkward way

shambles *noun* a scene of confusion and chaos; a mess ▶ *Our first rehearsal turned into a complete shambles.*

shame *noun* 1 a feeling of great sorrow or guilt because you have done wrong 2 something that you regret ▶ *It was a shame you couldn't come with us.*
shame *verb* (**shames**, **shaming**, **shamed**) to make someone feel ashamed

shameful *adjective* causing shame; disgraceful **shamefully** *adverb*

shampoo *noun* (*plural* **shampoos**) liquid soap for washing your hair
shampoo *verb* (**shampoos**, **shampooing**, **shampooed**) to wash your hair with shampoo

shamrock *noun* a small plant like clover, with leaves divided in three

shandy *noun* (*plural* **shandies**) a mixture of beer with lemonade or another soft drink

shan't short for *shall not* ▶ *I shan't be angry.*

shanty *noun* (*plural* **shanties**) 1 a sailor's song 2 a roughly-built hut

shape *noun* (*plural* **shapes**) 1 the outline of something or the way it looks 2 the condition that someone or something is in ▶ *They needed some exercise to put them in good shape for the run.* **shapeless** *adjective*

shape *verb* (**shapes, shaping, shaped**) to give something a shape **shape up** to develop well

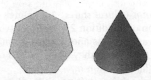

share *noun* (*plural* **shares**) 1 one of the parts into which something is divided between several people or things 2 a part into which a company's money is divided

share *verb* (**shares, sharing, shared**) 1 to divide something between several people or things 2 to use something when someone else is also using it ▶ *I'm sharing a room with Cathy.*

shark *noun* (*plural* **sharks**) a large sea fish with sharp teeth

sharp *adjective* (**sharper, sharpest**) 1 having an edge or point that can cut or make holes ▶ *a sharp knife* 2 quick to learn or notice things ▶ *sharp eyes* 3 sudden or severe ▶ *a sharp bend in the road* 4 slightly sour ▶ *The apples taste sharp.* 5 above the proper musical pitch **sharply** *adverb* **sharpness** *noun*

sharp *adverb* 1 sharply ▶ *Turn sharp right.* 2 punctually; exactly ▶ *Be there at six o'clock sharp.*

sharp *noun* (*plural* **sharps**) a musical note that is slightly higher than the natural note; the sign (#) that indicates this

sharpen *verb* (**sharpens, sharpening, sharpened**) to make something sharp or pointed **sharpener** *noun* a device for sharpening something

shatter *verb* (**shatters, shattering, shattered**) to break suddenly into tiny pieces **be shattered** to be very upset by something, or to be very tired

shave *verb* (**shaves, shaving, shaved**) 1 to remove hair from your skin with a razor 2 to cut or scrape a thin slice off something **shaver** *noun* an electric razor

shavings *plural noun* thin strips shaved off wood or metal

shawl *noun* (*plural* **shawls**) a large piece of material for covering your shoulders or wrapping a baby

she *pronoun* used as the subject of a verb to talk about a female person or animal already mentioned

sheaf *noun* (*plural* **sheaves**) a bundle of corn or papers

shear *verb* (**shears, shearing, sheared, shorn** or **sheared**) to cut the wool from a sheep

shears *plural noun* a tool like a large pair of scissors, for trimming grass and bushes or for shearing sheep

sheath *noun* (*plural* **sheaths**) a cover for the blade of a sword or dagger

shed[1] *noun* (*plural* **sheds**) a simple hut used for storing things or sheltering animals

shed[2] *verb* (**sheds, shedding, shed**) to let something fall off or drop ▶ *The trees are shedding their leaves.* ▶ *He was so badly hurt he was shedding blood.*

sheen *noun* a shine on a surface

sheep *noun* (*plural* **sheep**) an animal kept by farmers for its wool and meat

sheepdog *noun* (*plural* **sheepdogs**) a dog trained to guard and control sheep

sheepish *adjective* shy or embarrassed **sheepishly** *adverb* **sheepishness** *noun*

sheer *adjective* (**sheerer, sheerest**) 1 complete or thorough ▶ *It was sheer chance that Martha had been there at the same time.* 2 vertical or perpendicular ▶ *A few metres away was the top of a sheer cliff.* 3 (describing material) very thin or transparent

sheet *noun* (*plural* **sheets**) 1 a large rectangle of light material put on a bed 2 a flat piece of paper, glass, or metal 3 a wide area of water, snow, ice, or flame

sheikh *noun* (*plural* **sheikhs**) (*pronounced* shayk) an Arab leader

shelf *noun* (*plural* **shelves**) 1 a flat piece of hard material fitted to a wall or in a piece of furniture so that things can be put on it 2 a flat level surface that sticks out

shell *noun* (*plural* **shells**) 1 the hard outer covering round a nut or egg, or round an animal such as a snail or tortoise 2 a metal case filled with explosive, fired from a large gun 3 the walls or framework of a building or ship

shell *verb* (**shells, shelling, shelled**) to fire explosive shells at a building, ship, town, etc.

she'll short for *she will* ▸ *Margot says she'll take us to the station.*

shellfish *noun* (*plural* **shellfish**) a sea animal that has a shell

shelter *noun* (*plural* **shelters**) 1 a place that protects people from danger or from the weather 2 protection or safety

shelter *verb* (**shelters, sheltering, sheltered**) 1 to protect or cover something or someone ▸ *A hill shelters the house from the wind.* 2 to find shelter ▸ *We sheltered under the trees.*

shelve *verb* (**shelves, shelving, shelved**) 1 to leave an idea or plan for later ▸ *The council had been forced to shelve plans for a new swimming pool.* 2 to slope ▸ *The river bed shelves steeply.*

shepherd *noun* (*plural* **shepherds**) someone who looks after sheep

sherbet *noun* (*plural* **sherbets**) a fizzy sweet powder or drink
The word **sherbet** comes from an Arabic word meaning 'a drink'.

sheriff *noun* (*plural* **sheriffs**) the chief law officer of a county in America

sherry *noun* (*plural* **sherries**) a kind of strong wine

shield *noun* (*plural* **shields**) 1 a large piece of metal or wood carried by soldiers to protect their body in battle 2 a design in the shape of a shield 3 a protection

shield *verb* (**shields, shielding, shielded**) to protect someone or something

shift *noun* (*plural* **shifts**) 1 a change of position or condition 2 a group of workers who start work as another group finishes, or the time when they work ▸ *He's on the night shift this month.*

shift *verb* (**shifts, shifting, shifted**) to move or change position

shilling *noun* (*plural* **shillings**) an old British coin that was worth a twentieth of a pound (now 5 pence)

shimmer *verb* (**shimmers, shimmering, shimmered**) to shine with a quivering light ▸ *The sea shimmered in the sunlight.*

shin *noun* (*plural* **shins**) the front of your leg below your knee

shine *verb* (**shines, shining, shone** or, in 'polish' sense, **shined**) 1 to give out bright light 2 to polish something to make it shine ▸ *Have you shined your shoes?*

shine *noun* brightness

shingle *noun* pebbles on a beach

shiny *adjective* (**shinier, shiniest**) bright, gleaming

ship *noun* (*plural* **ships**) a large boat that goes on the sea

ship *verb* (**ships, shipping, shipped**) to send something on a ship

shipwreck *noun* (*plural* **shipwrecks**) 1 the destroying of a ship in a storm or accident at sea 2 the remains of a wrecked ship
shipwrecked *adjective* alive after your ship has been destroyed

shipyard *noun* (*plural* **shipyards**) a place where ships are built and repaired

shirk *verb* (**shirks, shirking, shirked**) to avoid doing a task or duty

shirt *noun* (*plural* **shirts**) a piece of clothing worn on the top half of your body, with a collar and sleeves and buttons down the front

shiver *verb* (**shivers, shivering, shivered**) to tremble with cold or fear **shivery** *adjective* trembling

shiver *noun* (*plural* **shivers**) an act of shivering

shoal *noun* (*plural* **shoals**) a number of fish swimming together

shock *noun* (*plural* **shocks**) 1 a sudden unpleasant surprise 2 a violent knock or jolt 3 a feeling of weakness that you can get if you are badly injured or get some very bad news 4 a harmful effect caused by a strong electric current passing through the body

shock *verb* (**shocks, shocking, shocked**) 1 to give someone a shock 2 to make someone feel upset or disgusted

shocking *adjective* upsetting or disgusting

shoddy *adjective* (**shoddier, shoddiest**) of poor quality; badly made

shoe *noun* (*plural* **shoes**) 1 a strong covering for your foot 2 a horseshoe

shoelace *noun* (*plural* **shoelaces**) a cord for fastening a shoe

shone past tense and past participle of **shine** *verb*

shook past tense of **shake**

shoot *verb* (**shoots, shooting, shot**) 1 to fire a gun or other weapon 2 to hurt or kill a person or animal with a gun 3 to move very fast ▶ *A sports car shot past.* 4 in football or netball, to kick or hit a ball at a goal 5 to take a photograph or make a film of a scene ▶ *The film was shot in Africa.*

shoot *noun* (*plural* **shoots**) a young branch or new growth of a plant

shooting star *noun* (*plural* **shooting stars**) a meteor

shop *noun* (*plural* **shops**) a place where you can buy things

shop *verb* (**shops, shopping, shopped**) to go and buy things in shops **shopper** *noun*

shopkeeper *noun* (*plural* **shopkeepers**) someone who owns or looks after a shop

shoplifter *noun* (*plural* **shoplifters**) someone who steals from shops **shoplifting** *noun*

shopping *noun* things you have bought in shops

shore *noun* (*plural* **shores**) the land along the edge of the sea or a lake

shorn past participle of **shear**

short *adjective* (**shorter, shortest**) 1 not long; occupying a small distance or time ▶ *I've been for a short walk.* 2 not tall ▶ *The man was short and aged about fifty.* 3 not enough; scarce ▶ *In a dry summer, water can be short.* ▶ *We are one person short.* 4 bad-tempered ▶ *He was rather short with me.* 5 (describing pastry) rich and crumbly, with a lot of fat **short of** not having enough of something ▶ *We seem to be short of butter.* **shortness** *noun*

short *adverb* suddenly or sharply ▶ *She stopped short.*

shortage *noun* (*plural* **shortages**) a lack of something you need

shortbread *noun* a rich crumbly biscuit made with butter, flour, and sugar

shortcoming *noun* (*plural* **shortcomings**) a fault or weakness

short cut *noun* (*plural* **short cuts**) a route or method that is quicker than the usual one

shorten *verb* (**shortens, shortening, shortened**) 1 to make something shorter 2 to become shorter

shorthand *noun* a way of writing words down quickly, using special signs

shortly *adverb* soon ▶ *The postman will be coming shortly.*

shorts *plural noun* trousers with legs that stop above the knee

short-sighted *adjective* 1 unable to see things clearly when they are further away 2 not thinking enough about what may happen in the future **short-sightedly** *adverb* **short-sightedness** *noun*

short-tempered *adjective* becoming angry easily

shot[1] *noun* (*plural* **shots**) **1** the firing of a gun or other weapon **2** something fired from a gun **3** a person judged by their skill in shooting ▸ *She is a great shot.* **4** a heavy metal ball thrown as a sport **5** a stroke in a game with a ball, such as tennis or snooker **6** a photograph or scene taken with a camera **7** an attempt to do something ▸ *I'm going to have a shot at the competition.*

shot[2] past tense and past participle of **shoot** *verb*

shotgun *noun* (*plural* **shotguns**) a gun that fires small lead pellets

should *verb* **1** used to express what you ought to do ▸ *You should have told me.* **2** used to express what you expect to happen ▸ *They should be here soon.*

shoulder *noun* (*plural* **shoulders**) the part of your body between your neck and the top of your arm

shoulder blade *noun* (*plural* **shoulder blades**) each of the two large flat bones at the top of your back

shout *verb* (**shouts, shouting, shouted**) to speak or call very loudly
shout *noun* (*plural* **shouts**) a loud cry or call

shove *verb* (**shoves, shoving, shoved**) (*pronounced* shuv) to push very hard
shove *noun* (*plural* **shoves**) a hard push

shovel *noun* (*plural* **shovels**) (*pronounced* shuv-el) a tool like a spade with the sides turned up, for lifting and moving things
shovel *verb* (**shovels, shovelling, shovelled**) to move something with a shovel

show *verb* (**shows, showing, showed, shown**) **1** to let people see something ▸ *Show me what you've done.* **2** to explain something ▸ *Gopal showed me how to mend a puncture.* **3** to guide or lead someone somewhere ▸ *I'll show them round the house.* **4** to be visible ▸ *It's only a scratch and it won't show.* **show off** to try to impress people
show *noun* (*plural* **shows**) **1** a display or exhibition ▸ *a boat show* ▸ *a fashion show* **2** an entertainment

shower *noun* (*plural* **showers**) **1** a brief fall of light rain **2** a device for spraying water to wash your body **3** a lot of small things coming or falling like rain ▸ *They were met by a shower of stones.*
shower *verb* (**showers, showering, showered**) **1** to fall like rain **2** to give someone a lot of something ▸ *She showered them with kisses.* **3** to wash yourself under a shower

showjumping *noun* a competition in which riders make their horses jump over fences and other obstacles **showjumper** *noun*

showy *adjective* (**showier, showiest**) bright or highly decorated

shrank past tense of **shrink**

shrapnel *noun* pieces of metal scattered from an exploding shell
Shrapnel is named after Henry Shrapnel, a British officer who invented it in about 1806.

shred *noun* (*plural* **shreds**) a small piece torn or cut off something
shred *verb* (**shreds, shredding, shredded**) to tear something or cut it into shreds

shrew *noun* (*plural* **shrews**) a small animal like a mouse

shrewd *adjective* (**shrewder, shrewdest**) having good sense **shrewdly** *adverb* **shrewdness** *noun*

shriek *verb* (**shrieks, shrieking, shrieked**) to give a shrill cry or scream
shriek *noun* (*plural* **shrieks**) the sound of someone shrieking

shrill *adjective* (**shriller, shrillest**) sounding very high and loud **shrilly** *adverb*

shrimp *noun* (*plural* **shrimps**) a small shellfish

shrine *noun* (*plural* **shrines**) an altar or other sacred place

shrink *verb* (**shrinks, shrinking, shrank, shrunk**) **1** to become smaller ▸ *My dress has shrunk.* **2** to avoid doing something because you are afraid or embarrassed ▸ *Neil always shrank from meeting strangers.*

shrinkage *noun* the amount that something shrinks

shrivel *verb* (**shrivels, shrivelling, shrivelled**) to become wrinkled and dry

shroud *verb* (**shrouds, shrouding, shrouded**) to cover or conceal something ▸ *The countryside was shrouded in mist.*

shroud *noun* (*plural* **shrouds**) a thing that covers or conceals something

shrub *noun* (*plural* **shrubs**) a bush or small tree

shrubbery *noun* (*plural* **shrubberies**) an area full of shrubs

shrug *verb* (**shrugs, shrugging, shrugged**) to raise your shoulders slightly as a sign that you do not care or do not know

shrug *noun* (*plural* **shrugs**) the act of shrugging

shrunk past participle of **shrink**

shrunken *adjective* smaller because it has shrunk

shudder *verb* (**shudders, shuddering, shuddered**) to shake from cold or fear

shudder *noun* (*plural* **shudders**) the act of shuddering

shuffle *verb* (**shuffles, shuffling, shuffled**) 1 to drag your feet along the ground as you walk 2 to mix playing cards before you use them

shun *verb* (**shuns, shunning, shunned**) to avoid seeing or meeting someone

shunt *verb* (**shunts, shunting, shunted**) to move a railway train or wagons from one track to another

shut *verb* (**shuts, shutting, shut**) 1 to move a door or window, or a lid or cover, so as to block up an opening 2 to become closed ▸ *The door shut suddenly.* **shut down** to stop work or business **shut up** (*informal*) to stop talking

shutter *noun* (*plural* **shutters**) 1 a panel or screen used to cover a window 2 the device in a camera that opens and closes to let light fall on the film

shuttle *noun* (*plural* **shuttles**) 1 the part of a loom that carries the thread from side to side 2 a train, bus, or aircraft that makes regular journeys between two places 3 a space shuttle

shuttlecock *noun* (*plural* **shuttlecocks**) a small rounded piece of cork or plastic with a ring of feathers fixed to it, used in the game of badminton

shy *adjective* (**shyer, shyest**) nervous about meeting or talking to other people **shyly** *adverb* **shyness** *noun* being shy

sibling *noun* (*plural* **siblings**) your brother or sister ▸ *Lucy has three siblings now.*

sick *adjective* (**sicker, sickest**) 1 ill or unwell 2 vomiting or likely to vomit ▸ *I feel sick.* **be sick of** to be tired of something or someone

sicken *verb* (**sickens, sickening, sickened**) 1 to start feeling ill 2 to disgust someone

sickly *adjective* (**sicklier, sickliest**) 1 often ill; unhealthy ▸ *Emma had been a sickly child.* 2 making you feel sick ▸ *The cake had a sickly taste.*

sickness *noun* (*plural* **sicknesses**) 1 an illness or disease 2 being ill or sick

side *noun* (*plural* **sides**) 1 a flat surface ▸ *There are six sides to a cube.* 2 a line that forms the edge of something ▸ *A triangle has three sides.* ▸ *There is a path on one side of the road.* 3 the outer part of something that is not the front or the back ▸ *There is no door on this side of the house.* 4 a group of people that is playing or fighting another group ▸ *They are on our side.*

side *verb* (**sides, siding, sided**) to support someone in a quarrel or argument ▸ *Dad always sides with Richard.*

sideboard *noun* (*plural* **sideboards**) a large piece of furniture with drawers and cupboards and a flat top, used in a dining room for plates, cutlery, and tablecloths

sideshow *noun* (*plural* **sideshows**) one of the entertainments at a fair

sideways *adverb* and *adjective* to or from the side ▸ *Crabs walk sideways.*

siding *noun* (*plural* **sidings**) a short railway line leading off a main line

siege *noun* (*plural* **sieges**) (*pronounced* seej) the action of surrounding a place with an army until it surrenders

sieve *noun* (*plural* **sieves**) (*pronounced* siv) a device made of mesh or perforated metal or plastic, used to separate harder or larger parts from liquid or powder

sift *verb* (**sifts**, **sifting**, **sifted**) to put a fine or powdery substance through a sieve

sigh *verb* (**sighs**, **sighing**, **sighed**) to breathe out heavily when you are sad or tired, or relieved about something

sigh *noun* (*plural* **sighs**) the action or sound of someone sighing

sight *noun* (*plural* **sights**) **1** the ability to see ▸ *She has very good sight.* **2** something that you see ▸ *The garden is a lovely sight in spring.* **3** something worth seeing ▸ *Visit the sights of Paris.* **4** a device that helps you to aim a gun

sight *verb* (**sights**, **sighting**, **sighted**) to see or observe something ▸ *The boy was sighted at a bus stop.*

sightseeing *noun* going round looking at interesting places **sightseer** *noun* a tourist

sign *noun* (*plural* **signs**) **1** a special mark or shape that means something ▸ = *is the sign for 'equals'.* **2** a board or notice with information on it ▸ *A no-entry sign had been put across the road.* **3** something that shows that a thing exists ▸ *There were no signs of life at the cottage.* **4** an action or signal that gives a command ▸ *She gave them a sign to be quiet.*

sign *verb* (**signs**, **signing**, **signed**) **1** to write your signature on something **2** to give someone a contract for a job ▸ *We have signed three new players.*

signal *noun* (*plural* **signals**) **1** a gesture or sound that gives someone information **2** a device, such as a set of lights, for controlling road or railway traffic **3** a series of radio waves sent out or received

signal *verb* (**signals**, **signalling**, **signalled**) to give someone a signal

signature *noun* (*plural* **signatures**) your name written in your own special way

significant *adjective* having a meaning or importance **significance** *noun* meaning or importance **significantly** *adverb* in an important way

signify *verb* (**signifies**, **signifying**, **signified**) to mean something or indicate it ▸ *A cross on the map signifies a church.*

signing or **sign language** *noun* a way of communicating by using expressions of the face and movements of the hands instead of sounds. Signing is used by deaf people and by people communicating with them.

signpost *noun* (*plural* **signposts**) a sign at a road junction showing the names and distances of the places that each road leads to

Sikh *noun* (*plural* **Sikhs**) (*pronounced* seek) someone who believes in **Sikhism**, one of the religions of India

silence *noun* (*plural* **silences**) a state of no sounds or talking

silence *verb* (**silences**, **silencing**, **silenced**) to make someone or something silent

silencer *noun* (*plural* **silencers**) a device for reducing the sound made by an engine or a gun

silent *adjective* not making any sound; not speaking **silently** *adverb*

silhouette *noun* (*plural* **silhouettes**) (*pronounced* sil-oo-et) a dark outline seen against a light background

silicon *noun* a substance found in rocks and used to make transistors and chips for microprocessors

silk *noun* **1** a fine soft thread produced by silkworms for making their cocoons **2** smooth shiny cloth made from this thread **silken** *adjective* **silky** *adjective*

silkworm *noun* (*plural* **silkworms**) a kind of caterpillar that covers itself with a cocoon of fine threads when it is ready to turn into a moth

sill *noun* (*plural* **sills**) a strip of stone or wood or metal underneath a window or door

silly *adjective* (**sillier**, **silliest**) foolish or unwise **silliness** *noun*

silver *noun* **1** a shiny white precious metal **2** coins made of this metal or a metal that looks like it **3** the colour of silver **silvery** *adjective* like silver

silver *adjective* having the colour of silver

similar *adjective* alike or almost the same **similarity** *noun* something similar **similarly** *adverb*

simile *noun* (*plural* **similes**) (*pronounced* sim-i-li) an expression that compares one thing with another, such as *bold as brass* or *as brave as a lion*

simmer *verb* (**simmers, simmering, simmered**) to boil gently **simmer down** to become calm after being anxious or angry

simple *adjective* (**simpler, simplest**) **1** not complicated or difficult ▶ *a simple question* ▶ *a simple idea* **2** plain ▶ *a simple dress* **simplicity** *noun* how simple something is

simplify *verb* (**simplifies, simplifying, simplified**) to make something simpler **simplification** *noun* something that has been made simpler

simply *adverb* **1** in a simple way ▶ *Explain it simply.* **2** completely ▶ *I simply love Italian food.* **3** only or merely ▶ *It's simply a question of time.*

simulate *verb* (**simulates, simulating, simulated**) **1** to imitate something or make a copy of it ▶ *The machine simulates a space flight.* **2** to pretend to be or feel something ▶ *He simulated illness.* **simulation** *noun* **simulator** *noun* a device that simulates something, so that you can try it out or practise on it

simultaneous *adjective* (*pronounced* sim-ul-tay-ni-us) happening at the same time **simultaneously** *adverb*

sin *noun* (*plural* **sins**) a bad action that breaks a religious or moral law

sin *verb* (**sins, sinning, sinned**) to commit a sin **sinful** *adjective* **sinner** *noun*

since *conjunction* **1** from the time when ▶ *I have not seen them since they moved to Scotland.* **2** because ▶ *Since we've missed the bus, we'll have to walk home.*

since *preposition* from a certain time

▶ *I have lived in this house since 1995.*

since *adverb* between then and now ▶ *He has not been seen since.*

sincere *adjective* (**sincerer, sincerest**) truly felt or meant; genuine ▶ *I gave them my sincere good wishes.* **sincerely** *adverb* **sincerity** *noun* being sincere

sing *verb* (**sings, singing, sang, sung**) to make musical sounds with your voice **singer** *noun*

singe *verb* (**singes, singeing, singed**) to burn something slightly

single *adjective* **1** only one ▶ *A single red rose stood in a vase.* **2** designed for one person ▶ *a single bed* **3** not married

single *noun* (*plural* **singles**) **1** a single person or thing **2** a record, tape, or CD with one song or short piece of music on it **3** a single ticket

single *verb* (**singles, singling, singled**) **single out** to pick someone from other people

single file *noun* **in single file** in a line, one behind the other

single-handed *adjective* by your own efforts; without any help

single ticket *noun* (*plural* **single tickets**) a ticket for a journey in one direction only

singly *adverb* one by one

singular *noun* the form of a word when it means only one person or thing, such as *house* and *child*

singular *adjective* (not an everyday word) extraordinary ▶ *It was a singular piece of luck that she was at home at the time.*

sinister *adjective* looking or seeming evil or harmful
This word comes from the Latin word *sinister* meaning 'left', because the Romans thought that the left side was unlucky.

sink *verb* (**sinks, sinking, sank** or **sunk, sunk**) **1** to go under water ▶ *The ship sank in a storm.* **2** to make something go under water ▶ *They fired on the ship and sank it.* **3** to go down gradually ▶ *He sank to his knees.* ▶ *The sun sank behind the trees.*

sink *noun* (*plural* **sinks**) a basin with a drain and with taps to supply water

sip *verb* (**sips, sipping, sipped**) to drink slowly in small mouthfuls

siphon *noun* (*plural* **siphons**) a tube for taking liquid from one container to another at a different level

siphon *verb* (**siphons, siphoning, siphoned**) to transfer liquid with a siphon

sir *noun* a word sometimes used when speaking politely to a man, instead of his name ▶ *Can I help you, sir?* **Sir** the title given to a knight ▶ *Sir Francis Drake*

siren *noun* (*plural* **sirens**) a device that makes a loud hooting or screaming sound

sister *noun* (*plural* **sisters**) 1 a girl or woman who has the same parents as you 2 a senior nurse in a hospital

sister-in-law *noun* (*plural* **sisters-in-law**) the sister of someone's husband or wife, or the wife of someone's brother

sit *verb* (**sits, sitting, sat**) 1 to rest on your bottom, as you do when you are on a chair 2 to take an exam 3 to be in a particular position ▶ *The house sits on top of a hill.* 4 to act as a babysitter for someone

site *noun* (*plural* **sites**) 1 the place where something has been built or will be built ▶ *a building site* 2 a place made for some activity ▶ *a camping site*

sitting room *noun* (*plural* **sitting rooms**) a room with comfortable chairs for sitting in

situated *adjective* in a particular place ▶ *They lived in a town situated in a valley.*

situation *noun* (*plural* **situations**) 1 a place or position; where something is ▶ *The house is in a pleasant situation near the shops.* 2 the things that are happening in a particular place or at a particular time ▶ *We saw a programme about the situation in Bosnia.* 3 a job or employment

six *noun* (*plural* **sixes**) the number 6 **sixth** *adjective* and *noun*

sixteen *noun* (*plural* **sixteens**) the number 16 **sixteenth** *adjective* and *noun*

sixty *noun* (*plural* **sixties**) the number 60 **sixtieth** *adjective* and *noun*

size *noun* (*plural* **sizes**) 1 how large a person or thing is 2 the measurement something is made in ▶ *I don't think this shoe is my size.*

sizeable *adjective* fairly large

sizzle *verb* (**sizzles, sizzling, sizzled**) to make a crackling or hissing sound

skate *noun* (*plural* **skates**) 1 a boot with a steel blade attached to the sole, used for sliding on ice 2 a roller skate

skate *verb* (**skates, skating, skated**) to move on skates **skater** *noun*

skateboard *noun* (*plural* **skateboards**) a small board with wheels, used for standing and riding on

skeleton *noun* (*plural* **skeletons**) the framework of bones in a person's or animal's body

sketch *noun* (*plural* **sketches**) 1 a quick or rough drawing 2 a short amusing play

sketch *verb* (**sketches, sketching, sketched**) to draw something quickly or roughly

sketchy *adjective* (**sketchier, sketchiest**) roughly drawn or described, without any detail

skewer *noun* (*plural* **skewers**) a long pointed pin that is pushed through meat to hold it together while it is being cooked

ski *noun* (*plural* **skis**) (*pronounced* **skee**) a long flat strip of metal or wood fastened to each foot for moving quickly over snow

ski *verb* (**skis, skiing, skied** or **ski'd**) to travel on skis **skier** *noun*

skid *verb* (**skids, skidding, skidded**) to slide sideways accidentally

skilful *adjective* having a lot of skill **skilfully** *adverb* cleverly or expertly

skill *noun* (*plural* **skills**) the ability to do something well **skilled** *adjective*

skim *verb* (**skims, skimming, skimmed**) 1 to move quickly over a surface 2 to remove something from the surface of a liquid
▸ *Skim the cream off the milk.*

skin *noun* (*plural* **skins**) 1 the outer covering of a person's or animal's body 2 the outer covering of a fruit or vegetable 3 a thin layer on the surface of a liquid

skin *verb* (**skins, skinning, skinned**) to take the skin off something

skinny *adjective* (**skinnier, skinniest**) very thin

skip *verb* (**skips, skipping, skipped**) 1 to jump or move along by hopping from one foot to the other 2 to jump with a skipping rope 3 to miss something out or ignore it
▸ *You'll have to skip a few pages to finish the book in time.*

skip *noun* (*plural* **skips**) a large metal container for taking away builders' rubbish

skipper *noun* (*plural* **skippers**) the captain of a ship or team

skipping rope *noun* (*plural* **skipping ropes**) a length of rope with a handle at each end, which you swing over your head and under your feet as you jump

skirt *noun* (*plural* **skirts**) a piece of clothing for a woman or girl that hangs down from the waist

skirt *verb* (**skirts, skirting, skirted**) to go round the edge of something

skittle *noun* (*plural* **skittles**) a piece of wood or plastic shaped like a bottle, which you try to knock down with a ball in a game of **skittles**

skull *noun* (*plural* **skulls**) the set of bones in your head

skunk *noun* (*plural* **skunks**) a black furry North American animal that makes an unpleasant smell when it feels threatened

sky *noun* (*plural* **skies**) the space above the earth, where you can see the sun, moon, and stars

skylark *noun* (*plural* **skylarks**) a small brown bird that sings as it hovers high in the air

skylight *noun* (*plural* **skylights**) a window in a roof

skyscraper *noun* (*plural* **skyscrapers**) a very tall building

slab *noun* (*plural* **slabs**) a thick flat piece of something hard

slack *adjective* (**slacker, slackest**) 1 loose; not pulled tight ▸ *The rope was slack.* 2 lazy; not busy or working hard
▸ *Business is often slack on Mondays.*

slacken *verb* (**slackens, slackening, slackened**) to become slack, or to make something slack

slain past participle of **slay**

slam *verb* (**slams, slamming, slammed**) 1 to shut something hard or loudly 2 to hit something with great force ▸ *He slammed the ball into the net.*

slang *noun* a kind of colourful language that you use when speaking to your friends but not in writing or when you want to be polite

slant *verb* (**slants, slanting, slanted**) to slope or lean

slant *noun* (*plural* **slants**) a sloping or leaning position

slap *verb* (**slaps, slapping, slapped**) 1 to hit someone with the palm of your hand 2 to put something somewhere forcefully or carelessly ▸ *We slapped paint on the walls.*

slap *noun* (*plural* **slaps**) a hit with the palm of your hand

slapdash *adjective* careless or messy

slash *verb* (**slashes, slashing, slashed**) 1 to make large cuts in something 2 to reduce prices or costs by a lot

slash (*plural* **slashes**) *noun* a diagonal line (/) used between letters and numbers

slat *noun* (*plural* **slats**) a thin strip of wood or plastic arranged with others

slate *noun* (*plural* **slates**) 1 a kind of grey rock that splits easily into flat plates 2 a piece of this rock used to cover roofs

slaughter *verb* (**slaughters, slaughtering, slaughtered**) **1** to kill an animal for food **2** to kill a large number of people or animals

slaughter *noun* slaughtering or killing

slave *noun* (*plural* **slaves**) a person who is owned by someone else and has to work for them without being paid **slavery** *noun* having slaves, or being a slave

slave *verb* (**slaves, slaving, slaved**) to work very hard

slay *verb* (**slays, slaying, slew, slain**) (old use) to kill someone

sledge or **sled** *noun* (*plural* **sledges** or **sleds**) a vehicle for travelling over snow, with strips of metal or wood instead of wheels

sledgehammer *noun* (*plural* **sledgehammers**) a large heavy hammer

sleek *adjective* (**sleeker, sleekest**) smooth and shiny ▸ *The cat has lovely sleek fur.*

sleep *noun* the state you are in when your body is relaxed, your eyes are closed, and your mind is unconscious, for example at night

sleep *verb* (**sleeps, sleeping, slept**) to have a sleep

sleeper *noun* (*plural* **sleepers**) **1** someone who is asleep ▸ *Lewis is a heavy sleeper.* **2** each of the wooden or concrete beams on which a railway line rests **3** a railway carriage for sleeping in

sleeping bag *noun* (*plural* **sleeping bags**) a warm padded bag for sleeping in

sleepless *adjective* unable to sleep; without sleep ▸ *We've had a sleepless night.*

sleepy *adjective* (**sleepier, sleepiest**) tired and ready to sleep **sleepily** *adverb* **sleepiness** *noun*

sleet *noun* a mixture of rain with snow or hail

sleeve *noun* (*plural* **sleeves**) the part of a piece of clothing that covers your arm **sleeveless** *adjective* not having sleeves

sleigh *noun* (*plural* **sleighs**) (*pronounced* slay) a large sledge pulled by horses

slender *adjective* (**slenderer, slenderest**) slim or thin

slept past tense and past participle of **sleep** *verb*

slew past tense of **slay**

slice *noun* (*plural* **slices**) a thin piece cut off something

slice *verb* (**slices, slicing, sliced**) to cut something into slices

slick *noun* (*plural* **slicks**) a patch of oil floating on water

slide *verb* (**slides, sliding, slid**) to move smoothly over a flat or smooth surface

slide *noun* (*plural* **slides**) **1** a sliding movement **2** a smooth slope for sliding down **3** a type of photograph that lets light through and that can be shown on a screen **4** a small glass plate that you use for examining things under a microscope **5** a large decorative clip for your hair

slight *adjective* (**slighter, slightest**) very small; not serious or important **slightly** *adverb*

slim *adjective* (**slimmer, slimmest**) **1** thin and graceful **2** small ▸ *We have a slim chance of succeeding.*

slim *verb* (**slims, slimming, slimmed**) to try to make yourself slimmer **slimmer** *noun* someone who is trying to lose weight

slime *noun* unpleasant wet slippery stuff ▸ *There was slime on the pond.* **slimy** *adjective*

sling *verb* (**slings, slinging, slung**) **1** to throw something forcefully or carelessly ▸ *They were slinging stones into the lake.* **2** to hang something up or support it so that it hangs loosely ▸ *He had slung the bag round his neck.*

sling *noun* (*plural* **slings**) **1** a piece of cloth tied round your neck to support an injured arm **2** a string with a strap in the middle, for throwing stones

slink *verb* (**slinks, slinking, slunk**) to move in a stealthy or guilty way ▸ *The burglar slunk past the window.*

slip *verb* (**slips, slipping, slipped**) **1** to slide or fall over without meaning to **2** to go somewhere quickly and quietly ▸ *We* *slipped out of the house.* **3** to put something somewhere quickly without being seen ► *Slip this in your pocket.* **4** to do something with a gentle or easy movement ► *I'll just slip on my coat.* **slip up** to make a mistake

slip *noun* (*plural* **slips**) **1** an accidental slide or fall **2** a small mistake **3** a small piece of paper **4** a petticoat **give someone the slip** to escape from someone

slipper *noun* (*plural* **slippers**) a soft light shoe for wearing indoors

slippery *adjective* smooth or wet so that it is difficult to stand on or hold

slit *noun* (*plural* **slits**) a long narrow cut or opening

slit *verb* (**slits**, **slitting**, **slit**) to make a slit in something

slither *verb* (**slithers**, **slithering**, **slithered**) to slip or slide unsteadily

sliver *noun* (*plural* **slivers**) (*rhymes with* river) a thin strip of wood, glass, or other material

slog *verb* (**slogs**, **slogging**, **slogged**) **1** to hit something hard or wildly **2** to work hard ► *I'm slogging away at my essay.* **3** to walk with effort ► *We slogged through the snow.*

slog *noun* a piece of hard work or effort

slogan *noun* (*plural* **slogans**) a catchy phrase used to advertise something

slop *verb* (**slops**, **slopping**, **slopped**) to spill liquid over the edge of its container

slope *noun* (*plural* **slopes**) a surface that has one end higher than the other

slope *verb* (**slopes**, **sloping**, **sloped**) to have one end higher than the other

sloppy *adjective* (**sloppier**, **sloppiest**) **1** liquid, and slopping or dripping easily ► *The paint was sloppy and dripped down the walls.* **2** careless or badly done ► *Their work is sloppy.* **3** weak and sentimental ► *What a sloppy story.* **sloppily** *adverb* **sloppiness** *noun*

slot *noun* (*plural* **slots**) a narrow opening to put things through

sloth *noun* (*plural* **sloths**) (*rhymes with* both) **1** a South American animal that lives in trees and moves very slowly **2** laziness

slouch *verb* (**slouches**, **slouching**, **slouched**) to stand, sit, or move in a lazy way with your shoulders rounded and your head bent forwards

slovenly *adjective* (*pronounced* **sluv**-en-li) careless or untidy

slow *adjective* (**slower**, **slowest**) **1** not quick; taking more time than usual **2** (describing a clock or watch) not showing the correct time, so you think it is earlier than it really is ► *I missed the train because my watch was slow.* **slowly** *adverb* **slowness** *noun*

slow *verb* (**slows**, **slowing**, **slowed**) **slow down** to go more slowly ► *You'll have to slow down at the traffic lights.*

slug *noun* (*plural* **slugs**) a slimy animal like a snail without a shell

slum *noun* (*plural* **slums**) an area where very poor people live, in houses that are overcrowded and in bad condition

slumber *verb* (**slumbers**, **slumbering**, **slumbered**) to sleep peacefully

slump *verb* (**slumps**, **slumping**, **slumped**) to fall heavily or suddenly

slung past tense and past participle of **sling** *verb*

slunk past tense and past participle of **slink**

slush *noun* snow that is melting on the ground **slushy** *adjective*

sly *adjective* (**slyer**, **slyest**) cunning or mischievous **slyly** *adverb* **slyness** *noun*

smack *verb* (**smacks**, **smacking**, **smacked**) to hit someone with the palm of your hand

smack *noun* (*plural* **smacks**) a slap

small *adjective* (**smaller, smallest**) not large; less than the normal size

smart *adjective* (**smarter, smartest**) 1 neat and well dressed 2 clever 3 fast ▸ *She set off at a smart pace.* **smartly** *adverb*

smart *verb* (**smarts, smarting, smarted**) to feel a stinging pain

smash *verb* (**smashes, smashing, smashed**) 1 to break into pieces noisily and violently 2 to hit something with great force ▸ *The lorry left the road and smashed into a wall.*

smash *noun* (*plural* **smashes**) a collision between road vehicles

smear *verb* (**smears, smearing, smeared**) to rub something sticky or greasy over a surface

smear *noun* (*plural* **smears**) a sticky mark or smudge

smell *verb* (**smells, smelling, smelt** or smelled) 1 to use your nose to sense something ▸ *I can smell coffee.* 2 to give out a smell ▸ *The room smells of roses.*

smell *noun* (*plural* **smells**) 1 something you can smell ▸ *There was a strong smell of burning.* 2 the ability to smell things ▸ *I have a good sense of smell.*

smelly *adjective* (**smellier, smelliest**) having an unpleasant smell

smelt *verb* (**smelts, smelting, smelted**) to melt ore in order to get metal from it

smile *verb* (**smiles, smiling, smiled**) to make an expression with your lips stretched and turning upwards at the ends, showing that you are pleased or amused

smile *noun* (*plural* **smiles**) a pleased or amused expression on your face

smith *noun* (*plural* **smiths**) someone who makes things out of metal

smock *noun* (*plural* **smocks**) a loose piece of clothing like a very long shirt

smog *noun* a mixture of smoke and fog

smoke *noun* the grey or blue mixture of gas and particles that rises from a fire **smoky** *adjective*

smoke *verb* (**smokes, smoking, smoked**) 1 to give out smoke ▸ *The fire is smoking.* 2 to breathe in the smoke of tobacco

smoker *noun* someone who smokes cigarettes or a pipe

smooth *adjective* (**smoother, smoothest**) 1 having an even surface without any marks or roughness ▸ *The top of the table was smooth and polished.* 2 having no lumps ▸ *Stir the mixture until it is smooth.* 3 moving without bumps or jolts ▸ *We had a smooth ride.* 4 not harsh; flowing easily ▸ *She spoke in a smooth voice.* 5 without any serious problems ▸ *The change to the metric system was quite smooth.* **smoothly** *adverb* in a smooth way; evenly **smoothness** *noun* being smooth

smooth *verb* (**smooths, smoothing, smoothed**) to make something smooth

smother *verb* (**smothers, smothering, smothered**) 1 to kill someone by stopping them from breathing 2 to cover something thickly ▸ *He brought in a cake smothered in icing.*

smoulder *verb* (**smoulders, smouldering, smouldered**) to burn slowly without a flame

smudge *noun* (*plural* **smudges**) a dirty mark made by rubbing something

smudge *verb* (**smudges, smudging, smudged**) to make a smudge on something

smug *adjective* too pleased with yourself **smugly** *adverb* **smugness** *noun*

smuggle *verb* (**smuggles, smuggling, smuggled**) to bring goods into a country illegally or secretly **smuggler** *noun*

smut *noun* (*plural* **smuts**) a small piece of soot or dirt

snack *noun* (*plural* **snacks**) a small meal eaten quickly

snag *noun* (*plural* **snags**) an unexpected difficulty or obstacle

snail *noun* (*plural* **snails**) a small animal with a soft body in a hard shell

snake *noun* (*plural* **snakes**) a reptile with a long narrow body and no legs

snap *verb* (**snaps, snapping, snapped**) 1 to break suddenly with a sharp noise 2 to bite fiercely at someone ▸ *The dog snaps at everyone.* 3 to say something quickly and angrily **4** to make a sharp sound with your fingers

snap noun (*plural* **snaps**) **1** the act or sound of snapping **2** a photograph **3** a card game in which you shout 'snap'

snappy adjective (**snappier, snappiest**) quick and lively

snare noun (*plural* **snares**) a trap for catching animals

snare verb (**snares, snaring, snared**) to catch an animal in a snare

snarl verb (**snarls, snarling, snarled**) (used about an animal) to growl angrily, showing the teeth **be snarled up** to become tangled or jammed ▸ *The motorway was snarled up for several miles.*

snarl noun (*plural* **snarls**) a snarling sound or expression

snatch verb (**snatches, snatching, snatched**) to grab something quickly ▸ *She snatched the bag and ran out of the house.*

sneak verb (**sneaks, sneaking, sneaked**) to move quietly and secretly ▸ *When they aren't looking we can sneak out of the house.*

sneak noun (*plural* **sneaks**) (informal) a person who tells tales

sneaky adjective (**sneakier, sneakiest**) dishonest or deceitful **sneakily** adverb

sneer verb (**sneers, sneering, sneered**) to curl your lip in a way that shows scorn or disapproval

sneeze verb (**sneezes, sneezing, sneezed**) to blow out air through your nose suddenly and uncontrollably

sneeze noun (*plural* **sneezes**) the action or sound of sneezing

sniff verb (**sniffs, sniffing, sniffed**) **1** to make a noise by drawing air in through your nose **2** to smell something by sniffing

sniff noun (*plural* **sniffs**) the action or sound of sniffing

snigger verb (**sniggers, sniggering, sniggered**) to give a quiet sly laugh

snigger noun (*plural* **sniggers**) the action or sound of sniggering

snip verb (**snips, snipping, snipped**) to cut a small piece or pieces off something

sniper noun (*plural* **snipers**) someone who shoots at people from a hiding place

snippet noun (*plural* **snippets**) a short piece of news or information

snivel verb (**snivels, snivelling, snivelled**) to cry or complain in a whining way

snob noun (*plural* **snobs**) someone who looks down on people who are poor, and admires people who are rich and powerful **snobbery** noun being a snob **snobbish** adjective

snooker noun a game played with long sticks (called *cues*) and coloured balls which you have to hit into pockets round the edge of a long cloth-covered table

snoop verb (**snoops, snooping, snooped**) to pry or try to find out about someone else's business **snooper** noun

snooze verb (**snoozes, snoozing, snoozed**) to sleep lightly or for a short time

snooze noun (*plural* **snoozes**) a short sleep

snore verb (**snores, snoring, snored**) to make loud breathing noises while you are sleeping

snorkel noun (*plural* **snorkels**) a tube for breathing through when you are swimming underwater

snort verb (**snorts, snorting, snorted**) to make a noise by forcing air out through your nose

snort noun (*plural* **snorts**) a noise of someone snorting

snout noun (*plural* **snouts**) the front part of an animal's head, with its nose and mouth

snow noun frozen drops of water falling from the sky as small white flakes **snowy** adjective

snow verb (**snows, snowing, snowed**) to fall as snow ▸ *It was still snowing when they went out.* ▸ *It might snow later.*

snowball noun (*plural* **snowballs**) a hard ball made by pressing snow

snowdrop *noun* (*plural* **snowdrops**)
a small white spring flower

snowflake *noun* (*plural* **snowflakes**)
a flake of snow

snowman *noun* (*plural* **snowmen**) a
figure of a person made of snow

snowplough *noun* (*plural* **snowploughs**)
a vehicle with a large blade at the front for
clearing snow from a road or railway track

snub *verb* (**snubs, snubbing, snubbed**) to be
unkind to someone who is trying to be
friendly

snug *adjective* (**snugger, snuggest**) warm
and comfortable **snugly** *adverb*

snuggle *verb* (**snuggles, snuggling,
snuggled**) to curl up close to someone or in
a comfortable place

so *adverb* 1 to such an extent ▸ *Why are
you so cross?* ▸ *It was so late we went to
bed.* 2 also ▸ *I was wrong but so were you.*
or so or about that number ▸ *We need
about fifty or so.* **so as to** in order to **so far**
up to now **so what?** (informal) what does
that matter?

so *conjunction* for that reason ▸ *It was
dark, so we took a torch.*

soak *verb* (**soaks, soaking, soaked**) to make
someone or something very wet **soak up** to
take in liquid in the way that a sponge
does

soap *noun* (*plural* **soaps**) a substance used
with water for washing and cleaning
things **soapy** *adjective*

soap opera *noun* (*plural* **soap operas**)
a television serial about the ordinary life
of a group of imaginary people

soar *verb* (**soars, soaring, soared**) 1 to rise
or fly high in the air 2 to increase a lot
▸ *Prices were soaring.*

sob *verb* (**sobs, sobbing, sobbed**) to cry with
gasping noises

sob *noun* (*plural* **sobs**) a sound of sobbing

sober *adjective* 1 not drunk 2 calm and
serious ▸ *Myra had a sober expression on
her face.* 3 not bright or showy ▸ *The
room was painted in sober colours.*

so-called *adjective* having the name but
perhaps not deserving it ▸ *Even his so-
called friends deserted him.*

soccer *noun* short for *Association football*, a
form of football played with a round ball
which only the goalkeeper may handle
during play

sociable *adjective* (*pronounced* **soh-sha-
bul**) liking to be with other people;
friendly

social *adjective* (*pronounced* **soh-shal**)
1 living in a community ▸ *Bees are social
insects.* 2 to do with society ▸ *a social
problem* 3 helping the people in a
community ▸ *a social worker* 4 helping
people to meet one another ▸ *a social club*
socially *adverb*

socialism *noun* a political system in which
all the people share the wealth and the
state controls the main industries **socialist**
noun and *adjective*

society *noun* (*plural* **societies**) 1 people
living together in a group or nation
2 a group of people organized for a
particular purpose ▸ *Harry was a member
of a local poetry society.*

sock *noun* (*plural* **socks**) a soft piece of
clothing that covers your foot

socket *noun* (*plural* **sockets**) a hole or set
of holes into which a device such as an
electric plug fits

soda *noun* 1 a substance made from
sodium, such as baking soda 2 soda water

soda water *noun* fizzy water used in
drinks

sodium *noun* a soft silvery-white metallic element that is found in salt

sofa *noun* (*plural* **sofas**) a long soft seat with sides and a back, for more than one person

soft *adjective* (**softer, softest**) 1 not hard or firm; easily pressed or cut into a new shape ▶ *soft clay* 2 smooth; not rough or stiff ▶ *soft fur* 3 gentle; not loud ▶ *a soft voice* **softly** *adverb* **softness** *noun*

soft drink *noun* (*plural* **soft drinks**) a cold drink that does not contain alcohol

soften *verb* (**softens, softening, softened**) to become softer, or make something softer

software *noun* computer programs and data

soggy *adjective* (**soggier, soggiest**) wet and soft

soil *noun* the loose earth that plants grow in

soil *verb* (**soils, soiling, soiled**) to make something dirty

solar *adjective* 1 to do with the sun 2 powered by the sun's energy

solar system *noun* the sun and the planets that revolve round it

sold past tense and past participle of **sell**

solder *noun* a soft alloy that is melted to join pieces of metal together

solder *verb* (**solders, soldering, soldered**) to join things with solder

soldier *noun* (*plural* **soldiers**) someone who belongs to an army

sole[1] *noun* (*plural* **soles**) the part of your shoe or foot that you walk on

sole[2] *noun* (*plural* **sole**) a flat sea fish used for food

sole[3] *adjective* single or only ▶ *A young child was the sole survivor of the attack.* **solely** *adverb*

solemn *adjective* serious and dignified **solemnity** *noun* being serious and dignified **solemnly** *adverb*

solicitor *noun* (*plural* **solicitors**) a lawyer who advises clients and prepares legal documents

solid *adjective* 1 not hollow; with no space inside 2 keeping its shape; not a liquid or gas 3 firm or strongly made ▶ *The house was well built with solid walls.* 4 strong and reliable ▶ *They gave solid support.* **solidly** *adverb* **solidity** *noun* firmness

solid *noun* (*plural* **solids**) something that is solid

solidarity *noun* keeping together and supporting each other

solidify *verb* (**solidifies, solidifying, solidified**) to become solid

solitary *adjective* 1 alone; on your own ▶ *He lived a solitary life.* 2 single ▶ *There was a solitary van in the car park.*

solitude *noun* being on your own

solo *noun* (*plural* **solos**) something sung or performed by one person **soloist** *noun*

soluble *adjective* able to be dissolved

solution *noun* (*plural* **solutions**) 1 the answer to a problem or puzzle 2 a liquid with something dissolved in it

solve *verb* (**solves, solving, solved**) to find the answer to a problem, puzzle, or mystery

sombre *adjective* gloomy and dark

some *adjective* 1 a few or a little ▶ *I'd like some biscuits and some jam.* 2 an unknown person or thing ▶ *Some animal has left a paw mark here.*

some *pronoun* a certain number or amount ▶ *Some of them were late.*

somebody *pronoun* someone; some person ▶ *Can somebody help me?*

somehow *adverb* in some way ▶ *We must get home somehow.*

someone *pronoun* some person ▶ *I saw someone in the garden.*

somersault noun (plural **somersaults**) (pronounced **sum-er-solt**) a movement in which you turn head over heels and land on your feet

something pronoun a thing ▸ *Something exciting has happened!*

sometime adverb at some uncertain time ▸ *I'll be seeing her sometime next week.*

sometimes adverb at some times but not always ▸ *We sometimes walk home.*

somewhat adverb to some extent; rather ▸ *It was somewhat late.*

somewhere adverb in or to some place ▸ *I put my coat down somewhere, and now I can't find it.*

son noun (plural **sons**) a boy or man who is someone's child

sonar noun a system using the echo from sound waves to locate objects underwater The word **sonar** comes from **so**und **na**vigation and **r**anging.

song noun (plural **songs**) 1 a piece of music with words for singing 2 singing ▸ *He burst into song.*

songbird noun (plural **songbirds**) a bird that sings sweetly

sonic adjective to do with sound or sound waves

sonnet noun (plural **sonnets**) a poem of 14 lines with a fixed rhyming pattern

soon adverb (**sooner**, **soonest**) 1 in a short time from now ▸ *It will be time to go soon.* 2 not long after something ▸ *She became ill, but was soon better.* 3 early or quickly ▸ *How soon will lunch be ready?*

soot noun the black powder left by smoke in a chimney or on a building **sooty** adjective

soothe verb (**soothes**, **soothing**, **soothed**) 1 to make someone calm 2 to make a pain or ache hurt less

sophisticated adjective 1 used to a fashionable or cultured life ▸ *sophisticated people* 2 able to do complex things ▸ *a sophisticated machine* **sophistication** noun being sophisticated

sopping adjective very wet; soaked

soppy adjective (**soppier**, **soppiest**) (informal) sentimental or silly

soprano noun (plural **sopranos**) (pronounced **so-prah-noh**) a singer with a high singing voice

sorcerer noun (plural **sorcerers**) someone who performs magic spells **sorcery** noun performing magic

sore adjective (**sorer**, **sorest**) painful or smarting **soreness** noun

sore noun (plural **sores**) a sore place

sorely adverb seriously; very ▸ *We were sorely tempted to run away.*

sorrow noun (plural **sorrows**) sadness or regret **sorrowful** adjective

sorry adjective (**sorrier**, **sorriest**) feeling regret or sadness

sort noun (plural **sorts**) a group of things or people that are similar; a kind ▸ *What sort of food do you like?*

sort verb (**sorts**, **sorting**, **sorted**) to arrange things in groups or kinds **sort out** to organize something or arrange it in order

SOS noun an urgent appeal for help or rescue

sought past tense and past participle of **seek**

soul noun (plural **souls**) 1 the invisible part of a person. Some people believe that your soul goes on living after your body has died. 2 a person ▸ *Don't tell a soul.*

sound^1 noun (plural **sounds**) something you can hear

sound verb (**sounds**, **sounding**, **sounded**) 1 to make a sound ▸ *A bell sounded.* ▸ *Sound your horn at the corner.* 2 to give a certain impression when someone hears it ▸ *He sounds pleased.* ▸ *The car sounds as if it needs a service.* **sound out** to try to find out what someone thinks about something

sound^2 adjective (**sounder**, **soundest**) 1 not damaged; in good condition 2 healthy 3 reasonable or correct ▸ *He says odd things but his ideas are sound.* 4 reliable or secure ▸ *They made a sound investment.* 5 thorough or deep ▸ *I could do with a sound sleep.* **soundly** adverb thoroughly or completely

sound effects *plural noun* special sounds produced to make a play or film more realistic

soundproof *adjective* preventing sound from passing through ▶ *a soundproof room*

soundtrack *noun* (*plural* **soundtracks**) the sound that goes with a cinema film

soup *noun* (*plural* **soups**) a liquid food made from vegetables or meat

sour *adjective* (**sourer, sourest**) 1 having a sharp taste like vinegar or lemons 2 unpleasant or bad-tempered **sourly** *adverb* **sourness** *noun*

source *noun* (*plural* **sources**) the place from which something comes ▶ *We're not sure what the source of the rumour is.*

south *noun* the direction to the right of a person facing east

south *adjective* and *adverb* 1 towards the south or in the south 2 (describing the wind) coming from the south

south-east *noun* and *adjective* and *adverb* midway between south and east

southerly *adjective* (*pronounced* **suth-er-lee**) 1 to the south or towards the south ▶ *We were travelling in a southerly direction.* 2 (describing the wind) blowing from the south

southern *adjective* (*pronounced* **suth-ern**) from or to do with the south

southerner *noun* (*plural* **southerners**) (*pronounced* **suth-er-ner**) someone who lives in the south of a country

southward or **southwards** *adjective* and *adverb* towards the south

south-west *noun* and *adjective* and *adverb* midway between south and west

souvenir *noun* (*plural* **souvenirs**) (*pronounced* **soo-ven-eer**) something that you keep to remind you of a person, place, or event
The word **souvenir** comes from a French word meaning 'to remember'.

sovereign *noun* (*plural* **sovereigns**) (*pronounced* **sov-rin**) 1 a king or a queen 2 an old British gold coin that was worth £1

sow[1] *verb* (**sows, sowing, sowed, sown** or **sowed**) (*rhymes with* go) to put seeds into the ground so that they will grow into plants

sow[2] *noun* (*plural* **sows**) (*rhymes with* cow) a female pig

soya bean *noun* (*plural* **soya beans**) a bean that is rich in protein, used to make kinds of oil and flour

space *noun* (*plural* **spaces**) 1 the whole area outside the earth, where the stars and planets are 2 an area or volume ▶ *There is plenty of space for a car.* 3 an empty area or gap ▶ *There is a space at the back of the cupboard.* 4 a period of time ▶ *They moved house twice in the space of a year.*

space *verb* (**spaces, spacing, spaced**) to arrange things with gaps or periods of time between them

spacecraft *noun* (*plural* **spacecraft**) a vehicle for travelling in outer space

space shuttle *noun* (*plural* **space shuttles**) a spacecraft that can travel into space and back to earth

space station *noun* (*plural* **space stations**) a satellite which orbits the earth and is used as a base for astronauts

spacious *adjective* having plenty of space **spaciousness** *noun*

spade *noun* (*plural* **spades**) 1 a tool with a long handle and a wide blade for digging 2 a playing card with the shape of a black upside-down heart printed on it

spaghetti *noun* (*pronounced* **spa-get-i**) pasta made in long strings, usually served with a sauce

span *noun* (*plural* **spans**) 1 the length of something from one end to the other 2 the distance between the tips of your thumb and little finger when your hand is spread out 3 a part of a bridge between two supports 4 a period of time

span *verb* (**spans, spanning, spanned**) to reach from one side or end of something to the other ▶ *Several bridges span the river.*

spaniel *noun* (*plural* **spaniels**) a breed of dog with long ears and silky fur

spank *verb* (**spanks, spanking, spanked**) to smack someone several times on the bottom as a punishment

spanner *noun* (*plural* **spanners**) a tool for tightening or loosening a nut

spare *verb* (**spares, sparing, spared**) **1** to afford something or be able to give it to someone ▸ *Sally needed some money, but her mother could only spare two pounds.* **2** to be merciful towards someone, or not harm them ▸ *The king was willing to spare his enemies.*

spare *adjective* not used but kept ready in case it is needed; extra ▸ *The lorry carries three spare wheels.* ▸ *I don't have any spare money.*

spark *noun* (*plural* **sparks**) **1** a tiny flash **2** a tiny glowing piece of something hot

spark *verb* (**sparks, sparking, sparked**) to give off sparks

sparkle *verb* (**sparkles, sparkling, sparkled**) to shine with tiny flashes of bright light

sparkler *noun* (*plural* **sparklers**) a firework that sparkles

sparrow *noun* (*plural* **sparrows**) a small brown bird

sparse *adjective* (**sparser, sparsest**) small in amount and thinly scattered **sparsely** *adverb*

spasm *noun* (*plural* **spasms**) a sudden jerking movement

spat past tense and past participle of **spit** *verb*

spatter *verb* (**spatters, spattering, spattered**) to splash something or scatter it in small drops or pieces ▸ *The lorry spattered mud all over the pavement.*

spawn *noun* the eggs of frogs, fish, and other water animals

speak *verb* (**speaks, speaking, spoke, spoken**) **1** to say something ▸ *She was too upset to speak.* ▸ *I spoke to Kelly this morning.* **2** to be able to talk in a language ▸ *Do you speak Spanish?*

speaker *noun* (*plural* **speakers**) **1** a person who is speaking **2** the part of a radio or music system that produces the sound

spear *noun* (*plural* **spears**) a long pole with a sharp point, used as a weapon for throwing

spear *verb* (**spears, spearing, speared**) to pierce something with a spear or something pointed

special *adjective* **1** different from other people or things; unusual **2** meant for a particular person or purpose ▸ *There's a special tool for taking out broken screws.*

specialist *noun* (*plural* **specialists**) an expert in a particular subject

speciality *noun* (*plural* **specialities**) something that you are especially good at doing

specialize *verb* (**specializes, specializing, specialized**) to study a particular subject or concentrate on a particular area in your work ▸ *She specializes in biology.*

specially *adverb* for a special purpose ▸ *I came specially to see you.*

species *noun* (*plural* **species**) (*pronounced* **spee**-shiz) a group of animals or plants that are similar in some way

specific *adjective* **1** definite or precise ▸ *We have to know the specific day it happened.* **2** to do with a particular thing ▸ *I was given the money for a specific purpose.*

specifically *adverb* for a special purpose ▸ *The car is designed specifically for taller drivers.*

specify *verb* (**specifies, specifying, specified**) to name someone or something precisely ▸ *The recipe specifies brown sugar, not white.*

specimen *noun* (*plural* **specimens**) a small amount or sample of something

speck *noun* (*plural* **specks**) a tiny piece of something

speckled *adjective* covered with small spots

spectacle *noun* (*plural* **spectacles**) something exciting to see

spectacles *plural noun* a pair of lenses in a frame, which you wear over your eyes if you need to improve your eyesight

spectacular *adjective* exciting to see

spectator *noun* (*plural* **spectators**) a person who watches a game or show

spectre *noun* (*plural* **spectres**) (*pronounced* **spek**-ter) a ghost

spectrum *noun* (*plural* **spectra**) the band of colours like those in a rainbow

speech *noun* (*plural* **speeches**) 1 the action or power of speaking 2 a talk given to a group of people

speechless *adjective* unable to speak, especially because you are surprised or angry

speed *noun* (*plural* **speeds**) how fast something or someone moves, or how quickly something happens

speed *verb* (**speeds, speeding, sped** or **speeded**) to go very fast or faster than is allowed ▶ *Drivers can be fined for speeding.* **speed up** to become quicker

speedboat *noun* (*plural* **speedboats**) a fast motor boat

speedometer *noun* (*plural* **speedometers**) (*pronounced* spee-**dom**-it-er) a gauge in a vehicle that shows how fast it is moving

speedy *adjective* (**speedier, speediest**) quick or fast ▶ *We need a speedy reply.* **speedily** *adverb*

spell[1] *verb* (**spells, spelling, spelt** or **spelled**) to say or write the letters of a word in the right order

spell[2] *noun* (*plural* **spells**) 1 a period of time or activity ▶ *We are going to spend a short spell in the country.* 2 in stories, a saying that is supposed to have magic power ▶ *The wizard looked in his book of spells.*

spelling *noun* (*plural* **spellings**) the way in which letters are put together to make a word

spend *verb* (**spends, spending, spent**) 1 to use money to pay for something 2 to pass time doing something ▶ *He spent a year in Singapore.*

sperm *noun* (*plural* **sperms** or **sperm**) a male cell that can fertilize a female egg

sphere *noun* (*plural* **spheres**) a round solid shape like a globe or ball **spherical** *adjective* shaped like a ball

spice *noun* (*plural* **spices**) a strong-tasting substance made from the dried parts of plants and used to flavour food **spicy** *adjective* having a strong flavour; full or spices

spider *noun* (*plural* **spiders**) a small animal with eight legs that spins webs to catch insects

spied past tense and past participle of **spy** *verb*

spike *noun* (*plural* **spikes**) a sharp point **spiky** *adjective*

spill *verb* (**spills, spilling, spilt** or **spilled**) 1 to let something fall out of a container by accident ▶ *A lorry had spilled its load on the motorway.* ▶ *Don't spill your drink.* 2 to fall out ▶ *The coins came spilling out.*

spin *verb* (**spins, spinning, spun**) 1 to turn round and round quickly 2 to make pieces of wool or cotton into thread by twisting them 3 to make a web or cocoon out of threads

spinach *noun* a vegetable with dark green leaves

spindle *noun* (*plural* **spindles**) a thin rod on which you wind something or round which something turns

spine *noun* (*plural* **spines**) 1 the line of bones down the middle of your back 2 a thorn or prickle 3 the back part of a book where the pages are joined together **spinal** *adjective* to do with your spine

spinning wheel *noun* (*plural* **spinning wheels**) a machine for spinning thread from wool or cotton

spinster *noun* (*plural* **spinsters**) a woman who is not married
The word used to mean 'a woman who spins wool or cotton', and that is what women who were not married often used to do.

spiral *adjective* going round in a series of circles that get larger and larger

spire *noun* (*plural* **spires**) a tall pointed part on top of a church tower

spirit *noun* (*plural* **spirits**) 1 a person's soul 2 a ghost or other supernatural being 3 courage or liveliness 4 a person's mood or the way they feel ▶ *She was in good spirits after the exam.* 5 a strong alcoholic drink, such as gin or whisky

spiritual *adjective* 1 to do with your soul 2 to do with religion or the Church **spiritually** *adverb*
spiritual *noun* (*plural* **spirituals**) a religious song originally sung by Black Americans

spit¹ *verb* (**spits, spitting, spat**) to shoot drops of liquid out of your mouth
spit *noun* (*plural* **spits**) 1 saliva from your mouth 2 a metal spike that you put through meat to hold it while it is roasted

spite *noun* a strong wish to hurt or annoy someone to get your own back **in spite of** although something has happened or is happening ▶ *They went out in spite of the rain.* **spiteful** *adjective* wanting to hurt or annoy someone **spitefully** *adverb*

splash *verb* (**splashes, splashing, splashed**) 1 to make someone or something wet by sending drops of liquid towards them ▶ *Ben stood there with the brush in his hand, splashing us with paint.* 2 to fly about in drops ▶ *The water splashed all over me.*
splash *noun* (*plural* **splashes**) the action or sound of splashing

splendid *adjective* magnificent; very fine **splendidly** *adverb*

splendour *noun* a brilliant display or appearance

splint *noun* (*plural* **splints**) a strip of wood or something else hard that is tied to a broken arm or leg to hold it firm

splinter *noun* (*plural* **splinters**) a thin sharp piece of wood or glass broken off a larger piece
splinter *verb* (**splinters, splintering, splintered**) to break into splinters

split *verb* (**splits, splitting, split**) to break or separate into parts **split up** to separate after being together for some time
split *noun* (*plural* **splits**) a place where something has split

splutter *verb* (**splutters, spluttering, spluttered**) to make a lot of spitting or coughing sounds ▶ *The smoke from the bonfire made us splutter.*

spoil *verb* (**spoils, spoiling, spoilt** or **spoiled**) 1 to make something less good or useful ▶ *Kevin didn't want to spoil the story by giving away the ending.* 2 to make someone selfish by always letting them have what they want

spoke¹ *noun* (*plural* **spokes**) one of the rods that go from the centre of a wheel to the rim

spoke² past tense of **speak**

spoken past participle of **speak**

sponge *noun* (*plural* **sponges**) 1 a sea creature with a soft body full of holes, which soaks up water 2 a lump of soft material containing lots of tiny holes, used for washing 3 a soft light cake or pudding **spongy** *adjective* soft, squashy, or full of holes, like a sponge
sponge *verb* (**sponges, sponging, sponged**) to wash with a sponge

sponsor *noun* (*plural* **sponsors**) someone who supports an activity with money, or who agrees to pay money to charity if someone completes a task, such as a walk **sponsorship** *noun* sponsoring someone or something

spontaneous *adjective* (*pronounced* spon-tay-ni-us) happening or done without being planned ▶ *A spontaneous cheer* greeted the visitors. **spontaneously** adverb **spontaneity** noun behaving in a spontaneous way

spooky adjective (**spookier, spookiest**) (informal) frighteningly strange or ghostly **spookily** adverb **spookiness** noun

spool noun (plural **spools**) a reel for winding on something long and thin such as thread or tape

spoon noun (plural **spoons**) a device with a small shallow bowl and a handle, used for lifting food to your mouth or for stirring or measuring

spoonful noun (plural **spoonfuls**) as much as a spoon will hold

sport noun (plural **sports**) a game that exercises your body, especially a game played out of doors

sportsman or **sportswoman** noun (plural **sportsmen** or **sportswomen**) a man or woman who takes part in sport **sportsmanship** noun behaving fairly and considerately

spot noun (plural **spots**) 1 a small round mark 2 a pimple on your skin 3 a small amount of something ▶ We've had a spot of difficulty. 4 a place ▶ Let's find a shady spot by the trees. **on the spot** immediately; there and then ▶ We can repair your bike on the spot. **spotty** adjective having spots

spot verb (**spots, spotting, spotted**) 1 to notice someone or something 2 to mark something with spots

spotless adjective completely clean **spotlessly** adverb

spotlight noun (plural **spotlights**) a strong light with a beam that shines on a small area

spout noun (plural **spouts**) a pipe or opening for pouring liquid

spout verb (**spouts, spouting, spouted**) to come out in a jet of liquid

sprain verb (**sprains, spraining, sprained**) to injure your ankle or wrist by twisting it

sprain noun (plural **sprains**) an injury of this kind

sprang past tense of **spring** verb

sprawl verb (**sprawls, sprawling, sprawled**) 1 to sit or lie with your arms and legs spread out 2 to be spread out loosely or untidily ▶ There were books and papers sprawled all over the floor.

spray verb (**sprays, spraying, sprayed**) to scatter liquid in tiny drops over something

spray noun (plural **sprays**) 1 tiny drops of liquid sprayed on something 2 a device for spraying liquid

spread verb (**spreads, spreading, spread**) 1 to lay or stretch something out to its full size ▶ I spread the newspaper on the table. 2 to make something cover a surface ▶ The butter was hard and difficult to spread. 3 to make news or information widely known 4 to reach a large number of people or a large area ▶ The disease began to spread.

spread noun (plural **spreads**) a soft food that you spread on bread

spreadsheet noun (plural **spreadsheets**) a table with columns of figures that you create on a computer

sprightly adjective (**sprightlier, sprightliest**) lively and energetic

spring verb (**springs, springing, sprang, sprung**) 1 to move quickly or suddenly ▶ She sprang to her feet. 2 to happen as a result of something ▶ The trouble has sprung from carelessness. 3 to surprise someone with something ▶ They sprang a new idea on us last night.

spring noun (plural **springs**) 1 a coil of metal that springs back to its full size after being squeezed 2 a sudden upward movement 3 a place where water rises out of the ground 4 the season of the year when most plants start to grow, between winter and summer

springy adjective (**springier, springiest**) able to spring back to its original position when you bend it or squeeze it and let it go

sprinkle verb (**sprinkles, sprinkling, sprinkled**) to make tiny drops of liquid or pieces of powder fall on something **sprinkler** noun a device for sprinkling water

sprint *verb* (**sprints, sprinting, sprinted**) to run very fast for a short distance **sprinter** *noun*

sprout *verb* (**sprouts, sprouting, sprouted**) to start to grow or to produce leaves

sprout *noun* (*plural* **sprouts**) a small green vegetable like a tiny cabbage

spruce *adjective* (**sprucer, sprucest**) neat and smart

sprung past participle of **spring** *verb*

spun past tense and past participle of **spin** *verb*

spur *noun* (*plural* **spurs**) a sharp spike on the heel of a rider's boot, used to urge a horse to go faster **on the spur of the moment** on an impulse

spur *verb* (**spurs, spurring, spurred**) 1 to urge a horse to go faster 2 to encourage someone to do something ▶ *Promise of a reward spurred us to action.*

spurt *verb* (**spurts, spurting, spurted**) 1 to come out in a fast stream ▶ *Water spurted from the tap.* 2 to speed up suddenly ▶ *The car spurted past us.*

spurt *noun* (*plural* **spurts**) 1 a jet of liquid 2 a sudden increase in speed ▶ *He put on a spurt and caught us up.*

spy *noun* (*plural* **spies**) someone who works secretly to find out things about another country

spy *verb* (**spies, spying, spied**) 1 to be a spy or to watch secretly ▶ *He was spying on us.* 2 to notice someone or something ▶ *We spied a house in the distance.*

squabble *verb* (**squabbles, squabbling, squabbled**) to quarrel about something unimportant

squabble *noun* (*plural* **squabbles**) a silly quarrel

squad *noun* (*plural* **squads**) a small group of people working or being trained together

squadron *noun* (*plural* **squadrons**) part of an army, navy, or air force

squalid *adjective* dirty and unpleasant ▶ *The old houses were cramped and squalid.* **squalor** *noun* a dirty, unpleasant state

squall *noun* (*plural* **squalls**) a sudden storm or strong wind **squally** *adjective*

squander *verb* (**squanders, squandering, squandered**) to waste money or time

square *noun* (*plural* **squares**) 1 a shape or object that has four equal sides and four right angles 2 in a town, an open space with buildings on all sides

square *adjective* 1 in the shape of a square ▶ *a square window* 2 used in measurements of area. A square metre is a unit of area that measures one metre along each side. 3 equal or even ▶ *The teams are square with six points each.*

square *verb* (**squares, squaring, squared**) 1 to multiply a number by itself ▶ *5 squared is 25.* 2 to match or agree with something else ▶ *His story doesn't square with yours.*

squarely *adverb* directly; exactly ▶ *The ball hit him squarely in the chest.*

square meal *noun* (*plural* **square meals**) a good satisfying meal

square root *noun* (*plural* **square roots**) the number that gives another number if it is multiplied by itself ▶ *5 is the square root of 25.*

squash *verb* (**squashes, squashing, squashed**) to squeeze something hard

squash *noun* (*plural* **squashes**) 1 a crowd or a crowded place ▶ *There was a tremendous squash outside the stadium.* 2 a fruit-flavoured drink 3 a fleshy vegetable that you can cook and eat 4 a game played with rackets and a small ball in a special indoor court **squashy** *adjective* soft and easy to squash

squat *verb* (**squats, squatting, squatted**) 1 to sit back on your heels 2 to live in an empty building without permission **squatter** *noun* someone who squats in a building

squat *adjective* (**squatter, squattest**) short and fat

squaw *noun* (*plural* **squaws**) a Native American woman

squawk *verb* (**squawks, squawking, squawked**) to make a loud harsh cry

squawk *noun* (*plural* **squawks**) a sound of squawking

squeak *verb* (**squeaks, squeaking, squeaked**) to make a high-pitched sound or cry

squeak *noun* (*plural* **squeaks**) a sound of squeaking **squeaky** *adjective*

squeal *verb* (**squeals, squealing, squealed**) to make a long shrill sound

squeal *noun* (*plural* **squeals**) a sound of squealing

squeamish *adjective* easily feeling sick or disgusted

squeeze *verb* (**squeezes, squeezing, squeezed**) 1 to press something from opposite sides, especially so as to get liquid out of it 2 to force a way into or through a small space ▸ *We squeezed into the car.* **squeezer** *noun* a device for squeezing lemons

squeeze *noun* (*plural* **squeezes**) the action of squeezing something

squelch *verb* (**squelches, squelching, squelched**) to make a sound like someone treading in thick mud

squelch *noun* (*plural* **squelches**) a sound of squelching

squid *noun* (*plural* **squid** or **squids**) a sea animal with tentacles

squint *verb* (**squints, squinting, squinted**) 1 to have eyes that look in different directions at the same time 2 to peer at something or look at it with half-shut eyes

squint *noun* (*plural* **squints**) a fault of the eyes that makes someone squint

squirm *verb* (**squirms, squirming, squirmed**) to wriggle about when you feel uncomfortable or embarrassed

squirrel *noun* (*plural* **squirrels**) a small animal with grey or red fur and a bushy tail

squirt *verb* (**squirts, squirting, squirted**) to send out liquid in a strong jet ▸ *The man was angry because Keith had squirted water at him.*

St short for **Saint** or **Street**

stab *verb* (**stabs, stabbing, stabbed**) 1 to hurt or kill someone by pushing a knife or pointed object into them 2 to poke a thin or sharp object at someone or something

stab *noun* (*plural* **stabs**) a sudden sharp pain

stabilize *verb* (**stabilizes, stabilizing, stabilized**) to make something stable **stabilizer** *noun* a small extra wheel on a bicycle to make it stable

stable *noun* (*plural* **stables**) a building where horses are kept

stable *adjective* (**stabler, stablest**) steady or firmly fixed ▸ *The bed isn't very stable.* **stability** *noun* how stable something is **stably** *adverb*

stack *noun* (*plural* **stacks**) 1 a neat pile 2 a single chimney or a group of chimneys

stack *verb* (**stacks, stacking, stacked**) to put things in a stack or pile

stadium *noun* (*plural* **stadiums** or **stadia**) a large sports ground surrounded by seats for spectators

staff *noun* (*plural* **staffs**) 1 the people who work in an office or shop 2 the teachers in a school or college 3 a thick walking stick

stag *noun* (*plural* **stags**) a male deer

stage *noun* (*plural* **stages**) 1 a raised platform for the performances in a theatre or hall 2 the point that you have reached in a process or journey ▸ *The next stage is to fix the handles on.*

stage *verb* (**stages, staging, staged**) 1 to present a performance on a stage 2 to organize an event ▸ *We are going to stage a protest.*

stagecoach *noun* (*plural* **stagecoaches**) a kind of horse-drawn coach that used to travel on regular routes

stagger *verb* (**staggers, staggering, staggered**) 1 to walk unsteadily 2 to surprise or confuse someone ▸ *I was* *staggered at the price.* **3** to arrange events so that they do not all happen at the same time ▸ *We stagger our holidays so that someone is always here.*

stagnant *adjective* (describing water) not flowing or fresh

stain *noun* (*plural* **stains**) a dirty mark on something

stain *verb* (**stains, staining, stained**) **1** to make a stain on something ▸ *Handling the fruit had stained his hands.* **2** to colour material or wood with a special liquid

stair *noun* (*plural* **stairs**) each of a series of steps that take you from one floor of a building to another

staircase *noun* (*plural* **staircases**) a series of stairs

stake *noun* (*plural* **stakes**) **1** a thick pointed length of wood that is driven into the ground **2** an amount of money used for a bet

stake *verb* (**stakes, staking, staked**) to use money on a bet **stake a claim** to claim something or get a right to it

stalactite *noun* (*plural* **stalactites**) a spike of rock hanging like an icicle from the roof of a cave

A **stalactite** comes down and a **stalagmite** (the next word in this dictionary) goes up. One way of remembering which is which is that **stalactite** has a c in it, like *icicle*.

stalagmite *noun* (*plural* **stalagmites**) a spike of rock standing like a pillar on the floor of a cave

stale *adjective* (**staler, stalest**) (describing food) not fresh

stalk *noun* (*plural* **stalks**) the main part of a plant, from which the leaves and flowers grow

stalk *verb* (**stalks, stalking, stalked**) to follow or hunt someone stealthily

stall *noun* (*plural* **stalls**) **1** a table or small open-fronted shop where things are sold **2** a place for one animal in a stable or shed

stall *verb* (**stalls, stalling, stalled**) **1** (used about an engine) to stop suddenly **2** to delay what you are doing to give yourself more time ▸ *They tried to stall until Roger returned.*

stallion *noun* (*plural* **stallions**) a male horse

stalls *plural noun* the seats on the ground floor of a theatre or cinema

stamen *noun* (*plural* **stamens**) (*pronounced* **stay-men**) the part of a flower that holds the pollen

stamina *noun* (*pronounced* **stam-in-a**) the ability to go on working or exercising for a long time

stammer *verb* (**stammers, stammering, stammered**) to keep repeating the sounds at the beginning of words

stammer *noun* (*plural* **stammers**) a stutter that you have all the time, or because you are nervous

stamp *noun* (*plural* **stamps**) **1** a small piece of gummed paper with a special design on it, which you stick on a letter or parcel to show you have paid the postage **2** a small block with raised letters for printing words or marks on something

stamp *verb* (**stamps, stamping, stamped**) **1** to bang your foot heavily on the ground **2** to print words or marks on something with a stamp **3** to put postage stamps on a letter or parcel

stampede *noun* (*plural* **stampedes**) a sudden rush of animals or people

stand *verb* (**stands, standing, stood**) **1** to be on your feet without moving ▸ *Are you going to stand there chatting all day?* **2** to place something upright ▸ *Michael stood the plant on the table.* **3** to remain available ▸ *The offer will stand for three weeks.* **4** to be able to endure or tolerate something difficult or unpleasant ▸ *She couldn't stand the thought of leaving without us.* **stand for** to mean something ▸ *'MP' stands for 'Member of Parliament'.* **stand out** to be clear or obvious **stand up** to rise to your feet **stand up to** to be ready to defend yourself against someone **stand up for** to support someone or defend them

stand *noun* (*plural* **stands**) **1** something made for putting things on ▸ *The statue had fallen off its stand.* **2** a stall where things are sold or displayed **3** a structure at a sports ground with seats for spectators

standard *noun* (*plural* **standards**) **1** the level by which you judge something ▶ *The work has been done to a high standard.* **2** a special flag **3** an upright pole

standard *adjective* of the usual or ordinary kind

standard of living *noun* (*plural* **standards of living**) the level of comfort and wealth that a person or country has

standstill *noun* a stop; an end to movement or activity ▶ *The traffic came to a standstill.*

stank past tense of **stink** *verb*

stanza *noun* (*plural* **stanzas**) a group of lines in a poem

staple¹ *noun* (*plural* **staples**) **1** a tiny piece of wire used to fix pieces of paper together **2** a U-shaped nail **stapler** *noun* a device for putting staples in things

staple² *adjective* main or normal ▶ *Rice is a staple food in many countries.*

star *noun* (*plural* **stars**) **1** a large mass of burning gas that you see as a bright speck of light in the sky at night **2** a shape with five or six points **3** a famous actor or entertainer **starry** *adjective* full of stars

star *verb* (**stars, starring, starred**) to be one of the main performers in a film or show

starboard *noun* the right-hand side of a ship or aircraft when you are facing forward

starch *noun* (*plural* **starches**) **1** a white substance found in bread, potatoes, and other food, which is an important part of the human diet **2** a substance used to stiffen clothes **starchy** *adjective* like starch, or containing starch

stare *verb* (**stares, staring, stared**) to look hard at someone or something without moving your eyes

starfish *noun* (*plural* **starfish** or **starfishes**) a sea animal shaped like a star with five points

starling *noun* (*plural* **starlings**) a common bird with dark shiny feathers

start *verb* (**starts, starting, started**) **1** to take the first steps in doing something **2** to begin a journey **3** to make a sudden movement of surprise ▶ *We all started when the train rushed past.*

start *noun* (*plural* **starts**) **1** the act of starting ▶ *We need to make an early start tomorrow.* **2** the place or time that something starts ▶ *Go back to the start.* ▶ *Saturday is the start of the new season.* **3** an advantage that someone starts with ▶ *We gave the young ones a 10 minutes' start.* **4** a sudden movement ▶ *She woke up with a start.*

startle *verb* (**startles, startling, startled**) to surprise or alarm a person or animal

starve *verb* (**starves, starving, starved**) **1** to suffer or die from not having enough food **2** to make someone suffer or die in this way ▶ *The prisoners had been starved to death.* **starvation** *noun* starving

state *noun* (*plural* **states**) **1** the way that someone or something is, or the condition that they are in ▶ *The room was in an untidy state.* **2** a country with its own government and laws **3** a division of a country ▶ *the state of California* **4** a dignified or grand style ▶ *The King was buried in state.*

state *verb* (**states, stating, stated**) to say something clearly or formally

stately *adjective* (**statelier, stateliest**) grand and dignified

stately home *noun* (*plural* **stately homes**) a grand house that a noble family has owned for many years

statement *noun* (*plural* **statements**) **1** words that state something **2** a formal account of something that has happened **3** a report made by a bank about the money in your account

statesman or **stateswoman** *noun* (*plural* **statesmen** or **stateswomen**) someone who is important or skilled in governing a state

static *adjective* not moving or changing

static electricity *noun* electricity which is present in something but does not flow as a current

station *noun* (*plural* **stations**) **1** a place where people get on or off trains or buses **2** a headquarters for police, firemen, or other public officials **3** a place from which radio or television broadcasts are made

station *verb* (**stations, stationing, stationed**) to put someone at a place for a special purpose ▶ *A man was stationed at the door to take the tickets.*

stationary *adjective* not moving; still

stationery *noun* paper, envelopes, and other things used for writing

statistics *plural noun* numbers that gives information about something ▶ *These statistics show that the population has doubled.* **statistical** *adjective* **statistically** *adverb*

statue *noun* (*plural* **statues**) a model of a person or animal made of stone or metal

status *noun* (*plural* **statuses**) a person's position or rank, or how important they are compared with other people

staunch *adjective* firm and loyal

stave *noun* (*plural* **staves**) a set of five lines on which music is written

stave *verb* (**staves, staving**) **stave off** to keep something unwelcome away ▶ *They staved off hunger by drinking a lot of water.*

stay *verb* (**stays, staying, stayed**) **1** to continue to be somewhere **2** to spend time as a visitor

stay *noun* (*plural* **stays**) a period of time spent somewhere ▶ *Did you enjoy your stay in Italy?*

steady *adjective* (**steadier, steadiest**) **1** not shaking or moving; firm **2** regular or continuous ▶ *The runners kept up a steady pace.* **steadily** *adverb* in a steady way; gradually **steadiness** *noun* being steady

steady *verb* (**steadies, steadying, steadied**) to make something steady ▶ *Steady yourself before you dive.*

steak *noun* (*plural* **steaks**) a thick slice of meat or fish

steal *verb* (**steals, stealing, stole, stolen**) **1** to take something that does not belong to you, and keep it **2** to move quietly without being noticed ▶ *When it was dark he stole out of the house.*

stealthy *adjective* (**stealthier, stealthiest**) secret and quiet, so as not to be noticed **stealth** *noun* quiet or secret movement **stealthily** *adverb*

steam *noun* gas or vapour that comes from boiling water **steamy** *adjective* full of steam

steam *verb* (**steams, steaming, steamed**) **1** to give out steam **2** to move using the power of steam ▶ *The boat steamed down the river.* **3** to cook food in steam

steam engine *noun* (*plural* **steam engines**) a railway engine driven by steam

steamer *noun* (*plural* **steamers**) a ship driven by steam

steamroller *noun* (*plural* **steamrollers**) a heavy vehicle with wide metal wheels, used to flatten surfaces when making roads
It is called **steamroller** because the first ones were powered by steam.

steel *noun* a strong metal made from iron and carbon **steely** *adjective* hard, cold, or grey like steel

steel *verb* (**steels, steeling, steeled**) **steel yourself** to find the courage to do something difficult

steel band *noun* (*plural* **steel bands**) a band of musicians who play steel drums

steep *adjective* (**steeper, steepest**) rising or sloping sharply **steeply** *adverb* **steepness** *noun*

steeple *noun* (*plural* **steeples**) a church tower with a spire

steeplechase *noun* (*plural* **steeplechases**) a race across country or over hedges and fences
It is called a **steeplechase** because races like this used to be run towards a steeple you could see in the distance.

steer[1] *verb* (**steers, steering, steered**) to make a vehicle go in the direction you want

steer[2] *noun* (*plural* **steers**) a young bull kept for its meat

steering wheel *noun* (*plural* **steering wheels**) a wheel used for steering a vehicle

stem *noun* (*plural* **stems**) the main long thin part of a plant above the ground, that the leaves and flowers grow from
stem *verb* (**stems, stemming, stemmed**) 1 to start from something or arise from it ▸ *Their interest in the area stems from yearly holidays spent there.* 2 to stop or control something that is flowing ▸ *I managed to stem the rush of water with a piece of rag.*

stench *noun* (*plural* **stenches**) a strong unpleasant smell

stencil *noun* (*plural* **stencils**) a piece of card or metal or plastic with pieces cut out of it, used to produce a picture or design

step *noun* (*plural* **steps**) 1 each movement you make with your foot when you are walking, running, or dancing 2 the sound you make when you put your foot down to walk ▸ *Mark thought he could hear steps on the path outside.* 3 each of the level surfaces on a stair or ladder 4 each of a series of actions ▸ *The first step is to make a plan.* **watch your step** to be careful
step *verb* (**steps, stepping, stepped**) to tread or walk **step up** to increase something

stepchild *noun* (*plural* **stepchildren**) a child that a husband or wife has from an earlier marriage. A boy is a **stepson** and a girl is a **stepdaughter**.

stepfather *noun* (*plural* **stepfathers**) a man who is married to your mother but is not your own father

stepladder *noun* (*plural* **stepladders**) a folding ladder with flat treads

stepmother *noun* (*plural* **stepmothers**) a woman who is married to your father but is not your own mother

stepping stone *noun* (*plural* **stepping stones**) each in a line of stones put in a stream to help people cross it

stereo *noun* (*plural* **stereos**) a system for playing recorded music using two speakers to spread the sound

sterile *adjective* 1 not able to have children or young 2 (describing land) not able to grow plants or crops 3 free from germs **sterility** *noun* being sterile

sterilize *verb* (**sterilizes, sterilizing, sterilized**) 1 to make something free from germs 2 to make a person or animal unable to bear young **sterilization** *noun* sterilizing something or someone

sterling *noun* British money ▸ *Prices are shown in sterling.*

stern[1] *noun* (*plural* **sterns**) the back part of a ship

stern[2] *adjective* (**sterner, sternest**) strict and severe **sternly** *adverb* **sternness** *noun*

stethoscope *noun* (*plural* **stethoscopes**) (*pronounced* **steth-o-skohp**) a device used by doctors to listen to a patient's heartbeat or breathing
The word **stethoscope** comes from Greek words meaning 'chest' and 'to look at'.

stew *verb* (**stews, stewing, stewed**) to cook food slowly in liquid
stew *noun* (*plural* **stews**) a dish of meat and vegetables cooked by stewing

steward *noun* (*plural* **stewards**) 1 a person who looks after the passengers on a ship or aircraft 2 an official who looks after the arrangements at a public event

stewardess *noun* (*plural* **stewardesses**) a woman who looks after the passengers on a ship or aircraft

stick[1] *noun* (*plural* **sticks**) 1 a long thin piece of wood 2 a long piece of wood used to hit the ball in some ball games ▸ *a hockey stick* 3 a long thin piece of something ▸ *a stick of dynamite*

stick[2] *verb* (**sticks, sticking, stuck**) 1 to push a sharp or pointed object roughly into something ▸ *He stuck a pin in the balloon.* 2 to fasten or join things ▸ *Leanne stuck a poster on her door.* 3 to become fixed or jammed ▸ *The door keeps sticking.* 4 (informal) to put up with something ▸ *I can't stick it any longer.* **stick out** or **stick up** to stand out or up from a surface or be noticeable **stick together** to stay loyal to one another **stick up for** (informal) to support or defend someone

sticker *noun* (*plural* **stickers**) a label with a picture or writing on it, for sticking on something

stickleback *noun* (*plural* **sticklebacks**) a small fish with sharp spines on its back

sticky *adjective* (**stickier, stickiest**) covered in something that will make it stick to things ▸ *I'll put a sticky label on the jar.* **stickiness** *noun* being sticky

stiff *adjective* (**stiffer, stiffest**) 1 not able to bend or change its shape easily ▸ *stiff cardboard* 2 harsh or difficult ▸ *a stiff penalty* ▸ *a stiff test* 3 formal; not friendly ▸ *a stiff telephone conversation* 4 strong or severe ▸ *a stiff breeze*

stiffen *verb* (**stiffens, stiffening, stiffened**) to become stiff or make something stiff

stifle *verb* (**stifles, stifling, stifled**) 1 to make it difficult or impossible for someone to breathe 2 to stop something happening or continuing ▸ *They tried to stifle their giggling.*

stile *noun* (*plural* **stiles**) a set of steps or bars in a fence, for people to climb over

still *adjective* (**stiller, stillest**) 1 not moving 2 quiet and peaceful ▸ *The guns stopped, and all was still.* 3 (describing a drink) not fizzy **stillness** *noun*
still *adverb* 1 up to this or that time ▸ *Are you still there?* 2 even more ▸ *It became still colder.* 3 even so ▸ *I lost my game but I still enjoyed it.*
still *verb* (**stills, stilling, stilled**) to stop something moving

stilts *plural noun* 1 a pair of poles with supports for your feet, for walking high above the ground 2 tall supports for a house built over water

stimulate *verb* (**stimulates, stimulating, stimulated**) to make someone excited or interested **stimulation** *noun*

stimulus *noun* (*plural* **stimuli**) something that makes you interested or excited enough to do something ▸ *The children used the story as a stimulus to make up their own play.*

sting *noun* (*plural* **stings**) 1 the part of an insect or plant that can cause pain or a wound 2 a painful area or wound caused by an insect or plant
sting *verb* (**stings, stinging, stung**) 1 to wound or hurt someone with a sting ▸ *She was stung by a wasp.* 2 to feel a sharp pain like a sting ▸ *The wound was beginning to sting.*

stingy *adjective* (**stingier, stingiest**) (*pronounced* stin-ji) mean; not generous **stinginess** *noun* meanness

stink *verb* (**stinks, stinking, stank** or **stunk, stunk**) to have a strong unpleasant smell
stink *noun* (*plural* **stinks**) a strong unpleasant smell

stir *verb* (**stirs, stirring, stirred**) 1 to move something liquid or soft round and round, for example with a spoon 2 to move slightly after being still **stir up** to excite or arouse something ▸ *They always seem to stir up trouble.*
stir *noun* 1 an act of stirring ▸ *Give it a stir.* 2 a fuss or disturbance ▸ *The news caused quite a stir.*

stir-fry *noun* (*plural* **stir-fries**) food that you fry quickly in a deep pan while stirring and tossing it

stirring *adjective* making you feel moved or excited ▸ *We were watching a stirring adventure serial.*

stirrup *noun* (*plural* **stirrups**) a metal loop that hangs from a horse's saddle to support the rider's foot

stitch *noun* (*plural* **stitches**) 1 a loop of thread made in sewing or knitting 2 a sudden pain in your side caused by running
stitch *verb* (**stitches, stitching, stitched**) to sew something with stitches

stoat *noun* (*plural* **stoats**) an animal like a weasel

stock noun (plural **stocks**) 1 a supply of things kept ready to be sold or used 2 a collection of farm animals 3 a liquid made by stewing meat, fish, or vegetables 4 a number of a company's shares
stock verb (**stocks, stocking, stocked**) to keep a supply of things to be sold or used

stocking noun (plural **stockings**) a close-fitting nylon covering for the leg and foot

stocks plural noun a wooden framework with holes for the legs and arms, in which criminals were locked as a punishment in the past

stocky adjective (**stockier, stockiest**) short and solidly built **stockily** adverb **stockiness** noun

stodgy adjective (**stodgier, stodgiest**) (describing food) thick and heavy

stoke verb (**stokes, stoking, stoked**) to add fuel to a furnace or fire

stole past tense of **steal**

stolen past participle of **steal**

stomach noun (plural **stomachs**) 1 the part of your body where food starts to be digested 2 the front of your body in the middle

stone noun (plural **stones**) 1 the hard solid mineral of which rocks are made 2 a piece of this mineral 3 a jewel 4 the hard seed in the middle of some fruits, such as a cherry, plum, or peach 5 (plural **stone**) a unit of weight equal to 14 pounds or 6.35 kilograms ▸ The machine says you weigh 8 stone.
stone verb (**stones, stoning, stoned**) 1 to throw stones at someone 2 to take the stones out of fruit

stone-deaf adjective completely deaf

stony adjective (**stonier, stoniest**) 1 full of stones 2 hard or cold like stone

stood past tense and past participle of **stand** verb

stool noun (plural **stools**) a small seat without a back

stoop verb (**stoops, stooping, stooped**) to bend your body forwards

stop verb (**stops, stopping, stopped**) 1 to finish doing something 2 to be no longer moving 3 to prevent something happening or continuing ▸ I must go out and stop that noise. 4 to fill a hole or gap 5 to stay at a place for a short time ▸ Where shall we stop for the night?
stop noun (plural **stops**) 1 stopping; an end 2 a place where a bus or train stops

stoppage noun (plural **stoppages**) 1 an interruption in the work of a business or factory 2 a blockage

stopper noun (plural **stoppers**) something that fits into a hole, such as the top of a bottle or jar to close it

stopwatch noun (plural **stopwatches**) a watch that can be started or stopped, used for timing races

storage noun the storing of goods

store verb (**stores, storing, stored**) to keep things until they are needed
store noun (plural **stores**) 1 a place where things are stored 2 a supply of things for future use 3 a large shop **in store** going to happen ▸ There was a surprise in store for us.

storey noun (plural **storeys**) one whole floor of a building

stork noun (plural **storks**) a large bird with long legs and a long neck and beak

storm noun (plural **storms**) 1 a period of bad weather with strong winds and rain, and often thunder and lightning 2 a violent attack or outburst ▸ There was a storm of anger at the decision. **stormy** adjective
storm verb (**storms, storming, stormed**) 1 to move or behave violently or angrily ▸ He stormed out of the room. 2 to attack a castle or other fortified place

story noun (plural **stories**) an account of real or imaginary events

stout adjective (**stouter, stoutest**) 1 rather fat 2 thick and strong 3 brave ▸ The defenders put up a stout resistance.

stove noun (plural **stoves**) a device that produces heat for cooking or for warming a room

stow *verb* (**stows, stowing, stowed**) to pack something or store it away

stowaway *noun* (*plural* **stowaways**) someone who hides on a ship or aircraft so they can travel without paying

straddle *verb* (**straddles, straddling, straddled**) to sit or stand across something ▸ *A long bridge straddles the river.*

straggle *verb* (**straggles, straggling, straggled**) 1 to grow or move in an untidy way ▸ *Black hair straggled down over her shoulders.* 2 to lag behind or wander on your own **straggler** *noun* someone who lags behind **straggly** *adjective* growing untidily

straight *adjective* (**straighter, straightest**) 1 going continuously in one direction; not curving or bending ▸ *The road seemed to go on for ever in a straight line.* 2 tidy; in proper order ▸ *We need to get the house straight for our visitors.* 3 honest or frank ▸ *She said she wanted a straight answer to a simple question.*

straighten *verb* (**straightens, straightening, straightened**) to become straight, or to make something straight

straightforward *adjective* 1 easy to understand or do 2 honest or frank

strain *verb* (**strains, straining, strained**) 1 to stretch or push something or pull it too hard ▸ *The doctor said I had strained a muscle in my back.* 2 to make a great effort ▸ *Colin was straining to keep his head above the water.* 3 to put liquid through a sieve to take out any lumps or other things in it

strain *noun* (*plural* **strains**) 1 the force of straining 2 an injury caused by straining 3 a bad feeling you get from too much work or worry

strainer *noun* (*plural* **strainers**) a device for straining liquids

strait *noun* (*plural* **straits**) a narrow stretch of water between two seas

strand *noun* (*plural* **strands**) each of the threads or wires twisted together to make a rope or cable

stranded *adjective* left in a difficult or helpless position ▸ *Carly took my bike and left me stranded at school.*

strange *adjective* (**stranger, strangest**) 1 unusual or surprising 2 not known or experienced before **strangely** *adverb* **strangeness** *noun*

stranger *noun* (*plural* **strangers**) 1 a person you do not know 2 a person who is in a place they do not know

strangle *verb* (**strangles, strangling, strangled**) to kill someone by pressing their throat so they can't breathe

strap *noun* (*plural* **straps**) a flat strip of leather or other material for fastening things or holding them in place

strap *verb* (**straps, strapping, strapped**) to fasten something with a strap

strategy *noun* (*plural* **strategies**) a plan or policy to achieve something **strategic** *adjective* useful as a way of achieving something

stratosphere *noun* a layer of air high above the earth's surface

stratum *noun* (*plural* **strata**) (*pronounced* **strah-tum**) a layer or level

straw *noun* (*plural* **straws**) 1 dry cut stalks of corn 2 a long narrow tube for drinking through

strawberry *noun* (*plural* **strawberries**) a soft red fruit with seeds on the outside

stray *verb* (**strays, straying, strayed**) to wander or become lost

stray *noun* a lost animal

streak *noun* (*plural* **streaks**) a long thin line or mark **streaky** *adjective*

streak *verb* (**streaks, streaking, streaked**) 1 to mark something with streaks ▸ *The sky was streaked with pink.* 2 to move very quickly ▸ *A ginger cat streaked past up the stairs.*

stream *noun* (*plural* **streams**) 1 a small river 2 a flow of liquid 3 a number of things moving in the same direction, such as traffic

stream *verb* (**streams, streaming, streamed**) 1 to flow ► *Blood was streaming from her cut hand.* 2 to move in a strong or fast flow ► *Traffic was streaming across the bridge.*

streamer *noun* (*plural* **streamers**) a long strip of paper or ribbon used as a decoration

streamlined *adjective* (describing a car, aircraft, or ship) having a smooth shape that helps it to move easily through air or water

street *noun* (*plural* **streets**) a road with houses beside it in a city or town

strength *noun* (*plural* **strengths**) 1 how strong a person or thing is 2 something that you are particularly good at

strengthen *verb* (**strengthens, strengthening, strengthened**) to become stronger, or to make something stronger

strenuous *adjective* needing a lot of effort **strenuously** *adverb*

stress *noun* (*plural* **stresses**) 1 a force or pressure that pulls or twists something 2 the strain caused by having many worries and difficulties 3 the extra loudness or emphasis you give to a word or part of a word when you say it
stress *verb* (**stresses, stressing, stressed**) to give importance to a point or idea ► *I must stress that the work is urgent.*

stretch *verb* (**stretches, stretching, stretched**) 1 to pull something so that it becomes longer or wider 2 to become longer or wider when pulled 3 to extend or continue ► *The road stretched ahead for miles.*
stretch *noun* (*plural* **stretches**) 1 the action of stretching something 2 a continuous period of time or area of land or water ► *a stretch of motorway*

stretcher *noun* (*plural* **stretchers**) a framework like a light folding bed with handles at each end, for carrying a sick or injured person

strew *verb* (**strews, strewing, strewed, strewn** or **strewed**) (not an everyday word) to scatter things over a surface ► *Flowers were strewn over the path.*

strict *adjective* (**stricter, strictest**) 1 firm in demanding obedience or good behaviour ► *Her parents have always been strict.* 2 complete or exact ► *I want the strict truth.* **strictly** *adverb*

stride *verb* (**strides, striding, strode, stridden**) to walk with long steps
stride *noun* (*plural* **strides**) a long step in walking or running

strife *noun* fighting or quarrelling

strike *verb* (**strikes, striking, struck**) 1 to hit something or someone 2 to attack people or a place suddenly ► *A hurricane struck the village.* 3 to light a match by rubbing it against something rough 4 to chime a certain number of times ► *The clock struck ten.* 5 to stop working as a protest 6 to find oil or gold by drilling or mining 7 to give you a certain impression ► *The story struck me as rather sentimental.*
strike *noun* (*plural* **strikes**) 1 a hit 2 a refusal to work, as a way of making a protest

striker *noun* (*plural* **strikers**) 1 a worker who is on strike 2 in football, an attacking player who tries to score goals

striking *adjective* impressive or interesting

string *noun* (*plural* **strings**) 1 thin rope or cord for tying things 2 a piece of stretched wire or nylon used in a musical instrument to make sounds 3 a line or series of things ► *A string of cars was queuing for petrol.*
string *verb* (**strings, stringing, strung**) 1 to tie something with string 2 to thread things on a string 3 to put strings on something

strings *plural noun* the violins and other instruments in an orchestra that have strings

stringy *adjective* (**stringier, stringiest**) 1 long and thin like string 2 containing tough fibres

strip *noun* (*plural* **strips**) 1 a long narrow piece of something 2 an outfit that members of a sports team wear
strip *verb* (**strips, stripping, stripped**) 1 to take a covering off something 2 to take

your clothes off **3** to take something away from someone ▸ *They could strip him of his championship title.*

stripe *noun* (*plural* **stripes**) a long narrow band of colour **striped** *adjective* **stripy** *adjective*

strive *verb* (**strives, striving, strove, striven**) (not an everyday word) to try hard to do something

strode past tense of **stride** *verb*

stroke *noun* (*plural* **strokes**) **1** a blow or hit ▸ *He knocked the man down with one stroke.* **2** a movement or action ▸ *a swimming stroke* **3** a sudden illness that can cause a person to be paralysed **4** something that happens unexpectedly ▸ *The fine weather was a stroke of luck.*

stroke *verb* (**strokes, stroking, stroked**) to move your hand gently along something

stroll *verb* (**strolls, strolling, strolled**) to walk along slowly

stroll *noun* (*plural* **strolls**) a short leisurely walk

strong *adjective* (**stronger, strongest**) **1** having a lot of power or energy ▸ *The little boy wasn't strong enough to lift the box.* **2** not easily broken or damaged ▸ *The gate was held by a strong chain.* **3** having a lot of flavour or smell ▸ *He made a pot of strong coffee.* **strongly** *adverb*

stronghold *noun* (*plural* **strongholds**) a place built with strong walls to resist attack

strove past tense of **strive**

struck past tense and past participle of **strike** *verb*

structure *noun* (*plural* **structures**) **1** something that has been built or put together **2** the way that something is built or made **structural** *adjective* to do with the structure of something **structurally** *adverb*

struggle *verb* (**struggles, struggling, struggled**) **1** to move your body about violently when you are fighting or trying to get free **2** to make strong efforts to do something ▸ *The family is struggling to earn enough money.*

struggle *noun* (*plural* **struggles**) a spell of struggling; a hard fight

strum *verb* (**strums, strumming, strummed**) to play a guitar or piano in a casual way

strung past tense and past participle of **string** *verb*

strut *verb* (**struts, strutting, strutted**) to walk in a proud or stiff way

strut *noun* (*plural* **struts**) a bar of wood or metal that strengthens a framework

stub *verb* (**stubs, stubbing, stubbed**) **stub your toe** to hit your toe against something hard

stub *noun* (*plural* **stubs**) a short piece of something left after the rest has been used or removed ▸ *Keep your ticket stubs.*

stubble *noun* **1** the short stalks of corn left in the ground after a harvest **2** short stiff hairs growing on a man's chin when he has not shaved recently

stubborn *adjective* not willing to change your ideas or ways; obstinate **stubbornly** *adverb* **stubbornness** *noun*

stuck past tense and past participle of **stick** *verb*

stuck-up *adjective* unpleasantly proud or conceited

stud *noun* (*plural* **studs**) **1** a small round piece of metal that is fixed to something ▸ *Yasmin has a gold stud in her nose.* **2** a peg or knob, such as the ones on the bottom of football or hockey boots

student *noun* (*plural* **students**) someone who studies at a college or university

studio noun (*plural* **studios**) 1 a place for making films, or for broadcasting radio or television programmes 2 the room where an artist or photographer works

studious *adjective* fond of studying; studying hard **studiously** *adverb* **studiousness** *noun*

study *verb* (**studies, studying, studied**) 1 to spend time learning about something 2 to look at something carefully ▸ *She lowered her head to study the menu.*

study noun (*plural* **studies**) 1 the process of studying 2 a room used for studying or writing

stuff noun 1 a substance or material 2 things; possessions ▸ *We have to go and collect our stuff from the house.*

stuff *verb* (**stuffs, stuffing, stuffed**) 1 to fill something tightly 2 to push something in carelessly ▸ *He stuffed the paper into his pocket.*

stuffing noun (*plural* **stuffings**) 1 soft material used to fill a cushion or pillow 2 a savoury mixture put into poultry before cooking it

stuffy *adjective* (**stuffier, stuffiest**) 1 not letting in fresh air ▸ *a stuffy room* 2 formal and old-fashioned **stuffiness** *noun*

stumble *verb* (**stumbles, stumbling, stumbled**) 1 to trip and almost fall over 2 to speak or act hesitantly or uncertainly **stumble across** or **stumble on** to find something by chance

stump noun (*plural* **stumps**) 1 the bottom of a tree trunk left in the ground when the tree has fallen or been cut down 2 in cricket, each of the three upright sticks forming the wicket

stump *verb* (**stumps, stumping, stumped**) 1 in cricket, to get the person who is batting out by touching the stumps with the ball 2 to be too difficult for someone ▸ *The last question stumped everyone.*

stun *verb* (**stuns, stunning, stunned**) 1 to knock someone on the head so they are unconscious for a short time 2 to shock someone ▸ *They were stunned by the news.*

stung past tense and past participle of **sting** *verb*

stunk past tense and past participle of **stink** *verb*

stunning *adjective* beautiful or impressive ▸ *Miriam looked stunning in her long red dress.*

stunt noun (*plural* **stunts**) something unusual or difficult done to attract attention or as part of a performance

stupendous *adjective* amazing; tremendous

stupid *adjective* (**stupider, stupidest**) not having any sense or intelligence **stupidity** *noun* being stupid **stupidly** *adverb*

sturdy *adjective* (**sturdier, sturdiest**) strong and solid **sturdily** *adverb* **sturdiness** *noun*

stutter *verb* (**stutters, stuttering, stuttered**) to keep repeating the sounds at the beginning of words

stutter noun (*plural* **stutters**) a habit of stuttering

sty noun (*plural* **sties**) 1 a sore swelling on your eyelid 2 a place for keeping pigs The first meaning also has the spelling **stye**, and the plural of this is **styes**.

style noun (*plural* **styles**) 1 the way that something is done, made, said, or written 2 fashion or elegance

style *verb* (**styles, styling, styled**) to give something a special style

stylish *adjective* fashionable and smart

subdue *verb* (**subdues, subduing, subdued**) to overcome someone or bring them under control

subdued *adjective* quiet and downcast

subject noun (*plural* **subjects**) (*pronounced* **sub**-jikt) 1 the person or thing that is being talked or written about 2 something that you can study 3 in language, the word naming the person or thing that performs the action of the verb, for example *Jim* in the sentence *Jim saw her.* 4 someone who must obey the laws of a particular ruler or government ▸ *a British subject*

subject *verb* (**subjects, subjecting, subjected**) (*pronounced* **sub**-jekt) to make someone submit to something ▸ *The audience subjected the speaker to a flood of questions.*

submarine *noun* (*plural* **submarines**) a type of ship that can travel under water

submerge *verb* (**submerges, submerging, submerged**) to go under water, or to put someone or something under water

submit *verb* (**submits, submitting, submitted**) 1 to let someone rule or control you 2 to give something to someone for their opinion or decision **submission** *noun* submitting

subordinate *noun* (*plural* **subordinates**) someone who is lower in rank or position than someone else

subscribe *verb* (**subscribes, subscribing, subscribed**) to pay money to receive something, such as a magazine, regularly or to belong to a club or society **subscriber** *noun*

subscription *noun* (*plural* **subscriptions**) money you pay to receive something, such as a magazine, regularly or to belong to a club or society

subsequent *adjective* (not an everyday word) coming after something else ▸ *Subsequent events proved that she was right.* **subsequently** *adverb* later

subside *verb* (**subsides, subsiding, subsided**) 1 to sink lower ▸ *After a few days the flood water began to subside.* 2 to become quiet or normal ▸ *The pain in her head began to subside.* **subsidence** *noun* subsiding, especially into the ground

subsidy *noun* (*plural* **subsidies**) money paid by a government to keep prices low or to support an industry or activity **subsidize** *verb* to help pay the cost of something

substance *noun* (*plural* **substances**) something that you can touch or see, especially something used for making things

substantial *adjective* 1 large or important 2 strong and solid **substantially** *adverb*

substitute *verb* (**substitutes, substituting, substituted**) to use one thing or person instead of another ▸ *After six months you*

should substitute a new battery for the old one. **substitution** *noun* something that is substituted

substitute *noun* (*plural* **substitutes**) a person or thing that is used instead of another

subtle *adjective* (**subtler, subtlest**) (*pronounced* **sut**-el) 1 faint and delicate, or not easy to notice ▸ *There was a subtle perfume in the room.* 2 clever but not obvious ▸ *It was a subtle plan to get more money.*

subtract *verb* (**subtracts, subtracting, subtracted**) to take one amount from another ▸ *If you subtract 2 from 7, you get 5.* **subtraction** *noun*

suburb *noun* (*plural* **suburbs**) an area of houses on the edge of a city or large town **suburban** *adjective* to do with suburbs

subway *noun* (*plural* **subways**) an underground passage for pedestrians

succeed *verb* (**succeeds, succeeding, succeeded**) 1 to do or get what you wanted 2 to be the next person to do what someone else did ▸ *James I succeeded Elizabeth to the throne of England.*

success *noun* (*plural* **successes**) 1 doing or getting what you wanted 2 a person or thing that does well ▸ *The trip was a great success.*

successful *adjective* having success; doing well **successfully** *adverb*

succession *noun* (*plural* **successions**) a number of people or things coming one after another ▸ *We heard a succession of explosions.* **in succession** one after another

successor *noun* (*plural* **successors**) someone who has a position or does a job after someone else

such *adjective* 1 of that kind; of the same kind ▸ *Try not to think about such things.* 2 so great or so much ▸ *It was such a funny story!*

suck *verb* (**sucks, sucking, sucked**) 1 to take in liquid or air through your mouth 2 to move something around inside your mouth so that you can taste it ▸ *Joanna* *was sucking a toffee.* **3** to draw something in or absorb it ▸ *A machine was sucking up the snow and hurling it out again.*

suction *noun* the process of drawing in liquid or air by creating a vacuum

sudden *adjective* happening quickly and unexpectedly **suddenly** *adverb* **suddenness** *noun*

suds *plural noun* froth on soapy water

sue *verb* (**sues, suing, sued**) to start a claim in a lawcourt to get money from someone

suede *noun* (*pronounced* swayd) leather with one side soft and velvety

suet *noun* hard fat from cattle and sheep, used in cooking

suffer *verb* (**suffers, suffering, suffered**) **1** to feel pain or sadness **2** to have to put up with something unpleasant

sufficient *adjective* enough **sufficiently** *adverb*

suffix *noun* (*plural* **suffixes**) a word or syllable joined to the end of a word to change its meaning, as in forge*tful*, lion*ess*, and rus*ty*

suffocate *verb* (**suffocates, suffocating, suffocated**) **1** to die because you cannot breathe **2** to kill someone by stopping them breathing **suffocation** *noun*

sugar *noun* a sweet food obtained from plants such as sugar beet or sugar cane **sugary** *adjective* sweet

suggest *verb* (**suggests, suggesting, suggested**) **1** to mention something as an idea that you think is good or useful **2** to give an impression of something ▸ *His tone of voice suggested he was angry.* **suggestion** *noun* something that someone has suggested

suicide *noun* (*plural* **suicides**) the act of killing yourself deliberately ▸ *to commit suicide* **suicidal** *adjective* wanting to kill yourself

suit *noun* (*plural* **suits**) **1** a set of matching clothes, such as a jacket and trousers or a jacket and skirt **2** a set of clothing for a particular purpose ▸ *a diving suit* **3** each of the four sets in a pack of playing cards:

spades, hearts, diamonds, and clubs

suit *verb* (**suits, suiting, suited**) **1** to be suitable or convenient for someone ▸ *What time would suit you?* **2** to look right for someone ▸ *The red hat suits you better.*

suitable *adjective* right or satisfactory for a particular person, purpose, or occasion **suitability** *noun* how suitable something is **suitably** *adverb*

suitcase *noun* (*plural* **suitcases**) a case with a lid and a handle, for carrying your clothes when you are travelling

suite *noun* (*plural* **suites**) (*pronounced* sweet) **1** a set of furniture or equipment ▸ *a bathroom suite* **2** a set of rooms ▸ *We stayed in the smartest suite in the hotel.*

sulk *verb* (**sulks, sulking, sulked**) to be silent because you are angry

sulky *adjective* (**sulkier, sulkiest**) sulking or moody **sulkily** *adverb* **sulkiness** *noun*

sullen *adjective* silent and moody **sullenness** *noun*

sulphur *noun* a yellow chemical used in industry and medicine

sultan *noun* (*plural* **sultans**) a ruler in some Muslim countries

sultana *noun* (*plural* **sultanas**) a dried grape with no seeds

sultry *adjective* hot and humid

sum *noun* (*plural* **sums**) **1** the amount you get when you add numbers together **2** an amount of money **3** a problem in arithmetic

sum *verb* (**sums, summing, summed**) **sum up** to give a summary of what has been said

summarize *verb* (**summarizes, summarizing, summarized**) to give a summary of something

summary *noun* (*plural* **summaries**) a statement of the main points of something that someone has said or written

summer *noun* (*plural* **summers**) the warm season between spring and autumn **summery** *adjective* like summer, or suitable for summer

summertime *noun* the season of summer

summit *noun* (*plural* **summits**) 1 the top of a mountain 2 an important meeting between world leaders

summon *verb* (**summons, summoning, summoned**) to order someone to be present ▸ *The king summoned his doctors.*

sun *noun* 1 the star round which the earth travels, giving us warmth and light 2 warmth and light from the sun ▸ *Shall we sit in the sun?*

sunbathe *verb* (**sunbathes, sunbathing, sunbathed**) to lie or sit in the sun, especially because you are trying to get a suntan

sunburn *noun* redness of the skin caused by being in the sun too long **sunburnt** *adjective*

Sunday *noun* (*plural* **Sundays**) the first day of the week
Sunday is an Anglo-Saxon name meaning 'day of the sun'.

sundial *noun* (*plural* **sundials**) a device like a small table with a dial on top, which shows the time by a shadow made by the sun

sunflower *noun* (*plural* **sunflowers**) a tall flower with a round yellow head

sung past participle of **sing**

sunglasses *plural noun* dark glasses that you wear to protect your eyes from strong sunlight

sunk past tense and past participle of **sink** *verb*

sunlight *noun* light from the sun **sunlit** *adjective*

sunny *adjective* (**sunnier, sunniest**) 1 having a lot of sunshine ▸ *The next day was warm and sunny.* 2 full of sunshine ▸ *Katie had a large sunny room to work in.*

sunrise *noun* the time when the sun rises in the morning

sunset *noun* (*plural* **sunsets**) the time when the sun sets in the evening

sunshine *noun* strong light and warmth from the sun

sunstroke *noun* an illness caused by being in strong sunlight for too long

suntan *noun* (*plural* **suntans**) a brown colour of the skin caused by the sun's rays **suntanned** *adjective*

super *adjective* (informal) excellent or very good

superb *adjective* magnificent or excellent **superbly** *adverb*

superficial *adjective* 1 on the surface only, not deep ▸ *It's only a superficial cut.* 2 only slight; not strong or thorough ▸ *I have a superficial interest in politics.* **superficially** *adverb*

superfluous *adjective* (not an everyday word) not necessary; no longer needed ▸ *We began to think a car might be superfluous in the big city.*

superintendent *noun* (*plural* **superintendents**) 1 someone who is in charge of a group of people 2 a police officer above the rank of inspector

superior *adjective* 1 better or more important 2 conceited or proud ▸ *He walked over with a superior look on his face.* **superiority** *noun* being superior

superior *noun* (*plural* **superiors**) someone who has a higher rank or position than another person

supermarket *noun* (*plural* **supermarkets**) a large self-service shop selling food and other goods

supernatural *adjective* not belonging to the natural world or having a natural explanation

supersonic *adjective* faster than the speed of sound

superstition *noun* (*plural* **superstitions**) a belief or action that is based on fear or feeling rather than reason ▸ *It is a*

superstition *that 13 is an unlucky number.*
superstitious *adjective* believing in
superstitions

supervise *verb* (**supervises, supervising,
supervised**) to be in charge of someone
supervision *noun* supervising someone
supervisor *noun* someone who supervises
you

supper *noun* (*plural* **suppers**) a meal or
snack that you eat in the evening

supple *adjective* (**suppler, supplest**)
bending easily, not stiff **suppleness** *noun*

supplement *noun* (*plural* **supplements**)
something added as an extra ▶ *The
newspaper has a colour supplement on
Saturdays.* **supplementary** *adjective*

supply *verb* (**supplies, supplying, supplied**)
1 to give or sell something to someone
who needs it 2 to give someone what they
need **supplier** *noun* someone who supplies
something

supply *noun* (*plural* **supplies**) 1 an amount
of something kept ready to be used when
needed 2 the action of supplying
something

support *verb* (**supports, supporting,
supported**) 1 to hold something so that it
does not fall down 2 to give someone help
or encouragement **supporter** *noun*
someone who supports a team or political
party

support *noun* (*plural* **supports**) 1 help or
encouragement 2 something that holds
another thing up

suppose *verb* (**supposes, supposing,
supposed**) to think that something is likely
or true ▶ *I suppose you must be right.* **be
supposed to** to have to do something as an
order or duty

suppress *verb* (**suppresses, suppressing,
suppressed**) 1 to put an end to something
using force 2 to keep something secret or
stop it happening **suppression** *noun*
suppressing something

supreme *adjective* highest or greatest;
most important **supremacy** *noun* being
supreme **supremely** *adverb*

sure *adjective* (**surer, surest**) 1 convinced
about something; not having any doubt
▶ *I'm sure I shut the door.* 2 likely to happen
▶ *They are sure to come.* 3 reliable ▶ *Karen
is a sure friend.* ▶ *Those clouds are a sure
sign of rain.* **make sure of** to find out
whether something is true **surely** *adverb*

surf *noun* the white foam of waves
breaking on rocks or the seashore

surface *noun* (*plural* **surfaces**) the outside
or the top part of something
surface *verb* (**surfaces, surfacing, surfaced**)
1 to give a road or path a hard covering
layer 2 to come up to the surface from
under water

surfing *noun* the sport of riding on surf
using a flat board **surfer** *noun*

surge *verb* (**surges, surging, surged**) to
move powerfully forwards or upwards

surgeon *noun* (*plural* **surgeons**) a doctor
who treats disease or injury by repairing
or removing parts of the body

surgery *noun* (*plural* **surgeries**) 1 the work
of a surgeon 2 a building or room where a
doctor or dentist sees patients **surgical**
adjective to do with surgery

surly *adjective* (**surlier, surliest**) bad-
tempered and rude **surliness** *noun*

surname *noun* (*plural* **surnames**)
a person's last name, which all the
members of a family have

surpass *verb* (**surpasses, surpassing,
surpassed**) to do better or be better than
someone

surplus *noun* (*plural* **surpluses**) an amount
left over after you have used what you
need

surprise *noun* (*plural* **surprises**)
1 something that you did not expect 2 the
feeling you have when something
unexpected happens
surprise *verb* (**surprises, surprising,
surprised**) 1 to be a surprise to someone
2 to catch or attack someone unexpectedly

surrender *verb* (**surrenders, surrendering, surrendered**) 1 to stop fighting an enemy and put yourself under their control 2 to hand something over to someone
surrender *noun* the act of surrendering

surround *verb* (**surrounds, surrounding, surrounded**) to be round someone or something or to come round them on all sides

surroundings *plural noun* the things or conditions around a person or place

survey *noun* (*plural* **surveys**) (*pronounced* ser-vay) 1 a general look at a topic or activity 2 a detailed inspection or examination of a building or area
survey *verb* (**surveys, surveying, surveyed**) (*pronounced* ser-vay) to inspect something or make a survey of it

surveyor *noun* (*plural* **surveyors**) someone who surveys buildings and land

survive *verb* (**survives, surviving, survived**) to stay alive after someone else has died or in spite of an accident or disaster **survival** *noun* surviving **survivor** *noun* someone who survives

suspect *verb* (**suspects, suspecting, suspected**) (*pronounced* su-spekt) 1 to think that someone has done something wrong or is not to be trusted 2 to think that something unwelcome will happen
suspect *noun* (*plural* **suspects**) (*pronounced* sus-pekt) someone who is thought to have done something wrong

suspend *verb* (**suspends, suspending, suspended**) 1 to stop something happening or continuing for a time 2 to take away someone's job or position for a time, as a punishment 3 to hang something up
suspension *noun* suspending something or someone

suspense *noun* an anxious or uncertain feeling while waiting for something

suspension bridge *noun* (*plural* **suspension bridges**) a bridge strengthened by cables attached to upright supports

suspicion *noun* (*plural* **suspicions**) 1 suspecting someone of doing wrong 2 an uncertain feeling that something is not right

suspicious *adjective* 1 suspecting someone or something ▸ *I'm suspicious about what happened.* 2 making you suspect someone or something ▸ *There are suspicious footprints along the path.* **suspiciously** *adverb*

sustain *verb* (**sustains, sustaining, sustained**) 1 to keep someone alive or healthy 2 to keep something going ▸ *It's difficult to sustain such an effort.*

swagger *verb* (**swaggers, swaggering, swaggered**) to walk or behave in a proud or conceited way

swallow[1] *verb* (**swallows, swallowing, swallowed**) to make food or drink go down your throat **swallow up** to use up all of something ▸ *A whole lot of unexpected bills swallowed up the extra money.*

swallow[2] *noun* (*plural* **swallows**) a small bird with a forked tail and long pointed wings

swam past tense of **swim** *verb*

swamp *verb* (**swamps, swamping, swamped**) 1 to flood an area of ground 2 to overwhelm someone with a large number of things ▸ *They have been swamped with complaints.*
swamp *noun* (*plural* **swamps**) a marsh **swampy** *adjective* full of swamps

swan *noun* (*plural* **swans**) a large white waterbird with a long neck and powerful wings

swap *verb* (**swaps, swapping, swapped**) (informal) to exchange one thing for another ▸ *The teams swapped jerseys.*
swap *noun* (*plural* **swaps**) 1 something swapped for something else 2 an exchange

swarm *noun* (*plural* **swarms**) a large number of bees or other insects flying or moving about together

swarm *verb* (**swarms, swarming, swarmed**) **1** to move in a swarm **2** to be crowded with people ▸ *The town is swarming with tourists in summer.*

swat *verb* (**swats, swatting, swatted**) (*pronounced* swot) to hit or crush a fly or other insect **swatter** *noun* an implement for swatting flies

sway *verb* (**sways, swaying, swayed**) to move gently from side to side

swear *verb* (**swears, swearing, swore, sworn**) **1** to make a solemn promise ▸ *He swore he would return.* **2** to use rude or coarse words **swear by** to have a lot of confidence in something

swear word *noun* (*plural* **swear words**) a word that is rude or offensive, used by someone who is angry or upset

sweat *verb* (**sweats, sweating, sweated**) (*pronounced* swet) to give off moisture through the pores of your skin, especially when you are hot or doing exercise

sweat *noun* moisture that comes out of your skin when you sweat **sweaty** *adjective* sweating, or covered with sweat

sweater *noun* (*plural* **sweaters**) (*pronounced* swet-er) a jumper or pullover

sweatshirt *noun* (*plural* **sweatshirts**) a loose thick top with long sleeves

swede *noun* (*plural* **swedes**) a large kind of turnip with purple skin and yellow flesh

sweep *verb* (**sweeps, sweeping, swept**) **1** to clean a room or floor with a broom or brush **2** to move something quickly ▸ *The flood swept away the bridge.* ▸ *I was swept along by the crowd.* **3** to move rapidly or grandly ▸ *She swept out of the room.* **sweeper** *noun* a machine for sweeping

sweep *noun* (*plural* **sweeps**) **1** a sweeping action or movement ▸ *I'll give the room a sweep.* **2** someone who cleans out a chimney

sweet *adjective* (**sweeter, sweetest**) **1** having a taste like sugar or honey **2** pleasant or attractive ▸ *The perfume has a sweet smell.* ▸ *The girl had a sweet*

nature. **sweetly** *adverb* **sweetness** *noun*

sweet *noun* (*plural* **sweets**) a small piece of sweet food made from sugar or chocolate

sweetcorn *noun* the juicy yellow seeds of maize, eaten as a vegetable

sweeten *verb* (**sweetens, sweetening, sweetened**) to become sweet, or to make something sweet **sweetener** *noun* a substance used instead of sugar to make a drink or food sweet

sweetheart *noun* (*plural* **sweethearts**) a person you love very much

swell *verb* (**swells, swelling, swelled, swollen** or **swelled**) to get bigger or louder

swell *noun* (*plural* **swells**) the rise and fall of the sea's surface

swelling *noun* (*plural* **swellings**) a swollen place on the body

sweltering *adjective* uncomfortably hot

swept past tense and past participle of **sweep** *verb*

swerve *verb* (**swerves, swerving, swerved**) to move suddenly to one side while going along ▸ *The car swerved to avoid a cyclist.*

swift *adjective* (**swifter, swiftest**) quick; moving or happening quickly and easily **swiftly** *adverb* **swiftness** *noun*

swift *noun* (*plural* **swifts**) a small bird like a swallow

swill *verb* (**swills, swilling, swilled**) to rinse or flush something with water

swill *noun* a sloppy mixture of waste food given to pigs

swim *verb* (**swims, swimming, swam, swum**) **1** to move yourself through the water with movements of your arms and legs **2** to be covered in liquid or full of it ▸ *Their eyes were swimming with tears.* **3** to feel dizzy ▸ *My head started to swim.* **swimmer** *noun*

swim *noun* (*plural* **swims**) a spell of swimming ▸ *Let's go for a swim.*

swimming bath or **swimming pool** *noun* (*plural* **swimming baths** or **swimming pools**) a specially built pool with water for people to swim in

swindle *verb* (**swindles, swindling, swindled**) to get money from someone by cheating them **swindler** *noun*

swine *noun* (*plural* **swine**) (not an everyday word) a pig

swing *verb* (**swings, swinging, swung**) **1** to move backwards and forwards or in a curve **2** to turn suddenly ▸ *The back of the vehicle swung round and nearly hit the hedge.*

swing *noun* (*plural* **swings**) **1** a swinging movement **2** a seat hung on chains or ropes so that someone can swing in it for fun **in full swing** with a lot happening ▸ *The party was in full swing.*

swipe *verb* (**swipes, swiping, swiped**) **1** to give someone or something a hard hit **2** to pass a credit card through a special reading device when you pay with it **swipe** *noun* (*plural* **swipes**) a hard hit

swirl *verb* (**swirls, swirling, swirled**) to move around quickly in circles

swish *verb* (**swishes, swishing, swished**) to make a hissing or rustling sound

switch *noun* (*plural* **switches**) **1** a device that you press or turn to start or stop an electrical device **2** a sudden change of opinion or methods

switch *verb* (**switches, switching, switched**) **1** to operate an electrical device with a switch ▸ *Shall I switch the light on?* **2** to swap or change something ▸ *We've switched from gas to electricity.*

switchboard *noun* (*plural* **switchboards**) a place in a large building or organization where telephone calls are connected

swivel *verb* (**swivels, swivelling, swivelled**) to turn or swing right round

swollen past participle of **swell** *verb*

swoop *verb* (**swoops, swooping, swooped**) **1** to dive or come down suddenly **2** to make a sudden attack or raid
swoop *noun* (*plural* **swoops**) a sudden dive or attack

swop *verb* (**swops, swopping, swopped**) another spelling of **swap**

sword *noun* (*plural* **swords**) (*pronounced* sord) a weapon with a long pointed blade and a handle

swore past tense of **swear**

sworn past participle of **swear**

swum past participle of **swim** *verb*

swung past tense and past participle of swing *verb*

sycamore *noun* (*plural* **sycamores**) a tall tree with winged seeds

syllable *noun* (*plural* **syllables**) a word or part of a word that has a separate sound ▸ *'Mouse' has one syllable, and 'el-e-phant' has three syllables.*

syllabus *noun* (*plural* **syllabuses**) (*pronounced* sil-a-bus) a list of subjects or topics to be studied

symbol *noun* (*plural* **symbols**) a mark or sign that has a meaning or stands for something ▸ *The crescent is a symbol of Islam.* **symbolic** *adjective* having a special meaning **symbolically** *adverb*

symbolize *verb* (**symbolizes, symbolizing, symbolized**) to be a symbol of something ▸ *Red symbolizes danger.*

symmetrical *adjective* (*pronounced* sim-et-rik-al) having two halves that are the same, but the opposite way round like an reflection in a mirror ▸ *A wheel and a butterfly are both symmetrical.* **symmetrically** *adverb* **symmetry** *noun* the quality of being symmetrical

sympathetic *adjective* feeling sympathy or understanding for someone **sympathetically** *adverb*

sympathize *verb* (**sympathizes, sympathizing, sympathized**) to show or feel sympathy for someone ▸ *Everyone sympathized with me when my cat was run over.*

sympathy *noun* the sharing or understanding of other people's feelings or difficulties

symphony *noun* (*plural* **symphonies**) a piece of music in several sections for an orchestra **symphonic** *adjective* like a symphony

symptom *noun* (*plural* **symptoms**) a sign or clue that you have an illness ▸ *Red spots are a symptom of measles.*

synagogue *noun* (*plural* **synagogues**) (*pronounced* **sin-a-gog**) a building where Jews meet to worship
The word **synagogue** comes from a Greek word meaning 'assembly'.

synchronize *verb* (**synchronizes, synchronizing, synchronized**) (*pronounced* **sink-ro-nyz**) 1 to make things happen at the same time 2 to make watches or clocks show the same time **synchronization** *noun* synchronizing things

synonym *noun* (*plural* **synonyms**) (*pronounced* **sin-o-nim**) a word that means the same as another word, such as *big* and *large* **synonymous** *adjective* meaning the same

synthesizer *noun* (*plural* **synthesizers**) an electronic musical instrument that can make many different sounds

synthetic *adjective* made artificially; not natural **synthetically** *adverb*

syringe *noun* (*plural* **syringes**) a device with a tube and a long needle, used for sucking in liquid and giving injections

syrup *noun* (*plural* **syrups**) a thick sweet liquid **syrupy** *adjective* thick and sweet

system *noun* (*plural* **systems**) 1 a set of parts that work together ▸ *the transport system* ▸ *your digestive system* 2 an organized way of doing something ▸ *a political system* ▸ *the metric system*

systematic *adjective* organized or planned **systematically** *adverb*

Tt

tab *noun* (*plural* **tabs**) a small strip or flap that is fixed to the edge of something to pull it out or identify it

tabby *noun* (*plural* **tabbies**) a grey or brown cat with dark streaks of fur
The word **tabby** originally meant a kind of striped cloth, and was named after a district of Baghdad called al-Attabiyya, where the cloth was made.

table *noun* (*plural* **tables**) 1 a piece of furniture with legs and a flat top to put things on 2 a list of facts arranged in rows and columns

tablecloth *noun* (*plural* **tablecloths**) a cloth for covering a table

tablespoon *noun* (*plural* **tablespoons**) a large spoon used for serving food

tablet *noun* (*plural* **tablets**) 1 a small hard piece of medicine that you swallow 2 a flat piece of stone or wood with words carved or written on it

table tennis *noun* a game played with bats and a small light ball on a table with a net across the middle

tack *noun* (*plural* **tacks**) a short nail with a flat head

tack *verb* (**tacks, tacking, tacked**) 1 to nail something with tacks 2 to sew material together quickly with long stitches 3 to sail a zigzag course to get the full effect of the wind

tackle *verb* (**tackles, tackling, tackled**) 1 to start doing a task 2 in football and other games, to try to get the ball from another player

tackle *noun* (*plural* **tackles**) 1 equipment for fishing or a sport 2 an act of tackling someone in football or rugby or hockey

tacky *adjective* (**tackier, tackiest**) sticky or not quite dry ▸ *The paint is still tacky.*

tact *noun* skill in not upsetting people

tactful *adjective* good at dealing with people without upsetting them **tactfully** *adverb*

tactics *plural noun* ways used to fight battles or play games **tactical** *adjective*

tactless *adjective* likely to upset people by saying the wrong thing **tactlessly** *adverb*

tadpole *noun* (*plural* **tadpoles**) a young frog or toad at a stage when it has an oval head and a long tail and lives in water

tag *noun* (*plural* **tags**) 1 a label tied or stuck to something 2 a chasing game

tag *verb* (**tags, tagging, tagged**) to fix a tag or label on something **tag along** to go along with other people

tail *noun* (*plural* **tails**) 1 the part that sticks out at the rear end of an animal or bird 2 the part at the back of an aircraft 3 the side of a coin opposite the head **tailless** *adjective* not having a tail

tail *verb* (**tails, tailing, tailed**) to follow someone without them seeing you **tail off** to become fewer or smaller

tailback *noun* (*plural* **tailbacks**) a long line of traffic stretching back from an obstruction

tailor *noun* (*plural* **tailors**) someone who makes trousers, jackets, and coats

take *verb* (**takes, taking, took, taken**) 1 to get hold of something or someone or bring them into your possession ▸ *The boy took his mother's hand.* ▸ *She took a cake from the plate.* ▸ *Who do you think took the money?* ▸ *The army took several prisoners.* 2 to carry or drive someone to a place ▸ *I'll take you to the station.* ▸ *Take this parcel to the post office.* 3 to make use of something useful or pleasant ▸ *Do you take sugar?* ▸ *You must take a holiday this year.* ▸ *Do take a seat.* 4 to need someone or something for a purpose ▸ *It took a lot of time to finish the job.* 5 to make a note of information ▸ *Take their names and addresses.* 6 to teach a subject to a class ▸ *Who takes you for English?* 7 to subtract one number from another ▸ *Take two*

from ten and you get eight. 8 to do an exam or test ▸ *I'm taking my maths exam today.* 9 to make a photograph with a camera **take after** to be like someone older in your family ▸ *Kelly takes after her Dad.* **take in** to fool or deceive someone **take off** (used about an aircraft) to leave the ground at the beginning of a flight **take over** to take control of something **take part in** to share in doing something **take place** to happen

takeaway *noun* (*plural* **takeaways**) cooked food that you can buy to take away

takings *plural noun* money that has been received by a shop

talc or **talcum powder** *noun* a perfumed powder for rubbing on the skin

tale *noun* (*plural* **tales**) a story **tell tales** to tell people about something wrong someone has done

talent *noun* (*plural* **talents**) an ability to do something well ▸ *She shows a great talent for acting.* **talented** *adjective* good at doing something
The word **talent** comes from an ancient Greek word *talanton*, which was a sum of money.

talk *verb* (**talks, talking, talked**) to speak or have a conversation

talk *noun* (*plural* **talks**) 1 a conversation or discussion 2 a lecture

talkative *adjective* talking a lot

tall *adjective* (**taller, tallest**) 1 higher than the average ▸ *The church has a tall steeple.* 2 measured from the bottom to the top ▸ *The bookcase is two metres tall.* **tall story** a story that is hard to believe

Talmud *noun* a collection of writings on Jewish religious law
Talmud is a Hebrew name meaning 'instruction'.

talon *noun* (*plural* **talons**) a strong claw

tambourine *noun* (*plural* **tambourines**) a musical instrument like a small drum with jingling metal discs round the edge

tame *adjective* (**tamer, tamest**) 1 (describing an animal) gentle and not afraid of people 2 dull or uninteresting **tamely** *adverb*

tame *verb* (**tames, taming, tamed**) to make an animal tame **tamer** *noun* someone who tames animals

tamper *verb* (**tampers, tampering, tampered**) to interfere with something ▸ *The television isn't working because someone tampered with it.*

tampon *noun* (*plural* **tampons**) a plug of soft material that a woman puts into her vagina to absorb the blood during her period

tan *noun* (*plural* **tans**) 1 a yellowish-brown colour 2 a suntan

tan *adjective* having a yellowish-brown colour

tan *verb* (**tans, tanning, tanned**) 1 to make your skin turn brown in the sun 2 to make the skin of a dead animal into leather

tandem *noun* (*plural* **tandems**) a bicycle for two riders, one behind the other

tandoori *noun* a type of Indian cookery in which you use a clay oven

tang *noun* a strong flavour or smell

tangent *noun* (*plural* **tangents**) (*pronounced* **tan**-jent) a straight line that touches the outside of a curve or circle

tangerine *noun* (*plural* **tangerines**) (*pronounced* tan-jer-**een**) a kind of small orange with a loose skin
The word **tangerine** is named after Tangier in Morocco, where the fruit originally came from.

tangle *verb* (**tangles, tangling, tangled**) to become twisted or muddled, or to make something twisted or muddled

tangle *noun* (*plural* **tangles**) a tangled state

tangy *adjective* (**tangier, tangiest**) having a strong sharp taste ▸ *a tangy tomato sauce*

tank *noun* (*plural* **tanks**) 1 a large container for a liquid or gas 2 a large heavy vehicle with guns, used in war

tankard *noun* (*plural* **tankards**) a large heavy drinking mug

tanker *noun* (*plural* **tankers**) 1 a large ship for carrying oil 2 a large lorry for carrying a liquid

tantalize *verb* (**tantalizes, tantalizing, tantalized**) to torment someone by showing them something good that they cannot have
The word **tantalize** comes from the name of Tantalus in Greek mythology. He was punished by having to stand near water and fruit which moved away when he tried to reach out for them.

tantrum *noun* (*plural* **tantrums**) a sudden outburst of bad temper

tap¹ *noun* (*plural* **taps**) a device for letting out liquid or gas in a controlled flow

tap *verb* (**taps, tapping, tapped**) 1 to take liquid out of a container through a tap 2 to fix a device to a telephone line so that you can hear someone else's conversation

tap² *noun* (*plural* **taps**) a quick light hit, or the sound it makes ▸ *I gave him a tap on the shoulder.*

tap *verb* (**taps, tapping, tapped**) to give something or someone a gentle hit

tap-dance *noun* (*plural* **tap-dances**) a dance in hard shoes that make sharp tapping sounds on the floor **tap-dancing** *noun* **tap-dancer** *noun*

tape *noun* (*plural* **tapes**) 1 a thin strip of cloth or paper or plastic 2 a thin plastic strip coated with a magnetic substance and used for recording sound or pictures

tape *verb* (**tapes, taping, taped**) 1 to fix or cover something with tape 2 to record sound or pictures on magnetic tape

tape-measure *noun* (*plural* **tape-measures**) a long strip of paper or plastic marked in centimetres or inches for measuring things

taper *verb* (**tapers, tapering, tapered**) to become narrower at one end

tape recorder *noun* (*plural* **tape recorders**) a machine for recording sound on magnetic tape and playing it back **tape recording** *noun*

tapestry *noun* (*plural* **tapestries**) (*pronounced* **tap-i-stri**) a piece of cloth with pictures or patterns woven into it

tar *noun* a thick black liquid made from coal or wood and used in making roads **tarry** *adjective*

tarantula *noun* (*plural* **tarantulas**) (*pronounced* **ta-ran-tew-la**) a large poisonous spider found in warm countries

target *noun* (*plural* **targets**) something that you aim at and try to hit or reach

tarmac *noun* a covering of tar mixed with small stones, used on roads

tarnish *verb* (**tarnishes, tarnishing, tarnished**) to become less shiny, or to make a metal less shiny

tarpaulin *noun* (*plural* **tarpaulins**) a large sheet of waterproof canvas

tart[1] *noun* (*plural* **tarts**) a pie containing fruit or jam

tart[2] *adjective* (**tarter, tartest**) tasting sour ▸ *The apples are tart.*

tartan *noun* (*plural* **tartans**) a Scottish woollen cloth with a special pattern of colours and stripes

task *noun* (*plural* **tasks**) a piece of work

tassel *noun* (*plural* **tassels**) a bundle of threads tied together at the top and used as a decoration

taste *verb* (**tastes, tasting, tasted**) 1 to eat or drink food and recognize its flavour 2 to have a particular flavour ▸ *The milk tastes sour.*

taste *noun* (*plural* **tastes**) 1 the flavour something has when you taste it ▸ *The fruit had a strange taste.* 2 the ability to taste things 3 the ability to enjoy beautiful things ▸ *Their choice of clothes shows good taste.* **tasteful** *adjective* stylish and pleasant to look at **tasteless** *adjective* having no taste

tasty *adjective* (**tastier, tastiest**) having a pleasant taste

tatters *plural noun* rags; badly torn pieces **tattered** *adjective* torn

tattoo[1] *noun* (*plural* **tattoos**) 1 a picture or pattern made on someone's skin with a needle and dye 2 an outdoor entertainment with military music and marching

tattoo *verb* (**tattoos, tattooing, tattooed**) to put a tattoo on someone's skin

tatty *adjective* (**tattier, tattiest**) in bad condition; shabby

taught past tense and past participle of **teach**

taunt *verb* (**taunts, taunting, taunted**) to jeer at someone or insult them

taut *adjective* (**tauter, tautest**) stretched tightly **tautly** *adverb* **tautness** *noun*

tavern *noun* (*plural* **taverns**) (old use) an inn or public house

tawny *adjective* (**tawnier, tawniest**) yellowish-brown

tax *noun* (*plural* **taxes**) an amount of money that people and businesses have to give to the government to pay for things like hospitals and schools

tax *verb* (**taxes, taxing, taxed**) to make someone pay a tax **taxation** *noun* making people pay taxes

taxi *noun* (*plural* **taxis**) a car with a driver which you can hire for short journeys

taxi *verb* (**taxis, taxiing, taxied**) (used about an aircraft) to move slowly along the ground before taking off or after landing

tea *noun* (*plural* **teas**) 1 a drink made by pouring hot water on the dried leaves of a shrub grown in Asia 2 the dried leaves of this shrub 3 a meal eaten in the afternoon

teach *verb* (**teaches, teaching, taught**) to give someone knowledge or skill about something

teacher *noun* (*plural* **teachers**) someone who teaches people at a school or college

teak *noun* a hard strong wood from Asia

team *noun* (*plural* **teams**) 1 a group of players who form one side in a game or sport 2 a group of people who work together

teapot *noun* (*plural* **teapots**) a pot with a handle and spout, for making and pouring out tea

tear[1] *verb* (**tears, tearing, tore, torn**) (*pronounced* **tair**) **1** to make a split in something or to pull it apart ▸ *Be careful not to tear your clothes on the fence.* **2** to pull or remove something with force ▸ *He tore the picture off the wall.* **3** to move very quickly ▸ *Children were tearing home down the street.*

tear *noun* (*plural* **tears**) a hole or split made by tearing something

tear[2] *noun* (*plural* **tears**) (*pronounced* **teer**) a drop of water that comes from your eye

tearful *adjective* in tears; crying easily **tearfully** *adverb*

tease *verb* (**teases, teasing, teased**) to annoy someone playfully or joke about them

teaspoon *noun* (*plural* **teaspoons**) a small spoon for stirring drinks

teat *noun* (*plural* **teats**) **1** a nipple through which a baby drinks milk **2** the cap of a baby's feeding bottle

technical *adjective* to do with machines or the way things work **technically** *adverb*

technician *noun* (*plural* **technicians**) someone who looks after scientific equipment and does practical work in a laboratory

technique *noun* (*plural* **techniques**) (*pronounced* **tek-neek**) a method of doing something

technology *noun* (*plural* **technologies**) using science to help you make things and do things **technological** *adjective*

teddy bear *noun* (*plural* **teddy bears**) a soft furry toy bear

tedious *adjective* (*pronounced* **tee**-di-us) long and slow; boring **tediously** *adverb*

teem *verb* (**teems, teeming, teemed**) **1** to be full of something ▸ *The river was teeming with fish.* **2** to rain very hard

teenage *adjective* in your teens; to do with teenagers

teenager *noun* (*plural* **teenagers**) a person aged between 13 and 19

teens *plural noun* the time of your life between the ages of 13 and 19 ▸ *They started playing tennis in their teens.*

teeth plural of **tooth**

teething *adjective* (describing a baby) starting to grow new teeth

teetotaller *noun* (*plural* **teetotallers**) someone who does not drink alcohol

telecommunications *plural noun* sending news and information by telephone, fax, television, radio, and satellite

telegram *noun* (*plural* **telegrams**) a short message sent by telegraph

telegraph *noun* (*plural* **telegraphs**) a way of sending messages by using electric current along wires or by radio

telepathy *noun* (*pronounced* til-**ep**-a-thi) understanding another person's thoughts without them speaking, writing, or making gestures **telepathic** *adjective* able to know what someone else is thinking

telephone *noun* (*plural* **telephones**) a device for speaking to people over long distances, using electric wires or radio

telephone *verb* (**telephones, telephoning, telephoned**) to speak to someone by telephone

telescope *noun* (*plural* **telescopes**) an instrument with a long tube and lenses at each end, for seeing distant objects more clearly

telescopic *adjective* **1** to do with telescopes **2** folding into itself like a portable telescope ▸ *a telescopic umbrella*

teletext *noun* a system that gives news and information on a television screen

televise *verb* (**televises, televising, televised**) to put a programme on television

television *noun* (*plural* **televisions**) **1** a system using radio waves to reproduce pictures on a screen **2** a device for receiving these pictures

tell *verb* (**tells, telling, told**) **1** to give someone information or instructions by speaking to them **2** to reveal a secret ▸ *Promise you won't tell.* **3** to recognize something ▸ *Can you tell the difference between butter and margarine?* **tell off** to tell someone severely that they have done wrong

temper *noun* (*plural* **tempers**) **1** a person's mood ▸ *Is John in a good temper?* **2** an angry mood ▸ *The bus driver was in a temper.* **lose your temper** to become very angry

temperament *noun* the way you are and the way you behave ▸ *Alison has a gentle temperament.*

temperamental *adjective* easily upset or excited

temperature *noun* (*plural* **temperatures**) **1** a measure of how hot or cold a person or thing is **2** a high body temperature ▸ *She's feverish and has a temperature.*

tempest *noun* (*plural* **tempests**) (old use) a violent storm

temple *noun* (*plural* **temples**) **1** a building where a god is worshipped **2** the flat part of your head between your forehead and your ear

tempo *noun* (*plural* **tempos**) the speed or rhythm at which a piece of music is played

temporary *adjective* only lasting or used for a short time **temporarily** *adverb*

tempt *verb* (**tempts, tempting, tempted**) **1** to try to make someone do something wrong or unwise **2** to try to persuade a person or animal to do something ▸ *Trevor tempted the kitten to come out of the cupboard by giving it some milk.* **temptation** *noun* tempting someone, or being tempted

ten *noun* (*plural* **tens**) the number 10 **tenth** *adjective* and *noun*

tenant *noun* (*plural* **tenants**) someone who rents a house or building **tenancy** *noun* the time when you are a tenant

tend *verb* (**tends, tending, tended**) **1** to be inclined or likely to do something ▸ *The older boys tend to go out on Friday evenings.*

2 to look after something or someone ▸ *The gardener was tending his plants in the greenhouse.*

tendency *noun* (*plural* **tendencies**) the way a person or thing is likely to behave ▸ *He has a tendency to lose his temper.*

tender *adjective* (**tenderer, tenderest**) **1** not tough or hard; easy to chew ▸ *We can have some tender green beans.* **2** delicate or sensitive ▸ *Some of the more tender plants need special treatment.* **3** gentle or loving ▸ *a tender smile* **tenderly** *adverb* **tenderness** *noun*

tendon *noun* (*plural* **tendons**) a piece of strong tissue that joins a muscle to a bone

tennis *noun* a game played with rackets and a ball on a marked court with a net across the middle

tenor *noun* (*plural* **tenors**) a male singer with a high voice

tenpin bowling *noun* a game in which you knock down sets of ten skittles with a ball

tense¹ *adjective* (**tenser, tensest**) **1** nervous; excited or exciting ▸ *Most of the runners felt tense before the race.* **2** tightly stretched ▸ *He felt stiff and his muscles were tense.* **tensely** *adverb*

tense² *noun* (*plural* **tenses**) the form of a verb that shows when the action happens. The past tense of *see* is *saw*; the present tense is *see*, and the future tense is *will see*

tension *noun* (*plural* **tensions**) **1** how tightly stretched a rope or wire is **2** a feeling of anxiety or nervousness about something about to happen

tent *noun* (*plural* **tents**) a shelter made of canvas or cloth supported by upright poles

tentacle *noun* (*plural* **tentacles**) a long bending part that some animals have for feeling

tepee *noun* (*plural* **tepees**) a Native American's tent made from animal skins

tepid *adjective* slightly warm; lukewarm

term *noun* (*plural* **terms**) 1 a part of the year when a school or college does its teaching 2 a definite period ▸ *a term of imprisonment* 3 a word or phrase with a special meaning ▸ *technical terms* 4 a condition offered or agreed ▸ *The contract has many terms.* **be on good terms** or **on bad terms** to be friendly or unfriendly with someone

terminal *noun* (*plural* **terminals**) 1 the place where something ends; a terminus 2 a building where air passengers arrive or depart 3 a place where a wire is connected to a battery or electric circuit 4 a monitor and keyboard for a computer

terminal *adjective* (describing an illness) causing death

terminate *verb* (**terminates**, **terminating**, **terminated**) (not an everyday word) to end or stop **termination** *noun* ending or stopping something

terminus *noun* (*plural* **termini**) the station at the end of a railway or bus route

terrace *noun* (*plural* **terraces**) 1 a level paved area beside a house 2 a row of houses joined together 3 a level area on a slope or hillside

terracotta *noun* 1 a brownish-red clay used for making pots and tiles 2 a brownish-red colour

terracotta *adjective* having a brownish-red colour

terrapin *noun* (*plural* **terrapins**) a kind of small turtle that lives in water

terrible *adjective* very bad; awful **terribly** *adverb*

terrier *noun* (*plural* **terriers**) a kind of small dog

terrific *adjective* (informal) 1 very great in size or amount ▸ *a terrific speed* 2 very good or excellent ▸ *a terrific idea* **terrifically** *adverb*

terrify *verb* (**terrifies**, **terrifying**, **terrified**) to make a person or animal very frightened

territory *noun* (*plural* **territories**) an area of land belonging to a country or person, or land of a special kind ▸ *They were moving into unexplored territory.* **territorial** *adjective*

terror *noun* (*plural* **terrors**) great fear

terrorist *noun* (*plural* **terrorists**) someone who uses violence for political purposes **terrorism** *noun*

terrorize *verb* (**terrorizes**, **terrorizing**, **terrorized**) to terrify someone with threats

test *noun* (*plural* **tests**) 1 a set of questions to find out how much you know about something 2 a medical examination ▸ *Greg went to have an eye test.* 3 a trial to find out what something is like ▸ *They will do a test to check the car's performance.*

test *verb* (**tests**, **testing**, **tested**) to give someone or something a test

testament *noun* (*plural* **testaments**) 1 a written statement 2 each of the two main parts of the Bible, the **Old Testament** and the **New Testament**

testicles *plural noun* the two glands below the penis of a man or male animal, which produce sperm

testify *verb* (**testifies**, **testifying**, **testified**) to give evidence in a lawcourt

test match *noun* (*plural* **test matches**) a cricket or rugby match between teams from different countries

test tube *noun* (*plural* **test tubes**) a glass tube closed at one end, used for experiments in chemistry

tether *verb* (**tethers**, **tethering**, **tethered**) to tie an animal so that it cannot move far

tether *noun* (*plural* **tethers**) a rope for tying an animal **at the end of your tether** unable to stand something any more

text *noun* (*plural* **texts**) the words of something printed or written

textbook *noun* (*plural* **textbooks**) a book used for teaching a subject

textiles *plural noun* kinds of cloth; fabrics

texture *noun* (*plural* **textures**) the way that the surface of something feels ▸ *Silk has a smooth texture.*

than *conjunction* used to compare one person or thing with another ▸ *Carol is taller than David.*

thank *verb* (**thanks, thanking, thanked**) to tell someone you are grateful for something they have given you or done for you **thank you** words that you say when thanking someone **thanks** *plural noun*

thankful *adjective* feeling glad or grateful for something **thankfully** *adverb*

that *adjective* the one there ▸ *Whose is that book?*
that *conjunction* used to introduce a statement or result ▸ *I hope that you are well.* ▸ *Do you know that it is one o'clock?* ▸ *The puzzle was so hard that no one could solve it.*
that *pronoun* **1** the one there ▸ *Whose book is that?* **2** which or who ▸ *This is the book that I wanted.* ▸ *Are you the person that I saw the other day?*

thatch *noun* a roof covering made of straw or reeds **thatched** *adjective* covered in thatch

thaw *verb* (**thaws, thawing, thawed**) to melt or become soft after being frozen ▸ *The ice has thawed.*

the *adjective* (called the *definite article*) a particular one; that or those ▸ *Have you brought the book with you?*

theatre *noun* (*plural* **theatres**) **1** a building where plays or shows are performed **2** a special room where you go to have an operation

theatrical *adjective* to do with plays or acting

theft *noun* (*plural* **thefts**) the crime of stealing

their *adjective* belonging to them ▸ *This is their house.*

theirs *pronoun* belonging to them ▸ *This house is theirs.*

them *pronoun* a word used for *they* when it is the object of a verb, or when it comes after a preposition ▸ *I like them.* ▸ *I gave it to them.*

theme *noun* (*plural* **themes**) **1** a subject for talking about **2** a short tune or melody

theme park *noun* (*plural* **theme parks**) an amusement park with rides and activities connected with a special subject or theme

themselves *plural noun* them and nobody else, used to refer back to the subject of a verb already mentioned as 'they' ▸ *They have hurt themselves.* **by themselves** on their own; alone ▸ *They did the work all by themselves.*

then *adverb* **1** at that time ▸ *I lived in London then.* **2** after that; next ▸ *Then they came home.* **3** in that case; therefore ▸ *If you are going, then I can stay.*

theology *noun* the study of God and religion **theological** *adjective* to do with theology

theory *noun* (*plural* **theories**) **1** an idea or set of ideas suggested to explain something ▸ *One theory is that the baby fell out of its pushchair.* **2** the principles of a subject ▸ *Do you understand the theory of how computers work?* **theoretical** *adjective* to do with theory, not practice

therapy *noun* (*plural* **therapies**) treatment of an illness of the mind or the body, usually without using surgery or medicines **therapist** *noun*

there *adverb* **1** in or to that place **2** a word that you say to call attention to someone or something or to talk about them ▸ *There's a spider in the bath.* ▸ *There's a good dog!*

therefore *adverb* (not an everyday word) for that reason; and so

thermal *adjective* to do with heat; using heat

thermometer *noun* (*plural* **thermometers**) an instrument for measuring temperature

thermostat noun (plural **thermostats**)
a device that automatically controls the
temperature of a room or piece of
equipment

thesaurus noun (plural **thesauri** or
thesauruses) a kind of dictionary in which
words with the same meaning are listed in
groups together
The word **thesaurus** comes from a Greek word
meaning 'storehouse' or 'treasure-house'.

these adjective and pronoun the people or
things here   ▶ Whose are these shoes?
▶ These are my brothers.

they pronoun 1 the people or things that
someone is talking about   ▶ Are Lucy and
Jack still here, or have they gone home?
2 people in general   ▶ They say it's a very
good film.

thick adjective (**thicker**, **thickest**)
1 measuring a lot from one side to the
other   ▶ The castle's outer walls were thick
and strong.   ▶ It would take a long time to
read such a thick book. 2 measured from
one side to the other   ▶ The wall is ten
centimetres thick. 3 crowded or dense
▶ The path was blocked by thick foliage.
4 (informal) stupid **thickly** adverb **thickness**
noun

thicken verb (**thickens**, **thickening**,
thickened) to become thicker, or to make
something thicker

thief noun (plural **thieves**) someone who
steals

thigh noun (plural **thighs**) the part of your
leg above your knee

thimble noun (plural **thimbles**) a small
cover you put on the end of your finger so
that you don't get pricked while you are
sewing

thin adjective (**thinner**, **thinnest**)
1 measuring a small amount from one side
to the other; not fat   ▶ The walls of my flat
are thin.   ▶ A thin young woman walked
into the room. 2 not thick or dense   ▶ a
thin soup **thinly** adverb **thinness** noun
thin verb (**thins**, **thinning**, **thinned**) to
become thin, or to make something thin

thing noun (plural **things**) 1 an object;
anything that can be touched or seen
2 something that happens or that you can
think about   ▶ A strange thing happened
yesterday.

think verb (**thinks**, **thinking**, **thought**) 1 to
use your mind to form ideas 2 to have
something as an idea or opinion   ▶ I think
that's a good idea. **thinker** noun

third adjective and noun the next after the
second **thirdly** adverb
third noun (plural **thirds**) each of three
equal parts into which something can be
divided

Third World noun the poor or developing
countries of Asia, Africa, and South and
Central America

thirst noun a feeling that you need to drink

thirsty adjective (**thirstier**, **thirstiest**)
feeling that you need a drink **thirstily**
adverb

thirteen noun (plural **thirteens**) the
number 13 **thirteenth** adjective and noun

thirty noun (plural **thirties**) the number
30 **thirtieth** adjective and noun

this adjective and pronoun the one here
▶ Take this pen.   ▶ This is the one.

thistle noun (plural **thistles**) a wild plant
with prickly leaves and purple flowers

thorn noun (plural **thorns**) a sharp point
growing on the stem of roses and other
plants **thorny** adjective

thorough adjective done or doing things
properly and carefully   ▶ The windows
needed a thorough clean inside and out.
▶ She is very thorough in all she does.
thoroughly adverb **thoroughness** noun

those adjective and pronoun the ones there
▶ Where are those cards?   ▶ Those are the
ones I want.

though conjunction in spite of the fact that;
even if   ▶ It is not true, though he says it is.
though adverb however; all the same
▶ She's right, though.

thought[1] *noun* (*plural* **thoughts**)
1 something that you think; an idea or opinion 2 a spell of thinking ▸ *I gave the matter some thought.*

thought[2] past tense and past participle of **think**

thoughtful *adjective* 1 thinking a lot ▸ *Danny looked thoughtful.* 2 thinking of other people and what they would like ▸ *Mark was a good son, always courteous and thoughtful.* **thoughtfully** *adverb*

thoughtless *adjective* not thinking of other people; selfish **thoughtlessly** *adverb* **thoughtlessness** *noun*

thousand *noun* (*plural* **thousands**) the number 1,000 **thousandth** *adjective* and *noun*

thrash *verb* (**thrashes, thrashing, thrashed**) 1 to keep hitting someone hard with a stick or whip 2 to defeat an opponent in a game or sport 3 to fling your arms and legs about wildly

thread *noun* (*plural* **threads**) 1 a long piece of cotton, wool, or other material used for sewing or weaving 2 a long thin piece of something 3 the spiral ridge round a screw or bolt
thread *verb* (**threads, threading, threaded**) 1 to put a thread through the eye of a needle 2 to put a strip of material through or round something 3 to put beads on a thread

threadbare *adjective* (describing clothes) worn thin with threads showing

threat *noun* (*plural* **threats**) 1 a warning that you will punish or harm someone if they do not do what you want 2 a danger

threaten *verb* (**threatens, threatening, threatened**) 1 to make threats to someone 2 to be a danger ▸ *The quarrel threatened to turn violent.*

three *noun* (*plural* **threes**) the number 3

three-dimensional *adjective* having three dimensions: length, width, and height or depth

thresh *verb* (**threshes, threshing, threshed**) to beat corn so that you separate the grain from the husks

threshold *noun* (*plural* **thresholds**) 1 a flat piece of stone or board under the doorway of a building 2 the beginning of something important ▸ *We are on the threshold of a great discovery.*

threw past tense of **throw** *verb*

thrifty *adjective* (**thriftier, thriftiest**) careful with money **thriftily** *adverb*

thrill *noun* (*plural* **thrills**) 1 a sudden feeling of excitement 2 something that gives you this feeling
thrill *verb* (**thrills, thrilling, thrilled**) to give someone a thrill

thriller *noun* (*plural* **thrillers**) an exciting story or film, usually about crime

thrive *verb* (**thrives, thriving, throve** or **thrived, thrived**) to grow strongly or do well ▸ *The family is thriving.*

throat *noun* (*plural* **throats**) 1 the front of your neck 2 the tube in your neck that takes food and air into your body

throb *verb* (**throbs, throbbing, throbbed**) to beat or vibrate with a strong rhythm
throb *noun* (*plural* **throbs**) a sound of throbbing

throne *noun* (*plural* **thrones**) a special chair for a king or queen

throng *noun* (*plural* **throngs**) a crowd of people
throng *verb* (**throngs, thronging, thronged**) to form a large crowd

throttle *verb* (**throttles, throttling, throttled**) to strangle someone
throttle *noun* (*plural* **throttles**) a device that controls the flow of fuel into an engine

through *adverb* and *preposition* 1 from one end or side to the other ▸ *I can't get through.* ▸ *Climb through the window.* 2 because of; by means of ▸ *We'll do it through hard work.*

throughout *preposition* and *adverb* all the way through

throve past tense of **thrive**

throw *verb* (**throws, throwing, threw, thrown**) 1 to send something or someone through the air ▸ *She threw the ball* against a tree. **2** to put something down carelessly ▸ *He came in and threw his coat on the chair.* **3** to move a part of your body quickly ▸ *She threw her head back and laughed.* **4** to affect someone in a particular way ▸ *We were thrown into confusion.* **throw away** to get rid of something

throw *noun* (*plural* **throws**) a throwing action or movement

thrush *noun* (*plural* **thrushes**) a songbird that has a white front with brown spots

thrust *verb* (**thrusts, thrusting, thrust**) to push something hard ▸ *Cathy thrust a book into my hand.*

thud *noun* (*plural* **thuds**) the dull sound of something heavy falling

thud *verb* (**thuds, thudding, thudded**) to fall with a thud

thug *noun* (*plural* **thugs**) a violent and brutal person

thumb *noun* (*plural* **thumbs**) the short thick finger at the side of each hand

thump *verb* (**thumps, thumping, thumped**) **1** to hit someone or something heavily **2** to make a dull heavy sound

thump *noun* (*plural* **thumps**) an act or sound of thumping

thunder *noun* **1** the loud noise that you hear after lightning during a storm **2** a loud heavy noise **thunderous** *adjective* very loud, like thunder

thunder *verb* (**thunders, thundering, thundered**) **1** to make the noise of thunder **2** to speak with a loud booming voice

thunderstorm *noun* (*plural* **thunderstorms**) a storm with thunder and lightning

Thursday *noun* (*plural* **Thursdays**) the fifth day of the week
Thursday is an Anglo-Saxon name meaning 'day of thunder'.

thus *adverb* (not an everyday word) **1** in this way ▸ *We did it thus.* **2** therefore ▸ *Thus, we must try again.*

tick *noun* (*plural* **ticks**) **1** each of the short sharp sounds that a clock or watch makes **2** a small mark (✓) used to show that something is correct or has been done

tick *verb* (**ticks, ticking, ticked**) **1** to make the sound of a tick, as a clock or watch does **2** to mark something with a tick ▸ *She ticked the correct answers.*
tick off (informal) to scold someone or tell them off

ticket *noun* (*plural* **tickets**) a piece of paper or card that allows you to do something such as see a film or travel on a bus or train

tickle *verb* (**tickles, tickling, tickled**) **1** to keep touching someone's skin lightly, giving them a tingling feeling that can make them laugh and wriggle **2** to have a tickling or itching feeling ▸ *My throat is tickling.* **3** to please or amuse someone ▸ *It tickled her to think of all those people waiting to see her.*

ticklish *adjective* likely to laugh or wriggle when you are tickled

tidal *adjective* to do with tides or affected by tides

tidal wave *noun* (*plural* **tidal waves**) a huge sea wave moving with the tide

tiddlywink *noun* (*plural* **tiddlywinks**) a small counter flipped into a cup with another counter in the game of **tiddlywinks**

tide *noun* (*plural* **tides**) the regular rising or falling of the sea, which usually happens twice a day
tide *verb* (**tides, tiding, tided**) **tide over** to give you what you need for the time being

tidings *plural noun* (old use) news

tidy *adjective* (**tidier, tidiest**) **1** neat and orderly, with things in the right place **2** (informal) fairly large ▸ *There was a tidy sum of money in the drawer.* **tidily** *adverb* **tidiness** *noun*

tie *verb* (**ties, tying, tied**) **1** to fasten something with string or ribbon **2** to make a knot or bow in a strip of material such as a ribbon **3** to finish a game or competition with an equal score or position **tie up** to secure an animal or boat

tie *noun* (*plural* **ties**) **1** a thin strip of material tied round the collar of a shirt with a knot at the front **2** an equal result in a game or competition **3** one of the matches in a competition

tiger *noun* (*plural* **tigers**) a large wild cat with yellow and black stripes, found in Asia

tight *adjective* (**tighter, tightest**) **1** fitting closely ► *He was wearing tight jeans and a jumper.* **2** firmly fastened ► *The lid is too tight to open.* **3** fully stretched ► *Make the rope tight.* **tightly** *adverb* **tightness** *noun*

tighten *verb* (**tightens, tightening, tightened**) to become tighter, or to make something tighter

tightrope *noun* (*plural* **tightropes**) a tightly stretched rope placed high above the ground, for acrobats to balance on

tights *plural noun* a piece of clothing that fits tightly over the lower parts of your body including your legs and feet

tigress *noun* (*plural* **tigresses**) a female tiger

tile *noun* (*plural* **tiles**) a flat piece of baked clay or other hard material used in rows to cover roofs, walls, or floors **tiled** *adjective*

till¹ *preposition* and *conjunction* until

till² *noun* (*plural* **tills**) a drawer or box for money in a shop

till³ *verb* (**tills, tilling, tilled**) to make land ready to grow crops

tilt *verb* (**tilts, tilting, tilted**) **1** to slope or lean **2** to make something lean

timber *noun* (*plural* **timbers**) wood used for building

time *noun* (*plural* **times**) **1** a measure of the passing of years, months, days, and other units **2** a particular moment or period ► *What time is it now?* ► *The best time to call is in the evening.* ► *There were fields here in past times.* **3** an occasion ► *I've been to Paris several times.* **4** a period for which something lasts ► *We only had a short time to wait.* ► *She spent a long time in the library.* **5** the rhythm and speed of a piece of music **from time to time** sometimes; occasionally **in time** or **on time** soon or early enough ► *Make sure you get to the station in time.*

time *verb* (**times, timing, timed**) **1** to measure how long something takes **2** to arrange the time when something will happen

timer *noun* (*plural* **timers**) a device for timing things

times *plural noun* multiplied by ► *6 times 4 is 24* $(6 \times 4 = 24)$.

timetable *noun* (*plural* **timetables**) a list of the times of buses and trains, or of school lessons

timid *adjective* nervous and easily frightened **timidity** *noun* nervousness **timidly** *adverb*

timing *noun* the choice of time to do something ► *Arriving at lunchtime was good timing.*

tin *noun* (*plural* **tins**) **1** a soft white metal **2** a metal dish or container ► *a cake tin* **3** a metal container for preserving food **tinned** *adjective* (describing food) preserved in a tin

tinged *adjective* slightly coloured ► *The sky was tinged with red towards the horizon.*

tingle *verb* (**tingles, tingling, tingled**) to have a slight stinging or prickling feeling

tinker *verb* (**tinkers, tinkering, tinkered**) to try to mend or improve something without really knowing how to

tinker *noun* (*plural* **tinkers**) (old use) someone who travelled around mending pots and pans

tinkle *verb* (**tinkles, tinkling, tinkled**) to make a gentle ringing sound

tinny *adjective* (**tinnier, tinniest**) making a unpleasant high-pitched sound

tinsel *noun* strips of glittering material used for decoration

tint *noun* (*plural* **tints**) a shade of colour
tint *verb* (**tints, tinting, tinted**) to colour something faintly

tiny *adjective* (**tinier, tiniest**) very small

tip *noun* (*plural* **tips**) **1** the narrow end of something long or tall **2** a useful piece of information or advice **3** a small present of money given to someone who has helped

you ► *We'd better give the waiter a tip.*
4 a place where rubbish is left

tip *verb* (**tips, tipping, tipped**) **1** to lean, or to make something lean **2** to empty something out of a container ► *Go and tip the rubbish into the bin.* **3** to give someone a small present of money **4** to name someone or something as likely to win or succeed

tiptoe *verb* (**tiptoes, tiptoeing, tiptoed**) to walk quietly or carefully on your toes

tiptoe *noun* **on tiptoe** walking or standing on your toes

tire *verb* (**tires, tiring, tired**) to become tired, or to make someone tired

tired *adjective* feeling that you need to sleep or rest **be tired of** to be fed up with something **tiredness** *noun*

tiresome *adjective* annoying or tedious

tissue *noun* (*plural* **tissues**) **1** thin soft paper for blowing your nose or cleaning things **2** the substance of which living things are made

title *noun* (*plural* **titles**) **1** the name of a book, film, piece of music, or something similar **2** a word that shows a person's position or profession, such as *Sir, Lady, Dr,* and *Ms.*

titter *verb* (**titters, tittering, tittered**) to giggle or laugh in a silly way

to *preposition* in the direction of ► *We are all going to Stratford.*
You also use **to** with a verb to make an infinitive, for example *I want to see him*, to show purpose, for example *He did that to annoy us*, and to show preference, for example *I prefer films to books.*

toad *noun* (*plural* **toads**) an animal like a large frog, which lives on land

toadstool *noun* (*plural* **toadstools**) a fungus that looks like a mushroom, and is often poisonous

toast *noun* (*plural* **toasts**) **1** bread that is heated and made brown by a grill or toaster **2** a call to honour someone or something with a drink

toast *verb* (**toasts, toasting, toasted**) **1** to cook food by heating it under a grill or in

front of a fire **2** to have a drink in someone's honour **toaster** *noun* a machine that makes toast

tobacco *noun* the dried leaves of certain plants, used for smoking in cigarettes, cigars, or pipes

toboggan *noun* (*plural* **toboggans**) a small sledge for sliding downhill **tobogganing** *noun*

today *noun* this day ► *Today is Monday.*
today *adverb* **1** on this day ► *I saw him today.* **2** nowadays ► *Today we don't have slaves.*

toddler *noun* (*plural* **toddlers**) a young child who has just started to walk

toe *noun* (*plural* **toes**) **1** each of the five separate parts at the end of your foot **2** the part of a shoe or sock that covers your toes

toffee *noun* (*plural* **toffees**) a sticky sweet made from butter and sugar

together *adverb* with another person or thing, or with each other ► *We went into town together.*

toil *verb* (**toils, toiling, toiled**) (not an everyday word) **1** to work hard **2** to move slowly and with difficulty ► *The old man toiled up the hill.*
toil *noun* hard work

toilet *noun* (*plural* **toilets**) **1** a bowl with flushing water, in which you get rid of urine and waste from your body **2** a room or building with a toilet in it

token *noun* (*plural* **tokens**) **1** a sign or signal of something ► *A white flag is a token of surrender.* **2** a special disc or voucher that can be used instead of money to buy things

told past tense and past participle of **tell**

tolerable *adjective* able to be tolerated; bearable **tolerably** *adverb*

tolerate *verb* (**tolerates, tolerating, tolerated**) to allow something or accept it although you do not approve of it **tolerant** *adjective* accepting other people's ideas and ways

toll[1] *noun* (*plural* **tolls**) **1** a payment charged for using a bridge or road **2** an amount of loss or damage ▸ *The death toll in the earthquake is rising.*

toll[2] *verb* (**tolls**, **tolling**, **tolled**) to ring a bell slowly

tomahawk *noun* (*plural* **tomahawks**) an axe used by Native Americans

tomato *noun* (*plural* **tomatoes**) a soft red fruit with seeds inside it, eaten as a vegetable

tomb *noun* (*plural* **tombs**) (*pronounced* toom) a place where a dead body is buried

tombstone *noun* (*plural* **tombstones**) a memorial stone set up over a grave

tomorrow *noun* and *adverb* the day after today

ton *noun* (*plural* **tons**) **1** a unit of weight equal to 2,240 pounds or about 1,016 kilograms **2** (informal) a large amount ▸ *There's tons of room.*

tone *noun* (*plural* **tones**) **1** the nature or quality of a sound ▸ *I didn't like the tone of his voice.* **2** a shade of a colour **3** a sound in music

tone *verb* (**tones**, **toning**, **toned**) **tone down** to make sounds softer or quieter

tongs *plural noun* a tool with two arms joined at one end, used for picking things up

tongue *noun* (*plural* **tongues**) **1** the long soft piece of muscle in your mouth, which you use for talking and eating, and for licking things **2** a language **3** the flap of material under the laces of a shoe

tongue-twister *noun* (*plural* **tongue-twisters**) something that is very difficult to say

tonic *noun* (*plural* **tonics**) something that makes you healthier or stronger

tonight *adverb* and *noun* this evening or night

tonne *noun* (*plural* **tonnes**) a unit of weight equal to 1,000 kilograms

tonsillitis *noun* a disease that makes your tonsils extremely sore

tonsils *plural noun* the two pieces of soft flesh inside your throat

too *adverb* **1** also; as well ▸ *I'd like to come too.* **2** more than is wanted or allowed ▸ *The box is too small.* ▸ *She drives much too fast.*

took past tense of **take**

tool *noun* (*plural* **tools**) a device that you use to help you do a particular job, such as a hammer or saw

tooth *noun* (*plural* **teeth**) **1** each of the hard white bony parts that grow in your gums, used for biting and chewing **2** each in a row of sharp parts, such as those on the blade of a saw **toothed** *adjective* having teeth

toothache *noun* a pain in a tooth

toothbrush *noun* (*plural* **toothbrushes**) a small brush on a long handle, for brushing your teeth

toothpaste *noun* (*plural* **toothpastes**) a creamy paste for cleaning your teeth

top *noun* (*plural* **tops**) **1** the highest part of something **2** the upper surface of something **3** the covering or stopper of a jar or bottle **4** a piece of clothing for the upper part of your body **5** a toy that can be made to spin on its point

top *adjective* highest ▸ *They live on the top floor.*

top *verb* (**tops**, **topping**, **topped**) **1** to put a top or covering on something ▸ *The cake was topped with icing.* **2** to be more than ▸ *The charity collection this year topped £100.* **top up** to fill something to the top

top-heavy *adjective* too heavy at the top, so that it falls over easily

topic *noun* (*plural* **topics**) a subject to talk or write about

topical *adjective* to do with things that are happening now

topmost *adjective* highest

topping *noun* (*plural* **toppings**) food that is put on the top of a cake, pudding, or pizza

topple *verb* (**topples, toppling, toppled**)
1 to fall over clumsily 2 to overthrow someone in power

topsy-turvy *adverb* and *adjective* in a muddle

torch *noun* (*plural* **torches**) 1 a small electric lamp that you hold in your hand 2 a piece of wood with burning material on the end, used as a light

tore past tense of **tear** *verb*

toreador *noun* (*plural* **toreadors**) (*pronounced* tor-i-a-dor) a bullfighter

torment *verb* (**torments, tormenting, tormented**) 1 to make someone suffer or feel pain 2 to keep annoying someone deliberately **tormentor** *noun*

torment *noun* (*plural* **torments**) great suffering

torn past participle of **tear** *verb*

tornado *noun* (*plural* **tornadoes**) (*pronounced* tor-**nay**-doh) a violent storm or whirlwind
The word **tornado** comes from a Spanish word *tronada* meaning 'thunder'.

torpedo *noun* (*plural* **torpedoes**) a long tube-shaped missile sent under water to destroy ships and submarines

torpedo *verb* (**torpedoes, torpedoing, torpedoed**) to attack a ship with a torpedo

torrent *noun* (*plural* **torrents**) a strong stream or fall of water **torrential** *adjective* falling in torrents

torso *noun* (*plural* **torsos**) the main part of your body, not including your head, arms, and legs
The word **torso** comes from an Italian word meaning 'stump'.

tortoise *noun* (*plural* **tortoises**) (*pronounced* tor-tus) a slow-moving animal with a shell over its body

torture *verb* (**tortures, torturing, tortured**) to make someone feel great pain, especially so that they will give information

torture *noun* (*plural* **tortures**) great pain or suffering **torturer** *noun*

Tory *noun* (*plural* **Tories**) a member of the British Conservative Party

toss *verb* (**tosses, tossing, tossed**) 1 to throw something into the air 2 to spin a coin to see which side lands uppermost, as a way of deciding something 3 to move about restlessly

toss *noun* (*plural* **tosses**) an act of tossing

total *noun* (*plural* **totals**) the amount you get by adding everything together

total *adjective* 1 complete; including everything ► *The total length of the walk was about seven miles.* 2 complete; utter ► *What happened next was a total mystery.* **totally** *adverb*

total *verb* (**totals, totalling, totalled**) 1 to add everything up 2 to reach an amount as a total ► *Next day we received a repair bill totalling more than £500.*

totem pole *noun* (*plural* **totem poles**) a large pole carved or painted by Native Americans
It is called **totem pole** because it shows the **totems** or symbols of Native American tribes and families.

totter *verb* (**totters, tottering, tottered**) to walk or move unsteadily

touch *verb* (**touches, touching, touched**) 1 to feel something lightly with your hand or fingers 2 to come into contact with something or hit it gently 3 to be next to something so that there is no space in between 4 to interfere or meddle with something ► *Don't touch anything in this room.* 5 to reach an amount or level ► *His temperature touched 104 degrees.* 6 to affect someone's feelings ► *She had been deeply touched by their friendship.* **touch down** to land in an aircraft or spacecraft **touch up** to improve something by making small changes or additions

touch *noun* (*plural* **touches**) 1 an act of touching 2 the ability to feel things by touching them 3 a small amount of something ▸ *The fresh air put a touch of colour into their cheeks.* **4** communication with someone ▸ *We have lost touch with them.* **5** the part of a football field outside the playing area

touchdown *noun* (*plural* **touchdowns**) the landing of an aircraft or spacecraft

touchy *adjective* (**touchier, touchiest**) easily upset or offended

tough *adjective* (**tougher, toughest**) **1** strong; hard to break or damage ▸ *You'll need tough shoes for the climb.* **2** (describing food) hard to chew **3** rough or violent ▸ *He is an actor who plays tough characters in films.* **4** hard or difficult ▸ *Farming can be tough work.* **toughness** *noun*

toughen *verb* (**toughens, toughening, toughened**) to become tougher, or to make something tougher

tour *noun* (*plural* **tours**) a journey visiting several places

tourist *noun* (*plural* **tourists**) someone who is travelling or on holiday abroad **tourism** *noun* organizing holidays for people

tournament *noun* (*plural* **tournaments**) a series of games or contests

tow *verb* (**tows, towing, towed**) (*rhymes with* go) to pull a vehicle or boat with another vehicle ▸ *The car moved slowly up the hill, towing a caravan.*

towards or **toward** *preposition* **1** in the direction of ▸ *The man starting walking towards the house.* **2** in relation to ▸ *She always behaved kindly towards us.* **3** as a contribution to ▸ *I'll put the money towards my holiday.*

towel *noun* (*plural* **towels**) a piece of soft cloth for drying things

tower *noun* (*plural* **towers**) a tall narrow building or part of a building

tower *verb* (**towers, towering, towered**) to be much taller than the things on each side ▸ *The skyscrapers towered above the city.*

town *noun* (*plural* **towns**) a place with many houses, shops, schools, offices, and other buildings

town hall *noun* (*plural* **town halls**) a building with offices for the local council and usually a hall for public events

towpath *noun* (*plural* **towpaths**) a path beside a canal or river
It is called a **towpath** because it was originally used for horses to walk along while towing barges.

toxic *adjective* poisonous

toy *noun* (*plural* **toys**) something for a child to play with

toy *verb* (**toys, toying, toyed**) to think about an idea casually or idly ▸ *Stephanie toyed with the idea of joining the police.*

trace *noun* (*plural* **traces**) **1** a mark or sign left by a person or thing ▸ *They vanished without any trace.* **2** a small amount of something ▸ *They found a trace of blood on the carpet.*

trace *verb* (**traces, tracing, traced**) **1** to find someone or something after a search **2** to copy a picture or map by drawing over it on paper you can see through

track *noun* (*plural* **tracks**) **1** a path made by people or animals **2** marks left by a person, animal, or vehicle walking or moving along **3** a set of rails for trains to run on **4** a road or area of ground prepared for racing **5** a metal belt used instead of wheels on a heavy vehicle such as a tank or tractor **6** one song or item on a record or CD **keep track of** to know where something or someone is or what they are doing

track *verb* (**tracks, tracking, tracked**) to follow someone or something by observing the signs or marks they leave **track down** to find someone or something that has been lost **tracker** *noun* someone who tracks a person or animal

tracksuit *noun* (*plural* **tracksuits**) a set of loose trousers and a top that athletes wear for jogging and warming up

tractor *noun* (*plural* **tractors**) a motor vehicle used for pulling farm machinery or heavy loads

trade *noun* (*plural* **trades**) **1** the business of buying or selling or exchanging things **2** a job or occupation, especially one needing skill

trade *verb* (**trades, trading, traded**) to buy and sell things **trade in** to give something towards the cost of something new ► *He traded in his motorcycle for a car.* **trader** *noun*

trademark *noun* (*plural* **trademarks**) a sign or name that only one manufacturer is allowed to use

trade union *noun* (*plural* **trade unions**) an organization of workers in a particular trade. Trade unions look after the workers and try to improve their pay and conditions.

tradition *noun* (*plural* **traditions**) a belief or custom that is passed down from one generation to the next **traditional** *adjective*

traffic *noun* 1 vehicles, ships, or aircraft moving along a route 2 an illegal trade ► *They were involved in the traffic in drugs.*
traffic *verb* (**traffics, trafficking, trafficked**) to trade in something illegally, especially in drugs

traffic lights *plural noun* a set of coloured lights used to control road traffic

traffic warden *noun* (*plural* **traffic wardens**) an official who controls the parking of vehicles in towns and cities

tragedy *noun* (*plural* **tragedies**) 1 a story or play with unhappy events or a sad ending 2 a very sad event

tragic *adjective* 1 very sad or distressing 2 to do with tragedy **tragically** *adverb*

trail *noun* (*plural* **trails**) 1 a path or track through the countryside 2 marks left behind by someone or something that has passed
trail *verb* (**trails, trailing, trailed**) 1 to follow an animal by looking for the scent or marks it has left behind 2 to drag something behind you 3 to follow someone, going more slowly than them ► *A few walkers trailed behind the others.* 4 to hang down loosely ► *She wore a long trailing scarf.*

trailer *noun* (*plural* **trailers**) 1 a container with wheels, which is pulled along by a car or lorry 2 a set of short pieces or extracts advertising a film or television programme

train *noun* (*plural* **trains**) 1 a set of railway coaches or trucks for carrying passengers or goods 2 a number of people or animals moving along together, especially in a desert ► *There was a camel train in the distance.* 3 a series of connected events or ideas ► *I can't follow your train of thought.* 4 a long part of a dress that trails behind on the ground

train *verb* (**trains, training, trained**) 1 to give someone skill or practice in something ► *Margaret is training me in judo.* 2 to practise, especially for a sporting event ► *She is training for the marathon.* 3 to make a plant grow in a particular direction ► *Roses can be trained up walls.* 4 to aim a gun at a target ► *He trained his rifle on the bridge.*

trainer *noun* (*plural* **trainers**) 1 a person who trains people or animals 2 a soft shoe with a rubber sole, worn for running and jogging

traitor *noun* (*plural* **traitors**) someone who betrays their country or friends

tram *noun* (*plural* **trams**) a passenger vehicle that runs along rails set in the road

tramp *noun* (*plural* **tramps**) 1 a person without a home or job who walks from place to place 2 a long walk 3 the sound of heavy footsteps
tramp *verb* (**tramps, tramping, tramped**) 1 to walk with heavy footsteps 2 to walk a long way

trample *verb* (**tramples, trampling, trampled**) to crush something by treading heavily on it

trampoline *noun* (*plural* **trampolines**) (*pronounced* **tramp-o-leen**) a piece of equipment for gymnasts to spring up and down on, made of a tight sheet of material joined to a frame by springs

trance *noun* (*plural* **trances**) a dreamy or unconscious state like sleep

tranquil *adjective* quiet and peaceful **tranquillity** *noun*

tranquillizer *noun* (*plural* **tranquillizers**) a drug used to make a person feel calm

transaction *noun* (*plural* **transactions**) a business deal

transfer *verb* (**transfers, transferring, transferred**) (*pronounced* trans-**fer**) to move someone or something from one place or person to another
transfer *noun* (*plural* **transfers**) (*pronounced* trans-**fer**) 1 the process of moving a person or thing to another place 2 a piece of paper with a picture or design that can be transferred to another surface by soaking or heating the paper

transform *verb* (**transforms, transforming, transformed**) to change the form or appearance of something ▸ *A new coat of paint would transform the bathroom.* **transformation** *noun* a complete change

transformer *noun* (*plural* **transformers**) a device which changes the voltage of an electric current

transfusion *noun* (*plural* **transfusions**) an injection of blood taken from one person into another person's body

transistor *noun* (*plural* **transistors**) 1 a small electronic device that controls the flow of an electric current 2 a portable radio that uses transistors

transition *noun* (*plural* **transitions**) a change from one thing to another

translate *verb* (**translates, translating, translated**) to say or write words from one language in another language **translation** *noun* **translator** *noun*

transmit *verb* (**transmits, transmitting, transmitted**) 1 to send out radio or television signals 2 to send or pass something from one person or place to another ▸ *We don't know how the disease is transmitted.* **transmission** *noun* **transmitter** *noun* a piece of equipment used to transmit radio or television signals

transparent *adjective* able to be seen through **transparency** *noun* how transparent something is

transpire *verb* (**transpires, transpiring, transpired**) to happen or become known ▸ *It transpired that he had never been to Rome.*

transplant *verb* (**transplants, transplanting, transplanted**) 1 to move a plant from one place to another 2 to take a body organ from one person and put it in the body of a person who is ill **transplantation** *noun*
transplant *noun* (*plural* **transplants**) an operation to transplant a body organ

transport *verb* (**transports, transporting, transported**) (*pronounced* trans-**port**) to take people or things from one place to another
transport *noun* (*pronounced* **trans**-port) 1 the process of transporting people or things 2 vehicles used to do this **transporter** *noun* a large vehicle used for moving cars and other things

trap *noun* (*plural* **traps**) 1 a device for catching and holding animals 2 a plan or trick to capture or fool someone 3 a two-wheeled carriage pulled by a horse
trap *verb* (**traps, trapping, trapped**) 1 to catch an animal in a trap 2 to capture or fool someone with a plan or trick

trapdoor *noun* (*plural* **trapdoors**) a door in a floor or ceiling

trapeze *noun* (*plural* **trapezes**) a piece of equipment for acrobats to swing from, made of a bar hanging from two ropes high above the ground

trapezium *noun* (*plural* **trapeziums**) a four-sided figure that has only two parallel sides, which are of different length

trash *noun* rubbish or nonsense **trashy** *adjective* worthless; badly made

travel *verb* (**travels, travelling, travelled**) to go from one place to another
travel *noun* travelling ▸ *Martha loves travel.* **traveller** *noun* someone who travels, or another word for a gypsy

trawler *noun* (*plural* **trawlers**) a fishing boat that pulls a large net behind it

tray noun (plural **trays**) a flat piece of hard material with handles, used for carrying food and drink

treacherous adjective 1 betraying people 2 dangerous or unreliable ▸ *It's been snowing and the roads are treacherous.* **treachery** noun betraying someone

treacle noun a thick sweet sticky liquid made from sugar

tread verb (**treads, treading, trod, trodden**) to walk on something or put your foot on it

tread noun (plural **treads**) 1 a sound or way of walking 2 the part of a tyre that touches the ground

treason noun betraying your country

treasure noun (plural **treasures**) 1 a collection of valuable things like jewels or money 2 a precious person or thing

treasure verb (**treasures, treasuring, treasured**) to treat something as very precious

treasurer noun (plural **treasurers**) someone in charge of the money belonging to an organization or club

treasury noun (plural **treasuries**) a place where treasure or money is stored **the Treasury** the government department in charge of a country's money

treat verb (**treats, treating, treated**) 1 to behave towards someone or something in a certain way ▸ *His stepmother always treats him very kindly.* 2 to give medical care to a person or animal ▸ *She was treated for rheumatism.* ▸ *The nurse treated his wound.* 3 to put something through a process to improve it ▸ *The woodwork needs treating so that it doesn't rot.* 4 to pay for someone's food or drink or entertainment ▸ *I'll treat you to a burger.*

treat noun (plural **treats**) something that you enjoy very much ▸ *Going to the cinema will be a treat.*

treatment noun (plural **treatments**) 1 the way you treat someone 2 medical care

treaty noun (plural **treaties**) a formal agreement between countries, for example to end a war

treble adjective three times as much or three times as many

treble noun (plural **trebles**) 1 a boy with a high singing voice 2 an instrument that uses a high range of notes ▸ *a treble recorder*

treble verb (**trebles, trebling, trebled**) 1 to make something three times as big or three times as many 2 to become three times as big

tree noun (plural **trees**) a tall plant with leaves, branches, and a thick wooden trunk

trek noun (plural **treks**) a long walk or journey

trek verb (**treks, trekking, trekked**) to go on a trek

trellis noun (plural **trellises**) a framework of crossing wooden or metal bars, used to support climbing plants

tremble verb (**trembles, trembling, trembled**) to shake gently from fear or excitement

tremble noun (plural **trembles**) a trembling movement or sound

tremendous adjective 1 very large or loud ▸ *Then they heard a tremendous explosion.* 2 excellent ▸ *We had a tremendous time.* **tremendously** adverb

tremor noun (plural **tremors**) a shaking or trembling

trench noun (plural **trenches**) a long hole or ditch dug in the ground

trend noun (plural **trends**) 1 the general direction in which something is going 2 a fashion

trendy adjective (**trendier, trendiest**) (informal) fashionable; trying to be up to date **trendily** adverb **trendiness** noun

trespass verb (**trespasses, trespassing, trespassed**) to go on someone's land or property without their permission **trespasser** noun

trial noun (plural **trials**) 1 a test or experiment to see how well something works 2 the process of trying someone in a lawcourt

triangle *noun* (*plural* **triangles**) **1** a flat shape with three straight sides and three angles **2** a musical instrument made from a metal rod bent into a triangle and played by striking it **triangular** *adjective* in the shape of a triangle

tribe *noun* (*plural* **tribes**) a group of families living together and ruled by a chief **tribal** *adjective* to do with a tribe **tribesman** *noun* **tribeswoman** *noun*

tributary *noun* (*plural* **tributaries**) a river or stream that flows into a larger river or a lake

tribute *noun* (*plural* **tributes**) something you say or do as a mark of respect or admiration for someone

trick *noun* (*plural* **tricks**) **1** something done to deceive or fool someone **2** a clever action you do to amuse someone ▸ *a card trick*
trick *verb* (**tricks, tricking, tricked**) to deceive or fool someone **trickery** *noun* tricks, or tricking someone

trickle *verb* (**trickles, trickling, trickled**) to flow slowly and in small quantities
trickle *noun* (*plural* **trickles**) a slow gradual flow

tricky *adjective* (**trickier, trickiest**) difficult; needing skill

tricycle *noun* (*plural* **tricycles**) a vehicle with pedals and three wheels

tried past tense and past participle of **try** *verb*

trifle *noun* (*plural* **trifles**) **1** a pudding made of sponge cake covered with custard, fruit, and cream **2** something that is very small or unimportant

trifling *adjective* unimportant

trigger *noun* (*plural* **triggers**) a lever on a gun, for firing it

trillion *noun* (*plural* **trillions**) a million million (1,000,000,000,000) or sometimes a million million million (1,000,000,000,000,000,000)
People often say **trillions**, meaning very many, and then the exact number does not matter.

trim *adjective* (**trimmer, trimmest**) neat and tidy
trim *verb* (**trims, trimming, trimmed**) **1** to cut the edges or unwanted parts from something **2** to decorate a piece of clothing
trim *noun* an act of trimming ▸ *Give it a quick trim.*

Trinity *noun* the Trinity in Christianity, the union of Father, Son, and Holy Spirit in one God

trio *noun* (*plural* **trios**) a group of three people or things

trip *verb* (**trips, tripping, tripped**) **1** to catch your foot on something and fall or stumble **2** to make someone fall or stumble **3** to move with quick gentle steps
trip *noun* (*plural* **trips**) **1** a short journey or outing **2** a fall

tripe *noun* **1** part of the stomach of an ox used as food **2** (*informal*) nonsense

triple *adjective* **1** three times as much or three times as many **2** having three parts
triple *verb* (**triples, tripling, tripled**) to make something three times as big

triplet *noun* (*plural* **triplets**) one of three children or animals born at the same time to the same mother

tripod *noun* (*plural* **tripods**) (*pronounced* **try-pod**) a stand with three legs, for supporting a camera

triumph *noun* (*plural* **triumphs**) **1** a great success or victory **2** a celebration of success ▸ *They returned home in triumph.*
triumph *verb* (**triumphs, triumphing, triumphed**) to win a great success or victory **triumphant** *adjective* happy because you have won

trivial *adjective* not important or valuable **trivially** *adverb*

trod past tense of **tread** *verb*

trodden past participle of **tread** *verb*

troll *noun* (*plural* **trolls**) in stories, a nasty creature that lives in a cave or under a bridge

trolley *noun* (*plural* **trolleys**) **1** a small table on wheels, for pushing food and drink around **2** a small cart or basket on wheels ▸ *a shopping trolley*

trombone *noun* (*plural* **trombones**) a large brass musical instrument with a sliding tube **trombonist** *noun* someone who plays the trombone

troop *noun* (*plural* **troops**) a group of soldiers or Scouts

troop *verb* (**troops**, **trooping**, **trooped**) to move along in large numbers

troops *plural noun* soldiers

trophy *noun* (*plural* **trophies**) a prize or souvenir for a victory or success

tropics *plural noun* the hot regions of the earth on each side of the equator as far as the latitudes of about 23° north and 23° south **tropical** *adjective* to do with the tropics, or from the tropics ▸ *tropical diseases.* ▸ *tropical fruit juice*

trot *verb* (**trots**, **trotting**, **trotted**) 1 (used about a horse) to run gently without cantering or galloping 2 (used about a person) to run gently with short steps **trot** *noun* a slow or gentle run

trouble *noun* (*plural* **troubles**) something that causes worry or difficulty **take trouble** to take care in doing something

trouble *verb* (**troubles**, **troubling**, **troubled**) 1 to cause someone trouble or worry ▸ *Something was troubling Gopal's mother.* 2 to make an effort to do something ▸ *Nobody troubled to ask us what we wanted.*

troublesome *adjective* causing trouble or worry

trough *noun* (*plural* **troughs**) (*pronounced* trof) a long narrow box for animals to eat or drink from

trousers *plural noun* a piece of clothing worn over the lower half of your body, with two parts to cover your legs

trout *noun* (*plural* **trout**) a freshwater fish used for food

trowel *noun* (*plural* **trowels**) 1 a tool for digging small holes 2 a tool with a flat blade for spreading cement or mortar

truant *noun* (*plural* **truants**) a child who stays away from school without permission **truancy** *noun* staying away from school in this way

truce *noun* (*plural* **truces**) an agreement between sides who are fighting to stop for a time

truck *noun* (*plural* **trucks**) 1 an open railway wagon for carrying goods 2 a lorry

trudge *verb* (**trudges**, **trudging**, **trudged**) to walk slowly and heavily

true *adjective* (**truer**, **truest**) 1 real or correct; telling what actually exists or happened ▸ *This is a true story.* 2 genuine or proper ▸ *He is the true heir to the estate.* 3 loyal and faithful ▸ *You are a true friend.* **truly** *adverb* really, genuinely

trump *noun* (*plural* **trumps**) a playing card of a suit that ranks above the others for one game or round of play ▸ *Hearts are trumps this time.*

trumpet *noun* (*plural* **trumpets**) a brass musical instrument with valves that are pressed down to make different notes **trumpeter** *noun* someone who plays the trumpet

trumpet *verb* (**trumpets**, **trumpeting**, **trumpeted**) to make a loud sound, as an elephant does

truncheon *noun* (*plural* **truncheons**) a short thick stick carried as a weapon by a police officer

trundle *verb* (**trundles**, **trundling**, **trundled**) (used about a cart or motor vehicle) to move along slowly and heavily

trunk *noun* (*plural* **trunks**) 1 the main part of a tree, coming out of the ground 2 an elephant's long flexible nose 3 a large box with a lid, for carrying or storing things 4 the main part of your body, not including your head, legs, and arms

trunk road *noun* (*plural* **trunk roads**) a main road

trunks *plural noun* shorts worn by men and boys for swimming or sports

trust *verb* (**trusts, trusting, trusted**) **1** to believe that someone is good or reliable ▶ *I trust you to do your work while I am out.* **2** to let someone use something or look after it ▶ *Liz trusted me with her new pen.*

trust *noun* **1** the feeling that a person or thing can be trusted **2** responsibility; being trusted **trustful** *adjective* having trust or confidence

trustworthy *adjective* able to be trusted; reliable

truth *noun* what is true or real ▶ *Please tell me the truth.*

truthful *adjective* **1** telling the truth ▶ *They are truthful people.* **2** true ▶ *They gave a truthful account of what happened.* **truthfully** *adverb* **truthfulness** *noun*

try *verb* (**tries, trying, tried**) **1** to make an effort to do something or to see if you can do it ▶ *Try to finish by tomorrow.* **2** to use something to see if it works ▶ *Try the lights again.* **3** to find out in a lawcourt if someone is guilty of a crime, by hearing all the evidence about it ▶ *They were tried and found guilty.* **4** to annoy someone over a long time ▶ *You really do try me with your constant complaining.* **try on** to put on clothes to see if they fit **try out** to use something to see if it works

try *noun* (*plural* **tries**) **1** a go at trying something; an attempt **2** in rugby football, a way of scoring by putting the ball down on the ground behind your opponents' goal

T-shirt *noun* (*plural* **T-shirts**) a shirt or vest with short sleeves

tub *noun* (*plural* **tubs**) **1** a round open container **2** a round container for liquids or soft food

tuba *noun* (*plural* **tubas**) (*pronounced tew-ba*) a large brass musical instrument that makes a deep sound

tubby *adjective* (**tubbier, tubbiest**) short and rather fat **tubbiness** *noun*

tube *noun* (*plural* **tubes**) **1** a long thin hollow piece of material such as metal, plastic, rubber, or glass, used for carrying liquids or gases **2** a long hollow container for something soft such as toothpaste **3** an underground railway

tuber *noun* (*plural* **tubers**) a thick rounded plant root or stem that produces buds

tubular *adjective* shaped like a tube

tuck *verb* (**tucks, tucking, tucked**) to push something into or behind something else so that it is tidy or hidden **tuck in** (informal) to eat heartily **tuck in** or **tuck up** to put the bedclothes snugly round someone

tuck shop *noun* (*plural* **tuck shops**) a shop in a school for children to buy sweets, cakes, crisps, and drinks

Tuesday *noun* (*plural* **Tuesdays**) the third day of the week
Tuesday is an Anglo-Saxon name honouring the god of war called *Tiw* (pronounced *tue*).

tuft *noun* (*plural* **tufts**) a bunch of soft or fluffy growing things such as grass or hair

tug *noun* (*plural* **tugs**) **1** a hard or sudden pull **2** a small powerful boat used for towing ships

tug *verb* (**tugs, tugging, tugged**) to pull something hard

tug of war *noun* (*plural* **tugs of war**) a sport in which two teams pull a rope from opposite ends

tulip *noun* (*plural* **tulips**) a plant with a bright cup-shaped flower that grows from a bulb

tumble *verb* (**tumbles, tumbling, tumbled**) to fall over or fall down clumsily

tumble-drier *noun* (*plural* **tumble-driers**) a machine that dries washing in warm air in a rotating drum

tumbler *noun* (*plural* **tumblers**) a drinking glass with straight sides

tummy *noun* (*plural* **tummies**) (*informal*) your stomach

tumour *noun* (*plural* **tumours**) (*pronounced* **tew**-mer) an abnormal growth on the body or inside it

tumult *noun* (*pronounced* **tew**-mult) an uproar or state of great confusion

tumultuous *adjective* noisy and excited ▶ *We got a tumultuous welcome.*

tuna *noun* (*plural* **tuna** or **tunas**) (*pronounced* **tew**-na) a large sea fish used for food

tundra *noun* in cold regions, an area of flat frozen land with no trees

tune *noun* (*plural* **tunes**) a short piece of music or a series of musical notes that you can sing **in tune** at the correct musical pitch **tuneful** *adjective* having a pleasant tune

tune *verb* (**tunes, tuning, tuned**) 1 to adjust a musical instrument to the correct pitch 2 to adjust a radio or television to receive a particular broadcasting station 3 to adjust an engine so that it works smoothly

tunic *noun* (*plural* **tunics**) (*pronounced* **tew**-nik) 1 a close-fitting jacket worn as part of a uniform 2 a loose piece of clothing without sleeves

tunnel *noun* (*plural* **tunnels**) a passage made underground or through a hill
tunnel *verb* (**tunnels, tunnelling, tunnelled**) to make a tunnel through the ground

turban *noun* (*plural* **turbans**) a covering for the head made by wrapping a strip of cloth round it

turbine *noun* (*plural* **turbines**) a machine or motor that is driven by a flow of water or gas

turbulence *noun* strong movement of the air or water, causing aircraft and ships to be tossed about **turbulent** *adjective* moving violently

turf *noun* (*plural* **turfs** or **turves**) a piece of short grass with the soil it is growing in

turkey *noun* (*plural* **turkeys**) a large bird kept for its meat
The word **turkey** comes from the name of the country Turkey, although it originally meant a different bird.

turmoil *noun* a great disturbance or confusion

turn *verb* (**turns, turning, turned**) 1 to move round in a circle, like a wheel 2 to change direction ▶ *Turn left at the lights.* 3 to make something move round or in a new direction ▶ *I'll turn the car round.* 4 to change appearance ▶ *When he heard the news he turned pale.* 5 to change into something ▶ *The frog turned into a prince.* 6 to make something change ▶ *You can turn milk into cheese.* 7 to use a switch to make something work or stop working ▶ *Shall I turn the television off?* ▶ *Please turn out the lights.* **turn down** to reject something or not want it **turn out** 1 to happen a certain way ▶ *The weather turned out fine after all.* 2 to empty something ▶ *She turned out her pockets.* **turn up** to appear or arrive suddenly ▶ *Dan turned up after lunch.*

turn *noun* (*plural* **turns**) 1 the action of turning; a turning movement 2 a place where a road bends; a junction 3 a person's task or duty ▶ *It's your turn to wash up.* 4 a short performance in a show 5 (*informal*) an attack of illness; a nervous shock ▶ *Seeing her like that after all this time gave me a funny turn.* **a good turn** something you do that is helpful

turning *noun* (*plural* **turnings**) a place where you leave a road to join another

turnip *noun* (*plural* **turnips**) a plant with a large round white root used as a vegetable

turnstile *noun* (*plural* **turnstiles**) a revolving gate that lets one person through at a time

turpentine *noun* (*pronounced* **ter**-pen-tyn) a kind of oil used to make paint thinner and to clean paintbrushes

turquoise *noun* (*pronounced* **ter**-kwoiz) 1 a greenish-blue colour 2 a jewel of this colour

turquoise *adjective* having a greenish-blue colour

turret *noun* (*plural* **turrets**) 1 a small tower in a castle 2 a revolving structure containing a gun

turtle *noun* (*plural* **turtles**) a sea animal with a hard shell **turn turtle** to capsize

tusk *noun* (*plural* **tusks**) a long pointed tooth that sticks out of the mouth of an elephant, walrus, or boar

tussle *noun* (*plural* **tussles**) a hard struggle or fight
tussle *verb* (**tussles, tussling, tussled**) to struggle or fight over something

tutor *noun* (*plural* **tutors**) a teacher who teaches students individually or in small groups

TV short for **television**

tweed *noun* a thick rough woollen cloth

tweezers *plural noun* a tool for picking up small objects

twelve *noun* (*plural* **twelves**) the number 12 **twelfth** *adjective* and *noun*

twenty *noun* (*plural* **twenties**) the number 20 **twentieth** *adjective* and *noun*

twice *adverb* two times; on two occasions

twiddle *verb* (**twiddles, twiddling, twiddled**) to turn something round in an idle way ▸ *Jan was twiddling a knob on the radio.*

twig *noun* (*plural* **twigs**) a short thin piece from a branch of a tree

twilight *noun* the time of dim light after the sun sets in the evening

twin *noun* (*plural* **twins**) one of two children or animals born at the same time to one mother

twine *noun* strong thin string

twinge *noun* (*plural* **twinges**) a sudden sharp pain

twinkle *verb* (**twinkles, twinkling, twinkled**) to sparkle or shine with flashes of bright light
twinkle *noun* (*plural* **twinkles**) a twinkling light

twirl *verb* (**twirls, twirling, twirled**) to turn round and round quickly
twirl *noun* (*plural* **twirls**) a twirling movement

twist *verb* (**twists, twisting, twisted**) 1 to turn the ends of something in opposite directions ▸ *You have to twist the lid to open it.* 2 to turn round or from side to side ▸ *The road twisted through the hills.* 3 to bend something out of its proper shape ▸ *My front wheel is twisted.*
twist *noun* (*plural* **twists**) a twisting movement or action

twitch *verb* (**twitches, twitching, twitched**) to jerk or move suddenly and quickly
twitch *noun* (*plural* **twitches**) a jerk or sudden movement

twitter *verb* (**twitters, twittering, twittered**) to make quick chirping sounds, as birds do

two *noun* (*plural* **twos**) the number 2

tying present participle of **tie** *verb*

type *noun* (*plural* **types**) 1 a kind or sort of people or things ▸ *What type of computer have you got?* 2 letters and figures designed for use in printing
type *verb* (**types, typing, typed**) to write something with a typewriter **typist** *noun* someone who uses a typewriter

typewriter *noun* (*plural* **typewriters**) a machine with keys that you press to print letters or figures on a sheet of paper **typewritten** *adjective*

typhoid *noun* a serious disease caused by bacteria, which gives you a fever and affects your intestines

typhoon *noun* (*plural* **typhoons**) a violent tropical storm with strong winds and rain

typical *adjective* 1 associated with a particular type of person or thing ▸ *The soldiers fought with typical courage.* 2 usual, normal ▸ *Her typical day would begin with a good breakfast.* **typically** *adverb*

tyrant *noun* (*plural* **tyrants**) (*pronounced* ty-rant) someone who rules people cruelly or unjustly **tyrannical** *adjective* cruel or unjust

tyre *noun* (*plural* **tyres**) a covering of rubber fitted round the rim of a wheel to make it grip the road and run smoothly

Uu

udder *noun* (*plural* **udders**) the bag-like part of a cow, goat, or ewe, from which milk is taken

UFO *noun* (*plural* **UFOs**) short for *unidentified flying object*, a flying object that no one can explain

ugly *adjective* (**uglier**, **ugliest**) 1 not beautiful; unpleasant to look at ▸ *What an ugly house it was.* 2 threatening or dangerous ▸ *He was usually kind but he had an ugly temper.* **ugliness** *noun* being ugly

ulcer *noun* (*plural* **ulcers**) a sore on your skin or inside your body

ultimate *adjective* last or final ▸ *His ultimate goal was to get a job in television.* **ultimately** *adverb*

ultraviolet light *noun* light beyond the violet end of the spectrum, which you cannot see with your eye

umbilical cord *noun* (*plural* **umbilical cords**) a cord connecting a baby to its mother in the womb. The baby gets oxygen and food through this cord.

umbrella *noun* (*plural* **umbrellas**) a folding frame covered with cloth, which you open out to form a protection from rain

umpire *noun* (*plural* **umpires**) a referee in cricket, tennis, and some other games

un- *prefix* meaning 'not', as in *unfriendly*, or added to verbs to make the action of the verb opposite to normal, as in *undo* There are hundreds of words beginning with **un-**. Those listed here are the ones that you will most often hear people use, and that you will read in books and want to use yourself. You can make many more words, especially by adding **un-** to an adjective, for example *unexplained*, *unripe*, *unsociable*.

unable *adjective* not able ▸ *She was unable to walk after her accident.*

unaided *adjective* without any help

unanimous *adjective* (*pronounced* yoo-nan-i-mus) agreed by everyone ▸ *It was a unanimous decision.* **unanimously** *adverb*

unavoidable *adjective* not able to be avoided; bound to happen

unaware *adjective* not aware

unawares *adjective* unexpectedly ▸ *His question caught me unawares.*

unbearable *adjective* not able to be borne or endured ▸ *The heat was unbearable.* **unbearably** *adverb*

unbeaten *adjective* not defeated

unbelievable *adjective* not able to be believed; amazing **unbelievably** *adverb*

unblock *verb* (**unblocks**, **unblocking**, **unblocked**) to clear something of a block or obstruction

uncalled for *adjective* not justified or necessary ▸ *Your rudeness was uncalled for.*

uncanny *adjective* (**uncannier**, **uncanniest**) strange and mysterious ▸ *There was an uncanny silence.* **uncannily** *adverb*

uncertain *adjective* 1 not certain ▸ *Jill and Judy are uncertain whether they can come.* 2 not reliable ▸ *The weather is rather uncertain at the moment.* **uncertainty** *noun* being uncertain

uncle *noun* (*plural* **uncles**) the brother of your father or mother, or your aunt's husband

uncomfortable *adjective* not comfortable; hard or awkward **uncomfortably** *adverb*

uncommon *adjective* not common; unusual

unconscious *adjective* 1 not conscious ▸ *The poor man lay unconscious on the pavement.* 2 not aware ▸ *We were entirely unconscious of the time.* **unconsciously** *adverb* **unconsciousness** *noun*

uncouth *adjective* (*pronounced* un-**kooth**) rude and rough in manner

uncover *verb* (**uncovers, uncovering, uncovered**) **1** to take the cover or top off something **2** to discover a secret or something unknown ▸ *The police have uncovered a huge fraud.*

undecided *adjective* uncertain what to do

undeniable *adjective* impossible to deny; certainly true **undeniably**

under *preposition* **1** lower than; below ▸ *Hide it under the desk.* **2** less than ▸ *They are under 5 years old.* **3** ruled or controlled by ▸ *The army is under his command.* **4** in the process of; undergoing ▸ *The road is under repair.* **5** using; moving by means of ▸ *The machine moves under its own power.*

under *adverb* in or to a lower place; below the surface ▸ *She tried to stop her head going under.*

underarm *adjective* and *adverb* with the arm kept below shoulder level and moving forward and upwards

undercarriage *noun* an aircraft's wheels and the supports for them

underclothes *plural noun* clothes you wear next to your skin, under your main clothes

undercover *adjective* working or done secretly

underdog *noun* (*plural* **underdogs**) a competitor who is unlikely to win

underdone *adjective* not properly done or cooked

underestimate *verb* (**underestimates, underestimating, underestimated**) to estimate something or someone to be smaller or less important than they really are

underfoot *adverb* on the ground, where you walk ▸ *There was a thick carpet of leaves underfoot.*

undergo *verb* (**undergoes, undergoing, underwent, undergone**) to experience something or have to do it

undergraduate *noun* (*plural* **undergraduates**) a student at a university who has not yet taken a degree

underground *adjective* and *adverb* **1** under the ground **2** done or working in secret

underground *noun* (*plural* **undergrounds**) a railway that runs through tunnels under the ground

undergrowth *noun* bushes and other plants growing closely under tall trees

underhand *adjective* secret and deceitful

underline *verb* (**underlines, underlining, underlined**) **1** to draw a line under something you have written **2** to show that something is important ▸ *Ali's accident underlines the need to be careful.*

undermine *verb* (**undermines, undermining, undermined**) to make someone's efforts or plans weaker

underneath *preposition* and *adverb* below or beneath

underpants *plural noun* a piece of men's or boys' underwear worn under trousers

underpass *noun* (*plural* **underpasses**) a place where one road or path goes under another

underprivileged *adjective* not having the same rights or standard of living as most people

understand *verb* (**understands, understanding, understood**) **1** to know what something means or how it works **2** to have heard a piece of information ▸ *I understand Jill has measles.* **understandable** *adjective* easy to understand

understanding *noun* **1** the power to understand or think; intelligence **2** agreement; harmony ▸ *In the end the two brothers came to an understanding.* **3** sympathy or tolerance ▸ *You need a lot of understanding to look after young children.*

understanding *adjective* sympathetic and helpful ▸ *Sheila was very understanding when I was ill.*

understudy *noun* (*plural* **understudies**) an actor who learns another actor's part and can take over the role if needed

undertake *verb* (**undertakes, undertaking, undertook, undertaken**) to agree or promise to do something

undertaker *noun* (*plural* **undertakers**) someone who arranges funerals

undertaking *noun* (*plural* **undertakings**) something that you agree to do

underwater *adjective* below the surface of water

underwear *noun* clothes you wear next to your skin, under your main clothes

underworld *noun* **1** in legends, the place where the spirits of dead people go **2** people who are regularly involved in crime

undesirable *adjective* not wanted or liked

undeveloped *adjective* not yet developed

undo *verb* (**undoes, undoing, undid, undone**) **1** to take the wrapping off a package or parcel **2** to cancel or reverse the effect of something already done ▸ *He didn't want the huge dog to undo all his good work in the garden.*

undoubted *adjective* definite or certain **undoubtedly** *adverb*

undress *verb* (**undresses, undressing, undressed**) to take your clothes off, or someone else's clothes off

unearth *verb* (**unearths, unearthing, unearthed**) to dig something up, or to find it by searching

unearthly *adjective* supernatural; strange and frightening

uneasy *adjective* (**uneasier, uneasiest**) anxious or worried **uneasily** *adverb* **uneasiness** *noun*

unemployed *adjective* not having a job **unemployment** *noun* being unemployed

uneven *adjective* not level or regular **unevenly** *adverb* **unevenness** *noun*

unexpected *adjective* not expected; surprising **unexpectedly** *adverb*

unfair *adjective* not fair; unjust **unfairly** *adverb* **unfairness** *noun*

unfaithful *adjective* not faithful or loyal

unfamiliar *adjective* not familiar or well known

unfasten *verb* (**unfastens, unfastening, unfastened**) to open something that has been fastened

unfit *adjective* **1** not fit or fully healthy **2** not suitable ▸ *He is unfit for the job.*

unfold *verb* (**unfolds, unfolding, unfolded**) **1** to open something or spread it out **2** to become known gradually ▸ *Listen as the story unfolds.*

unforeseen *adjective* unexpected

unforgettable *adjective* not able to be forgotten

unforgivable *adjective* not able to be forgiven

unfortunate *adjective* **1** unlucky **2** unsuitable or regrettable ▸ *It was an unfortunate thing to say and he was sorry for it.* **unfortunately** *adverb*

unfounded *adjective* not true or justified ▸ *Their fears were unfounded.*

unfriendly *adjective* (**unfriendlier, unfriendliest**) not friendly or welcoming **unfriendliness** *noun*

unhappy *adjective* (**unhappier, unhappiest**) **1** not happy **2** unfortunate or regrettable ▸ *It was an unhappy coincidence that both parents lost their jobs in the same month.* **unhappily** *adverb* **unhappiness** *noun*

unhealthy *adjective* (**unhealthier, unhealthiest**) not healthy **unhealthily** *adverb*

unheard-of *adjective* not known or done before; extraordinary

unicorn *noun* (*plural* **unicorns**)
(*pronounced* **yoo**-ni-korn) in stories, an
animal like a horse with a long straight
horn growing from its head

uniform *noun* (*plural* **uniforms**) the
special clothes worn by members of an
army or school or organization

uniform *adjective* always the same; not
changing **uniformity** *noun* being the same
uniformly *adverb*

unify *verb* (**unifies, unifying, unified**) to
become one, or make several things into
one **unification** *noun* unifying things

unintentional *adjective* not intentional or
deliberate **unintentionally** *adverb*

uninterested *adjective* not interested

uninteresting *adjective* not interesting;
dull, boring

uninterrupted *adjective* continuing
without any interruption

union *noun* (*plural* **unions**) 1 the joining
together of people or organizations
2 a trade union

Union Jack *noun* (*plural* **Union Jacks**) the
flag of the United Kingdom

unique *adjective* (*pronounced* **yoo-neek**)
being the only one of its kind or very
unusual ▸ *This jewel is unique.* **uniquely**
adverb **uniqueness** *noun*

unisex *adjective* suitable for men and
women

unison *noun* (*pronounced* **yoo**-ni-son) in
unison making the same sound together

unit *noun* (*plural* **units**) 1 an amount used
in measuring or counting, such as a
centimetre or a pound 2 a single person or
thing 3 a group of people or things that
belong together

unite *verb* (**unites, uniting, united**) to join
several people or things into one thing or
group

unity *noun* being united or having
agreement

universal *adjective* including everyone and
everything **universally** *adverb*

universe *noun* everything that exists,
including all the stars and planets

university *noun* (*plural* **universities**)
a place where people go to study for a
degree after they have left school

unjust *adjective* not fair or just **unjustly**
adverb

unkempt *adjective* untidy

unkind *adjective* (**unkinder, unkindest**) not
kind **unkindly** *adverb* **unkindness** *noun*

unknown *adjective* not known; not heard
of

unleaded *adjective* (describing petrol) not
containing lead

unless *conjunction* except when; if not
▸ *We cannot go unless we are invited.*

unlike *preposition* 1 not like ▸ *Unlike me,
she enjoys reading.* 2 not typical ▸ *It was
unlike you to be so nasty to her.*

unlikely *adjective* (**unlikelier, unlikeliest**)
not likely to happen or be true

unload *verb* (**unloads, unloading,
unloaded**) to remove the load from a
container or vehicle

unlock *verb* (**unlocks, unlocking, unlocked**)
to open a door or container with a key

unlucky *adjective* (**unluckier, unluckiest**)
not lucky; unfortunate **unluckily** *adverb*

unmistakable *adjective* not likely to be
mistaken for another; clear and definite
unmistakably *adverb*

unnatural *adjective* not natural or normal
unnaturally *adverb*

unnecessary *adjective* not necessary
unnecessarily *adverb*

unoccupied *adjective* not occupied; empty

unofficial *adjective* not official **unofficially**
adverb

unpack *verb* (**unpacks, unpacking, unpacked**) to take things out of a suitcase or container

unpleasant *adjective* not pleasant or agreeable **unpleasantly** *adverb* **unpleasantness** *noun*

unplug *verb* (**unplugs, unplugging, unplugged**) to disconnect an electrical device by taking its plug out of the socket

unpopular *adjective* not popular

unravel *verb* (**unravels, unravelling, unravelled**) to unwind something or disentangle it

unreal *adjective* not real; existing only in the imagination

unreasonable *adjective* not reasonable or fair **unreasonably** *adverb*

unreliable *adjective* not reliable

unrest *noun* trouble caused by people feeling unhappy

unroll *verb* (**unrolls, unrolling, unrolled**) to open something that has been rolled up

unruly *adjective* (**unrulier, unruliest**) (*pronounced* un-**roo**-li) behaving badly **unruliness** *noun*

unscathed *adjective* unharmed; undamaged

unscrew *verb* (**unscrews, unscrewing, unscrewed**) to undo something that has been screwed up

unscrupulous *adjective* not having any conscience about the way you behave

unseen *adjective* not seen; invisible

unsettled *adjective* anxious or upset about something

unsightly *adjective* not pleasant to look at; ugly

unsteady *adjective* (**unsteadier, unsteadiest**) not steady **unsteadily** *adverb*

unsuccessful *adjective* not successful **unsuccessfully** *adverb*

unsuitable *adjective* not suitable **unsuitably** *adverb*

unthinkable *adjective* too unlikely or too bad to be worth thinking about

untidy *adjective* (**untidier, untidiest**) not tidy; in a mess **untidily** *adverb* **untidiness** *noun*

untie *verb* (**unties, untying, untied**) to undo something that has been tied

until *preposition* and *conjunction* up to a particular time or event ▸ *The shop is open until 8 o'clock.* ▸ *We will stay with you until the bus comes.*

untold *adjective* not able to be counted or measured ▸ *They enjoyed untold wealth.*

untrue *adjective* not true

untruthful *adjective* not telling the truth **untruthfully** *adverb*

unused *adjective* (*pronounced* un-**yoozd**) not yet used

unusual *adjective* not usual; strange or rare **unusually** *adverb*

unwell *adjective* not well; ill

unwieldy *adjective* awkward to handle or move

unwilling *adjective* not willing **unwillingly** *adverb*

unwind *verb* (**unwinds, unwinding, unwound**) (*rhymes with* find) **1** to undo something that has been wound in a roll or a ball **2** to relax after hard work

unwrap *verb* (**unwraps, unwrapping, unwrapped**) to take something out of its wrapping

unzip *verb* (**unzips, unzipping, unzipped**) to undo something that has been zipped up

up *adverb* and *preposition* **1** in or to a standing or upright position ▸ *Stand up.* **2** in or to a high or higher place or level ▸ *Put it up on the shelf.* ▸ *Prices are going up.* ▸ *Let's climb up the hill.* **3** completely ▸ *Eat up your carrots.* **4** out of bed ▸ *It's time to get up.* **5** finished ▸ *Your time is up.* **6** happening ▸ *Something is up.* **be up to** to be doing something suspicious ▸ *What are they up to?*

upbringing *noun* the way a child is brought up and educated

update *verb* (**updates, updating, updated**) to bring something up to date

upgrade *verb* (**upgrades, upgrading, upgraded**) to improve a machine by installing new parts in it

upheaval *noun* (*plural* **upheavals**) a violent change or disturbance

uphill *adjective* and *adverb* 1 sloping upwards 2 difficult ▸ *Coping with the garden was an uphill struggle.*

uphold *verb* (**upholds, upholding, upheld**) to support a decision or belief or agree with it

upholstery *noun* covers and padding for furniture

upkeep *noun* the cost of keeping something in good condition

uplands *plural noun* the highest part of a country or region

upon *preposition* on

upper *adjective* higher in position or rank

uppermost *adjective* highest

upright *adjective* 1 standing up; vertical 2 honest

uprising *noun* (*plural* **uprisings**) a rebellion against the people in power

uproar *noun* a loud or angry disturbance

upset *verb* (**upsets, upsetting, upset**) 1 to make someone unhappy or anxious 2 to knock something over and spill its contents

upset *adjective* anxious or unhappy about something

upside down *adjective* and *adverb* 1 with the top part underneath 2 very untidy ▸ *Everything in the room was upside down.*

upstairs *adverb* and *adjective* to or on a higher floor in a building

upstream *adjective* and *adverb* in the direction opposite to the flow of a river or stream

uptight *adjective* upset or nervous about something

up to date *adjective* modern or fashionable
You spell it **up-to-date** (with hyphens) when you use it in front of a noun: ▸ *She likes to wear up-to-date clothes.*

upward or **upwards** *adverb* towards a higher place

uranium *noun* (*pronounced* yoor-**ay**-ni-um) a radioactive metal used as a source of atomic energy

urban *adjective* to do with a town or city

Urdu *noun* a language related to Hindi, spoken in northern India and Pakistan

urge *verb* (**urges, urging, urged**) 1 to try to persuade someone to do something 2 to drive people or animals forward

urge *noun* (*plural* **urges**) a sudden strong desire or wish

urgent *adjective* needing to be done or dealt with immediately **urgently** *adverb* **urgency** *noun* seriousness or importance

urinate *verb* (**urinates, urinating, urinated**) (*pronounced* **yoor**-i-nayt) to pass urine out of your body **urination** *noun*

urine *noun* (*pronounced* **yoor**-in) waste liquid that collects in your bladder and is passed out of your body

urn *noun* (*plural* **urns**) 1 a large metal container with a tap, in which water is heated 2 a vase for holding the ashes of a person who has been cremated

us *pronoun* a word used for *we* when it is the object of a sentence or when it comes after a preposition ▸ *She likes us.* ▸ *She gave it to us.*

usable *adjective* that you can use

usage *noun* (*plural* **usages**) (*pronounced* **yoo**-sij) the way that something is used, especially the way that words and language are used

use *verb* (**uses, using, used**) (*pronounced* yooz) to perform an action or task with something ▸ *His grandfather had to use a hearing aid.* **used to** did in the past ▸ *They used to live in London.* **be used to** to be familiar with doing something ▸ *We're used to hard work.* **use up** to use all of something

use *noun* (*plural* **uses**) (*pronounced* yooss) 1 the action of using something or being used 2 the purpose or value of something ▸ *I'm sure I can find a use for this jar.*

used *adjective* (*pronounced* yoozd) not new ► *We're buying a used car.*

useful *adjective* able to be used a lot or do something that needs doing **usefully** *adverb* **usefulness** *noun*

useless *adjective* not having any use **uselessly** *adverb* **uselessness** *noun*

user-friendly *adjective* designed to be easy to use **user-friendliness** *noun*

usher *noun* (*plural* **ushers**) someone who shows people to their seats in a cinema or theatre

usherette *noun* (*plural* **usherettes**) a woman who shows people to their seats in a cinema or theatre

usual *adjective* happening often or all the time; expected **usually** *adverb*

utensil *noun* (*plural* **utensils**) (*pronounced* yoo-ten-sil) a tool or device used in the house

uterus *noun* (*plural* **uteri**) (not an everyday word) a woman's womb

utilize *verb* (**utilizes, utilizing, utilized**) (not an everyday word) to use something

utmost *adjective* greatest ► *Look after it with the utmost care.*

utter[1] *verb* (**utters, uttering, uttered**) to say something clearly or loudly ► *He uttered a loud yell.* **utterance** *noun* something that you say

utter[2] *adjective* complete or absolute ► *People rushed along in utter panic.* **utterly** *adverb*

U-turn *noun* (*plural* **U-turns**) 1 a turn a vehicle makes when it is driven round in one movement to face the opposite direction 2 a complete change of ideas

vacant *adjective* 1 empty; not occupied ► *The house had been vacant for several months.* 2 not showing any expression ► *He gave a vacant stare.* **vacancy** *noun*

vacate *verb* (**vacates, vacating, vacated**) (not an everyday word) to leave a place empty

vacation *noun* (*plural* **vacations**) (*pronounced* va-**kay**-shon) a holiday, especially between the terms at a university

vaccinate *verb* (**vaccinates, vaccinating, vaccinated**) (*pronounced* **vak**-si-nayt) to give someone a vaccine so that they do not get a disease **vaccination** *noun*

vaccine *noun* (*plural* **vaccines**) (*pronounced* **vak**-seen) a type of medicine injected into people to protect them from disease
It is called **vaccine** from the Latin word *vacca* meaning 'cow', because the first vaccine was taken from cows.

vacuum *noun* (*plural* **vacuums**) a space without any air in it

vacuum cleaner *noun* (*plural* **vacuum cleaners**) an electrical device that sucks up dust and dirt from the floor

vacuum flask *noun* (*plural* **vacuum flasks**) a container with double walls that have a vacuum between them, for keeping liquids hot or cold

vagina *noun* (*plural* **vaginas**) (*pronounced* va-**jy**-na) the passage in a woman's body that leads from the vulva to the womb

vague *adjective* (**vaguer, vaguest**) not definite or clear **vaguely** *adverb* **vagueness** *noun*

vain *adjective* (**vainer, vainest**) 1 too proud of yourself, especially of how you look 2 unsuccessful ► *They made vain attempts to save him.* **in vain** with no result; unsuccessfully **vainly** *adverb*

valentine *noun* (*plural* **valentines**) 1 a card sent on St Valentine's Day (14 February) to someone you love 2 the person you send a valentine to

valiant *adjective* brave or courageous **valiantly** *adverb*

valid *adjective* able to be used or accepted; legal ► *My passport is no longer valid.* **validity** *noun* how valid something is

valley *noun* (*plural* **valleys**) an area of low land between hills

valour *noun* bravery, especially in fighting

valuable *adjective* worth a lot

valuables *plural noun* things that are worth a lot of money

value *noun* (*plural* **values**) 1 the amount of money that something could be sold for 2 how useful or important something is **valueless** *adjective*

value *verb* (**values, valuing, valued**) 1 to think that something is valuable or useful ▸ *They valued our advice.* 2 to estimate what something is worth ▸ *The estate agent is coming to value the house.* **valuation** *noun* a judgement about what something is worth

valve *noun* (*plural* **valves**) a device used to control the flow of a gas or liquid

vampire *noun* (*plural* **vampires**) in stories, a dead person who comes to life to suck people's blood

van *noun* (*plural* **vans**) a small covered lorry for carrying goods

vandal *noun* (*plural* **vandals**) someone who deliberately breaks or damages things **vandalism** *noun* **vandalize** *verb* to break or damage something deliberately
The word **vandal** comes from the name of the Vandals, a German tribe who invaded the Roman Empire in the 5th century, destroying many books and works of art.

vanilla *noun* a flavouring for sweet food, made from the pods of a tropical plant

vanish *verb* (**vanishes, vanishing, vanished**) to disappear completely

vanity *noun* being vain or conceited

vanquish *verb* (**vanquishes, vanquishing, vanquished**) to defeat or conquer someone

vaporize *verb* (**vaporizes, vaporizing, vaporized**) to turn into vapour

vapour *noun* (*plural* **vapours**) a gas that you can see, usually one that has been changed from a liquid or a solid

variable *adjective* able or likely to change

variation *noun* (*plural* **variations**) a different form of something

varied *adjective* of various kinds; full of variety

variety *noun* (*plural* **varieties**) 1 a number of different kinds of things ▸ *There was a large variety of magazines to choose from.* 2 a particular type of something ▸ *There are many rare varieties of butterfly.* 3 a lot of interesting changes ▸ *We have a life full of variety.*

various *adjective* of different kinds ▸ *The loudspeakers are sold in various sizes.*

varnish *noun* (*plural* **varnishes**) a liquid that you paint on wood or other surfaces to make it hard and glossy

varnish *verb* (**varnishes, varnishing, varnished**) to put varnish on a surface

vary *verb* (**varies, varying, varied**) 1 to keep changing something ▸ *She varies the way she does her hair.* 2 to be different ▸ *The cars are the same, although the colours vary.*

vase *noun* (*plural* **vases**) (*pronounced* vahz) a jar used for holding flowers or as an ornament

vast *adjective* very large or wide **vastly** *adverb* **vastness** *noun*

VAT short for *value-added tax*, a tax on goods and services

vat *noun* (*plural* **vats**) a large container for holding liquid

vault *verb* (**vaults, vaulting, vaulted**) to jump over something using your hands or a pole to support you

vault *noun* (*plural* **vaults**) 1 a jump done by vaulting 2 an underground room for storing money and valuables

VCR short for **video cassette recorder**

VDU short for **visual display unit**

veal *noun* the meat of calves

vector *noun* (*plural* **vectors**) in mathematics, a quantity that has size and direction, such as velocity (which is speed in a certain direction)

Veda *plural noun* the ancient writings of the Hindu religion
Veda is an ancient Sanskrit name meaning 'sacred knowledge'.

veer *verb* (**veers, veering, veered**) to change direction suddenly

vegan *noun* (*plural* **vegans**) (*pronounced* **vee**-gan) someone who does not use or eat any products made from animals

vegetable *noun* (*plural* **vegetables**) a plant that can be used for food

vegetarian *noun* (*plural* **vegetarians**) (*pronounced* vej-i-**tair**-i-an) someone who does not eat meat

vegetation *noun* the plants that are growing in a place

vehicle *noun* (*plural* **vehicles**) a machine with wheels for carrying people and things, such as a car, lorry, bus, or bicycle

veil *noun* (*plural* **veils**) (*rhymes with* nail) a piece of thin material to cover your face or head **veiled** *adjective* covered with a veil, or hidden

vein *noun* (*plural* **veins**) (*rhymes with* main) **1** one of the tubes that carry blood towards your heart **2** a line or streak on a leaf or rock or insect's wing

velocity *noun* (*plural* **velocities**) (*pronounced* vil-**os**-i-ti) speed in a particular direction
The word **velocity** comes from a Latin word *velox* meaning 'swift'.

velvet *noun* a soft material with short thick fibres on one side **velvety** *adjective*

vendetta *noun* (*plural* **vendettas**) a long-lasting quarrel or feud
Vendetta is an Italian word, and comes from a Latin word *vindicta* meaning 'vengeance'.

vending machine *noun* (*plural* **vending machines**) a machine containing things you can buy, which you operate by putting in coins

veneer *noun* (*plural* **veneers**) a thin layer of fine wood used to cover wood of a poorer quality

venerable *adjective* old and worthy of respect or honour

venereal disease *noun* (*plural* **venereal diseases**) (*pronounced* vin-**eer**-i-al) a disease that is passed on by sexual intercourse

venetian blind *noun* (*plural* **venetian blinds**) a window blind made of thin horizontal pieces which control the light coming through

vengeance *noun* something you do to harm someone who has harmed you

venison *noun* the meat of deer

Venn diagram *noun* (*plural* **Venn diagrams**) in mathematics, a diagram using circles to show how sets of things relate to one another

venom *noun* the poison of some snakes, spiders, and scorpions **venomous** *adjective* poisonous

vent *noun* (*plural* **vents**) an opening to let out smoke or gas

ventilate *verb* (**ventilates, ventilating, ventilated**) to let fresh air move freely in and out of a place **ventilation** *noun* **ventilator** *noun* a machine that breathes for someone in hospital

ventriloquist *noun* (*plural* **ventriloquists**) (*pronounced* ven-**tril**-o-kwist) an entertainer who speaks without moving the lips, so that it looks as though a dummy is speaking **ventriloquism** *noun*

venture *verb* (**ventures, venturing, ventured**) to do something difficult or adventurous ▶ *Shall we venture out into the snow?*

venture *noun* (*plural* **ventures**) something adventurous or risky

veranda *noun* (*plural* **verandas**) (*pronounced* ver-**an**-da) a covered terrace along one side of a house

verb *noun* (*plural* **verbs**) a word that shows what someone or something is doing, such as *do, exist,* and *talk*

verbal *adjective* **1** spoken and not written **2** expressed in words **verbally** *adverb*

verdict *noun* (*plural* **verdicts**) the decision reached by a judge or jury about whether someone is guilty of a crime

verge *noun* (*plural* **verges**) a strip of grass beside a road or path **on the verge of** just about to do something ▶ *She was on the verge of leaving.*

verify *verb* (**verifies, verifying, verified**) to find or show whether something is true or correct **verification** *noun* verifying something

vermin *noun* animals or insects that damage crops or food or carry disease, such as rats and fleas

verruca *noun* (*plural* **verrucas**) (*pronounced* ver-oo-ka) a kind of wart on the sole of your foot

versatile *adjective* (*pronounced* ver-sa-tyl) **1** able to do different things **2** useful for many things **versatility** *noun* being versatile

verse *noun* (*plural* **verses**) **1** writing in the form of poetry **2** a group of lines in a poem or song **3** one of the short numbered sections of a chapter in the Bible

version *noun* (*plural* **versions**) **1** one person's account of something that happened ▶ *Mandy's version of the incident was a lot different from Emma's.* **2** a book or writing that is translated or rewritten from something else ▶ *We looked at an English version of the Koran.* **3** a particular form of a thing ▶ *I bought the wide-screen version of the video.*

versus *preposition* against or competing with, especially in sport ▶ *The final will be Brazil versus Germany.*

vertebra *noun* (*plural* **vertebrae**) (*pronounced* ver-ti-bra) one of the bones that form your backbone

vertebrate *noun* (*plural* **vertebrates**) (*pronounced* ver-ti-brit) an animal with a backbone

vertical *adjective* going directly upwards, at right angles to the ground **vertically** *adverb*

very *adverb* to a great amount; extremely ▶ *It was a very warm afternoon.*
very *adjective* **1** exact or actual ▶ *Those were her very words.* **2** extreme ▶ *We've reached the very end.*

Vesak *noun* (*pronounced* ves-ak) an important festival of Buddhism, held in April to May

vessel *noun* (*plural* **vessels**) **1** a boat or ship **2** a container **3** a tube inside an animal or plant, carrying blood or another liquid

vest *noun* (*plural* **vests**) a piece of underwear worn on the top half of your body

vestment *noun* (*plural* **vestments**) a piece of outer clothing worn by a priest or the choir at a church service

vestry *noun* (*plural* **vestries**) a room in a church where the clergy and choir prepare for a service

vet *noun* (*plural* **vets**) a person trained to treat sick animals
The word **vet** is short for **veterinary surgeon.**

veteran *noun* (*plural* **veterans**) a person with long experience, especially as a soldier

veteran car *noun* (*plural* **veteran cars**) a car made before 1916

veto *noun* (*plural* **vetoes**) (*pronounced* vee-toh) **1** a refusal to let something happen **2** the right to reject or stop something
veto *verb* (**vetoes, vetoing, vetoed**) to refuse or forbid something

vex *verb* (**vexes, vexing, vexed**) to annoy or worry someone **vexation** *noun* being annoyed

via *preposition* (*pronounced* vy-a) going through; stopping at ▶ *The train goes from Paris to Venice via Milan.*

viaduct *noun* (*plural* **viaducts**)
(*pronounced* **vy-a-dukt**) a long bridge with
arches, carrying a road or railway over low
ground

vibrate *verb* (**vibrates, vibrating, vibrated**)
to shake very quickly, often with a rattling
or quivering sound **vibration** *noun*

vicar *noun* (*plural* **vicars**) a minister of the
Church of England who is in charge of a
parish

vicarage *noun* (*plural* **vicarages**) the
house where a vicar lives

vice *noun* (*plural* **vices**) 1 evil or
wickedness 2 a wicked or bad habit 3 a
device with jaws for holding something
tightly in place while you work on it

vice-president *noun* (*plural* **vice-
presidents**) a deputy to a president. The
vice-president helps the president and
takes over if the president is ill.

vice versa *adverb* (*pronounced* **vys-ver-sa**)
the other way round ▸ *We need them and
vice versa' means 'We need them and they
need us'.*

vicinity *noun* (*plural* **vicinities**)
a neighbourhood or surrounding district
▸ *There are few shops in this vicinity.*

vicious *adjective* (*pronounced* **vish-us**)
1 cruel and aggressive 2 severe or violent
viciously *adverb* **viciousness** *noun*

victim *noun* (*plural* **victims**) a person who
suffers or is harmed by someone or
something

victimize *verb* (**victimizes, victimizing,
victimized**) to treat someone unfairly

victor *noun* (*plural* **victors**) (not an
everyday word) the winner of a battle or
contest

victory *noun* (*plural* **victories**) success in a
battle or contest or game **victorious**
adjective successful, triumphant

video *noun* (*plural* **videos**) (*pronounced*
vid-i-oh) 1 the recording on tape of
pictures and sound 2 a video recorder
3 a television programme or a film
recorded on a video cassette
video *verb* (**videoes, videoing, videoed**) to
record something on videotape

video recorder or **video cassette
recorder** *noun* (*plural* **video recorders** or
video cassette recorders) a machine for
recording television programmes and
playing them back

videotape *noun* (*plural* **videotapes**)
a magnetic tape used for video recording

view *noun* (*plural* **views**) 1 what you can
see from one place ▸ *There's a fine view
from the top of the hill.* 2 a person's opinion
▸ *She has strong views about smoking.* **in
view of** because of something
view *verb* (**views, viewing, viewed**) 1 to
look at something carefully 2 to think
about something or someone in a certain
way ▸ *They seemed to view us with
suspicion.*

viewer *noun* (*plural* **viewers**) someone
who watches a television programme

vigilant *adjective* (*pronounced* **vij-i-lant**)
watching carefully for something **vigilance**
noun careful watching

vigorous *adjective* full of strength and
energy **vigorously** *adverb*

vigour *noun* strength and energy

Viking *noun* (*plural* **Vikings**)
a Scandinavian pirate or trader in the
8th to 10th centuries

vile *adjective* (**viler, vilest**) disgusting or
bad ▸ *What a vile smell.*

villa *noun* (*plural* **villas**) a large country
house, especially one in Roman times or
one used for holidays

village *noun* (*plural* **villages**) a group of
houses and other buildings in the country,
smaller than a town **villager** *noun* someone
who lives in a village

villain *noun* (*plural* **villains**) a wicked person or criminal **villainous** *adjective* wicked **villainy** *noun* wicked behaviour

vine *noun* (*plural* **vines**) a plant on which grapes grow

vinegar *noun* a sour liquid used to flavour food

vineyard *noun* (*plural* **vineyards**) (*pronounced* **vin-yard**) an area of land where vines are grown to produce grapes for making wine

vintage *noun* (*plural* **vintages**) 1 the wine made in a particular year 2 the period from which something comes

vintage car *noun* (*plural* **vintage cars**) a car made between 1917 and 1930

vinyl *noun* (*pronounced* **vy-nil**) a kind of plastic

viola *noun* (*plural* **violas**) (*pronounced* **vee-oh-la**) a stringed instrument slightly larger than a violin and with a lower pitch

violate *verb* (**violates, violating, violated**) 1 to break a promise or a law 2 to treat a person or place without respect **violation** *noun* violating something

violent *adjective* using force that does harm or damage **violence** *noun* **violently** *adverb*

violet *noun* (*plural* **violets**) 1 purple 2 a small plant that usually has purple flowers
violet *adjective* having a purple colour

violin *noun* (*plural* **violins**) a musical instrument with four strings, played with a bow **violinist** *noun*

VIP short for *very important person*

viper *noun* (*plural* **vipers**) a small poisonous snake

viral *adjective* (describing a disease) caused by a virus

virgin *noun* (*plural* **virgins**) a person who has not had sexual intercourse **virginity** *noun*

virtual reality *noun* a computer image or environment that imitates the real world and that you can be part of

virtually *adverb* in effect; nearly ▸ *He comes here so often he's virtually a member of the family.*

virtue *noun* (*plural* **virtues**) 1 doing what is morally right and good ▸ *They all admired her virtue.* 2 a particular kind of goodness ▸ *Honesty is a great virtue.* **virtuous** *adjective* good; morally right

virus *noun* (*plural* **viruses**) (*pronounced* **vy-rus**) 1 a tiny living creature that can cause disease 2 a hidden set of instructions in a computer program that is designed to destroy data

visa *noun* (*plural* **visas**) an official stamp put in a passport to show that someone has permission to enter a country

visibility *noun* the distance to which you can see clearly ▸ *Visibility is down to 20 metres.*

visible *adjective* able to be seen ▸ *The house was visible through the trees.* **visibly** *adverb*

vision *noun* (*plural* **visions**) 1 the power to see 2 something that you see or imagine, especially in a dream 3 imagination and understanding ▸ *They need a leader with vision.*

visit *verb* (**visits, visiting, visited**) to go and see a place or person or stay there
visit *noun* (*plural* **visits**) a short stay at a place or with a person

visitor *noun* (*plural* **visitors**) someone who is visiting or staying at a place

visor *noun* (*plural* **visors**) (*pronounced* **vy-zer**) 1 the part of a helmet that you lower to cover your face 2 a shade that you lower to protect your eyes from the sun

visual *adjective* to do with seeing; used for seeing **visually** *adverb*

visual display unit *noun* (*plural* **visual display units**) a screen on which a computer displays information

visualize *verb* (**visualizes, visualizing, visualized**) to imagine something or someone as a picture in your mind

vital *adjective* 1 needed in order to live 2 extremely important; essential ▶ *It is vital that we catch the last bus.* **vitally** *adverb*

vitality *noun* liveliness or energy

vitamin *noun* (*plural* **vitamins**) one of the substances which are present in some foods and which you need to stay healthy

vivid *adjective* bright and clear ▶ *The colours are very vivid.* ▶ *She gave a vivid description of the storm.* **vividly** *adverb* **vividness** *noun*

vivisection *noun* doing surgical experiments on live animals as part of scientific research

vixen *noun* (*plural* **vixens**) a female fox

vocabulary *noun* (*plural* **vocabularies**) 1 a list of words used in a language 2 the words that a person knows and uses

vocal *adjective* to do with your voice; using your voice

vocalist *noun* (*plural* **vocalists**) a singer

vocation *noun* (*plural* **vocations**) a job or activity that you feel strongly you want to do **vocational** *adjective* to do with a job
The word **vocation** comes from a Latin word *vocare* meaning 'to call', because the job or activity is thought of as something that calls you. You will also find the word **calling** in this dictionary, with nearly the same meaning.

vodka *noun* (*plural* **vodkas**) a strong clear alcoholic drink

vogue *noun* (*plural* **vogues**) a fashion or craze that does not last very long **in vogue** fashionable or popular

voice *noun* (*plural* **voices**) 1 the sound you make in speaking or singing 2 the power to speak or sing ▶ *I seem to have lost my voice.*

void *noun* (*plural* **voids**) an empty space

volcano *noun* (*plural* **volcanoes**) a mountain with a crater at the top through which molten lava can erupt

volcanic *adjective*
The word **volcano** is Italian and comes from Vulcan, the name of the Roman god of fire.

vole *noun* (*plural* **voles**) a small animal like a rat

volley *noun* (*plural* **volleys**) 1 a number of bullets or shells fired at the same time 2 in ball games, hitting or kicking the ball back before it touches the ground

volleyball *noun* a game in which two teams hit a large ball to and fro over a net with their hands

volt *noun* (*plural* **volts**) a unit for measuring the force of an electric current
Volt is named after an Italian scientist called Alessandro Volta, who invented the electric battery.

voltage *noun* (*plural* **voltages**) electric force measured in volts

volume *noun* (*plural* **volumes**) 1 the amount of space filled by something 2 an amount ▶ *The volume of traffic has increased.* 3 the loudness produced by something that makes sound 4 a book, especially one of a set

voluntary *adjective* done because you want to do it, not for money or because you are forced to **voluntarily** *adverb*

volunteer *noun* (*plural* **volunteers**) someone who offers to do something ▶ *Susan volunteered to make the sandwiches.*

volunteer *verb* (**volunteers, volunteering, volunteered**) 1 to offer to do something that you do not have to do 2 to provide something willingly ▶ *Several people generously volunteered their time.*

vomit *verb* (**vomits, vomiting, vomited**) to bring food back from your stomach through your mouth; to be sick

vote *verb* (**votes, voting, voted**) 1 to show which person or thing you prefer by putting up your hand or making a mark on a piece of paper 2 to say that you want to do something ▶ *They voted for an outing to London.* ▶ *I vote we see a film.* **voter** *noun*

vote *noun* (*plural* **votes**) 1 the act of voting 2 the right to vote

voucher *noun* (*plural* **vouchers**) a piece of paper allowing you to get something in exchange

vow *noun* (*plural* **vows**) a solemn promise

vow *verb* (**vows, vowing, vowed**) to make a vow

vowel *noun* (*plural* **vowels**) any of the letters a, e, i, o, u, and sometimes y

voyage *noun* (*plural* **voyages**) a long journey by ship or in space

vulgar *adjective* rude; without good manners or good taste **vulgarity** *noun* being vulgar

vulgar fraction *noun* (*plural* **vulgar fractions**) a fraction shown by numbers above and below a line (such as ½ and ⅞), not by a decimal

vulnerable *adjective* able to be harmed or attacked easily

vulture *noun* (*plural* **vultures**) a large bird that eats the flesh of dead animals

Ww

wad *noun* (*plural* **wads**) a pad or bundle of soft material

waddle *verb* (**waddles, waddling, waddled**) to walk with short rocking steps, like a duck

wade *verb* (**wades, wading, waded**) to walk through water

wader *noun* (*plural* **waders**) a bird with long legs that wades through water

wafer *noun* (*plural* **wafers**) a thin kind of biscuit, often eaten with ice cream

waffle¹ *noun* (*plural* **waffles**) a crisp square cake made from batter

waffle² *verb* (**waffles, waffling, waffled**) to speak or write for a long time without saying anything important

wag *verb* (**wags, wagging, wagged**) to move quickly from side to side or up and down

wage *noun* or **wages** *plural noun* the money paid to someone for the job they do

wage *verb* (**wages, waging, waged**) to fight a war or campaign ▸ *The country waged a long war against its neighbours.*

wager *noun* (*plural* **wagers**) (*pronounced* **way**-jer) a bet

waggle *verb* (**waggles, waggling, waggled**) to move something quickly from side to side or up and down ▸ *Can you waggle your ears?*

wagon *noun* (*plural* **wagons**) 1 a cart with four wheels, pulled by a horse or ox 2 an open railway truck

wagtail *noun* (*plural* **wagtails**) a small bird with a long tail that it moves up and down

wail *verb* (**wails, wailing, wailed**) to make a long sad cry

wail *noun* (*plural* **wails**) a sound of wailing

waist *noun* (*plural* **waists**) the narrow part of your body between your chest and your hips

waistcoat *noun* (*plural* **waistcoats**) a close-fitting jacket without sleeves, worn over a shirt

wait *verb* (**waits, waiting, waited**) 1 to stay in a place or situation until something happens 2 to be a waiter

wait *noun* (*plural* **waits**) a period of time spent waiting ▸ *We had a long wait for the bus.*

waiter *noun* (*plural* **waiters**) a person who serves food in a restaurant

waitress *noun* (*plural* **waitresses**) a woman who serves food in a restaurant

wake *verb* (**wakes, waking, woke, woken**) 1 to be awake again after sleeping 2 to make someone awake after sleeping ▸ *A noise in the street woke her early in the morning.*

wake *noun* (*plural* **wakes**) 1 the trail left on the water by a ship 2 a time when people come to sit by someone who has recently died

wakeful *adjective* unable to sleep

walk *verb* (**walks, walking, walked**) to move along on your feet at an ordinary speed
walker *noun*
walk *noun* (*plural* **walks**) 1 a journey on foot 2 the way that someone walks ▸ *He has a funny walk.* 3 a path or route for walking ▸ *There are lovely walks here.*

walkie-talkie *noun* (*plural* **walkie-talkies**) a radio transmitter and receiver that you carry around with you, so that you can talk to someone far away

walkover *noun* (*plural* **walkovers**) an easy victory

wall *noun* (*plural* **walls**) a structure built of brick or stone and forming one side of a building or room, or going round a space
walled *adjective* surrounded by walls

wallaby *noun* (*plural* **wallabies**) (*pronounced* **wol**-a-bi) a kind of small kangaroo

wallet *noun* (*plural* **wallets**) a small folding case for paper money and credit cards

wallflower *noun* (*plural* **wallflowers**) a sweet-smelling garden plant

wallop *verb* (**wallops, walloping, walloped**) (*informal*) to hit someone or something hard

wallow *verb* (**wallows, wallowing, wallowed**) 1 to roll about in water or mud 2 to enjoy something very much ▸ *We wallowed in the luxury of our hotel room.*

wallpaper *noun* (*plural* **wallpapers**) paper used to cover the walls of rooms

walnut *noun* (*plural* **walnuts**) 1 a kind of nut with a wrinkled surface 2 the tree from which this nut comes

walrus *noun* (*plural* **walruses**) a large Arctic sea animal like a large seal, with two long tusks

waltz *noun* (*plural* **waltzes**) a kind of dance
waltz *verb* (**waltzes, waltzing, waltzed**) to dance a waltz

wan *adjective* looking tired and pale ▸ *The illness made Steffi look wan.*

wand *noun* (*plural* **wands**) a short thin rod like the one that a conjurer uses

wander *verb* (**wanders, wandering, wandered**) 1 to go about without trying to reach a particular place 2 to stray or get lost ▸ *Don't let the dogs wander.* **wanderer** *noun*

wane *verb* (**wanes, waning, waned**) to become smaller or less powerful

wangle *verb* (**wangles, wangling, wangled**) (*informal*) to get something by trickery or clever planning

want *verb* (**wants, wanting, wanted**) 1 to feel that you would like to have something or do something 2 to need something ▸ *Your hair wants cutting.*
want *noun* (*plural* **wants**) 1 a wish to have something 2 a lack of something ▸ *They died for want of water.*

wanted *adjective* being looked for by the police as a suspected criminal

wanton *adjective* done without a good reason ▸ *wanton damage*

war *noun* (*plural* **wars**) 1 a period of fighting between countries or armies 2 a serious struggle against an evil such as crime or disease

warble *verb* (**warbles, warbling, warbled**) to sing gently, as some birds do

ward *noun* (*plural* **wards**) 1 a room with beds for patients in a hospital 2 an area of a town or city represented by a councillor 3 a child looked after by a guardian
ward *verb* (**wards, warding, warded**) **ward off** to keep something or someone away

warden *noun* (*plural* **wardens**) an official in charge of a hostel, college, or other building

warder *noun* (*plural* **warders**) an official who guards prisoners in a prison

wardrobe *noun* (*plural* **wardrobes**)
1 a cupboard to hang clothes in
2 a stock of clothes or costumes

warehouse *noun* (*plural* **warehouses**)
a large building where goods are stored

wares *plural noun* goods offered for sale

warfare *noun* fighting or waging war

warhead *noun* (*plural* **warheads**) the part
of a missile that explodes

warlike *adjective* fond of fighting; ready
for war

warm *adjective* (**warmer, warmest**) 1 fairly
hot 2 enthusiastic or friendly ▶ *They gave
us a warm welcome.* 3 close to the right
answer ▶ *You're getting warm now.*
warmth *noun*

warm *verb* (**warms, warming, warmed**) to
become warm, or to make something or
someone warm

warm-hearted *adjective* kind or loving

warn *verb* (**warns, warning, warned**) to tell
someone about a danger or difficulty that
might affect them

warning *noun* (*plural* **warnings**)
something that tells someone about a
danger

warp *verb* (**warps, warping, warped**)
(*pronounced* **worp**) to become bent or
twisted out of shape because of dampness
or heat

warrant *noun* (*plural* **warrants**)
a document that gives a person the right
to do something ▶ *The police arrived with
a search warrant.*

warren *noun* (*plural* **warrens**) a piece of
ground with many rabbit burrows

warrior *noun* (*plural* **warriors**) someone
who fights in battles

warship *noun* (*plural* **warships**) a ship
designed for use in war

wart *noun* (*plural* **warts**) a small hard
lump on your skin

wary *adjective* (**warier, wariest**) cautious
and careful **warily** *adverb* **wariness** *noun*

was a form of the verb **be** used when
referring to another person in the past

wash *verb* (**washes, washing, washed**) 1 to
clean something with water 2 to flow over
or against something ▶ *Waves were
washing over the rocks.* 3 to carry someone
or something along in moving liquid
▶ *The boxes were washed overboard.* **wash
up** to wash the dishes and cutlery after a
meal

wash *noun* (*plural* **washes**) 1 the action of
washing 2 the disturbed water behind a
moving ship

washable *adjective* able to be washed
without being damaged

washer *noun* (*plural* **washers**) a small ring
of metal or rubber placed between two
surfaces so that they fit tightly together

washing *noun* clothes that need washing
or have been washed

washing machine *noun* (*plural* **washing
machines**) a machine for washing clothes

washing-up *noun* washing the dishes and
cutlery after a meal, or the things that
need to be washed

wasn't short for *was not* ▶ *I wasn't
listening.*

wasp *noun* (*plural* **wasps**) a stinging insect
with black and yellow stripes across its
body

wastage *noun* something lost by waste

waste *verb* (**wastes, wasting, wasted**) 1 to
use more of something than you need to,
or to use it without getting much value
from it 2 to fail to use something ▶ *We
have wasted a good opportunity.* 3 to
become weak or useless ▶ *The dog became
ill and began to waste away.*

waste *adjective* 1 left over or thrown away
because it is not wanted ▶ *What shall we
do with all this waste paper?* 2 not used or
usable ▶ *Waste land stretched for miles.*

waste *noun* (*plural* **wastes**) 1 wasting
something or not using it well ▶ *It's a
waste of time.* 2 things that are not wanted
or used

wasteful *adjective* wasting things or not
using them well **wastefully** *adverb*
wastefulness *noun*

watch *verb* (**watches, watching, watched**)
1 to look at someone or something closely
2 to be on guard or ready for something to
happen ▸ *Watch for the lights to change.*
3 to look after someone ▸ *Jason watched
the children while I went into a shop.*

watch *noun* (*plural* **watches**) 1 a device
like a small clock, which you wear on your
wrist 2 the action of watching 3 a period of
duty on a ship

watchdog *noun* (*plural* **watchdogs**) a dog
kept to guard buildings

watchful *adjective* alert and watching
carefully

water *noun* (*plural* **waters**) a transparent
liquid that falls as rain or is found in seas,
rivers, and lakes

water *verb* (**waters, watering, watered**) 1 to
sprinkle water over something ▸ *Have
you watered the garden?* 2 to give an
animal water to drink 3 to produce water
or tears or saliva ▸ *The smell of food made
my mouth water.*

watercolour *noun* (*plural* **watercolours**)
1 a paint that can be mixed with water
2 a painting done with this kind of paint

watercress *noun* a kind of cress that
grows in water

waterfall *noun* (*plural* **waterfalls**) a place
where a river or stream falls from a height
over a cliff or large rock

watering can *noun* (*plural* **watering
cans**) a container with a long spout, for
watering plants

waterlogged *adjective* completely soaked
or filled with water

watermark *noun* (*plural* **watermarks**)
a faint design you can see in some types of
paper when you hold it up to the light

waterproof *adjective* able to keep water
out

water-skiing *noun* the sport of skiing on
water while being towed by a motor boat

watertight *adjective* made so that water
cannot get into it

waterway *noun* (*plural* **waterways**)
a river or canal that ships or boats can
travel on

waterworks *noun* (*plural* **waterworks**)
a place with pumping machinery for
supplying water to a district

watery *adjective* 1 like water ▸ *The paint
is too watery.* 2 full of water ▸ *Mary came
in with eyes watery from the wind.*

watt *noun* (*plural* **watts**) a unit of electric
power
Watts are named after a Scottish engineer called
James Watt, who studied energy.

wave *verb* (**waves, waving, waved**) 1 to
move your hand about in the air as a signal
meaning hello or goodbye 2 to move
something from side to side or up and
down 3 to make hair wavy

wave *noun* (*plural* **waves**) 1 a moving
ridge on the surface of water, especially on
the sea 2 a curling piece of hair 3 a sudden
increase in something strong ▸ *a wave of
anger.* ▸ *a wave of violence* 4 one of the
vibrations in which sound and light and
electricity travel 5 the action of waving
your hand

wavelength *noun* (*plural* **wavelengths**)
1 the size of a sound wave or electric wave
2 the wavelength used by a broadcasting
station

waver *verb* (**wavers, wavering, wavered**)
1 to be unsteady or move unsteadily 2 to
hesitate or falter

wavy *adjective* (**wavier, waviest**) full of
waves or curves **waviness** *noun*

wax[1] *noun* a soft substance that melts
easily, used for making candles, crayons,
and polish **waxed** *adjective* covered with
wax **waxy** *adjective* like wax

wax[2] *verb* (**waxes, waxing, waxed**) (used
about the moon) to appear larger

waxwork *noun* (*plural* **waxworks**) a full-
size wax model of a person

way *noun* (*plural* **ways**) **1** a road or path that takes you to a place **2** the direction or distance to a place ▸ *Do you know the way to London?* **3** how something is done; a method ▸ *I know a good way of making paper aeroplanes.* **4** a condition or state ▸ *Things were in a bad way.* **get your own way** to make people let you have what you want **in the way** blocking your path so that you can't move or see properly

ways *plural noun* habits or customs

WC short for *water closet*, used on a sign to show where a public toilet is

we *pronoun* a word used by someone to talk about them and someone else

weak *adjective* (**weaker**, **weakest**) not strong; easy to break, bend, or defeat **weakly** *adverb* **weakness** *noun*

weaken *verb* (**weakens**, **weakening**, **weakened**) to become weaker, or to make something weaker

weakling *noun* (*plural* **weaklings**) a weak person

wealth *noun* **1** a lot of money or property **2** a large amount of something ▸ *The picture has a wealth of detail.*

wealthy *adjective* (**wealthier**, **wealthiest**) having a lot of money or property

weapon *noun* (*plural* **weapons**) something used to harm or kill people in a battle or fight

wear *verb* (**wears**, **wearing**, **wore**, **worn**) **1** to be dressed in something **2** to become damaged by use ▸ *The carpet has worn in several places.* **3** to last ▸ *We'll need to use a cloth that wears well.* **wear off** to become less strong or intense ▸ *The pain began to wear off.* **wear out** to become weak or useless

wear *noun* **1** what you wear; clothes ▸ *Where can I find men's wear?* **2** gradual damage done by rubbing or using something

weary *adjective* (**wearier**, **weariest**) not having any more energy; tired **wearily** *adverb* **weariness** *noun*

weasel *noun* (*plural* **weasels**) a small fierce animal with a long slender body

weather *noun* the rain, snow, wind, sunshine, and temperature at a particular time or place **under the weather** feeling ill or depressed

weather *verb* (**weathers**, **weathering**, **weathered**) **1** to become worn because of being exposed to the weather **2** to come through a difficulty successfully ▸ *They weathered the storm.*

weathercock or **weathervane** *noun* (*plural* **weathercocks** or **weathervanes**) a pointer that turns in the wind and shows which way the wind is blowing

weave *verb* (**weaves**, **weaving**, **wove**, **woven**) **1** to make material or baskets by crossing threads or strips over and under each other **2** to move in and out of other people or things ▸ *He weaved his way skilfully through the traffic.* **weaver** *noun* someone who weaves cloth

web *noun* (*plural* **webs**) **1** a cobweb **2** a computer network, especially the internet

webbed *adjective* having the toes joined by pieces of skin, as ducks do

wed *verb* (**weds**, **wedding**, **wedded** or **wed**) (not an everyday word) to marry someone

wedding *noun* (*plural* **weddings**) the ceremony at which people are married

wedge *noun* (*plural* **wedges**) a piece of hard material that is thick at one end and thin at the other

wedge *verb* (**wedges**, **wedging**, **wedged**) to hold something in place with a wedge

Wednesday *noun* (*plural* **Wednesdays**) the fourth day of the week
Wednesday is an Anglo-Saxon name honouring the god Odin or Woden.

wee *adjective* small

weed *noun* (*plural* **weeds**) a wild plant that grows where it is not wanted

weed *verb* (**weeds**, **weeding**, **weeded**) to remove weeds from the ground

weedy *adjective* (**weedier**, **weediest**) **1** full of weeds **2** weak or thin

week *noun* (*plural* **weeks**) a period of seven days, especially from Sunday to the following Saturday

weekday *noun* (*plural* **weekdays**) any day except Saturday and Sunday

weekend *noun* (*plural* **weekends**) Saturday and Sunday

weekly *adjective* and *adverb* happening once a week or every week

weep *verb* (**weeps, weeping, wept**) to cry or shed tears

weigh *verb* (**weighs, weighing, weighed**) 1 to find out how heavy something or someone is 2 to have a certain weight ▶ *Helen's dad weighs twelve stone.* **weigh anchor** to raise the anchor and start a voyage **weigh down** to hold a thing down with something heavy **weigh up** to think hard about something

weight *noun* (*plural* **weights**) 1 the measure of how heavy something is 2 a piece of metal that you know the weight of, used on scales to weigh things 3 a heavy object used to hold things down **weightless** *adjective* not weighing very much **weightlessness** *noun*

weighty *adjective* (**weightier, weightiest**) 1 heavy 2 important or serious

weir *noun* (*plural* **weirs**) (*pronounced* weer) a dam across a river or canal to control the flow of water

weird *adjective* (**weirder, weirdest**) (*pronounced* weerd) very strange or unnatural **weirdly** *adverb*

welcome *noun* (*plural* **welcomes**) a kind or friendly greeting or reception

welcome *adjective* 1 that you are glad to get or see ▶ *The money was a welcome surprise.* 2 allowed or free to do or take something ▶ *You are welcome to try the strawberries.*

welcome *verb* (**welcomes, welcoming, welcomed**) to show someone or something that you are pleased when they arrive

weld *verb* (**welds, welding, welded**) to join pieces of metal by using heat or pressure **welder** *noun* someone whose job is to weld metal

welfare *noun* people's health, happiness, and comfort

well[1] *noun* (*plural* **wells**) a deep hole dug or drilled to get water or oil out of the ground

well[2] *adverb* (**better, best**) 1 in a good way or in the right way ▶ *He swims well.* 2 actually; probably ▶ *It may well be our last chance.* **well off** rich or fortunate

well *adjective* 1 in good health ▶ *They returned looking fit and well.* 2 good or satisfactory ▶ *I hope everything is well.*

we'll short for we shall or we will ▶ *We'll be going now.*

well-being *noun* health or happiness

wellingtons *plural noun* rubber or plastic waterproof boots
Wellingtons are named after the Duke of Wellington, the British statesman and soldier who defeated Napoleon at the Battle of Waterloo in 1815.

well-known *adjective* known to many people; famous

went past tense of **go** *verb*

wept past tense and past participle of **weep**

were past tense of **be**

we're short for we are ▶ *We're very sorry.*

werewolf *noun* (*plural* **werewolves**) in stories, a person who sometimes changes into a wolf

west *noun* the direction in which the sun sets

west *adjective* and *adverb* 1 towards the west or in the west 2 (describing the wind) coming from the west

westerly *adjective* 1 to the west or towards the west ▶ *We were travelling in a westerly direction.* 2 (said of the wind) blowing from the west

western *adjective* from or to do with the west

western *noun* (*plural* **westerns**) a film or story about American cowboys

westward or **westwards** *adjective* and *adverb* towards the west

wet *adjective* (**wetter, wettest**) 1 covered or soaked in water or other liquid ▶ *The ground was too wet for cutting the grass.* 2 not yet set or dry ▶ *The paint is still wet.* 3 rainy ▶ *The weather has turned wet.*

wetness *noun*

wet *verb* (**wets, wetting, wetted**) to make something wet

wetsuit *noun* (*plural* **wetsuits**) a rubber suit that clings to your skin, worn by skin divers and windsurfers

we've short for *we have* ▸ *We've got something to tell you.*

whack *verb* (**whacks, whacking, whacked**) to hit someone hard

whack *noun* (*plural* **whacks**) a hard hit or blow

whale *noun* (*plural* **whales**) a large sea animal

whaler *noun* (*plural* **whalers**) a person or ship that hunts whales

whaling *noun* hunting whales

wharf *noun* (*plural* **wharves** or **wharfs**) (*pronounced* worf) a place by the water where ships are loaded or unloaded

what *adjective* and *pronoun* 1 used to ask questions ▸ *What street do you live in?* ▸ *What did she say to you?* 2 used in exclamations ▸ *What a horrid man!* 3 used to mean 'the thing or things that' ▸ *Tell me what you bought.*

whatever *pronoun* and *adjective* 1 anything or everything ▸ *Do whatever you like.* 2 no matter what ▸ *Whatever happens, I am going.*

wheat *noun* a cereal plant from which flour is made

wheel *noun* (*plural* **wheels**) a circular device that turns round on an axle passing through its centre

wheel *verb* (**wheels, wheeling, wheeled**) 1 to push something along on its wheels 2 to move in a curve or circle ▸ *The soldiers wheeled to the right.*

wheelbarrow *noun* (*plural* **wheelbarrows**) a small cart with one wheel at the front and two handles for pushing it

wheelchair *noun* (*plural* **wheelchairs**) a chair on wheels for a person who cannot walk

wheeze *verb* (**wheezes, wheezing, wheezed**) to make a whistling or gasping noise as you breathe

whelk *noun* (*plural* **whelks**) a shellfish that looks like a snail

when *adverb* and *conjunction* 1 at what time ▸ *When did the children arrive?* 2 at the time that ▸ *The bird flew away when I moved.* 3 because; considering that ▸ *Why are you wearing a coat when it's so hot?*

whenever *conjunction* 1 at any time ▸ *You can do it whenever you like.* 2 every time ▸ *Whenever I see him, he's smiling.*

where *adverb* and *conjunction* 1 in or to what place ▸ *Where have you put my book?* ▸ *Where did they go?* 2 in or to the place that ▸ *Leave it where it is.*

whereabouts *adverb* roughly where; in what area ▸ *Whereabouts is Tanya's house?*

whereabouts *noun* the place where something is ▸ *Have you any idea of her whereabouts?*

whereas *conjunction* but on the other hand ▸ *Some people like sailing, whereas others hate it.*

whereupon *adverb* (not an everyday word) after that; and then ▸ *The man shouted angrily, whereupon the little boy burst into tears.*

wherever *adverb* and *conjunction* in or to whatever place; no matter where ▸ *Ruth goes wherever her sister goes.*

whether *conjunction* used to mean 'if' when there is more than one choice ▸ *I don't know if they are here or not.*

whey *noun* (*pronounced* way) the watery part of milk that separates from the curds when cheese is made

which *adjective* and *pronoun* 1 what person or thing ▸ *Which way did he go?* ▸ *Which is your house?* 2 used to talk about a person or thing just mentioned ▸ *They heard a noise, which made the windows rattle.*

whichever *pronoun* and *adjective* **1** any one which ▸ *Take whichever you like.* **2** no matter which ▸ *I'll come, whichever day you say.*

whiff *noun* (*plural* **whiffs**) a slight smell of something

while *conjunction* **1** during the time that; as long as ▸ *She was singing while she worked.* **2** but; although ▸ *She is fair, while her sister is dark.*
while *noun* a period of time ▸ *We have waited all this while.*
while *verb* (**whiles, whiling, whiled**) while away to pass time doing something leisurely ▸ *We whiled away the afternoon by doing puzzles.*

whim *noun* (*plural* **whims**) a sudden idea or wish

whilst *conjunction* while

whimper *verb* (**whimpers, whimpering, whimpered**) to cry with a low trembling voice
whimper *noun* (*plural* **whimpers**) a sound of whimpering

whine *verb* (**whines, whining, whined**) **1** to make a long high piercing sound **2** to complain in a feeble way
whine *noun* (*plural* **whines**) a sound of whining

whinny *verb* (**whinnies, whinnying, whinnied**) to neigh gently, as a horse does

whip *noun* (*plural* **whips**) a cord or strip of leather fixed to a handle and used for hitting people or animals
whip *verb* (**whips, whipping, whipped**) **1** to hit a person or animal with a whip **2** to beat cream or eggs until they become thick whip out to take something out quickly or suddenly

whirl *verb* (**whirls, whirling, whirled**) to turn or spin very quickly
whirl *noun* (*plural* **whirls**) a whirling movement

whirlpool *noun* (*plural* **whirlpools**) a strong current of water going round in a circle and pulling things towards it

whirlwind *noun* (*plural* **whirlwinds**) a very strong wind that whirls around in a spiral

whirr *verb* (**whirrs, whirring, whirred**) to make a continuous buzzing sound
whirr *noun* (*plural* **whirrs**) a sound of whirring

whisk *verb* (**whisks, whisking, whisked**) **1** to move or take something suddenly ▸ *A waiter whisked away my plate.* **2** to beat cream or eggs until they are thick
whisk *noun* (*plural* **whisks**) a device for whisking eggs or cream

whisker *noun* (*plural* **whiskers**) a hair growing on the face of a person or animal

whisky *noun* (*plural* **whiskies**) a strong alcoholic drink
The word **whisky** come from Scottish Gaelic words meaning 'water of life'.

whisper *verb* (**whispers, whispering, whispered**) to speak softly or secretly
whisper *noun* (*plural* **whispers**) a whispering voice or sound

whist *noun* a card game for four players

whistle *verb* (**whistles, whistling, whistled**) to make a shrill sound by blowing through your lips
whistle *noun* (*plural* **whistles**) **1** a sound of whistling **2** a device that makes a shrill sound when you blow into it

white *adjective* (**whiter, whitest**) **1** of the very lightest colour, like snow or milk **2** having light skin **whiteness** *noun*
white *noun* (*plural* **whites**) the white liquid round the yolk of an egg

whiten *verb* (**whitens, whitening, whitened**) to become white, or to make something white

whitewash *noun* a white liquid used to paint walls and ceilings

Whit Sunday or **Whitsun** *noun* the seventh Sunday after Easter
The name **Whit** comes from an old word meaning 'white', because people used to be baptized on Whit Sunday and wore white clothes.

whiz *verb* (**whizzes, whizzing, whizzed**) **1** to move very quickly **2** to sound like something rushing through the air

who *pronoun* **1** which person or people ► *Who threw that?* **2** used to talk about a person just mentioned ► *These are the people who did it.*

whoever *pronoun* **1** anyone or everyone ► *Whoever comes is welcome.* **2** no matter who ► *Let them come in, whoever they are.*

whole *adjective* complete; without anything missing ► *He ate a whole packet of biscuits.* ► *That is the whole truth.*

whole *noun* (*plural* **wholes**) a complete thing **on the whole** considering everything; mainly

wholefood *noun* (*plural* **wholefoods**) food that has been produced without using artificial fertilizers

wholemeal *adjective* made with flour from the whole grain of wheat

whole number *noun* (*plural* **whole numbers**) a number without a fraction

wholesale *adjective and adverb* **1** selling goods in large quantities to shops, who then sell them to customers **2** on a large scale; including everybody or everything ► *the wholesale slaughter of infected animals*

wholesome *adjective* good for your health ► *You need wholesome food.*

wholly *adverb* completely or entirely ► *She said she was wholly to blame for the situation.*

whom *pronoun* a word used for *who* when it is the object of a verb or comes after a preposition, as in *the person whom I met* or *the person to whom I spoke*

whooping cough *noun* (*pronounced* **hoop**-ing-kof) an illness that makes you cough and gasp as you breathe in

who's short for *who has* or *who is* ► *Who's taken my pen?* ► *We don't know who's to blame.*

whose *adjective and pronoun* **1** belonging to what person ► *Whose bike is that?* **2** of which; of whom ► *The girl whose party we went to.*

why *adverb* for what reason or purpose ► *Why have you come?* ► *Tell me why you have come.*

wick *noun* (*plural* **wicks**) the string that goes through the middle of a candle, which you light at the top

wicked *adjective* (**wickeder, wickedest**) **1** very bad or cruel; doing things that are wrong **2** mischievous ► *He gave a wicked smile.* **wickedly** *adverb* **wickedness** *noun*

wickerwork *noun* things made of reeds or canes woven together

wicket *noun* (*plural* **wickets**) **1** in cricket, each set of three stumps with two bails on top of them **2** the part of a cricket ground between or near the wickets

wicketkeeper *noun* (*plural* **wicketkeepers**) the fielder in cricket who stands behind the batsman's wicket

wide *adjective* (**wider, widest**) **1** measuring a lot from one side to the other ► *We had a view across a wide river.* **2** from one side to the other ► *The room is 4 metres wide.* **3** covering a large range ► *There is a wide choice.*

wide *adverb* (**wider, widest**) **1** completely; fully ► *Her eyes were wide open.* **2** far from the target ► *The shot went wide.*

widely *adverb* **1** in many places ► *The story is widely known.* **2** far apart ► *The trees were widely spaced.*

widen *verb* (**widens, widening, widened**) to become wider, or make something wider

widespread *adjective* existing in many places; common

widow *noun* (*plural* **widows**) a woman whose husband has died

widower *noun* (*plural* **widowers**) a man whose wife has died

width *noun* (*plural* **widths**) a measure of how wide something is

wield *verb* (**wields, wielding, wielded**) (*pronounced* **weeld**) to hold something and use it ► *The knight wielded a sword.*

wife *noun* (*plural* **wives**) the woman that a man is married to

wig *noun* (*plural* **wigs**) a covering of artificial hair that you wear on your head

wiggle *verb* (**wiggles, wiggling, wiggled**) to move something from side to side

wigwam *noun* (*plural* **wigwams**) a tent made by a Native American

wild *adjective* (**wilder, wildest**) 1 living or growing in its natural state and not looked after by people ▸ *wild animals* ▸ *wild flowers* 2 very foolish or unreasonable ▸ *a wild guess* ▸ *a wild idea* 3 rough or violent ▸ *It was a wild night, with heavy rain and strong winds.* **wildly** *adverb* **wildness** *noun*

wilderness *noun* (*plural* **wildernesses**) an area of wild country; a desert

wildlife *noun* wild animals in their natural setting

wilful *adjective* 1 determined to do what you want ▸ *George is a wilful child.* 2 deliberate ▸ *She was accused of wilful disobedience.* **wilfully** *adverb* **wilfulness** *noun*

will¹ *verb* (*past tense* **would**) used to talk about the future ▸ *They will arrive tomorrow.* ▸ *They said they would arrive in the evening.*

will² *noun* (*plural* **wills**) 1 the power to use your mind to decide what you do 2 what someone chooses or wants ▸ *He did it against his mother's will.* 3 a legal document saying what is to be done with your property when you die

willing *adjective* ready to help or to do something **willingly** *adverb* **willingness** *noun*

willow *noun* (*plural* **willows**) a tree with long thin branches, often growing near water

wilt *verb* (**wilts, wilting, wilted**) to lose freshness and droop, as plants do

wily *adjective* (**wilier, wiliest**) crafty or cunning **wiliness** *noun*

win *verb* (**wins, winning, won**) 1 to do better than your opponents in a battle or contest 2 to get something by using effort or skill ▸ *She has won a prize.*

win *noun* (*plural* **wins**) a success or victory

wince *verb* (**winces, wincing, winced**) to make a slight movement when something hurts you

winch *noun* (*plural* **winches**) a device for lifting or pulling things with a rope or cable that goes round a cylinder

wind¹ *noun* (*plural* **winds**) (*rhymes with* tinned) 1 a current of air 2 gas in your stomach or intestines that makes you uncomfortable 3 breath used for a purpose, such as running **windy** *adjective* having a lot of wind

wind² *verb* (**winds, winding, wound**) (*rhymes with* find) 1 to move in curves or circles 2 to tighten the spring of a clock or watch so that it works

winded *adjective* out of breath

windfall *noun* (*plural* **windfalls**) 1 fruit that has been blown off a tree by the wind 2 a piece of unexpected good luck, such as a gift of money

wind instrument *noun* (*plural* **wind instruments**) a musical instrument played by blowing into it, such as a flute or clarinet

windmill *noun* (*plural* **windmills**) a mill with large sails which are turned by the wind

window *noun* (*plural* **windows**) an opening in a wall or roof to let in light and air, usually filled with glass

windpipe *noun* (*plural* **windpipes**) the tube through which you breathe air into your lungs

windscreen *noun* (*plural* **windscreens**) the window at the front of a motor vehicle

windsurfing *noun* the sport of gliding across water on a board with a sail fixed to it **windsurfer** *noun*

wine *noun* (*plural* **wines**) an alcoholic drink made from grapes or other fruit

wing *noun* (*plural* **wings**) 1 one of the parts of a bird or insect, which it uses for flying 2 one of the long flat parts that support an aircraft in the air 3 a part of a building that is built at the side and is joined to the main part 4 each side of a theatre stage, out of sight of the audience 5 the part of a car's body above each wheel 6 a player in football and other ball games whose position is at the side of the field **winged** *adjective* having wings

wink *verb* (**winks, winking, winked**) 1 to close and open your eye quickly 2 to flicker or twinkle

winkle *noun* (*plural* **winkles**) a shellfish that you can eat

winner *noun* (*plural* **winners**) a person who wins something

winnings *plural noun* money that you have won in a game or by betting

winter *noun* (*plural* **winters**) the coldest season of the year, between autumn and spring **wintry** *adjective* cold, like winter

wipe *verb* (**wipes, wiping, wiped**) to dry or clean something by rubbing it **wipe out** to destroy something ▶ *The town was wiped out by bombing during the war.*

wire *noun* (*plural* **wires**) a thin length of covered metal used to carry electric current

wire *verb* (**wired, wiring, wired**) to connect a device with wires to carry electricity

wiring *noun* a set of wires carrying electric current ▶ *The fire was caused by faulty wiring.*

wiry *adjective* (**wirier, wiriest**) 1 thin and tough like wire 2 lean and strong **wiriness** *noun*

wisdom *noun* knowledge and understanding of many things

wisdom tooth *noun* (*plural* **wisdom teeth**) a tooth that grows at the back of your mouth much later than the other teeth

wise *adjective* (**wiser, wisest**) knowing and understanding many things and having good sense **wisely** *adverb*

wish *verb* (**wishes, wishing, wished**) 1 to think or say that you would like to do something or have something ▶ *I wish we could stay a bit longer.* ▶ *The children all wished for snow at Christmas.* 2 to say that you hope someone will get something ▶ *They wished us luck.*

wish *noun* (*plural* **wishes**) 1 something you want 2 the action of wishing ▶ *Make a wish.*

wishbone *noun* (*plural* **wishbones**) a forked bone from the breast of a chicken or other bird

wisp *noun* (*plural* **wisps**) a thin piece of something light or fluffy **wispy** *adjective* thin and fluffy

wistful *adjective* sadly longing for something **wistfully** *adverb* **wistfulness** *noun*

wit *noun* (*plural* **wits**) 1 intelligence or cleverness 2 a clever kind of humour 3 a person who has wit **keep your wits about you** to stay alert

witch *noun* (*plural* **witches**) a woman who is believed to use magic powers

witchcraft *noun* using magic powers, especially to make bad things happen

with *preposition* 1 having something ▶ *We saw a house with a thatched roof.* 2 in the company of or accompanied by ▶ *I have come with a friend.* 3 using something ▶ *He hit the nail with a hammer.* 4 against another ▶ *They fought with each other.* 5 because of ▶ *He shook with laughter.*

withdraw *verb* (**withdraws, withdrawing, withdrew, withdrawn**) 1 to take something away or take it back ▶ *She withdrew some money from her account.* 2 to decide not to join in with something ▶ *Several people have withdrawn from the trip.* 3 to leave or move back ▶ *The troops have withdrawn from the frontier.* **withdrawal** *noun* moving back, or taking something back

wither *verb* (**withers, withering, withered**) to shrivel up and die

withhold *verb* (**withholds, withholding, withheld**) (not an everyday word) to refuse to give something to someone ▶ *It is important not to withhold any information.*

within *preposition* and *adverb* inside; not beyond something

without *preposition* not having something ▶ *They passed a car without any lights.*

withstand *verb* (**withstands, withstanding, withstood**) to resist something ▶ *Few animals and plants can withstand such high temperatures.*

witness *noun* (*plural* **witnesses**) a person who sees something happen and can give information about it later, especially in a lawcourt
witness *verb* (**witnesses, witnessing, witnessed**) to be a witness of something that happens ▶ *A young girl had witnessed the whole incident.*

witty *adjective* (**wittier, wittiest**) clever and amusing **wittily** *adverb*

wizard *noun* (*plural* **wizards**) a man who is believed to use magic powers **wizardry** *noun* something done in a clever way or by magic

wizened *adjective* shrivelled or dried up

wobble *verb* (**wobbles, wobbling, wobbled**) to move unsteadily from side to side **wobbly** *adjective*

woe *noun* (*plural* **woes**) (not an everyday word) sorrow or misfortune **woeful** *adjective* full of sorrow **woefully** *adverb*

wok *noun* (*plural* **woks**) a deep bowl-shaped frying pan used in Chinese cookery

woke past tense of **wake** *verb*

woken past participle of **wake** *verb*

wolf *noun* (*plural* **wolves**) a wild animal like a large dog

woman *noun* (*plural* **women**) a grown-up female human being

womb *noun* (*plural* **wombs**) (*pronounced* woom) the part of a female's body where babies develop before they are born

won past tense and past participle of **win** *verb*

wonder *noun* (*plural* **wonders**) 1 a feeling of surprise and admiration 2 something that gives you this feeling
wonder *verb* (**wonders, wondering, wondered**) 1 to be curious about something or try to decide about it ▶ *I wonder what's for dinner.* ▶ *I wondered what to do next.* 2 to feel surprise and admiration about something ▶ *The audience wondered at the acrobats' daring.*

wonderful *adjective* marvellous or excellent **wonderfully** *adverb*

won't short for *will not* ▶ *They won't tell us.*

wood *noun* (*plural* **woods**) 1 the substance that trees are made of 2 a lot of trees growing together

wooded *adjective* covered with growing trees

wooden *adjective* made of wood

woodlouse *noun* (*plural* **woodlice**) a small crawling creature with seven pairs of legs, living in rotten wood or damp soil

woodpecker *noun* (*plural* **woodpeckers**) a bird that taps tree trunks with its beak to find insects

woodwind *noun* musical instruments that you play by blowing into them, such as the clarinet and oboe. They can be made of wood, metal, or plastic.

woodwork *noun* 1 making things with wood 2 things made of wood, such as the doors and window frames in a building

woodworm *noun* (*plural* **woodworm** or **woodworms**) the larva of a beetle that bores into wood

woody *adjective* (**woodier, woodiest**) 1 like wood or made of wood ▶ *a woody plant* 2 full of trees

wool *noun* 1 the thick soft hair of sheep or goats 2 thread or cloth made from this hair

woollen *adjective* made of wool

woolly *adjective* (**woollier, woolliest**) 1 made of wool or covered with wool 2 vague and not clear ▸ *He has a few ideas but they are rather woolly.* **woolliness** *noun*

word *noun* (*plural* **words**) 1 a set of sounds or letters that has a meaning and is written with a space before and after it 2 a promise ▸ *He gave me his word.* 3 a command or order ▸ *Start when I give the word.* 4 a message or piece of information ▸ *We sent word that we had arrived safely.*

word *verb* (**words, wording, worded**) to express something in words ▸ *I'm not sure how to word my letter.*

wording *noun* the words used to say something

word processor *noun* (*plural* **word processors**) a computer used for writing and editing letters and documents **word processing** *noun*

wore past tense of **wear** *verb*

work *noun* (*plural* **works**) 1 an activity that needs effort or energy ▸ *Cleaning up the kitchen was hard work.* 2 a person's job ▸ *What work do you do?* 3 something produced by work ▸ *I have to hand in my work on Monday.* 4 a piece of writing or music or painting **at work** working

work *verb* (**works, working, worked**) 1 to do work ▸ *I've been working on my nature project.* 2 to have a job or be employed ▸ *She works in a bank.* 3 to operate correctly or successfully ▸ *Is the lift working?* ▸ *My idea doesn't work.* 4 to make something act or operate ▸ *Can you work the lift?* **to work loose** to become gradually loose **to work out** 1 to happen in a certain way ▸ *Things have worked out well for them.* 2 to find the answer to something ▸ *I'm trying to work out how much I owe you.* 3 to exercise ▸ *Philippa works out in the gym every day.*

workable *adjective* able to be done

workbench *noun* (*plural* **workbenches**) a bench for doing carpentry or other work

worker *noun* (*plural* **workers**) 1 someone who does work 2 a bee or ant that does the work in a hive or colony but does not produce eggs

workout *noun* (*plural* **workouts**) a session of physical exercise or training

works *plural noun* 1 the moving parts of a machine 2 a factory or industrial site

workshop *noun* (*plural* **workshops**) a place where things are made or mended

world *noun* (*plural* **worlds**) 1 the earth with all its countries and peoples 2 everything to do with a particular subject or activity ▸ *She enjoyed working in the world of television.*

worldly *adjective* (**worldlier, worldliest**) 1 to do with life on earth 2 only interested in money and possessions 3 practical and knowing a lot about life

worldwide *adjective* and *adverb* over the whole world

worm *noun* (*plural* **worms**) a small thin wriggling animal without a backbone or legs

worm *verb* (**worms, worming, wormed**) to move along slowly when people or things are in your way ▸ *He wormed his way through the crowd.*

worn past participle of **wear** *verb*

worry *verb* (**worries, worrying, worried**) to be anxious or troubled about something, or to make someone anxious or troubled

worry *noun* (*plural* **worries**) 1 worrying or being anxious 2 something that makes you worry

worse *adjective* and *adverb* less good or less well

worsen *verb* (**worsens, worsening, worsened**) to become worse, or to make something worse

worship *verb* (**worships, worshipping, worshipped**) 1 to give praise to God or a god 2 to adore someone or have great respect for them **worshipper** *noun* someone who is worshipping God or a god

worship *noun* religious ceremonies or services

worst *adjective* and *adverb* least good or least well

worth *adjective* 1 having a certain value ▸ *I have a stamp worth £100.* 2 deserving something; good or important enough for something ▸ *The book is worth reading.*

worth *noun* value or usefulness

worthless *adjective* having no value or use

worthwhile *adjective* important or good enough to do; useful

worthy *adjective* (**worthier, worthiest**) deserving respect or support **worthy of** deserving something ▸ *The charity is worthy of your support.*

would *verb* 1 past tense of the verb **will** ▸ *We said we would do it.* ▸ *He said he would come if he could.* 2 used in polite questions or requests ▸ *Would you mind closing the window?*

wouldn't short for *would not* ▸ *I wouldn't do that if I were you.*

wound[1] *noun* (*plural* **wounds**) (*pronounced* woond) an injury done to a part of your body

wound *verb* (**wounds, wounding, wounded**) to give someone a wound

wound[2] (*pronounced* wownd) past tense and past participle of **wind** *verb*

wove past tense of **weave**

woven past participle of **weave**

wrap *verb* (**wraps, wrapping, wrapped**) to put paper or some other covering round something

wrapper *noun* (*plural* **wrappers**) a piece of paper or cloth for wrapping round something

wrapping *noun* (*plural* **wrappings**) material used to wrap something

wrath *noun* (*rhymes with* cloth) (not an everyday word) anger **wrathful** *adjective* angry

wreath *noun* (*plural* **wreaths**) (*pronounced* reeth) a circle of flowers and leaves woven together

wreck *verb* (**wrecks, wrecking, wrecked**) to damage or ruin something so badly that it cannot be used again **wrecker** *noun*

someone or something that destroys things

wreck *noun* (*plural* **wrecks**) a wrecked ship, car, or building

wreckage *noun* the pieces of a wreck

wren *noun* (*plural* **wrens**) a small brown bird

wrench *verb* (**wrenches, wrenching, wrenched**) to pull or twist something suddenly or violently ▸ *He fetched a screwdriver and wrenched the lid off.*

wrench *noun* (*plural* **wrenches**) 1 a wrenching movement 2 a tool for gripping and turning bolts or nuts

wrestle *verb* (**wrestles, wrestling, wrestled**) 1 to fight with someone by grasping them and trying to throw them to the ground 2 to struggle to solve a problem or difficulty **wrestler** *noun* **wrestling** *noun*

wretch *noun* (*plural* **wretches**) someone who is very poor or miserable

wretched *adjective* (*pronounced* **rech**-id) very poor or miserable

wriggle *verb* (**wriggles, wriggling, wriggled**) to twist and turn your body **wriggle out of** to avoid doing something you do not like

wring *verb* (**wrings, wringing, wrung**) 1 to squeeze or twist something wet to get the water out of it 2 to squeeze something very hard **wringing wet** very wet; soaked

wrinkle *noun* (*plural* **wrinkles**) a small crease or line in your skin or on a surface

wrinkle *verb* (**wrinkles, wrinkling, wrinkled**) to make wrinkles in something

wrist *noun* (*plural* **wrists**) the joint that connects your hand to your arm

write *verb* (**writes, writing, wrote, written**) 1 to make words or signs on paper or some other surface 2 to be the author of a story or play or the composer of a piece of music 3 to send someone a letter ▸ *I wrote to my cousin in Paris.* **write off** to think something is lost or useless **writer** *noun*

writhe *verb* (**writhes, writhing, writhed**) (*pronounced* ryth) to twist your body about, especially because you are in pain

writing *noun* (*plural* **writings**) something you write, or the way you write

wrong *adjective* **1** not fair or morally right ▶ *It is wrong to cheat.* **2** incorrect ▶ *The answer was wrong.* **3** not working properly ▶ *There's something wrong with the engine.* **wrongly** *adverb*

wrong *adverb* wrongly ▶ *You guessed wrong.*

wrong *noun* (*plural* **wrongs**) something that is wrong **in the wrong** having done or said something wrong ▶ *She knew she was in the wrong, so she apologized.*

wrong *verb* (**wrongs, wronging, wronged**) to do wrong to someone

wrote past tense of **write**

wrung past tense and past participle of **wring**

wry *adjective* (**wryer, wryest**) slightly mocking or sarcastic ▶ *He has a wry sense of humour.* **wryly** *adverb*

Xx

Xmas *noun* (*plural* **Xmases**) (informal) Christmas

X-ray *noun* (*plural* **X-rays**) a photograph of the inside of something, especially a part of your body, made by a kind of radiation that can pass through something solid

X-ray *verb* (**X-rays, X-raying, X-rayed**) to make an X-ray of something

xylophone *noun* (*plural* **xylophones**) (*pronounced* zy-lo-fohn) a musical instrument made of a row of bars of different lengths, which you hit with small hammers

The word **xylophone** comes from Greek words *xylon* meaning 'wood' and *phone* meaning 'sound' (the same word as in *telephone*).

Yy

yacht *noun* (*plural* **yachts**) (*pronounced* yot) **1** a light sailing boat used for racing **2** a private ship used for cruising

yak *noun* (*plural* **yaks**) a long-haired ox from Tibet

yam *noun* (*plural* **yams**) a tropical vegetable that grows underground

yank *verb* (**yanks, yanking, yanked**) to pull something strongly and suddenly

yap *verb* (**yaps, yapping, yapped**) to make a shrill barking sound, as a small dog does

yap *noun* (*plural* **yaps**) a shrill bark

yard *noun* (*plural* **yards**) **1** a measure of length, 36 inches or about 91 centimetres **2** a piece of ground beside a building

yarn *noun* (*plural* **yarns**) **1** thread spun by twisting fibres together **2** a long complicated story

yashmak *noun* (*plural* **yashmaks**) a veil that Muslim women wear in public in some countries

yawn *verb* (**yawns, yawning, yawned**) to open your mouth wide and breathe in deeply when you are tired or bored

yawn *noun* (*plural* **yawns**) the action of yawning

year *noun* (*plural* **years**) **1** the time that the earth takes to go right round the sun, about 365 ¼ days or twelve months **2** the period of time from 1 January to 31 December, or any period of twelve months

yearly *adjective* and *adverb* happening once a year or every year

yearn *verb* (**yearns, yearning, yearned**) to long for something

yeast *noun* a substance used to make bread rise and to form alcohol in beer and wine

yell *verb* (**yells, yelling, yelled**) to cry or shout loudly

yell *noun* (*plural* **yells**) a loud cry or shout

yellow *adjective* (**yellower, yellowest**) 1 having the colour of ripe lemons and buttercups 2 cowardly

yellow *noun* the colour of ripe lemons and buttercups

yelp *verb* (**yelps, yelping, yelped**) to make a shrill bark or cry, as a dog does when it is hurt

yelp *noun* (*plural* **yelps**) a shrill bark or cry

yes *interjection* a word used for agreeing to something

yesterday *noun* and *adverb* the day before today

yet *adverb* 1 up to now; by this time ▸ *Has the postman come yet?* 2 at some time in the future ▸ *I'll get even with him yet.* 3 in addition; even ▸ *She became yet more excited.*

yet *conjunction* nevertheless ▸ *It is strange, yet it is true.*

yeti *noun* (*plural* **yetis**) (*pronounced* **yet-ee**) a large hairy animal that some people think lives in the Himalayas

yew *noun* (*plural* **yews**) an evergreen tree with red berries and dark leaves like needles

yield *verb* (**yields, yielding, yielded**) 1 to surrender or give in ▸ *In the end they yielded to persuasion.* 2 to produce something ▸ *These trees yield good apples.*

yield *noun* (*plural* **yields**) an amount produced by something

yodel *verb* (**yodels, yodelling, yodelled**) to sing with your voice changing rapidly from low to high notes

yoga *noun* a set of exercises based on a Hindu system of meditation

yoghurt *noun* (*plural* **yoghurts**) (*pronounced* **yog-ert**) thickened milk with a sharp taste, made by adding bacteria

yoke *noun* (*plural* **yokes**) a curved piece of wood put across the necks of animals pulling a cart

yoke *verb* (**yokes, yoking, yoked**) to harness or link animals with a yoke

yolk *noun* (*plural* **yolks**) (*rhymes with* **soak**) the yellow part of an egg

Yom Kippur *noun* the Day of Atonement, a Jewish day of fasting and prayer

you *pronoun* 1 the person or people someone is speaking to ▸ *Who are you?* 2 people; anyone ▸ *You can never be too sure.*

you'd short for *you had* or *you would* ▸ *I didn't know you'd been abroad.* ▸ *You'd better take your muddy boots off.*

you'll short for *you will* ▸ *I expect you'll have a good time.*

young *adjective* (**younger, youngest**) having lived or existed only a short time; not old

young *plural noun* children or young animals ▸ *The film showed a lioness taking care of her young.*

youngster *noun* (*plural* **youngsters**) a young person

your *adjective* belonging to you ▸ *Is this your book?* ▸ *I like your Dad.*

you're short for *you are* ▸ *You can vote when you're 18.*

yours *pronoun* belonging to you ▸ *Is this pen yours?*

yourself *pronoun* (*plural* **yourselves**) used to talk about the person already mentioned as 'you' ▸ *Have you hurt yourself?* **by yourself** or **yourselves** on your own; alone ▸ *Try to finish the work by yourself.*

youth *noun* (*plural* **youths**) 1 being young, or the time when you are young ▸ *There were no computers in my youth.* 2 a young man 3 young people ▸ *The youth of today are much more serious.* **youthful** *adjective* looking young or behaving like a young person

youth club *noun* (*plural* **youth clubs**) a club with leisure activities for young people

youth hostel *noun* (*plural* **youth hostels**) a hostel where young people can stay cheaply

you've short for *you have* ▸ *You've got my book.*

yo-yo *noun* (*plural* **yo-yos**) a round wooden or plastic toy that moves up and down on a string which you hold

Yuletide *noun* (old use) Christmas

Zz

zany *adjective* (**zanier**, **zaniest**) funny in an odd or crazy sort of way

zap *verb* (**zaps**, **zapping**, **zapped**) (slang) to attack or destroy people or things, especially in electronic games

zeal *noun* enthusiasm or eagerness to do what you believe is right

zealous *adjective* (*pronounced* **zel**-us) enthusiastic or keen **zealously** *adverb*

zebra *noun* (*plural* **zebras**) an African animal like a horse with black and white stripes

zebra crossing *noun* (*plural* **zebra crossings**) a strip across a road marked with white stripes where pedestrians can cross

zero *noun* (*plural* **zeros**) nought; the figure 0

zero hour *noun* (*plural* **zero hours**) the time when something is planned to start

zest *noun* 1 great enjoyment or interest 2 the peel of a lemon, lime, or orange, shredded and used as a flavouring

zigzag *noun* (*plural* **zigzags**) a line or route full of sharp turns

zigzag *verb* (**zigzags**, **zigzagging**, **zigzagged**) to move with sharp turns

zinc *noun* a white metal

zip *noun* (*plural* **zips**) 1 a device with two rows of small teeth that fit together, used to join two pieces of material 2 liveliness or energy

zip *verb* (**zips**, **zipping**, **zipped**) 1 to fasten something with a zip 2 to move along quickly

zodiac *noun* an area of the sky divided into twelve equal parts, called **signs of the zodiac**, each named after a group of stars

zombie *noun* (*plural* **zombies**) a dead person said to be brought back to life by witchcraft

zone *noun* (*plural* **zones**) a special district or area ▸ *This is a pedestrian zone.*

zoo *noun* (*plural* **zoos**) a place where wild animals are kept for people to look at or study

zoology *noun* (*pronounced* zoo-ol-o-jee) the study of animals **zoological** *adjective* **zoologist** *noun* someone who studies animals

zoom *verb* (**zooms**, **zooming**, **zoomed**) to move very quickly with a buzzing or humming sound

zoom lens *noun* (*plural* **zoom lenses**) a camera lens that you can use to make distant objects appear closer

A Wheatley